PARTY, PROCESS,
AND POLITICAL CHANGE
IN CONGRESS

SOCIAL SCIENCE HISTORY

Edited by Stephen Haber and David Brady

PARTY, PROCESS, AND POLITICAL CHANGE IN CONGRESS

New Perspectives on the History of Congress

Edited by

DAVID W. BRADY

AND MATHEW D. MCCUBBINS

STANFORD UNIVERSITY PRESS

Stanford, California 2002

Stanford University Press
Stanford, California

© 2002 by the Board of Trustees of the
Leland Stanford Junior University

Printed in the United States of America
on acid-free, archival-quality paper

Library of Congress Cataloging-in-Publication Data

Party, process, and political change in Congress : new
perspectives on the history of Congress / edited by
David W. Brady and Mathew D. McCubbins.
        p. cm.—(Stanford series in social science history)
    Includes bibliographical references and index.
    ISBN 0-8047-4570-6 (cloth : alk. paper)—
    ISBN 0-8047-4571-4 (pbk. : alk. paper)
    1. United States. Congress—History. 2. United
States—Politics and government. I. Brady, David W.
II. McCubbins, Mathew D. (Mathew Daniel), date
III. Series.

JK1021 .P38 2002
328.73-dc21   2002003104

Original Printing 2002

Last figure below indicates year of this printing:
11   10   09   08   07   06   05   04   03   02

Typeset by G&S Typesetters in 10.5/13 Bembo

CONTENTS

Afterword: History as a Laboratory

John H. Aldrich is the Pfizer-Pratt University Professor of Political Science at Duke University. He is the author of *Before the Convention* and *Why Parties?* and coauthor of *Change and Continuity in the 2000 Elections*. He has been a fellow at the Center for Advanced Study in the Behavioral Sciences, has served as coeditor of the *American Journal of Political Science*, and is a past president of the Southern Political Science Association and is also a fellow of the American Academy of Arts and Sciences.

Mark M. Berger received his Ph.D. from Duke University. His research interests include American politics and elections.

David W. Brady is the Bowen H. and Janice Arthur McCoy Professor of Business and a professor of political science at Stanford University and a senior fellow at the Hoover Institution.

Andrea C. Campbell is an assistant professor of political science at the University of Illinois at Urbana-Champaign. She received her Ph.D. in 2001 from the University of California at San Diego. Her research interests include Congress, political organizations, and public policy.

Joseph Cooper is a professor of Political Science at Johns Hopkins University. He has served as Autrey Professor of Social Sciences and dean of social sciences at Rice University, staff director of the U.S. House Commission on Administrative Review (Obey Commission), and provost at Johns Hopkins University. His publications include several books and articles on the institutional development of Congress, party voting in Congress, changing patterns of congressional leadership, and presidential-congressional relationships. His most recent book is an edited volume, *Congress and the Decline of Public Trust* (1999), sponsored by the Dirksen Congressional Center.

Gary W. Cox is a professor of political science at the University of California at San Diego. In addition to numerous articles in the areas of legislative and electoral politics, Cox is the author of such prizewinning works as *The Efficient Secret*, *Making Votes Count: Strategic Coordination in the World's Electoral Systems*, and (with Mathew D. McCubbins) *Legislative Leviathan*. A former

Guggenheim fellow, Cox was elected to the American Academy of Arts and Sciences in 1996.

Kenneth Finegold is a senior research associate with the Urban Institute's Assessing the New Federalism project. His current research is on the U.S. federal system, state policy, race and ethnicity, and fiscal issues. Finegold previously taught political science at Eastern Washington University, Rutgers University, and Vanderbilt University.

Evelyn C. Fink is the author of several political science articles, including "Institutional Change as a Sophisticated Strategy: The Bill of Rights as a Political Solution" in the *Journal of Theoretical Politics* and "Representation by Deliberation: Changes in the Rules of Deliberation in the U.S. House of Representatives, 1789–1844" in the *Journal of Politics*.

Gerald Gamm is an associate professor of political and history and chair of the Department of Political Science at the University of Rochester. He received his Ph.D. in history and political science from Harvard University in 1994. Gamm is author of *Urban Exodus: Why the Jews Left Boston and the Catholics Stayed* and *The Making of New Deal Democrats: Voting Behavior and Realignment in Boston, 1920–1940*, as well as articles on congressional committees, Senate leadership, voluntary associations, and state and local government.

Brian D. Humes is an associate professor of political science at the University of Nebraska at Lincoln. He has published numerous articles in scholarly journals and is the coauthor (with Scott Gates) of *Games, Information, and Politics: Applying Game Theoretic Models to Political Science* and (with Evelyn C. Fink and Scott Gates) of *Game Theory Topics: Incomplete Information, Repeated Games, and N-Player Games*.

Jeffery A. Jenkins is an assistant professor of political science at Northwestern University. He received his Ph.D. from the University of Illinois at Urbana–Champaign. His interests involve the study of American political institutions, roll call voting analysis, and American political development. He has written numerous articles and is currently working on two book projects.

Calvin C. Jillson taught at Louisiana State University and the University of Colorado before joining the faculty of Southern Methodist University, where he teaches and writes in the areas of American political thought, development of American political institutions, and democratization more generally. With Rick K. Wilson, he wrote *Congressional Dynamics: Structure, Coordination, and Choice in the First American Congress, 1774–1789* and is the author of a widely used text titled *American Government: Historical Change and Institutional Development*.

Nolan McCarty's areas of interest include U.S. politics, democratic political institutions, and political methodology. He is the recipient of the Robert Eckles Swain National Fellowship from the Hoover Institution and the John M. Olin Fellowship in Political Economy. McCarty is the author of numerous scholarly articles and is the coauthor (with Keith T. Poole and Howard Rosenthal) of *The Realignment of National Politics and the Income Distribution*.

Mathew D. McCubbins is a professor of political science at the University of California at San Diego. He has taught at the University of Texas, Stanford University, and Washington University in St. Louis. He is the coauthor of several award-winning books, including *The Logic of Delegation* (with D. Roderick Kiewiet) and *Legislative Leviathan* (with Gary W. Cox), and author of many more. He is also editor or coeditor of seven books and has published more than sixty scientific articles. McCubbins was a fellow at the Center for Advanced Study in the Behavioral Science and currently serves as a coeditor of the *Journal of Law, Economics and Organization*.

Timothy P. Nokken is an assistant professor of political science at the University of Houston. He received his Ph.D. from the University of Illinois at Urbana-Champaign in 1999. His current research centers on the study of roll call voting behavior in lame-duck sessions of the House of Representatives. He has published articles in *Legislative Studies Quarterly* and the *Journal of Theoretical Politics*.

Keith T. Poole is the Kenneth L. Lay Professor of Political Science at the University of Houston. He received his Ph.D. in political science from the University of Rochester. His research is concerned with the political and economic history of American institutions and methodology. He is the coauthor (with Howard Rosenthal) of *Congress: A Political-Economic History of Roll Call Voting* and (with Nolan M. McCarty and Howard Rosenthal) *Income Redistribution and the Realignment of American Politics*. Poole serves on the editorial boards of *Social Science Quarterly*, *Journal of Politics*, and the *American Journal of Political Science*.

David W. Rohde is the University Distinguished Professor of Political Science at Michigan State University. His research deals with various aspects of American national politics, particularly the politics of the U.S. Congress. He is the author of *Parties and Leaders in the Postreform House* and coauthor of *Change and Continuity in the 2000 Elections* (with Paul R. Abramson and John H. Aldrich).

Howard Rosenthal is the Roger Williams Straus Professor of Social Sciences and a professor of politics at Princeton University. He is the coauthor of *Prediction*

Analysis of Cross Classifications; *Partisan Politics, Divided Government and the Economy* (with Alberto Alesina), and *Congress: A Political Economic History of Roll Call Voting* (with Keith T. Poole). He has contributed to the study of agenda control, divided government, and legislative and electoral behavior in both the United States and France. He is a member of the American Academy of Arts and Sciences.

Brian R. Sala is an assistant professor of political science at the University of California at Davis. His published works have appeared in leading political science journals and include "Careerism, Committee Assignments and the Electoral Connection" (written with Jonathan N. Katz) and "The Spatial Theory of Voting and the Presidential Election of 1824" (Jeffery A. Jenkins). His current research focuses on the rise of "candidate-centered campaigns" for Congress in the early twentieth century.

Barbara Sinclair is the Marvin Hoffenberg Professor of American Politics at the University of California at Los Angeles. She received her Ph.D. from the University of Rochester. Her publications on the U.S. Congress include articles in the *American Political Science Review*, the *American Journal of Political Science*, the *Journal of Politics*, and *Legislative Studies Quarterly* and the following books: *Congressional Realignment; Majority Leadership in the U.S. House; The Transformation of the U.S. Senate; Legislators, Leaders, and Lawmaking: The U.S. House of Representatives in the Postreform Era;* and *Unorthodox Lawmaking: New Legislative Processes in the U.S. Congress.*

Steven S. Smith is the Kate M. Gregg Professor of Social Sciences, a professor of political science, and director of the Weidenbaum Center on the Economy, Government, and Public Policy at Washington University in St. Louis. He has taught at George Washington University, Northwestern University, and the University of Minnesota. He was a senior fellow at the Brookings Institution and a congressional fellow of the American Political Science Association. He has authored, coauthored, or edited seven books, including *Call to Order: Floor Politics in the House* and *Senate, Politics or Principle: Filibustering in the United States Senate*, and *The Politics of Institutional Choice: The Formation of the Russian State Duma.*

Charles H. Stewart III is a professor of political science and associate dean of humanities, arts, and social sciences at the Massachusetts Institute of Technology. He has written extensively on congressional history, budgetary politics, and congressional elections. His most recent book is *Analyzing Congress*. Stewart received his Ph.D. from Stanford University in 1983.

Randall Strahan is an associate professor of political science at Emory University. His publications include *New Ways and Means*; "The Clay

Speakership Revisited," published in *Polity*; and "Personal Motives, Constitutional Forms, and the Public Good: Madison on Political Leadership" in *James Madison: The Theory and Practice of Republican Government* (edited by Samuel Kernell). He is currently completing a study of the influence of four leaders (Henry Clay, Thomas Reed, James Wright, and Newt Gingrich) on the politics and development of the U.S. House of Representatives.

Elaine K. Swift is a study director at the National Academy of Sciences, where she works on health policy issues. She coedited (with Margarita P. Hurtado and Janet M. Corrigan) *Envisioning the National Health Care Quality Report* and coauthored (with Christopher Koepke, Jorge Ferrer, and David Miranda) "Which Messages in Patient Safety Should the Federal Government Promote?," an award-winning paper delivered at the 2000 Patient Safety Conference. Swift is also the author of *The Making of an American Senate* and numerous articles and book chapters on American national political institutions.

Sean M. Theriault is an assistant professor of government at the University of Texas at Austin. In addition to historical research on the U.S. Congress, Theriault studies the relationship between public pressure and member voting on the floor of the House and Senate. He has published articles in the *Journal of Politics*, *Legislative Studies Quarterly*, and *Presidential Studies Quarterly*.

Richard M. Valelly is a professor of political science at Swarthmore College. He is the author of *Radicalism in the States: The Minnesota Farmer-Labor Party and the American Political Economy* and *Political Parties and Voting Rights: The Making of African-American Suffrage and Officeholding*.

Barry R. Weingast is a senior fellow at the Hoover Institution and the Ward C. Krebs Family Professor in the Department of Political Science at Stanford University. He was elected to the American Academy of Arts and Sciences in 1996. His research focuses on the political foundation of markets, economic reform, and regulation in American, comparative, and historical perspectives.

Rick K. Wilson is a professor of political science at Rice University. He is involved in a number of research projects that use experimental methods to explore strategic choice. He has designed experiments that reveal the development of cooperation in numerous bargaining games. Wilson is also an expert on the evolution of American political institutions. He is the coauthor of *Congressional Dynamics: Structure, Coordination, and Choice in the First American Congress, 1774–1789* and has published articles in a wide range of scholarly journals.

Garry Young is an assistant professor of political science at the University of Missouri at Columbia. His primary focus is legislative organization and politics, with an emphasis on the impact of political parties in legislative settings. His work has appeared in such forums as *Congress Reconsidered*, the *Journal of Theoretical Politics*, *Legislative Studies Quarterly*, and *Political Research Quarterly*, and he has received research support from such organizations as the National Science Foundation and the Dirksen Congressional Center.

TABLES

FIGURES

ACKNOWLEDGMENTS

This volume evolved out of two conferences on the history of Congress, one held at the University of California, San Diego, in June of 1998 and the other at Stanford University in January of 1999. Without the initial funding for these conferences, this project would not have been possible. Hence, we gratefully acknowledge the support of Dick Attiyeh, Vice Chancellor of Research and Dean of Graduate Studies at UCSD, who allocated funds for the Public Policy Research Project to put on the initial conference. Stanford deans Stephen Haber and John Shoven provided the bulk of the funding for the second conference and the publication of this volume. The Social Science History Institute at Stanford University under Stephen Haber provided guidance and encouragement throughout the project. Mathew McCubbins gratefully acknowledges the support of NSF grant #SES 9905224 and UCSD COR grants RW 237G, RX 218G, and RZ 587G, which helped fund the research in Chapters 1, 5, and 6 of this volume. Finally, we would like to thank Scott Basinger, Melanie Beamer, Greg Bovitz, Chris Den Hartog, James Druckman, and Nathan Monroe for their editorial and research assistance.

We owe a special thanks to the Social Science History Institute at Stanford University for generous support of the production of this volume.

PARTY, PROCESS,
AND POLITICAL CHANGE
IN CONGRESS

Incorporating the history of the U.S. Congress into the tests of our theories allows the authors here to observe greater variation in their independent variables, thereby providing additional tests for their theories. Many features of Congress and American politics have not varied much in the postwar era but varied greatly in the past. To the extent that congressional theories involve parameters that do not vary in recent times but *do* vary in the past, a historical approach gives us opportunities for testing the importance and roles of such parameters—opportunities that are missed without looking at history.

A similar advantage of historical studies is that they can capture variation of a subtly different kind: many features of modern politics are constant across recent decades and so are not (explicitly) treated as variables; rather, they are modeled as exogenous and permanent institutional features of congressional politics. For example, we often take for granted the standing committee system, the existence of party leadership, or the two-party system. Yet these constant features of recent decades *are not* constant as one goes back through history; there have been times in the past when each of these "givens" was flatly false. In striking contrast to the modern era, which is marked by only modest partisan realignment and institutional change, the period preceding the New Deal was a time of tremendous partisan and institutional change. During the nation's first 150 years, parties emerged, developed, realigned, and disappeared; standing committees emerged and evolved; the standing rules of the House and Senate expanded and underwent many changes; Congress's workload increased dramatically; and both houses grew sharply in size. In short, the early House and Senate were so different from the contemporary House and Senate that they were in many ways more akin to the legislature of a foreign country than to the modern U.S. Congress. In a sense, then, this variation provides tests not only of explicitly modeled variables but also of many assumptions that go into our theories.

This suggests the second broad reason that testing our theories in the laboratory of American history is desirable: it holds great promise as an avenue toward theoretical advances. A historical approach pushes us to recognize and confront the limits of our theories and ideally to provide better theories as a result. By broadening our perspective and being forced to think more carefully about our assumptions, we stand to learn a great deal. Moreover, trying to understand the limits of our assumptions promises to raise interesting new research questions. In sum, incorporating history gives us a more dynamic view of Congress and its behavior than the relatively static picture that emerges from a strict focus on the recent past.

The chapters in this volume synthesize contemporary congressional organization scholarship and congressional history in a wide variety of ways.
Each chapter addresses one of three general questions that have animated the
literature on congressional politics in recent years: What is the role of party
organizations in policymaking? In what ways have congressional processes
and procedures changed? And how do congressional processes and procedures affect congressional politics and policy? Let us discuss each of these
questions briefly.

The Role of Parties

Originally, of course, there were no political parties in the United States.
The framers of the Constitution considered political parties an unwanted
by-product of the governmental process, the deleterious effects of which
they sought to control. Nonetheless, legislative factions amounting to proto-
parties sprang up in the first Congress, and political parties have shaped
American politics ever since. Throughout the nineteenth century, the American party system evolved steadily, from the first party system—Federalist
versus Republican-Democrat—of the first three decades of the Republic to
the Jacksonian Democrat–versus–Whig party system of the later antebellum
period to the Democrat-versus-Republican alignment that emerged on the
eve of the Civil War and has persisted ever since.

A great deal of research addresses the role of party organizations in policymaking. Essentially, most of it attempts to determine if political parties
have an independent effect on congressional behavior and policy. In other
words, does the majority party amount to more than just a set of like-
minded legislators who present themselves to the electorate using the same
label? Or does the concept of party add to our theoretical or empirical understandings of Congress? And in what ways, if any, do parties make Congress different from what it would be if there were no parties?

Typically, debate centers on two ways in which parties might alter the
political landscape. First, parties may influence how their members vote in
Congress. Voting divisions in Congress are rarely as neat and uniform as they
are in Britain or Canada, where deviation from party-line voting rarely occurs (which explains the dearth of legislative voting studies on those countries). The fact that there is no strict party-line voting in the U.S. Congress
allows scholars to study roll call votes to determine the level of party effect.
Second, parties may exert influence by structuring the legislative process
(for example, by controlling committees and the bills they propose, by implementing special rules, by structuring the standing rules, or by controlling

the legislative agenda) in ways that bias congressional decisions in particular ways.

Interestingly, two major modern theories of congressional organization, the *distributive* and the *informational*, assume that parties are irrelevant to explanations of congressional organization.[3] We will discuss these theories in greater detail shortly; for now, we focus on a third major theory, the *partisan*, which puts parties at the center of congressional organization. There are two overlapping yet distinctive versions of the partisan model, each of which figures prominently in recent debates. The first is the conditional party government (CPG) model (Cooper and Brady 1981; Rohde 1991; Aldrich and Rohde 1998, 2000a); the second is the partisan cartel model (Cox and McCubbins 1993, 1994a; see also Cox 1987; Kiewiet and McCubbins 1991).

According to the CPG model, the House alternates between periods of strong parties and strong party government and periods of weak parties and committee government. The key variable that determines which type of government obtains is the extent to which the two parties are internally cohesive and in conflict with each other. When conditions favor party government (i.e., when both parties are highly cohesive internally and the parties have very different goals), committees still have important powers, but they are not autonomous fiefdoms. Committee chairs can be removed, legislation can be referred to multiple committees, and the majority leadership has significant say over who is awarded the most prized committee slots. Conversely, when there is significant dissonance within parties, the House will be organized more along committee government lines—that is, party leadership will be weak relative to committee leadership.

By contrast, the cartel model suggests that parties are *always* the principal organizing force in the House. Cox and McCubbins (1993, 1994a) argue that incumbents' probability of reelection is in part a function of their party's reputation among voters and that maintaining that reputation requires collective action by members of the party caucus. So party members delegate to party leaders the authority to enforce cooperation and maintain the party's "brand name." Toward this end, the majority party *cartelizes* the legislative process in the House—it uses its ability to make the rules to organize the House such that the structure and process favor the party's interests. It is through this capture of the rulemaking power, and in particular its control over the order of business and the legislative agenda, that the majority party influences policy outputs.

Regardless of their approach, most scholars of Congress see party as an important explanatory variable.[4] This view of the centrality of parties does not go unchallenged, however. In a series of works, Krehbiel (1991, 1993,

1998) argues that legislators' preferences are the fundamental explanatory variable in determining congressional behavior and decisions. He argues that party is correlated with preferences and that on the basis of that correlation, we often attribute to party an effect that is more simply explained by preferences alone. He proposes a test of party strength in which, to prove that party has an independent effect, members would have to vote with their party's median voter, or adopt their leaders' position, rather than their own preferred position. Unless such a test can be met, the problem of observational equivalence (i.e., that party and preferences are highly correlated) cannot be solved; in other words, we will be unable to reject the hypothesis that party effects are in reality only preference effects. A number of chapters in this book address this problem.

The Evolution of Congressional Processes and Procedures

The structure and institutions of congressional politics have evolved dramatically over the course of U.S. history, especially in the nineteenth century. At the beginning of the Republic, there were no party organizations, no standing committees, and only minimal standing rules to govern procedures in the two houses of Congress. In the House, there was a Speaker, but initially this was an unimportant and largely ceremonial position. Select agents of the president, whether cabinet members or members of the House, served as informal leaders of the majority party (Galloway 1976) until Henry Clay transformed the Speakership into the leadership position of the majority party following the War of 1812. Other House majority party leadership positions, such as majority leader and whip, did not emerge until the late nineteenth and early twentieth century, respectively. In the Senate, as discussed in Chapter 11 of this book, there was no formal or informal leadership position until after the Civil War, and formal positions did not emerge until very late in the nineteenth century. Control over the order of business also evolved in both the House and the Senate, with major changes occurring at the turn of the twentieth century.

In its first two decades, the House relied almost exclusively on ad hoc select committees to draft bills—and even then, most work on bills was done on the floor, with specific instructions given to committees about how the floor wanted certain technical details ironed out. Not until the time of Henry Clay, twenty-five years into the Republic, did the system of permanent standing committees begin to emerge. In the Senate, creation of a standing committee system occurred virtually overnight in 1816 (Cooper 1970).

The most obvious question about changes in the processes and procedures of lawmaking is, What drives these changes? Presumably, changes represent attempts by members to achieve their goals . . . but *how* do institutions help achieve goals? And what goals do they help achieve? Throughout the literature, congressional institutions are seen as solutions to social choice and collective action problems that threaten legislators' productivity and hence their electoral fortunes. Indeed, one of the key distinctions among the various theories of congressional organization is that they posit differing problems for which changes in congressional organization are seen as a solution.

The distributive perspective (Shepsle and Weingast 1987a; Weingast and Marshall 1988) sees the primary collective action problem as creating a stable policy distribution. From this viewpoint, the committee system is a solution to problems of collective action and collective choice instability described by early chaos theories.[5] In the informational model (Gilligan and Krehbiel 1989; Krehbiel 1991, 1998), the collective action problem that drives organization is the production and dissemination of information about policy. Because acquiring policy expertise is costly but expertise is beneficial to all members, legislators face a collective action problem in trying to gain information about policy. The legislature therefore organizes the committee system in a manner that gives committees incentives to acquire expertise and pass it along to the legislature as a whole. The aforementioned partisan models are not inherently contradictory to the distributional and informational models on the topic of collective action problems; to some extent, they merely posit that it is *members of the majority party*, rather than the House as a whole, whose collective action problems are solved by congressional organization. Nonetheless, the partisan models emphasize particular goals of the majority. Aldrich (1995) argues that the majority has faced a series of collective action problems—beginning with social choice cycling problems in early Congresses, continuing with the need to win a majority in the electoral college in the later antebellum period, and later progressing to the need for extensive extralegislative organizations in order to win legislative majorities. As mentioned previously, Cox and McCubbins (1993) emphasize the problem of maintaining the party's electoral reputation, as well as coordinating the actions of copartisans, as the central goal of parties.

Another way in which the theories differ is in their implications about the identity of the key actor or actors involved in institutional change. The distributive theory suggests that institutional change should serve the interests of committees, the informational theory treats the member of the legislature with the median ideal point as the key actor, and the partisan model makes the majority party the driving force behind change.

A third way in which the theories differ is in the economic analogies that they employ. Each relies on an analogy in which congressional organization is an equilibrium resulting from some combination of supply and demand considerations faced by legislators (Shepsle and Weingast 1995).[6] However, the different theories emphasize different aspects of this analogy. The distributive and conditional party government theories rely heavily on the "demand" aspect. So in the distributive model, the committee system results from legislators' desire to give constituents what they want—especially particularistic benefits. Similarly, under the CPG theory, the array of legislator preferences determines the strength or weakness of party government. In contrast, the informational and cartel theories emphasize supply as well as demand. In the former, committees facilitate production by providing legislators with better information about how to bring supply in line with demand;[7] in the latter, the majority party acts as a cartel (or firm), internalizing many transactions that would otherwise inhibit or reduce production.

Finally, there is another strand of literature arguing that institutional change is the result of exogenous changes in the demands on Congress. Polsby (1968) emphasizes the role of external factors in explaining the "institutionalization" of the House, while others argue that changes in workload (especially during the industrial expansion of the late nineteenth century) drove changes in legislative practice (Cooper and Young 1989).[8]

Policy Choice and Congressional Institutions

A common assumption throughout the positive, institutional, and rational choice literatures is that political institutions affect policy choices. Despite the widespread acceptance of this premise, however, this simple hypothesis is actually tested only infrequently.[9] Often scholars have linked policy changes not to institutional change but to political changes that follow from the alternation of political power between Democrats and Republicans, partisan realignments, and so forth.[10] Some of the chapters in this book explicitly demonstrate the effects of institutional change on policy choices in particular policy areas.

If changes in rules have predictable policy consequences, then we should expect politicians to try to choose institutions that are likely to produce desired policy outcomes (Riker 1980). Indeed, many changes in congressional rules and procedures seem to be directed toward facilitating particular policy goals; such changes often coincide with the arrival of a new majority party, particularly in the House. The proponents of change are sometimes party elites, as in the case of Henry Clay, and are sometimes backbenchers, as with the revolt against Joe Cannon.

Regardless, important questions follow: Do changes in institutions, procedures, and rules affect policy choices and influence actual legislative decisions? *How* do institutions affect policy? The collective choices of Congress are the dependent variable of ultimate interest throughout the congressional organization literature, explicitly or implicitly.

Plan of the Book

The chapters in this volume are organized into three parts, corresponding to the three broad questions outlined in this chapter.

Part I, "Parties, Committees, and Political Change in Congress," addresses the role of parties. This part begins with Chapter 2, in which John Aldrich, Mark Berger, and David Rohde explore the conditional party government model of congressional organization by operationalizing and measuring the extent of party government in Congress from 1877 to 1994. As previously noted, the CPG model posits that party government is conditional upon *homogeneity within* the majority party and *heterogeneity between* the two parties; in other words, when the members of a party want the same things and those things are most at odds with the goals of the other party, party government will be strongest. In this chapter, the authors use various measures to operationalize the extent to which this condition is met, as well as the extent of party government. They show that broadly speaking, these various measures track one another; moreover, they reveal surges and declines in partisanship that comport with conventional wisdom regarding periods of increased and decreased party strength.

In Chapter 3, Barbara Sinclair studies the effects of various factors on the choice of rules that govern floor consideration of bills in the House; her argument centers around the notion that such procedural choices affect the decisions that are made by the floor on final passage. The reasoning is straightforward: by regulating the number and nature of possible amendments and also by placing an upper limit on delaying tactics, rules can play an integral role in manipulating the agenda and thus outcomes. Using both anecdotal illustrations and statistical methods, Sinclair shows that the majority party chooses rules strategically in order to pursue its agenda, primarily by means of restrictive rules that limit opportunities for the agenda to be hijacked (or at least derailed) and taken in an unfavorable direction.

Joe Cooper and Garry Young, in Chapter 4, consider the variability of partisanship over time. Unlike Aldrich, Berger, and Rohde, who focus on legislators' preferences, these authors examine party unity on roll call votes over the period 1889–1999. This emphasis on aggregate, vote-based measures of partisanship has a long history in political science, and Cooper and Young contribute to this work in multiple ways. First, they provide an extensive and insightful overview of party voting literature, explaining in great detail the different operational measures that have been used over the years, as well as the pros and cons of various approaches; second, they study a longer time series than has typically been used for this type of work, thereby broadening the conditions under which party voting is studied; third, they introduce new measures of roll call partisanship designed in part to avoid the pitfalls of past efforts and also in part to answer the following three questions: To what extent is voting partisan? How extensive is the effect of party on the passage of legislation? And does party have an independent causal effect on floor voting? As the authors acknowledge, answering any one of these questions is challenging; nonetheless, this ambitious chapter provides new ways for measuring the role of party in roll call voting and suggests many fruitful avenues of future research in this area.

Chapters 5 and 6 are companion pieces to each other, dealing with majority party control of the agenda in each house of Congress. Chapter 5, by Gary Cox and Mathew McCubbins, deals with the House; Chapter 6, by Andrea Campbell, Gary Cox, and Mathew McCubbins, deals with the Senate. Cox and McCubbins steer the congressional organization debate away from questions about *if* or *when* parties matter, instead focusing on what it means for a party to matter. In contrast to work that focuses on whether parties influence members' votes on the floor of the House, they focus on how parties matter through *agenda control*—specifically, by controlling which bills are or are not voted on by the floor (they label the ability to prevent passage of bills that party members dislike "negative agenda control"). This chapter employs a simple spatial model of bill enactment on the floor and varies one key assumption about agenda control in order to produce two competing models of Congress. One model features majority party control of the agenda, and the other features agenda control by the floor median, or pivot. The models yield different implications about expected patterns of voting in Congress, which are then tested with House roll call data from the period 1877–1986. The results support the partisan model; in addition, they show that negative agenda control is an aspect of majority party power that is constant over time, contrary to the common belief that party power waxes and wanes.

In Chapter 6, Campbell, Cox, and McCubbins apply the same models to the Senate. As before, the models skirt questions of party influence on floor votes and the amendment process in order to focus on the importance of controlling floor access. By assuming that party *does not* influence either floor voting or floor amendments, the authors underscore the prediction that even in the absence of such power, party still matters by using its gatekeeping power to block unfavorable bills from the floor. In both chapters, the authors modify the models in order to incorporate the "gridlock zone" produced by the filibuster and the presidential veto (Krehbiel 1998). As in Chapter 5, the empirical results in Chapter 6 support the partisan model over the floor or pivot model. In the Senate, however, there is an interesting exception to majority negative agenda control: divided government appears to have a weakening effect on negative agenda control.[11]

Concluding Part I, Brian Sala shows in Chapter 7 that despite the high-profile changes of the so-called Cannon revolt in 1910 that appeared to weaken parties, there is ample evidence that parties remained important in subsequent decades. Congressional scholarship has long held that the high-water mark of party government in the House (at least prior to 1994) ended with the 1910 revolt against Cannon and the accompanying decrease in the formal powers and authorities of the Speaker; the "textbook" Congress of autonomous, independent committees and committee chairs, as well as weak parties, is thought to have begun at this point. Sala challenges the textbook view. The evidence presented shows that in the 1920s and 1930s, committee chairs did not significantly differ from rank-and-file party members in terms of support for party leaders on important votes; those members of the House who *did* oppose the leadership, moreover, did *not* receive committee chairmanships. These findings comport more closely with the conventional picture of strong party government of earlier decades than with the textbook, committee-based image. Thus Sala demonstrates that in at least some respects, institutional changes did not produce notably different results.

Part II, "The Evolution and Choice of Congressional Institutions," deals with changes in partisan and congressional institutions. It begins with Chapter 8, in which Jeffery Jenkins and Charles Stewart explore the advent of the full-blown standing committee system in the House in the early nineteenth century. Initially, for more than two decades, the House had few standing committees; rather, it relied primarily on ad hoc select committees to do its business. Then, in the short period from the mid-1810s to the early 1820s, this pattern was supplanted by a system of standing committees—that has formed the basic internal structure of the House ever since. The standing

stant; they then spell out the logic of the different sets of rules, showing that the Articles of Confederation restricted Congress's decision-making capacity to a greater degree than the Constitution did.

In Chapter 13, Sean Theriault and Barry Weingast confront a similar puzzle: Why did the Compromise of 1850 initially fail to pass through the Senate, only to be approved soon thereafter by essentially the same set of legislators? The compromise represents one of the most momentous pieces of legislation in U.S. history; it was a package of several different policies intended as a compromise between North and South and meant to temper the rapidly escalating tensions between the two. When first considered by the Senate, Henry Clay presented the various elements of the compromise as an omnibus bill, only to see it rejected; soon after, Daniel Webster successfully pushed the several elements through the Senate as separate bills. This chapter is an impressive demonstration of the potential for fruitfully blending historical and social science methods: it first draws on different historical answers to the puzzle in order to generate competing hypotheses; it then uses both historical and social science evidence to test these competing explanations. By blending social choice arguments, spatial theory, historical detail, and roll call data, the authors show that by making marginal changes to the various components of the compromise, Webster manipulated the agenda so as to garner the support of pivotal senators on each component.

Chapter 14, by Nolan McCarty, Keith Poole, and Howard Rosenthal, differs somewhat from the chapters before it in that it falls at the nexus of the endogeneity between preferences and institutions. The purpose of the chapter is to explain the addition of new states to the union in the nineteenth century. According to the authors, the policy decision at hand—whether or not to add a new state—was simultaneously a decision to change the institutions that aggregate preferences by adding new actors to the process, and a decision to change the composition and distribution of preferences within Congress. Using extensive roll call data and D-NOMINATE scores (Poole and Rosenthal 1997), they argue that short-term partisan interests drove both the antebellum battles over "balancing," and the post–Civil War attempts to establish Republican dominance. An additional theme of the chapter is that this type of instrumental institutional manipulation proved unwieldy and met with limited success, largely due to the number of "moving parts" involved in gauging the effects of adding new states and the attendant uncertainty about how they would ultimately affect preferences within Congress.

Part III concludes with a chapter by Brian Humes, Elaine Swift, Richard Valelly, Ken Finegold, and Evelyn Fink, who take a novel approach to comparing the effects of institutions. Rather than comparing outcomes at two different times, they compare an actual outcome to the counterfactual outcome that would have resulted under an alternative set of rules. They address an interesting topic that, as they point out, remains, surprisingly, unexplored: the effects of congressional overrepresentation of a Southern white minority prior to the Civil War. They begin by noting that Southern black disfranchisement—via the three-fifths clause of the Constitution—in effect granted overrepresentation to Southern whites. They then make two types of counterfactual comparisons. First, using population data, they reconstruct what congressional apportionment would have looked like had the South not been treated differently from the North and the West. Then they project how this different apportionment would have affected partisan balance in Congress, as well as outcomes on roll call votes. Tempering their comments due to the inherent uncertainty involved in making counterfactual arguments, they nevertheless conclude that American history would have been radically different had representation in the North and South been on an equal basis.

Finally, we follow these essays with a brief afterword in which we recap some of the major findings of the individual chapters and discuss their implications for the larger congressional organization literature.

Part I

Parties, Committees, and Political Change in Congress

Chapter 2

The Historical Variability in Conditional Party Government, 1877–1994

JOHN H. ALDRICH, MARK M. BERGER,
AND DAVID W. ROHDE

Congress is the crossroads of democracy in the United States. All power flows to it directly from the great body of the people, to paraphrase Madison. The people exercise this power through their selection of those whom they most want to serve them in the two chambers. Power, prestige, and policy are then forged in and allocated from its committee rooms, lobbies, and chamber floors.

Many people seek to instruct legislators in ways that extend beyond the exercise of the franchise. Political parties, organized interest groups, and members of executive agencies are only among the most prominent of these. Of all the many groups seeking to work at this crossroads, the political party holds a unique position. The two major parties are organizations seeking to shape the allocation of power, prestige, and policy. The two parties, along with self-proclaimed independents, nearly partition the electorate. But what makes them unique, in addition to organizing both these special and general interests, is that (virtually) every representative and senator is publicly affiliated with, an active participant in, and a leader of a political party. Any history of congressional politics is thus at the same time in part a history of party politics.

The purpose of this chapter is to assess a substantial swath of this joint history of party and Congress. By examining more than a century of their joint history, we hope to learn more about this crossroads of democracy. It is our belief that studying variation in partisan politics, both in the electorate and in Congress, will help us understand variation in congressional politics and policy. We reserve for later the complementary task of considering how variation in congressional politics in turn illuminates partisan politics. In any event, it is our more general belief that recent politics is better understood if placed in historical context. And so we assess variation in the congressional party and its politics from 1877 to 1986 and, to a less complete degree, to 1994.

This book is a testament to the substantial and growing interest in historical analyses of Congress. Because it has electoral and organizational in addition to governmental components, the political party has its own historical dynamic, and that, too, has received considerable (if still too little) study. Roughly speaking, the past 125 or so years of party history are typically understood in one of two ways (see Aldrich 1995 for further consideration). Some (e.g., Brady, 1988; Burnham, 1970) point to the dynamic of critical elections and partisan realignments. Those taking this tack give special attention to the realignment of the periods around 1896 and 1932, along with the partisan realignment that did *not* happen in the 1960s (or, in the case of Aldrich and Niemi [1993], a realignment in the 1960s that went largely unnoticed). Burnham (1970) also developed the major account of the second dynamic associated with the political parties, as he pointed to the onset of their decline, a decline most evident in the party-in-the-electorate. He places the onset of this decline around 1888 or so and argues that except for a brief resurgence during the New Deal, the mass party has been in more or less continual decline since then. To put it most simply, electoral politics is today candidate-centered rather than party-centered. Most analysts claim that there has been no significant resurgence since Burnham wrote in 1970 in that aspect of the party, although there are some signs of resurgence in that quintessential measure of the electoral party, party identification (contrast Aldrich 1999 with Shea 1999; see also Abramson, Aldrich, and Rohde 1999; Bartels 2000).

To turn to the historical patterns of the party in Congress, Brady, Cooper, and Hurley (1979) examined the party in the U.S. House from 1887 through 1968, as Hurley and Wilson (1989) did for the party in the Senate from 1877 to 1986. They found a basic pattern of decline in party voting on the floor of both chambers that seemed to parallel Burnham's observation of this decline of the party in the public. While there were differences between the two chambers (in part due to the differing time periods), both sets of authors argued that the decline of party voting in House and in Senate was due primarily to electoral forces.

In this chapter, we seek to consider the status of a measure of what we have called "conditional party government" (CPG) over roughly the same historical era covered by the Brady, Cooper, and Hurley and Hurley and Wilson studies, across the two chambers (see Aldrich 1995; Berger 1999; Rohde 1991). Our theoretical argument is that there is variable strength to the party in government and in this case to the party in legislature in particular. This strength varies over time due to variability in the preferences legislators seek to reveal publicly and enact legislatively. Presumably (although we do not estimate this effect ourselves), the preferences legislators seek to reveal publicly are those that they bring with them to Congress, with a heavy dose of inducement of those preferences from their constituencies.

The greater the extent to which legislators' preferences satisfy the GPC condition, the more (potential) incentive they have to empower their party in the chamber. The more similar the preferences of party members—that is, the greater the internal homogeneity of preferences of party affiliates and the greater the divergence in preferences between members of the two parties—the more completely the condition is satisfied. That being the case, we would anticipate that members of each party would seek to strengthen the powers and resources of their party and its leadership. Doing so would increase the party's ability to overcome collective action problems inherent in group politics, possibly by "internalizing externalities" (to borrow from Cox and McCubbins 1993). The joint effect of preferences distributed increasingly like those of the CPG account with enhanced resources of party organizations would lead, we argue, to increasingly partisan-based determination of outcomes. While less relevant to the present chapter, we also argue that with increasing CPG, the majority is disproportionately advantaged and therefore able to achieve more favorable outcomes than it would otherwise (e.g., "pull" outcomes away from the center on the floor toward the center of the party).

We observe, in this chapter, a pattern of results over a long time span and across the two chambers that is broadly consistent with the theory of conditional party government. We also claim that there is a different pattern to the variability of the party in government than found by Brady, Cooper, and Hurley (1979) and Hurley and Wilson (1989). In some significant part, the differences are due to the fact that we have the advantage of viewing a longer sweep to the historical patterns. In particular, we will find that the partisan patterns of legislator preferences were largely unvarying over time from the end of Reconstruction until the early 1920s (Senate) or late 1930s (House). We then find that the condition in CPG sagged dramatically in the late

1930s, with a near linear decline in the House, bottoming out around 1970. In the Senate, the decline is less perfectly linear than in the House, but it also reaches a nadir around 1970. After 1970, the measure shows dramatic increases in both chambers, ending nearly back at the starting level, fifty years earlier. Thus the period centered around 1970 stands out (at least from a vantage point of more than thirty years later) as a lengthy, singular exception to what had typically been essentially constant before World War II. Finally, we will see that the pattern in the House (and, with more limited data, apparently the Senate) in the past decade is more like that of the post-Reconstruction period—consistent and (at least in relative terms) high levels of CPG. After developing the theory and measurement of CPG used here and observing the historical patterns, we will conclude by considering possible explanations of those patterns.

Data and Measurement

Aldrich and Rohde (1998) developed four specific measures designed to capture a wide range of aspects of the condition in CPG and used them in assessing the post–World War II House of Representatives. Two of those measures were also created to cover the postwar period in the Senate. In this chapter, we examine these four measures, for both chambers, back to the end of Reconstruction.

The theoretical condition in CPG concerns distribution of congressional partisans' preferences over policy (or ideological) dimensions. Here we use the first, or basic, dimension estimated via the Poole and Rosenthal (1985, 1997) procedure. Poole and Rosenthal use the entire set of roll call votes cast to estimate both the dimensionality of legislative policy spaces over the Congresses and the location of legislators' ideal points on those dimensions. As they have argued, most, but not all, Congresses are estimated to be essentially unidimensional, with a distinct but clearly less consequential second dimension. In a few Congresses (including some of those in the time period studied here), the second dimension is considerably more substantial, especially in the Senate. What is more important for our purposes, however, is that the first dimension is consistently the one that is most strongly associated with party. Using it would thus capture nearly all of the relevant portions of preferences for assessing the condition in CPG.

The "Poole measures" (as we shall refer to the Poole-Rosenthal first-dimension estimates) of ideal points are based on votes taken at the end of the democratic (i.e., electoral and legislative) process. Thus these measures of roll call voting include within their determination all those elements that go into the preferences legislators would like to express in voting. But they *also* include the impact, if any, of institutional structure, such as those induced by, say, committee structures, effects of partisan actions within the House, the consequences from bicameralism, or the influence of the president. Any one set of observations, such as roll call votes, must therefore be considered a complex mix of preferences and institutional considerations, among other things. This point becomes more important when relating the Poole estimates to measures such as party votes. Both are based on large numbers of the same roll call votes. As we shall see, these two summary measures are distinct, and we shall examine the relationship between them.

Our interests are in the historical comparisons. It is therefore important to build measures that can be as fully comparable from one Congress to another, over a century or more. As a result, we use the Poole-Rosenthal D-NOMINATE ideal point estimates that are derived from the entire set of all roll calls ever cast in all Congresses. The disadvantage is that D-NOMINATE estimates are available only through the 99th Congress (1985–86). Aldrich and Rohde (1998) used W-NOMINATE estimates, which are those derived from roll call votes cast within each Congress individually. They developed these measures of the condition in CPG to facilitate comparing across Congresses. We will report those data and measures so that we can assess to some degree what we would expect to observe if we had the D-NOMINATE estimates to go beyond the 99th Congress.

Aldrich and Rohde (1998) developed the following measures:

1. *Median*: The difference between the location of the median Democrat and the median Republican.[1] This measure captures one aspect of interparty heterogeneity.
2. *SD*: The ratio of the standard deviation of ideal points in the majority party to that of the full House, which indicates variation in intraparty homogeneity.[2]
3. R^2: The R^2 resulting from regressing the member's ideal point estimate on party affiliation.
4. *Overlap*: The proportion of overlap between the two parties' distribution of ideal points, subtracted from 1. Overlap is measured as the minimum number of ideal points that would have to be changed to yield a complete separation of the two parties, with all Democrats' ideal points being to the left of all Republicans' ideal points on the first Poole dimension. This number is then converted to the proportion of the relevant chamber and subtracted from 1, to put it in the same scale as the other measures.

Each of these taps different aspects of the condition, and collectively they cumulate to a reasonably full picture of how well or poorly the condition is satisfied in each congress.

The Four Measures of the Condition of CPG

Figures 2.1 and 2.2 present the basic distribution of the four measures for the House and Senate, respectively, over the full set of congresses (the 45th to 99th). The four measures for the House fluctuate, but within reasonably confined bounds, from 1877 (the 45th Congress) until approximately the 76th Congress (elected in 1938). To be sure, there are exceptions, such as the difference between the two parties' medians, especially during the New Deal. Still, all four measures seemingly vary at random over time and are constrained—rather highly constrained—in their variation until late in the New Deal. At that point, each of the four measures begins to decline, led especially by the decline in relevance of party affiliation to align with the first dimension (as measured by R^2) and, even more clearly, the standard deviation measure.

The conditions for the Senate are reasonably similar. Perhaps the most striking similarity in both chambers is that there is absolutely *no* overlap between the two estimated ideal point positions of the affiliates of the two parties for the first fifty years—literally (and longer) in the House and very nearly so in the Senate. That means, of course, that the Republican most "like" a Democrat was still distinct in his or her voting on the floor, and vice versa. Party effectively distinguished Republicans from Democrats in their voting choices and, as Poole and Rosenthal assume in the model that generates their estimates, in their policy preferences that lead (along with institutional features) to the observed voting choices.

The Senate differs from the House most clearly in the steep decline in the standard deviation measure and, to a lesser extent, the R^2. This decline started at about the same time as nationwide direct elections to the Senate. The decline continued until a dramatic reversal in 1932. The other major difference between the House and Senate is that a clearly defined V-shaped decline and resurgence mark variation in the House on each of these measures in the last fifty years we consider. In the Senate, there appear to be sharp changes during the New Deal, but not a House-like continuous decline to about 1970. Instead there appears to be a change at the end of the New Deal that remains at that lower level until about 1980. At that point, there is a resurgence of most of the measures, in some cases nearing pre–New Deal levels.

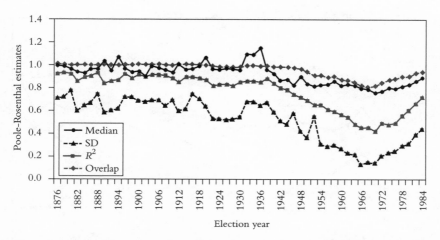

Figure 2.1. Four measures of conditional party government (45th–99th Congresses), House of Representatives.

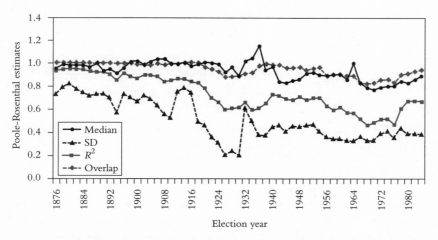

Figure 2.2. Four measures of conditional party government (45th–99th Congresses), Senate.

The data in Figures 2.3 and 2.4 are drawn from Aldrich and Rohde (1998) and extend the CPG measures to more recent Congresses using the W-NOMINATE estimates. Figure 2.3, reporting all four measures for the House, demonstrates that the *V*-shaped pattern continued its climb in the 100th and following Congresses. Figure 2.4 compares the House and

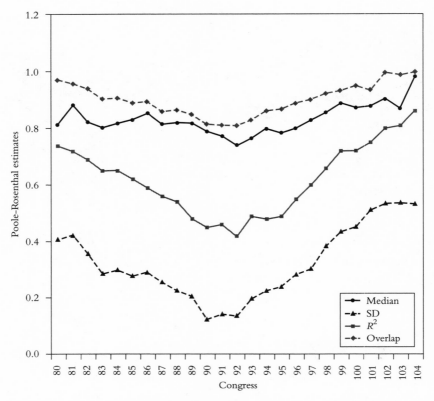

Figure 2.3. Four measures of conditional party government (80th–104th Congresses), House of Representatives.

Senate on the two measures reported by Aldrich and Rohde. The figure indicates that the climb in these measures in the Senate, already observed to have begun in the 1970s, continued into the 1990s, and it did so apparently at a greater rate than in the House. Insofar as we can judge, therefore, these measures suggest that by the mid-1990s, the two chambers had returned to levels of these four measures more typical of eras preceding the Depression.

A Single Measure of CPG

The four measures tap different aspects of the condition, but they are not, nor were they intended to be, separate or independent measures. We consider CPG a single, if complex, condition. To show the relationship among

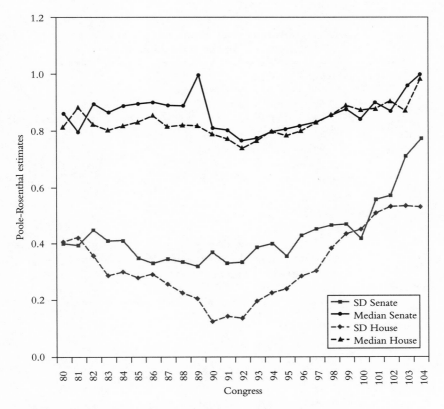

Figure 2.4. Two measures of conditional party government: House and Senate compared.

the four measures, we report their intercorrelations for the House and Senate for the 1877–1986 period in Tables 2.1 and 2.2. We also include the correlation with time to demonstrate the extent of the visually apparent party decline over time. The last row ("CPG") for each chamber will be explained shortly.

The correlations in the House are very high, dipping only as low as .81. Conversely, their negative correlations with time are by now considerably smaller than the nearly linear decline in party voting found by Brady, Cooper, and Hurley (1979). Recall that their data ended in 1969, essentially the bottom of the long-term decline. Our measures would also show a higher correlation if ended in 1969. Essentially the same story is true for the Senate, even though the Senate correlations tend to be lower throughout.

Table 2.1

Correlations Among Four Measures of Conditional
Party Government in the House

	Median	SD	R^2	Overlap	Time	CPG
Median	1.00					
SD	.80	1.00				
R^2	.82	.97	1.00			
Overlap	.82	.94	.98	1.00		
Time	−.68	−.84	−.85	−.79	1.00	
CPG	.83	.97	1.00	.98	−.84	1.00

Table 2.2

Correlations Among Four Measures of Conditional
Party Government in the Senate

	Median	SD	R^2	Overlap	Time	CPG
Median	1.00					
SD	.48	1.00				
R^2	.58	.88	1.00			
Overlap	.64	.77	.92	1.00		
Time	−.67	−.78	−.89	−.78	1.00	
CPG	.63	.88	.99	.95	−.88	1.00

This is especially true with the median measures. Still, even the Senate correlations with the median measure are robust. This high degree of internal structure suggests that the various measures are in fact alternative measures of one underlying factor, the condition in conditional party government. Therefore, a single measure was created from the factor scores.[3] The two sets of factor loadings of each individual measure are reported in Table 2.3.

We call this measure CPG. For ease of comparison, the two CPG variables were set to have the same mean and variance as the four individual measures. This recalibration simply puts CPG, when graphed, on the same metric as the individual measures from which it was composed. The two CPG measures are correlated with the four component measures as reported in Tables 2.1 and 2.2. In the House, the correlations are extremely high,

Table 2.3

Factors Scores for Each Condition:
House and Senate

	House	Senate
Median	.828	.617
SD	.968	.868
R^2	.992	.974
Overlap	.979	.936

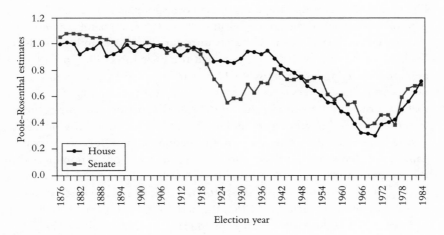

Figure 2.5.   CPG: House and Senate compared.

dipping under .98 only to .85 with the median measure. Again, the Senate figures are lower, although only substantively smaller (.63), with the median measure.

In Figure 2.5, we graph the two CPG measures for the two chambers over time. Here the weighted combination of the four measures smoothes considerably the Congress-by-Congress variation in the individual component measures. In both chambers, the CPG measure is virtually at a constant high value from the end of Reconstruction through the end of World War I. The Senate variable then declines noticeably in the 1920s, climbs back to its former level in the New Deal, and then displays a relatively consistent decline until about 1970 and resurgence thereafter, as we saw in the measures for the House.

The House CPG is high and nearly flat for the first fifty years. This plateau is followed by a nearly smooth and linear decline from about its peak in 1936 to 1970, with an equally smooth and linear (although steeper) resurgence thereafter. As we noted earlier and as Figures 2.3 and 2.4 indicate, it can reasonably be assumed that had we extended these measures through the 104th Congress, the increase would have continued in both chambers, ending in the mid-1990s at nearly the level found in the first fifty years of our data.

Comparing CPG in the House and the Senate

Figure 2.5 illustrates that there is a close correspondence between the degree of satisfaction of the condition in CPG in the two chambers. Indeed, the correlation between the CPG measure for the two chambers is .847. Such a close correspondence suggests that the basic forces that shape CPG are forces shared in common by the House and the Senate. Although we do not measure these forces directly, we believe that it is reasonable to assume that the similarity is primarily due to the role that parties play in elections. It is the partisanship among the public that affects members of Congress's voting choices, in the first instance. In the second instance, it is the party organizations that structure those choices (e.g., in selection of nominees, in the resources and activists they provide, and in the alliances struck with interest groups). To put it simply, the party in elections and the party as organization combine to affect, via CPG, the party in government.

Hurley and Wilson (1989) raise an additional question about the relationship between the two chambers, in their case with respect to various party voting measures. Their question was whether one chamber could be said to be the leading chamber and the other the lagging chamber. They found, primarily by inspection of figures comparable to our Figure 2.5, that each appeared to lead at times.

Visual inspection of Figure 2.5 is ambiguous in these terms. The decline in the Senate CPG in the 1920s clearly separates the two bodies, but not evidently in a lead-lag sense, because the pattern is not replicated in the House.[4] There is some indication that the House led in the long-term decline, especially in the post–World War II years. One probably would expect that the House would lead in reflecting changing partisan tastes among the public, having all members elected every two years. Conversely, it is not visually evident which chamber is leading or lagging in the increase in the CPG measure over the last three decades. Substantively, one might argue that the degree of partisanship is higher today in the House, at a relative maximum in the CPG measure, than in the Senate.

Complicating this question is the commonality of external political and partisan forces that are presumably driving both houses of Congress at more or less the same time. Although, of course, voting for representatives to the House and to the Senate is not identical, the role of party is typically similar in both (see, for example Gronke 2000). We investigated this question of the relationship between chambers a bit further by performing a vector autoregression analysis (necessarily limited by number of time points). In this way, we can study the relationship between CPG across the chambers, controlling for the driving forces that shape each chamber's own dynamics. In effect, removing the commonality of partisan electoral dynamics allows us to assess how closely the two chambers track each other beyond what elections would lead us to expect and whether one chamber is more responsive to the leadership of the other.

Fortunately (at least for degrees of freedom), a one-period lag appeared sufficient to explain each chamber's CPG time path. The resulting regression of CPG on its own last-period value is presented in the top half of Tables 2.4 and 2.5 for the House and the Senate, respectively. The bottom halves then report the VAR estimates for the two chambers. As seen in Table 2.4, the Senate is completely irrelevant for the House. The results reported in Table 2.5 suggest that there might be some impact of prior House patterns on those in the Senate, controlling for the Senate's own time dynamics (which we understand as controlling for the commonly shared electoral forces). The coefficient estimate for the lagged House CPG variable is of reasonable magnitude for VAR results and significant at the .10 level. Assuming for the moment that there is a causative effect of the House CPG on that in the Senate, two interpretations suggest themselves. First, the House may be "leading" only because the structure of elections makes it quicker to respond to changes in electoral forces than the Senate. A second possibility is that in fact (and perhaps because of its closer proximity to the "heats and passions" of the public) the House and its leadership are more important, more of the time, in congressional politics. Think how much more often the Speaker of the House is known, compared to the Senate leadership.

Conclusion

The historical patterns of CPG in the House and the Senate revealed especially in Figures 2.3 and 2.5 lead to several conclusions.

Table 2.4

Vector Autoregression for the House

($N = 54$)

Dependent Variable: CPG in House	Coefficient (Standard Error)
Constant	.017
	(.023)
House CPG Lag 1	.973*
	(.028)

*Indicates coefficient statistically significant at $p < .05$

Adj. $R^2 = .959$

$F(1, 52) = 1248.26$

Dependent Variable: CPG in House	Coefficient (Standard Error)
Constant	.018
	(.024)
House CPG Lag 1	.980*
	(.050)
Senate CPG Lag 1	−.008
	(.052)

*Indicates coefficient statistically significant at $p < .05$

Adj. $R^2 = .959$

$F(2, 51) = 612.46$

Perhaps the most remarkable is the regularity, even the smoothness, of the pattern over time in the two CPG measures, especially in the measure for the House. In that instance, the degree of party polarization is nearly constant from 1877 through about 1937. After those sixty years of consistently high degrees of party polarization, the House CPG began a thirty-year decline that was nearly linear, followed by a twenty-year resurgence that was also nearly linear and led the measure to rebound to very near its earlier high constant value. Insofar as we can compare the W-NOMINATE with D-NOMINATE scores for the House (as in Figure 2.3), it appears that the

Table 2.5

Vector Autoregression for the Senate

$(N = 54)$

Dependent Variable: CPG in Senate	Coefficient (Standard Error)
Constant	.038
	(.033)
Senate CPG Lag 1	.943*
	(.040)

*Indicates coefficient statistically significant at
$p < .05$
Adj. R^2 = .911
$F(1, 52)$ = 547.19

Dependent Variable: CPG in Senate	Coefficient (Standard Error)
Constant	.026
	(.033)
Senate CPG Lag 1	.853*
	(.072)
House CPG Lag 1	.104
	(.070)

*Indicates coefficient statistically significant at
$p < .05$
Adj. R^2 = .914
$F(2, 51)$ = 281.17

final decade of our time series represents a return to the long-term, historically high, and virtually constant level. The Senate CPG measure is less regular and less vividly *V*-shaped but is otherwise quite similar, with one exception. Around the 1920s, the Senate measure dipped noticeably for about a decade and then recovered until the end of the 1930s, when it, like that for the House, began its long decline and resurgence.

A second observation is of the post-Depression decline and resurgence *V* that is very vivid and strong. In the House, in fact, it is the only important variation in a century and a quarter. We will consider an explanation for this pattern shortly. Before doing so, however, these figures provide one more major conclusion.

As Figure 2.5 illustrates clearly, excepting only the 1920s, the House and Senate measures of CPG track each other closely (and even with the 1920s included, the correlation between chambers is .85). This striking similarity provides one set of clues for understanding the origin and nature of the historical patterns: look for explanations among those factors that affect the two chambers similarly. The most prominent factor of this sort is the political party, especially the party in the electorate. All theories of partisanship predict impacts of partisanship on voter choice, especially for elections to different chambers of the same legislature (and Gronke 2000 provides strong evidence for this prediction).

A fourth conclusion is that the most obvious possible explanations help us understand the observed patterns in CPG over time, at least in part. The most likely sources of variation in the Poole measures are changes in the electorate, changes in institutional structures that affect the party in Congress, or both. We will propose such an electoral-institutional explanation for the key time dynamic, the V decline and resurgence in the 1940s through 1980s. It is not clear, however, that these factors can easily explain the nearly complete lack of variation in the House measure at all other times. It also seems reasonable to propose that it was just such an amalgam of institutional and electoral changes that explains the dip in the Senate CPG measure in the 1920s. It is easy to imagine that direct election of senators would generate a decline from the highest levels of party polarization as senators competed in their individual states for a personal vote (to use more contemporary language). Less clear but possible within this explanation is the resurgence of polarization in Senate CPG in the New Deal era. The problem with this explanation is that it is very similar to that used by Katz and Sala (and others, see their citations, 1996) for the origin of a personal vote in the House. They pointed to the introduction of the secret ballot as the starting point for the rise of the personal vote for members of the House of Representatives. The House CPG measure, however, appears to be unaffected by the rise of a personal vote in the House in this time period. If so, we must conclude at least that if Katz and Sala are correct, it does not follow that the creation of a personal vote will necessarily affect the CPG measure, even though it might be a major explanation for the Senate patterns around the 1920s.

There is a relationship between chamber CPG and the internal organization of the chamber. Brady, Cooper, and Hurley (1979) describe three periods of internal institutional change characterizing the 50th to 90th Con-

Table 2.6

Party-Line Voting in the House
(amended percentages, Brady, Cooper, and Hurley periods)

Years	Characterization of Leadership	Percent Party-Line Voting
1890–1910	Centralized leadership plus caucus	68
1911–1939	Caucus	56
1940–1974	Neither	48
1975–1986	Caucus	45
1987–1994	Centralized leadership plus caucus	58

gresses (1890–1968); see Table 2.6. They describe 1890 to 1910 as a time of centralized party leadership and a strong party caucus, the House from 1911 to 1939 as having a strong party caucus but not strong leadership, and the House from 1940 to 1968 as having neither strong leadership nor a strong party caucus. In Table 2.6, we have extended the Brady, Cooper, and Hurley classification through the 103rd Congress (1993–94). We believe it reasonable to extend the "neither" category to run through 1974. We have divided the post-Watergate election period into two categories. The first, 1975 to 1986, we mark as a return to a strong caucus but lacking strong leadership in the majority party. In the remainder (1987–94), and thus beginning with Speakership of Jim Wright, the role of party leadership increased. In Table 2.6, we have also reported the percentage of party line votes in each of these periods (the measure Brady and colleagues employed —reporting a summary of CPG, which one can infer from Figure 2.3, yields similar conclusions).

Hurley and Wilson (1989) find many more changes in the party leadership structure of the Senate, as reported in Table 2.7. They consider three basic categories: centralized, decentralized, and individualized. Centralized has the strongest level of party leadership, while individualized has the least. Thus we would expect that centralized leadership should lead to relatively higher levels of party voting. Hurley and Wilson find ten periods from 1877 to 1986, the last period being one of intense individualization from 1969 to 1986. We modified the last, arguing that the election of Reagan and the Republican majority of 1981 began a period of centralized leadership from 1981 to the end of the data in 1994. While centralization may have been less than in the House under, say, Newt Gingrich, it was high for the more in-

Table 2.7

Party-Line Voting in the Senate
(amended percentages, Hurley-Wilson periods)

Years	Characterization of Leadership	Percent Party-Line Voting
1877–1885	Individualized	71
1885–1905	Centralized	72
1905–1911	Decentralized	70
1911–1917	Centralized	63
1917–1933	Individualized	53
1933–1937	Centralized	61
1937–1955	Decentralized	57
1955–1961	Decentralized/Individualized	42
1961–1969	Individualized	42
1969–1980	Intensely individualized	41
1981–1994	Centralized	48

dividualized Senate. That leads to the eleven-period categorization reported in Table 2.7.

We can use the over-time variation in the partisan institutional structures (as measured by periodizing dummy variables) to determine if they explain variation in CPG. The multiple correlation coefficient between CPG and the House institutional time periods is .87, while the comparable figure for the (more finely periodized) Senate is .98. This is a perhaps surprisingly high pair of correlations. Our belief is that it is not merely a relationship between floor voting and internal organization of the chambers but a relationship that is due primarily to the impact of the expression of preferences in partisan terms by the electorate.

By far the most interesting question, however, is the source of the dramatic decline and resurgence in CPG in both chambers in the 1938–94 period. Previous research (Aldrich and Rohde 1997a, 1997b, 1998; Berger 1999) has demonstrated how the condition in conditional party government has changed in the years following World War II. In this chapter, we have expanded the analysis to include the last 125 years and have confirmed that the postwar era, when examined within the context of the full time sample, is quite anomalous. As argued elsewhere (e.g., Rohde 1991), the results here are consistent with the dramatic changes in partisan forces in the postwar

South. Only with the breakup of the solid Democratic South, the creation of the Conservative Coalition cutting across party lines, and the emergence of civil rights on the national agenda would the partisan nature of congressional politics be disrupted. And with the diminishing place of civil rights on the national agenda, that disruption ended, and gradually, the more traditional pattern of partisan cleavages reemerged. It thus appears that a Congress divided more or less sharply, but almost invariably divided, by parties is the historical norm. The relative absence of party cleavages in the 1960s and 1970s is therefore the more anomalous circumstance.

Although changing preferences are very important, they do not tell the complete story about partisan outcomes such as the party voting measure considered here. When the condition in conditional party government is increasingly well satisfied, the evidence suggests that it is due to both preferential and internal institutional changes. The evidence thus supports the inference that it is precisely when the CPG condition is better satisfied that members have incentives to strengthen their partisan institutions so that the combination of preferences and institutions enhances satisfaction of the collective goals of their party.

Chapter 3

Do Parties Matter?

BARBARA SINCLAIR

Do parties matter? Congressional scholars have for decades assumed that parties do matter; they have written about Congress as if parties are important and have provided what they believed was ample evidence that parties affect how Congress operates and, to varying extents, influence the substance of the legislation produced. Yet a number of prominent political scientists, notably Keith Krehbiel, have contested what seemed obvious. Krehbiel (1991, 1993, 1997a, 1998) argues that little to no evidence of significant party behavior, as he defines it, can be found and that theories of congressional institutional arrangements and of lawmaking in the United States gain nothing, theoretically or in predictive power, by positing parties.

My purpose here is to critically assess Krehbiel's argument, suggest an alternative perspective, and test some hypotheses derived therefrom. My tests focus primarily on special rules in the House. I argue that indeed Congress cannot be understood in the absence of parties and that parties do affect outcomes. I focus on Krehbiel's formulations because they are so much more precise than those of others in the "parties don't matter" school.

The Controversy

Do parties in Congress matter? During the founding decades of modern political science, no scholar would have asked that question. Renowned political scientists like E. E. Schattschneider and James McGregor Burns might lament that parties didn't matter more, but they never questioned that they affect how Congress legislates. Many of the important congressional scholars of the 1960s such as Richard Fenno, Charles Jones, and John Manley, might focus on entities other than parties, especially committees, but they too saw parties as significant. Then, in 1974, in the enormously influential book *Congress: The Electoral Connection*, David Mayhew wrote that "no theoretical treatment of the United States Congress that posits parties as analytic units will go very far" (27). Rational choice theorists constructed models of congressional structure and decision making in which parties played no role (see Shepsle and Weingast [1994] for an authoritative review of this literature). And in 1991, Mayhew published another influential book, *Divided We Govern*, claiming that divided partisan control of the presidency and the Congress was irrelevant for legislative productivity.

In contrast, another group of congressional scholars wrote extensively about what they reported as a resurgence of partisanship and of party leadership activism in Congress, especially in the House of Representatives, during the 1980s (see Sinclair 1983, 1989a, 1992a, 1992b, 1995; Rohde 1991; Bach and Smith 1988; Smith 1989). Cox and McCubbins made parties the central feature of their formal model of Congress; they see parties as solutions to collective dilemmas and leaders as agents chosen by their members to further the collective goals of the party membership (1993: 107–36). Other less formal theoretical formulations in which parties play a major role appeared (Rohde 1991; Sinclair 1995). Rohde proposes a theory of conditional party government; he argues that when legislative preferences within each party are homogeneous and differences between the parties are substantial, political parties in the House exert predominant influence over policymaking and the majority party deflects outcomes from the chamber median toward the majority party median (Rohde 1991; Aldrich and Rohde 1997a: 2–4).

Like Cox and McCubbins and Rohde, I conceptualize leadership in legislatures as having been instituted to ameliorate problems of collective action (see Sinclair 1995, chap. 2). Since at least some of the time, the passage of legislation is necessary to advance their goals, members of Congress have an interest in developing and maintaining organizational forms that will allow them to overcome collective action problems and legislate. The House long ago decided to organize itself along both party and committee lines. The benefits of delegation to committees and party leaders can be great. Specifically, a party leadership well endowed with powers and resources can significantly facilitate the passage of legislation that furthers its membership's policy, reelection, and power goals. Yet delegation also carries risks; agents may use the powers they have been granted to pursue interests different from those of their principals.

Members can change the rules that delegate tasks, powers, and resources, and they have done so from time to time. They do so, I argue, when the costs and benefits of existing arrangements change and as a result, those arrangements no longer serve to advance their goals. A change in the homogeneity of party members' legislative preferences alters the costs and benefits to members of assertive versus restrained party leadership and consequently may lead members to increase or decrease the powers and resources delegated to the party leadership. Changes within the institution or in its political environment that alter the difficulty of enacting the legislation members need to advance their goals may thereby also alter the perceived costs and benefits to members of an assertive or restrained leadership and thus may lead members to expand or diminish the powers and resources they delegate to their party leadership.

Rohde and I differ from Cox and McCubbins (1993)—and considerably more from the formal distributive and informational theorists (Shepsle and Weingast, Krehbiel)—by focusing on and attempting to explain change over time. We contend that in the 1980s and 1990s, parties became increasingly consequential to how the House operates and to the legislative outcomes it produces.

A Critique of Krehbiel

How can similarly trained scholars look at the same phenomenon and see it so differently? Almost certainly the basis of the scholarly disagreement must lie in definitions and assumptions. Of the formulations denying the significance of parties, Krehbiel's work is by far the most precise and fully developed and has become increasingly influential (see Aldrich and Rohde 1997a; Evans and Oleszek 1997). Consequently, this is the work on which I focus.

Krehbiel defines and operationalizes "*significant* party behavior . . . as behavior that is independent of preferences" (1993: 235, emphasis in the original) and writes that a test of whether parties are important is if they "govern by passing laws that are different from those that would be passed in the absence of parties"(235). Critically, he asserts that the former is a necessary condition for the latter—only if the party induces members to behave independently of their preferences will the legislation that is passed be different from what would be passed in the absence of parties. I argue that this follows only if one accepts Krehbiel's basic assumptions.

Krehbiel assumes that the policy space is unidimensional and that "each player has an *ideal point* on the policy space, that is, a policy that yields greater benefits to the player than all other policies" (1998: 2, emphasis in the original). This formulation thus takes members' preferences as given; the determination of preferences is not considered in the model. It also regards the policy space as exogenously determined and does not deal with how the alternatives from which members choose are formulated and mapped into the policy space. All models must, of course, simplify. These simplifying assumptions are, however, problematic for the question at issue, as I shall argue; they assume away much of the political process in Congress and in the broader national political arena that is consequential for outcomes and in which parties may play a role.

If parties don't matter, how does Krehbiel explain the fact that members of Congress tend to vote along party lines, very strongly so in recent years? Krehbiel readily concedes that members of the two parties differ in their legislative preferences. His argument is that preferences, not party, drive the vote.

Krehbiel does not contest the influence of constituency on members' legislative preferences. He argues that constituency (and any other determinants) produce legislative preferences that are stable, at least over the course of a Congress, and that including party in one's model adds nothing theoretically or statistically.

Even if preferences are as stable as Krehbiel asserts, leaving out party leads to skewed as well as incomplete understanding, for it leaves out a key mechanism in the production of the distribution of preferences in Congress, as I argue elsewhere (Sinclair 1998a). If we do not know how legislative preferences are shaped, we can say little to nothing about the circumstances under which they—and therefore policy—are likely to change. However, if legislative preferences and how issues map into the policy space are less stable and more manipulable than Krehbiel contends and if the people in the best position to manipulate them are party leaders in and out of Congress, then the problem is even more basic.

Krehbiel argues that significant party behavior is manifest when "individual legislators vote with fellow party members *in spite of their disagreement* about the policy in question" (1993: 238, emphasis in the original). Thus only instances in which the party, presumably working through its elected leaders, induces a member to vote differently than he or she would if he or she voted on the basis of personal policy views and constituency opinion would qualify as significant party behavior according to Krehbiel. Under what circumstances might behavior meeting Krehbiel's definition arise? A member might change his or her vote in return for a party leader's promise of a good committee assignment or help obtaining a district project. If being liked and trusted by fellow party members is necessary for attaining an elected party position, peer pressure might on occasion induce a member to vote contrary to the dictates of constituency opinion and personal policy views. A same-party president might employ other inducements to sway a member's vote.

Such side payments as a major determinant of member behavior would be incongruent with Krehbiel's model. Although they certainly play some role, I do not contend that explicit quid pro quos are a major route of party influence on members' behavior, and in any case, data for testing that proposition would be difficult to gather. Another mechanism is, I believe, more important and more likely to yield convincing tests. The majority party, through its leaders, can sometimes influence the mapping of alternatives into the policy space and can sometimes structure the choices members confront so that members in voting their preferences vote in a way that is consistent with the party position.

Krehbiel purports to show that members' preferences predict their behavior and that knowing their party adds little or no predictive power (1998). Of course, if one conceptualizes legislative preferences as the members' preferences on the matter at issue, all things considered and immediately prior to the vote, the prediction is trivial. Krehbiel does not fall into that trap; he views legislative preferences as stable and as a function of constituency preferences and perhaps personal policy views but not of party influence. Krehbiel uses Poole and Rosenthal's (1985) NOMINATE scores as his measure of preferences. Since no direct measure of member preferences is available, various roll call–based measures are regularly used. However, in doing so, one must remember that all these measures are actually measures of behavior: roll call voting is public behavior by members of Congress. If party does influence members' behavior, roll call–based measures incorporate party effects. Without a more explicit model of party influence that to some extent deals with the formation of the legislative preferences immediately proximate to the vote, we cannot disentangle and test for party effects.

A Model of Party Influence

I posit that members' legislatively relevant behavior is a weighted function of (1) the member's own views of what constitutes good public policy, (2) the preferences of his or her electorally relevant constituents, and (3) the prefer-

ences of other career- and influence-relevant political actors (Fenno 1973).
I assume that factors 1 and 2 are more important than factor 3 and further
that the greater the likelihood that a given behavior will significantly affect
a member's reelection chances, the more heavily factor 2 will be weighted
vis-à-vis factor 1.

What determines the likelihood that some legislatively relevant behavior
will significantly affect a member's reelection? The exposition that follows
applies to all forms of such behavior, but for ease of exposition and con-
creteness, I will talk in terms of voting behavior. Arnold (1990: 84) has provided a convincing and nuanced but still tractable answer. In simplified
form, constituents' preferences or potential preferences on the alternatives at
issue, the intensity of their preferences or potential preferences, and the likelihood that potential preferences will become actual preferences must be
considered.

Can majority party leaders affect any of these components of the member's decision? Leaders, including, of course, the president, certainly try,
through their message strategies, to influence public preferences (see Sinclair
1998b; Stid 1996; Peters 1996; Drew 1996). They do not attempt to persuade directly; rather, great effort goes into attempts to define issues and
frame the debate. The mapping of issues and alternatives into the policy
space is a key part of the political process; treating it as exogenous severely
limits the scope of any model. Yet any sort of comprehensive examination of
that process is a major undertaking and is beyond the scope of this chapter.

Majority party leaders can be shown to influence the alternatives at issue
and may be able to influence the effective preferences of their members'
constituents by how alternatives are shaped. In particular, by bundling proposals into indivisible packages, leaders may be able to shape a package that
the constituents of a majority of party members (and usually much more
than a majority) prefer to the status quo, even if many of the components
individually are not preferred to the status quo. Packaging assumes a multidimensional issue space (though if packages are regularly party-sponsored,
voting may still fall along a unidimensional continuum; see Poole and Rosenthal, 1997: 35, 115–17). Even if one assumes a unidimensional issue space,
leaders can influence the impact of constituents' preferences by the choice
of the alternatives that come to a vote. If leaders can exclude certain alternatives from coming to a vote—those preferred by their members' constituents to the party position—then members can vote for the alternative most
preferred by their constituents *of those available*, and that will be the party
position.

Can leaders influence the intensity of constituents' preferences, the second component of concern to their members? Packaging can potentially be used to reduce constituents' intensity; leaders may produce a package that for the constituents of some of their members is not preferable to the status quo but is close enough that it reduces their intensity—they don't like it, but they don't hate it either. By adding alternatives, the leadership may also be able to reduce constituents' intensity. Leaders may construct and offer an alternative that, while not the constituents' most preferred, is more acceptable than the status quo. Such an alternative provides "cover" for members.

Finally, can leaders affect the likelihood that potential preferences become actual preferences and intense ones? Some of the determinants of this likelihood are inherent to policy design, which I do not consider here (but see Arnold 1990, esp. chaps. 2 and 5); others, such as the actions of their opponents, are clearly beyond the control of the party leaders. Yet to the extent that procedure affects the likelihood, majority party leaders do have considerable control. Information is central for potential preferences to become actual preferences; constituents are more likely to receive sufficient information if the policy battle is clear-cut and highly visible. Through procedure, leaders can affect clarity and visibility. When procedures are structured so that key decisions come on procedural rather than substantive votes, clarity and visibility are reduced; when the vote is on big packages rather than individual policy proposals, clarity is less; "diversionary" alternatives can also reduce clarity.

Leaders may be able to affect the impact of constituents' preferences and the likelihood of potential preferences' becoming actual preferences by keeping certain issues off the floor of the House. Even if one assumes a unidimensional issue space on which all possible policy proposals on all possible issues can be arrayed, no legislature will consider all possible issues; it simple lacks the time. Majority party leaders in the House schedule legislation for floor consideration and thus act as gatekeepers, at least in the literal sense. If leaders keep a policy proposal that their members' constituents prefer to the status quo off the floor, those constituent preferences have no effect on outcomes. What happens in the prefloor legislative process is less well understood by most citizens and less public than floor action, so when proposals are blocked before they get to the floor, the reasons and the responsibility are often unclear. Furthermore, since floor consideration is likely to raise the visibility of a policy proposal, keeping it off the floor is likely to decrease the likelihood that potential preferences become actual.

Proponents of the majoritarian model will immediately object that any such attempts to "manipulate" members' behavior will be foiled by the

House's majoritarian rules; if leaders attempt to induce members to act against their preferences, they can and will be voted down or circumvented (Krehbiel 1991). Thus if leaders attempt to block majority-preferred proposals from getting to the floor by refusing to schedule them, the majority can force floor consideration through a discharge petition, which simply requires the signatures of a majority of House members. If leaders attempt through special rules to manipulate members' choices on the floor so as to prevent members from voting on their most preferred alternative, a majority can defeat the rule or, by defeating the previous question, amend the rule to its liking. The infrequency of successful discharge petitions or of rules defeated on the floor, pure majoritarians would argue, indicates that leaders do not attempt to block majority-supported proposals or alternatives from floor consideration.

Why might members of the House majority party assent to having their choices constrained or otherwise manipulated? Why might members willingly allow their leaders to keep certain issues off the floor? Why might members agree to having their choices constrained by restrictive special rules? In a model in which preferences are exogenous and fixed, a majority should allow leaders to keep off the floor only those proposals that they prefer less than the status quo; even then, the majority should not prefer that the proposal be kept off the floor since, were it brought up, it would be defeated; only time considerations would favor keeping such proposals off the floor. In the fixed, exogenous preferences model, a majority should favor a closed rule only if the bill at issue is at the majority's ideal point, and if that is the case, the closed rule should be unnecessary, since that bill should be able to defeat all alternatives. Similarly, majorities should oppose restrictive rules if in fact the rule makes a difference in outcome.

Krehbiel does offer a rationale for restrictive rules within the majoritarian model. He argues that they are inducements offered to committees to specialize and share their expertise. Within this formulation, rules are tools of the House majority, not of the majority party. Members approve restrictive rules for expert, representative, heterogeneous committees, especially on legislation with minority party support; and restrictive rules do little to deflect the outcome from the chamber median (Krehbiel 1991: 151–92).

My formulation offers a different answer. Members might well vote for procedures that aid them in successfully balancing their sometimes competing goals; specifically, members may vote for procedures that allow them to weight their own policy preferences or those of actors they need to satisfy to further their power goal more heavily vis-à-vis their constituents' preferences. (For scholars uncomfortable with positing that members have personal policy goals, one could substitute the policy goals of their activist supporters, which they are in fact likely to share, and the logic would be much the same.)

Rules and Parties

To reiterate and state more concretely, I contend that the majority party in the House, through its elected party leaders, uses procedural strategies to affect legislative outcomes. The leaders do this through their scheduling powers by, for example, keeping certain proposals from reaching the floor. Instances of such strategic behavior can be cited—the minimum wage increase in 1999–2000, for example. Cox and McCubbins's study of majority party roll rates on passage votes in Chapter 5 strongly suggests that majority leaders commonly keep off the floor legislation opposed by a majority of their members. Still, studying such negative agenda control directly raises difficulties. Leaders also use packaging, the exclusion of alternatives (rather than entire proposals), and providing cover to affect legislative outcomes. Since most of these procedural strategies require special rules to implement, they can be more easily studied. Most major legislation is brought to the floor under a special rule from the Rules Committee and requires majority assent from the House for approval. Thus the number of cases is substantial, and recorded votes provide some basis for inferences about members' preferences on both the procedure and the substance of the proposals at issue.

To support my contention, three questions must be answered in the affirmative. Do special rules have the effect of implementing the procedural strategies of packaging, exclusion of alternatives, and providing cover? Are special rules tools of the majority party? Do special rules make a difference in legislative outcomes?

Do Special Rules Structure Choices?

Toward the end of the nineteenth century, special rules from the Rules Committee developed as a device for controlling and thus rationalizing the order in which legislation was considered on the House floor (Oppenheimer 1994). Rules could also regulate the amending process, but until the 1970s, most were simple open rules that allowed all germane amendments; a small proportion were closed rules barring all but committee-sponsored amendments. In the late 1970s, rules began to become more complex, and since

Table 3.1

Change in the Character of House Special Rules

Congress	Years	% Restrictive	% Closed
95th	1977–78	15	3
96th	1979–80	25	5
97th	1981–82	25	5
98th	1983–84	32	0
99th	1985–86	43	4
100th	1987–88	46	12
101st	1989–90	55	14
102nd	1991–92	66	16
103rd	1993–94	70	9
104th	1995–96	54	15

NOTE: Totals include rules for initial consideration of legislation, except rules on appropriations bills, which only waive points of order. SOURCES: Compiled by Donald Wolfensberger, minority counsel, House Committee on Rules. Data for 104th Congress from House Committee on Rules, "Survey of Activities of the House Committee on Rules 104th Congress," Report 104-868, Washington, D.C.: Government Printing Office, 1996.

then, rules that restrict amending activity in some way have become the norm rather than the exception (see Table 3.1). However, most restrictive rules are not closed rules but so-called modified closed rules, which restrict amendments to a specified and limited list, or modified open rules, which restrict amendments to a specified but long list, place a time limit on the amending process, or place some requirement on amendments, such as submitting them to the Rules Committee by a certain time or preprinting them in the *Congressional Record*.

Do these special rules in fact have the effect of implementing the procedural strategies of packaging, exclusion of alternatives, and providing cover? My examination of special rules focuses on special rules for major measures, defined as legislation *Congressional Quarterly* identified as such in its contemporaneous lists plus measures on which key votes occurred, again according to *Congressional Quarterly*. If rules are strategic tools of the majority party leadership, as I am arguing, one would expect them to be employed as such on major legislation more frequently than on less important and presumably

Table 3.2

Excluding Alternatives: Rule Type on Major Legislation (%)

	CONGRESS			
Rule Type	*100th*	*101st*	*103rd*	*104th*
Open	28.6	27.9	18.6	27.8
Modified open	28.6	27.9	20.9	16.7
Modified closed	31.4	32.6	48.8	44.4
Closed	11.4	11.6	11.6	11.1
N	35	43	43	54
Modified closed, non-appropriations bills	33.3	36.8	51.4	47.1

less contentious legislation. My data consist of all major measures considered on the House floor under special rules in the 100th (1987–88), 101st (1989–90), 103rd (1993–94), and 104th (1995–96) Congresses.[1]

EXCLUDING ALTERNATIVES

Restrictive rules, by definition, exclude alternatives that would otherwise be in order. As Table 3.2 shows, in each of these Congresses, more than 70 percent of the rules for major measures did restrict alternatives to some extent. In the 100th and 101st, about 43 percent of rules were either closed or modified closed and thus restricted alternatives substantially; in the 103rd and 104th, over 55 percent of rules did so. Closed rules were no more frequent in the latter pair of Congresses than in the former; the increase in the restrictiveness of rules occurred in the modified closed category. If regular appropriations bills, which have traditionally been considered under open rules, are excluded, the proportion of modified closed rules and the increase in such rules is even greater.

What sort of alternatives are excluded by restrictive rules? Were alternatives excluded that an appreciable number of members favored or wanted a vote on or just time-wasting amendments supported by a tiny fringe? Were there amendments that might well have passed? No systematic analysis of all 175 cases is possible; for most of the examples I provide, these questions cannot be answered definitively. Yet the answers are suggestive.

In the 100th Congress, the modified closed rule for the omnibus trade bill excluded all product-specific amendments. The closed rule for the highway bill of course barred all amendments, including one to raise the speed limit that a number of members wanted to offer and that a vote soon thereafter showed to have majority support (*Congressional Quarterly Weekly Report*, January 24, 1987: 169–70). The modified closed rule for the welfare reform bill did not allow a vote on the Carper amendment severely cutting spending, even though most Republicans and an appreciable number of Democrats—probably enough to make a majority—seemed to support it (*Congressional Quarterly Weekly Report*, December 19, 1987: 3157). The modified open rule for the AIDS policy bill nevertheless excluded amendments requiring physicians to notify the spouse of anyone diagnosed as having AIDS and requiring mandatory testing of all Americans (*Congressional Quarterly Weekly Report*, September 17, 1988: 2585). In the 101st Congress, the modified closed rule for the minimum wage bill barred the Petri amendment to substitute an increase in the earned income tax credit for the increase in the minimum wage. In the 103rd, the closed rule for Clinton's stimulus program barred the Stenholm amendment, which would have required offsetting spending increases, an amendment probably supported by a majority. In the 104th, the modified closed rule for the welfare reform bill barred several amendments supported by antiabortion Republicans that softened the bill and thus would probably have garnered Democratic support (*Congressional Quarterly Weekly Report*, March 18, 1995: 814; March 25, 1995: 872–75). The modified closed rule for the tax bill disallowed a vote on an amendment to reduce the income ceiling on families eligible for the $500-per-child tax credit to $95,000, even though 102 Republicans had signed a letter asking for such a vote and most Democrats favored it. The modified closed rule for the defense authorization bill allowed no amendments that would trim any of the National Security Committee's add-ons to President Clinton's budget request, not even those proposed by Republicans (*Congressional Quarterly Weekly Report*, May 11, 1996: 1310).

STRATEGIC PACKAGING

Are restrictive rules used to hold together complex legislative packages? Or to be more cautious in phrasing, are such packages more likely to be considered under restrictive rules than other legislation? Table 3.3 shows that omnibus legislation is much more likely to be considered under restrictive rules; during these four Congresses, not a single omnibus measure was considered under an open rule, and nearly 88 percent were considered under either modified closed or closed rules. Omnibus measures include budget resolutions, reconciliation bills, continuing resolutions and some other big bills, such as the omnibus trade and drug bills in the 100th Congress. Thus most

Table 3.3

Holding Packages Together:

Rule Type on Major Omnibus Legislation (%)

	RULE TYPE				
Omnibus	*Open*	*Modified open*	*Modified closed*	*Closed*	*N*
Yes	0	12.5	70.8	16.7	24
No	29.1	24.5	35.8	10.6	151
All bills	25.1	22.9	40.6	11.4	175

of the measures that derived from presidential-congressional summits are included (Sinclair 1997). However, not all bills that resulted from high-level
negotiations were classified as omnibus measures, though all were complex
packages. Thus the compromise Contra aid package worked out by Congress and President Bush in 1989 was not an omnibus measure. Nor are two
other packages worked out in high-level bargaining between the Democratic and Republican congressional leaderships—a compromise Contra aid
package in 1988 and an ethics and pay raise package in 1989. All three of
these deals were considered on the House floor under closed rules.

PROVIDING COVER

A rule or other procedure provides cover to members when it makes it easier or less likely to be necessary for them to explain their legislative behavior to their constituents. For example, if a procedure makes a decision less
visible to constituents, it might provide cover for members who want, for
whatever reason, to support the decision but fear it will be unpopular with
their constituents. Self-executing rules, which are rules that provide for the
automatic adoption of an amendment or other matter upon the adoption of
the rule, are possible tools for providing cover because they eliminate the
need for a separate vote on the substance of the matter. The open rule for
the Department of Transportation appropriations bill in 1989 contained a
self-executing provision providing for the adoption of the Durbin amendment making permanent the ban on smoking on flights lasting two hours or
more. According to *Congressional Quarterly*, tobacco-state members, convinced that the Durbin amendment would pass on the floor, asked for the
self-executing procedure to be used to avoid a vote (*Congressional Quarterly
Almanac*, 1989: 754). Self-executing rules were rarely used until recently;

they averaged two per Congress from the 95th through the 98th (1977–84); the Congresses since the mid-1980s, in contrast, have averaged about twenty self-executing rules each (see source note to Table 3.1; data are for the 99th through the 104th Congresses but excluding the 103rd).

Packaging can also provide cover for members. The big reconciliation bills of the 1990s and before have included less than popular provisions—tax increases in 1993 and entitlement cuts in 1995, for example. Restrictive rules protected supporters from having to vote on such provisions individually.

Cover can also take the form of giving members something to vote for that will make explaining their behavior easier. When something very popular is packaged with something less palatable, members can explain the vote for the package containing the latter in terms of their desire for the former. For example, in 1996, the line-item veto was added as a sweetener to the debt limit increase, which Republicans had to pass but hated voting for. One of the three amendments made in order by the modified closed rule for the 1990 civil rights bill stated that "nothing in the act shall be construed to require an employer to adopt hiring or promotion quotas" (*Congressional Quarterly Weekly Report*, August 2, 1990: 2517). When a furor over two arts grants for supposedly obscene art gave opponents of the National Endowment for the Arts ammunition for seeking to cut funding drastically, supporters offered an amendment cutting the exact amount of the controversial grants—less than $200,000. In 1994, a time of intense concern about the deficit, the supplemental appropriations bill for disaster aid was a target of budget hawks, who intended to offer amendments for large offsetting cuts. In response, supporters offered their own amendment for a much more modest offset, thus providing members who wanted to show fiscal discipline a less draconian way of doing so (*Congressional Quarterly Weekly Report*, February 5, 1994: 272).

The so-called king-of-the-hill procedure offers another means of providing cover. A king-of-the-hill provision in a rule specifies that a series of amendments or substitutes are to be voted on in order, and the last one that receives a majority prevails. This device makes possible a direct vote on each of several alternatives; in ordinary parliamentary procedure, if an amendment or substitute receives a majority, no vote on the original (unamended) version of the legislation ever occurs. Clearly, when this procedure is employed, the amendment or substitute voted on last is advantaged. The procedure also makes it possible for members to vote for more than one version, which is sometimes politically advantageous.

The first such rule was crafted for consideration of the budget resolution in 1982. Thereafter, during the period of Democratic control of the House, budget resolutions were often considered under a king-of-the-hill rule. Members were thus guaranteed a vote on each of the substitute versions of the resolution made in order by the rule—usually a Black Caucus version, which provided liberals with an opportunity to go on the record for a version they and many of their constituents preferred to the less generous committee majority version, and two Republican substitutes. The House Budget Committee version was always placed in the advantageous last position.

The rule for the 1991 civil rights bill also contained a king-of-the-hill procedure. The rule gave liberals a vote on their much stronger version but put that substitute first in line. Having cast a vote in favor of the tough bill civil rights activists favored, these members then could support the leadership compromise. The rule next gave House Republicans and the Bush administration a vote on their preferred version. It put the Democratic compromise last in the advantaged position.

In 1993, Republican Benjamin Gilman invoked the War Powers Act to force House consideration of his resolution calling on President Clinton to withdraw U.S. troops from Somalia by January 31, 1994, rather than March 31, as Clinton had promised. The resolution was considered under a king-of-the hill procedure, with Gilman's provision to change the date to January 31 voted on first and the substitute amendment of Lee Hamilton, chairman of the House Foreign Affairs Committee, to change the deadline back to March 31 voted on second. The Gilman amendment passed, with the support of fifty-five Democrats. It was then superseded by the Hamilton amendment, which also passed; twenty-four Democrats voted for both amendments (*Congressional Quarterly Weekly Report*, October 30, 1993: 2987–88; November 13, 1993: 3139).

To this point, I have attempted to discuss the impact of special rules without prejudging who is responsible or even if the impact was calculated. This discussion was intended and, I believe, has shown that special rules can have the effect of excluding alternatives, holding packages together, and providing cover. It is usually but not always restrictive rules that do so.

Are Special Rules Party Leadership Tools?

To show that special rules are indeed party leadership tools, I need to answer three questions in the affirmative: Can majority party leaders control the form that rules take? Does the pattern of restrictive rule use conform with what we would expect if majority party leaders used rules to advance the majority party's interests (and conflict with what we would expect under

Krehbiel's information theory)? Does the pattern of member behavior on rule and passage votes conform to what we would expect if rules are used to advance majority party interests?

CAN PARTY LEADERS INFLUENCE RULES?

Changes in party rules have given majority party leaders the power to influence the crafting of special rules. In 1974, new Democratic caucus rules granted the Democratic Speaker the right, at the beginning of each Congress, to nominate the Democratic members and the chairman of the Rules Committee, subject only to caucus ratification. The Republicans followed suit in the 1980s, giving their party leader power to choose Republican Rules Committee members. Party leaders choose and can remove their party's members of Rules, which remains a coveted assignment. In interviews, Rules Committee members and party leaders freely attest to leadership influence on the form of rules, and other House members and close observers uniformly report that as well. Thus majority party leaders can and do influence the crafting of special rules (Sinclair 1995: 136–62). Those rules must, of course, be able to command a majority on the House floor.

The majority party leadership may be able to influence the form of the special rules the Rules Committee reports, but does it use that influence to further the interests of the majority party? Or as Krehbiel posits, are restrictive rules used to induce committee members to specialize and to share their knowledge with other members?

WHEN ARE RESTRICTIVE RULES USED?

Hypotheses. If majority party leaders attempt to use restrictive rules to further the interests of their party, they will employ them on measures that are both especially important to the party and face a potential problem on the floor. One would thus expect restrictive rules to be used on omnibus legislation, much of which is centrally important to the majority party's governing reputation and which, as a big package, is vulnerable to being picked apart on the floor. The same considerations would dictate the use of restrictive rules on other package deals between the majority party leadership and either the president or the leaders' minority party counterparts. If the reporting committee or committees split along partisan lines, the measure is likely to face more problems on the floor than if committee action was consensual, and the issues that split committee members along party lines are likely to be of importance to party members. So one would expect restrictive rules to be more frequently employed when committee action was partisan. Majority party leadership involvement on a measure signals that the measure is important to party members and, usually, that there is some expectation of problems (Sinclair 1995). (The leadership has far too much to do to involve itself, especially in a major way, on legislation expected to have completely smooth sailing.) One would thus expect the frequency in the use of restrictive rules to vary with the extent of majority party leadership involvement. Legislation on the majority party leadership's agenda and, to a lesser extent, that on the president's agenda also meet the criterion of being important to the majority party. However, such legislation can vary considerably in its vulnerability, so predictions are less certain.

To choose between two theories, one needs a critical test: a pair of cleanly testable hypotheses that predict clearly opposing results in the two theories. Some of my indicators of importance to the majority party and vulnerability lend themselves to alternative interpretations and thus do not provide that test. Omnibus legislation is complex legislation, and one could argue that it is the complexity per se that triggers restrictive rule use, a claim not inconsistent with Krehbiel's information theory. An adherent to nonpartisan information theory might even argue that majority party leaders really act as chamber leaders and that their involvement in legislation is triggered solely by chamber, not partisan, concerns. Committee partisanship does provide the critical test.

The Impact of Committee Partisanship. The committee partisanship hypothesis provides a direct test of the partisan theory versus Krehbiel's informational theory. A key hypothesis Krehbiel derives from his theory states, "The greater the minority party's support for a committee's bill, the greater will be the probability that the bill receives a restrictive rule" (1991: 166). As Krehbiel points out:

> The clearest example of competing empirical and theoretical claims in the context of restrictive rules is provided by the (empirical) partisanship claim and the (theoretical) confirmatory signaling hypothesis. The partisanship claim holds that restrictive rules are often, if not always, tools of the majority party. . . . We would expect a positive relationship between majority support for bills and the propensity of majority leaders to [use restrictive rules]. The confirmatory signaling hypothesis, in contrast, holds that rules are tools of chamber majorities that are deliberately deployed to elicit committees' private information. We would expect then to see a positive relationship between minority support for

Table 3.4

Relationship Between Committee Partisanship
and Rule Type (%)

Rule Type	ALL MAJOR BILLS COMMITTEE PARTISAN		OMNIBUS MEASURES COMMITTEE PARTISAN	
	No	*Yes*	*No*	*Yes*
Open	36.2	13.8	0	0
Modified open	27.7	17.5	33.3	0
Modified closed	24.5	58.8	55.6	80.0
Closed	11.7	10.0	11.1	20.0
N	94	80	9	15

bills and the use of restrictive rules. Why? Because minority support is a credible confirmatory signal. . . . (167)

Clearly, Krehbiel's theory predicts that legislation that committees' report by bipartisan or consensual action should be more likely to receive a restrictive rule than legislation reported by partisan action.

Because committee partisanship provides a crucial test between the theories, a look at the bivariate relationship between that variable and rule type is warranted before proceeding to the multivariate analysis. Committee action on a measure was coded as having been partisan if the committee's approval vote on the measure was a party vote or, when the bill was reported by a voice vote, minority party committee leaders spoke against and opposed the bill during general debate and all minority party committee members who spoke during general debate opposed the legislation.[2]

Committee action was partisan on 46 percent of the measures, with the frequency increasing over the course of these four Congresses. In the 100th and 101st Congresses, committees were partisan in only one-third of the cases; by the 104th, committee action was partisan almost two-thirds of the time. Committee action was more likely to be partisan on omnibus measures than on other measures; nearly 63 percent of all omnibus measures were partisan at the committee stage.

As Table 3.4 shows, measures on which the committee was partisan were much more likely to be considered under restrictive rules than those on which the committee was not partisan. Note especially that a quarter of

Table 3.5

Models of Rule Choice

Independent Variables	Model 1	Model 2
Leadership involvement	.92*	.55*
	(.25)	(.25)
Committee partisanship	1.26*	1.29*
	(.38)	(.38)
Omnibus/Summit	1.85*	1.96*
	(.67)	(.68)
Leaders' agenda	−.56	—
	(.44)	
President's agenda	.47	—
	(.45)	
Special	—	1.55*
		(.40)
Constant	−1.96*	−1.80*
	(.42)	(.40)
Percent correctly predicted	72	73
Cox&Snell R^2	.27	.29
Nagelkerke R^2	.36	.38

NOTE: Numbers in parentheses are standard errors.
*Significant at the .05 level or better.

nonpartisan measures but almost 60 percent of partisan measures were considered under modified closed rules. The same pattern holds for omnibus measures; although all omnibus measures were likely to be considered under restrictive rules, those that emerged from partisan committee processes received more restrictive rules than those that did not.

Multivariate Analysis. For the multivariate analysis, I dichotomize rule type as Krehbiel does by combining open and modified open into an unrestrictive category (49 percent of the cases) and combining modified closed and closed into a restrictive category (51 percent of the cases). Table 3.5 shows the results of the first tentative model proposed previously in the text. Committee partisanship, leadership involvement,[3] and the omnibus variable (which includes the top-level deals as mentioned in the text)[4] are correctly signed and robustly significant and the overall fit is quite good. The agenda

Table 3.6
Evaluating the Model's Accuracy of Prediction

Rule Type	Mean Predicted Probability Restrictive	Percent Accurately Predicted
Open	.298	82.2
Modified open	.424	52.5
Modified closed	.640	74.3
Closed	.729	89.5

variables, however, are not significant. Multicolinearity is something of a problem, but the conceptualization may also be. One should not expect the leadership to use restrictive rules on a party or presidential agenda item, regardless of its importance to the party, unless there was a need to do so. To capture both importance and need, a variable that is the interaction between major leadership involvement and the president's agenda was constructed. As I argued, majority party leadership involvement on a measure signals that the measure is important to party members and, usually, that there is some expectation of problems. When in addition, the measure is an item on the president's agenda, the stakes are heightened. The variable is also coded 1 for measures on the leadership's agenda that the leaders declare as urgent at the beginning of a Congress.[5]

Model 2 in Table 3.5 shows the results. All the explanatory variables are correctly signed and significant. The fit is quite good, with the model decreasing errors of prediction by about 45 percent over the null model (1 minus 47/85). Given the imprecision of my measures of legislative vulnerability and the fact that modified open and even sometimes open rules can be strategically used, the 73 percent correct prediction seems quite respectable.

Because underlying the dichotomous dependent variable is an ordered four-category variable, some further tests of the adequacy of the model are possible. An examination of the relationship between the four types of rules and mean probability of the rule's being restrictive predicted by model 2 shows that the model does distinguish among all four types of rules; the mean probability of restrictiveness is considerably less for open rules than for modified open rules; it is higher for closed than for modified closed rules (see Table 3.6). The model predicts open and closed rules very well and modified closed rules quite well; it is least successful in its prediction of modified open rules, which are a borderline category.

Can we also show that the pattern of member behavior conforms to what we would expect if rules are used to advance the majority party's interests? What are our expectations about how members vote on rule and passage votes if, on the one hand, Krehbiel is correct or if, on the other hand, rules are tools used to advance majority party interests?

In Krehbiel's informational theory, members do cast procedural votes, on rules, for example, that may be independent of or at least not totally dictated by their preferences on the underlying bill. According to Krehbiel, since rules are not and cannot be use to deflect outcomes (much) from the chamber median, members do not base their rule votes on their preferences about whether the procedure does so (or only to vote down rules that attempt to deflect outcomes from the chamber median). Members may cast procedural votes to encourage specialization and information sharing. However, since party membership does not affect members' behavior independent of their fixed preferences, party membership should not affect members' rule votes independent of their preferences on the underlying bill. In Krehbiel's theory, partisan voting on rules must simply reflect member preferences on the underlying bill.

An analysis of the range of possible interpretations of members' rule votes within the context of the partisan and informational theories provides the basis for some testable propositions. If a member votes for a rule, he or she may do so because the member (1) supports the bill (prefers it over the status quo) in its present form, (2) does not prefer the bill in its present form over the status quo but believes there is some chance it will be changed on the floor in such a way that he or she will support it or (3) supports the procedure even though he or she does not support the bill, perhaps for party-related reasons. If a member votes against a rule, he or she may do so because (1) the member opposes the bill (prefers the status quo to the bill) and does not believe there is a real chance it will be changed on the floor in such a way that he or she will support it or (2) opposes the procedure, perhaps for party-related reasons, even though he or she supports the bill. To make inferences possible, I assume that members vote sincerely on passage: they vote for the bill if they prefer it over the status quo and against it if they prefer the status quo to the bill.

The voting patterns of members who vote for the rule and for the bill or against the rule and against the bill are consistent with the simple bill preference scenario. If all members simply voted their bill preferences, the rule vote and the passage vote should be identical, at least for measures not changed on the floor, and that should be true for both the partisan majority and the partisan minority. Regressing the rule vote (percent yes) on the passage vote (percent yes) provides a test. For the majority party, the relationship for all measures is significant but weak ($R^2 = .03$); the relationship is somewhat stronger for the minority party, but still not impressive ($R^2 = .16$). Of course, legislation may be changed, even drastically, on the floor. Are the relationships as expected if only those measure not significantly altered on the floor are examined? The relationships are stronger ($R^2 = .07$ for the majority party and $R^2 = .28$ for the minority party), but clearly, rule votes and passage votes are not simply duplicates.

Substantial numbers of members vote for a rule and against the bill or against the rule and for the bill. What can we infer from these patterns? If a member votes for the rule and against the bill *and the bill was not substantially changed on the floor*, then the member cannot have preferred the bill to the status quo. So either the changes the member hoped for did not occur on the floor, or the member cast a procedural vote, that is, a vote based on preferences over procedures rather than over substance. If the rule was closed, then the member knew no changes could be made on the floor and so cast a procedural vote. Party theory contends that restrictive rules are majority party leadership tools and can affect floor outcomes and thus predicts that members should cast procedural votes as here defined along party lines. Thus majority party members should be more likely to vote for the rule and against the bill than minority party members, and the more restrictive the rule is, the more likely they should be to do so. Minority party members who oppose the bill as it came to the floor should be more likely to vote for a rule the more nearly open it is either because they believe they can make desired changes or because they are casting a vote based on preferences about procedure.

If a member votes against the rule and for the bill *and the bill was not substantially changed on the floor*, then the member cannot have preferred the status quo to the bill. Therefore, the member cast a procedural vote. Party theory predicts that minority party members should more often evince this pattern than majority party members and that minority party members who favor the bill as it came to the floor over the status quo should be less likely to vote for a rule the more restrictive it is (see Table 3.7).

To summarize, I expect majority party members to be more likely to vote for the rule and against the bill than minority party members, and minority party members to be more likely to vote against the rule and for the bill than majority party members. In both cases, the differences should increase as the restrictiveness of the rules increases (see Table 3.8).

Table 3.7

Possible Interpretations of Rule Votes

Motion	Vote	Possible Interpretations
Rule	Yes	(1) MC supports the bill (prefers it over the status quo) in its present form.
		(2) MC does not prefer the bill in its present form over the status quo but believes there is some chance it will be changed on the floor in such a way that MC will support it.
		(3) MC supports the procedure even though he or she does not support the bill, perhaps for party-related reasons.
Rule	No	(1) MC opposes the bill (prefers the status quo to the bill) and does not believe there is a real chance it will be changed on the floor in such a way that he or she will support it.
		(2) MC opposes the procedure, perhaps for party-related reasons, even though he or she supports the bill.
Passage	Yes	MC prefers bill to the status quo (by assumption)
Passage	No	MC prefers status quo to the bill (by assumption)

NOTE: MC = Member of Congress

In contrast, Krehbiel's informational theory predicts that the frequency of neither pattern should be causally related to members' party identification. However, since party is related to members' policy preferences, one might reasonably infer from Krehbiel's theory that the "yes on rule, no on passage" pattern should be more frequent among minority than majority party members. Assuming that the passage vote reflects a member's policy preferences and that the rule vote reflects the member's information-based procedural preferences, minority party members, who will often be members of a policy minority as well, should more often be faced with rules that they favor for informational reasons for the consideration of bills they oppose on policy preference grounds.

Table 3.9 shows that the data largely bear out expectations of the party theory and not those of the informational theory. Using the difference in percentage yes on the rule vote and percentage yes on the passage vote for bills not changed on the floor as the indicator, one finds that majority party members are likely to vote at a higher rate for the rule than for passage and that the difference does tend to increase with the restrictiveness of the rule.[6] When the proportion of bills on which the majority voted at a higher

Table 3.8

Inferences from Rule and Passage Vote Patterns when the Bill Was Not Substantially Changed on the Floor

Rule	Pass	Deductions About Rule Vote	Relationship to/Predictions from Theories
Y	Y	Simple bill preference vote (pro)	Consistent with Krehbiel; not inconsistent with party
N	N	Simple bill preference vote (anti)	Same
Y	N	MC did not prefer bill to the status quo. So either (1) The changes the MC hoped for did not occur on the floor, or (2) The MC cast a procedural vote (pro-procedure). If the rule was closed, the MC knew no changes could be make on the floor, so the MC cast a procedural vote.	Krehbiel: Pattern not related to MC's party Party theory: Majority party pattern If MCs believe restrictive rules are majority party leadership tools, majority party MCs should be more likely to vote for the rule and against the bill than minority party MCs, and the more restrictive the rule is, the more likely they should be to do so. Minority party MCs (who oppose the bill as it comes to the floor) should be more likely to vote for a rule the more nearly open it is because either (1) they are more likely to believe they can make desired changes or (2) they are casting a vote based on preferences about procedure.
N	Y	The MC did not prefer the status quo to the bill. So the MC cast a procedural vote (anti-procedure).	Krehbiel: Pattern not related to MC's party Party theory: Minority party pattern If MCs believe restrictive rules are majority party tools, minority party MCs more often than majority party MCs should vote against the rule even though they favor the bill, and the more restrictive the rule, the more likely minority party MCs (who favor the bill as it comes to the floor over the status quo) should be to vote against the rule.

NOTE: MC = Member of Congress.

Table 3.9

Majority and Minority Party Patterns on Rule and Passage Votes
(on measures not significantly changed on House floor*)

	% YES ON RULE − % YES ON PASSAGE		% CONFORMING CASES**	
Rule Type	*Majority*	*Minority*	*Majority*	*Minority*
Open	4.5	25.1	64.5	71.0
Modified open	3.5	−8.4	71.4	71.4
Modified closed	5.4	−5.4	81.3	60.4
Closed	17.6	−11.9	85.0	55.0

*N = 120.

**Conforming cases are for the majority, cases on which percent yes on the rule is greater than percent yes on passage; for the minority, if rule is open, cases on which percent yes on the rule is greater than percent yes on passage; if rule is MO, MC, or C, cases on which percent yes on the rule is less than percent yes on passage. Nonconforming cases include those on which percent yes on the rule equal percent yes on passage.

rate on the rule than on passage is examined, the pattern is similar; in only 11 percent of the cases did the reverse pattern appear. These patterns hold whether the majority is Democratic or Republican. Note especially that the difference is much greater for closed than for other rules (17.6 percentage points and 85 percent of the bills). These are procedural votes; knowing that the bill could not be changed on the floor and preferring the status quo to the bill, majority party members nevertheless voted for the rule. This would seem to fit Krehbiel's definition of party behavior.

In contrast and again as predicted by party theory, minority party members tended to vote for passage at a higher rate than they voted for the rule so long as the rule was at all restrictive. These patterns hold whether the minority is Democratic or Republican. The difference between rule and passage vote was greatest on closed rules, which, as I have argued, can be interpreted as procedural votes. However, minority party members were a great deal more likely to vote for the rule than for final passage when the rule was completely open. Either they believed they had a reasonable chance of altering these bills, something they did not believe about bills brought up under modified open or modified closed rules, or they cast a vote indicating approval of the procedure. Both strongly suggest these members believe procedure affects outcomes.

Do Rules and Parties Affect Outcomes?

I contend that the majority party in the House, through its elected party leaders, uses procedural strategies to affect legislative outcomes. To support my contention, I have shown that special rules do have the effect of implementing the procedural strategies of packaging, exclusion of alternatives, and providing cover and that the data are consistent with special rules' being tools of the majority party. Finally, is it possible to show that special rules make a difference in legislative outcomes? And more broadly, what can one conclude about the influence of parties on outcomes?

In Krehbiel's conceptualization, the expected outcome is that preferred by the median voter and hence to show that a special rule had an impact on outcomes, one would need to show that the rule resulted in an outcome different from that most preferred by the median voter. To do so requires reliable information about the preferences of most members on a specific issue that is independent of their vote on that issue (and in fact in conflict with that vote), and this is seldom available. In my discussion of the strategic effects of rules, I described a number of instances in which it seems reasonable to infer that a nonmedian outcome did occur. The Republican tax bill in the 104th Congress provides a rare example in which the evidence is conclusive. Almost half of the Republican membership—102—had signed a letter to Speaker Gingrich supporting a reduction to $95,000 in the income limit of families eligible for the $500-per-child tax credit. Most Democrats were on the record as supporting the reduction. If an amendment reducing the cap in the bill had been offered on the floor, it would have passed; reducing the cap was clearly the median position. Yet because the rule did not allow that amendment, the bill passed with its $200,000 cap (Rubin 1995).

Although 102 Republicans publicly declared their support for reducing the cap, only one voted against the previous question on the rule, a motion that, if successful, would have allowed the rule to be altered so as to make that amendment in order, and only 11 voted against the rule. Krehbiel argues that significant party behavior is manifest when "individual legislators vote with fellow party members *in spite of their disagreement* about the policy in question" (1993: 238, emphasis in the original). The rule votes on the tax bill certainly seem to fit that definition. More generally, the strong tendency of members of the majority party to vote for rules even on legislation they then vote against is best explained as party behavior.

Poole and Rosenthal scores for the party switchers during the 104th Congress provide another bit of strong evidence for party behavior. Because the five House party switchers changed party during the course of the 104th

Congress, Poole and Rosenthal could compute NOMINATE scores for each for both the period before and the period after the member switches. The five's mean NOMINATE score as Democrats in the 104th was .22; their mean NOMINATE score as Republicans in the 104th was .71. Thus the switchers on averaged moved .49 units, about a quarter of the issues space, to the right after they switched, with the minimum move being .36 and the maximum being .73. Parker (Miss.), who was furthest to the right as a Democrat, moved least; the two leftmost members, Deal (Ga.) and Laughlin (Tex.), moved most.

Although examples of nonmedian outcomes and of party behavior as Krehbiel defines it can be documented despite the difficulties of obtaining the necessary data, concentrating one's energies on doing so seems a misplaced effort. The Krehbiel formulation of the problem leads us to ask the wrong questions, I believe. Members' legislative preferences, those directly proximate to their vote choice, are a good deal more contingent on context than Krehbiel's formulation allows. Two propositions, both in my view theoretically and empirically compelling and centrally important to the understanding of the legislative process and American politics more generally, account for the contingency. First, members have multiple goals, and the factors, such as issue saliency, that determine the relative weight members give the different goals can and often do vary over periods of time shorter than the two-year electoral cycle. Second, where new proposals fall on the issue space is not an exogenous given; the process by which proposals get mapped into the issue space is a complex political process the results of which affect members' legislative preferences. Both processes are susceptible to manipulation by political actors, including prominent party leaders— through special rules and in other ways as well.

The battle over Clinton's health care plan and that over the Republicans' overhaul of Medicare in the 104th Congress provide examples of struggles to determine where in the issue space a proposal is mapped. Opponents' success in defining each as "far out" largely determined the policy outcome. Public relations wars like those so prevalent in policy contests in the 1980s and 1990s revolve around the definition and framing of the policy proposal at issue, which in effect is about where the proposal is perceived on the issue space (Sinclair 1998b). If the location of proposals is assumed to be a given that cannot be affected by political actors, much of recent American politics becomes inexplicable.

Unless one assumes that members have multiple goals and that the factors, such as issue saliency, that determine the relative weight members give the different goals can vary, much congressional behavior is inexplicable.

Why were 177 members, 160 of them Democrats, willing to vote against a constitutional amendment banning flag burning in 1990 (Sinclair 1995: 284–85)? Why did Marjorie Margolies-Mezvinsky, a Democrat from a Republican district who had promised her constituents she would oppose all tax increases and who had voted against the budget resolution because it contained tax increases, then vote for the reconciliation bill actually enacting Clinton's economic program with its tax increases? Why did many Democrats vote for a welfare reform bill in 1996 that they would never have voted for in 1994? Why did the first Republican House in forty years approve an increase in the minimum wage?

The key question is not "Do parties and party leaders somehow induce their members to vote against their preferences, and do nonmedian policy outcomes results?" Rather, we should be asking, "Can and do party leaders affect the mapping of proposals into the issue space and influence the factors that determined the weights their members place on their different goals, and, if so, under what circumstances?"

Chapter 4

Party and Preference in Congressional Decision Making: Roll Call Voting in the House of Representatives, 1889-1999

JOSEPH COOPER AND GARRY YOUNG

Recent decades have witnessed a resurgence of interest in the historical analysis of Congress among political scientists (Swift and Brady 1994; Cooper and Brady 1981). The aim has been to expand understanding of the U.S. Congress and democratic legislatures generally by using historical evidence to perfect and apply theories that enhance our knowledge and explanatory power. Our focus in this chapter is on the role of parties in Congress, and we will use history as a laboratory for improving our understanding of their role and importance.

In so doing, we will restrict our analysis to policy outcomes and roll call voting. These limits are necessary to preserve theoretical tractability and to impose boundaries on the length of this chapter. For similar reasons, we will focus our analysis on the House of Representatives. However, we will introduce and rely on Senate evidence as well when it is helpful to reinforce our argument or put it in broader perspective. Finally, in bringing historical evidence to bear, the period we will deal with is the period from 1889 to 1999. Our reasons are again both substantive and practical. The adoption of the Reed Rules at the start of the 51st House (1889–91) marks the culmination of institutional development in the nineteenth-century House and provides an appropriate point of demarcation for a historical analysis of House roll call voting.

Issues and Approach

Our guiding assumptions are that understanding, theory, and measurement of the role of congressional parties are interdependent—that we cannot understand what history has to tell us without theories that provide explanatory power and that theory and measurement are and must be mutually informative. Therefore, the fact that we have limited the scope of our inquiry does not mean that its purview is narrow. On the contrary, the theoretical issues we wish to address are pivotal and profound, the related measurement issues are multiple and complex, and the time period to be examined is more than a century. Given such goals, it is essential that we first briefly explore the theoretical and measurement issues we will address through the use of history and broadly outline the approach we will take.

THEORETICAL ISSUES

The primary theoretical issue in the literature on congressional parties concerns the conflict between theorists who argue that party has a causal role in congressional decision making and those who argue that it does not. Both sides of the debate have been dominated by scholars with rational choice perspectives who accept the premises of formal theory. The debate thus turns on whether there are independent party effects in roll call voting, not on the assumptions regarding fixed preferences, cutpoints, and proximity voting that underlie spatial analysis. The most prominent defenders of independent party effects are Cox and McCubbins (1993, 1994a) and Aldrich and Rohde (1994b, 1997a, 1997b, 2000a, 2000b). Both pairs of theorists emphasize the importance of party in legislative decision making. However, Cox and McCubbins do so comprehensively in terms of a theory of party that sees it as a cartel that operates to solve Congress's collective action problems, whereas Aldrich and Rohde do so contingently in terms of a theory of party that sees "party government" as dependent on high degrees of partisan unity and conflict over legislative programs. In contrast, Krehbiel (1998) favors and seeks to develop a preference-based theory of legislative voting rather than a party-based theory (see also Krehbiel 1993). In his view roll call voting, like all aspects of politics, is best explained simply through reliance on the preference and proximity assumptions of spatial analysis, and the concept of party is seen as unneeded superstructure. His theory of pivotal politics is thus an extension of median voter theory adjusted to the supermajority requirements established by the veto power and the cloture rule.

These theories have raised and highlighted a number of fundamental issues in explaining legislative decision making that traditional party theory did not recognize (Cooper and Wilson 1994). However, the result has not only been to shatter the old consensus but also to spawn an intense debate over conflicting theoretical and empirical claims. At heart, the conflict between party-based theory and preference-based theory is about the explanatory value of the concept of party and data based on it. Krehbiel's (1998) desire to proceed simply in terms of preferences is tied to a stricter and more pristine view of the demands of deduction, determinism, and universality in providing "scientific" or valid knowledge.[1] As a consequence, he is far more insistent on reductionism and simplicity in theory building than his opponents both within and without the rational choice camp.

MEASUREMENT ISSUES

If knowledge is tied to explanation, explanation to theory, and theory to measurement, then the manner in which we identify and measure "facts" is critical. With respect to the role of parties, a number of basic issues exist. One such issue concerns the merits of aggregate measures of party voting as opposed to dimensional measures. In recent decades, dissatisfaction with traditional aggregate measures has led to the invention of a new type of dimensional measure—the Poole and Rosenthal NOMINATE scores (1997, 2001).[2] These new scores have not merely posed a challenge to traditional party scores; they have largely replaced them in research on congressional parties. It is not surprising that this is so. The NOMINATE scores reflect and respond to the dominant orientation toward scientific analysis in recent decades, that is, the individualistic and egoistic assumptions of rational choice theory.

Nonetheless, whether the NOMINATE scores are superior measures of the role and impact of party remains questionable. These scores represent a form of multidimensional scaling that uses roll call data to identify and measure patterns of ideological coherence in voting choices in both the House and the Senate. They are indeed far better measures of the ideological underpinnings of party coherence and conflict than aggregate party scores are. But they have weaknesses that traditional scores do not possess (Heckman and Snyder 1997; Snyder and Groseclose 2000).[3] They involve a host of assumptions regarding scalability on voting dimensions as well as commensurability across time and across the House and the Senate. In addition, for good and substantial reasons related to the underlying rationale of this measure, reliance is placed on first-dimension scores alone. However, this generally leaves about 20 percent of yea–nay votes to be accounted for by other dimensions that, in effect, are then disregarded because individually they are difficult to interpret and add little explanatory power. Finally, the NOMI-NATE scores indiscriminately merge votes in which parties agree and disagree in measuring voting patterns. It is equally true that aggregate party voting scores possess advantages that the NOMINATE scores do not. They provide a way of measuring the role of party that is direct and inclusive, allows comparison among different types of votes, is readily serviceable as a measure of success or effectiveness, and is free of the assumptions required to treat voting data in a dimensional manner both in particular Congresses and over time. Be that as it may, what matters in the end is the utility of these two types of scores, and that is an issue we can use history to explore.

A second issue concerns the adequacy of existing aggregate measures of party voting.[4] Our regard for such measures does not mean that we believe that traditional measures of party voting and recent variants are flawless in their construction or application. On the one hand, we see party voting as involving a number of components and therefore as something that is complex and variegated, not simple and uniform. These components include not only unity and divisiveness but also the size or margin of the majority party relative to the minority party and the stability or fluidity of party support across issues within both parties. The construction and application of measures of party voting thus need to be sensitive to the existence of multiple components and to the interrelationships between them. On the other hand, the construction and application of aggregate measures also has to be sensitive to the object of analysis. The degree to which partisan allegiance structures voting is not the same question as the degree of party success in passing programs. The former is a matter of the impact of partisanship in both parties on structuring patterns of voting, and the latter is a matter of the effectiveness of the majority party in mobilizing majorities on the basis of support from its own partisans and minority defection.

Current use of aggregate measures of party voting too often errs on both counts. Increased attention has been given in recent years to combining components, but we still lack comprehensive measures and any developed sense of how these components interrelate. Equally important is to define a measure of effectiveness that is independent of party structure. These two objects of analysis raise similar issues regarding how to define the scope or arena of party voting. Moreover, they both involve the same components of party voting. Nonetheless, measurement needs to be sensitive to differences in the manner in which these components participate and interact in the case of partisan structuring as opposed to partisan effectiveness. A host of difficult issues are involved that have not been confronted but sidestepped on the basis of the assumption that votes can be treated and components used indiscriminately. We do not agree. Although we do not pretend that we can resolve all the difficulties, we do believe that better aggregate measurement is required, and we will devote much of this chapter to the design of new measures and their application over time.

A third and final issue concerns the interpretation and significance of measures of party voting, whether aggregate or dimensional (see Krehbiel 2000). Advocates of preference theory claim that at best, traditional measures of party voting reduce to nothing more than measures of preferences. By implication, the same claim applies to the Poole and Rosenthal scores. In contrast, advocates of party effects must and do see both types of scores as reflecting party as well as preference effects (Aldrich and Rohde 1998). However, since both types of scores are based on roll call votes, that is, on choices and not preferences, they may or may not contain party effects as well as preference effects. The ambiguous significance of existing scores has led to a confounding of theoretical and measurement issues. Party theorists with rational choice orientations have begun to prefer dimensional scores because of their apparent tie to preferences while continuing to argue for independent party effects. Preference theorists have rejected party scores as much, if not more, for theoretical reasons as measurement defects. Because party is seen as without causal effect, the relevance and significance of party scores have also been dismissed. Such a situation does not serve the interests of either theory or measurement, and the issues that pertain to each need to be approached in a manner that clarifies, not confuses, their interrelationship.

APPROACH

The nature of these issues provides guidelines on how to approach them. The basic strategy we will follow in organizing our analysis is to separate the task of assessing the utility of party scores from assessing the causal effects of party. What we explore first is whether party scores provide useful information for explaining patterns of voting and outcomes on votes. In so doing, we proceed on the assumption that conceptualizing and measuring structuring or patterning is different from conceptualizing and measuring success or effectiveness and that better measures of both are needed. The new measures we devise and apply serve a variety of ends. They clarify trends in party structuring and effectiveness over the course of the twentieth century; aid in assessing the three theoretical approaches we have identified, since these trends have important implications for the claims of these approaches; and aid in assessing the merits of party versus dimensional scores. Having analyzed the utility and advantages of party scores, in the final section we address the issue of independent party effects. We do so primarily with respect to theoretical issues and primarily by surveying current research findings, although we also attend to the measurement implications. We conclude by assessing the deeper epistemological and methodological conclusions that can be drawn regarding how best to frame inquiry into the role of congressional parties.

Thus our analysis is organized around three basic questions.

First, to what degree does the historical evidence indicate that congressional voting is partisan? In short, aside from the question of whether party is a factor with independent causal force, to what degree do partisan labels or allegiance serve as a basis for identifying consistencies in voting patterns? We will equate such consistencies with an ordering or structuring of the vote but without any assumptions of causal effect, much as a thermometer can be seen as a measure of heat without assuming that it is the cause of heat.

Second, if party does order or structure voting to some significant degree, to what degree does the historical evidence indicate that party voting is involved in the success or failure of policy outcomes on the floor? In short, again aside from the question of whether party has an independent causal effect on voting choices, what role has partisan voting played in passing legislation on the floor, and what components of party voting are associated with party success or effectiveness?

Third, if on the basis of historical evidence, party can be seen to order or structure voting patterns and to play a role in the passage of legislation, does it have an independent causal effect in doing so? Equally, if not more important, given our answer to this question, what should we conclude about the explanatory value of the concept of party and the best way to frame the analysis and measurement of legislative voting in Congress?

Partisan Structuring

The first question we wish to address is the question of whether partisanship structures congressional voting. As noted, in asking this question we do not wish to raise the issue of cause. All we want to ask is whether partisanship is a sufficiently important aspect or facet of legislative voting that measures of its strength provide useful information in distinguishing differences in patterns of legislative voting.

PROBLEMS AND GUIDELINES

In seeking to answer this question, we will not rely on existing measures of partisan structuring. These include the traditional party vote, unity, cohesion, and unlikeness scores, developed by Lowell, Rice, and Turner, as well as more recent measures, such as the Cooper-Brady-Hurley score, which multiplies cohesion by the party vote; the Cox and McCubbins party agenda and leadership scores; and various scores developed by Poole and Rosenthal and Aldrich and Rohde based on first-dimension NOMINATE scores.[5] None of these measures, traditional or recent, is adequate to the task.

What we need is a measure that captures the degree to which party labels or allegiance orders patterns of voting but takes both parties into account simultaneously and is sensitive to differences in the direction of the vote. The latter consideration is as critical as the former, though often ignored. To measure partisan structuring correctly, the type of ordering that occurs when majorities of both parties vote together must not be equated with the type of ordering that occurs when majorities of both parties vote in opposition to one another. When party majorities vote in the same direction, that is, both vote yea or nay, partisanship does not structure the vote. It is rather structured by some bipartisan motive or principle that unites the parties. Partisan structuring must therefore be restricted to cases in which party majorities vote in opposite directions and both unity and divisiveness are taken into account in measuring it. Only in this way can we find measures that will allow us to weigh and compare partisan structuring with structuring based on rival principles in a comprehensive fashion.

In developing a new set of structuring scores that do meet our requirements, we shall rely on the party vote score both to identify the domain of party voting and to standardize vote scores in that domain so that they can be weighted relative to voting in all domains. Given the concerns that exist regarding the weight or significance that should be attributed to the party vote score, it is appropriate to ask, even before we present our new measures, whether such reliance will produce arbitrary or artificial results.[6] In addressing this question, once again we must be careful not to predetermine it by requiring that there be demonstrable nonpreference effects for party scores to be regarded as reliable measures. Rather, the arbitrariness or artificiality of our structuring scores should be determined in terms of their validity and utility as measures of voting patterns, not in terms of whether their results can be distinguished from preferences so as to confirm the independent impact of party. Indeed, unless one assumes from the start that partisanship has little or nothing to do with preferences, the utility of our scores is bolstered, not undercut, by their ability to reflect preferences. Moreover, party scores can hardly improve on preferences if one assumes, as preference-based theory does, that preferences are exogenous, fixed, and revealed in roll call votes. In short, although causal issues are critical ones, they are not controlling here.

Hence concerns about the party vote measure that stem directly or indirectly from a prior commitment to preference-based theory can be easily dismissed. The claim that the party vote measure fails as an indicator of party voting because it does not always attain perfection in the sense of a 100 percent score, when perfect party voting in the sense of 100 percent unity in each party occurs, derives from a definition of party voting that disregards the direction of the vote (Krehbiel 2000).[7] Votes on which 100 percent of each party vote in the same direction are bipartisan, not partisan, votes; unity by itself does not provide party voting. Ironically enough, analyzing this claim sustains rather than undercuts the rationale for defining the point at which each party is split 50–50 as a zero or midpoint in a continuum that stretches from perfect partisanship at one end to perfect bipartisanship at the other. Similarly, the claim that party scores are artificial because party voting is highly variable and not distinguishable from preference voting rests on the assumption that party voting is based on discipline, not preferences, and thus should be clearly distinguishable from preference voting and by implication also perfect or close to perfect when present. The dismissal of party scores because they do not meet these requirements thus derives from prior premises, including the premise that votes are merely revealed preferences. Moreover, as noted, this claim, even if sustainable, would still not mean that party scores were not useful measures of preference distributions (Krehbiel 1993; 1998: 167–72, 202; 1999a; 2000).[8]

The more serious concerns relate to doubts about the validity of using a 50–50 split within the two parties as a demarcation point for constructing scores (Cox and McCubbins 1993: 139–45). There are, however, good theoretical and empirical reasons for choosing to do so. What we seek to measure is structuring on the basis of party as opposed to rival principles. Hence what we need to measure is the degree to which partisanship structures voting on issues that are ordered by goals that divide the parties and bipartisanship structures voting on issues that are ordered by goals that unite the parties. To the degree that parties are incohesive on party issues so that party minorities vote with opposing majorities or incohesive on bipartisan issues so that party minorities vote in concert against allied party majorities, structuring on the basis of partisanship or bipartisanship does not occur. Rather, varying forms of cross-party voting occur. Given that our objective is to measure structuring in terms of partisanship as opposed to rival principles, a sound theoretical basis thus exists for relying on the party vote score as well as its obverse, the bipartisan vote score, to delineate the domains within which the strength of structuring or cohesiveness can be measured and to standardize the scores that are obtained so that they can be assessed relative to one another. In sum, reliance on the party vote provides not only a preferable alternative to leadership scores but also the only feasible alternative for measuring structuring both absolutely in particular domains and relatively across all domains.

Even so, a critical empirical issue remains. If some sizable number of party votes fall with the range of 50 to 60 percent of one party opposed to 50 to 60 percent of another party or a sizable number of bipartisan votes fall within the range of 50 to 60 percent of one party joining 50 to 60 percent of the other, the justification for distinguishing these two domains as we have done may be questioned. In theory, this should not happen if there is even a modicum of structuring power in partisanship or bipartisanship. Indeed, if the power of these principles is extremely weak, our scores should show that voting is highly cross-partisan or, in other words, not highly structured by either partisan or bipartisan motivations. And in fact, in certain Houses before 1860, this is what our scores do show. But none of this is an issue for any House after 1860. In our time period, as we shall see shortly, there are no Houses or Senates in which the cross-partisan score exceeds the sum of the partisan and bipartisan scores. Thus in the Congresses we study, House and Senate unity scores on individual roll calls do not cluster in the 50 to 60 percent range either when party majorities oppose one another or when they vote together. For example, a study of four partisan Congresses, the 102nd–105th (1991–99), and five bipartisan ones, the 90th–94th (1967–77), conducted by Cooper and Hering (2001), reveals that in the House, the average percentage of votes in which both parties were united less than 60 percent on bipartisan votes was 0.5 percent in the partisan 102nd–105th Congresses and 1.3 percent in the bipartisan 90th–94th Congresses. The corresponding figures on party votes are 0.5 percent and 4.6 percent. The results for the Senate are very similar: 0.8 percent and 1.9 percent, respectively, on bipartisan votes and 0.5 percent and 4.6 percent, respectively, on party votes. It is accordingly no surprise that the average party and bipartisan unity scores in our time period are never below 70 percent, rarely below 75 percent for both parties, and often above 80 percent for at least one of the parties. In short, then, one cannot conclude that partisan and bipartisan votes often fall so close to a 50–50 split that little difference exists between them. Indeed, the correlation between the overall partisan structuring and overall bipartisan structuring scores we will soon present is −.925, a finding that indicates that our reliance on the boundaries set by the party vote in constructing a more comprehensive measure captures the realities of vote structuring very well.

MEASURING PARTY STRUCTURING

We may now confront the task of developing a new set of measures that meet our requirements (for an earlier formulation, see Cooper and Young 1997). It is best to begin by further developing the rationale that underlies our new scores. At one extreme, one can conceive of a situation in which 100 percent of one party votes against 100 percent of the other party. Such a vote can be seen as a perfect partisan vote. At the other extreme, one can conceive of a situation in which 100 percent of one party votes with 100 percent of the other. Such a vote can be seen as a perfect bipartisan vote. Finally, a situation that is exactly between these two situations can also be conceived in which 50 percent of each party votes yea and is opposed by 50 percent of each party voting nay. Such a situation may be conceived as perfect cross-partisan vote. Now, to be sure, there are few, if any, perfect partisan, bipartisan, or cross-partisan votes. However, by adopting a 50 percent versus 50 percent split between and within the parties as the midpoint between votes that perfectly unite or divide the parties, we can measure the degree to which votes are partisan within the parameters set by a perfect partisan vote and a perfect cross-partisan vote as well as the degree to which votes are bipartisan within the parameters set by a perfect bipartisan vote — and a perfect cross-partisan vote. At the same time, we can measure the degree of cross-party voting when votes are partisan but not perfectly partisan and the degree of cross-party voting when votes are bipartisan but not perfectly bipartisan.

In other words, in terms of this logic, partisan votes that are less than perfect combine an element of partisan structuring in which majorities of varying size in the two parties oppose one another and an element of cross-partisanship in which minorities of varying size within each party vote with the majority of the other party rather than with a majority of their fellow partisans. For example, in the case of the 73rd House (1933–35), 85.2 percent of the Democrats, on average, voted against 88.4 percent of the Republicans on votes that split the parties. However, a minority of 14.8 percent of the Democrats and 11.6 percent of the Republicans voted in a cross-partisan manner with majorities of the opposing party. Similarly, bipartisan votes that are less than perfect combine an element of bipartisanship in which majorities of varying size in both parties vote together and an element of cross-partisanship in which minorities of varying size in both parties vote together in opposition to majorities in both parties. For example, in the case of the 73rd House, 81.4 percent of the Democrats, on average, voted with 77.2 percent of the Republicans on votes that united majorities of the two parties. However, a minority of 18.6 percent of the Democrats and 22.8 percent of the Republicans voted together in a cross-partisan manner in opposition to their own party majorities.

Given these distinctions, a simple structuring score can be constructed to measure the degree to which partisanship structures voting on party votes and bipartisanship structures voting on bipartisan votes in any House or Senate. In essence, the simple partisan structuring score measures the degree to which the potential for partisan structuring has been realized on party votes, taking both parties into account. The party unity scores are key to the construction of the simple partisan structuring score. However, these scores need to be indexed, since by definition they range only from 50 percent to 100 percent, whereas structuring by definition varies from zero partisan structuring (a 50–50 split within and between each party) to 100 percent partisan structuring (a split in which 100 percent of each party opposes 100 percent of the other). The unity scores thus have to be indexed to a 0 to 100 percent range and averaged to secure a figure that encompasses both parties. When indexed, a score of 100 percent represents the total amount of partisan structuring possible and results when each party is perfectly united or cohesive. Less than perfect unity or cohesion results in less than perfect structuring. The total amount of actual partisan structuring, subtracted from 100 percent, the total amount of partisan structuring possible, provides the cross-partisan residual and reflects the degree of incohesion or failure in partisan structuring.

For example, in the 73rd House, the partisan structuring score is 73.6 percent and the cross-partisan residual is 26.4 percent. The first figure can be derived by subtracting 50 percent from each of the two unity scores (85.2 percent and 88.4 percent), multiplying each result by 2 to index them to a 100-point scale (70.4 percent and 76.8 percent), and then averaging the two scores to secure the simple structuring score (73.6 percent). What is not structured represents the combined amount of incohesion in both parties as opposed to cohesion. The cross-partisan residual (26.4 percent) is thus simply the sum of the portions not structured by voting cohesion in each party and can be secured by subtracting the simple structuring score (73.6 percent) from 100 percent. The same results for the structuring score can be obtained simply by subtracting 50 percent from each unity score (35.2 percent and 38.4 percent) and adding them together and for the cross-partisan residual by adding together the unstructured portions (14.8 percent and 11.6 percent). See Figure 4.1 for a graphic representation. Finally, it should be

	UNITY		SIMPLE STRUCTURING	
	Democrat	*Republican*	*Partisan structuring*	*Cross-partisan residual*
Voted with majority of own party	85.2%	88.4%	73.6%	26.4%
Voted against majority of own party	14.8%	11.6%		

A. Unity

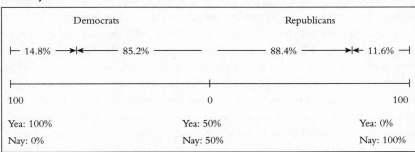

B. Partisan structuring

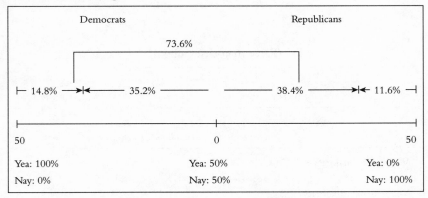

Figure 4.1. Vote structuring on party votes, 73rd House (1933–35).

noted that the partisan structuring score is equivalent to the unlikeness score between the parties as well as to the average of the party cohesion scores on votes that split the parties.

Similarly, the simple bipartisan structuring score measures the degree to which the potential for bipartisan structuring has been realized on bipartisan votes. Again because the bipartisan unity score varies only from a 50– 50 split within and between the parties to a split in which 100 percent of each party vote together, the unity scores for each party have to be indexed to a 100-point scale and averaged to secure the structuring score. This total subtracted from 100 percent provides the cross-partisan residual that pertains. For example, in the 73rd House, the bipartisan structuring score is 58.6 and the cross-partisan residual is 41.4. The first figure can be derived by subtracting 50 percent from the two unity scores (81.4 percent and 77.2 percent), multiplying each result by 2 (62.8 percent and 54.4 percent), and averaging them or else by subtracting 50 percent from each bipartisan unity score (31.4 percent and 27.2 percent) and adding them together. The cross-partisan residual can be secured by subtracting this figure from 100 percent or by adding together the unstructured portions (18.6 percent and 22.8 percent). See Figure 4.2 for a graphic representation of the latter method. It should be noted that the structuring score in this instance is not equal to the unlikeness score on these votes or to the likeness score. In this case, the structuring score continues to measure the combined difference from a 50– 50 break, but the unlikeness and likeness scores measure the amount of difference or similarity between the scores of the parties. What the structuring score continues to be equivalent to is the average of the party cohesion scores on bipartisan votes.

Scores
(Party majorities allied)

| | UNITY | | SIMPLE STRUCTURING | |
| | | | | |
	Democrat	Republican	Bipartisan structuring	Cross-partisan residual
Voted with majority of own party	81.4%	77.2%	58.6%	41.4%
Voted against majority of own party	18.6%	22.8%		

A. Unity

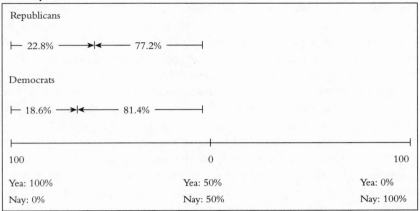

B. Bipartisan structuring

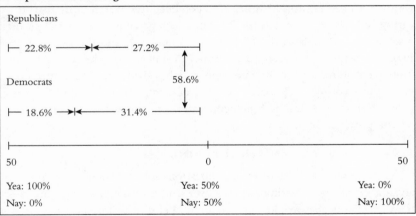

Figure 4.2. Vote structuring on bipartisan votes, 73rd House (1933–35).

The simple structuring scores, as we shall see, are valuable scores. They capture cohesion and incohesion on party and bipartisan votes and allow us to analyze trends in each domain. However, they present a bifurcated picture of structuring and thus do not provide a basis for comparing the strength of structuring in one domain as opposed to the other. In short, we must be able to measure shifts in the proportion of partisan and bipartisan votes, together with shifts in cohesion in these votes, if we are to compare the overall strength of structuring principles in different Houses or sets of

Houses. For example, if all votes were always party votes, in the 73rd House we could simply conclude that the overall partisan structuring score was 73.6 percent, the overall bipartisan structuring score was 0 percent, and the overall cross-partisan structuring score was 26.4 percent, and compare these results with other Houses. A similar point applies to simple bipartisan structuring. However, in the 73rd House, as in all Houses, party votes are less than 100 percent of the total and vary from House to House. We must therefore construct an overall structuring score that standardizes the simple scores in terms of variation in the party vote if we are to measure the influence of partisan structuring as compared to bipartisan and cross-partisan structuring. This can be done by multiplying the simple partisan and bipartisan scores as well as the two cross-partisan residuals by the percentage of party votes and the percentage of bipartisan votes as appropriate.[9] In the 73rd House, the percentage of party votes was 72.7 and the percentage of bipartisan votes was 27.3. The overall partisan structuring score for the 73rd House is thus 53.5 percent (0.727 times 73.6 percent), the overall bipartisan structuring score is 16.0 percent (0.273 times 58.6 percent), the overall partisan residual is 19.2 percent (0.727 times 26.4 percent), and the overall bipartisan residual is 11.3 percent (0.273 times 41.4 percent). The sum of the two cross-partisan residuals is 30.5 percent, which provides an overall measure of cross-party voting. The three overall structuring scores are thus 53.5 percent, 16.0 percent, and 30.5 percent, and they sum to 100 percent, the total amount of structuring possible.

TRENDS IN PARTISAN STRUCTURING

Given these scores, the determining questions are how useful they are in analyzing variations in voting patterns over time and whether there are alternative measures that would be more useful. Let us therefore now turn to our data and findings. Figure 4.3 displays overall structuring scores for the House from 1889 to 1999. Table 4.1 presents mean structuring scores, both simple and overall, for four distinct periods over the course of that time period. We have, in addition, in Table 4.2 classified all Houses in that period in terms of the relationships between components of the overall structuring scores. Our criteria are as follows.

Our initial distinction is between Houses in which the overall cross-partisan score is less than the sum of the overall partisan and bipartisan scores and Houses in which it is greater. We consider Houses in which it is greater to be factional. As noted earlier, there are no such Houses in the years from 1899 to 1999. When the sum of the overall partisan and bipartisan scores

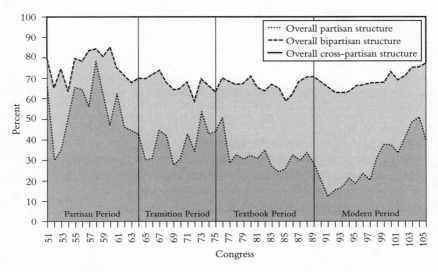

Figure 4.3. House overall structuring scores, 1889–1999.

Table 4.1

House Structuring Scores, 1889–1999

	Partisan Period 51st–65th (1889–1919)	Transition Period 66th–76th (1919–1941)	Textbook Period 77th–90th (1941–1969)	Modern Period 91st–105th (1969–1999)
I. Simple Scores				
Mean partisan structuring	76.6	67.9	61.4	59.7
Mean partisan residual	23.4	32.1	38.6	40.3
Mean bipartisan structuring	68.8	64.6	71	74.8
Mean bipartisan residual	31.2	35.4	29	25.2
II. Overall Scores				
Mean party vote	66.9	58.9	47.7	47.9
Mean partisan structuring	52.0	40.3	29.3	29.8
Mean bipartisan structuring	23.1	26.7	37.2	38.9
Mean cross–partisan structuring	24.9	33.0	33.5	31.3
Mean type	Dominant partisan	Strong partisan	Constrained bipartisan	Constrained bipartisan

Table 4.2

Types of Houses, 1889–1999

	Partisan Period 51st–65th (1889–1919)	Transition Period 66th–76th (1919–1941)	Textbook Period 77th–90th (1941–1969)	Modern Period 91st–105th (1969–1999)
Partisan				
Dominant partisan	8	3	0	2
Strong partisan	4	4	0	0
Constrained partisan	0	0	0	2
Total	*12*	*7*	*0*	*4*
Bipartisan				
Dominant bipartisan	0	0	1	1
Strong bipartisan	1	0	1	6
Constrained Bipartisan	1	1	6	1
Total	*2*	*1*	*8*	*8*
Cross-partisan				
Strong cross-partisan	0	1	1	0
Constrained cross-partisan	0	0	1	0
Total	*0*	*1*	*2*	*0*
Other				
Mixed	1	2	3	2
Truncated	0	0	0	1
Hybrid	0	0	1	0
Total	*1*	*2*	*4*	*3*
Period Totals	*15*	*11*	*14*	*15*

does exceed the overall cross-partisan score, we classify Houses in terms of 50 percent and 10 percent parameters. We do so because a 50 percent difference in scores, given the fact that the sum total of our three scores must be 100 percent, represents a substantial difference, whereas differences of less than 10 percent may be regarded as inconsequential.

Thus in cases in which the highest score is 50 percent greater than either of the other two scores, we classify the House as dominant partisan (DP), dominant bipartisan (DB), or dominant cross-partisan (DX), depending on the highest score. In cases in which the highest score is 50 percent higher than the third score but only between 10 and 49 percent higher than the second score, we classify the House as strong partisan (SP), strong bipartisan (SB), or strong cross-partisan (SX), depending on the highest score. In cases in which the highest score is not 50 percent higher than either of the two other scores but at least 10 percent higher than each, we classify the House as constrained partisan (CP), constrained bipartisan (CB), or constrained cross-partisan (CX), depending on the highest score.

However, these three categories do not exhaust the possibilities. They all concern cases in which the highest score is at least 10 percent greater than the other two scores. Another set of cases exists in which this feature does not obtain. In cases in which the highest score is 50 percent greater than the third score but not 10 percent greater than the second score, we classify the House as truncated (T). In cases in which the highest score is only 10 to 49 percent greater than the third score and not 10 percent greater than the second score, we classify the House as mixed (M). In cases in which the highest score is not 10 percent higher than either of the other two scores, we classify the House as hybrid (H). Finally, in the case of truncated and mixed Houses, we included the two highest scores in parentheses because our classification scheme regards neither one as preeminent—for example, M(PB) or T(PB) when the highest score is the partisan one and the next highest score is the bipartisan one.

Our structuring scores and classifications enlarge our analytical capacities in a number of ways. First, they refine and enlarge our capacity to understand trends in House voting patterns in ways beyond the reach of traditional party scores or NOMINATE scores. As indicated by Tables 4.1 and 4.2 and Figure 4.3, the role of partisanship in structuring voting patterns in the House is substantially different in our first two time periods as compared to the second two, despite an upsurge of partisanship at the end of the last period. The mean overall partisan structuring scores are 52.0 and 40.3 in the first two periods and 29.3 and 29.8 in the last two. Similarly, of the 23 Houses of 55 that qualify as dominant, strong, or constrained partisan, 19 occur before 1941 and only 4 after 1941, and 3 of these 4 in the 1990s. In contrast, 16 of 19 bipartisan Houses occur after 1941, as do 7 of 10 mixed, hybrid, or truncated Houses. The reasons for these differences pertain, in part, to the fact that the average party vote declined from 66.9 percent and 58.9 percent in the periods 1911–19 and 1919–41 to 47.7 percent and 47.9 percent in the periods 1941–69 and 1969–99, respectively. However, our simple structuring scores indicate that changing patterns of cohesiveness were also a major factor. The average partisan residual on party votes increased from 23.4 percent in our first period to 32.1, 38.6, and 40.3 percent in the three periods that follow. In contrast, the corresponding figures for the average bi-partisan residual on bipartisan votes are 31.2, 35.4, 29, and 25.2 percent, re-spectively. To place these scores in perspective, it may be noted that an av-erage residual of 50 percent is equivalent to an average voting division of 75 percent–25 percent in both parties, and an average residual of 25 percent is equivalent to an average voting division of 87.5 percent–12.5 percent in both parties.

Second, our scores can assist in making more precise comparisons among similar sets of Houses across the periods. As Figure 4.3 indicates, the broadly defined periods in Table 4.1 mask some important elements of variation within the periods. For example, high levels of partisan structuring are pres-ent in three of our periods but are not easily pinned down in Table 4.1 or even in Figure 4.3. However, if we attend to scores within the periods, we can compare the five most partisan Houses of the twentieth century. These are the Reed-Henderson Houses (1895–1903), the Cannon Houses (1903–11), the Clark Houses (1911–19), the New Deal Houses (1933–41), and the Foley-Gingrich Houses (1989–99). Our scores indicate that the first two, with average simple structuring scores of 79.4 and 82.0 and overall par-tisan structuring scores of 58.7 and 62.1, are clearly more partisan than the other three, whose simple structuring scores are 71.1, 70.9, and 71.4 and whose overall structuring scores are 40.8, 47.5, and 42.6, respectively. They also indicate that although the Foley-Gingrich Houses are far more partisan than others in their period, they are not on a par with the most partisan Houses of the Party Period. Rather, they are quite comparable to the Clark and New Deal Houses. It may be noted that differences between party me-dians in the DW-NOMINATE scores provide rankings that are similar in a number of respects. However, these scores, in contrast to our scores, rank the New Deal Houses significantly lower in partisanship than the Clark and Foley-Gingrich Houses and rank the Republican Houses of the 1920s (1919–29) as their equals, if not superiors.[10]

Third, our structuring scores and classifications refine and enlarge our ability to compare the House and Senate in ways beyond the reach of tradi-tional party scores or the NOMINATE scores. Overall, the Senate has been far more cross-partisan than the House. Of our 55 cases, 23 qualify as dom-inant, strong, or constrained cross-partisan as compared to only 3 in the House. However, 17 of these occur in the middle two periods. The first pe-riod is quite similar to that in the House, and the last is characterized by a larger variety of forms than in any other period in either body, including mixed, truncated, and hybrid. Underlying the differences between the four periods are trends similar to the House—a decline in the party vote and growing partisan incohesion on party votes and bipartisan cohesion on bipartisan votes. However, growth in bipartisan cohesion is more pronounced in the Senate.[11]

Last but not least, our structuring scores and classifications allow us to distinguish among individual Houses and Senates in ways beyond the reach of traditional party scores or NOMINATE scores. Take, for example, the 104th (1995–97) and 105th (1997–99) Houses of Speaker Gingrich. Whereas the differences in partisanship between the 104th and 105th Houses may seem hard to unravel, our scores cast considerable light on them. Both the majority and minority party unity scores in the two House are quite close—92 and 90 percent and 84 and 85 percent, respectively. As a result, the simple partisan structuring scores are virtually the same—75 percent. However, the party vote score drops from 67 percent in the 104th House to 52 percent in the 105th House, and the simple bipartisan structuring score increases from 75 percent to 80 percent. So whereas the 104th can be seen as a dominant partisan (DP) Congress, the scope and strength of bipartisanship in the 105th is enhanced so that overall it rivals partisanship as a source of structuring. Its classification as truncated—T(PB)—thus reflects the realities of decision making in this House. Partisanship does not dominate bipartisanship, but both are strong enough to keep cross-partisanship under control. What occurred is that in a context of a slim majority margin and divided government, intraparty divisions stimulated bipartisan action. Again, these nuances are not captured by differences in DW-NOMINATE party medians, which lead us to see these two Houses as essentially the same (0.78 in the 104th versus 0.80 in the 105th). In contrast, our overall structuring scores pinpoint critical differences. They are 50.8 partisan, 24.3 bipartisan, and 24.8 cross-partisan for the 104th with corresponding scores of 39.3, 37.3, and 22.8 for the 105th.

SUMMARY

We may conclude that the answer to the first question we posed is yes. Party scores are useful in analyzing and understanding voting patterns. Moreover, the structuring scores we have devised go beyond the reach of current measures of party structuring. Among other advantages, they help us understand why the current House is not comparable in partisan structuring to the House at the turn of the twentieth century, despite the increase in party voting in recent years, and how the House and Senate differ both in recent decades and over time.

Our findings have important implications for the theoretical and measurement issues identified at the start of this chapter as well. In the case of Cox and McCubbins's theory of party as a cartel, our data support their claim that party structures voting in the Congress. Nonetheless, the variable strength of party as a structuring principle in comparison to other structuring principles indicates that it is not the only basis on which decision making is organized in the House and Senate. Variations in the ability of parties to structure the vote both in individual Houses and between the House and Senate therefore need to be taken into account, and the logic and importance of solving collective action problems through bipartisanship and cross-partisanship must also be explored (see Schickler, 2001; see also Collie, 1988a; Schickler and Rich, 1997). Indeed, such variation calls into question the aptness of viewing party as a "cartel," even metaphorically. The notion of party as a cartel thus needs to be reconsidered, and the case for doing so, as we shall see, also derives from the presumption implicit in the concept of a cartel that structuring and effectiveness covary. In the case of Aldrich and Rohde's theory of conditional party government, our data certainly sustain the notion that party structuring of the vote in the House varies greatly over time. They do not, however, indicate that a state of "party government" can be identified that is distinguishable in kind from all other states of party or that such a state is conditioned only by high levels of unity and divisiveness. Such claims not only make differences in states of party structuring more dichotomous than they appear but also assume that party structuring and party success or effectiveness are associated in close to a one-to-one manner at high levels of structuring. In short, here again, the theory rests on claims that need further examination and refinement. In the case of Krehbiel, none of our findings contradict his belief that party voting is little more than a shadow of preferences. That claim, of course, rests on the underlying nature of causality, an issue that cannot be resolved simply and directly on the basis of roll call votes and will be considered in the last section of this chapter.

As for measurement issues, our structuring scores have a number of advantages over their leading rival, the NOMINATE scores, as measures of voting patterns. Even aside from the fact that they are free of the assumptions needed to produce and compare NOMINATE scores, they reflect all votes, not simply those that can be classified successfully along a single dimension, and they can distinguish and measure bipartisan and cross-partisan voting as well as partisan voting. Consequently, they provide a basis for analyzing changing rates of cohesion and incohesion in voting patterns and changing relationships among different types or forms of voting. As a result, they refine and enlarge our ability to analyze differences between Houses and sets of Houses as well as trends over time.[12] Nor, as we have argued, can our scores be dismissed as arbitrary or artificial. Indeed, in more recent work, Krehbiel (2000) sees the party cohesion score as a simple transformation of the party vote score and the party vote score as a mere reflection of the distribution of preferences. Although his aim is to downgrade the importance of party scores, his claims implicitly sustain their reliability as measures in the very process of explicitly denying them causal import.

Nonetheless, in defending our structuring scores against charges of irrelevance and artificiality, we do not mean to claim that they rest on any deep grasp of the dynamics of vote structuring. In fact, quite aside from more basic issues of causality, we lack adequate understanding of the differences in patterns of interaction that can occur. A good illustration is provided by comparison of the following two sets of Houses. In the first set, majority margin is 12 percent higher in the 74th House (1935–37) than in the 71st (1929–31) House—74 percent to 62 percent. But majority party unity is virtually the same—84.7 percent and 85.7 percent, despite Douglas Dion's (1997) contention that unity and margin vary inversely. Similarly, minority party unity is virtually the same—86.0 percent to 85.3 percent. Hence the two simple structuring scores are also virtually the same—70 percent and 71 percent. In the second set of Houses, majority margin is 14.5 percent higher in the 54th House (1895–97) than in the 80th House (1947–49)—71.1 percent to 56.6 percent. However, in line with Dion's contention, majority unity increases as its proportion of the House decreases—82.1 percent to 89.1 percent—and minority unity decreases as its proportion of the House increases—87.2 percent to 82.4 percent. Since the changes in unity mirror one another, the simple structuring scores are virtually the same in both these Houses as well—69 percent and 71 percent—and they closely match the scores in the other two Houses. However, the patterns of interaction between unity and margin are quite different. In sum, then, though our structuring scores substantially improve our ability to capture the dynamics of vote structuring, it is also clear that we have significant gaps in our understanding of the dynamics of vote structuring. In important ways, they continue to elude us, and as we shall also argue in the case of effectiveness, improving our understanding of these relationships constitutes one of the prime immediate needs of perfecting party theory.

Partisan Effectiveness

The second question we have posed concerns partisan effectiveness or success. Our problem is to assess the benefits of analyzing legislative outcomes in terms of party programs and party voting. Once again, we focus on the utility of party scores, not the underlying relationship between party voting and preferences. What we wish to examine is whether party, in the sense of the labels that members freely choose to identify and distinguish themselves, has utility in explaining policy outcomes as well as voting patterns, not whether party has causal force of its own apart from preferences. This in turn requires more careful attention than has been given in the party literature both to measuring partisan effectiveness or success and to delineating the tie between success and the components of party voting.

MEASURING PARTISAN EFFECTIVENESS

We begin by constructing measures of partisan effectiveness that capture success in the achievement of partisan goals and using them to trace trends in partisan effectiveness in the House and to some degree the Senate over the past century. The tasks of conceptualizing and measuring partisan effectiveness raise a number of difficult issues. One set concerns how to conceptualize effectiveness. Here we opt for a formal approach because of the immense difficulties of a substantive approach. Though ideally we would prefer to measure effectiveness in terms of the actual content of bills, we do not know how to solve the problems of subjectivity and complexity that bar operationalizing the notion of importance in any comprehensive and consistent way. Our concept of effectiveness is thus simply the ability of the majority party to pass its programs. A second set of issues relates to whether partisan effectiveness should be measured in absolute or relative terms. It can, for example, be argued that partisan effectiveness should be assessed only on issues that can properly be deemed partisan. The rationale for this approach is that not all issues are matters of party policy or program and that partisan effectiveness should be assessed only where partisan goals are involved. Nonetheless, it can be argued equally persuasively that partisan effectiveness should be assessed relative to all areas of legislation and not restricted to areas where matters of party program are at issue. The rationale here is that the scope of partisan issues varies from Congress to Congress and hence that measures of effectiveness should take account of such variation in assessing the role of party in passing legislation. Given the fact that both approaches are pertinent to the question of effectiveness, we shall adopt both and call one simple partisan effectiveness and the other overall partisan effectiveness. In short, we will follow the same logic we employed in our structuring scores.

These choices guide but do not resolve questions regarding the concrete measures we should apply. In implementing a formal approach to effectiveness, they suggest two obvious measures. One is a *win score* that measures the percentage of the time a majority of the majority party is on the winning side on issues that are party issues. The second is a *party rule score* that measures the percentage of the time the majority party wins simply on the basis of the votes of its own partisans on issues that are party issues. Each of these scores has limitations. The win score is not immune to the watering down of party objectives to attract support, while the party rule score imposes a very harsh test. We shall therefore make use of both to parameterize the range of possibilities in a formal approach to effectiveness.

More serious difficulties pertain to the question of how to identify and distinguish the issues or votes that constitute party programs—in other words, how to define the domain of party. As in the case of measuring structuring, two broad alternatives exist in the literature. One is to use the party vote criterion to identify party issues. The other is to use patterns of leadership choice—for example, the Cox and McCubbins (1993, 1994b) measures of party program based on patterns of disagreement and agreement among party leaders or measures framed in terms of presidential position taking. However, once again, neither of these two measures of partisan issues or domain is superior to the party vote. Whatever the appeal of the intuitions on which the Cox and McCubbins approach is based, the majority party agenda is not captured by voting agreement between the majority party leader and whip and opposition on the part of at least one minority leader. As noted earlier, disagreement between the majority leader and whip does not necessarily mean an issue is not partisan if the parties split. It is equally true that voting agreement between the majority party leaders and the opposition of one but not both of the minority party leaders does not necessarily mean an issue is partisan if the parties vote in concert. Similarly, issues on which the president takes a position may or may not evoke party divisions. On the whole, then, more is lost than gained by confounding party and bipartisan votes on the basis of patterns of leadership choice. Followers must count at least as much as leaders. In addition, neither presidential positions nor patterns of congressional leadership choice provide as flexible an instrument for measuring partisan effectiveness both relatively in terms of all issues and absolutely in terms of party issues alone. Nor are these approaches as serviceable over long periods of time as the party vote score.

We therefore again rely on the party vote score in identifying partisan votes or issues. Once we do so, we can easily specify our measures of simple and overall partisan effectiveness. The method we adopt in constructing these scores is the same we have followed in calculating our structuring scores. In measuring simple partisan effectiveness, we calculate the win score and party rule score entirely on the basis of votes that split the parties. In measuring overall partisan effectiveness, we adjust our simple win and party rule scores by multiplying them by the party vote score to enable us to measure wins and party rule relative to all votes, not just partisan votes. For all the reasons identified earlier, we do not regard reliance on a 50–50 benchmark as arbitrary; here too, the validity and utility of our approach hinge on the results we obtain.

TRENDS IN PARTISAN EFFECTIVENESS

If we turn now to our scores, House party majorities appear to have had substantial success in controlling outcomes on party votes. In 50.9 percent of our fifty-five cases, the win score is 80 or higher, and the median win score is 80.1. However, these figures do not tell the whole story. Table 4.3 presents data on both simple and overall partisan effectiveness in the House over the course of the twentieth century, organized again in terms of the same four broad but distinct periods previously identified.[13] The simple effectiveness scores in Table 4.3 reveal a number of important features. First is the distinctiveness of the Textbook House. In three of the four periods identified, the average win score varies only from 75.7 percent to 79.3 percent, but in that of the Textbook House (1941–69), it drops to 69.4 percent. In effect, this means that average cross-partisan wins on party votes increase to 30.6 percent as compared to 21.3, 20.7, and 24.3 percent in the other periods, respectively. Similarly, the average party rule score in the period of the Textbook House is 37.8 percent as compared to 64.8, 58.4, and 47.8 in the other periods, respectively. A second feature is even more important. Differences between these scores testify to a greater degree of partisan effectiveness in the first two periods than in the last two. This is true not only because the averages for both scores are higher in the first two than the last two periods but, even more important, also because the sharper and more consistent decline in the party rule score suggests that a large part of the greater stability and strength in the win score is attributable to compromises that watered down the achievement of party goals, even though the parties still split on these votes.

Our findings with respect to overall partisan effectiveness are even more informative. The overall or adjusted scores in Table 4.3 allow us to compare the effectiveness of party relative to other structuring principals. As might be expected given the greater sensitivity of this measure to the declining proportion of party votes, the decline in partisan effectiveness is more pronounced. The median score on adjusted wins is 40.97, and only 38.2 percent of our fifty-five cases have adjusted win scores over 50. Again, however,

Table 4.3

House Effectiveness Scores, 1889–1999

	Partisan Period 51st–65th (1889–1919)	Transition Period 66th–76th (1919–1941)	Textbook Period 77th–90th (1941–1969)	Modern Period 91st–105th (1969–1999)
I. Simple Scores				
Partisan wins				
Mean	78.7	79.3	69.4	75.7
Range	90.0–33.9	95.2–50.4	90.9–33.4	87.8–50.2
Cross-partisan wins				
Mean	21.3	20.7	30.6	24.3
Range	66.1–10.0	49.6–4.8	66.6–9.1	49.8–12.2
Party rule				
Mean	64.8	58.4	37.8	47.8
Range	83.4–0	87.5–0	73.1–7.7	75.1–10.3
II. Adjusted Scores				
Party vote				
Mean	66.9	58.9	47.7	47.9
Range	90.8–45.7	72.7–44.7	59.1–35.4	67.4–28.4
Partisan wins				
Mean	53.4	46.9	32.9	37.5
Range	75.0–15.8	69.2–30.6	42.9–16.7	59.1–16.2
Cross-partisan wins				
Mean	13.5	12.0	14.8	10.4
Range	30.8–5.7	31.3–3.1	33.7–4.3	16.0–7.6
Bipartisan wins				
Mean	33.1	41.1	52.3	52.1
Range	54.3–9.2	55.3–27.3	64.6–40.9	71.6–32.6
Party rule				
Mean	44.7	35.2	18.1	25.3
Range	66.6–0	63.6–0	35.0–3.8	47.9–3.2

such data are insufficient to identify the trends, and Table 4.3 fills the gap. As in the case of simple effectiveness, the period of the Textbook House provides the lowest scores. In terms of the adjusted win score, the averages for our four periods are 53.4, 46.9, 32.9, and 37.5 percent, respectively. In terms of the adjusted party rule score, the averages for our four periods are 44.7, 35.2, 18.1, and 25.3 percent. Once again, the decline in both scores,

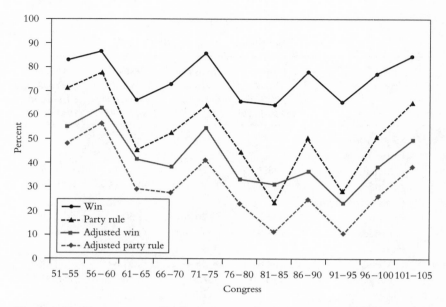

Figure 4.4. House mean effectiveness scores by ten-year periods, 1889–1999.

and especially the party rule score, speaks to the diminished role of party in the passage of legislation. This can be seen even more clearly if we analyze the implications of the adjusted win score in greater detail. For example, if, as in the first period, the average party vote is 66.9 percent, an overall or adjusted average win score of 53.4 percent means that on average, 53.4 percent of total wins were partisan wins on party votes, 13.5 percent were cross-partisan wins on party votes, and 33.1 percent were bipartisan wins on bipartisan votes. Given this, we may note that whereas the average proportion of cross-partisan wins has declined somewhat over our four periods, the average proportion of partisan wins has substantially declined, and the average proportion of bipartisan wins has substantially increased. Our last period is thus virtually a mirror image of the first, with scores of 37.5 percent partisan wins, 10.4 percent cross-partisan wins, and 52.1 percent bipartisan wins.

As in the case of partisan structuring, more detailed analysis of differences within our four broad periods provides additional insights into these periods and improves comparisons across periods. Figure 4.4, which displays mean effectiveness scores by decade, thus refines our understanding of the broad trends identified in Table 4.3. For example, the mean win score for the last decade of the Textbook Period (86th–90th Houses) is higher (78.4 percent) than the scores in each of the two preceding decades (roughly 65 percent) and similar to the score (73.6 percent) in the 1920s (66th–70th Houses) and the score (77.4 percent) in the 1980s (96th–100th Houses). Similarly, although differences in mean adjusted wins between different decades in the Textbook Period are more muted, the score in the 1960s (37.4 percent) remains comparable to the score in the 1920s (38.2 percent) and the score in the 1980s (38.7 percent). In at least some important respects, then, the classic form of the Textbook House seems to have ended by 1960. As for partisan trends, the mean party rule score (65.1 percent) for the 1990s (101st–105th Houses) is much higher than in the other decades of the Modern Period and matches the score (64.2 percent) in the 1930s (71st–75th Houses). But it does not match the scores (71.2 percent and 78.1 percent) in the first two decades of the Party Period (51st–60th Houses). The 1990s are also quite different from the preceding decades of the Modern Period in terms of adjusted wins and adjusted party rule. But the adjusted win score (50.3 percent) in this decade does not match the 1930s (54.9 percent) or the decades from 1889 to 1909 (55.3 percent and 63.4 percent, respectively). Nor does the mean adjusted party rule score in the 1990s (39 percent) match the scores in the latter two decades (48 percent and 57 percent). In short, once again, despite the stability in the mean win score, levels of partisan effectiveness in the 1990s are distinguishable from those at the turn of the twentieth century and to a lesser extent those of the 1930s.

Results for the Senate are inclined in the same direction but are more extreme than in the House. Simple partisan effectiveness is lower with the median win score at 72.5 percent and only 29 percent of the scores higher than 80 percent. The period that stands out is that of the Party Senate. Though its average win (77.2 percent) and party rule scores (51.5 percent) are lower than those for the House, they are much higher than those for the Senates of the other periods, and these periods are not very different from one another.[14] In terms of overall partisan effectiveness, the median adjusted win score is 34.5 percent, and only 25.5 percent of our fifty-five cases have adjusted win scores of 50 percent or more. Again, only the period of the Party Senate stands out, with an average adjusted win score of 50.5 percent and an average adjusted party rule score of 37 percent. Although the decline in the Senate party vote is roughly comparable to that in the House, adjusted scores in the remaining periods fall to lower levels than in the House.[15] Thus the overall scores for the Modern Period in the Senate are the lowest of all (33.3 percent for adjusted wins and 16.1 percent for adjusted party rule). This translates into only 33 percent of total wins being partisan wins on partisan votes. Here too, the scores for this period are virtually a mirror image of the first period. In sum, although partisan structuring has not been weaker in the Senate than in the House, partisan effectiveness has. This is not unexpected, given the differences in culture and rules.

ANALYZING PARTISAN EFFECTIVENESS

To find that partisan effectiveness declined in both houses over the course of the twentieth century is important in that it confirms that variation in outcomes can be viewed and understood in terms of the role of party. However, it does not speak to another prime facet of the problem we have identified—the nature of the relationship between the components of party voting and variation in partisan effectiveness. Let us turn first to simple partisan effectiveness. Given our approach to conceptualizing effectiveness, simple partisan effectiveness is necessarily a matter of the strength of mobilization in the majority party plus the strength of disaffection in the minority party. This has consequences for measurement. Although a focus on unity and divisiveness suffices to measure the determinants of structuring, it does not suffice to measure the determinants of effectiveness. In measuring mobilization, all the components of party voting must be taken directly into account and treated appropriately.

The need to combine components in measuring effectiveness has been widely recognized since publication of the Hurley, Brady, and Cooper article (1977) and is now a common feature of attempts to measure party strength in the sense of what is best conceptualized as mobilization rather than structuring (see Binder 1997; Gamm and Smith 1998). However, that article and current approaches based on party scores rely on traditional cohesion scores, which are insensitive to the direction of the vote. Recently, scholars such as Binder (1999) and Schickler (2000) have turned to first-dimension NOMINATE scores and in one way or another combined them with size.[16] Whatever the merits of these analyses for explaining gridlock or rules change, the benefits provided for measuring partisan effectiveness in terms of policy outcomes are limited. Although the manner in which both treat and measure the role of party is open to challenge, the more important point for us at this stage of our analysis is that both authors focus on causality, downgrade the role of party, and end by questioning the utility of partisan measures of effectiveness, whether measured in party scores or NOMINATE scores. In contrast, in regression models constructed by Sieberer (2001) including all Houses since 1889, size, majority party unity, and minority party unity explain 74 percent of the variance in the win score and 90 percent of the variance in the party rule scores, whereas inclusion of the standard polarization score based on first-dimension DW-NOMINATE scores contributes little and is statistically insignificant.

Questions of causality aside, then, we need not discard reliance on partisan measures of effectiveness. Our problem is rather to improve our ability to measure the ties between party voting and partisan effectiveness by devising more appropriate and more comprehensive measures. In terms of appropriateness, our approach is governed by the same rationale we followed in the case of simple partisan structuring. As in the case of analyzing structuring, we need to be sensitive to the impact of differences in the direction of the vote, to whether majorities are aligned or opposed. In terms of the components included in a measure, however, our approach must be quite different. As we have suggested, in the case of structuring, unity and divisiveness mediate the impact of the other components; in the case of effectiveness, they do not. We therefore need to include size and fluidity or stability in voting in a far more prominent manner than in the case of structuring because their impact on effectiveness is more direct and influential. The same is true of a facet of structuring that ties closely to the impact of majority size with far more direct consequences than in the case of structuring. That facet is minority defection, and an ideal measure would include this factor as well.

Although we do not know how to satisfy all these requirements in a single measure, we do have a new comprehensive measure to offer that supports our claim that the determinants of effectiveness are multiple. We call it the *semicertainty score* because high scores on this measure substantially bolster the chances of success. This score combines unity, fluidity, and size. In essence, it is a measure of the percentage of an absolute majority that majority party members who support the party 80 percent or more of the time supply on average on party votes. Though it does not adequately take divisiveness or minority defection into account, it performs quite well. We may note that the correlations between the simple partisan structuring score and the win and party rule scores are .49 and .69, respectively. In contrast, the correlations between the semicertainty score and the win and party rule scores are .81 and .89.

These results show that the relationship between the strength of the components of party voting, correctly combined and measured, and simple partisan effectiveness is very strong. They indicate as well that there is a relationship between structuring and effectiveness. This is not surprising. All the components of party voting are involved in each, and in unity and divisiveness, quite directly. However, the data also indicate that the relationship between structuring and effectiveness, though not weak, is not controlling. This too is not surprising. As we have argued, the components of party vot-

Table 4.4

Partisan Effectiveness by Levels
of Simple Partisan Structuring, 1889–1999

SIMPLE PARTISAN STRUCTURING	WIN		PARTY RULE	
Level	*Range*	*Median*	*Range*	*Median*
80+ (*n* = 7)	90.0–84.8	87.6	83.4–73.4	79.3
70–79.9 (*n* = 14)	95.2–63.6	83.8	87.5–38.0	68.2
60–69.9 (*n* = 21)	93.1–33.3	78.1	82.2–0	55.4
50–59.9 (*n* = 9)	90.9–43.0	66.7	73.1–0	21.7
40–49.9 (*n* = 4)	73.2–50.2	62.6	45.6–10.9	12.2

ing play different roles and interact in different ways in determining effectiveness as opposed to structuring. After all, partisan structuring is a matter of the degree of partisanship in both parties, and our measure of it necessarily provides an average measure of partisanship across both parties that may not fully capture the ability of the majority party to mobilize a majority, especially in combination with other components. As a result, variation in the levels of particular components can easily have different effects in determining effectiveness than in determining structuring.

The large amount of unexplained variance in the relationship between simple partisan structuring and simple partisan effectiveness therefore tells us something important. It testifies to the fact that the impact of structuring on effectiveness is complex. There thus can be substantial variation among individual Houses in the strength of their simple effectiveness scores even when their simple structuring scores are comparable. As Table 4.4 indicates, the range in win and party rule scores at similar levels of simple partisan structuring is quite wide. Indeed, this is true even at high levels of structuring. In addition, the fact that the medians are generally roughly in the middle of these ranges testifies to the presence of considerable dispersion, and such dispersion also prevails across levels as the inconsistencies in the boundaries of the ranges indicate. There is, in short, much that the relationship cannot explain.

Similar problems characterize our ability to understand the determinants of overall partisan effectiveness. We have argued that partisan effectiveness can and should be assessed in relation to all the business of Congress, not just

Table 4.5

Overall Partisan Effectiveness by Levels
of Overall Partisan Structuring, 1889–1999

OVERALL PARTISAN STRUCTURING	ADJUSTED WIN		ADJUSTED PARTY RULE	
Level	Range	Median	Range	Median
60+ (*n* = 6)	77.0–51.0	67.9	66.7–39.6	63.9
50–59.9 (*n* = 4)	69.2–50.7	59.2	63.6–42.3	49.5
40–49.9 (*n* = 12)	59.5–31.8	50.9	52.5–16.8	48.3
30–30.9 (*n* = 17)	50.0–15.8	40.2	38.8–0	25.1
20–20.9 (*n* = 11)	42.9–23.4	33.3	34.5–5.4	21.3
10–19.9 (*n* = 5)	27.3–16.2	22.4	17.0–3.2	5.2

the business that splits the parties. The overall partisan effectiveness scores thus adjust the simple scores to the scope of partisanship by multiplying them by the party vote. As in the case of simple partisan effectiveness, our semicertainty score performs creditably. It correlates at .87 with adjusted wins and .90 with adjusted party rule.

Nonetheless, once again, evidence from our scores supports our belief that the high correlation between structuring and effectiveness masks a great deal of complexity in the relationship. As Table 4.5 indicates, there is significant variation in overall effectiveness scores at the same levels of structuring, as well as inconsistencies in the boundaries of the ranges at different levels of structuring.

SUMMARY

We may conclude that the answer to our second question is also yes. Our win, party rule, and semicertainty scores testify to the utility of party scores in analyzing legislative policy outcomes. Substantively, these scores pinpoint trends in both simple and overall partisan effectiveness in the House and differences with the Senate. In addition, they aid in differentiating and accounting for variations in levels of success in particular periods and across periods. More generally, they indicate that structuring and effectiveness, while related, are also too divergent to be treated as if they were one and the same. What is clear is that variations in party success over time as well as with respect to particular sets of Houses cannot be explained simply in terms of the relationship between structuring and effectiveness. As a matter of logic, we have argued from the beginning of this chapter that the problem of vote structuring needs to be distinguished from the problem of party effectiveness, and the empirical evidence confirms the value of such an approach.

Once again, these findings have importance both for current theory and for measurement. In the case of Cox and McCubbins, they confirm and extend the point we made earlier. The ability of the majority party to serve as a cartel, to serve as a vehicle for solving the collective action problems of the House and Senate, is highly variable both when effectiveness is viewed simply in terms of party votes and when it is viewed overall in terms of all votes. Such variation needs to be explained, not simply ignored or discounted. In the case of Rohde and Aldrich, they see effectiveness, as Hurley, Brady, and Cooper did before them, as a variable that is contingent on high levels of structuring. Much in our data confirms that view. Both kinds of effectiveness do tend to increase as structuring increases. However, once again, our data indicate that the structuring and effectiveness can and do diverge to significant degrees.[17] This is because effectiveness is not contingent simply on unity and divisiveness, as many theorists with a conditional view have assumed. It rather responds to complex forms of interaction, among all the components of party voting, that differ in character and impact in determining effectiveness as opposed to structuring. Finally, despite the fact that the origins of the theory of conditional government are closely linked to the analysis of electoral change, the theory thus far has only begun to grapple in any deep and integrated way with the external determinants of the components of party voting—for example, the state of the electoral system, the role of the president, and changes in the technology of communication. Yet in the end, any adequate theory of party in the legislative process must be tied to and dependent on a broader theory of party that encompasses exogenous forces as well.[18]

In the case of Krehbiel, his preference-based approach leads him to transform the explanation of effectiveness into the explanation of stalemate. In essence, the ability to pass legislation becomes a matter of the ability to overcome two pivot points—the three-fifths required to impose cloture in the Senate and the two-thirds required to override a presidential veto in both houses. Such a theory does have the great advantage of recognizing the importance of the president and the filibuster as determinants of legislative success. However, it also suffers from some serious disadvantages that flow from an emphasis on preferences and the allied consequences of relying on proximity voting in analyzing voting outcomes. For what such a theory of stalemate assumes is that failure is not a matter of the lack of a majority but the lack of a supermajority, when in fact legislative effectiveness hinges as much on the ability to organize a majority as to achieve a supermajority when it is required. In sum, even though a majority is a necessary but not always a sufficient condition of success, it constitutes an equally important if not more important hurdle, and party theory is more open to including both contingencies than a theory of preferences and pivot points that simply assumes the existence of majorities.

In terms of measurement issues, once again, our new measures have advantages over traditional party measures and NOMINATE scores. The win scores and party rule scores provide a formal approach to defining the dependent variable in measuring policy success that is very difficult to address substantively, whether reliance is placed on party scores or NOMINATE scores. Our semicertainty score provides a more sensitive mix of the components of party voting than other partisan measures of effectiveness and, as a party score, escapes the limitations of first-dimension NOMINATE scores. Nonetheless, as in the case of structuring, in arguing that the concept of party can be relied on to provide useful measures for understanding legislative outcomes, we do not mean to imply that substantial problems do not continue to exist. Our understanding of the dynamics of party effectiveness remains inadequate, perhaps even more inadequate than our understanding of structuring.

Party as a Causal Force

We have deliberately addressed our first two questions without raising the issue of whether party has independent causal significance in the legislative process. Our reason for doing so was simply to prevent causal positions from preempting and confusing measurement issues. But clearly, the issue of whether party has effects independent of preferences is an issue of great importance, whose resolution necessarily expands or narrows the significance of our findings in the preceding sections of this chapter. What we wish to do now is to move beyond a focus on the utility of party scores and draw on existing literature to sketch an answer to the third question we posed—the issue of whether party has an independent effect on voting patterns and policy outcomes.

PARTY AND PREFERENCES

To start, we must first consider the relationship between party and preferences. As formulated by Krehbiel, preference-based theory argues that if party has an independent effect, it must be demonstrable in nonpreference

Table 4.6

Relationships Between Structuring Scores
and NOMINATE Scores, 1889–1999

I. PARTISAN HOUSES

	N	*Mean Overall Partisan Structuring*	*Mean Distance Between Party Medians (DW-NOMINATE)*
Dominant partisan	13	57.7	.839
Strong partisan	8	44.2	.742
Constrained partisan	2	39.2	.609

II. BIPARTISAN HOUSES

	N	*Mean Overall Bipartisan Structuring*	*Mean Distance Between Party Medians (DW-NOMINATE)*
Dominant bipartisan	2	51.2	.429
Strong bipartisan	8	44.1	.514
Constrained bipartisan	9	39.1	.565

III. CROSS–PARTISAN HOUSES

	N	*Mean Overall Cross-partisan Structuring*	*Mean Distance Between Party Medians (DW-NOMINATE)*
Strong cross-partisan	2	41.5	.562
Constrained cross-partisan	1	37.6	.479

(continued)

terms. Thus party effects either must not be related to preferences or, if they are related, must necessarily become mere reflections of preferences. The result is to set the barrier artificially high for party effects. Party effects, to be recognized, must involve voting against preferences or become mere preference effects.

Table 4.6
(continued)

IV. MIXED–HYBRID HOUSES

	N	Mean Overall Mixed-Hybrid Structuring	Mean Distance Between Party Medians (DW-NOMINATE)
Mixed partisan–bipartisan	1	36.4	.617
Mixed bipartisan–partisan	2	34.8	.544
Mixed bipartisan–cross-partisan	2	35.6	.764
Mixed cross-partisan–partisan	1	35.8	.494
Mixed cross-partisan–bipartisan	2	34.6	.632
Truncated partisan–bipartisan	1	38.6	.706
Hybrid	1	33.3	.555

There can be little doubt that parties are instruments of preferences. A variety of forms of evidence confirm this fact. First, as noted earlier, Krehbiel (2000) himself in recent work develops a model of preference-based voting that ties party to preferences. Second, whatever their differences and relative advantages, our structuring scores and first-dimension DW-NOMINATE scores are broadly in alignment, especially with respect to party voting. The correlation between overall partisan structuring and the distance between the party medians is .798, and the correlation between bipartisan structuring and the distance between the party medians is −.665. Moreover, although the NOMINATE scores blur differences among the various types of Houses, they do track our partisan and bipartisan structuring scores fairly well when organized in terms of our classifications (see Table 4.6). Third, measures based on the NOMINATE scores alone suggest a strong relationship between partisan structuring and ideological consistency in patterns of preferences. As members become more divided on ideological grounds, partisan divisions between Democratic and Republican members become more consistent and compartmentalized (Poole and Rosenthal 1997). In short, the fact that NOMINATE scores, which measure ideological orientations, can be organized and interpreted in terms of party strongly suggests that preference coherence underlies partisan cohesion in roll call voting. Ironically enough, if no relationship between party and preferences could be found in roll call votes, both the case for and the case against the causal importance of party would be undermined. On the one hand, if there were no relationship between party and preferences, how could party leaders manipulate cutpoints around the status quo so as to maximize the attainment of party policy goals? On the other hand, if there were no relationship between preferences and party, how could preference-based theory account for and discount the empirical relationships that exist between party and actual voting patterns and outcomes? Such anomalies disappear only if one assumes that party voting does reflect regularities in patterns of preferences.

CAUSAL RELATIONSHIPS

The question that remains is whether the fact that parties reflect preferences means that they are merely a mirror of preferences with no independent effect. In sum, the issue is whether voting patterns generally and party voting specifically should be seen as mere reflections of preferences or as something involving both party and preference effects. In considering this question, what needs to be remembered is something we pointed out at the start of this chapter—that roll call evidence, whether in terms of party scores or NOMINATE scores, is based on vote choices, not preferences, and thus masks underlying determinants. The fact that NOMINATE scores identify patterns of ideological consistency in voting behavior on the basis of an analysis premised on the concepts of ideal points and cutpoints does not mean that they are pure measures of preferences. Indeed, if this were so, it would be self-defeating for those who believe that party has independent effects to rely on them, as is their current wont. It is equally true that the fact that party scores and NOMINATE scores can be used to demonstrate changes in partisan strength or structuring does not mean that party has an independent effect. Again, the basic evidence relates to vote choices that mask underlying determinants.

Hence the problem cannot be solved by assuming that vote choices are merely revealed preferences or that the role of party in influencing vote choices is too obvious empirically to be denied. In either case, that is to solve the problem by assumption or definition. Rather, what is required are innovative research strategies for teasing out evidence from roll calls that does speak to the issue, even if indirectly. Nor should we accept the presumption that party effects must be based entirely on something other than preferences or the conclusion that follows—that all preference effects testify to the determinative role of preferences and the subordinate role of party. That too is to decide the issue by assumption or definition, and with very rigid consequences. For not only does this threaten to make all strategic voting for reasons of policy or personal power a party effect, but it also fails to adequately recognize that in reality, different types of preferences exist, both substantive and political. Recognizing this duality, in turn, has important consequences. It means that the case for the causal primacy of preferences, if it is to be true by more than assumption or definition, must rest on the role of substantive policy preferences, not political preferences tied to electoral or power considerations. In other words, advocates of preference theory cannot hide behind the cloak of agnosticism as to the source or character of preferences. Political preferences testify to endogenous impacts on voting within the legislative process, which preference-based theory assumes do not exist and which party theory must insist do exist. The question, then, of whether party has an independent effect on voting does not reduce to a dichotomous choice between preference and party effects. Rather, the question is better framed by asking whether party effects might combine preferences and organizational factors in such a way as to make the impact of party something more than simply a shadow of preferences.

Admittedly, such reframing is no less an exercise in deductive logic than preference-based theorizing and proves little about the "real world." However, the brunt of the recent empirical evidence does lend support to such a view. A variety of studies indicate that party does indeed have an independent effect on legislative voting patterns. Researchers have approached the difficult task of getting behind data that directly reflect only choices to analyze determinants in a number of ingenious ways. Some have dealt with changes in voting behavior; some have dealt with the distribution of incentives or the manipulation of formal powers by party leaders; some have found ways to treat roll call data so as to test the proposition that party has an independent effect; and some have relied on simulations to test the independent effect of party.[19] Though there continue to be discussion and criticism of the methodologies involved in these studies, all confirm the proposition that party does have an independent effect on voting.

The work of several authors is of special interest for our argument. In a recent paper, Rick Wilson (1998) has taken seriously both the claim that the lack of a status quo point makes party measures and data spurious and our findings regarding the relationship between our overall structuring scores and the nominate scores. He therefore seeks to test whether the actual majority party medians on all votes in the House are divergent from a simulation of those medians based on the assumption that voting is driven entirely by preferences. He tests this question in Houses from the 46th (1879–81) through the 105th (1997–99) and finds that in most instances, there is a statistically significant difference between the observed and simulated majority party medians. This paper is not without some problems for advocates of the role of party, but it does impose a severe test by including all votes. In general, it confirms both that party has an independent effect and that the absence of a status quo point in aggregate roll call data does not mean that party cannot be shown to have such an effect. Another recent paper, by Eric Lawrence, Forrest Maltzman, and Steven Smith (1999), comes to the same conclusions on the basis of a cross-sectional analysis of recent Houses and Senates. It also tests and rejects the proposition that the absence of status quo points vitiates the utility of party scores or the causal importance of party. Finally, Jeffery Jenkins (1999, 2000) has published articles comparing Confederate Houses and the last two antebellum U.S. Houses. He finds not only that party has an independent effect but also that without the support or reinforcement that party provides, ideological consistency in the distribution of preferences withers away. In short, his work provides sophisticated empirical support for our earlier point about disorder and factional Houses and develops their implications regarding the interdependence of party and preference.

These findings all support the claims of party theory, as developed in the cartel approach of Cox and McCubbins and the conditional party approach of Aldrich and Rohde. More important, they suggest that these theories are reinforcing in ways that have not been fully recognized. To start, we may note that Aldrich (1994, 1995) provides good theoretical reasons in rational choice terms for recent findings that party does have an independent effect. From the beginning, their case for independent party effects has been largely an extension of the chaos theorems of rational choice theory. In contrast to Krehbiel, who for heuristic reasons assumes that voting is unidimensional, they argue that legislative voting is multidimensional—that in reality, the distribution of policy preferences can be ordered and mobilized in different ways. The independent causal force of party thus derives from the ability of party leaders, given their sources of organizational leverage, to map the policy preferences of their followers onto choice, to order and aggregate preferences among fellow partisans in a stable and consistent manner across issue areas. Similarly, the theoretical contributions of Cox and McCubbins (1993, 1994a) are substantial and reinforcing. By emphasizing the imperatives of collective action and highlighting the role of political preferences instead of substantive or policy preferences, they contribute another important piece of the puzzle. Indeed, it is a piece that Aldrich and Rohde (1997a, 2000b) have incorporated into their theory of conditional party government as well (see also Rohde 1994). What Cox and McCubbins argue is that the power of party leaders derives from the desire of members for reelection and majority status, two goals that are promoted by action in common and whose achievement involves political, policy, and psychological benefits for members. The result is to add a very new and different facet of dimensionality in support of the role of party. For now party has independent causal force, not simply because party leaders discipline the potential for disorder in underlying substantive preferences but also because party leaders use political incentives to unite partisans. Party leaders can thus be seen as agents who manage conflicts between the substantive and political preferences of party members in the process of mobilizing support to realize the benefits of collective action. In a sense, then, the answer to Krehbiel's challenge that the independent role of party requires that it be shown that members vote against their preferences is not only that this cannot be determined from roll call votes but also that members may and do vote against their substantive preferences in support of their political preferences and that in part this is what party is all about.

Nonetheless, two caveats in defense of preference-based theory are necessary. First, Krehbiel's approach to legislative voting captures an important part of the truth that theories of legislative decision making ignore at their peril. The role of substantive preferences is very powerful and, though not always congruent with political preferences, must still on balance provide a foundation for them. Otherwise, there would be little basis for the variations in party voting that do occur. In sum, then, party voting cannot derive simply from the role of party leaders in manipulating their agenda power or the other forms of leverage the organizational structure places in their hands. It must also be based on and constrained by the underlying constellation of preferences. This pattern both energizes partisan behavior on the basis of its commonalities and impedes it on the basis of the overlaps that exist among members of the two parties. So even though we may not be convinced by Krehbiel's case for preference-based theory, this does not mean that his intuitions on the importance of preferences or the dependence of party on them can be ignored.

Second, Krehbiel is quite correct in arguing that congressional party theory is inadequate, despite the application of rational choice theory to support it. It can well be argued that traditional party theory, whatever its merits, failed to provide us with an adequate empirical theory of congressional parties. Nonetheless, it is also arguable that the contributions Aldrich and Rohde and Cox and McCubbins have made to building such theory accept too many of the premises that underlie preference theory to provide a viable alternative. Whereas preference theory can be built on premises of fixed preferences and proximity voting, it is far from clear that party theory can.

Whatever the benefits of reintroducing multidimensionality in policy choices or emphasizing political preferences, they cannot provide an adequate basis for a theory of congressional parties until the former is given a firmer theoretical base with respect to organizational effects and the latter is integrated with the former. Both cartel theory and conditional party theory take large steps in these direction. But in the end, it is questionable whether such needs can be satisfied in a theory that continues to assume that human motives are fixed and uniform and therefore treatable as ideal points in a spatial model. Indeed, in effect, by introducing multidimensionality, Aldrich and Rohde render the concept of fixed preferences moot, and by introducing the concept of political preferences, Cox and McCubbins complicate the notion of ideal points so seriously as to undermine analysis based on proximity voting. It is thus reasonable to suspect that in the end, any adequate theory of congressional parties must abandon the anarchistic and egoistic assumptions of classical economics and replace them with an emphasis on organizational effects, rooted in structural leverage, ends-means uncertainty, variable intensity, and mixed motivation, or else suffer enduring problems in avoiding the reduction of party to preferences.[20] Given their continuing attachment to rational choice premises regarding preferences, it is no accident that Aldrich and Rohde have great difficulties formally demonstrating that party strength moves the party median in ways that preference theory cannot account for or that the empirical case they and Cox and McCubbins make for party rests on arguments and evidence that derive their persuasive power from assumptions of mixed motivation and organizational leverage and clash with the assumptions of the spatial model. Nor is it an accident that when opponents accept the basic assumptions of fixed preferences and spatial analysis, Krehbiel (1997a, 1997b, 1999b, 2000) has easily held his own.[21]

SUMMARY

What the current state of the debate over the role of party suggests to us is that the issue needs to be reframed and congressional party theory needs to be further developed. In the first regard, the evidence suggests that party both depends on preferences and has an independent impact and that the aim of research should be to clarify the complexities in the relationship, not to make dichotomous choices. We should ask not whether party has an independent effect but how party and preferences interact to determine patterns of voting and outcomes. In the second regard, analysis suggests that we need to develop a more adequate theory of congressional parties. Indeed, if the unidimensionality of the Poole-Rosenthal scores derive, as their originators believe, from ideology in the sense of overarching belief systems, then we need not conclude that the translation of broad ideological inclinations into concrete voting choices is automatic and smooth (Poole and Rosenthal 2001). We can rather conclude that the translation of policy dispositions into voting choices is open, within limiting but variable parameters, to party influences stemming from organizational leverage, conflicting facts, variations in intensity, and mixed motivations.

If we are to focus inquiry on the relationship between preferences and party and build a more adequate form of congressional party theory, we must begin to probe the relationship between exogeneity and endogeneity far more seriously than in the past. In other words, we must begin to seek ways of conceptualizing and measuring the potential for partisan agreement as it enters the legislative process from the electoral process and the conditions that shape its translation into partisan action. In so doing, we must come to a far better understanding of both the parameters imposed by exogenous forces and the trade-offs between substantive and political preferences than has been the case to this point. In short, we must come to a far better understanding of how external processes, both electoral and executive, affect the legislative process, how various types of endogenous effects are generated in the legislative process, and how the components of party voting interact to structure voting patterns.

As we suggested at the start of this chapter, all this speaks to very fundamental issues. Our critique of both preference and party theory in their current forms has important implications for the character of the epistemological and methodological premises that should guide inquiry. It is not for idle purposes that Krehbiel assumes that voting is an anarchistic process of aggregating preferences; that choice rests on and reveals fixed, exogenous, and uniform preferences; that voting can and should be approached in unidimensional terms; and that reduction to basic units of analysis is to be preferred. Many, if not all, these premises are assumed to be necessary to derive lawlike statements, and lawlike statements, according to the precepts of positivism, are the hallmark of valid knowledge. Krehbiel is thus more pristine methodologically than his critics in the rational choice camp. His preference-based approach to explaining legislative decision making rests on strict adherence to the goals of universalism and determinism and the canons of reductionism and simplicity thought necessary to achieve them. Nonetheless, the thrust of our conclusions regarding reframing the issue and reformulating the theory of party is that traditional positivist premises should not underlie and constrain inquiry. If the key to better understanding is to seek to deal with endogeneity and exogeneity in a measured fashion with respect to both external impacts and internal outcomes, then contingency and com-

plexity, not universalism and determinism, should be the premises that en-
ergize and guide analysis.

We will, admit, in closing, that we cannot know for certain whether the
search for universalism and determinism errs by underestimating the limits
that the complexity of human nature and the social world impose on simplicity. What does seem clear, in terms of both logic and evidence, is that a
search for universalism and determinism leads to assumptions in orienting
research that are not only unrealistic but also not as useful as assumptions of
contingency and uncertainty. In the natural world, the quest for lawlike
statements has in recent decades been constrained by an increasing recognition that the conditions of relationships need to be uncovered and specified
and that even then, elements of uncertainty may remain and be inherent in
the complex ways in which variables combine. In the social world, the case
for such an approach is even stronger, given the embeddedness of intention
and action in social contexts (Scharpf 1997). We conclude, then, by recom-
mending it in the study of legislative decision making. In our view, the way
to knowledge is to focus on the conditions of relationships and not to shape
the lenses we apply to make sense of the empirical world to fit the assumption that knowledge, to be valid or useful, must be universalistic and deter-
ministic in character.

Chapter 5

Agenda Power in the U.S. House
of Representatives, 1877–1986

GARY W. COX AND MATHEW D. MCCUBBINS

Congressional organization and politics seem to change roughly every generation. The literature has identified twelve eras of congressional organization—outlined in Table 5.1 (see Galloway 1976 and Hinckley 1988)—that
can be classified by their degree of centralization of power. In some eras,
strong party leaders (such as Joe Cannon or Newt Gingrich) control legislative organization and policy outputs. In other eras, control is decentralized
to committee chairs, subcommittee chairs, nonpartisan coalitions, and so on.

The fifth and tenth eras listed in Table 5.1 are good examples of the more
decentralized end of the spectrum of congressional organization. Indeed,
Richard Fenno's (1973: xiii) summary of conventional wisdom on congressional organization in the tenth era reached back to Gilded Age commentary for the appropriate touchstones (see also Cater 1964; Fenno 1966, 1973;
Davidson 1981; Eulau and McCluggage 1984; Shepsle and Weingast 1984a,
1987a, 1987b; Dodd 1989; Shepsle 1989a; Weingast 1989):

> The oldest and most familiar [characterization of congressional organi-
> zation] is Woodrow Wilson's book-length assertion that committees
> dominate congressional decision making. A corollary states that com-
> mittees are autonomous units, which operate quite independently of
> such external influences as legislative party leaders, chamber majorities,
> and the President of the United States. Other staples of committee
> commentary hold . . . that each committee is the repository of legisla-

Table 5.1

The Twelve Partisan "Arrangements"
in Congress

Name	Years
1) Federalist-Democrat	1789–1816
2) "Era of Good Feelings"	1817–1824
3) Multiparty Competition	1825–1860
4) Republican Hegemony	1861–1874
5) "The Gilded Era"	1875–1895
6) Republican Hegemony II	1896–1908
Pivotal Progressives	1909–1910
7) Democratic Interlude	1911–1920
8) Republican Hegemony III	1921–1932
9) New Deal Democratic Hegemony	1933–1936
10) Conservative Coalition	1937–1972
*11) Liberal Hegemony	1973–1994
*12) Republican Revolution?	1995–

SOURCE: Except for the asterisked eras, which we have
added, the eras are drawn from Galloway 1976.

tive expertise within its jurisdiction; that committee decisions are usually accepted and ratified by other members of the chamber; that committee chairmen can (and usually do) wield a great deal of influence
over their committees.

Both of these eras of decentralization—the fifth and the tenth—ended
when power was transferred away from committee chairs—mostly to party
leaders after the Gilded Age, to both party leaders and subcommittee chairs
in the 1970s.

How should we understand the shifts in congressional organization listed
in Table 5.1? One possible perspective is that parties have never been of
much independent force in congressional politics, so that the eras sometimes
described as party government—such as Republican Hegemony II—are
at best tending in that direction. Another perspective is that party government is conditional on the homogeneity of preferences within the majority
party (see, e.g., Brady, Cooper, and Hurley 1979; Collie and Brady 1985;
Collie 1988b, Rohde 1991; Aldrich and Rohde 1997a, 1998).[1] From this
perspective, the periods labeled "party government" really evinced party

government and the periods labeled "committee government," such as the Conservative Coalition, really evinced committee government. A third perspective is that important aspects of party government are ubiquitous throughout congressional history. From this perspective, one might talk of decentralized party government in era 10, but talk of bipartisan committee government would be misleading.

This last perspective is closest to that articulated in our previous work (Cox and McCubbins 1993, 1994b), and especially because this seems to have caused the most confusion—or outright disbelief—among our readers, we wish to explain and defend it here. We begin by noting that at least if one focuses on the post–Civil War organizational eras, there are some noticeable constants in legislative organization. In particular, the majority party (1) selects *all* institutional leaders such as the Speaker, committee chairs, and subcommittee chairs (Hinckley 1988; Oleszek 1989; Sinclair 1994); (2) holds a supermajority on the Rules Committee (see Oleszek 1989: 131–32); (3) controls appointments of its own members to standing, select, and conference committees (Oleszek 1989; Kiewiet and McCubbins 1991; Cox and McCubbins 1993); (4) controls a disproportionate share of staff and other legislative resources; and (5) because of the first four points, controls access to the floor agenda.[2] This suggests that while some aspects of party government may be conditional, other aspects are not.

Indeed, we will argue the following points:

1. The majority party's formal agenda powers allow it to, and are used to, keep issues off the floor agenda that would foreseeably displease significant portions of the party. This *negative agenda power* is *unconditional*, in the sense that its exercise should not theoretically and does not empirically vary with the similarity of the party's members' (constituency-induced or personal) ideas of good public policy.

2. In addition to its power to stop new legislation, thereby preserving past gains, the majority can also propose changes to existing policy. However, the size of the majority party's agenda (i.e., the volume of new policies it seeks to implement) waxes and wanes, depending on how similar party members' policy goals are (cf. Rohde 1991; Aldrich and Rohde 1998; Peters 1990: 11; Cox and McCubbins 1993), because leaders do not wish to waste their time leading where their followers will not (or cannot be induced to) follow. That is, *positive agenda control* is ever present, but the frequency with which the party uses this power varies with the degree to which the party membership agrees on what the party's collective reputation should

be and hence on what should be done (Cox and McCubbins 1993: 154–55).

The formal basis for these conclusions is a garden-variety spatial model of legislative procedure onto which we graft two starkly different assumptions about who controls the floor agenda. In one model, we assume that the floor agenda is determined by majority vote on the floor and hence by the median legislator on the floor. We call this the *floor agenda model*, and its predictions about what the floor agenda will look like form our null hypothesis. We contrast the floor agenda model with an alternative we call the *cartel agenda model* (Cox and McCubbins 1993, 1994b), which contends that agenda control is partisan in nature. It asks, if the majority party leadership determines the floor agenda, what would that agenda look like?

Simply put, we present two polar models of agenda power. In what follows, we contrast these two models with each other and test their predictions head to head. Using outcomes from the 45th to 99th Congresses (1877 to 1986), we find that we can reject the floor agenda model. In contrast, there is substantial and credible evidence supporting the cartel agenda model. In particular, we show that negative agenda control is indeed a largely *invariant* advantage of majority status and that positive agenda control is variable, changing with the internal homogeneity of the majority party. Variations in these two aspects of agenda control, we suggest, explain some of the basic tensions and historical fluctuations in congressional organization.

Modeling the Floor Agenda

BACKGROUND ASSUMPTIONS

In pathbreaking research, Shepsle (1979) and Shepsle and Weingast (1981, 1987a, 1987b) modeled the House agenda process and examined the consequences of agenda power. They relied on a spatial analogy wherein policy choices correspond to points in a multidimensional Euclidean space (cf. Black 1958; Downs 1957). For simplicity and ease of exposition, we will adapt their well-known model to our purposes.

We use the following five assumptions to model agenda setting in the House:

- *Dimensions of policy choice.* First, there are *n* policy instruments that can be adjusted by the legislature. For example, the minimum wage can be increased or decreased, the criteria to qualify for welfare payments can be loosened or tightened, and so forth. A status quo point for each instrument (or dimension) is commonly known.

- *Legislators.* Second, there are N members in the legislature, whose preferences over the policy dimensions are additively separable and who vote strategically. Specifically, on any given dimension j, legislator k has a unique ideal point on that dimension, x_j^k, which is common knowledge. The utility that legislator k derives from a given policy vector, $z = (z_1, \ldots, z_n)$, declines with the sum of the distances between x_j^k and z_j: $u_k(z) = -\Sigma_j \mid x_j^k - z_j \mid$. We assume that members seek to maximize the utility that they derive from the final policy choice of the House (i.e., to minimize the summed distances between their ideal points and the final choices on each dimension).[3] A consequence of this assumption is that the model of policy choice is, in essence, reduced to a series of independent unidimensional choices.

- *Agenda setters.* Third, there exist agenda-setting agents who have the right to propose bills to the floor within their (fixed) jurisdictions; for convenience, we assume that the bills they offer can propose changes in only one dimension at a time.

- *Legislative sequence.* Fourth, the legislative sequence consists of only three stages: (1) some agent selects (or some agents select) the bills that the floor will consider; (2) the floor then considers the bills presented to it, amending them as it sees fit; (3) the floor then votes on final passage of the amended bill.

- *Open rules.* Fifth, we consider the special case in which all bills are considered under open rules, subject only to a germaneness restriction. Extending the model to include closed rules only increases the majority party's agenda power.

Shepsle (1979: 350) suggests that there are three possible agenda-setting agents in the House: the Committee of the Whole, legislative parties, and committees. The third possibility, wherein autonomous and independent committees set the floor agenda, is the topic of Shepsle and Weingast's (1981, 1987a, 1987b) classic analyses. Our focus is on the agenda-setting powers of the first two of the agents listed: the floor as a whole and the parties—in particular, the majority party.

In one of the models to follow, the median legislator of the majority party has the unilateral power to put bills on the floor agenda, directly or through committees. Alternatively, one can think of the agenda setter in this model as the majority party leader, whose reelection incentives ensure a centrist-within-the-majority-party stance. In our second model, parties are not appropriate "analytic units," and the floor agenda is determined as if by majority vote on the floor (in the spirit of Mayhew 1974 and Krehbiel 1998).

For ease of exposition only, and without loss of generality, we also incorporate in our model an assumption that members of the majority party are generally to the left of members of the minority party (we are thinking of the long period of Democratic dominance from the early 1930s to the mid-1990s). More formally, let m_j denote the location of the median member of the minority party on dimension j. Let M_j denote the location of the median member of the majority party on dimension j. Finally, let F_j denote the location of the median member of the House on dimension j. We assume that $M_j < F_j < m_j$ for all j.[4] Note that the assumption allows some Democrats to be to the right of some Republicans, or even to the right of a majority of them, on some (or even all) dimensions. Similarly, some Republicans may be to the left of some Democrats, or even a majority, on some (or even all) dimensions. Note also that no assumption is made that the same member of Congress is the median on all dimensions, although this too is possible within our model.

We also assume that the location of the status quo on any given dimension—which we also assume is the reversion—may vary. The world deals out "shocks" that upset the best-laid plans of previous legislatures, so that the status quo outcome on any given dimension may have drifted over a number of years (e.g., a once generous minimum wage erodes with inflation) or experienced a sudden shift (e.g., various foreign policy dimensions looked quite different after the fall of the Berlin Wall). Formally, we assume that the status quo on dimension j at time t, denoted SQ_{jt}, is such that $SQ_{jt} = SQ_{j,t-1} + \varepsilon_{jt}$, where $SQ_{j,t-1}$ is the status quo as it was at the end of the previous legislature and ε_{jt} is the shock (thought of as arriving at the beginning of Congress t) dealt out by nature.[5]

The model is simplest if one assumes that the policy shocks chosen by nature become common knowledge at the beginning of the game. With this assumption, the location of the status quo on each dimension is also common knowledge.

All told, the sequence of moves in the model is as follows. First, nature chooses the policy shock ε_{jt} for each dimension j, which then becomes common knowledge. Second, the agenda setting agent or agents decide to put various bills on the floor agenda (where all bills must deal with a single dimension). Third, the floor considers all bills reported, amending them as the members see fit. Fourth, the floor then either passes or rejects the amended bill by majority vote.

VOTING ON THE FLOOR

Regardless of how the floor agenda is set, the following observations hold. At final passage, some bill b_j (possibly an amended version of the bill originally reported to the floor) will be pitted against the status quo SQ_j on dimension j. Because the vote at this stage is binary, a member with ideal point x will vote for the bill if and only if b_j is closer to x than SQ_j is.

This conclusion can be restated with some further notation. Let $R_j(x) = 2x - b_j$ denote the point that is equally far from x as b_j is but on the opposite side of x from b_j. If $x < b_j$, then $R_j(x)$ is just as far to the left of x as b_j is to the right of x. If $x > b_j$, then $R_j(x)$ is just as far to the right of x as b_j is to the left of x. In either case, $R_j(x)$ is utility-equivalent to b_j for the member with ideal point x. Then

> *Lemma 1*: Consider a member with ideal point x on dimension j voting on final passage of bill b_j.
>
> a.   If $x < b_j$, the member votes in favor of b_j if and only if $SQ_j \notin [R_j(x), b_j]$;
> b.   If $x > b_j$, the member votes in favor of b_j if and only if $SQ_j \notin [b_j, R_j(x)]$.

Proof: Omitted.

THE CARTEL AGENDA MODEL

Legislators face a number of collective action problems—allocating scarce legislative time and resources, cooperating to secure their own personal as well as their party's reputation for the next election, coordinating so that work gets done, and so forth. We have argued elsewhere (cf. Cox and McCubbins 1993) that parties overcome these collective action problems through the institutionalization of a central authority, much as Alchian and Demsetz (1972) have argued that firms overcome similar problems.[6] In the case of the U.S. House, the central authority is the majority party leadership, to which significant authority is delegated to ensure coordination and cooperation among individual legislators. The majority party leadership controls various mechanisms, such as appointments to control committees and the scheduling of plenary time, to keep party members in line. Party members, in turn, maintain ultimate control through the power to select and remove their own leaders. For this reason, we assume that the majority party leadership is strongly responsive to the median member of the majority party.

In the cartel agenda model, we assume that the leader of the majority party is the median of his or her party (or acts in the median's interests) and has the unilateral power to put bills on the floor agenda or keep them off. Equivalently, we can assume that the agenda is set as if by majority vote in the majority party's caucus.

What should happen in this model? Lemma 1 leads to the following results. We only sketch the proofs, as they are fairly transparent given the simple model constructed so far. We discuss plausible wrinkles to the model —including uncertainty about the location of the status quo or about member ideal points—later.

Result 1: No dimension j on which SQ_j is preferred to F_j by a majority of the majority party is ever scheduled for floor consideration.

Proof: The median majority party agent can anticipate that if he or she puts a bill dealing with dimension j on the floor agenda, this bill will be amended to the floor median. The agenda–setting agent will therefore report only dimensions on which he or she prefers F_j to SQ_j. But this is equivalent to never reporting a dimension on which SQ_j is preferred to F_j by a majority of the majority party.

Corollary: Every bill b_j passed results in policy being moved closer to M_j, the median majority party agent's ideal point.

Proof: In light of Result 1, all status quo points in the interval $[M_j - |M_j - F_j|, M_j + |M_j - F_j|]$ are not reported to the floor. In other words, all status quo points in an interval centered on the median member of the majority party's ideal point are stabilized, while all others are brought closer to this point.

Result 2: No bill opposed by a majority of the majority party's members ever passes.

Proof: From Result 1, the median majority party agent will report to the floor only bills concerning dimensions on which the party prefers F_j to SQ_j. Thus the bill, as amended, will always pass, and a majority of the majority party will always favor passage.

Figure 5.1 helps illustrate these results. If the status quo lies anywhere between $2M - F$ and F (indicated by the solid line), then a majority of the majority party will oppose putting the issue on the floor agenda. Hence, per Result 1, dimensions with status quo points in the solid-line region will never be scheduled for floor consideration; all others will be. Thus a bill to change SQ_2 will be reported to the floor (as F is preferred by M to SQ_2), while a bill to change SQ_1 will *not* (as SQ_1 is preferred by M to F).

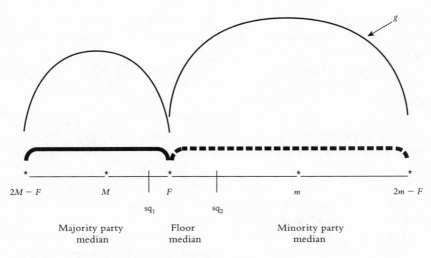

Figure 5.1.   Spatial model of legislative voting.

Results 1 and 2 both have testable implications that can be stated in terms of the concept of a "roll." We say that a party is rolled at the agenda-setting stage when a majority of the party unsuccessfully opposes the placement on the floor agenda of a particular bill. A party is rolled at final passage when a majority of its members unsuccessfully oppose a particular bill's final passage. In terms of rolls, Result 1 says the majority party is never rolled at the agenda-setting stage, while Result 2 says it is never rolled at final passage.

We should hasten to note that these "majority party never gets rolled" predictions are similar in analytic status to other predictions drawn from complete information models, such as "there is never any war" or "there are never any vetoes" (cf. Cameron 2000). These sorts of results should be viewed as baselines illustrating the extreme case of zero uncertainty. Add a little uncertainty into these models, and it is well known that one begins to get "mistakes"—in the present context, mistakes in which the agenda setter schedules a bill that a majority of majority party agents dislike (because, for example, the status quo point turns out not to be where it was most likely to be). We plan to extend the model to include uncertainty, but for now, this simple model—similar to that in Krehbiel (1998) and many other applications of the unidimensional spatial model—yields the main insights: (1) if the majority party controls the agenda, then bills that (are likely to) lead to policy changes opposed by a majority of majority party agents never (rarely) make it onto the floor agenda, and (2) if the majority party controls the agenda, policy changes (almost) always bring policy closer to M, the median majority party agent's ideal point.

We make four further observations about these results. First, they are not automatic consequences of the majority party's having a majority of seats in the legislature, as will be seen in the next section.

Second, aspects of the same results survive into multidimensional models in which legislators have spherical indifference contours. In particular, if the agenda is set as if by majority vote in the majority caucus, then the only bills that are scheduled move policy closer to the majority party yolk (the smallest hypersphere that intersects all majority party median hyperplanes). In the unidimensional model, the yolk collapses to the median, and so it is the median that acts as the "policy attractor."

Third, the standard unidimensional spatial model assumes that there are no opportunity, consideration, or proposal costs. Changing any of these zero-cost assumptions would not centrally affect the majority party's negative agenda-setting success.

Finally, we should note that the (complete information) model yields no clear predictions about the exact bills that will be put on the floor agenda and whether they will be amended. If the median majority party agent prefers (1) reporting a bill at its own ideal point, seeing that bill amended to the floor median and then passed, to (2) reporting a bill at the floor median and having the bill as reported passed, there can be amendments and they will always go *against* a majority party majority. But this story implicitly assumes that agents care about the positions they are associated with and not just about the final outcome. Although we certainly think that legislative agents do care about position-taking payoffs, and we intend to explore models with such act-contingent utilities (cf. Sinclair 1998a), we do not elaborate that point here.

THE FLOOR AGENDA MODEL

In the floor agenda model, we assume that the bills to be considered on the floor are determined by majority vote on the floor. It is simplest to imagine that the median legislative agent moves that a bill implementing F be put onto the floor agenda. (If some other bill is put on the agenda, it will be amended to F before passage in any event.)

Under this agenda structure, *all* dimensions j with SQ_j not equal to F_j are considered on the floor. (Recall that there are no opportunity, proposal, or consideration costs in the standard unidimensional spatial model on which we are building.) If SQ_j is to the left of F_j, then the median and all to his or her right will vote to consider a bill and then to pass it (as amended if amended). If SQ_j is to the right of F_j, then the median and all to his or her left will vote to consider a bill and then to pass it (as amended if amended).

Will a majority of majority party agents ever vote against the placement of a bill on the floor agenda in this model? Will they ever oppose a bill on final passage? The following results give the answers:

> *Result 1*: A majority of the majority party will vote against putting a particular dimension j on the floor agenda (but will lose) if and only if SQ_j is closer to M_j than F_j is.
>
> *Corollary*: The probability with which a majority of the majority party unsuccessfully opposes placing an issue j on the floor agenda is a function of (1) how large the interval between M_j and F_j is and (2) the distribution of SQ_j.
>
> *Result 2*: A majority of the majority party will vote against a bill pertaining to dimension j on final passage (but will lose) if and only if SQ_j is closer to M_j than F_j is.
>
> *Corollary*: The probability with which a majority of the majority party unsuccessfully opposes a bill on final passage is a function of (1) how large the interval between M_j and F_j is and (2) the distribution of SQ_j.

Note that similar results hold for the minority party. Just substitute *minority party* for *majority party* and m_j for M_j in these claims.

LOCAL VERSUS GLOBAL AGENDA CONTROL

In our discussion of the cartel model, we assumed that the majority party's median member (or the leadership acting in that member's interest) set the floor agenda. Another variant of the cartel model, slightly more nuanced, assumes that the majority party contingent on each committee in the House sets the floor agenda in the committee's jurisdiction. The first model assumes that the floor agenda is set by the majority party's global median, whereas the second assumes that it is set, in each jurisdiction, by the majority party's local median. A similar distinction between a global majoritarian model (agenda set by floor median) and a local majoritarian model (agenda in each jurisdiction set by the relevant committee median) can be made.

The predictions of the local models are similar to those made by the global models. For example, when considering just one committee, the local cartel model predicts that the majority party contingent will never be rolled, while the rate at which the minority party contingent is rolled depends on the distance between the minority's local median and the interval between the floor and committee median. (The reason that the relevant distance is that between the minority median and the interval between floor and committee medians can be indicated by considering a status quo point that lies between the floor and committee medians. A bill proposing to change such a status quo will never be reported from committee, because the committee median will correctly anticipate that such a bill would end up at F, worse than the current status quo from his or her perspective. Thus the minority cannot be rolled on such bills; only those outside the intermedian interval can generate minority rolls. See Cox 1999 for details.)

In the next section, we use final passage votes on the floor to pit global versions of the cartel and floor agenda models against one another, and we use committee reports to pit local versions of the two models against one another. This leaves for another time the task of judging whether a global cartel (floor) model outperforms a local cartel (floor) model.

Comparing the Two Models

The floor agenda model and the cartel agenda model produce distinct point estimates and distinct comparative statics regarding the frequency of certain legislative outcomes. While we ultimately rely more on comparative statics to test the veracity of our models, we begin by examining the models' competing point estimates.

POINT ESTIMATES

Here we look at how often the majority party fails to stop legislation of which a majority of its members disapprove at either of two critical junctures in the legislative process. First, how often does the majority party get rolled on final passage votes on the House floor? That is, how often does a majority of the majority party oppose a bill that nonetheless passes? Second, how often does the majority party get rolled on committee votes? That is, how often does a majority of the majority party contingent on the relevant committee oppose a bill that nonetheless passes?

The cartel agenda model says that the majority party never gets rolled. The floor agenda model says that the majority party may be rolled less often than, as often as, or even more often than the minority, depending on where M_j, m_j, and F_j are and on how the status quo points are distributed on each dimension j. Assuming that the distribution of status quo points has no areas of zero density, a necessary and sufficient condition for the majority party to have a zero probability of losing under the floor agenda model is: $M_j = F_j$ for all j. This might happen, for example, if the majority party consisted of a single unitary party that successfully imposed a single ideal point on its members. But it should be a rare event in cases where parties cannot be taken as "analytic units."

FINAL PASSAGE VOTES

We look first at final passage votes on the House floor. The set of final passage votes that we analyze is drawn from roll call votes for the 45th Congress through the first session of the 99th Congress.[7] We coded each final passage vote as either ordinary (only a majority required for passage) or extraordinary (a supermajority of two-thirds required for passage), excluding the latter from analysis. The analysis is restricted to H.R. bills.

We identify rolls by examining how the membership of each party voted on each final passage votes. If the nay votes exceeded the aye votes for one party (on committee or on the floor) but the measure passed nonetheless, we code that party as having been rolled on that vote. As shown in Table 5.2, the modal number of times, by Congress, that the majority party was rolled on final passage votes on the House floor is *zero*, as the majority party is not rolled at all in eighteen of the fifty-five Congresses in our study. The average number of times the majority party is rolled in a congress is 1.5, and the median number is 1. By contrast, the average number of rolls of the minority party is 13, with a median of 10. The average number of ordinary final passage votes per Congress is 51, and the median is 32.

Consider next the party roll rates (the number of times a party was rolled in a Congress divided by the total number of ordinary final passage votes). Roll rates for the majority and minority parties are given in Figure 5.2. The (weighted) average roll rate for the majority party in the fifty-five Congresses under study here is less than 3 percent. By contrast, the (weighted) average for the minority party is 25 percent.

The differences between the frequency of rolls on final passage votes and the roll rates for the majority and minority party meet our expectations very well. Nonetheless, the majority party was rolled 84 times in 2,826 votes in fifty-five Congresses (compared to 713 for the minority party), and we can reject the hypothesis that the average roll rate was zero for both the majority and minority parties. Is this close enough to our expectations to motivate further examination of the cartel agenda idea?

We believe so. To dispel one potential point of confusion that might convince some readers otherwise, we stress that there is no reason to expect the majority party to have a low roll rate merely because it has a majority. Let us elaborate this point before moving on to more systematic tests of the floor and cartel models.

Table 5.2
House Rolls on Final Passage Votes for Majority and Minority Parties, by Congress

Congress	Majority Rolls	Minority Rolls	Total Final Passage Votes	Majority Party
The Gilded Era/1877−1897				
45	5	7	21	Democrats
46	6	19	56	Democrats
47	5	15	45	Republicans
48	1	8	46	Democrats
49	6	4	27	Democrats
50	4	3	11	Democrats
51	1	17	25	Republicans
52	1	4	18	Democrats
53	1	11	25	Democrats
54	0	8	12	Republicans
Republican Hegemony II/1897−1909				
55	1	12	18	Republicans
56	0	6	7	Republicans
57	3	4	13	Republicans
58	0	3	4	Republicans
59	1	5	11	Republicans
60	0	3	5	Republicans
Pivotal Progressives/1909−1911				
61	1	10	11	Republicans
Democratic Interlude/1911−1921				
62	0	10	24	Republicans
63	1	10	23	Democrats
64	2	7	27	Democrats
65	0	6	37	Democrats
66	1	11	38	Republicans
Republican Hegemony III/1921−1933				
67	0	16	34	Republicans
68	1	7	22	Republicans
69	0	6	20	Republicans
70	0	2	10	Republicans
71	0	5	10	Republicans
72	1	8	16	Democrats

(continued)

Table 5.2

(continued)

Era/Congress	Majority Rolls	Minority Rolls	Total Final Passage Votes	Majority Party
New Deal Democratic Hegemony/1933−1937				
73	0	13	27	Democrats
74	2	12	31	Democrats
Conservative Coalition/1937−1973				
75	0	10	22	Democrats
76	2	10	32	Democrats
77	0	9	38	Democrats
78	4	1	29	Democrats
79	2	5	41	Democrats
80	0	7	35	Republicans
81	2	14	41	Democrats
82	0	7	23	Democrats
83	0	8	38	Republicans
84	2	3	43	Democrats
85	2	5	43	Democrats
86	2	16	49	Democrats
87	1	19	56	Democrats
88	2	29	81	Democrats
89	0	34	114	Democrats
90	1	16	121	Democrats
91	4	12	150	Democrats
92	4	7	150	Democrats
Liberal Hegemony/1973−1989				
93	1	30	236	Democrats
94	3	57	227	Democrats
95	2	44	187	Democrats
96	1	31	157	Democrats
97	2	24	96	Democrats
98	3	44	103	Democrats
99	0	19	40	Democrats

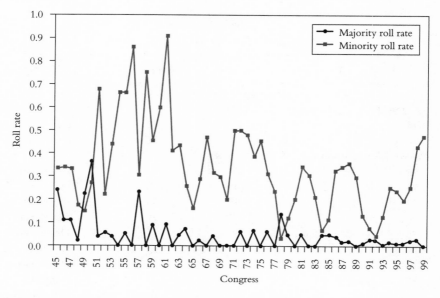

Figure 5.2.   Majority and minority roll rates, by Congress.

Imagine a majority party that holds less than 100 percent of the seats in the House, and suppose that each legislator has a distinct ideal point. For any such majority, it is necessarily true that a majority of the party members' ideal points lie either to the left of the median legislator's ideal or to the right. Suppose that they lie to the left and a bill moving a status quo SQ to F is proposed, where $M < SQ < F$ (i.e., the status quo lies between the majority party and floor medians). Under the floor agenda model, the bill will pass despite the fact that a majority of the majority party will vote against it. In other words, the mere fact that the majority party has a majority, even a very big one, does not guarantee that it will not get rolled. The frequency of majority rolls depends on how many status quo points there are in the interval between M and F relative to the total number of status quo points altered in the session, not on the majority's size.

COMMITTEE REPORTS

We can also ask how often the majority party gets rolled in committee (that is, how often does a majority of the majority party contingent on a committee oppose reporting a bill to the floor but lose?). To do so, we employ a data set from Cox and McCubbins (1993) that contains 5,628 committee reports on bills introduced to the House in the 84th, 86th, 88th, 90th,

Table 5.3

Democrats' and Republicans' Roll Rates
on Committee Reports, by Congress

Congress	Number of Committee Reports	Democrats' Roll Rate (%)	Republicans' Roll Rate (%)	Notes
84	905	0.11	0.55	Democrats rolled once, in Post Office Committee
86	782	0.13	2.56	Democrats rolled once, in Judiciary Committee
88	671	0	3.58	
90	621	0.16	3.22	Democrats rolled once, in HUAC
92	622	0	1.61	
94	672	0	7.44	
96	663	0.15	6.33	Democrats rolled once, in Interior Committee
98	686	0	9.04	
	Sum: 5628	Average: 0.07 (4/5628)	Average: 4.14 (233/5628)	

NOTE: Democrats were majority party in all Congresses.

92nd, 94th, 96th, and 98th Congresses. We count the majority contingent as being rolled when a majority of them file a dissent to the committee's report.

The data are summarized in Table 5.3. We find that the majority party was rolled on the committee report only 0.07 percent of the time (4 reports out of 5,628).

We also examined rolls on House-Senate conference reports (as evidenced by who signed and who did not sign the report). We found that the majority party in the House was rolled on final passage of the conference committee report only once in 240 times from the 96th through the 101st Congresses (data from Hennig 1996).[8]

The paucity with which the House majority party is rolled at the agenda-setting and final passage stages seems to fit nicely with the predictions of the cartel agenda model. Indeed, there are far fewer majority party rolls at all levels then we anticipated. This evidence is somewhat ambiguous, however, when it comes to choosing which model—the floor agenda or the cartel agenda—is better at explaining the history of congressional behavior. First, the floor agenda model merely predicts a positive roll rate for the majority, the exact size depending on how many dimensions have status quo points between M and F. The distribution of (unobserved) status quo points just might be such that very few status quo points lie between M and F. Thus the floor agenda model is also potentially consistent with the low roll rates for the majority that we observed. Second, while the (complete information) cartel model predicts no majority rolls, there are a few. That the roll rate for the majority is low but not zero suggests that some omitted considerations—such as uncertainty or divided government (which we explore more fully later in this chapter)—are producing an occasional roll of the majority party. It is to more definitive tests that we now turn.

COMPARATIVE STATICS

To bolster our confidence that the cartel model outperforms the floor model, we now examine the two models' competing comparative statics predictions, beginning with final passage votes. Under the floor agenda model, the probability that the majority party loses a final passage vote increases with the distance between M_j and F_j for all j, while the probability that the minority loses an agenda-setting or final passage vote increases with the distance between m_j and F_j for all j.[9] Under the cartel agenda model, the second of these comparative statics expectations holds—the opposition should lose more often the more distant its median member is from the floor median—but the first does not: the majority party should never lose, and any fluctuations in its roll rate should be unrelated to the distance between the majority party and floor medians.

We cannot observe the distance between party medians and the floor median on a dimension-by-dimension basis. But we can use multidimensional scaling results, such as the NOMINATE scale produced by Poole and Rosenthal (1985, 1997), to estimate the average location of the party and floor medians across all dimensions in a Congress. If we denote party c's estimated median in Congress t by P_{ct}, the estimated floor median by F_t, and the distance between these two by $D_{ct} = |P_{ct} - F_t|$, then the foregoing discussion suggests estimating the following regression to test the two models:

$$Pr[ROLL_{cjt} = 1] = G[\alpha_c + \beta_c \times D_{ct}] \qquad (1)$$

where $ROLL_{cjt}$ is a dummy variable that takes on a value of 1 if party c was rolled on ordinary final passage vote j in Congress t and 0 otherwise; α_c and β_c are parameters; and G is a cumulative distribution function.

Note that while our dependent variable takes on a value of 0 or 1 for each vote, our independent variables do not vary by vote but rather by Congress. This presents special estimation problems. Although we have many votes in a Congress, they may not be independent. While we might believe that votes are independent if the floor agenda model is true, the cartel agenda model implies that they are not. But if votes are not independent, estimating Equation 1 for each observation of $ROLL_{cjt}$ may exaggerate our true number of observations and make our standard errors seem smaller than they really are. We therefore estimate Equation 2:

$$ROLL\_RATE_{ct} = \chi_c + \beta_c D_{ct} + \varepsilon_{ct} \tag{2}$$

where $ROLL\_RATE_{ct}$ is the roll rate for each party c in Congress t.

Equation 2 can be estimated by ordinary least squares (OLS) because the number of observations that make up the denominator in the proportion, $ROLL\_RATE_{ct}$, averages more than 50 and thus $ROLL\_RATE_{ct}$ should approximate a normal distribution asymptotically. We expect that Equation 2 will suffer from heteroskedasticity as the number of votes per Congress varies by two orders of magnitude. Examining roll rates in Figure 5.2 leads us to believe that our estimation will also suffer serial correlation. We found evidence of both problems. We corrected for this using the Huber-White sandwich estimator of variance. To correct for autocorrelation, we included one and two term lags of the dependent variables as right-hand side variables. Further diagnostics of our regression suggested no other problems for our estimation.

Maddala (1983: 18–30) suggests the minimum logit chi square (MLCS) technique of Berkson (1953) as an alternative method to estimate Equation 2. In this technique, the dependent variable is the smoothed logit of the roll rate:

$$\log\left[\frac{ROLL\_RATE_{ct} + (2TOTAL\_FPV_t)^{-1}}{1 - ROLL\_RATE_{ct} + (2TOTAL\_FPV_t)^{-1}}\right]$$

where $TOTAL\_FPV_{ct}$ is the total number of final passage votes for Congress t. One estimates the model using weighted least squares with weights $TOTAL\_FPV_t \times [ROLL\_RATE_{ct} + (2TOTAL\_FPV_t)^{-1}] \times [1 - ROLL\_RATE_{ct} + (2TOTAL\_FPV_t)^{-1}]$. This technique should approximate a logit regression on $ROLL_{cjt}$ without exaggerating our number of observations and biasing our tests.[9]

The floor agenda model predicts that the coefficient β_c in Equation 2 will be positive and significant for both the majority and minority parties. That is, the floor agenda model predicts that as D_{ct} increases, the likelihood that the majority (minority) party is rolled on vote j increases.

The cartel agenda model, in contrast, predicts that the coefficient β_c for the majority party will be zero: the likelihood that the *majority* party is rolled on vote j is not systematically related to D_{ct}. However, β_c is predicted to be positive for the minority party.

Which of these two stark models better fits the observed data? Table 5.4 provides an answer.

FINAL PASSAGE ROLLS

The results from an OLS estimation of $ROLL\_RATE_{ct}$ for final passage floor votes is reported in the middle of the table. As the cartel agenda model predicts, the estimated coefficient $\hat{\beta}_c$ for the majority party is statistically indistinguishable from zero ($p < .324$, two-tailed test), while the estimated coefficient for the minority party is positive and highly significant ($p < .00$, two-tailed test). This implies that the likelihood of rolling the majority party on the floor is unrelated to the distance between the majority party and floor medians; but the likelihood of rolling the minority increases the more distant its median member is from the floor median. This flatly refutes the floor agenda model.

The MCLS estimates for final passage floor votes are also reported in the middle of Table 5.4. The results are quite similar to the Huber-White OLS estimates: we cannot reject the null hypothesis that $\hat{\beta}_c$ for the majority party ($p > .418$) is equal to zero, but we can reject the null hypothesis that $\hat{\beta}_c = 0$ for the minority party ($p > 0$). This too flatly rejects the floor agenda model.

COMMITTEE ROLLS

In our analysis of the House committee data, the unit of observation is a Congress-committee-party vote. Thus the dependent variable, $ROLL^l_{cjt}$, is whether or not party c was rolled on vote j in committee l in Congress t. Unlike the situation with final passage votes, the number of observations per committee is often relatively small. We cannot rely on large numbers to produce normally distributed proportions. Accordingly, OLS is not an attractive estimation procedure in the case of the committee data. Here we present estimates from an MLCS model. (Estimating the model directly as a logistic regression produces comparable results, as it does in the case of final passage votes.)

Our sample of committee votes was restricted to even-numbered Congresses from the 84th to the 98th (inclusive). The main independent variable

Table 5.4
Effect of Distance from Floor Median on Party Roll Rates: Cartel Model vs. Floor Model

Predicted Coefficients from the Cartel and Floor Models

	Majority $\hat{\beta}$	Minority $\hat{\beta}$
Cartel agenda control model	0	+
Floor agenda control model	+	+

Estimated OLS and MLCS Coefficients, House Final Passage Votes

	Majority $\hat{\beta}$	Minority $\hat{\beta}$
Effect of D_{ct} on roll rates for House final passage votes, estimated using OLS[a]	0.091 (0.091)	0.514 (0.096)
Effect of D_{ct} on roll rates for House final passage votes, estimated using MLCS[b]	1.569 (1.92)	2.108 (0.412)

Estimated MLCS Coefficients, Committee Bill Reports

	Majority $\hat{\beta}$	Minority $\hat{\beta}$
Effect of D_{ct}^{l} on roll rates for House committee bill reports	−0.378 (0.481)	1.436 (0.394)

[a] The estimated constant term is .022 (majority) and .036 (minority). The estimated coefficients for the autoregressive terms are $\gamma_1 = -.006$ (majority) and .250 (minority) for the first lag of the dependent variable and $\gamma_2 = .029$ (majority) and −.067 (minority) for the second lag of the dependent variable. A joint test of the null hypothesis that $\gamma_1 + \gamma_2 = 0$ can be rejected in both cases. $N = 53$, $F(3, 49) = .61$ (majority) and 12.8 (minority), Prob $> F = .614$ (majority) and .000 (minority), $R^2 = .013$ (majority) and .50 (minority).

[b] The estimated constant term is −2.15 (majority) and −1.68 (minority). The estimated coefficients for the autoregressive terms are $\gamma_1 = .130$ (majority) and .243* (minority) for the first lag of the dependent variable and $\gamma_2 = .247*$ (majority) and −.145* (minority) for the second lag of the dependent variable (*$p > |.05|$). A joint test of the null hypothesis that $\gamma_1 + \gamma_2 = 0$ can be rejected in both cases. $N = 53$, $F(3, 49) = 4.64$ (majority) and 15.8 (minority), Prob $> F = .006$ (majority) and .000 (minority), Adjusted $R^2 = .174$ (majority) and .461 (minority).

in our estimation of committee rolls is the distance between the median Democrat on the committee and the interval between the committee median and floor median, D_{a}^{l}.

Because the number of bills considered by a committee can differ widely, we expected, and found, our regression estimates to suffer from heteroskedasticity. We corrected for this using the Huber-White sandwich estimator of variance. Further diagnostics of our regression suggested no other problems for our estimation.

The results from our MLCS estimation of $ROLL_{a}^{l}$ is reported at the bottom of Table 5.4. As the cartel agenda model predicts, the estimated coefficient $\hat{\beta}$ is statistically indistinguishable from zero for the majority party ($p = .43$, two-tailed test), while the coefficient is positive and highly significant for the minority party ($p < .001$, two-tailed test). These results clearly support the cartel agenda model and refute the floor agenda model.

DISCUSSION: CONDITIONAL VERSUS UNCONDITIONAL PARTY GOVERNMENT

Our research shows that the majority party is very rarely rolled on (1) votes to report a bill from committee (0.07 percent of the time in our sample), (2) votes to report a bill from a conference committee (0.04 percent of the time in our sample), and (3) final passage votes on bills (about 3 percent of the time in our sample). We also find no systematic relationship between (1) the distance between the majority party median and the House median and (2) the party's roll rate on final passage votes. Similarly, we found no systematic relationship between (1) the distance between the majority-party median on a committee and the interval between committee and floor medians and (2) the party's roll rate on committee reports.

These results support the cartel agenda model and the simple view of negative agenda control it proposes. As our analysis spans more than a century of congressional history, this in turns suggest that the majority party's negative agenda power has been a constant feature of congressional organization during that time. In terms of the notion of conditional party government (see, for example, Rohde 1991 and Aldrich and Rohde 1997a, 1998), *the majority party's negative agenda control is not conditional*: in other words, it does not vary with the party's heterogeneity.

To verify this point, we regressed the majority party $ROLL\_RATE_{a}$ for each Congress from the 73rd through the 99th on the party's heterogeneity (measured by the standard deviation for majority party members from the party mean on the first dimension of D-NOMINATE scores).[10] We found that heterogeneity had no effect on the majority party's roll rates ($\hat{\beta}$ = $-.041$; SE = 0.117; $p < .73$, two-tailed test; R^2 = $.005$; constant term = $.033$; $N = 27$).

The majority party's consistent ability to keep things off the legislative agenda, at least under single-party control of both chambers of Congress, means that any social agent wishing to enact new legislation must deal with the majority party. This fact is very useful in raising campaign finance (see, for example, Cox and Magar 1999). Indeed, the dollar value of secure agenda control provides one reason to expect procedural powers to be stably cartelized.

DISCUSSION: DISRUPTING THE MAJORITY'S
AGENDA CONTROL

Because the majority party's roll rate is not actually zero, as the complete-information model presented previously would have it, what explains majority rolls? Three important actors might compete with the House majority in setting the House agenda: the Senate; the president; and an alternative majority coalition in the House, such as the Conservative Coalition. We found that divided government, comprising either a division of partisan control between the House and the Senate or between the House and the president had no systematic effect on party roll rates.[11] We found, however, that the activity of the Conservative Coalition did have a significant effect on roll rates, and it is to a report of these activities that we now turn.

It is conventional wisdom that the Conservative Coalition (an alliance of conservative Republicans with conservative Southern Democrats) was extremely influential in the House from its first appearance in 1937 through the mid-1970s. Indeed, it is not uncommon to hear that this coalition, rather than the Democratic party, really ruled the roost during this period. Our results pose a direct challenge to this view.

First, consider all the committees chaired by conservative Southern Democrats during this period. Suppose that one of these chairs decided to push a bill through his committee with Republican and Southern Democratic votes, in the teeth of Northern Democratic opposition—in other words, to activate the Conservative Coalition at the committee stage. Had any chair done so, one should have found Republicans and Southern Democrats on the committee signing the majority report of the committee, with Northern Democrats filing a dissenting report. Assuming that the North held a majority of the Democratic seats on the committee, as it did on most committees most of the time during this period, such an episode would necessarily have appeared in our data as a roll of the majority (Democratic) party. However, from the 84th Congress (1955–56) through the 92nd (1972–73), no Southern chair *ever* pushed a bill out of their committee on the basis of the Conservative Coalition—a surprising finding if one believes that the Conservative Coalition was the real power in the House.[12]

This is not surprising from our perspective: our model implies that the majority party should never get rolled in committee, which necessarily entails a "ban" on the appearance in committee of the Conservative Coalition. The ban, evidently, held throughout the heyday of the Conservative Coalition, despite the many opportunities (temptations) that Southern chairs must have faced.

Our model also implies that the Conservative Coalition should have been "banned" at the final passage stage: if the only bills put on the agenda changed a status quo that a majority of Democrats agreed needed changing, then at final passage one should not find a majority of Democrats voting against (in the complete-information version of the story presented here). So how often did the Conservative Coalition appear on final passage votes, as opposed to earlier floor votes (amendments mostly)?

The vast majority of the Conservative Coalition's appearances came at the amendment stage, rather than at final passage or procedural stages.[13] Of the 11,211 votes from the 84th to 100th Congresses, 3,686 were final passage votes on bills and resolutions.[14] Of these, the Conservative Coalition formed (a majority of Southern Democrats voting with a majority of Republicans) and opposed the Democratic majority on 305 (8.3 percent). There were 1,999 votes involving suspension of the rules or special rules, both procedures the majority party typically controls. Of these, the Coalition formed in opposition to the Democrats on 89 occasions (4.3 percent). What remains are 5,449 "prefinal votes," mostly concerning amendments and parliamentary maneuvers of various sorts.[15] Of these, the Conservative Coalition formed in opposition to a majority of Democrats on 1,303 (or 23.9 percent). Thus the Conservative Coalition appeared about four times as often (and at a rate that was three times higher) on prefinal as opposed to final votes, and the contrast is even greater with the key procedural steps that the majority controls.

How often was the Conservative Coalition successful on final passage votes for ordinary bills? How often did it hijack the House agenda and roll the Democratic majority? The data to answer these questions are given in Table 5.5. The rows in Table 5.5 indicate whether the Conservative Coalition was active (i.e., a majority of Southern Democrats voted with a major-

Table 5.5

Influence of the Conservative Coalition
on Final Passage Votes

Voting on Final Passage Overall

	DEMOCRATIC MAJORITY VOTED	
	Against	*In favor*
Conservative coalition		
Did not form	16	477
Voted against	16	143
Voted in favor	38	1623

Voting on Final Passage When the Bill Passed

	DEMOCRATIC MAJORITY VOTED	
	Against	*In favor*
Conservative coalition		
Did not form	9	463
Voted against	0	110
Voted in favor	33	1623

ity of Republicans) and in what sense (favoring or opposing passage). The columns indicate whether a majority of the Democratic party favored or opposed passage. The top portion of the table looks at all 2,313 final passage votes on ordinary bills from the 84th to 100th Congresses; the bottom portion is restricted to ordinary bills that actually passed (2,238 in all).

A look at Table 5.5 shows that the Conservative Coalition was for the most part either inactive (493 times) or in agreement with the Democratic majority (1,639 times) on final passage votes. On only 181 such votes (7.8 percent of the total) did the Coalition oppose the Democrats, and most of these (143) were cases where the Coalition opposed while the Democrats favored passage. There were 38 occasions (an average of twice per Congress) on which the Coalition favored while the Democrats opposed passage. Of these, the Democrats were rolled 33 times (about twice per Congress). These Democratic rolls represented about 1.5 percent of all final passage votes. Democratic roll rates on procedural votes were even lower—1.2 percent on votes on special rules and 0 percent on votes on suspension of the rules (which require a two-thirds majority to pass).

In our view, the Conservative Coalition was mostly a *substantive floor alliance*. It was a *floor* alliance in that it appeared almost never in committee. It was a *substantive* alliance in that it appeared rarely on procedural votes and then with little success. It appeared most often prior to the final passage vote stage and on nonprocedural votes—such as amendments and dilatory motions. The Democratic party, in contrast, was a procedural alliance that appeared almost always (in the negative sense of preventing rolls) in committee, on floor procedural votes, and at final passage.

Contrasting the Cartel Agenda Model and Pivot Models

So far we have tested two models of how the plenary agenda in the U.S. House of Representatives is set: one in which it is set as if by majority vote on the floor of the House (the floor agenda model) and one in which it is set as if by majority vote in the majority party's caucus (the cartel agenda model). We now contrast the cartel agenda model not with the pure majority rule floor model but instead with the pivot model recently advanced by Krehbiel (1998).

Krehbiel's pivot model differs from pure majority rule in that it incorporates two nonmajoritarian features of U.S. policymaking: the filibuster in the Senate and the presidential veto. Because of these features, the pivot model, unlike the floor agenda model, features a "gridlock zone." If the status quo policy lies in this zone, the model predicts no policy change.

Here we ask the following questions: Does the presence of these nonmajoritarian features in the pivot model produce predictions similar to those of the cartel model (which also has a zone of "protected" status quo points)? How do the two models differ in their observable implications? In particular, do they predict different roll rates?

PARTY ROLL RATES: THEORETICAL BACKGROUND

Under the cartel model, the majority party never loses on agenda-setting or final passage votes. How often the minority party gets rolled increases as the distance between m_{jt} (the median ideal point of the minority party) and F_{jt} (the median ideal point of the legislature) increases.

What about the pivot model? In this model, any status quo point in the gridlock interval is left alone, while those outside the interval are brought inside it. If a status quo point happens to lie *outside* the gridlock interval but *inside* the majority party roll region, the majority party will be rolled on the dimension in question. So what are the gridlock zone and the majority roll zone precisely?

In the case of a left-wing majority and right-wing president, for example, the gridlock zone extends from f_{jt} (the filibuster pivot, on the left) to v_{jt} (the veto pivot, on the right). Any status quo point to the left of the filibuster pivot will be sufficiently far left that there exists a bill to change it that can overcome a filibuster—that is, one that can attract the support of three-fifths or more of the Senate. Any status quo point to the right of the veto pivot will be sufficiently far right that there exists a bill to change it that can overcome a presidential veto—that is, one that can attract the support of at least two-thirds of the House and Senate. (In principle, the two-thirds point in the House and Senate could differ. Krehbiel's model ignores this potential complication.)

The majority party roll region is $(2M_{jt} - F_{jt}, F_{jt})$. Here M_{jt} is the median ideal point of the majority party's members and F_{jt} is, as noted before, the median ideal point of the legislature.

All told then, in the pivot model, the majority party is rolled on dimension j if and only if SQ_{jt} is in the interval $(2M_{jt} - F_{jt}, f_{jt})$. If $f_{jt} \leq 2M_{jt} - F_{jt}$, then this interval will be null, leading to the same prediction—that the majority is never rolled—as in the cartel model. If $f_{jt} > 2M_{jt} - F_{jt}$, in contrast, then the pivot model predicts that the majority party's roll rate will be positive.

Should one expect $f_{jt} > 2M_{jt} - F_{jt}$, so that the model predicts a positive roll rate for the majority? By way of answer, note that M_{jt} will be about the 25th percentile of the House ideal points for a party with a bare majority of seats (larger for larger parties), while f_{jt} is the ideal point of the 40th percentile in the Senate. If the quantiles of the distribution of ideal points in the Senate and House are identical, then any status quo point lying in the interval from M_{jt} (the 25th percentile) to f_{jt} (the 40th percentile) of ideal points in the House will produce a majority party roll.[16]

AN INITIAL CONTRAST BETWEEN THE PIVOT
AND CARTEL MODELS

Before considering party roll rates, we consider here how often the median legislator gets rolled on final passage votes on the House floor, compared to the median member of the majority party. Recall that in our model, each member's ideal point can vary from dimension to dimension so that the member who is the median on one dimension may not be the median on all others. It is possible, therefore, that there is no median legislator, if by that one means a legislator whose ideal point is the median on all dimensions. Nonetheless, suppose that there is a member who is usually at or near the median on each dimension, and compare this legislator to one who is usually at or near the majority party median on each dimension.

Operationally, we shall define the median legislator as the member—denoted F—whose Poole-Rosenthal D-NOMINATE score (first dimension) is the median in a particular Congress. We can similarly define the median majority party member—denoted M—for each Congress from the 85th to the 94th. Let us suppose that the operationally defined median members just identified—F and M—are typically *near* the relevant median on all dimensions but not necessarily *at* the median. More precisely, assume that F's ideal point on dimension j, x_j^F, is symmetrically distributed with mean F_j and variance s_j^2, and that M's ideal point on dimension j, x_j^M, is symmetrically distributed with mean M_j and variance t_j^2.

Under the cartel model, M should be rolled less often than F. This is because M's expected ideal point is in the middle of the majority party's block zone. M will be rolled only if his or her ideal point on a dimension is far enough from expected as to lie outside the zone $(2M_j - F_j, F_j) = (M_j - |F_j - M_j|, M_j + |F_j - M_j|)$. In contrast, F's expected ideal point is on the right-hand edge of the majority's block zone. Thus F's actual ideal point will lie outside the majority's block zone about half the time (assuming that the distribution of x_j^F is continuous), and thus F will not be protected from rolls by the majority agenda setter's preferences.

Under the pivot model, one expects exactly the opposite: M should be rolled more often than F. This is because F is now expected to be near the center of the gridlock zone on each dimension and hence will be protected from rolls by the fact that bills that the member would oppose will not be scheduled. In contrast, M is now outside the gridlock zone (for small enough majorities) and will not be protected.

So which is it? Is the majority party median (M) rolled more often or less often than the overall median (F)? To answer this question, we examined how M and F voted on each final passage vote and compared this to actual outcomes, thereby calculating roll rates for each. As shown in Table 5.6, we found that the median voter (F) was rolled between 4 percent and 29 percent of the time, for an average of more than 10 percent for the whole pe-

Table 5.6

Number of Rolls and the Roll Rates on Final Passage
Votes for Floor Median, by Congress

Congress	Median Rolls	Median Roll Rate (%)	Majority Roll Rate (%)
85	9	21	5
86	14	29	4
87	10	18	2
88	18	22	2
89	11	10	0
90	18	15	1
91	9	6	3
92	6	4	3
93	22	9	0
94	11	5	1
Average	12.8	10	2

riod. By comparison, the median of the majority party (M) was rolled less than one-sixth as often (20 times out of 1,227 final passage votes from the 84th to 94th Congresses, or 1.6 percent).

PARTY ROLL RATES WHEN PREFERENCES SHIFT: THEORY

Let us turn now to consider some differing predictions that the cartel and pivot model make regarding how party roll rates should react when congressional preferences shift. Suppose bills are passed at $t - 1$ in accordance with the pivot model and that these bills establish the status quo on each dimension at the end of period $t - 1$ (call this $Q_{j,t-1}$). Suppose also that nature adds a "policy shock" to each dimension ($\varepsilon_{j,t}$) at the beginning of period t. The status quo at the beginning of period t is then $SQ_{jt} = Q_{j,t-1} + \varepsilon_{j,t}$. The distribution of SQ_{jt} thus depends on (1) what Congress did at $t - 1$ and (2) the distribution of $\varepsilon_{j,t}$. We can make similar assumptions about the cartel model, with the $Q_{j,t-1}$ values established in accord with that model, then perturbed by nature.

With these assumptions about how status quo points are generated, what can we say? Consider nine cases, depending on whether the policy shocks tend to push things left, right, or in neither direction and whether preferences, as measured by the floor median's ideal point at time t, F_{jt}, shift left, right, or in neither direction. Formally, the policy shock tendency can be captured by the expected value of $\varepsilon_{j,t}$. If $E(\varepsilon_{j,t}) < 0$, nature tends to push the status quo leftward. If $E(\varepsilon_{j,t}) > 0$, nature tends to push the status quo rightward. Finally, if $E(\varepsilon_{j,t}) = 0$, nature pushes neither left nor right. With respect to preference shifts, the simplest case to consider is one in which the entire distribution of ideal points shifts left or right by a fixed amount, δ_{jt} (so that $\delta_{jt} = F_{jt} - F_{j,t-1}$). Preferences shift left, right, or in neither direction as δ_{jt} is less than, greater than, or equal to zero.

In what follows, we shall first consider how the pivot and cartel models differ in terms of their point estimates of the majority and minority roll rates. We shall then examine the more important subject of the models' competing comparative statics predictions.

POINT ESTIMATES

To explore the models' point estimates, let us consider the special case in which $E(\varepsilon_{j,t}) = 0$ and $\text{var}(\varepsilon_{j,t}) = 0$. In this case, nature does not shock any policy, and everything depends on how preferences shift. There are thus only three cases to consider: $\delta_{jt} < 0$, $\delta_{jt} = 0$, and $\delta_{jt} > 0$ (preferences shift left, stay the same, or shift right).

If preferences shift toward the right ($\delta_{jt} > 0$), the only status quo points that fall outside the new (time t) gridlock zone are those on the left. If $2M_{jt} - F_{jt} < f_{jt}$, some of these points will produce majority party rolls (see Figure 5.3, where the shaded area indicates the status quo policies produced at $t - 1$). In contrast, the minority party will *never* be rolled in this case because there are no status quo points to the right of the new gridlock zone (the gridlock zone has shifted right, and all status quo points to the right of the old gridlock zone were dealt with by the $t - 1$ Congress). This prediction—that the majority will be rolled at a positive rate, while the minority is never rolled—contrasts strongly with the cartel model's prediction in this case that neither party will be rolled.[17]

If preferences do not shift at all ($\delta_{jt} = 0$), the pivot model predicts that there will be no new legislation at time t. The cartel model predicts the same. Both these predictions would of course soften were one to allow policy shocks by nature.

Finally, if preferences shift left ($\delta_{jt} < 0$), the only status quo points that fall outside the new (time t) gridlock zone are those on the right. If $2m_{jt} - F_{jt} > v_{jt}$, some of these points will produce minority party rolls (see Figure 5.3). In contrast, the majority party will never be rolled in this case because

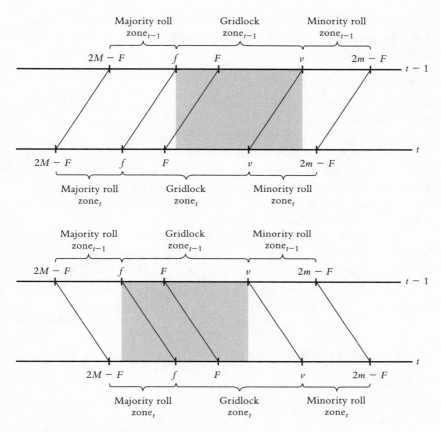

Figure 5.3. Gridlock zone and shifting preferences.

there are no status quo points to the left of the new gridlock zone (the grid-lock zone has shifted left, and all status quo points to the left of the old grid-lock zone were dealt with by bill by the $t - 1$ Congress). This prediction—that the minority will be rolled at a positive rate, while the majority is never rolled—agrees with the cartel model's prediction in this case.

All told, then, the predictions of the pivot and cartel models differ only in the case where preferences shift toward the minority party ($\delta_{jt} > 0$). Their difference in this case is stark and is not due simply to our considering the special case of $E(\varepsilon_{j,t}) = 0$ and $\text{var}(\varepsilon_{j,t}) = 0$. For leftist majorities, as long as the distribution of the policy shocks is symmetrical, the pivot model predicts that the majority roll rate will exceed the minority roll rate after rightward preference shifts, whereas the cartel model predicts the opposite. This difference provides us with an empirical wedge, a means to test the cartel agenda model against another prominent theory, the pivot model.

COMPARATIVE STATICS

What about the two models' comparative statics predictions? The pivot model predicts that the roll rates of both the majority party and the minority party should be sensitive to congressional preference shifts. The majority party, for example, should be rolled more often after preferences shift away from it (to the right in our case), but be rolled less often after preferences shift toward it (to the left). In contrast, the cartel model agrees that preference shifts will affect the minority party's roll rate but claims that such shifts will have no effect on the majority party's roll rate.

To explain the pivot model's predictions regarding the majority party, recall that the probability (before nature's policy shock is realized) that the majority party will be rolled on dimension j can be expressed as $P = Pr[SQ_{jt} \in (2M_{jt} - F_{jt}, f_{jt})]$. Because $SQ_{jt} = Q_{j,t-1} + \varepsilon_{jt}$, $M_{jt} = M_{j,t-1} + \delta_{jt}$, $F_{jt} = F_{j,t-1} + \delta_{jt}$, and $f_{jt} = f_{j,t-1} + \delta_{jt}$, P can be rephrased as $P = Pr[Q_{j,t-1} + \varepsilon_{jt} \in (2M_{j,t-1} - F_{j,t-1} + \delta_{jt}, f_{j,t-1} + \delta_{jt})]$. Subtracting $Q_{j,t-1}$ throughout gives $P = Pr[\varepsilon_{jt} \in (2M_{j,t-1} - F_{j,t-1} + \delta_{jt} - Q_{j,t-1}, f_{j,t-1} + \delta_{jt} - Q_{j,t-1})]$. If we denote the cumulative distribution function of ε_{jt} by G, then $P = G(f_{j,t-1} + \delta_{jt} - Q_{j,t-1}) - G(2M_{j,t-1} - F_{j,t-1} + \delta_{jt} - Q_{j,t-1})$.

Differentiating P with respect to δ yields $\partial P/\partial \delta(\delta) = g(f_{j,t-1} + \delta_{jt} - Q_{j,t-1}) - g(2M_{j,t-1} - F_{j,t-1} + \delta_{jt} - Q_{j,t-1})$, where g is the probability density function associated with G. We know that $Q_{j,t-1} \in (f_{j,t-1}, \nu_{j,t-1})$ because Congress will have altered any status quo points lying outside the $t-1$ gridlock zone. Thus $\partial P/\partial \delta(0) = g(f) - g(f - d)$, where $f = f_{j,t-1} - Q_{j,t-1} \leq 0$ and $d = f_{j,t-1} - (2M_{j,t-1} - F_{j,t-1}) > 0$—so that $f - d < f$. If g is single-peaked about zero, then $f - d < f \leq 0$ implies $g(f) - g(f - d) > 0$; hence $\partial P/\partial \delta(0) > 0$. Since $\partial P/\partial \delta(\delta)$ is a continuous function of δ, this suffices to show that $\partial P/\partial \delta(\delta) > 0$ for all δ in an interval I around zero. [It can be shown that $I = (-\infty, -f + 0.5d)$.] In words, the probability P of a majority party roll increases as preferences in Congress shift more to the right—that is, away from the majority, which is presumed to be leftist.[18]

Thus the pivot model's prediction—$\partial P/\partial \delta > 0$—is in stark contrast to the cartel model's prediction that $\partial P/\partial \delta = 0$. It can be shown, however, that both models predict $\partial p/\partial \delta(\delta) < 0$ for all δ in an interval including zero; that is, the minority party's roll rate decreases with larger rightward shifts in congressional preferences.[19]

PARTY ROLL RATES: EVIDENCE

To test the competing comparative statics claims just made, we again analyzed final passage roll rates for both the minority and majority parties on
the House floor. The unit of analysis is thus a party Congress, and we estimate separate regressions for the majority and minority parties. Our dependent variable is again $ROLL\_RATE_{ct}$.

The main independent variable is $PrefShift_{ct}$, a variable capturing the preference shift away from party c between Congress t and $t - 1$ (so rightward
shifts are positive if c is the Democratic party, and leftward shifts are positive
if c is the Republican party).[20] We also include, as a control in our analysis,
the measure of Conservative Coalition activity used earlier.

The cartel model predicts that (1) the constant term will be positive and
significant in the minority party regression (the minority party should be
rolled significantly often, preference shift and conservative coalition activity held constant) but insignificant in the majority party regression and that
(2) the coefficient on $PrefShift_{ct}$ will be insignificantly different from zero in
the majority party regression but positive and significant in the minority
party regression.

The pivot model predicts that the constant term in both the majority and
minority regressions will be insignificantly different from zero: if $PrefShift_{ct}$
is zero, there should be no status quo points outside the gridlock zone and
hence no rolls of either party. It also predicts that the coefficient on $PrefShift_{ct}$
will be positive and significant for both parties. Thus the pivot model agrees
with the cartel model regarding the constant term in the majority party regression (it should be zero) and the slope term in the minority regression (it
should be positive). But the two models disagree regarding the slope term in
the majority regression and the constant term in the minority regression.

The results of OLS and MLCS regression,

$$ROLL\_RATE_{ct} = \chi_c + \beta_c PrefShift_t + \gamma_c CC\_SCORE_t + G_t \qquad (3)$$

are reported in Table 5.7.

The results conform closely to the predictions of the cartel agenda model
and refute the predictions for the pivot model. In particular, while $\hat{\beta}_c$ is positive and significant in the regression for the minority party, we cannot reject the null hypothesis that it is zero for the majority party.[21] Interestingly,
the analysis also shows that the greater the activity of the Conservative
Coalition in a Congress, the greater the roll rates for both parties. These results give us added confidence that the cartel agenda model captures, at least

Table 5.7

Effect of Shifting Preferences on Roll Rates:
Cartel Model vs. Pivot Model

Predicted Coefficients from the Cartel
and Pivot Models

	Majority $\hat{\beta}$	Minority $\hat{\beta}$
Cartel agenda control model	0	+
Pivot control model	+	+

Estimated OLS Coefficients[a]

	Majority $\hat{\beta}$	Minority $\hat{\beta}$
Effect of *PrefShift*$_{ct}$ on roll		
rates for House	0.08	0.33
final passage votes	(0.09)	(0.16)

Estimated MLCS Coefficients[b]

	Majority $\hat{\beta}$	Minority $\hat{\beta}$
Effect of *PrefShift*$_{ct}$ on roll		
rates for House	1.53	1.90
final passage votes	(0.84)	(0.58)

[a]$N = 53$ (for both regressions), $F(4, 48) = 2.00$ (majority) and 6.98 (minority), Adjusted $R^2 = -.12$ (majority) and .42 (minority), CC_SCORE (majority) $= .02$ (.01)* and CC_SCORE (minority) $= .03$ (.02)* ($p > .05$).
[b]$N = 53$ (for both regressions), $F(4, 48) = 14.36$ (majority) and 10.49 (minority), Adjusted $R^2 = .54$ (majority) and .42 (minority), CC_SCORE (majority) $= .60$ (.12)* and CC_SCORE (minority) $= .11$ (.60)* ($p > .05$).

partly, some of the underlying principles of legislative organization and some of the important forces that animate congressional history.

Positive Agenda Power

On the one hand—the dominant hand—we view the majority party as a procedural cartel dedicated to preserving vetoes over policy change. On the other hand, the majority party is also a substantive coalition capable of taking positive action. Here we examine features of this other hand of agenda power.

In *Legislative Leviathan* (Cox and McCubbins 1993), we argued that the heterogeneity of the majority party determines the size of what we called the "party agenda," defined as the set of bills on which the party leadership takes a united stand (see also Sala 1999). Our argument—consistent with that of Rohde (1991) and others—was that majority parties whose members' core constituencies are more similar tend also to be those whose leaders use party resources to push a wider range of issues, while majority parties whose members' core constituencies are less similar tend also to be those whose leaders use party resources to push a narrower range of issues. We also noted that members' support of their leadership, conditional on the leadership's presenting a united front, varies little from Congress to Congress—typically hovering around the 90 percent mark.

If one imagines that party leaders take a united stand on a bill if and only if it is favored by at least T percent of the party, then the complete information cartel agenda model sketched in this chapter conforms to our previous work. For $T = 9$, for example, the model predicts that the party agenda consists of every dimension j on which the status quo is outside the interval $[R(M_{10}), \max(F, R(M_{90}))]$, where M_{10} is the position such that 10 percent of the majority party's members' ideal points lie to the left of M_{10}, and similarly for M_{90}. If we knew the "correct" value of T, we might take the distance between M_{100-T} and M_T as a measure of the party's heterogeneity, in which case the model would predict an inverse relation between heterogeneity and the size of the party agenda.

Note that the model does not assume that party leaders can pressure their members into voting for the party line (something we believe indeed happens) but instead assumes that they accurately aim for a minimum threshold of party support. We believe that this aiming is an important phenomenon not just in the United States but worldwide; thus the present model stresses "aiming in light of what the leaders think followers will like" rather than "aiming in light of how many followers leaders think can be pressured into support." Even if we were to allow for some pressuring in our model, however, the amended model would still predict an inverse relationship between the size of the party agenda and party heterogeneity, assuming that it is more costly to "buy" support from those more emphatically opposed to any given change in the status quo.

Not knowing T, we here try two alternative measures of the majority party's heterogeneity: first, the distance between F and M, and second, the

Table 5.8

Effects of Party Heterogeneity on Size of Positive Party Agenda

	Coefficient	*Standard Error*	*t*	*p*
Party heterogeneity	−0.656	0.242	−2.710	0.012
Constant	0.389	0.054	7.204	0.000
$N = 26$				
$R^2 = 0.234$				
Adjusted $R^2 = 0.202$				
Root MSE = 0.107				
$F(1, 24) = 7.34$				
Prob $> F = 0.012$				

NOTES: Coefficients are OLS coefficients.
Dependent variable is size of the majority party's positive agenda, which is measured as the number of roll calls (in a given Congress) on which (1) the majority leader and majority whip vote the same way, *and* (2) the minority leader and/or the minority whip vote in opposition to the position of the majority leaders (Cox and McCubbins 1993: p. 145−6).

standard deviation of NOMINATE scores within the party. The relation between d and the size of the party agenda is given in Table 5.8.

There are three points to make about the results. First, we tested the same model with an alternative operationalization of the independent variable, using instead the standard deviation about the majority party median; this produced the same qualitative results.

Second, our results show an inverse relationship between party heterogeneity (d) and the size of the party agenda for the majority party. Specifically, as predicted, the sign of the estimated coefficient for party heterogeneity is negative and significant ($p < .01$, one-tailed test). Thus positive agenda control is a *conditional* aspect of party government: the number of bills the party seeks to push through the House depends directly on the party's heterogeneity. But as we have argued previously (Cox and McCubbins 1993, 1994a) and as we showed earlier in this chapter, negative agenda control is an *unconditional* aspect of party government: the party's ability to keep issues off the legislative agenda, thereby preventing substantive change on those issues, is consistently strong and unrelated to party heterogeneity.

It is because of the constancy of the majority party's procedural advantages that we emphasized in *Legislative Leviathan* the image of parties as procedural cartels. It is because of the variability of the majority party's sub-

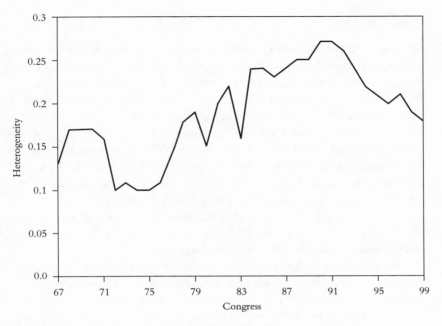

Figure 5.4. Major party heterogeneity, 1921–89.

stantive achievements that we, following Rohde (1991) and others, have emphasized the importance of party heterogeneity.

Finally, as can be seen in Figure 5.4, changes in the heterogeneity of the
majority party correspond to the changes in congressional organization that
scholars have observed (outlined earlier in Table 5.1). The majority party
was becoming decreasingly heterogeneous prior to the 72nd Congress. Majority party heterogeneity was at its ebb during the first two New Deal
Congresses, when the Democratic party was able to translate increased homogeneity of preferences among its members into a sizable party agenda.
This went hand in hand with the reemergence of the Democratic caucus and
a recentralization of agenda setting. Starting in the 75th Congress, with the
rise of the Conservative Coalition, we see a swift increase in heterogeneity
until the 92nd Congress. This corresponds to the era of "committee government" and the decentralization of agenda power in the House and, as we
have shown in our previous work (Cox and McCubbins 1993), a decrease
in the size of the party agenda. This is followed by a swift decrease in heterogeneity, corresponding to the modern period, with a recentralization of
agenda setting and an increase in the size of the party agenda.

Conclusion

Postwar congressional history is often described as a transition from "committee government" to "party government" (e.g., Rohde 1991). This viewpoint, probably dominant in the literature, has been attacked from two different directions. One set of scholars (e.g., Krehbiel 1993, 1998) argue that party government is always more illusory than real in the United States. By this view, the transition was from committee government to more of the same. In contrast, we (Cox and McCubbins 1993) have essentially argued that committee government is best thought of as a decentralized form of party government. By this view, the transition was from decentralized party government to a more centralized form of party government.

In this chapter, we have defended the latter view over a wider range of congressional history, one that includes many episodes of decentralization and recentralization. We stress the following points.

First, consistent with the notion of conditional party government, more homogeneous majority parties have systematically undertaken larger substantive agendas (see Table 5.7). We also believe that more homogeneous majorities have delegated more power to their leaders to prosecute their (larger) agendas. Here the case study evidence is compelling (Rohde 1991; Brady and Epstein 1997), but some analysts have argued that the idea does not explain the full range of rules changes observed in the House (Schickler and Rich 1997). Despite the latter work, it does seem that what distinguishes the conventional periods into which congressional history is divided are the differing levels of homogeneity of the majority party in each era.

Second, throughout all periods of congressional history from the end of Reconstruction to the present, the majority party has maintained a secure grip on the floor agenda. Access to the floor agenda has always been sufficiently stacked in the majority's favor that it is rarely unsuccessful when it opposes bills at the agenda-setting or final passage stage. Examining a wide range of Congresses, we find that the majority unsuccessfully opposes the report of a bill in committee only 0.07 percent of the time, while it unsuccessfully opposes final passage of a bill on the floor about 3 percent of the time. Negative agenda control—the ability to keep issues off the floor—is an *unconditional* power of the majority (not dependent on the party's internal homogeneity).

In contrast to these figures for the majority party, we find that the minority unsuccessfully opposes the report of a bill in committee about 4 percent of the time, while it unsuccessfully opposes final passage of a bill on the floor about 25 percent of the time. The minority's negative agenda power is weaker.

Third, the extremely low rates at which the majority party loses, when it attempts to prevent either the appearance of a bill on the floor agenda or a bill's final passage, has important consequences for how we understand phenomena such as the Conservative Coalition. This coalition (of conservative Southern Democrats and conservative Republicans) is best thought of as an occasional floor voting alliance that was most active and successful at the amendment stage. As such, it significantly limited what the Democratic party could do. But it was not a procedural alliance. Yes, Judge Smith stood as a bulwark against civil rights legislation. But Judge Smith was a leader of the Southern Democrats, who exploited the anticipated support of Republicans on the floor, not a leader of a bloc interested the usual sorts of coalition maintenance activities one associates with party leaders.

Fourth, the majority's ability to keep things off the floor agenda has important policy implications. If only bills favored by the majority party leadership (assumed to serve the majority party's median legislator) are considered on the floor of the House, then even if not all of them pass, the only policy changes actually made will be those palatable to the majority. Other issues, that the minority might have preferred to take up, languish. Thus policy drifts in the direction of the majority because only problems that need fixing from the majority's viewpoint are addressed.

If one were to ask, "Where's the Party?" the answer would not lie in an analysis of roll call votes, where ideological and partisan voting are hard to distinguish (Krehbiel 1993; but see Groseclose and Snyder 1996 and Cox and Poole 2001). Rather, by controlling the agenda, the party controls what gets voted on to begin with, which influences what ultimately passes the House. Where the party is is mostly in the setting of the agenda and control over rules, procedure, and organization. The party manifests itself through its control of the agenda and scheduling of rules and procedure (Sinclair 1998b); of committee assignments and chairmanship appointments (Cox and McCubbins 1993); of the procedures for establishing reversionary policy, reconciliation, budgeting, and appropriations (Kiewiet and McCubbins 1991, Stewart 1989); and of leadership selection.

Chapter 6

Agenda Power in the U.S. Senate, 1877–1986

ANDREA C. CAMPBELL, GARY W. COX,

AND MATHEW D. MCCUBBINS

There are numerous dissimilarities between the two chambers of the U.S. Congress. Aside from the basic differences in chamber size, member term lengths, and constituencies, the Senate's internal decision-making procedure is distinguished by its uniquely open rules governing floor debate and bill amending. The permissibility of the Senate's internal decision-making procedure is said to make it atomistic and far less partisan than the House of Representatives. In contrast to the House, these rules empower the individual and make even fairly small minorities formidable antagonists to the majority party. Ripley (1969: 16), for example, has argued that "the Senate naturally gravitates toward individualism. Changes generated by large numbers of senators are almost always aimed at spreading power" (see also Davidson 1985, 1989; Smith 1989; and Smith and Flathman (1989). Since that time, these rules have changed little.[1] More recently, Binder (1997) has argued that "unlike the House—in which partisan majorities have been able to mold chamber rules to their liking—no such majoritarian character has taken root in the Senate. *Control of the Senate agenda . . . has never been structured to reflect the interests of a partisan majority*" (168, emphasis added).

The following analysis is an attempt to better understand the processes and implications of agenda control within the U.S. Senate. In particular, we study the extent to which the Senate majority party exercises *negative agenda control*—the ability to prevent bills that the party dislikes from being approved by the Senate. We look at Senate-originated bills and executive nominations that make it to the chamber floor for a final passage vote. The *cartel agenda model* presented in Chapter 5 provides the theoretical framework for our analysis (henceforth, we refer to this as the "cartel model"). We extend this model to the Senate and perform tests similar to those presented in Chapter 5 on the House of Representatives.

The Senate presents a hard case for the cartel model. The Senate's lack of restrictions on floor debate and relevance of amendments has far-reaching effects. Possibly the most important of these effects is the constraint the Senate places on simple majorities. It is difficult for a simple majority to gain control over the chamber's rules and use the rules to stack the deck procedurally in its favor. In the House, the majority party obtains much of its power at the beginning of each congressional session by using the rule-making power to design the legislature's structure and processes in a self-benefiting manner. Simple majorities in the Senate are not so privileged. Because the Senate is considered a continuing body (no more than one-third of its membership can change with each national election), its rules continue from one session to the next. In other words, these legislators do not begin each new congressional session with a new set of rules. This makes cartel-like behavior by the majority party more difficult (see Cox and McCubbins 1993), as there is always a minority with an incentive to protect minority-empowering prerogatives. Because Senate rules have remained more consensual, majority party domination of the legislative agenda is, at least theoretically, much more of a challenge in the upper chamber.

Upon closer inspection of the current procedure to attain floor consideration of a bill or resolution, we can see just how the Senate's consensus-favoring rules challenge the majority party. After a committee reports out a bill, it automatically goes on the Senate's calendar. Unlike the House's Speaker, the Senate lacks a powerful presiding officer. Any senator has the right to make a motion to consider; however, by precedent, it is the majority leader, in consultation with the minority leader, who decides the order in which bills on the calendar should come to the floor for action. The majority leader, or someone acting at his or her behest, makes the motion. Under the Senate's standing rules, however, even the motion to consider is debatable, and with the Senate's lack of debate restrictions, it is vulnerable to a filibuster.[2] Furthermore, Rule 14 permits a senator to bypass the committee system altogether and have a bill placed directly on the calendar if he or she fears that the relevant committee will be unsympathetic. The same rule also provides that if a committee fails to act on a referred bill, the sponsoring senator may reintroduce a new bill with exactly the same provisions and get it directly on the calendar. Finally, the general lack of restrictions on germaneness of amendments permits senators to present issues to the Senate floor with what appears to be little regard for the committee system or preferences of the majority leader. A senator can do this by offering his or her bill in the form of an amendment to a bill already under consideration. This list of methods by which a senator can bring something to the Senate floor suggests that the chamber's agenda is extremely permeable.

Given what appears to be an open agenda-setting process, it would seem that a model positing universal control of the floor agenda might best describe the process. Universal control means that there is no particular group with privileged access to the agenda and that the agenda is determined by majority vote on the chamber floor and thus by the median legislator (Krehbiel 1993). We refer to this model as the *floor agenda model* (henceforth, the "floor model").

Access to the floor calendar is important, but an item still needs to be scheduled in order to pass the Senate. The power to schedule lies with the majority leader. While it is true that the majority leader typically acts in concert with or consults the minority leader when determining if, when, and how something will be brought up for debate and vote, it is the majority leader or someone acting at his or her behest who makes the motion. There is one exception to this rule: nongermane amending. An item can be brought up as an amendment to something already receiving floor consideration. The majority leader, however, is not without recourse should there be attempts to commandeer the floor agenda in this manner. The leadership has two tools to manage this problem: the motion to table and the motion to recommit. The motion to table takes precedence over a motion to amend, and it is not debatable. In fact, only a few motions take precedence over the motion to table: motions to adjourn, motions to recess, and motions to proceed to executive business. Tiefer (1989: 660) notes, "The rules and practices for the motion to table may be summed up thusly: it evokes a considerable degree of majority party loyalty, and it is procedural, privileged, and nondebatable." Alternatively, after all amendments have been offered and voted on, the majority leader may make a motion to recommit—which is used to strip all amendments from a bill. Another common technique used by the leadership is filling the amendment tree. If the majority leader fears that there may be unwanted amendments offered, he may use his right of first recognition to exhaust all of the available slots in the amendment tree and then release them to loyal senators as need be. Finally, the option to filibuster is available to majority party members just as it is available to the minority. A filibuster can be orchestrated to potentially kill an unwanted amendment. These are just a few examples of options available to the majority leadership to deal with nongermane amending. The point is that we should be wary of exaggerating the power of the minority prerogative to the filibuster. The question at issue for the partisan model remains: Can majority leaders in the Senate control the agenda? If agenda control in the Senate centers on the power to manipulate floor scheduling, a contrasting theoretical perspective emphasizing party control might be in order.

In sum, we have two opposing models of agenda control. If access to the floor and the ability to place something on the calendar are more important in setting the Senate agenda, the floor model will better explain the process. If control over floor scheduling—the if, when, and how things are brought up—is more relevant factor in Senate agenda setting, the cartel model will better explain the process. In the following analysis, we find that agenda setting in the modern Senate is quite similar to agenda setting in the House, inasmuch as the majority party exercises substantial control. The set of bills and nominations that make it to the floor for final passage in the "modern" (post–Seventeenth Amendment) Senate is largely consistent with the cartel model and inconsistent with the floor model. Despite much dissimilarity between the two chambers, the House and Senate have a number of important characteristics in common. It is these basic similarities that we believe engender the majority party's desire and ability to influence the legislative agenda in a self-benefiting manner. Before turning to each model's predictions, we briefly delineate the emergence and evolution of Senate floor leadership as it changes dramatically during the period under study, 1877–1986, which substantially affects the potential for partisan versus universal control of the floor agenda.

Emergence and Evolution of the Senate Floor Leadership

The modern Senate's majority party leadership institutions are much like those of the House. The locus of party power lies with the party caucus. Until about the 1870s, strict party allegiance in the Senate was confined to organizational matters. Lacking a partisan floor leader, party in caucus and party on the floor often acted discretely on substantive policy matters. While it took the Senate nearly thirty years to formally establish the positions of majority and minority leader, the origin of Senate party leadership can be traced to the 1890s with William Allison (R-Ia.) and Nelson Aldrich (R-R.I.) for the Republicans and Arthur Gorman (D-Md.) for the Democrats (Rothman 1966; see also Chapter 11).

Elected as the Republican caucus chairman in the late 1890s, William Allison, working closely with Nelson Aldrich, began using Senate institutions, such as the committee system and the Republican Steering Committee, to further the Republican party's control and engender loyalty in ways previously unseen. Arthur Gorman, Democratic caucus chairman in the 1890s, pioneered early floor leadership for his party. Like his Republican counterpart, Allison, Gorman controlled the Democratic Committee on Committees and Steering Committee, which gave him command over both committee assignments and the legislative agenda. Together, Allison, Aldrich, and Gorman set the precedent of increasing party unity and strength by extending the elected position of caucus chair to the Senate floor.

Unlike the emergence of a standing committee system, which occurred rather quickly in the Senate (Gamm and Shepsle 1989), the floor's formal leadership positions formed in stages over a number of years. By the mid-1920s, however, these positions were firmly in place. Since these changes, the modern Senate leadership structure looks remarkably similar to that of the House.

In what follows, we lay out a simple spatial model of partisan agenda control applied to the U.S. Senate. We then look at the model's point estimates for data on majority and minority rolls and roll rates.[3] We next present comparative statics for the partisan model along with the null hypothesis, the pivot model. This is followed by our regression results for predictions of these two competing theories governing the Senate agenda-setting process.

Modeling Agenda Control in the Senate

Building on Cox and McCubbins's analysis of agenda control in the House of Representatives in Chapter 5, we seek to determine who, if anyone, has primary control over what bills and nominations are permitted to come up for final passage vote on the Senate floor.

Cox and McCubbins distinguish between two types of agenda control, *positive* and *negative*, which is particularly useful in understanding the role of parties in the Senate. The Senate's minority-protecting features should have a greater impact on *positive* agenda control than on *negative* agenda control. Conditional on the characteristics of the majority party, changing the status quo policy—that is, *positive* agenda control—may require supermajority coalitions. The case of the Democrats and the Southern-Northern split over civil rights legislation is such an example. Because of the Senate's lack of restrictions on debate, a small minority was able to mount formidable opposition, and the Senate was not able to pass civil rights legislation until there was supermajority bipartisan support to do so and invoke cloture. Conversely, we expect that majority party *negative* agenda control—its ability to keep bills it dislikes from being passed by the Senate—will be unaffected by majority party heterogeneity.

To summarize, Cox and McCubbins argue two main points:

1. The majority party's formal agenda powers allow it to, and are used to, keep issues off the floor agenda that would foreseeably displease significant portions of the party. This *negative agenda power* is *unconditional*, in the sense that its exercise should not theoretically and does not empirically vary with the similarity of the party's members' (constituency-induced or personal) ideas of good public policy.

2. In addition to its power to stop new legislation, thereby preserving past gains, the majority can also propose changes to existing policy. However, the size of the majority party's agenda (i.e., the volume of new policies it seeks to implement) waxes and wanes, depending on how similar party members' policy goals are, because leaders do not wish to waste their time leading where their followers will not (or cannot be induced to) follow. That is, *positive agenda control* is ever present, but the frequency with which the party uses this power varies with the degree to which the party membership agrees on what the party's collective reputation should be and hence on what should be done.

In this analysis, we will be conducting an initial test of the first of these two claims—that the majority party should have relatively unconditional *negative* control over the legislative agenda in the Senate.

CARTEL AGENDA MODEL

Cox and McCubbins deduce their claims from a simple spatial model of agenda control, adapted from Shepsle (1979) and Shepsle and Weingast (1981, 1987a, 1987b). In this model, space is Euclidean and each point represents separate policy positions along any number of policy dimensions. Individual legislator utility is a function of the distance between his or her ideal point, or preference, and the final policy position. Legislators seek to maximize the utility that they derive by minimizing the sum of the distances between their ideal points and the final policy outcomes along the various issue dimensions. Individual preferences, as well as the status quo points, are assumed to be common knowledge, as is strategic voting.

Using the same juxtaposition performed in the House analysis in Chapter 5, we can address this question about the two competing, polar conclusions about who controls the legislative agenda. In one model, Cox and Mc-Cubbins assumed that the floor agenda is determined by majority vote on the floor, hence by the chamber's median legislator. This is the floor model, and its predictions about what the floor agenda will look like form the null hypothesis to their theory. In contrast to the floor model, the cartel model contends that agenda control is partisan. The party-driven model asks, "If the majority party leadership determined the floor agenda, what might that agenda look like?"

To restate, in the cartel model, Cox and McCubbins argue that the majority party is in control of the agenda, acting through its leadership. For modeling purposes, they assume that the majority party leader is the median of his or her party (or acts in the median's interests) and has the unilateral power to put bills on or keep them off the chamber floor. In the Senate, as in the House, an equivalent assumption would state that the agenda is set as if by majority vote in the majority party's caucus. Cox and McCubbins submit the following results for the cartel agenda model:

> *Result 1*: No dimension on which a majority of the majority party prefers the status quo to the floor median's ideal point is ever scheduled for floor consideration.
> *Corollary*: Every bill passed results in policy being moved closer to the median majority party agent's ideal point.
> *Result 2*: No bill opposed by a majority of the majority party's members ever passes.

FLOOR AGENDA MODEL

The floor model provides the null hypothesis. Cox and McCubbins assume that the bills to be considered on the floor are determined by majority vote of the floor. Under the floor model, all dimensions with status quo points not equal to the floor median are considered. If the status quo is to the left of the floor median, the median and legislators to the right will vote to consider a bill and then to pass it (as amended if amended). The inverse would be true if the status quo is to the right of the floor median.

Where might the predictions of these two models diverge? In other words, will a majority of the majority party ever vote against the placement of a bill on the floor agenda in the floor model? Will they ever oppose a bill on final passage? Cox and McCubbins submit the following results:

> *Result 1*: For a given dimension, a majority of the majority party will vote against putting a bill on the floor agenda (but will lose) if and only if the status quo is closer to the ideal point of the median member of the majority party than the ideal point of the floor median is.

Corollary: The probability that a majority of the majority party unsuccessfully opposes placing an issue on the floor agenda is a function of (1) how large the interval is between the ideal point of the median member of the majority party and the ideal point of the floor median and (2) the distribution of status quo points.

Result 2: A majority of the majority party will vote against a bill pertaining to a policy dimension on final passage (but will lose) if and only if the status quo on that dimension is closer to the ideal point of the median member of the majority party than the ideal point of the floor median is.

Corollary: The probability that a majority of the majority party unsuccessfully opposes a bill on final passage is a function of (1) how large the interval is between the ideal point of the median member of the majority party and the ideal point of the floor median and (2) the distribution of status quo points on that dimension.

Note that similar results hold for the minority party; just substitute *minority party* for *majority party* in the claims.

CARTEL AND FLOOR AGENDA MODEL POINT ESTIMATE PREDICTIONS

The cartel and floor models have testable implications that can be stated in terms of a legislative roll. A Senate roll is identified by examining how the membership of each party voted on final bill passage and nomination votes. Because this is solely an analysis of Senate agenda control, bills are confined to Senate-originated bills. If the nay votes exceeded the aye votes for one party and the bill or nomination passed regardless, the vote is coded as a roll for that party.

The cartel model predicts that the majority party never gets rolled and that how often the minority party gets rolled increases as the distance between the median ideal point of the minority party and the median ideal point of the legislature increases. The floor model says that the majority party may be rolled less often than, as often as, or even more often than the minority, depending on the location of the majority, minority, and floor medians and on how the status quo points are distributed on each dimension. To demonstrate the contrast between the two models, according to the floor model, the majority and minority medians would have to be in the exact same location on each dimension to predict that the majority party never gets rolled (assuming that there are no areas of zero density in the distribution of status quo points). Although such a situation is in principle possible, it seems unlikely. As Cox and McCubbins note, "This might happen, for example, if the majority party consisted of a single unitary party that successfully imposed a single ideal point on its members. But it should be a rare event in cases where parties cannot be taken as 'analytic units,'" as a theory positing universal control must argue.

We should note that these models admittedly do not capture important variables, such as opportunity costs, consideration costs, and proposal costs, as well as uncertainty or incorrect information about preferences and the location of policy. The two models and resulting predictions are meant to be understood as baselines for evaluating the underlying theoretical arguments with respect to predominant locus of agenda power and legislative organization.

Majority and Minority Party Roll and Roll Rate Results

To assess the predictions, we turn first to final passage on Senate bills only and nomination votes on the Senate floor. This set of votes is taken from votes receiving a roll call between the 45th and 99th Congresses, inclusive.[4] Each final bill passage and nomination vote was coded as either ordinary (only a majority required for passage) or extraordinary (a supermajority of two-thirds required for passage). We excluded the latter from the analysis, as the models' claims are based on simple majority requirements. The analysis begins in 1877, before the emergence of formal Senate floor leadership and popular election of senators. Both are crucial elements to the cartel model and hence provide an interesting comparative static between these very different institutional environments in addition to the juxtaposition of the cartel and floor models—a point we will return to later in our discussion.

The first cut at the data generally supports the cartel model. For Congresses 45–99, the number of majority and minority party rolls, as well as their respective roll rates, are shown in Table 6.1. The modal number of times, by congressional session, that the majority party was rolled on a final passage or nomination vote on the Senate floor is *zero*. Between Congresses 45 and 99 (1877–1986), the majority party was not rolled on a single final passage or nomination vote in twenty-six of the fifty Congresses. By contrast, the minority party had no rolls in only four Congresses (62nd, 66th, 70th, and 72nd).

Looking at the *roll rates* (the number of times a party was rolled in a session divided by the total number of ordinary final passage or nomination votes), we see that majority party has a weighted average roll rate of 6.4 percent. When compared to the minority party's weighted average roll rate of 31.6 percent, we see that the minority party's roll rate is nearly five times that of the majority party's.

Table 6.1

Senate Rolls on Final Passage and Nomination Votes
for Majority and Minority Parties, by Congress

Congress	Majority Rolls	Majority Roll Rate	Minority Rolls	Minority Roll Rate	Total Votes	Majority Party
45	11	17.7%	15	24.2%	62	Republicans
46	3	12.5%	4	16.7%	24	Democrats
47	11	15.7%	24	34.3%	70	Republicans
48	5	12.5%	20	50.0%	40	Republicans
49	11	18.6%	9	15.3%	59	Republicans
50	2	10.0%	9	45.0%	20	Republicans
51	1	2.6%	23	59.0%	39	Republicans
52	2	10.0%	7	35.0%	20	Republicans
53	3	12.5%	13	54.2%	24	Democrats
54	4	44.4%	1	11.1%	9	Republicans
55	0	0.0%	8	40.0%	20	Republicans
56	0	0.0%	2	50.0%	4	Republicans
57	0	0.0%	5	83.3%	6	Republicans
58	0	0.0%	2	40.0%	5	Republicans
59	0	0.0%	2	40.0%	5	Republicans
60	0	0.0%	3	75.0%	4	Republicans
61	0	0.0%	3	50.0%	6	Republicans
62	0	0.0%	0	0.0%	6	Republicans
63	0	0.0%	1	33.3%	3	Democrats
64	0	0.0%	4	36.4%	11	Democrats
65	1	10.0%	2	20.0%	10	Democrats
66	2	40.0%	0	0.0%	5	Republicans
67	0	0.0%	4	26.7%	15	Republicans
68	0	0.0%	2	13.3%	15	Republicans
69	0	0.0%	1	16.7%	6	Republicans
70	1	14.3%	0	0.0%	7	Republicans
71	1	4.8%	8	38.1%	21	Republicans
72	0	0.0%	0	0.0%	10	Republicans
73	1	9.1%	5	45.5%	11	Democrats
74	0	0.0%	6	50.0%	12	Democrats
75	0	0.0%	7	70.0%	10	Democrats
76	1	4.5%	7	31.8%	22	Democrats
77	0	0.0%	2	25.0%	8	Democrats
78	0	0.0%	7	41.2%	17	Democrats

(continued)

Table 6.1

(continued)

Congress	Majority Rolls	Majority Roll Rate	Minority Rolls	Minority Roll Rate	Total Votes	Majority Party
79	0	0.0%	2	15.4%	13	Democrats
80	4	25.0%	2	12.5%	16	Republicans
81	1	4.8%	6	28.6%	21	Democrats
82	1	10.0%	3	30.0%	10	Democrats
83	0	0.0%	3	23.1%	13	Republicans
84	3	15.0%	4	20.0%	20	Democrats
85	3	13.6%	4	18.2%	22	Democrats
86	0	0.0%	7	31.8%	22	Democrats
87	0	0.0%	11	40.7%	27	Democrats
88	0	0.0%	11	57.9%	19	Democrats
89	0	0.0%	4	12.1%	33	Democrats
90	0	0.0%	4	13.8%	29	Democrats
91	0	0.0%	4	8.0%	50	Democrats
92	1	1.4%	1	1.4%	74	Democrats
93	4	2.9%	10	7.3%	137	Democrats
94	7	8.3%	10	11.9%	84	Democrats
95	0	0.0%	6	10.2%	59	Democrats
96	0	0.0%	8	9.1%	88	Democrats
97	0	0.0%	7	10.1%	69	Republicans
98	0	0.0%	5	17.9%	28	Republicans
99	0	0.0%	11	29.7%	37	Republicans
Weighted Average:		1.68 6.40%		6.58 31.62%	29.54	
Congressional Average:		5.82%		28.74%		

The average number of times the majority party is rolled in a Congress is 1.68, and the median number is again 0. Yet the average number of rolls for the minority party is 6.58, with a median of 4. The average number of ordinary final passage votes and nominations per Congress is 29.54, and the median is 16.5.

Given the received wisdom about the Senate's decentralized power, individualistic senator behavior, and permeable agenda-setting process, the majority party's rolls and roll rates should have been much higher. The data here suggest that there may be something to our claim that what is really important is control over scheduling rather than just access to the Senate calendar. The differences between the frequency of rolls on final passage and nomination votes for the majority and minority party meet the expectations of the cartel model quite well.

Since the beginning of the twentieth century, the majority party roll rates rarely exceed 10 percent, only five Congresses (the 66th, 70th, 80th, 84th, and 85th) being exceptions. Moreover, even in these exceptional cases, only eleven rolls were observed. Looking at the data over the entire time series, we see that the big drop in majority party rolls occurred shortly before the end of the nineteenth century, as numerous states introduced popular control of senators and the concomitant emergence of Senate floor leadership. Prior to the emergence of formal leadership positions, we see partisan floor management as early as the mid-1890s through the Republican Steering Committee. As Gamm and Smith (2000b: 2) note, "With the development of steering committees, control over day-to-day business shifted from the caucus itself to a relative handful of senators."

We argue that this transition of senatorial accountability from the state legislatures to the popular voters was a key episode in the Senate's history and critical to understanding its internal dynamics and organization. The Seventeenth Amendment, mandating the direct election of senators, in addition to being a key event in the development of the modern Senate, significantly affects a crucial premise to the cartel model—that legislators care about their collective party reputation.

As part of the Progressive Era reforms, the push for a constitutional amendment on the direct election of senators took root in the 1870s.[5] By 1905, thirty-one of the forty-five state legislatures had formally requested that Congress consider a constitutional amendment on direct election. Long before its enactment, numerous legislatures in the western and north central states self-imposed some form of popular control, such as a binding primary or referendum, on the senators they sent to Congress. Moreover, by the 1890s, the nonbinding direct primaries of one-party states, as in the South, had nearly the same effect as general popular elections. Even though the legislature was not legally bound to the primary decisions, it rarely deviated from the popular choice in these one-party states. Furthermore, Haynes (1960: 104) notes, citing the December 26, 1910, *Boston Herald*, "So rapid became the sweep of senatorial primaries under Oregon's lead that in December, 1910, before the state legislatures had been convened which were to elect senators, it was declared: '*Fourteen out of thirty Senators who take the oath of office at the beginning of the next Congress, have already been designated by popular vote*'" [emphasis added].[6] The enactment of the Seventeenth Amendment in 1913, rather than a clear demarcation between two different methods of choosing U.S. senators, was instead the official confirmation of a transition that was nearly complete.

Assuming that senators are purposeful actors and that they desire to be reelected, this change in their means of reelection implies a change in their incentives and behavior, all else remaining constant. The popular election of senators increased the value of having a strong collective reputation, also known as brand name or party label. A strong party label requires collective action by party members within the chamber. Collective action is most often difficult. Moreover, the increasing demand for strong party reputations came at the same time as the increase in legislative workload, in terms of individual demands for legislation, and the resulting scarcity of floor time at the turn of the century (see Chapter 11). The evolving process of senatorial accountability, from the legislatures to popular voters, and the evolution of the Senate's leadership positions go hand in hand. We argue that the party leaders provided the coordination mechanism needed to address the newly developing collective action problems that senators were facing. Until the formal leadership positions were in place, the steering committees became the coordinating mechanism and clearinghouse through which party members must navigate their proposals.

In short, according to the *cartel partisan model*, it is this need to maintain a strong, consistent collective party reputation that engenders delegation to a central authority. With popular elections, senators developed a need for a strong, consistent party reputation in the legislature. This motive caused them to delegate authority to a central authority, the majority party leadership, and thus provide the leadership with the means to influence the Senate floor agenda. Shortly thereafter, we see the institutionalization of formal floor leadership positions.

Turning back to the data, the significant drop in the majority party roll rate near the end of the nineteenth century is exactly what the cartel model would have predicted given the changing electoral environment. This drop was not mirrored by the minority party, providing further evidence in support of the notion that party status is quite relevant in the modern Senate.

Received wisdom aside, the data here suggest that the cartel model merits further investigation in the Senate. To perform a more systematic test, we now turn to a comparative statics analysis. Before doing so, however, we expand briefly on the theoretical discussion to improve its applicability to the Senate case.

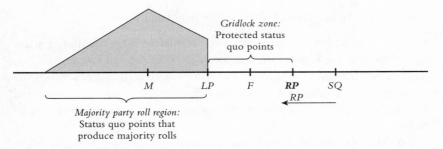

Figure 6.1. The pivot model.

The Pivot Model

Recently, Krehbiel (1998) has advanced a refined account of the floor agenda model. In the case of the Senate, this model is more appropriate since it incorporates two nonmajoritarian features of U.S. policymaking: the Senate filibuster and the presidential veto. Because of these features, the *pivot model*, unlike the floor model, features a "gridlock zone." Similar to the cartel model, the pivot model has a zone of protected status quo points.

The pivot model works much like the floor model. Now, only bills and nominations that fall outside the gridlock zone should make it onto the floor agenda. If the status quo policy lies in this zone, the model predicts no policy change. Instead of focusing on the floor median, we look at the left and right pivot points with the pivot model. This is illustrated by Figure 6.1. In this diagram, let *M* be the majority party median; *LP*, the left pivot point; *RP*, the right pivot point; *F*, the floor median; and *SQ*, the status quo. In this example, because *SQ* lies to the right of the right pivot point, policy would be brought inside of the *LP–RP* range.

Because the pivot model and the cartel model both have zones of "protected" status quo points, it's important to clarify how they differ in their empirical implications, that is, in their predicted roll rates. If a status quo point falls outside the gridlock zone and inside the majority party roll region, the majority party will be rolled on that dimension according to the pivot model.[7] Using the spatial example in Figure 6.1, in a session where the majority party has a slim majority, the majority party median will fall at approximately the 25th percentile of Senate ideal points and the left pivot will fall at the 40th percentile ideal point. This being the case, the pivot model predicts that the majority party's roll rate will be positive.

Comparative Statics Tests of the Cartel Agenda and Pivot Models

While the (complete information) cartel model *predicts* no majority party rolls, there are a few, as we discussed earlier. That the roll rate for the majority is low but not zero suggests that some omitted considerations—such as uncertainty or divided government (which will be more fully explored later in this chapter)—may be producing an occasional roll of the majority party.

Like the floor model, the pivot model predicts that the probability of the majority party's losing a final passage or nomination vote increases with the distance between the majority and floor median for all dimensions, while the probability of the minority party's losing such a vote increases with the distance between the minority and floor medians for all dimensions.[8] Under the cartel model, only the second of these comparative statics expectations holds—the opposition should lose more often the more distant its median member is from the floor median. The first comparative static is not true for the cartel model. The majority party should never lose, and any fluctuations in its roll rate should be unrelated to the distance between the majority party and floor medians.

To measure the distance between the party medians and the floor median, Poole and Rosenthal's (1985, 1997) D-NOMINATE multidimensional scaling was used to estimate the average location of the party and floor medians across all dimensions in a congressional session. Because of the estimation problems implied by simply estimating the probability of a roll on the distance between party medians and floor median,[9] the following equation was estimated:

$$ROLL\_RATE_{ct} = \chi_c + (\beta_c \times D_{ct}) + \varepsilon_{ct} \tag{1}$$

where $ROLL\_RATE_{ct}$ is the roll rate for each party c in Congress t and D_{ct} is the distance between the floor and party medians' D-NOMINATE scores for party c in Congress t.

Equation 1 can be estimated by ordinary least squares (OLS) because the number of observations that make up the denominator in the proportion, $ROLL\_RATE_{ct}$, averages more than 50 and thus $ROLL\_RATE_{ct}$ should approximate a normal distribution asymptotically. The data suffered from both heteroskedasticity, as the number of votes per Congress varies by two orders of magnitude, and serial correlation, which was dealt with by using the Huber-White sandwich estimator of variance. To correct for autocorrelation, one and two term lags of the dependent variable was included as

Table 6.2

Predicted Coefficients from the Cartel
and Pivot Models

	Majority $\hat{\beta}$	Minority $\hat{\beta}$
Cartel agenda model	0	+
Pivot model	+	+

right-hand side variables. Further diagnostics of the regression suggested no other estimation problems.

To estimate the equation, we performed the minimum logit chi square (MLCS) technique, suggested by Maddala (1983: 18–30). In this technique, the dependent variable is the smoothed logit of the roll rate:

$$\log\left[\frac{ROLL\_RATE_{ct} + (2TOTAL\_FPV_t)^{-1}}{1 - ROLL\_RATE_{ct} + (2TOTAL\_FPV_t)^{-1}} \right]$$

where $TOTAL\_FPV_{ct}$ is the total number of final passage votes for Congress t. One estimates the model using weighted least squares with weights $TOTAL\_FPV_t \times [ROLL\_RATE_{ct} + (2TOTAL\_FPV_t)^{-1}] \times [1 - ROLL\_RATE_{ct} + (2TOTAL\_FPV_t)^{-1}]$. This technique should approximate a logit regression on $ROLL_{cjt}$ without exaggerating our number of observations and biasing the tests.

Table 6.2 summarizes the hypotheses for both models. The pivot model predicts that the coefficient β_c in Equation 1 will be positive and significant for both the majority and minority parties. That is, the pivot model predicts that as D_{ct} increases, the likelihood that the majority (minority) party is rolled on vote j increases. The cartel model, in contrast, predicts that the coefficient β_c for the majority party will be zero: the likelihood that the *majority* party is rolled on vote j is not systematically related to D_{ct}. However, β_c is predicted to be positive for the *minority* party.

While we have decided that the MLCS technique is the most appropriate technique to estimate the model, we present the OLS results below as well. In the tables that follow, the results for the majority and minority parties are presented by technique along the rows.

The results presented in Table 6.3 agree with the predictions of the cartel model and differ with the pivot model's predictions. Specifically, $\hat{\beta}_c$ is positive and significant in both the OLS and MLCS regressions for the mi-

Table 6.3

Estimated OLS and MLCS Coefficients,
Senate Final Passage and Nomination Votes:
Cartel Model vs. Pivot Model

	Majority $\hat{\beta}$	Minority $\hat{\beta}$
Effect of D_{ct} on roll rates for Senate final passage votes, estimated using OLS	0.136 (0.068)	0.453 (0.094)
Effect of D_{ct} on roll rates for Senate final passage votes, estimated using MLCS	0.281 (0.385)	1.134 (0.488)

nority party. We cannot reject the null hypothesis that $\hat{\beta}_c$ is zero for the majority party in either the OLS or MLCS estimations. As predicted by the cartel agenda model, the distance between the majority party median member and the floor median is not significantly related to the incidence of being rolled for the majority party, however, it is significant for the minority party. That is to say, party status matters. If the floor model's predictions bore out, the $\hat{\beta}_c$ for both majority and minority party regressions should have been positive and significant.

With our system of separated powers, and the closer inspection of majority rolls in the preceding section, it has been suggested that divided government might be an important variable affecting agenda control, particularly with the Senate's unique responsibilities regarding nominations. Especially since our data includes executive nominations, we explore this further.

Next we add a variable to examine the effect of divided government on majority and minority party rolls. The results are presented in Table 6.4. As before, majority $\hat{\beta}$ and minority $\hat{\beta}$ are the coefficients for D_{ct} for the minority and majority parties. In addition, majority $\hat{\alpha}$ and minority $\hat{\alpha}$ are the coefficients for divided government. The divided government variable identifies division between the Senate and the president (divided government between the House and Senate was never significant in any of the regressions).

The inclusion of divided government affected the OLS results. Presenting the same coefficients as in Table 6.3, we now see that $\hat{\beta}_c$ for the majority party is positive and significant (upper left cell at the top of Table 6.4).[10] However, when we look at the more appropriate technique for our data in the row for MLCS, we see that the majority coefficient is no longer

Table 6.4

Estimated OLS and MLCS Coefficients
when Divided Government Is Included:
Cartel Model vs. Pivot Model

Effect of Distance

	Majority $\hat{\beta}$	Minority $\hat{\beta}$
Effect of D_{ct} on roll rates for Senate final passage votes, estimated using OLS	0.145 (0.068)	0.444 (0.093)
Effect of D_{ct} on roll rates for Senate final passage votes, estimated using MLCS	0.732 (0.367)	1.307 (0.440)

Effect of Divided Government on Roll Rates

	Majority $\hat{\alpha}$	Minority $\hat{\alpha}$
For Senate final passage votes, estimated using OLS	0.083 (0.030)	−0.119 (0.052)
For Senate final passage votes, estimated using MLCS	0.714 (0.200)	−0.847 (0.241)

significant. As before, the $\hat{\beta}_c$ for the minority party is always positive and significant.

Turning to the results for the divided government variable, Table 6.4 presents the coefficients for the minority and majority parties in the OLS and MLCS regressions. Divided government is among the Senate and president. In both the OLS and MLCS estimations, the incidence of divided government has a *negative* and significant effect on the minority party's roll rate. By contrast, the incidence of divided government has a *positive* effect on the majority party's roll rate. In other words, divided government increases the majority party's and decreases the minority party's respective roll rates. These results suggest, as we might expect, that owing to the Senate's unique institutional responsibilities (e.g., executive nominations) and internal rules, there are some things that the majority party has a hard time keeping off the floor. Despite these limitations, however, the majority party does remarkably well with negative agenda control.

We end this discussion by emphasizing the role of votes on nominations in agenda control. In measuring our dependent variable—whether or not the majority is rolled on final votes—we have included votes on whether or not to approve presidential nominations. In fact, there is ample reason to believe that in many cases, such as cabinet appointments, it is *not* feasible for the Senate majority to prevent the nominee from receiving a vote on the Senate floor. This suggests that when the executive and the Senate are controlled by opposite parties, the president can sometimes use nominations as a way of circumventing majority party gatekeeping to bring a matter to a floor vote.

Indeed, when executive nominations excluded from the dependent variable, the significant positive relationship between divided government and majority roll rates disappears.[11] Shared agenda control with the executive is apparently confined to executive nominations and does not extend to bills.

Conclusion

With a few exceptions, the Senate has fallen to the wayside in the contemporary congressional organization debate, which has been predominantly a debate about House organization. In this analysis, we have attempted to bring the Senate into the mainstream, and in doing so, we discovered a few interesting things.

First, in contrast to the conventional wisdom and a few of the claims made at the start of this chapter, it appears that the Senate majority party *does* have the ability to affect the floor agenda. We saw this in a direct comparison of majority and minority party rolls and roll rates as well as in the comparative statics results.

Second, consistent with partisan models of Congress—those that believe they are useful units of analysis—the majority party rolls dropped dramatically at the end of the nineteenth century, concomitant with the popular control of senators and the emergence of formal Senate party leadership. This drop in rolls was *not* paralleled by the minority party.

Finally, divided government may have an effect on the Senate's majority party's ability to control the agenda in ways unseen in the House. We saw that divided government had a positive effect on the majority party's roll rate and a negative effect on the minority party's, despite the cartel model's predicted comparative statics. So even though it is quite strong, majority party negative agenda control may not be *unconditional*, as Cox and McCubbins found it to be in the House.

Returning to the broader issue of whether or not characterizations of the Senate as atomistic, individualistic, and unresponsive to partisan control are justified, the data here suggest otherwise. In comparison to the House, party control of the Senate is definitely more challenging. Despite the challenge, however, the majority party in the modern Senate does a remarkably good job of keeping matters that may be offensive to a majority of its membership off of the chamber floor for final vote.

Chapter 7

Party Loyalty and Committee Leadership in the House, 1921-40

BRIAN R. SALA

Warren G. Harding opened his presidential campaign in 1920 with a call for a return to "normalcy" in America. For Congress, "normalcy" meant a return to unified Republican party control of government but not necessarily a rolling back of the clock to the days prior to Woodrow Wilson's presidency. Divisions within the Republican House contingent blocked the reinstitution of full-blown "Cannonism" when the party regained majority control of the House in the 66th Congress (1919–21). The golden age of party government in the U.S. Congress that ended with the 1910–11 revolt against House Speaker Joseph Cannon (R-Ill.) would not return. What, then, would arise in its place?

The literature on the evolution of the modern U.S. Congress has emphasized the 1890–1910 interval as a "takeoff" period for the modernization of the House. It was during this period that member return rates soared and careers lengthened (Fiorina, Rohde, and Wissel 1975; Polsby 1968; Polsby, Gallaher, and Rundquist 1969; Price 1971), committee assignment "property rights" solidified (Katz and Sala 1996; Polsby 1968; Price 1975, 1977), and party and chamber leadership positions were institutionalized (Polsby 1968).

Nonetheless, the modern or "textbook Congress"–era U.S. House of weak party leaders, strong committee leaders, and frequent cross-party floor coalitions did not emerge fully formed from the revolt against Cannon. In this chapter, I explore two aspects of the relationship among party leaders, committee leaders, and rank-and-file members in the House during the 1920s and 1930s, with an eye toward reexamining the thesis that the Cannon revolt destroyed the institutional conditions that made party government possible. I argue that the evidence from recorded votes in the 1920s and 1930s offers very little persuasive support for the thesis of party decline. Most floor motions, both before and after the revolt, were offered by senior members of the majority party. Motions offered by these members almost always passed, often on highly partisan votes, whereas those offered by minority party members almost always failed, often on highly partisan votes as well. Motions opposed by the majority floor leader and whip usually failed, even when offered by senior members of the majority party. While there is substantial evidence of factional strife within both the Republican majority in the 1920s and the Democratic majority in the 1930s, that strife did not translate into compelling evidence in favor of "committee government" in the House during the interwar period.

First, I examine the extent to which the majority party appears to have controlled access to the legislative agenda by examining *who* made motions on the floor of the House that receive recorded votes and *how* those motions were disposed. While important legislation can be (and often is) considered without the benefit of recorded votes, the conditions that must be met to force a roll call are mild, and these actions are one of the chief ways through which individual legislators can take publicly accountable stands on questions of public significance. The standing rules of the House confer considerable discretion on the Speaker to bestow recognition to make floor motions in the House. Hence patterns of recognition may reveal information about the distributions of loyalty and influence in the House.

Second, I examine the extent to which committee status affords members slack on important legislative votes, by looking at the party loyalty of committee leaders and rank-and-file members on a subset of recorded votes that proxied for "whipped votes," votes identified as important by party leaders. Many scholars have argued that the committee system offers an alternative source of power and influence in the House that stands independent of the powers of the post-Cannon Speakership. Was committee leadership in the 1920s and 1930s associated with independence or with (public) agreement on the party program?

Next, I briefly review the literature on party cohesion and on the committee system in the 1920s and 1930s. I then discuss the distribution of motion authorship on the floor of the House during that period and discuss the relationship between motion authorship and standard measures of partisanship. Next, I examine the track record of committee leaders' collective support for party leadership positions in the 1921–40 period and contrast that record with the support levels offered by rank-and-file members. A conclusion brings the chapter to a close.

Party Government After Cannon

"Party government" in the United States is the idea that the majority party organization bears primary responsibility for the outcomes generated by a legislative chamber. The primary outcomes of interest are, of course, legislative. The notion of party government thus rests critically on the majority party caucus's ability to regulate the content of floor activities. Majority party agents must gain timely access to the floor to bring up caucus-favored legislative proposals for consideration. Rank-and-file members must be mustered to the floor and cued as to how to vote. Internal party conflict must be held to a minimum if the majority is to present a coherent collective image to the attentive public.

On these dimensions, the period 1890–1909 was a golden age for party government in the U.S. House. "Czarist" House Speakers and their lieutenants closely managed the floor agenda, delivered clear voting cues on issues of central concern to the majority party's leadership, and intimidated potential dissenters within the party. Two key authorities—proposal power for special rules to circumvent the regular order and proposal power for committee assignments—were to a great extent centralized in the hands of the Speaker. As chairman of the Committee on Rules, the Speaker could largely determine whether a public bill would be considered out of its turn (or at all). And as the central agent for assigning members to committees, the Speaker could directly affect the welfare of individual members of Congress (MCs) by extending or withholding desired assignments.[1]

Republican Speakers Joseph Cannon (Ill., 1903–10), David Henderson (Ia., 1899–1903), and Thomas Reed (Me., 1889–91, 1895–99) and to a lesser extent, Democratic Speaker Charles Crisp (Ga., 1891–95) used this authority to great effect during the 1890–1910 period to mold policy outcomes to their own views (Jones, 1968; Polsby, 1968; Chiu, 1928). The Speaker used committee assignments and discretionary recognition as carrots and sticks to help maintain party discipline on important agenda items. Leaders could arrange the floor agenda via special rules adopted by simple majority vote.

But the Speaker's discretion was curtailed in the revolt against Cannon and its aftermath. The House stripped Speaker Cannon of his chairmanship of and membership on the Committee on Rules in March 1910. Simultaneously, the House also expanded the committee to ten members from its previous five. Following the fall elections, in which "Cannonism" seems to have been an important issue, the new Democratic majority approved rules changes that removed the Speaker's primacy in making committee assignments. Instead, they provided that committees were to be elected by the House. This meant in practice that a committee on committees appointed by the majority caucus would present a resolution naming the committees (see Hasbrouck, 1927; Binder, 1997).

Many scholars, following the lamentations of Joseph Cannon's friends and apologists, argued that by stripping the Speaker of so much authority, the House crippled "party government" as well. The conventional view of party influence in the U.S. Congress holds that a transition occurred in the House "from a hierarchical pattern of leadership" under Speaker Cannon "to a bargaining pattern" under Speakers beginning with Sam Rayburn in the 1940s and 1950s (Cooper and Brady 1981: 411). There developed a "marked tendency for [committee] chairmen to be comparatively uninterested in party matters when compared to rank-and-file party members" (Morrow 1969: 112). Committee chairmen in the post–World War II "textbook Congress" era were "chieftains to be bargained with, not lieutenants to be commanded" (Huitt 1961: 335).

Each committee was stylized as a nearly autonomous entity, firmly controlling the legislative gates within its jurisdiction. Committees became "little legislatures" (Goodwin 1970) as committee assignments became "routinized" (Gertzog 1976), and the seniority system took hold. Cox and McCubbins (1993: 47) summarized the conventional view neatly: "Most descriptions of seniority . . . see it as 'sovereign and inviolate'—and infer that committee chairs must, therefore, have been largely autonomous. Indeed, the customary right of reappointment (with seniority rank preserved) has generally been construed as insulating *all* committee members, not just chairs, from the wishes of party leaders."

The relationship between chairmen and party in the late nineteenth and early twentieth centuries was quite different from this "textbook" view, however. Contrary to the standard "czarist" view of the period, Speakers before and after Cannon appear to have worked closely with a small set of key committee leaders, whereas chairmen of lesser committees had to struggle to gain floor access for their committees' bills (Alexander 1916; Brady and Morgan 1987; Hasbrouck 1927; McConachie 1998).[2] This union of major committee and party leadership was clearest in the Democratic party after the revolt but was true of the Republicans after 1918 as well.

Beginning with the 62nd House (1911–13) and continuing until 1975, the Democrats used their contingent on Ways and Means as "a Board or Committee of Committees" to recommend a slate of committee assignments to the party caucus and then the House (Alexander 1916: 82–83; see also Shepsle 1978).[3] This group, together with the elected Democratic party leaders, continued to serve as the caucus's policy committee throughout the 1910s and 1920s (Brown 1974: esp. chap. 14). This latter practice can be viewed as little more than a broadening of the leadership set from the prior use of the chairman of Ways and Means as the majority floor leader.

Similarly, the postrevolt Republicans began to rely on a caucus Steering Committee to coordinate the legislative agenda. Moderate Republican leaders inside and out of the House apparently feared that Cannonism would become an issue in the 1920 elections (a presidential election year) if James R. Mann (R-Ill.) were elevated to the Speakership in 1919. Chiu (1928: 26–27), citing *New York Times* articles on Jan. 16 and Jan. 20, 1919, states that both the Republican National Committee chairman and a prominent Republican senator took "an active part" in the Speakership contest on behalf of the current "dean" of the House—and ranking Republican on the Appropriations Committee—Frederick Gillett (R-Mass.).

Republicans responded by restructuring their leadership institutions. Progressive and moderate Republicans struck a deal to elect Gillett as Speaker. Gillett was no reformer—his voting record in the 62nd–65th Houses (1911–19) was decidedly centrist within the Republican coalition.[4] The Republicans then separated the chairmanship of the Ways and Means Committee from its traditional association with the function of majority floor leader (electing Franklin Mondell of Wyoming floor leader after Mann declined the position) and created a new Committee on Committees to make up committee slates and a new Steering Committee to coordinate the party's agenda. According to the *New York Times* (February 28, 1919: 4), the adoption of the new committee on committees "was interpreted as indicating that the movement initiated by Representatives Longworth and Fess of Ohio and others with a view to breaking down and overthrowing the domination of the House committees under the seniority rule of service has been blocked and defeated."

The charge of "seniority rule" domination of the House is difficult to assess. Wary of Mann's loss in the Speakership race, the leaders of the "old guard" moved to confirm every returning ranking Republican (other than now-Speaker Gillett) as chair of his committee. This allowed some of Mann's critics within the caucus to assume committee chairmanships. George Brown (1974) comments that the Mann forces made a conscious effort to minimize criticism that the Republicans had returned to Cannonism. Hence new caucus rules also prohibited members of the Steering Committee from chairing "exclusive" standing committees. Given the acknowledged authority wielded by committee chairmen, this institutional change had the effect of creating new veto gates through which proposed policy changes must flow before becoming law.

The new House power structure was more hierarchical than had been true under Cannonism, not less so. Cannon's House formally centralized a great deal of authority in the hands of the Speaker (and in practice relied on the Speaker and his closest advisers to run the chamber). The Cannon-era Speaker could wave carrots such as the promise of better future committee assignments, a special rule to schedule a bill, or recognition to make unanimous consent requests to induce members to bring forward and support bills he desired.

In the new environment, party leaders' carrots were less apparent. The consequence of this restructuring was not a flood of legislative proposals antithetical to party leaders' positions because such disloyal proposals had never been inhibited greatly by the carrot supply per se. Rather, these proposals simply never made it onto the legislative agenda. After Cannon, a legislative proposal would have to satisfy a larger set of majority party actors to reach the floor for consideration than had been true before the revolt. Hence the most plausible adverse effect of these institutional changes should have been a shrinking of the positive portion of the majority party's partisan agenda, as though intraparty heterogeneity had increased. This would manifest itself in fewer motions supported by the majority party leaders and opposed by the minority leaders. At the same time, however, the size of the negative agenda may have increased if majority leaders found themselves less able to block floor access to measures sponsored by their own party's members.

Motion Sponsorship, 1921– 40

The "insurgent" critics of Speaker Joseph Cannon argued that Cannon's discretionary control over floor scheduling, amendment procedures, and the distribution of resources was too great. They sought and eventually achieved several rules changes that reduced the Speaker's discretion and influence. But it is not obvious that these rules changes necessarily had a great impact on observable floor activities in the House.

In particular, the rules changes should have had little effect on the majority party's ability to cue rank-and-file members about how they should vote on floor questions. Rather, the impact should have appeared in the responsiveness of members to those cues. If the rules changes broke the back of strong party government and created the conditions for committee government, leadership voting cues should have declined as a predictor of rank-and-file voting behavior. I explore this implication in the next section.

Furthermore, if leaders' policy preferences were declining in relevance in the 1920s and 1930s, rank-and-file members who disagreed with the majority leaders' policy preferences should have become better able to offer and gain approval of motions opposed by majority leaders. I shall now explore the relationship between motion sponsorship and leadership approval during the 1920s and 1930s.

MOTION SPONSORSHIP UNDER CANNON

To gain leverage on the sponsorship-approval relationship in the 1920s and 1930s, I first look briefly at the relationship near the end of Speaker Cannon's regime, in the 60th House (1907–09). The uses to which minority party members were to put floor votes in the 1920s and 1930s were dramatically different from those employed in that earlier Congress. Floor votes changed functions for the minority party. During the strong-Speaker era, the minority coalition enjoyed few opportunities to frame recorded votes for its own purposes. Instead, the minority often used House procedures for dilatory purposes—to delay passage of bills favored by the majority coalition.

After the revolt, the minority regained its ability to make clear policy statements via floor votes on legislation. Among the changes that would arise from the 1909 rules fight would be a provision guaranteeing to opponents of a bill the right to offer one motion to recommit the bill with or without instructions. Only two motions to recommit received recorded votes in the 60th House, out of 319 recorded votes. In contrast, recommittal motions constituted 12.4 percent of all recorded votes during 1921–40 and nearly half of all recorded-vote motions offered by minority party members during the period.[5]

The roots of this change can be found in the strategic maneuvering between Democrats and Republicans during the 60th Congress (1907–09). Democrats in the 60th House sponsored only thirteen recorded-vote motions (on eleven separate bills or resolutions), but they forced recorded votes on a number of other questions as part of a presidential-election-year dilatory campaign led by minority leader John S. Williams (D-Miss.). Republican leaders responded first (on April 4, 1908) by imposing a gag rule to make it easier to cut off debate on bills in the Committee of the Whole and to appoint conference committees on appropriations bills (*Congressional Record* 1908: 4368). Four days later, they imposed a second restrictive rule, which permitted majority rule suspension of the rules to pass appropriations bills reported favorably from the Committee of the Whole (4514). Both resolutions passed on straight party-line votes.

Suspension motions are self-executing "closed rule" motions that cut off debate and amendment and pass the associated measure. They rule out recommittal motions because such motions are to be made after amendments have been voted on and before a final passage vote is held. A vote to reject the suspension motion also defeats the underlying measure. Hence this rules change was designed to force the minority Democrats either to accept appropriations bills as written in the Committee of the Whole or bear responsibility for shutting down the government. Forty-two percent of all recorded votes (135 of 319) held during the 60th Congress were consumed by motions to suspend the rules, most of which involved appropriations bills. All but three of these motions were offered by Republicans.

Party discipline among Republicans appears to have been well maintained during the 60th House. Motions offered by committee chairmen (or Speaker Cannon's chief lieutenant on Rules, John Dalzell, R–Pa.) almost invariably led to highly cohesive party-line votes or to "hurrah" votes, in which most members voted the same way. More than half of the motions offered by Republican committee leaders in the 60th House led to highly cohesive party-line votes (two-thirds or more of voting Republicans opposing two-thirds or more of voting Democrats—127 of 225 votes). Another 40 percent of the motions offered by these members induced nonparty votes (more than half of the voting members from each party voting together— 91 of 225). Republican committee leaders got rolled on only ten recorded votes they sponsored.

In contrast, motions offered by other Republicans were much less likely to induce highly partisan votes. More than half were nonparty votes, while 37 percent were highly cohesive party votes. The difference can largely be explained by reference to the treatment of motions to suspend the rules. A higher percentage of suspension motions offered by Republican committee leaders were highly partisan votes compared to those offered by other Republicans (37 percent versus 27 percent), while a higher proportion of total motions offered by rank-and-file Republicans were consumed by suspension motions (52 percent versus 40 percent).

The recorded-vote evidence is consistent with there having been a close relationship between committee leaders and majority party leaders in the 60th House. Speaker Cannon worked closely with a cadre of committee leaders, such as Dalzell (second ranking member on Rules), Sereno Payne (R–N.Y., chairman of Ways and Means and majority floor leader), Franklin

Mondell (R-Wyo., chairman of the Committee on Public Lands), James Tawney (R-Minn., chairman of Appropriations), James Mann (R-Ill., chair of the Committee on Elections No. 1), and James Sherman (R-N.Y., chairman of Indian Affairs and vice-presidential candidate on the Taft ticket in 1908). Together, these six committee leaders offered 143 of the 319 motions that received recorded votes in the 60th House, accounting for 96 of the 164 highly partisan votes.

MOTION SPONSORSHIP IN THE 1920S

Conventional wisdom holds that the revolt against Cannon began a transition to "committee government" in the U.S. House (Brady 1973; Polsby 1968; Polsby, Gallaher, and Rundquist 1969). The hallmarks of committee government were said to be property rights in committee assignments and committee "independence" from party leaders.

I showed earlier that motions offered by majority party committee leaders dominated the floor agenda at the end of the Cannon era. Although minority party leaders often were responsible for forcing a recorded vote on a question, the majority of the motions resulting in recorded votes were made by majority party committee leaders, and a large share of such motions resulted in highly partisan recorded votes. How did patterns of floor activity change in the 1920s and 1930s? I examine first the evidence from the 67th–71st Houses (1921–31), an era of Republican majorities in Congress.

The Republicans in the 1920s endured persistent, internal partisan divisions (Schickler and Rich 1997; Binder 1997). The "progressive" or "insurgent" wing of the party—successor to the insurgents integral to the revolt against Cannon in 1909–10—held or nearly held the balance of power between Democrats and regular Republicans in 66th (1919–21) and 68th (1923–25) Houses. This splinter group helped defeat James Mann's bid for the Speakership in the 66th House (Brown 1974; Chiu 1928; Hasbrouck 1927) and forced procedural and committee assignment concessions from the party hierarchy in return for supporting the reelection of Speaker Frederick Gillett in the 68th (Binder, 1997; Hasbrouck, 1927).

In light of these internal dynamics—similar in many respects to the factional divisions that struck the House Republicans in the Cannon years—what should one expect of motion sponsorship? The floor agenda in the Cannon era was dominated by motions made by committee leaders and supported strongly by both party leaders and the majority rank-and-file membership.[6] But Cannonism had become political anathema by the 1920s. The committee government approach implies that committee leaders' motions should increasingly be independent of party leaders' preferences as power was transferred from party leaders to committee chairmen. Cross-party support coalitions should increasingly overcome the opposition of majority party leaders on floor motions. In other words, where there was a fusion of committee leadership and party leadership during the Cannon era, there should have developed an observable separation between the two in the committee government era.

I can find very little evidence in support of this expectation, however. Committee leaders rarely offered motions opposed by party leaders. Of the 817 recorded votes (excluding ballots for Speaker) held during the Republican 67th–71st Houses (1921–31), 577 were on motions made by Republicans, 288 of which were offered by committee chairs or the floor leader and 289 by rank-and-file Republicans. Democrats sponsored 172 motions (the sponsorship of the remaining observations could not be determined), 80 offered by ranking minority committee members and 92 by rank-and-file Democrats.

During the 1920s, Republican committee leaders sponsored a total of thirteen floor motions that were opposed by the party's floor leaders (out of the 288 motions sponsored). Seven of these motions passed: two each in the 67th, 68th, and 70th and one in the 71st. Of the six that failed, the Republican committee-leader sponsors actually opposed the motions five times.[7] In other words, during the 1920s, Republican committee leaders tried to roll the party leaders on eight occasions that led to recorded votes, failing twice.

Rank-and-file Republicans sponsored 32 floor motions during the period that were opposed by Republican floor leaders (out of 306 total motions), passing 17. Meanwhile, of 407 motions offered by Republicans and supported by the floor leaders (not including 46 offered by the majority leader) during the 1920s, 380 passed; only 27 failed.

Table 7.1 details the distribution of floor motions receiving recorded votes during the 1920s. Both parties' rank-and-file members were relatively active in offering motions that received votes in this period, unlike the 60th House. The table does suggest three procedural changes from the 60th House: more frequent final passage votes, recommittal votes, and separate votes on amendments being moved by rank-and-file Republicans. Separate votes on amendments previously accepted in the Committee of the Whole may have given motion sponsors and their allies opportunities to claim credit for their legislative achievements in the Committee of the Whole.

The modal category for minority-sponsored motions is that of votes on recommittal, and that for majority motions, votes on final passage. Final pas-

Table 7.1
Floor Motions by Party, 67th–71st Houses (1921–31)

Floor Motion	Democrats	Republican Rank-and-File	Republican Committee Chairs	Totals
Adjourn	13	6	20	39
Amend	30	52	13	95
Approve Senate amendment	8	35	17	60
Consider	5	28	35	68
Pass	6	85	96	187
Previous question	4	19	17	40
Recommit	77	19	6	102
Suspend rules	0	29	27	56
Table	3	4	6	13
Other	26	29	34	89
Totals	172	306	271	749

NOTE: Excludes one motion to instruct conferees offered by a Socialist member and 67 motions for which authorship could not be determined (including thirty-five motions to approve conference reports).

sage votes were more frequent than in the 60th House but were largely non-partisan in the 1920s, whereas they had usually been partisan in the 60th. Democrats typically used their recommittal motions to state a Democratic alternative to the majority's bill, thus often leading to highly partisan results. Fifty-seven percent of the Democratic recommittal motions during the 1920s resulted in highly partisan votes (at least two-thirds of the participating Democrats voting in opposition to at least two-thirds of the participating Republicans), whereas only 23 percent resulted in nonpartisan votes. In contrast, Republican-sponsored recommittal motions tended to divide the progressive Republicans against the bulk of the party.

Not surprisingly, given the historiography of the period, there is substantial evidence in this period in favor of active cross-party coalitions (Schickler and Rich 1997), particularly on votes to amend, where Republican leaders were rolled on 21 of 26 amendments offered by Republicans but opposed by the floor leader or whip. Nonetheless, it seems hard to argue that party leaders had become increasingly irrelevant in the House. Republican leaders opposed about 10 percent of the recorded-vote motions offered by

Republicans; half of those passed despite leaders' opposition. In contrast, more than 82 percent of Democratic floor motions opposed by the Republican leaders failed.

MOTION SPONSORSHIP IN THE 1930S

The Democrats regained control of the House in the 1930 midterm elections. They held very large majorities for most of the decade as the Republican party nearly disappeared as a viable national party in the wake of the Great Depression. Standard interpretations of House politics in the 1930s argue that Democratic party leaders in the House lost influence over the decade to committee leaders and to a Southern Democrat–Republican "conservative coalition" (Patterson 1967). The record on motion sponsorship offers little support for the thesis of committee government, however.

House members voted 636 times in 1931–38 (excluding votes to elect the Speaker).[8] Democrats passed 356 of 443 motions, whereas Republicans passed only 31 of 107 (authorship of the balance could not be determined from the ICPSR codebooks). Democratic committee leaders offered 18 motions opposed by their party leaders during the period, only 6 of which passed. Other Democrats were somewhat more active (and successful) in opposing the leaders: offering 72 motions, 31 of which passed (see Table 7.2).

In other words, just as was the case with Republicans during the 1920s, the roll call voting evidence is scant supporting the notion that committee leaders grew independent of majority party leaders. Party leaders almost always took positions consistent with those taken by their committee leaders, and those positions almost always prevailed on the floor of the House. When committee leaders offered motions that their party leaders opposed, the motions failed more often than they passed.

Neither the process of generating motions nor the process by which motions become recorded votes is well understood. I have offered a preliminary glimpse at the empirics of motion sponsorship in the pre–World War II House. That glimpse suggests that open conflict between House majority party leaders and committee chairs or the party's rank-and-file members was very rare.

Rank-and-file members were much more likely to offer motions receiving votes in this period than had been true in the 60th House. This is consistent with an interpretation of the revolt against Cannon as a dismantling of "party government." Yet this broader distribution of motion authorship was not accompanied by any substantively impressive decline in majority leaders' success rates on recorded votes. When the majority floor leader and whip both supported a motion receiving a recorded vote, it passed more

Table 7.2

Floor Motions by Party, 72nd–75th Houses (1931–38)

Floor Motion	Democratic Rank-and-File	Democratic Committee Chairs	Republicans	Totals
Adjourn	6	2	3	11
Amend	53	7	23	86
Approve senate amendment	26	7	5	38
Consider	11	10	3	24
Pass	82	96	9	187
Previous question	9	13	0	22
Recommit	18	3	53	77
Suspend rules	20	20	1	41
Table	10	7	0	17
Other	29	14	10	53
Totals	264	179	107	556

NOTE: Excludes three motions to amend and three motions to recommit offered by Progressive members and seventy-six motions for which authorship could not be determined (including fifty-five motions to pass a bill or resolution).

than 90 percent of the time. When both opposed, minority-sponsored motions failed more than three-quarters of the time, and majority-sponsored motions failed more than half the time.

Without a fully articulated theory of why certain motions receive recorded votes, it is impossible to confirm or refute either a "committee government" model or a "party government" model (or a "preferenceship" model, for that matter) for this period. But one can reasonably conclude that party affiliation remained relevant in the 1920s and 1930s for floor success.

Committee Leader Support for Party Leaders

I shall now review additional empirical evidence on the apparent responsiveness of committee leaders to voting cues from party leaders. My data set includes all recorded votes (other than votes to elect the Speaker) in the U.S. House from the 67th Congress (1921–23) through the 76th Congress (1939–40). This period spans the Republican "return to normalcy" period of the early 1920s, the internecine battles between progressive and regular

Republicans through the middle part of the decade, the New Deal, and the rise of the Conservative Coalition at the end of the period.

The bottom line of this analysis is that there was very little difference between the three classes of MCs in terms of their support for party agenda positions. I do not find impressive support for the argument that committee leaders gained independence from their party's leaders during this period. If anything, committee leaders as a class may have been slightly more loyal partisans than the typical rank-and-file party member.

Following Cox and McCubbins (1993), I code as party leaders the two parties' respective floor leaders and whips. I code a member as a committee leader for the majority if the member held a standing committee chairmanship at any time during a given Congress. Analogously for the minority party, I code a member as a committee leader if the MC was listed as the ranking minority member for a standing committee at any time during a Congress. The number of standing committees ranged from a high of 66 in the 68th House to a low of 49 in the 70th and 75th Houses. The number of Democratic committee leaders ranged from a low of 28 in the 71st House to a high of 41 in the 68th and 69th Houses; the number of Republicans ranged from 28 in the 75th House to 59 in the 67th House.

As noted, I partitioned members in each party into three groups: members who were committee leaders for a major committee, members who were committee leaders for a nonmajor committee (and no major committee), and rank-and-file members. I then examined the aggregate voting behavior of these groups on Democratic agenda votes for Democrats and Republican agenda votes for Republicans. For the purposes of this chapter, I define a Democratic agenda vote as a recorded vote on which *both* the Democratic floor leader and the Democratic whip voted the same way (e.g., both yea), while *at least one* of the analogous Republican leaders voted the opposite. Thus Democratic agenda votes arise when both Democrats vote yea (or both nay) and the Republicans are split (one yea and one nay), when both vote opposite the Democrats, or when one votes opposite and the other is absent.[9] Table 7.3 lists the frequencies of Democratic and Republican agenda votes for the period. The table shows that nearly two-thirds of the roll calls held from the 68th House through the 76th House fell into at least one party agenda—that is, one party's leaders took a united stand while at least one of the other party's leaders voted opposite.

For the most part, committee leaders strongly supported party leaders on *party agenda* votes. This is not entirely surprising, given that committee leaders were said to hold a veto over the reporting of bills to the floor and frequently serve as bill managers for bills they report from their own commit-

Table 7.3

Democratic and Republican Agenda Votes, 1921–40

House	Nonagenda Votes	Democrat Agenda Votes	Republican Agenda Votes	Leadership Votes (in both agendas)	Party Agenda Votes as pct of Total	Total
67	258	0	102	2	28.7	362
68	84	20	18	57	53.1	179
69	57	8	16	33	50.0	114
70	37	4	11	20	48.6	72
71	40	10	20	33	61.1	103
72	54	16	16	37	56.1	123
73	40	29	17	57	72.0	143
74	112	20	60	20	47.2	212
75	55	32	16	55	65.2	158
76	88	28	34	77	61.2	227
Total	825	167	310	391	51.3	1693

NOTE: The Democratic floor leader in the 67th House, Claude Kitchin (NC), was ill throughout much of that Congress and cast only 2 of 362 possible votes.

tees. Figures 7.1 and 7.2 display histograms of committee leader support levels throughout the period. The average Democratic major committee leader during the period supported the party agenda 75.9 percent of the time; the average nonmajor committee leader supported the agenda 71.2 percent (a difference that is statistically significant at the .05 level in a two-tailed test), and the average rank-and-file Democrat supported the agenda 70.6 percent of the time.[10] Overall, the average Democratic committee leader supported the agenda 72.6 percent of the time. Again, this was statistically different from the rank-and-file Democratic mean in a two-tailed test.[11]

For the Republicans, the average major committee leader supported his party's agenda 74.6 percent of the time; nonmajor committee leaders, 73.7 percent; and rank-and-file members, 74.8 percent. None of the differences in means were statistically significant in pairwise tests.

The histograms displayed in the two figures illustrate the point that the average support scores reported here are indeed typical scores for committee leaders.

Are these numbers indicative of high levels of party loyalty or not? Cox

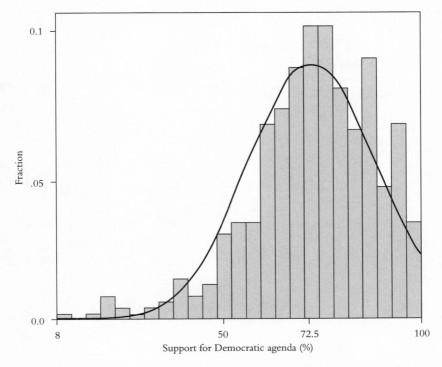

Figure 7.1.   Democratic committee leader loyalty on Democratic agenda votes, 1921–40.

and McCubbins (1993) show that Democratic leadership support scores on the Democratic party agenda bounced around between roughly 75 and 85 percent for most of the 1933–88 period (the 73rd–100th Congresses), with little evidence of any significant trend. Average Republican leadership support on Republican party agenda votes declined during the same period from the mid-90s to the low 80s.

Cox and McCubbins argued that agenda vote–based statistics of party loyalty help identify questions that are of low importance to the party as a party. In other words, we are relatively confident that votes outside the parties' respective agendas are *not* votes important to the parties. It is less easy to argue that agenda votes *are* important to one or both parties. Party leaders' vote choices may have very little marginal effect on members' vote choices, once those members' own policy preferences are taken into account. We lack any method for identifying votes important to a congressional party that is both independent of recorded votes and available for a long time period.

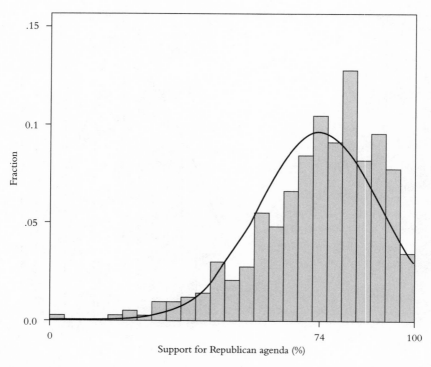

Figure 7.2. Republican committee leader loyalty on Republican agenda votes, 1921–40.

The agenda vote concept was intended to evoke the image of "whipped" votes—questions on which the party machinery was employed to cue MCs' behavior. Unfortunately, the fit between the party agenda concept and its operationalization is less than ideal.

Hidden in these aggregate numbers are numerous interesting stories. During the New Deal period, four Democratic chairs of major committees supported their party agenda less than 50 percent of the time in a Congress: Henry Steagall (D-Ala.), chairman of the Committee on Banking and Currency, in the 74th House (40 percent); Edward T. Taylor (D-Colo.), chairman of the Committee on Appropriations, in the 75th (20.5 percent) and 76th (34.7 percent) Houses; Samuel McReynolds (D-Tenn.), chairman of the Committee on Foreign Affairs, in the 76th House (17.8 percent);[12] and Hatton W. Sumners (D-Tex.), chair of the Judiciary Committee, in the 76th House (41.5 percent). These cases conceal the degree of actual opposition

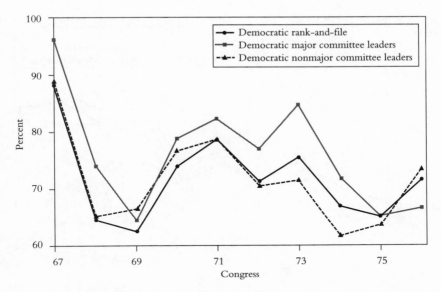

Figure 7.3.   Average Democratic agenda support, 1921–40.

raised by members, however. Steagall opposed the party leaders only 2 percent of the time on agenda votes in the 74th House, Taylor opposed the
leaders 1 percent of the time in the 75th and 5 percent in the 76th,
McReynolds never voted opposite the party leaders in the portion of the
76th he served, and Sumners opposed the leaders only 11.8 percent of the
time on agenda votes. The difference was made up in absenteeism by these
members.

The leading opponents (among committee chairs) of the Democratic
leadership in the New Deal period were Raymond J. Cannon (D-Wis.),
chair of the Committee on Revision of the Laws in the 74th and 75th
Houses, who voted against 22 percent of agenda items in the 74th and
22.7 percent in the 75th; Allan H. Gasque (D-S.C.), chairman of the Committee on Pensions during the 72nd through 75th Houses, who opposed
17 percent of agenda items in the 75th House; and William Connery (D-
Mass.), chairman of the Committee on Labor from the 72nd House to his
death during the 75th House, who opposed 16.7 percent of the agenda
items offered before his death during the 75th.

Figures 7.3 through 7.8 summarize the key findings of this section. They
plot the proportions of rank-and-file party members, nonmajor committee leaders, and major committee leaders, respectively, who supported or

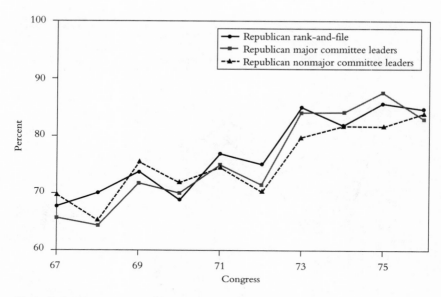

Figure 7.4. Average Republican agenda support, 1921–40.

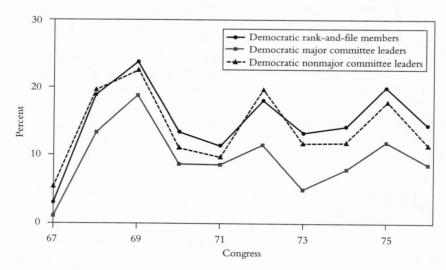

Figure 7.5. Average Democratic agenda opposition, 1921–40.

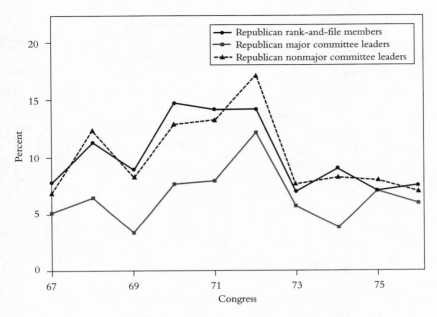

Figure 7.6. Average Republican agenda opposition, 1921–40.

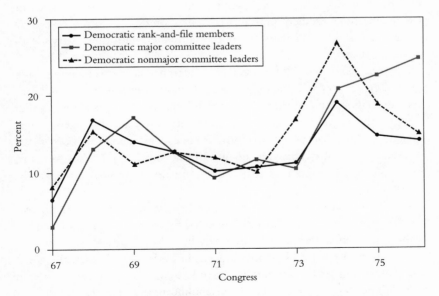

Figure 7.7. Average Democratic agenda abstention, 1921–40.

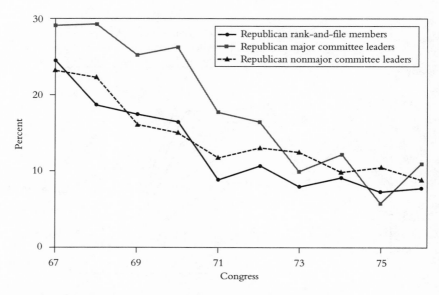

Figure 7.8. Average Republican agenda abstention, 1921–40.

opposed their respective party's position on party agenda votes and the proportion who abstained on those votes, by Congress. I express support as the proportion of *eligible* party members who voted with their party's leaders on the vote.

These data show very little systematic differences across the three groups of members, contrary to the expectations I drew from the "textbook Congress" description of committee leader indifference to party preferences. For example, the correlation between Democratic rank-and-file agenda support and Democratic nonmajor committee leader's agenda support is .94; between Democratic rank-and-file and major committee leaders' support, .90; and between Democratic major and nonmajor committee leaders' support, .80.

The figures clearly reveal a rising trend in Republican agenda support over the period, matched, curiously, by a downward trend in Republican abstention on agenda items and less strongly by a downward trend in Republican opposition on agenda items. Indeed, in both parties' cases, the over-time pattern of average support for agenda items is negatively correlated with both nonsupport categories. The Republicans most clearly shifted from relatively low levels of agenda support and relatively high levels of nonsupport in the early 1920s to relatively high levels of support and relatively low levels of nonsupport in the 1930s as progressive and moderate members left the party and the caucus shrank to a core of stalwart conservatives.

The Republicans during the 1920s suffered from internal divisions, fueled most prominently by the Wisconsin progressives (Hasbrouck 1927; Chiu 1928; Hicks 1960). Wisconsin members were strong opponents of the Republican leadership throughout the 1920s, averaging 42.9 percent support and 37.8 percent opposition on Republican agenda votes from the 67th House (1921–23) through the 71st (1929–31), abstaining 19.3 percent of the time. Not surprisingly, only two Wisconsonites held committee leadership positions during the 1920s: Florian Lampert, chair of the Committee on Patents in the 67th and 68th Houses, and John M. Nelson, chair of the Committee on Elections No. 2 in the 68th House and of the Committee on Invalid Pensions in the 71st.

The progressives held the balance of power between the parties in the 68th House (1923–25) and used that position to extract policy and procedural concessions from regular Republicans. Among the changes pushed through, Nelson was appointed to the Rules Committee, the chairman of that committee was denied his previous "pocket veto" authority over special rules proposals, and the new Committee on World War Veterans' Legislation was created (Hasbrouck 1927: 19–21). Perhaps most important of all, the Republican hierarchy tolerated frequent progressive opposition on agenda votes. But the progressives were otherwise mostly shut out of positions of authority within the House. That tolerance ended in the 69th House, when Speaker Nicholas Longworth (R-Ohio) banished thirteen progressive members from the Republican caucus for having supported Sen. Robert La Follette's presidential bid in 1924.

For their part, Democrats faced growing factionalism of their own during the 1930s as some conservative Southern members chafed at the liberalism of many of their Northern colleagues. But these factional fights do not show up prominently in these data. Southern Democratic chairs of major committees supported Democratic agenda items 74.3 percent of the time and opposed 8.5 percent of the time during the 1931–40 period, abstaining 17.2 percent of the time.[13] Southern rank-and-file Democrats supported 73 percent, opposed 14.4 percent, and abstained 12.5 percent of the time on agenda votes. These numbers do not differ significantly from the support and opposition levels offered by Northern party members.

For 71 of the 391 leadership votes (out of 1,693 total votes) held in 1921–

40, at least half of the participating committee leaders for at least one of the parties failed to support their respective party's position.[14] These votes tend to be somewhat quixotic struggles on the part of the losing party's leaders. The average margin in these 71 votes was 33 percent (i.e., 66 percent yea), as compared to 24 percent on the other 320 votes. Eleven occurred in the 68th House, all due to defections by (minority party) Democratic committee leaders. Recall that the progressive faction of the Republican party was pivotal in the 68th House. A number of these votes may reflect the efforts of progressives to shape the policy agenda during that Congress.

These votes provide some stark examples of the occasional idiosyncrasies of the Cox-McCubbins approach. For example, recorded vote 41 in the 75th House, June 1, 1937, was a 372–13 vote to override President Roosevelt's veto of H.R. 5478, a bill extending authority for government-sponsored term insurance for World War I veterans (New York Times, June 2, 1937). Despite the decisions by Majority Leader Sam Rayburn (D-Tex.) and whip Patrick Boland (D-Pa.) to support Roosevelt's veto of the bill, Democratic committee leaders voted 34–3 in favor of the override. Thankfully, this sort of overwhelming opposition to leaders' positions is quite rare. But it illustrates an empirical concern about the Cox-McCubbins measures. In this instant, the House Democratic party leaders appear to have been acting as agents of the president rather than of the majority party caucus. If the formal party leaders carry water for same-party presidents, their vote choices on such questions may not provide credible statements of the degree to which party regularity will be demanded of rank-and-file members. In other words, such votes may well be accompanied by a wink and a nod by leaders to party members that loyalty is neither expected nor required of them, even though the leaders feel compelled to support the president. In these cases, committee leaders' behavior may provide a better indicator of whether regularity is expected of the rank-and-file.

More typical, and more troubling, were leadership and agenda votes on which committee leaders were sharply divided. Committee leaders' support fell below 50 percent on 47 Democratic agenda votes (27 of which were also leadership votes), accounting for nearly 7 percent of the observations, and 12 Republican agenda votes (6 leadership votes) in the period (1.7 percent of all Republican agenda items). Average Democratic committee leader loyalty on these Democratic agenda votes was 37.9 percent, which strongly suggests that these votes are being misclassified by the Cox-McCubbins measure.

During the Republican 1920s, Democratic committee leaders split with their party leaders most often on tax, banking, and agriculture bills. In the 68th House, for example, Rep. John Nance Garner (D-Tex.), the ranking member of the Ways and Means Committee, offered a motion to amend the 1924 Revenue bill by increasing the tax on cigarettes. Republican committee chairmen opposed the motion 34–18, and Democratic ranking members voted 25–16 against, suggesting that this was a vote that did not separate the two parties from one another, even as it stressed each internally. Overall, Republicans opposed the amendment 130–83, Northern Democrats opposed 56–31, and Southern Democrats opposed 72–37, even as it separated the two parties' leaders, with Democrats Finis J. Garrett (Tenn.) and William Oldfield (Ark.) supporting Garner's motion. Republican leaders Nicholas Longworth (Ohio) and Albert Vestal (Ind.) voted against the motion even though Ways and Means Committee chairman Rep. William Green (Ia.) supported it.[15]

In contrast, the controversial leadership votes of the New Deal period tended to divide Democrats into Northern and Southern factions. Roll call 20 in the 75th House, April 7, 1937, a motion by Rep. Hamilton Fish (R-N.Y.) to bring up H.R. 2251, an antilynching bill, wreaked havoc on the Democratic coalition. A majority of House members had signed a discharge petition for H.R. 1507 (the Gavagan bill), another antilynching measure. In an effort to head off the more radical bill, the Judiciary Committee moved during Calendar Wednesday proceedings to bring up H.R. 2251, which was sponsored by Arthur Mitchell (Ill.), a black Democrat. Fish, after failing in an attempt to filibuster the motion, demanded a vote on consideration, which failed due to "conservative coalition" opposition (Southern Democrats opposed consideration 90–13, Northern Democrats supported it 102–82, and Republicans opposed it 74–7). Democratic committee chairs opposed the motion 28–10 even though the Democratic party leaders both supported the motion (and Republican leaders Snell and Englebright opposed).

Republican opposition and Northern Democratic support, however, were quite clearly strategic. The rule for consideration of the Gavagan bill was subsequently discharged from the Rules Committee on April 12 (Rayburn opposing, Boland abstaining, and committee chairs voting 23–20 against the discharge motion) and passed on the floor without significant amendment by a 286–129 vote, Southern Democrats voting 101–6 against while Republicans overwhelmingly joined Northern Democrats in support (Altman 1937: 1081).

In a sense, votes such as this one illustrate Cox and McCubbins's claim that one of the major functions of Democratic party leaders in the post–New Deal era was to protect party members from having to vote on issues that would threaten the stability of the coalition. Rayburn, though a Texan, had been elected floor leader on the strength of liberal, New Dealer support over John J. O'Connor (N.Y.), an archconservative by reputation—although his D-NOMINATE scores suggest that he became steadily more liberal throughout his career—and chairman of the Rules Committee (Altman 1937). In this case, Rayburn voted with his fellow Southerners while Boland, one of the most liberal members of the House in D-NOMINATE terms, chose not to participate.

Thus the Cox-McCubbins measures, while improving on some dimensions over traditional, "natural" measures of party voting and cohesion, are not without flaws of their own. Cox and McCubbins motivate their measures by arguing that House party leaders are delegated important gatekeeping and agenda-setting powers by their respective party caucuses. Their behavior should therefore provide us with important clues as to the issues on which the party caucus takes positions meant to reflect on the collective reputations of all party members. But because leaders in the president's party during this period also tended to act as the president's liaisons to the House, caucus positions and presidential preferences may be difficult to disentangle via the party agenda measures. Further, stochastic events, such as a leader's extended illness, can render the Cox-McCubbins measure almost meaningless for assessing interparty conflict and intraparty cohesion in some sessions of Congress.

The main point of this discussion—and this chapter—however, is that committee leaders' voting behavior on party agenda votes closely tracks that of rank-and-file members. Contrary to the "textbook Congress" claims that committee chairs showed little regard for party positions on votes, I found the collective behavior of committee leaders to be highly representative of their respective parties' rank-and-file.

Following the revolt against Cannon, both parties formally shifted the committee assignment function from the Speaker to more broadly based party committees. Even so, assignments were not handed out without regard for "party regularity." Hasbrouck (1927), for example, states that well into the twentieth century, leaders frequently withheld appointment of committee slates until days or even weeks into the first session of a new Congress: ". . . Only the members of a few important committees, which must begin work immediately, are usually on the slate [on the first day]" (36). Others would have to await further evidence of their party regularity before assignments would be finalized. "Thus on the first day of the 69th Congress, the Republican leaders desired to eliminate from the rules the discharge provision which had been inserted in the preceding Congress. The preliminary slate of committee nominations ready for presentation later in the day provided for only seven committees. . . . The remaining 54 were not named until nine days later," following the adoption of the desired rules change (36–37).

Thus even in the post-Cannon period, committees and committee leaders were not the aloof, imperious warlords they are sometimes made out to be. Certain aspects of party regularity were demanded of members, particularly those receiving the more desired assignments or chairmanships.

Conclusion

In this chapter, I have explored the relationships between party leadership vote cues and the collective voting behaviors of committee leaders and rank-and-file members. For the 1920s and the 1930s, allegedly the formative years for the postwar, "textbook Congress" era of committee government in the United States, committee leaders of both parties were virtually indistinguishable from rank-and-file party members in their levels of support for, opposition for, and abstention from party agenda votes. For the most part, serious opponents of the party leaders did not receive positions of committee leadership (particularly for "major" committees), or if they did, they tended not to express systematically their opposition on agenda votes.

Neither the Republicans in the 1920s nor the Democrats in the 1930s systematically promoted members to committee leadership positions who were strongly opposed to the agendas pursued by their party's leaders. The factional strife between progressive and regular Republicans of the 1920s manifested itself in strong opposition to the party program by a handful of "insurgent" members, but none achieved a position of committee leadership in the House. The factional strife between liberal Northern Democrats and conservative Southern Democrats in the 1930s, by contrast, is even more difficult to tease out of these data.

Nothing in these data either validates or destroys the "textbook Congress" view of committee power arising out of the ashes of Cannonism. But the strongest claim—that committee chairs were largely indifferent to party interests on policy—seems largely to have been refuted. Committee chairmen rarely offer motions that their party leaders oppose on the floor—and when they do, they usually lose. Committee chairmen's voting records also closely mirror the behavior of party rank-and-file members. Committee government did not emerge whole from the ashes of Cannonism. It appears that at worst, there was a high degree of policy agreement between party leaders, committee chairmen, and rank-and-file majority party members in the 1920s and 1930s.

Part II

The Evolution and Choice
of Congressional Institutions

Chapter 8

Order from Chaos: The Transformation of the Committee System in the House, 1816-22

JEFFERY A. JENKINS AND CHARLES H. STEWART III

The early decades of the nineteenth century are the primordial soup from which modern congressional features have evolved. The roots of today's political parties were set down (McCormick 1966, 1982; Chambers and Burnham 1967; Burnham 1970; Hoadley 1980; Aldrich 1995), majoritarian rules of procedure were imposed (Binder 1995, 1997), and the business of Congress was put into the hands of its standing committees (Harlow 1917; Cooper 1970, 1988; Skladony 1985; Swift 1996; Gamm and Shepsle 1989; Cooper and Young 1989; Strahan 1994; Stewart and others 1995; Jenkins 1998).

This last evolutionary development, the rise of congressional standing committees, has attracted the most recent attention from scholars. In the first three decades of the nineteenth century, the transformation of the congressional committee system was stunning. In both the House and Senate, the basic flow of business changed from a path dominated by ad hoc select committees to one dominated by permanent standing committees.

What do we make of this transformation? We propose to address this question by exploring two important reform episodes in the transformation of the House committee system of the 1810s and 1820s. These episodes are, first, the establishment of a dozen standing committees to oversee executive branch expenditures (1816) and second, the elevation of three important long-standing select committees (Foreign Affairs, Military Affairs, and Naval Affairs) to the ranks of the standings (1822).

In forging ahead with our investigation of early-nineteenth century-standing committee development, we will pay special attention to the goals and preferences of individual members of Congress (MCs) during that period. In general, MCs face a series of social choice problems individually and collectively that arise from their service in a majority rule institution. Some of these problems pertain to the provision of public goods, such as well-informed decision making and political stability. Some of these problems stem from MCs' private political goals, such as reelection and assisting political supporters, that can sometimes be achieved only by fashioning majority coalitions out of a set of particular interests—coalitions that theory tells us are inherently unstable. The rational choice literature on Congress gives us four views of why committees provide an effective means of overcoming these collective and private problems:

1. Committees allow "high demanders" on various issues to control policies on those dimensions while trading influence across other policy dimensions. This "gains from trade" system works to the individual benefit of all members (Weingast and Marshall 1988).

2. Committees provide the overall chamber with specialized information on particular policy issues, which prevents "outlier" policies from being adopted and leads instead to majoritarian outcomes (Krehbiel 1991).

3. Committees provide majority party leaders with tools to generate policy outputs that correspond to the collective interests of the majority party faithful (Cox and McCubbins 1993).

4. Committees, with defined jurisdictions and agenda-setting prerogatives, embody the most easily implemented form of "structure-induced equilibrium" by reducing the dimensionality of policy choice and keeping off the agenda policies of which a committee majority disapproves but which might enjoy majority chamber support (Shepsle 1979; Shepsle and Weingast 1981).

Our interest here is in journeying back to the early construction of this committee system. Just like students of the modern congressional committee system, we assume that the most salient features of early congressional organization evolved out of a desire to overcome a set of social choice problems MCs faced, collectively and individually. Unlike students of the modern committee system, however, the subject of our research was only just emerging. Indeed, most contemporary theories and practices of legislating were inimical to the creation of standing committees with the attributes we take for granted today, such as a permanent membership, the right to initiate legislation, gatekeeping authority, and closed rule protection (Cooper 1970, 1988; Cooper and Young 1989). The wide array of uses to which a standing committee system could be put were only dimly appreciated, if they were appreciated at all. Finally, contemporary observers were wont to comment directly on their motivations for reforming the committee system. The apotheosis of this disinterest in addressing structural reform head on came in 1822 when, following a protracted struggle over a major reform of the House rules, the closest and most astute observer of congressional politics of the time simply noted that "the matters are not of interest enough to our readers to detail . . ." (*Niles' Weekly Register*, March 16, 1822: 47).

Scholarship in this field has not reached the point where we can propose many meaningful theory-generated hypotheses and test them with a rich array of data. What we propose doing in this chapter is preliminary to such an effort—illustrating the plausibility of the claim that the early committee system was transformed out of a desire to confront a series of social choice problems that in their generic form persist across time and space among all legislatures.

First, we provide an overview of the evolution of the House committee system in the antebellum era. That overview takes two forms. First, we use broad brush strokes to sketch out the basic contours of the House committee system and how it changed. Second, we suggest themes that emerge in this broad history that link social choice theoretical concerns with that development. Next, we examine our first case, the creation of six expenditure oversight committees in the aftermath of the War of 1812. This case most obviously raises the principal-agent problem between Congress and the executive in the implementation of legislation.[1] At the same time, members of the House faced short-term political goals as they created these committees. The most obvious were responding to constituents' complaints about the reluctance of the federal government to pay its suppliers and reassuring skittish holders of federal government debt that Congress had a firm hand on the purse strings.

After that, we turn our attention to the elevation of the Foreign Affairs, Military Affairs, and Naval Affairs committees to standing committee status in 1822. This committee system change draws our attention to a wider array of rules reforms that occurred simultaneously in 1822, all intended to overcome the legislative chaos that had infected the 17th Congress. In a sense, these three standing committees were finally written into the rules almost as an afterthought. The overall thrust of the rules changes proposed by

a counsel of elders strengthened the hand of the Speaker in directing the referral of legislation and its subsequent debate. In the process, anomalies, such
as the existence of three semistanding committees outside the scope of the
formal rules, had to be cleared away. We end with our conclusion.

The Ascent of Standing Committees: An Overview

At the House of Representatives' first meeting in 1789, it adopted a set of
rules that delineated a simple set of expectations for the Speaker to follow in
exercising his duties and for the full body to follow in deliberating on legislation (see *House Journal*, 1789: 8–11). Very little was written about committees, except that Speakers would appoint small ones (with three or fewer
members) and the whole body would ballot to appoint larger ones. No
standing committees were mentioned. An additional set of rules was ap-
pended less than a week later. The first of these allowed "any member" to
"excuse himself from serving on any committee, at the time of his appointment, if he is then a member of two other committees" (*House Journal*,
1789: 13). Another provided for a standing committee on elections whose
duty it was to judge the credentials of newly elected members. Early in the
meeting of the second session of the 1st Congress, the provision for appointing large committees by ballot was rescinded, giving over to the
Speaker the duty of appointing these committees, too (*House Journal*, 1790:
140).

Consistent with a set of rules that were devoid of the mention of legislative standing committees, the House routinely appointed ad hoc committees to consider every piece of legislation that came before the body. This
led to the appointment of 220 select committees in the 1st Congress (Stewart and others 1995: tab. 1).[2] If we fast-forward to the eve of the Civil War,
the prominence of committees within the standing rules of the House was
quite different. By the 35th Congress (1857–59), six pages of the Standing
Rules and Order were devoted to committees, most of which was devoted
to the chamber's thirty-four standing committees (*House Journal*, 1857:
1157–62). Select committees were still used, but infrequently. The House
appointed select committees only 23 times in the 35th Congress, almost all
of which were investigatory.

This transformation of the rules and practices of the House from 1789 to
1861 is what needs explaining. Unlike the Senate, where the onset of a
standing committee system was sudden (see Swift 1998; Canon and Stewart
1998), the supplanting of ad hoc committees by standing committees in the
House was gradual. This is illustrated through a simple set of statistics. The

most basic is the number of standing and select committees appointed during each Congress, along with the fraction of House members appointed to each, which are reported in Figure 8.1. Though some Congresses were more innovative than others, on the whole the movement toward standing committees was unrelenting during the first half-century of the House's history.

Skladony's (1985) article on the distribution of legislative work between standing and select committees tells a similar story, even though his statistics cover only single sessions from five Congresses during this period. By his accounting, as the decades progressed, standing committees were the source of an increasing share of the bills reported to the House floor. Once reported to the floor, standing committee bills were much more successful (in terms of percentage of bills passing) than select committees. Thus by the first session of the 20th Congress (1827–28), 90 percent of all bills reported to the House came from standing committees, and the passage rate of bills coming from standing committee was about twice that of select committee bills (Skladony 1985: tabs. 5, 7).

The domain of standing committees, which in the earliest Congresses tended to be focused on housekeeping matters, gradually expanded to encompass the entire range of business that might come before the House. One method of illustrating this is shown in Table 8.1, which delineates the founding Congresses of the various standing committees, organizing them into four crude categories—housekeeping/internal, claims/private legislation, general legislation, and executive oversight. Displaying the standing committees in this way also helps illustrate how much of the organization of the House was aimed at establishing the national government's firm grip on the continent and handling the claims that individual citizens had against the federal government (see also Cooper and Young 1989). Still, this cataloging of committees deemphasizes the particularized nature of the House's work in the antebellum period, since so much of the work of the committees categorized as "general legislation" was also given over to handling private claims from individuals.[3]

In describing the broad contours of the growth of the House standing committee system and its eclipse of the select committees, one important detail must be mentioned in passing. Around the 12th Congress (1811–13), the House began regularly appointing a series of select committees, charging them with taking under consideration broad subjects contained in the president's annual message. These committees "on the president's message" came to be reappointed at the beginning of each session. Starting with the 14th Congress, they were authorized to sit for the entire session and to

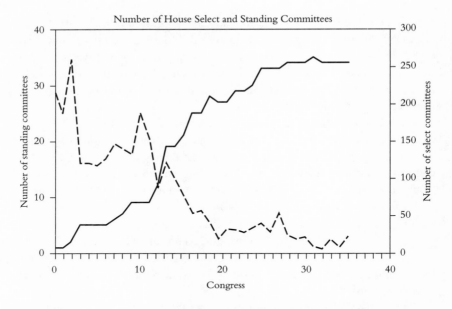

Number of House Select and Standing Committees

Percentage of House Members Holding at Least
One Standing or Select Committee Assignment

Figure 8.1. Number of House standing and select committees and percentage
of House members holding appointments on them, 1789–1855.

Table 8.1

Creation Dates of House Standing Committees, 1789–1855

Congress	Speaker	Housekeeping/ Internal	Claims/Private Legislation	General Legislation	Executive Oversight
1	Muhlenberg	Elections			
2	Trumbull				
3	Muhlenberg		Claims		
4	Dayton	Revisal and Unfinished Business		Commerce and Manufactures* Ways and Means	
5	Dayton/Dent				
6	Sedgwick				
7	Macon				
8	Macon	Accounts		Public Lands	
9	Macon				
10	Varnum	District of Columbia		Post Office and Post Roads	
11	Varnum				
12	Clay				
13	Clay/Cheves		Pensions and Revolutionary Claims**	Judiciary	Public Expenditures

(continued)

Table 8.1
(continued)

Congress	Speaker	Housekeeping/Internal	Claims/Private Legislation	General Legislation	Executive Oversight
14	Clay		Private Land Claims		Expenditures in the Departments of State, Treasury, War, Navy, P.O., and in Public Buildings (six committees)
15	Clay				
16	Clay/Taylor				
17	Barbour			Agriculture Indian Affairs Foreign Affairs Military Affairs Naval Affairs	
18	Clay				
19	Taylor		Military Pensions	Territories	
20	Stevenson				
21	Stevenson		Revolutionary Pensions Invalid Pensions		

#	Speaker				
22	Stevenson				Roads and Canals
23	Stevenson/ Bell				Militia
24		Mileage			
25	Polk		Polk	Patents	
				Public Buildings and Grounds	
26	Hunter				
27	White				
28	Jones	Engraving			
29	Davis				
30	Winthrop				
31	Cobb	Rules***			
32	Boyd				
33	Boyd				
34	Banks				
35	Orr				

*Separate committees on Commerce and Manufactures were appointed in the 16th Congress.

**Name changed to Revolutionary Claims in the 19th Congress.

***When the Rules Committee was designated a standing committee in the 31st Congress, the rules change was not codified. The House again elevated Rules to standing status in the 46th Congress.

report by bill on any subject within their domain (*Annals of the Congress of the United States*, 1815: 376–77; Cooper 1988: 58). Thus even though they were not formally standing committees, they were practically treated as such by the House membership, earning them the label "semistanding" by Skladony.

Three of these "semistanding" committees—Foreign Affairs, Military Affairs, and Naval Affairs—will become the focus later in this chapter. For the moment, suffice it to say that the fact that the House tolerated the existence of three important committees in this sort of parliamentary limbo begs the question of whether the distinction between select and standing committees was considered all that important among early-nineteenth-century parliamentarians. The fact that we have been unable to find any contemporary political actor or commentator to expound on this distinction gives us pause as we move ahead and try to understand why the early committee system evolved as it did.

Because "Congress in committee is Congress at work," the transformation of the House committee system in the early nineteenth century demands an accounting. Noting that the greatest expansion of the standing committee system corresponded roughly with Henry Clay's Speakership, three wide-ranging explanations have emerged that suggest ways to map Clay's political ambitions onto changes among the committees. These explanations are associated with Gerald Gamm and Kenneth Shepsle (1989; see also Rohde and Shepsle 1987), Jeffery A. Jenkins (1998), and Randall Strahan (1994; Strahan and others 1998).

Our approach in this chapter is to deemphasize the role that Henry Clay played in the House committee system's early development. As we have argued elsewhere (Jenkins and Stewart 1997, 1998; Jenkins 1998; Stewart 1998), this focus on Clay not only encourages a "great man" understanding of the House's early development but, even more important, encourages a "supply side" view of institutional development when we believe that the "demand side" deserves equal attention.

By a "supply side" view, we mean an understanding of institutional development that emphasizes the actions taken by political leaders to mold the institution to achieve their own purposes. By a "demand side" view, we mean an understanding of institutional development that draws its energy from the political desires of the rank-and-file. Cooper's (1970) analysis of standing committee development, for example, is largely from the demand side: he argues that changes in national environmental conditions produced a greater workload within the House, which led the membership to call for and adopt an organizational structure that was more conducive to the new legislative demands.[4] For instance, Clay championed the creation of a previous question motion at the beginning of the 12th Congress not simply because it would be an important tool for him to achieve his goals as Speaker but also because the War Hawks who worked so strongly for Clay's election insisted that ways be found to overcome the dilatory tactics of Quids like John Randolph (Harlow 1917).

Modern theories of committee behavior are, at root, demand-side views. Such theories can be divided into two major flavors: the *structure-induced equilibrium* (SIE) perspective, associated with Kenneth Shepsle and Barry Weingast, and the *information theory* perspective, associated with Keith Krehbiel. We consider them demand-side views because for both, the impetus for committee organization comes from the rank-and-file's policy and political goals.[5] They are also comprehensive theories of committee organization, since they account for the dual reality of committee behavior, contending that they simultaneously supply public goods to all members while also serving to distribute private political goods to legislators and their supporters.

It seems prudent to us to engage in a preliminary exploration of the creation of the standing committee system without being wedded to any one particular variant of rational choice theory. This is not to say that the following explorations are unguided by theory. In the following cases, we assume that the leaders and rank-and-file were contending with a general set of collective choice problems that stand above all modern research into congressional committees. The simple organization of the chamber to do business, the expert application of relevant information to legislation, the expeditious resolution of legislative business, and the passage of broadly beneficial national policies were all public goods House members tried to provide for themselves. There were certainly private political goods that House members sought to secure for themselves as well, and we assume that committees were seen as an important vehicle for that too. For the most parochial of House members, there were claims made by constituents against the government to be adjudicated, public lands to be distributed, import duties to be levied (or exempted), river snags to be cleared away, post offices established, and postal roads built. For the less parochial of legislators, whose future lay in the realm of large-scale partisan contestation, there was the business of using the federal government to bolster the image of one's party (or faction) at the expense of the opposition.

The politicians who set the House committee system along a path that leads to today were astute students of practical politics. In the cases that follow, we observe them piecing together a modern, complex legislative institution that serves many different political ends simultaneously. By understanding how they coupled institutional forms with pressing political goals, we will have laid the foundation for understanding how fundamental problems of social choice are addressed in a context in which practical and theoretical knowledge of how majority rule institutions function on a continental scale was in its infancy.

The Control of Expenditures

The greatest expansion of the House standing committee system during the antebellum period, measured by the sheer number of committees, occurred in 1816 (14th Congress), when six committees were appointed and charged with reporting to the House

> whether the expenditures of the respective Departments are justified by the law; whether the claims from time to time satisfied and discharged by the respective Departments are supported by sufficient vouchers . . . ; whether such claims have been discharged out of funds appropriated therefor; and whether all moneys have been disbursed in conformity with appropriation laws; and whether any and what provisions are necessary to be adopted to provide more perfectly for the proper application of the public moneys, and to secure the government from demands unjust in their character or extravagant in their amount.

They were further charged with reporting

> from time to time, whether any and what retrenchments can be made in the expenditures of the several Departments without detriment to the public service; whether any and what abuses at any time exist in the failure to enforce the payment of moneys which may be due to the United States from public defaulters, or others, and to report from time to time such provisions and arrangements as may be necessary to add to the economy of the several departments and the accountability of their officers. (*House Journal*, 1816: 411–12)

The genealogy of these six committees (associated with the State, Treasury, War, Navy, and Post Office Departments, plus public buildings) stretches back to the House Committee on Public Expenditures, which had been created in the previous Congress, and the Ways and Means Committee before that, which had been installed as a standing committee in the 3rd Congress. The proximate cause for their creation can plausibly be laid at the feet of the financial distress following the War of 1812. Yet the creation of these six committees, and their subsequent use, is more than simply a story of the House deciding to exercise due diligence in overseeing the executive. Nonetheless, the best place to start exploring the creation of these committees is the financial struggle the House contended with as it waged war against England earlier in the decade.

The consequences of the decision made by the 12th Congress (1811–13) to go to war with England were faced in the 13th and 14th Congresses. Among the most critical issues facing the national government, and thus Congress, were how to raise the money to fight the war and how to ensure that funds were properly applied. Prior to the War of 1812, the apparatus in the House for overseeing national finances was rudimentary: the small (seven-member) Ways and Means Committee was responsible for overseeing spending and taxing, investigating the executive branch to ensure that expenditures were properly applied, regulating the banking system, and generally exercising oversight wherever a dollar might be spent or raised. The war challenged the efficacy of this simple organizational setting.

Wars have put the greatest strains on the congressional executive oversight system, however constructed, whether by fire alarms or police patrols (McCubbins and Schwartz 1984). Even under the best of circumstances, wars challenge the control capacities of the executive. This in turn generates strains between the executive and Congress. Although Congress is always loath to reform the budgetary process during wartime, postwar periods of American politics are replete with examples of Congress reforming the budgetary process in light of wartime experience. Three cases of war-inspired reform have been highlighted in modern scholarship: the post–Civil War creation of the House Appropriations Committee, the post–World War I passage of the Budget and Accounting Act, and the post-Vietnam Congressional Budget and Impoundment Control Act (Fisher 1975; Sundquist 1981; Wander 1984; Brady and Morgan 1987; Stewart 1989; Kiewiet and McCubbins 1991).

Modern students of budget reform have focused their attention on the episodes that followed the Civil War and the twentieth century wars. Earlier generations of scholars, however, were equally acquainted with the War of 1812 as a spur for budget reform (see Powell 1939; Wilmerding 1943; White 1951). Within this older literature, the creation of the Public Expenditures Committee in the 13th Congress and the six agency-specific auditing committees in the 14th, along with a reorganization of the Treasury Department in 1817, are central organizational developments.

The government's handling of the War of 1812 has been widely regarded as a military, administrative, and financial disaster. Before war was declared against England, Congress undermined preparedness by retrenching the army and navy, abolishing internal revenues, and failing to recharter the Bank of the United States. Not only did these actions delay the buildup of American military forces when war *was* declared, but it also seriously undermined the ability of Congress to mobilize the financial resources to back up the military mobilization. It is on the fiscal, rather than military, mobilization that we focus our attention.[6]

As hostilities between the United States and Europe mounted, Congress began to authorize the call-ups of state militia units and the expansion of the regular army. Still, the same Congress that was intent on sponsoring a military buildup was unwilling to raise taxes to pay for it. An unwillingness to raise taxes to pay for war preparations was probably just as well: once hostilities began in earnest, imports plummeted and with them tariff revenues. Consequently, Treasury Secretary Albert Gallatin was compelled to borrow to meet the country's rapidly expanding financial obligations. Spending quickly outstripped the proceeds from borrowing, requiring Gallatin and his successor, Alexander Dallas, to return regularly to Congress, asking for authority to borrow on the government's behalf.

Gallatin and Dallas persuaded Congress to authorize federal government borrowing on the open market five times between 1812 and 1815. Attempting to borrow a total of $80 million during this period, the Treasury was in the end only able to net $34 million. The secondary market signaled its uneasiness with the national government's finances by the prices investors were willing to pay in the stock exchanges for these bonds, favoring the debt of some states above that of the national government (Martin 1871: 89–90).

Because the regions of the country that were most supportive of the war were capital-poor while bankers in capital-rich regions were much more skeptical, significant portions of the government's bonds were bought purely through the individual action of bankers and prominent politicians. For instance, John Jacob Astor himself personally subscribed to $2 million of the $16 million loan authorized in 1813 (Bolles 1894: 227).

In the midst of debating the largest wartime borrowing request from the Treasury, John W. Eppes, chair of the House Ways and Means Committee, took advantage of a break in the debate to introduce a resolution to create a committee, styled the Committee on Public Expenditures, specifying a jurisdiction for the committee that was taken verbatim from the jurisdictional statement of the Ways and Means Committee: "to examine into the state of the several Departments, and particularly into the laws making appropriations of money, and to report whether the moneys have been disbursed conformably with such laws; and also to report, from time to time, such provisions and arrangements as may be necessary to add to the economy of the Departments, and the accountability of their officers" (*Annals of the Congress of the United States*, 1814: 1627).

The resolution was considered on the House floor two days later, during another break in the debate over borrowing. Neither the *Annals of Congress* nor *Niles' Register* records any real debate arising from the resolution. Both do record Eppes's brief justification for it: "the duties contemplated to be assigned to this committee would fully occupy it during the session, and [were] necessary to relieve the Committee of Ways and Means from much of the business at present referred to it, and which it was unable properly to consider, etc." (*Annals of the Congress of the United States*, 1814: 1695; *Niles' Weekly Register*, March 5, 1814: 15). The motion itself was passed without opposition. Immediately upon passage of the motion, all "related matters being considered" by the Ways and Means Committee were referred to it. Neither the *Annals of Congress* nor the *House Journal* specifies which matters these were. The committee made no reports to the House in the 13th Congress.

At the same time the government was having difficulties raising the necessary money to fight the war, it was also facing the problem of not being able to pay its suppliers fast enough. Each of the cabinet departments had a skeleton staff of accountants and auditors in Washington who were responsible for examining and paying financial claims incurred by that department. This system was a legacy of the Hamilton years. Stated simply, bonded officials were issued warrants by the Treasury secretary and were in turn responsible for settling accounts between the government and suppliers. Because these individual officials were personally responsible for any errors in their accounts, they were exceptionally meticulous but also painfully slow in settling up.

This creaky payment system was unchanged for the duration of the war, resulting in federal government arrearages worth millions of dollars. And of course, the war effort had crowded out attempts to clear up outstanding pre-1812 warrants, resulting in arrearages reaching back into the eighteenth century. Government suppliers, also being constituents, complained loudly to their representatives, who responded by appointing a committee to investigate.

The House appointed a select committee in 1816 to examine the problem of the payment of government contractors, which was chaired by Benjamin Huger, a Federalist from South Carolina (*House Journal*, February 27, 1816: 408). The subsequent report of the committee laid out, in painful detail, the difficulties it encountered in trying to untangle the web of federal finances. The report began:

> At an early period after their appointment the committee proceeded to turn their attention to the subject submitted to them. Although prepared to meet many difficulties, in the proposed investigation of unsettled balances, they had by no means anticipated that these difficulties would have been so serious, or to the extent they experienced. They found themselves advancing into a labyrinth, the intricacies of which increased at every step they progressed. Little versed in the laws under which they were established, and still less in the rules, regulations, and modes of proceeding adopted by the different departments, it became necessary that they should, in the first instance, to endeavor to obtain some information on these points, and having no particular clue to guide them in making an investigation, the labor, zeal, and attention they were able to devote to this or that particular object of research not infrequently turned out to have been unnecessary, or of little or no avail. (American State Papers, *Finance*, vol. 3, p. 123, reprinted in Powell, 1939: 363)

The best Huger and his committee could do was outline the severity of the problem. They reported that neither the Indian nor the War Department had settled its accounts since 1798, that the Post Office had not settled since 1810, and that even the Treasury Department, the best of the lot, was two years behind in settling accounts with its suppliers (White 1951: 165–66).

The Huger Committee was composed of seasoned House veterans. Its report that they were clueless about where to begin their investigation and the estimate that their efforts had been a waste of time made an impression.

When the resolution creating the Huger Committee was passed, a competing resolution, offered by a rookie, Henry St. George Tucker (R-Va.) had been tabled. Tucker's resolution called for the creation of six new committees for the audit of the various executive departments. While the Huger Committee was still deliberating, the Tucker resolution was taken off the table and called up in the House (*House Journal*, March 30, 1816: 411–12). As originally proposed, it called for the creation of six "Committees on Accounts and Expenditures" pertaining to six objects: the State, Treasury, War, Navy, and Post Office Departments, plus public buildings.

The proposed jurisdictions were those that were noted at the beginning of this section. In addition, Tucker's resolution had two unusual features. First, he specified that these committees would be appointed for the entire

Congress, not just for the session, as was the case for all other committees. Second, they were authorized to meet between sessions of Congress, including the period between the adjournment of one Congress and the convening of the next.

As is characteristic of the time, very little in the official record or secondary press accounts provides good evidence about who supported and opposed this resolution and why. Tucker was a rookie member of the House and not especially prominent. The only opposition to the motion was registered in the remarks of Samuel Smith (R-Md.), a six-term House member who would go on to chair the Ways and Means Committee in the next three Congresses. Supporting speeches were noted by Tucker, Joseph Desha (R-Ky.), Richard Stanford (R-N.C.), Robert Wright (R-Md.), and William Lowndes (R-S.C.). Lowndes was singled out in the *Annals of Congress* as arguing "that the experiences of other States, particularly Virginia, proved the utility of such committees" (1816: 1298).

The creation of these six committees was not the only organizational innovation for the oversight of executive expenditures that was enacted during this Congress. The Huger Committee's one concrete recommendation in its report to the House was a request that the Treasury secretary draw up a plan for how the cabinet departments might be reorganized and the federal system of accounts better managed. Apparently, the House never actually passed such a resolution. However, four days before the Huger Committee made its formal report to the House, Senator Nathaniel Macon, former Speaker of the House and an original member of the House Committee on Public Expenditures, got the Senate to pass a resolution that was worded virtually identically to the Huger Committee's later recommendation. Macon's resolution directed the four cabinet secretaries to report to the Senate on plans to "insure the annual settlement of the public accounts, and a more certain accountability of the public expenditure, in their respective Departments" (*Senate Journal*, April 20, 1816: 506–07). The report from the four secretaries in December 1816 set in motion a chain of events quickly leading to the passage of a law that reorganized how the executive branch paid public accounts and how it reported its actions to Congress (see Act of March 3, 1817, 3 Stat. L, 366).

The law established five auditors within the Treasury Department with ultimate authority over the payment of public accounts. The auditors were given responsibility for specific departments. They were also responsible for reporting annually to the secretary of the Treasury about the details of all public accounts. The secretary, in turn, was responsible for reporting annually to Congress on the state of public finances. This law formed the basis of the reporting relationship between Congress and the Treasury secretary until the Budget and Accounting Act was passed in 1921 (Stewart 1989).

Creating committees to give greater attention to overseeing executive accounts was only the first step in actually overseeing those accounts. At the very least, it was necessary to populate the committees with members who had sufficient experience and knowledge to oversee the executive. Whether these committees had to be *active* is debatable, however. Political scientists have traditionally equated the inactivity of congressional oversight committees with the abdication of congressional oversight responsibilities. Our view of the "best" oversight regime is closer to that associated with the work of Mathew McCubbins and his collaborators, however, who argue that if Congress designs its appropriations oversight regime properly, automatic procedures may be sufficient to keep the executive in line (see McCubbins and Schwartz 1984; Kiewiet and McCubbins 1991). Such an argument could easily apply to control of the executive after 1814. In that case, what is most important is not whether these committees met regularly to pore over the Treasury Department's books but whether the committees were *capable* of facing down the Treasury if necessary—serving as a sort of fire alarm rather than a police patrol.

The committees that were initially appointed to oversee the executive expenditures appear to have been capable of handling their task at first, though in every case that level of capacity was not sustained. Speaker Cheves appointed seven members to the Committee on Public Expenditures immediately upon its creation (*House Journal*, February 26, 1814: 368). Two of the seven, Nathaniel Macon (R–N.C.) and William Findley (R–Pa.), had served in the House for over two decades. Macon had served as Speaker of the House from the 7th to the 9th Congress. The chair, James Pleasants (R–Va.), was a sophomore but had served on the Ways and Means Committee in both his Congresses. Of the remaining members, only two were rookies. In a House in which three-fifths of its members were in their first term, the Committee on Public Expenditures had an unusual level of legislative experience embodied in its membership.

Yet this exalted status for Public Expenditures did not last. Upon returning to the House in the 14th Congress, Speaker Clay reappointed only one of the seven members whom Cheves had previously tapped for service on the committee—Epaphroditus Champion, a Federalist from Connecticut. Still, with that single holdover from the previous Congress, the committee's membership was more experienced in Washington than the House as a whole: only two committee members were serving their first term in the

House, compared to 50 percent of the House as a whole. Its chair, William Murfree (R–N.C.), had risen to the second-ranked position on the Commerce and Manufacturers Committee in the previous Congress, and he retained that additional appointment in the 14th.

As time went on, the membership of Public Expenditures became even less distinguished. In the second session of the 14th Congress, for instance, its experienced chairman was replaced by Israel Pickens, a newcomer to the committee altogether who had not especially distinguished himself in his three terms in Congress. From that point on, its membership tended to be as inexperienced as the rest of the House (see Table 8.2). Exceptions to this generalization occurred in the few Congresses when either the chamber as a whole or the leadership in particular had a special-interest executive-branch economy. We will return to this point shortly.

The membership patterns on the six expenditure committees created in 1816 paralleled that of the single Public Expenditures Committee. When first appointed, they were all, with one exception, experienced House members. Three of the five members of the Huger Committee, which suspended its work in deference to the creation of these committees, were appointed to one of them—Huger himself as the sole Federalist on the Navy Department committee, Lewis Condict (R–N.J.) to chair Public Buildings, and Daniel Forney (R–N.C.) to the War Department. (Philip Barbour, a Republican from Virginia, was already on the Public Expenditures Committee. Asa Lyon, a Federalist from Vermont, was the only Huger Committee member not appointed to an agency-specific expenditures committee.) Each of the committees, except the one appointed to oversee the State Department, which had three rookies, was composed of two veterans and one rookie.

As with the single Public Expenditures Committee, the degree of legislative experience exhibited on these six committees plummeted rapidly after their initial creation (see Table 8.2). In quick order, they tended to be heavily populated with rookie House members. It was not uncommon for the chair to be the only experienced member of an agency-specific expenditures committees. Indeed, rookies were even occasionally assigned to chair them.

DISCUSSION

What can we conclude about the early evolution of the House standing committee system from the creation of committees to audit and review the executive departments? The most direct conclusion is that the early story of executive oversight of executive finances is the application of the combined insights from McCubbins and Schwartz (1984; see also Kiewiet and McCubbins 1991), in their explication of fire-alarm versus police-patrol over-

Table 8.2

Percentage of Public Expenditures Committee Members Who
Were Rookies, 13th–35th Congresses (1814–59), Compared
to the Ways and Means Committee and the Entire House

	COMMITTEES			
		Department-Specific		
	Public	*Expenditure*	*Ways and*	*House of*
Congress	*Expenditures*	*Committees*	*Means*	*Representatives*
13	33	—	29	58
14	29	44	14	50
15	71	46	29	65
16	57	53	0	51
17	71	50	57	56
18	57	44	0	55
19	43	39	0	39
20	29	39	0	40
21	43	44	29	48
22	29	56	0	42
23	67	80	22	56
24	44	47	3	46
25	89	77	33	53
26	33	53	11	55
27	44	47	22	51
28	56	70	33	75
29	78	83	0	56
30	44	57	22	57
31	78	87	11	59
32	78	60	22	59
33	78	87	0	64
34	78	72	33	62
35	56	83	0	50

sight, and from Fiorina's (1977) "keystone" argument about the relationship between Congress and executive agencies.

Even though it could be argued that the earliest flowering of the party system grew out of Jeffersonian distrust of Treasury Secretary Hamilton, and it is certainly the case that the Ways and Means Committee was made a permanent feature of the House rules because of that distrust, the internal capacity of the House to diligently oversee executive branch practices was always rudimentary. Nonetheless, as Kiewiet and McCubbins (1991: chap. 1) point out, even the earliest Congresses witnessed the House use a variety of tactics in an effort to guide executive behavior in the appropriations process. Within the annual appropriations process, Congress, through its committees, was unable to scrutinize every account closely. But it could scrutinize enough accounts sufficiently closely that the fear of random attention to different parts of the annual budget, year after year, would keep the executive branch on course without Congress having to devote too many of its scarce resources to oversight.

Still, the system that was set up during the Hamilton years to settle accounts between the federal government and suppliers would seem to have been prone to the same type of constituency work that Fiorina discusses in *Congress: Keystone of the Washington Establishment* and due to the same logic. Clutching the mantle of financial prudence, Congress designed an accounting system such that if a settling clerk made a mistake, it was the clerk's problem. This encouraged great conservatism on the part of agency clerks. Although this system may have prevented undue expenditures within executive agencies, it also encouraged suppliers (i.e., constituents) to petition Congress for relief from the overly stingy accountants in the departments. Almost two centuries before the rise of the welfare state encouraged members of Congress to have it both ways by creating entitlement programs crying out for congressional casework, Congress created a government accounting system that encouraged the same thing.

How pervasive was this double-dealing on the part of Congress? To our knowledge, no comprehensive analysis has been done of the claims that private citizens filed against the federal government for accounting arrearages in the antebellum era (but see Hill and Williams 1993). Our own preliminary analysis suggests that the practice may have been nontrivial. For example, roughly half the bills reported by the Ways and Means Committee in the 20th Congress were for the relief of individuals who had a revenue or expenditure claim against the government. Although the bulk of private claims petitions filed with the House that were cataloged in 1851 requested payment of a pension or back pay for military service, still 3 percent of all private petitions sought relief under an appropriations or tariff bill (*Congressional Serial Set*, ser. 653–55, 32nd Cong., 1st sess.). Constituency service opportunities in the realm of account settlements would seem a ripe topic for a student of Congress who wanted to apply modern research techniques to the past.

The expenditures committees did not seem to be highly active bodies. In the years immediately following their creation, most sessions of Congress might see one report issued by one of these committees, at the most (see the index of the *House Journal*, various years). The lack of activity on the part of these committees caused them to be quickly scorned by many members of the House. The low regard for these committees no doubt helps explain why over the next two decades, whenever the House got serious about retrenchment and expenditure controls, it resorted to separate *select* committees, bypassing the existing standing committees.[7]

The few reports that emanated from the six agency-specific committees often carried more complaints about their inability to perform their assigned tasks than detailed information about government accounts. One such plaint was seen in the 1819 report of the Committee on Expenditures in the Post Office: "[We] were convinced, from research, that to examine the immense mass of receipts and other vouchers, offered for their inspection, to compare them with the corresponding entries in the books of the office, and make the necessary computations, could only be effected by many months' vigilant attention and labor. This part of the inquiry, therefore, which your committee had marked out for themselves, was abandoned as impracticable." (quoted in Wilmerding, 1943: 214). Two years later, the committee on Expenditures in the Navy Department made a similar report:

> To investigate the various subjects referred to them, to enquire minutely into the expenditure of all public moneys appropriated for the naval service, and to ascertain whether these expenditures have been made with economy, and in strict conformity with the objects of Congress, in making them, would require greater time and research than could be bestowed by any committee, without a total abandonment of all legislative duties. Indeed, the investigation of any considerable item of expenditure, when pursued in all its details, would be a work of time and labor. (214–15)

Furthermore, confusion was sown over the conflicting jurisdictions of Ways and Means, Public Expenditures, the six agency-specific committees, and the occasional select committees. Although the jurisdiction initially granted the Committee on Public Expenditures in 1814 was taken verbatim from the jurisdiction of the Ways and Means Committee, the jurisdiction of the Ways and Means Committee itself was not changed in deference to the new committee. And of course, the jurisdictions of the six committees created in 1816 overlapped significantly with the jurisdictions of Ways and Means *and* Public Expenditures. The Committee on Public Expenditures made a report to the House in 1828, proposing a division of labor among these committees—particularly among the six agency committees and the Committee on Public Expenditures—but it was not adopted. Not having a clearly distinct jurisdiction, members of the Committee on Public Expenditures submitted a resolution in 1840 to abolish it, which the House debated for three days and then rejected by an overwhelming vote of 6–148 (*House Journal*, April 23, 1840: 817).

Representative Isaac Leet made a McCubbinsian point about the deterrent value of these committees when he argued in 1840 against abolishing the Public Expenditures Committee: "Sir, I would, keep the committee; I would preserve the board of visitors, in order that every Administration, in time to come, may at all times keep its 'house in order,' not knowing 'the day nor the hour when they may be called upon to give an account of their stewardship'" (*Congressional Globe*, April 22, 1840: 348–50). In the next breath, however, Leet made a justification for these committees that would seem to fit in quite well with the Mayhewian world of "position taking, credit claiming, and advertising" (Mayhew 1974):

> Would [my constituents] be satisfied with my telling them there was
> no necessity for this Committee on Public Expenditures? Would they
> agree that the *only* committee, which had a jurisdiction commensurate
> with all the departments of Government; which could march into any
> of the places where the public treasure was kept, and detect abuses,
> if any prevailed; would they, I say, agree to have that committee abol-
> ished? I think not. (*Congressional Globe*, April 22, 1840: 350)

Thus it is quite possible that these expenditure oversight committees helped keep the federal accounts in order through the operation of a system of random terror. More likely, however, the very existence of these committees and their episodic activity served as a signal to outsiders that Congress was being diligent in overseeing the nation's business. Whether these committees were in fact effective is subject to debate. To the progressive reformers of the early twentieth century, it was clear they were not.

The Foreign, Military, and Naval Affairs Committees

In 1822, during the 17th Congress, the House of Representatives made several changes to its internal organization by modifying its standing rules. New rules of procedure were enacted that tightened up floor procedures, clarified the order of priority for the referral of bills to committees, and added three existing select committees (Foreign Affairs, Military Affairs, and Naval Affairs) to the list of standing committees.[8]

Students of the committee system have tended to regard this episode as marking the denouement in the struggle between select and standing committees. These three committees were holdouts, remaining select committees long after panels with lesser jurisdictions had been moved permanently into the House rules.[9] The most plausible explanation for this tardiness is that Henry Clay, while Speaker, regarded them as his own "virtual state department" and thus a tool to needle the Madison and Monroe administrations and a springboard to the presidency (Jenkins 1998). Nonetheless, the totality of the 1822 rules changes were substantial, going well beyond changing the status of these three committees. Thus their elevation was much more than simply a case of the mice playing while the Speaker cat was away in Kentucky, and so the committee reforms that first drew our attention need to be understood in the context of a thick catalog of organizational issues.

We advance two complementary arguments to explain why these three committees were elevated to standing committee status in 1822. The first applies generally to the Era of Good Feelings (1815-22) and to the desire of political leaders to fashion large-scale political coalitions that were capable of governing, possibly forming the basis of a new set of political parties. The second is particular to the 17th Congress (1821–23). Here we suggest that organizational chaos had reached such a fevered pitch by 1822 that a portfolio of rules changes was supported by a large majority of House members in order to stem that chaos. Before wading into our narrative, we outline further both strains of this argument.

The first argument, which encompasses the entire decade following the War of 1812, can be summarized as follows. Amid the partisan instability of the Era of Good Feelings, two distinct factions had developed by the 16th Congress (1819–21) around the two major presidential candidates at the moment, John C. Calhoun and William H. Crawford. Crawford's faction was larger, which led his supporters to use the select committee on Military Affairs to undermine the policy desires of Calhoun, who was secretary of war. A protracted battle for the Speakership ensued in the 17th Congress, which was finally resolved, we believe, by a deal constructed by Martin Van Buren that affected the distribution of seats on standing and important select committees. Van Buren was attempting to rebuild the old interregional Jeffersonian party around the presidential candidacy of Crawford, but the institutional deal proved unstable. Three additional presidential aspirants—John Quincy Adams, Andrew Jackson, and Henry Clay—announced their candidacies in the 17th Congress, heightening multifactional divisions within the House and upsetting Van Buren's fragile institutional equilibrium. The legislative agenda nearly ground to a halt, spurring a majority of MCs to alter House rules in order to adjust to the new political environment. One consequence of the rules change elevating the status of Foreign Affairs, Military Affairs, and Naval Affairs was that standing committees became a more stable currency to use in resolving disputes over the Speakership.

Our second argument adheres more closely to the events particular to the 17th Congress. In her analysis of the suppression of minority rights in the House during the nineteenth century, Sarah Binder (1997) is generally successful in explaining that suppression in terms of partisan conflict that periodically erupted on the House floor in the 1800s. She is unsuccessful, however, in fitting the rules reforms in the 17th Congress into her general story, concluding that the 17th Congress "clearly is an outlier" from the perspective of her theory and her statistical estimation (78–79, n. 12).

Binder's failure to fit the rules changes of 1822 into her general story of minority rights suppression provides a clue, however, for why the Foreign Affairs, Military Affairs, and Naval Affairs committees were elevated to standing committee status in the 17th Congress. Binder's account rests heavily on measures of party strength, party competition, and obstructionism by the minority party to explain minority party suppression. However, there *was* no meaningful partisanship to structure institutional choice in the 17th Congress, nor was there a bipolar ideology available to structure debate and voting. In fact, Poole and Rosenthal (1997: 52) find that the 17th Congress is the worst-fitting House in American history for their model, one that resembles "spatial chaos." National politics had devolved into regionally based, multipolar factionalism in which electorally derived party labels were useless for identifying internal voting alliances in Congress. Thus there was no *one* minority being suppressed through the tightening of floor rules in the 17th Congress, if *suppressed* is even the right word. The disintegration of partisan ties encouraged a legislative free-for-all on the House floor whenever legislation was discussed. It also encouraged House members, in the rush to extract particularistic benefits for their localities, to pull business away from committees that had already been established. In the midst of the ensuing chaos, a counsel of elders proposed a set of rules changes to rein in this chaos.

Thus the elevation of the status of Foreign Affairs, Military Affairs, and

Naval Affairs occurred not so much to protect the position of these three committees but rather to protect the position of standing committees in general.

SPEAKERSHIP BATTLES IN THE ERA OF GOOD FEELINGS

Behind the leadership of Speaker Henry Clay and his so-called War Hawk allies, the Jeffersonian coalition had united around war-related policies during the War of 1812. After the war, however, the coalition's unity began to disintegrate. In the wake of the Hartford Convention, the Federalist party ceased to be a viable electoral opponent, and no new, salient national issues emerged around which the coalition might coalesce. Consequently, when sectional issues arose, they threatened to tear the party apart (Heale 1982: 38; Greenstone 1993: 161). With partisan sanctions no longer a "credible threat" in the one-party environment, rifts within the coalition began to develop, and instability within the chamber became the norm (Poole and Rosenthal 1997: 30–31, 38–39). The party hierarchy weakened during the Era of Good Feelings, and regional factions emerged to vie for power.

Despite the growing instability within the House, Clay was able to maintain some semblance of order within the chamber (Gamm and Shepsle 1989; Jenkins 1998). After the completion of the first session of the 16th House, however, Clay resigned from the Speakership, due to personal problems (Peterson 1987: 66–68; cf. Adams 1875: 59). The leadership vacuum created by Clay's relinquishment was filled in the second session by John W. Taylor of New York, who was elected to the Speakership on the twenty-second ballot, after securing the support of the "Bucktail" (anti-Clinton) faction from his home state (*Annals of the Congress of the United States*, 1822: 434–38; Spann 1960: 384; Leintz 1978: 69–71).

Before taking the Speakership, Taylor's policy views were well known. He was a fiscal conservative and an advocate for the restriction of slavery in the Western territories (Fuller 1909: 51; Spann 1960: 381–82). Both of these policy views would critically shape his performance as Speaker. The Missouri debates were still raging within the Republic, and Taylor's election was viewed in the North and South alike as a victory for slavery opponents (Jenkins and Stewart 1998; Stewart 1998).

Taylor's Speakership was hamstrung over the deadlock within the chamber over Missouri. In the end, Taylor became so associated with restrictionist forces that he had to turn to Clay (who remained a frequently absent member of the House) to provide leadership out of the Missouri quagmire (Brown 1926: 35–43, 65; Peterson 1987: 62–66). The Missouri Compromise was considered a slight victory for proslavery advocates. Still, Southern MCs maintained their distrust of Taylor and vowed to elect one of their own to the Speakership in the next Congress (Brown 1926: 67; Spann 1960: 391).

Although the Missouri question was a defining issue, Taylor's future as Speaker also hinged on his relationship with various members of the Monroe administration. The depression that followed the Panic of 1819 led to a 40 percent decline in government revenues (Dewey 1934: 164; White 1951: 121), forcing Congress, in an era before deficit spending, either to raise taxes or to cut spending. Raising taxes to mount a war against England had been impossible; doing so during a financial panic was equally difficult. Treasury Secretary William H. Crawford identified the military as a logical source for reductions.

Despite their widespread appeal, these proposed military cuts were also connected to political maneuvering within various Jeffersonian factions. Crawford publicly supported the cuts for fiscal purposes but privately supported them as a way to weaken his presidential rival, War Secretary Calhoun (Peterson 1987: 92–93). The Crawfordites took to the floor at the outset of the session to protest that a standing army threatened the liberties of the people, maintaining that militias were as effective and efficient without such dangers, being made up of "the great body of the American people" (see *Annals of the Congress of the United States*, 1821: 715–34, 767–94, 810–21, 823–41, 865–72, 891–901, 925–30). After much debate, the House considered legislation reported by the Military Affairs select committee to cut the size of the standing army by 40 percent (from ten thousand to six thousand soldiers) and slash appropriations for military fortifications by nearly 75 percent (from $800,000 to $202,000). Speaker Taylor supported the proposed military reductions (Spann 1960: 389–90). The legislation was passed by a vote of 109–48 and eventually signed into law (*Annals of the Congress of the United States*, 1821: 936–37).

Calhoun was infuriated. He viewed this defeat as a case of Crawford treachery abetted by Taylor's parliamentary engineering. Calhoun accused Taylor of being a tool of Crawford by appointing opponents of the War Department to the Military Affairs select committee (Adams 1875: 314–15, 428; Spann 1960: 390). Although Taylor asserted that he simply maintained the same committee appointments that Clay had made in the previous session (Adams 1875: 438–39), he in fact made several new appointments. Three of the seven members that he appointed to Military Affairs in the second session of the 16th House were his own (*House Journal* 1819: 20–21; 1820: 18).

Did Taylor stack Military Affairs with Crawford supporters, as Calhoun

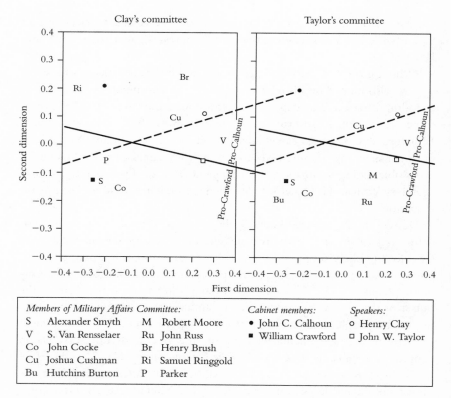

Figure 8.2. Ideological location of members of the select committee on Military Affairs, 16th Congress, 2nd session, using Poole W-NOMINATE scores.

contended? Rather than depend on historical anecdotes for evidence,[10] we employ common-space W-NOMINATE scores developed by Poole (1998) to examine Taylor's appointees and identify their spatial proximities to Calhoun and Crawford.[11] We will consider an MC either to be a Crawford or a Calhoun supporter based on measures of Euclidean distance: if an MC is closer spatially to Crawford than to Calhoun, we will presume him to be a Crawford supporter, and vice versa.

Figure 8.2 shows ideal-point estimates for Calhoun and Crawford, as well as for Taylor's appointees to the Military Affairs select committee. (The left-hand panel shows Clay's appointments, and the right-hand panel shows Taylor's appointments.) Each of Taylor's three "non-Clay" appointees— Hutchins G. Burton of North Carolina, Robert Moore of Pennsylvania, and John Russ of Connecticut—is closer to Crawford than to Calhoun. In ad-

Table 8.3

1821 Vote to Approve Cutting the Standing Army
by 40 Percent and Slashing Appropriations for
Military Fortifications by Nearly 75 Percent

Variable	Coefficient (s.e.)
Constant	0.33
	(0.13)
W-NOMINATE, first dimension	2.46
	(0.78)
W-NOMINATE, second dimension	−9.26
	(1.45)

dition, two of the three committee members whom Taylor replaced—
Henry Brush of Ohio and Samuel Ringgold of Maryland—are closer spatially to Calhoun than to Crawford. So Taylor took a committee that leaned
4–3 in favor of Calhoun and transformed it into one where Crawford held
a 5–2 advantage.

Further evidence that the retrenchment of the army was decided along
an agenda set by the Military Affairs committee is found in explaining the
vote on final passage of the bill in terms of the W-NOMINATE scores.
Table 8.3 reports the results of this analysis. The dotted lines in Figure 8.2
mark the estimated "cut line"—the line separating members predicted to
vote yea from those predicted to vote nay—of this vote in terms of W-
NOMINATE scores. First, the vote tended to divide mostly along the second dimension, which is the dimension on which Crawford and Calhoun
supporters were distinguished. Second, the side that prevailed is the pro-
Crawford side, which is the direction in which the committee had been
stacked. Therefore, had Taylor not altered the composition of Military Affairs, it is unlikely that the committee would have opened the gates for legislation so despised by Calhoun.

Clearly, sectarian maneuvers were afoot within the committee system
during the 16th House. The Crawford-dominated Military Affairs select
committee used its influence to scuttle Calhoun's position on the size of the
army. Taylor, through his appointments, made a significant contribution toward Crawford's success.

Taylor's behavior on the Missouri issue and army retrenchment set the
stage for the battle in the next Congress over its organization. He had alien-

ated the South in the Missouri debate by his tacit support of slavery restrictionists. However, if it had simply been a question of his stance on slavery, Taylor could have counted on reelection as Speaker. The North, after all, had a majority of seats in Congress. Taylor's stance on the second dimension, therefore, may have been crucial. Having sided with Crawford over Calhoun by stacking Military Affairs with Radicals, he left himself open to attack from other players on the national stage who had presidential ambitions.

Taylor's reelection hopes were dealt another serious blow in 1821 when his primary base of support in the North crumbled. His Clintonian faction had traditionally been the majority power in New York State, and Taylor believed its continued support was crucial to his reelection hopes as Speaker. The Clintonians, however, were routed by the Bucktails in the congressional elections of 1821, and Martin Van Buren, the Bucktail leader and freshman senator from New York, was determined to lead his partisans against Taylor's reelection bid. First, Van Buren believed that Taylor had been sympathetic to the Clintonians while Speaker, and he preferred to install someone who would favor his Bucktails (Spann 1960: 391–92; Niven 1983: 104–05). Second, Van Buren intended to rebuild the old intersectional Jeffersonian party from before the Era of Good Feelings—principally, a New York–Virginia alliance—in order to set and control the national political agenda into perpetuity (Nichols 1967: 264; Cole 1984: 104; Greenstone 1993: 155).

Van Buren planned to begin his party-building efforts around the Speakership election of 1821, which he believed would have powerful implications for the presidential election of 1824. Based on Taylor's performance in the 16th House, it was clear that the Speaker could be a major player in the presidential drama, as he was in a position (1) to mobilize the legislative powers of the House behind a favored candidate and (2) to use his appointive and bill-referral powers to harass the remaining candidates. Van Buren planned to use the Speakership election and the resulting congressional session as opportunities to rebuild alliances, which he would then use to reestablish the validity of the congressional nominating caucus (Spann 1960: 391; Nichols 1967: 254; Niven 1983: 104).

Van Buren saw Crawford as the candidate most likely to win in 1824 and eventually emerged to manage Crawford's presidential campaign (Mooney 1974: 220–21). To pave the way for his candidate's success, Van Buren arrived in Washington and approached Taylor's enemies, Calhoun and Secretary of the Navy Smith Thompson.[12] Calhoun and Thompson were unsure about Van Buren's political stripes—it was not yet clear that he was operating for Crawford—but were nevertheless eager to aid in defeating Taylor (Hemphill 1971: vol. 6, p. xvii; Niven 1983: 105–106).

While Van Buren was building support against Taylor's candidacy, Taylor went to work rebuilding bridges. He persuaded Adams that given another opportunity, he would be a willing friend to the administration. Though not premeditatedly, as Calhoun claimed, Taylor admitted that he made some poor committee appointments (Adams 1875: 428–29, 432, 439). Adams took Taylor's apologetic offer at face value and believed he would serve the administration well in the next Congress. Unfortunately for Taylor, Adams could not convince President James Monroe to voice his support, as Monroe instead "concluded to take no part whatsoever in the election of the Speaker" (Adams 1875: 436).

Without Monroe's support and unable to draw on a stable of Clintonians as before, Taylor entered the balloting without the support necessary for a quick victory. Caesar Rodney, a first-term MC from Delaware, was chosen by Van Buren, with the approval of Calhoun and Thompson, to oppose Taylor (Niven 1983: 107). Samuel Smith of Maryland and Louis McLane of Delaware also threw their hats into the ring.

On the first day of balloting, Rodney received a large bloc of Northern votes but could not attract the support of Southern MCs because he supported the restriction of slavery in Missouri and because "they considered him a Clayite" (Adams 1875: 437). Smith was unable to build any momentum throughout the day, while McLane, who voted with the South on the Missouri issue, could not overcome his Federalist background. Thus the day ended without the election of a majority winner.

That evening, Van Buren met with various state delegations and conferred with Calhoun and Thompson, which led to the selection of Philip P. Barbour of Virginia as his new "white knight" (Niven 1983: 107–108; 1988: 94–95). After five ballots on the second day, Barbour was elected Speaker, with 88 out of 172 votes cast (*Annals of the Congress of the United States*, 1821: 516; Leintz 1978: 71). Van Buren's choice of a Southern candidate proved to be decisive only in concert with Thompson's and Calhoun's lobbying (Adams 1875: 451; *Niles' Weekly Register*, vol. 21: 243). Although Barbour's allegiance to states' rights and traditional Jeffersonian maxims was instrumental in capturing Southern support, contemporary press accounts reported that Thompson and Calhoun finished the deal: Thompson, in concert with Van Buren, used his influence in New York to draw fifteen votes from Taylor, while Calhoun exercised his connections in Pennsylvania to

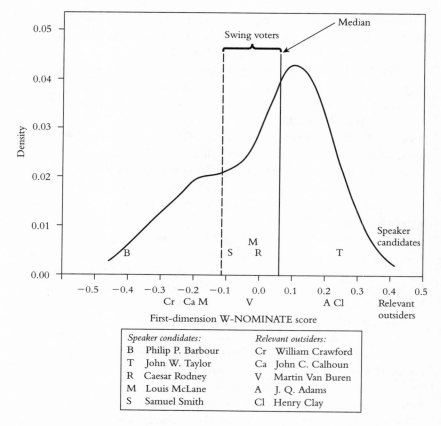

Figure 8.3.   Spatial summary of the 1821 Speakership fight.

siphon an additional eighteen votes from the New Yorker (*Niles' Weekly Register*, vol. 21: 242).

We can supplement this traditional narrative account of the 1821 Speakership battle by using W–NOMINATE scores to illustrate the puzzling nature of the final coalition that emerged to elect Barbour Speaker. In Figure 8.3, we show the overall House distribution of first-dimensional W–NOMINATE scores, the location of all the major Speaker candidates who emerged over the twelve ballots, and the spatial location of the principal outsiders who had an interest in the outcome of the balloting. (The location of the House median and the Taylor/Barbour cut line will come into play shortly.)

The balloting started with Taylor, Rodney, McLane, and Smith each receiving at least 20 votes (Leintz 1978: 71).[13] Taylor was alone on the "right" side of the issue space—the part occupied by slavery restrictionists in the previous Congress. The three remaining candidates split the "anyone but Taylor" vote, with two (Smith and McLane) occupying more moderate positions and Rodney occupying a more radical position.

This spatial accounting would lead us to predict that Taylor would win a plurality of the vote, with the other three candidates getting the rest. This is exactly what happened. On the first ballot, Taylor received 60 votes; Rodney, 45; McLane, 29; and Smith, 20. (Seven votes scattered.) McLane eventually dropped out, leaving the tally on the last ballot of the day at Taylor, 77 votes; Rodney, 59; and Smith, 26. On the first ballot of the second day, Barbour had entered the fray, but the anti-Taylor vote was almost evenly split: Taylor received 64 votes to Rodney's 36, Smith's 25, Barbour's 35, and a scattering of 12 votes going to other candidates. It was on the *next* ballot in which Rodney's and Smith's totals began marching steadily downward in favor of Barbour until Barbour bested Taylor, 88–67, with 17 scattered votes.

The spatial accounting of the Speakership contest leaves a significant puzzle: how could Philip Barbour, the most extreme Radical Southerner in the 17th House, defeat John Taylor, who was much closer to the House's ideological center? The historical account, of course, has emphasized nonspatial considerations—the coalition building that centered around Van Buren. How, precisely, did Van Buren pull off this deal?

Although the historical details are sketchy, we posit the following explanation. Barbour was given the Speakership with the understanding that he could not stack the standing committees with his ultra followers. In his effort to construct a new national party, Van Buren, we contend, could not allow Barbour to appoint outlier committees; rather, if collective goals were to be fostered, a heterogeneously distributed, centrist coalition needed to be created. Therefore, we investigate whether committees were representative of the underlying House population by applying two common techniques in the literature, a Wilcoxon difference-in-medians test and an F test for variance (see Krehbiel 1991; Cox and McCubbins 1993).

For each set of tests, we use first-dimension D-NOMINATE scores as our measure of preferences. First, we apply the Wilcoxon test to compare Barbour-created committee medians to noncommittee medians in the first session of the 17th Congress, with the null hypothesis being representative committees. Because we have priors regarding Barbour's location in the space (far to the left), we use a one-tailed test. If committees were composed of Radical extremists like Barbour—that is, preference outliers on the

Table 8.4

Wilcoxon Test p-Values Reflecting the Representativeness
of House Committees in the 17th Congress

	HOUSE MODEL		REPUBLICAN MODEL	
	$Med_{House} = Med_{Com}$	$\sigma^2_{House} = \sigma^2_{Com}$	$Med_{Rep} = Med_{Com}$	$\sigma^2_{Rep} = \sigma^2_{Com}$
Agriculture	0.18	0.71	0.31	0.71
Claims	0.66	0.65	0.71	0.61
Commerce	0.45	0.41	0.37	0.24
District of Columbia	0.85	0.43	0.98	0.18
Elections	0.30	0.66	0.34	0.62
Judiciary	0.20	0.65	0.02	0.11
Manufactures	0.27	0.34	0.34	0.29
Post Office	0.59	0.55	0.62	0.51
Private Land Claims	0.57	0.39	0.59	0.44
Public Expenditures	0.68	0.43	0.16	0.42
Public Lands	0.56	0.62	0.45	0.61
Revolutionary Claims	0.19	0.18	0.25	0.15
Ways and Means	0.22	0.60	0.26	0.55

NOTE: Tests were conducted using D-NOMINATE scores. All test results are one-tailed. The alternative hypotheses are: $Med_{House} > Med_{Com}$; $\sigma^2_{House} > \sigma^2_{Com}$; $Med_{Rep} > Med_{Com}$; and $\sigma^2_{Rep} > \sigma^2_{Com}$.

left side of the spectrum—then committee medians should be significantly smaller than noncommittee medians, allowing us to reject the null hypothesis of representativeness. Second, we use a one-tailed F test to compare the spreads of committees against the spread of the underlying population. If committees were representative, they should be composed of a heterogeneous group of members, and their spreads should therefore reflect the spreads of their noncommittee counterparts. If committees were nonrepresentative—composed entirely of one group, like the Radicals—they should appear homogeneous relative to the underlying population—that is, their spreads should be significantly smaller than the spreads of their noncommittee counterparts.

Our findings are presented in Table 8.4, in two separate forms. We test, first, whether committees were representative of the entire House and, second, whether the Republican contingents on committee were representative of the overall Republican contingent in the House.[14] Wilcoxon test results indicate that *none* of the thirteen committees in the House model and only *one* of the thirteen committees in the Republican model were composed of preference outliers, as the null hypothesis of representative committees cannot be rejected at the 5 percent level (one-tailed test), except in one case (Judiciary).[15] Even stronger results are discovered from the variance-based tests. *None* of the thirteen committees in *either* model have spreads that are significantly less heterogeneous than their noncommittee counterparts, as the null hypothesis of representative distributions cannot be rejected at the 5 percent level (one-tailed test) in *any* of the cases. Moreover, increasing the level of significance to 10 percent does not result in the rejection of the null (whether medians or spreads) in *any* additional cases. Thus despite the election of a *distinct* ideological outlier to the Speakership, the composition of committees was representative of the preferences and distribution of the underlying population.

Looking at committee rosters more closely, we also note that all of the major Speaker candidates received an important assignment, including Taylor. The two centrists who, historians note, overtly gave up support in favor of Barbour were rewarded with chairmanships: McLane chaired Naval Affairs, and Smith chaired Ways and Means. In addition, both Rodney and Taylor were placed on Foreign Affairs.

That a deal involving committee composition was constructed around the Speakership election is consistent with developments to come later in the first session, to which we now turn. For the moment, we treat the possibility of a deal to be potentially a critical link in understanding how the standing committee system became further entrenched during the 17th Congress.

The issue that had dominated the 16th Congress was Missouri. In the first session of the 17th, it was the census. The apportionment bill dashed all hopes that the House had moved beyond regionally based gridlock and prompted the creation of a "Grand Committee," consisting of a member appointed from each state (*House Journal*, 1821: 81). Such a committee, which was common in the early days of the Republic when great matters of state were under consideration and factional distrust ran high, had not been seen since the 11th Congress. The reapportionment committee reported out a bill that proposed an apportionment ratio of one member per forty thousand residents, which would result in some states losing members. Furthermore, the mathematically astute realized that with only the slight tweaking of the formula, one's state could do better under alternative arrangements. Consequently, the House endured a protracted legislative battle, lasting nearly a month and producing 16 of the 95 roll calls that occurred for the entire Congress.[16] The endless debate and voting inflamed tempers. Infinitesimal differences among succeeding motions not only exacerbated tensions but also encouraged one of John Randolph's patented filibusters, which was always guaranteed to raise the collective blood pressure of the House.

At the same time as committee consideration of the apportionment bill began, tensions flared over the referral of legislation in which certain constituents and local governments had a keen interest. John Rhea (R-Tenn.) and former Speaker Taylor found themselves at loggerheads over whether the reform of the pension system for Revolutionary War veterans should be referred to a select committee or to the standing committee on Pensions and Revolutionary Claims (*Annals of the Congress of the United States*, 1821: 519, 523–24). The motion of John Nelson, of Maryland, to create a select committee to craft a bill providing for the use of public land sales for the benefit of education in the "old" states met with a protracted debate, with opponents of the motion insisting that such a bill should be referred to the Public Land Committee (537, 710–15). A motion to refer a general inquiry into the state of Indian treaties to an existing select committee that had been charged with investigating the American occupation of the Pacific Northwest met resistance from those who wanted it referred to a separate select committee (550–51). The motion to create a select committee to inquire into the fugitive slave issue met resistance from those who wanted it sent to the Judiciary Committee (557).

These skirmishes on matters of bill referral finally came to a head on February 2, 1822, when a lengthy debate took place about the issue of a grant of land to be used for missionary efforts among the Indians. Henry Baldwin (R-Pa.), a Calhounite, requested that the issue be referred to the Committee on Public Lands, while John Floyd (R-Va.), a Crawford supporter, proposed to amend the motion to refer it instead to the newly established standing committee on Indian Affairs (*Annals of the Congress of the United States*, 1822: 878–90; *Niles' Weekly Register*, February 9, 1822: 378). Floyd emerged victorious.

Three days later, perhaps in response to his defeat over the referral of the Indian missionary bill, Baldwin submitted the following resolution adding to the standing rules:

> Whenever a resolution shall be offered, or a motion made, to refer any subject whatever to a committee, and different committees shall be proposed to which such reference shall be made, the question shall be taken upon the reference to such one of the committees which shall be proposed as is first in the following order or arrangement, that is to say:

the Committee of the Whole on the state of the Union; the Committee of the Whole; a standing committee of the House; and between two or more standing committees, the one first proposed; a select committee. (*Annals of the Congress of the United States*, 1822: 911)

On February 6, the same day the House passed the apportionment bill, it also considered Baldwin's resolution to alter the rules. Hugh Nelson of Virginia moved to amend Baldwin's resolution, to which Baldwin assented, "so as to raise a Select Committee, to revise the standing rules of the House generally" (*House Journal*, 1822: 239; *Annals of the Congress of the United States*, 1822: 920). The motion was adopted by the House, and Speaker Barbour appointed a seven-member select committee pursuant to the rules: Nelson was appointed chair and was joined by Baldwin, former-Speaker Taylor, Burwell Bassett of Virginia, Lewis Condict of New Jersey, Samuel Smith of Maryland, and Charles Rich of Vermont (*House Journal*, 1822: 239).

This was a group of highly experienced men during a time of high turnover in the chamber. The average member of this committee had served 5.4 terms, compared to the House average of 2.2 terms in the 17th Congress. Baldwin was the least senior member, having served only three terms in the House. The committee was balanced as well, representing the commercial (Taylor, Rich, Smith), manufacturing (Condict and Baldwin), and agrarian (Nelson and Bassett) interests of the nation. Two members (Taylor and Smith) had been principal vote-getters in the Speakership contest. Ideologically, the committee was not stacked in favor of either Crawford or Calhoun, nor did Barbour stack it with Southern partisans. In fact, a spatial analysis suggests that the committee slightly favored the Adams-Clay-Taylor side of the political spectrum.

The House Select Committee on Modifications to the Standing Rules of the House took a month to make recommendations. It eventually suggested four procedural changes and several structural changes that were adopted by the House. The changes were "intended primarily to lend greater structure and predictability to management of chamber business" (Binder 1997: 89; see also Cooper and Young 1989; Bach 1990). The first three, proposed and adopted on March 13, 1822, are discussed by Binder (1997: 89–92). These were rules intended to reduce the effectiveness of dilatory tactics and to expedite institutional outcomes: debate on the motion to table was prohibited and limits on other motions were instituted, precedence was given to a motion to strike out the enacting clause of a bill over motions to amend, and a two-thirds vote was required from among the MCs present in order to suspend the rules.

The fourth procedural change is more of interest to us: the select committee recommended giving standing committees full rights of bill referral within their jurisdictions; that is, they could report bills to the floor at their own discretion (Cooper 1988: 58). The committee also recommended that three new standing committees—Military Affairs, Naval Affairs, and Foreign Affairs—be created, changing the status of three select committees that had been routinely appointed for over a decade (*House Journal*, 1822: 351).

Why was this latter change important? The factional fights that erupted at the beginning of the 17th Congress over whether to refer legislation to select or standing committees had the potential to undermine coalitions that were built around distributing committee assignments during Speakership contests. If the carefully crafted standing committees could be evaded, then they could not serve as a credible commitment mechanism to resolve Speakership contests.[17] The adoption of procedural rules to protect the jurisdictional claims of standing committees was necessary to stabilize the outcomes of Speakership elections. Consequently, the codification of standing committee prerogatives went hand in hand with the conversion of Foreign Affairs, Military Affairs, and Naval Affairs to standing committee status. As standing committees, they would benefit from the assumption in the rules that they would have "first dibs" on legislation within their domains.

DISCUSSION

The 17th Congress witnessed the most significant long-term rules reform during the early nineteenth century. Yet as is the case with all other such rules changes of this era, we have no direct testimony from the principals involved about what was motivating these changes. Hezekiah Niles's judgment in his *Weekly Register* that these "matters were not of interest enough to our readers to detail" was already noted. Hence we must speculate about the motivations behind these changes. The two arguments we have put forward to explain the presence of this reform in the committees are distinct yet complementary speculations that are consistent with theory and the evidence.

Probably the most fundamental notion of social choice theory as applied to legislatures is found in McKelvey's (1976) "chaos results" of pure majority rule voting in a multidimensional issue space. Most of us regard the chaos result as an important theoretical construct of little practical relevance to the modern Congress. To the Congresses we are exploring, McKelvian chaos was palpable: It had already consumed one entire Congress over the question of Missouri and nearly consumed the first half of the next with the question of apportionment. Without the basis for some sort of structure-induced equilibrium, the House had devolved into substantive chaos over the two questions. It had flirted with institutional chaos too. The two most recent Speakership elections, absent the dominating personality of Henry Clay, had required numerous ballots to resolve. Without the glue of party to structure the organizing equilibrium in the 17th Congress particularly, the organization of the House that had been effected with the election of Speaker Barbour was, in effect, being renegotiated every time a new item of business was brought to the House floor or the question of issue referral arose.

From our preliminary analysis of committee appointments made by Taylor in the 16th Congress and Barbour in the 17th, it seems clear that the resolution of those contests involved distributing assignments to desirable committees. Of course, the strategies employed by Taylor and Barbour were different: Taylor used assignments to favor his faction explicitly, whereas Barbour more carefully placated different factions among the fractious Republicans. So we certainly cannot say that there was a *single* best way to organize the committee system during the Era of Good Feelings from the perspective of establishing a legislating equilibrium. But of this much we are certain: if the House rules did not give to the Speaker the authority to channel legislation once he had been elected, then no deal that produced a majority coalition to elect a Speaker would be credible. Likewise, if the House rules did not provide for attractive institutional positions in the form of standing committee assignments, which were immune to select committee "end runs" and could be distributed among pretenders to the Speakership and their followers in return for standing aside in favor of a single dominant Speaker candidate, Congress would have been incapable of legislating.

Such concerns seem foreign to modern sensibilities, where no multiballot contest for the Speakership has occurred in living memory of any practicing political scientist. Looking from the perspective of the 17th Congress, however, the House had just experienced a cycling of the Speakership from a Western proto-Whig to a Northern slavery restrictionist to a Southern slavery expansionist. This occurred within the span of two years without an appreciable shift in House membership. Looking ahead from the 17th Congress (and, of course, with the benefit of knowing what the future would bring), we also know that of the next twenty antebellum Speakership elections, seven would require multiple ballots to resolve. Institutional chaos was real.

Another factor lurking around the corner throughout this case is the even larger problem of organizing the federal government beyond Congress. Parties had disintegrated. Not only did this have implications for legislating, but it had implications for electing presidents as well. For a generation, presidents had emerged out of agreements among the congressional caucuses about how the party faithful should coordinate their behavior each quadrennium. No more. If Congress was to be involved, it appeared in the late 1810s that it would be through the constitutional process of breaking deadlocks through voting in the House. Elsewhere, we have provided evidence that Speaker Henry Clay, assuming that the next presidential election would be decided in the House and wanting to be elected, doled out institutional favors toward that end (Jenkins and Stewart 1998; Jenkins 1998). Although he was eliminated from the 1824 election, he did preside over the House that broke the deadlock in favor of Adams. One of the reasons that charges of a "corrupt bargain" between Clay and Adams seems so believable is that Clay had not been shy about using his institutional position to try to influence the outcome of the 1824 presidential contest long before his behavior became the subject of close scrutiny (but see Jenkins and Sala 1998).

And of course, along with chaos in Congress and within the presidential selection process came new efforts to try to reconstruct durable coalitions capable of winning elections—in other words, parties. In light of Aldrich's (1995) compelling argument concerning Van Buren's spearheading of the old Jeffersonian coalition, we find Van Buren's important behind-the-scenes tactical role in the Speakership contest of 1821 suggestive that he regarded a stable House to be a linchpin of his overall plan.

Given the paucity of direct evidence about motivations, all these must be regarded as, at best, plausible conjectures. Yet they also suggest future directions of research—research that either attempts to delve even deeper into the archival materials of the period we cover here or addresses issues of congressional organization moving forward. For instance, beginning with the 26th Congress (1839), Speakership ballots began to be cast publicly. If committee assignments were the key resource that was distributed on the way to constructing a majority coalition to organize the House, that should be evident as the data get better.

Conclusion

At the outset, we noted that a comprehensive view of why the House began to rely on standing committees is still in its preliminary formative stages. Now, at the end, we can conclude that not only is scholarship about the subject preliminary, but the standing committees themselves were also preliminary. At the point where we leave the committee system, the House was only just settling on the principle that the standing committees should dominate the review of legislation in earnest. It would be another half-century before the standing committees would secure most of the basics—such as the closed rule—on which their modern influence rests. And it would be another century and a quarter before other bases of that influence, such as staff resources and carefully delineated formal jurisdictions, would be codified (cf. King 1997).

Even though the standing committees of the 1820s did not possess the full array of parliamentary privileges and attendant power that we ascribe to modern committees, they were key ingredients in efforts among antebellum representatives who sought to manufacture coherence within a national legislature. That the antebellum committees did not possess the qualities assumed by modern rational choice students of committees does not mean that the organization of these committees is beyond the analysis of scholars who work in the rational choice tradition. Quite the contrary. The social choice dilemmas faced by early-nineteenth-century legislators were in many ways more fundamental than those faced today. This fact makes the study of early committee organization using modern social science techniques all the more important.

We introduced this chapter by noting that the rational choice literature has produced four views of the committee system in the modern Congress. By way of closing, we can offer some comments about how each of those views holds up in light of the narratives we have explored and make some suggestions intended to guide future research.

1. *Committee high demanders.* The cases we examined were not oriented toward studying whether the composition of House committees in the 1810s and 1820s facilitated a "gains from trade" system often attributed to the modern Congress. However, we do note that many of the committees that were created before, during, and after this period seem like candidates for this type of institutional arrangement. Many of the committees were framed around regional (e.g., Indian Affairs), economic (Agriculture, Manufactures), and local (Claims) constituency interests. Whether the committees in fact functioned this way would be a perfect topic for future research.

2. *The informational approach.* Committee creation during this period contains many elements that are perfectly consistent with Krehbiel's (1991) informational view. In particular, we note that the House was quite willing to further expand its committee system during the War of 1812 in order to confront the informational overload the war induced. That these committees may also have been useful for addressing constituency complaints or that many of them may have lay dormant periodically should not lead us to underappreciate the value of the committee system in channeling expertise in

the right direction. At the same time, it should also be noted that the parliamentary arsenal that is now available to protect the work of committees was mostly lacking in the early nineteenth century. Therefore, another topic of future empirical research must be understanding whether the House took full advantage of the informational potential of its committees.

3. *Majority party legislative cartel.* The existence of the legislative cartel that Cox and McCubbins (1993) posit for the modern Congress is an empirical claim—theory does not *require* such a cartel to exist always. In the period covered by this chapter, the turmoil of the party system itself—inside and outside government—calls into question whether this view is apt for the Era of Good Feelings. Nonetheless, it is clear that some legislative leaders understood an antimajoritarian potential of committees. They just didn't understand that potential fully, and at any rate, the House was still too majoritarian to use committees in the service of any sort of legislative cartel. Yet before the century was out, members of the House *had* figured out how to use committees to aid the majority party. Thus a topic of future research should be understanding how this came about in the mid-nineteenth century.

4. *Institutional equilibrium.* The House we have explored was largely a majoritarian institution, still mightily influenced by the Jeffersonian notions that had guided its earliest development (Cooper 1970, 1988). This commitment to majoritarianism had come at a price in the institution's short history, and we have explored a period when legislative leaders were beginning to reexamine that price. Early in the 1810s, the House had strengthened the powers of the Speaker to rein-in debate (Stewart 1998). In the early 1820s, we have witnessed the House beginning to strengthen its committee system so that debilitating levels of conflict could be transferred off the floor and into the committee rooms. This is, of course, precisely where Woodrow Wilson found Congress at work when he studied the institution half a century later. The largest research project that remains is understanding how and why the House continued to strengthen its committee system over the ensuing century and how that strengthened committee system contributed to its remarkable strength in the face of the political crises it later faced.

Chapter 9

Leadership and Institutional Change in the Nineteenth-Century House

RANDALL STRAHAN

Conventional wisdom about congressional history holds that two leaders stand out for having left an imprint on the nineteenth-century House of Representatives. Henry Clay of Kentucky is said to have transformed House politics in the early decades of the century, and Thomas Brackett Reed of Maine, to have done so again at the century's end. However, some of the most influential recent theorizing by political scientists about congressional leadership seems to call into question whether Clay and Reed—or for that matter any leader—could actually have played such an important role in the history of Congress. This approach to understanding leadership, which can be described as contextual theory, portrays leaders as having limited leeway to act independently of followers' expectations or preferences, which in turn reflect the political or institutional context of the times. From this perspective, individual leaders may reflect or respond to changes in congressional institutions but seem very unlikely to be an important cause of those changes. The goal of this chapter is to make the case that serious students of congressional history should take the conventional wisdom about the importance of leaders—or at least a qualified version of it—seriously. I will argue that theories seeking to explain the development of congressional institutions will have to take into account not only changes in contextual factors but also the contributions of congressional leaders.

This chapter addresses leadership and institutional change in the nineteenth-century House of Representatives as follows. First, I provide a brief overview of recent scholarship on leadership in Congress, focusing on those scholars who have developed the most influential contextual theories. Then I consider the cases of Speakers Henry Clay and Thomas B. Reed, both of whom served as leaders during important periods in the development of the nineteenth-century House. Clay's tenure coincides with the emergence of the Speakership as the central leadership institution in the House as well as the development of important features of the modern standing committee system. Reed's Speakership corresponds with the creation of the strongest party government regime ever established in the House. The politics of two of these three important nineteenth-century institutional developments, I will propose, simply do not fit very well with the political logic of the contextual theories of leadership. Specifically, while certain contextual conditions were probably necessary for these institutional changes to have occurred, contextual factors alone were not sufficient. Neither the emergence of a new type of Speakership by the 1820s nor the creation of such a strong party government regime in the 1890s can be fully explained without taking into account the contributions of an individual leader who had the personal motivation and political skill to act during a critical moment in House politics. In the third section of the chapter, I propose an alternative theoretical perspective on congressional leadership. This framework differs from the newer contextual approaches by proposing that theories of congressional leadership need to incorporate a more realistic understanding of leaders' goals and be more attentive to variation in the constraints and opportunities leaders encounter over time. Neither a theory that focuses on contextual factors to the exclusion of characteristics of individual leaders nor a "great man" theory of leadership can fully explain the contributions of leaders to congressional history. Both contextual factors *and* characteristics of individual leaders will need to be taken into account.

Explaining House Leadership

The House of Representatives was intended by its designers to have "an immediate dependence on, and an intimate sympathy with, the people" (Hamilton, Madison, and Jay 1961: 326–27). Students of the House have long recognized that its politics and leadership cannot be understood independently of the broader contours of American political life. As Barbara Sinclair (1990) noted in a survey of congressional leadership studies, "Congressional scholars agree that congressional leadership is best understood from a contextual perspective. The external context and the institutional environment shape and constrain leadership styles and strategies" (148–49). If congressional scholars have agreed that congressional leadership must be understood in light of political and institutional context, an important question remains how, and how much, contextual factors constrain or determine how leaders lead.

Among contemporary students of Congress, Charles O. Jones (1968) offered one of the earliest and most influential statements of the contextual view of leadership. Drawing on the cases of early-twentieth-century Speaker Joseph G. Cannon and midcentury Rules Committee Chair Howard W. Smith, Jones called attention to the limits imposed on all House leaders by the need to maintain a "procedural majority," a chamber majority in support of the rules and organizational arrangements on which the leader's authority is ultimately based. Scholars who followed Jones were drawn to the puzzle of why the House has witnessed such different leadership styles over its history. The most influential of this next generation of leadership studies was Joseph Cooper and David W. Brady's "Institutional Context and Leadership Style: The House from Cannon to Rayburn" (1981). Cooper and Brady concluded that institutional context, rather than qualities of individual leaders, was the primary determinant of both leadership power and style in the House. By institutional context, Cooper and Brady meant primarily party strength, which they viewed as partly a product of House rules but ultimately determined by the state of electoral politics *outside* the House. Strong leadership in Congress becomes possible primarily because partisan alignments have created two parties with polarized electoral constituencies. Within this framework, the power and leadership styles of House leaders are determined primarily by the state of party politics in the country at large, with individual leaders having limited opportunities to alter leadership institutions or innovate in matters of leadership style.

Contextualism in Recent Leadership Studies

Partly in response to the emergence of stronger leadership in the contemporary House, a new wave of congressional leadership studies has appeared in recent years. The most influential of these add some new twists to the contextual perspective. David W. Rohde's *Parties and Leaders in the Postreform House* (1991) attributed the more active leadership of late-twentieth-century Democratic Speakers primarily to contextual changes, especially increased polarization between the two parties, and greater party unity (preference homogeneity) among congressional Democrats as a consequence of the declining electoral fortunes of the party's Southern conservative wing. Barbara Sinclair's work (1992a, 1992b, 1995, 1999) on leadership shares this strong contextualist orientation in explaining the emergence of more active leadership. For Sinclair, changes in leadership institutions and power also reflect contextual factors: "What members consider the optimal balance will vary over time as a function of the costs and benefits to members of assertive versus restrained central leadership. Those costs and benefits, in turn, are a function of the political and institutional context"(1995: 18).

Sinclair, Rohde, and others have also introduced a new element to the contextual perspective by borrowing terminology from principal-agent theories developed in organizational economics. "Within this framework," Sinclair explains, "congressional party leaders are seen as agents of the members who select them and charge them with advancing members' goals, especially (though not exclusively) by facilitating the production of collective goods" (1995: 9; see also Sinclair 1997: 2). Rohde incorporates similar language in his analysis: leaders "are strong because (and when) they are agents of their memberships, who want them to be strong" (1991: 172; see also Rohde and Shepsle 1987).

While the proponents of these newer contextual theories of leadership sometimes characterize their approach as "principal-agent theory," it is worth noting that political scientists differ regarding the implications of economic principal-agent theories when these are applied to legislative politics. Kiewiet and McCubbins (1991), for example, also employ principal-agent theory in their work on legislative politics but draw somewhat different implications from that body of theory for the politics of leader-follower relationships. As they point out, in economic theory, control of agents by principals is always less than perfect. In addition, these "agency losses" can be even greater in situations—like that in the U.S. House—where collective principals are involved (24–27). While noting that legislative principals do exert control over their agents through careful selection and various institutional checks, Kiewiet and McCubbins also emphasize that agents retain significant strategic and informational advantages in relation to followers, including the ability under some conditions to use agenda powers to manipulate decision-making processes (27, 48–55). Hence, they advise, it is "unwise . . . to become preoccupied with what party leaders cannot do, especially given that there are so many things they can do to shape the content of major legislative proposals and to assemble the majorities needed to enact them"(44). In light of this divergence in opinion regarding the implications of principal-agent theory for the degree of autonomy legislative leaders enjoy, it is probably better to describe the more recent leadership theories advanced by Sinclair and Rohde as contextual theories than to place them in the broader category of principal-agent theory.

As the term *contextual theories* suggests, in explaining the politics of congressional leadership, these authors assign relatively little weight to characteristics of individual leaders. Instead, these theories rely almost entirely on followers' preferences to explain leadership behavior. Sinclair summarizes this perspective: ". . . Members' expectations shape the functioning of the leadership. Changes in that functioning should then be traceable to changes in what members want or to changes in what, within a given context, members need in order to get what they want" (1995: 10). "If party leaders are agents of their members as posited, they will respond to changes in members' expectations, which are themselves traceable to alternations in the political and institutional context" (1999: 423).[1]

While the newer contextual theories differ slightly on the specific factors that may affect members' expectations of leaders, they share a central theoretical claim regarding the conditions under which leaders will actively use their powers to direct legislative outcomes. Strong or active leadership, in this view, occurs only when the followers want or expect it of the leader-agent to whom they have delegated authority. And the most important determinant of followers' expectations of leaders is the extent to which followers themselves are in agreement on the political ends for which leadership powers are to be employed. Only when followers substantially agree on political ends (homogeneous follower preferences) should leaders be able to exercise strong leadership of the chamber. "When there is a high degree of homogeneity of preferences, party leaders tend to be granted a high degree of central control to pursue the common objectives . . . and the leaders vigorously use the tools they have been granted. As preference homogeneity declines, institutional arrangements tend to be altered to reduce the capacity of leadership for independent and forceful action, and leaders tend to respond with caretaker or housekeeping strategies". . . . (Rohde and Shepsle 1987: 122–23; see also Rohde 1991: 35–36, 163, 172). When partisan followers' preferences are homogeneous, Sinclair likewise contends, leaders will have "great latitude in the means they employ," while during periods when followers are divided or factionalized over political ends, "members' heterogeneity tends to limit [leaders] more stringently in the means they can use" (1999: 447).[2]

If followers' expectations of leaders are determined primarily by the degree of preference homogeneity, leaders have a powerful incentive to respond to those expectations—because they wish to remain leaders. Under these theories, leaders are assumed to be motivated primarily by that goal—remaining leader. Therefore, in situations where followers' preferences are heterogeneous, leaders will shun aggressive use of leadership prerogatives.

Aggressively wielding leadership powers independently of agreement among followers would jeopardize that goal by alienating members whose preferences were not being advanced. As Sinclair puts it, "Party leaders are directly elected and biennially reelected by the party members. To the extent that leaders value their positions and want to retain them, they have an incentive to try to fulfill members' expectations" (1995: 18; see also Rohde and Shepsle 1987: 117–18; Rohde 1991: 35–36, 172).

Leadership and Institutional Change

Although some of the most influential recent work on congressional leadership has taken this type of contextual approach, other scholars have continued to argue that greater weight should be assigned to individual leaders' characteristics (see Palazzolo 1992; Peters 1997). In addition, some recent works by political scientists on the historical development of Congress have also made the case for incorporating the influence of individual leaders in theories of institutional change. Aldrich and Shepsle (2000), for example, have argued that students of congressional history need to develop explanations that can account for patterns of institutional development "dotted with transforming events and occasions . . . in which a bold, unexpected, or imaginative interpretation or action moves events off in an entirely unpredicted direction"(38). Citing actions by leaders such as Clay, Reed, Sam Rayburn, and Mike Mansfield, they contend that explanations of how institutions develop will have to incorporate "exogenous interventions of imaginative individuals" (41). In a recent study of institutional development in Congress from the late nineteenth century to the present, Eric Schickler (2000) likewise finds that entrepreneurial leaders played an important role in more than one-third of the major institutional changes that occurred during these years (14–15, 250–52). While the new contextual theories are undoubtedly helpful for understanding some of the broad patterns in leadership politics in Congress, there is reason to believe that these theories may not tell the whole story of the contributions leaders have made to the history and development of the institution.

In the next section, I examine some important institutional changes that occurred during the Speakerships of Henry Clay and Thomas Reed. The purpose of these case studies is to consider the extent to which the actions of these leaders fit the patterns we would expect from the basic political logic that provides the foundation for the new contextual theories. These theories assume that leaders are motivated primarily by the goal of being re-elected leader and therefore imply that leaders will avoid the aggressive use of leadership prerogatives unless followers' preferences are homogeneous in support of the ends being pursued. If this logic holds for the politics of leadership in the nineteenth-century House, we would expect leaders to show restraint in acting on major policy or institutional questions about which their followers were divided and avoid taking actions that might place their leadership positions at risk. Activist leadership should occur only on issues about which followers are largely in agreement. Otherwise, the central claim that leaders are constrained by the degree of preference homogeneity among followers would not seem to have any clear empirical implications (and be very difficult to falsify). The Clay and Reed Speakerships may therefore provide some important evidence from which to consider the applicability of these new contextual leadership theories to congressional history.[3]

Before looking at these cases of institutional change during the Speakerships of Clay and Reed, a brief methodological comment may be in order. My main objective in analyzing these cases is theory development. I focus on the evidence to be found in the historical record regarding each leader's motivations and the extent to which he appears to have been constrained by his followers' preferences. In each case, there is considerable evidence that the leader was pursuing goals beyond merely continuing to occupy the Speaker's chair and in pursuit of those goals acted independently of followers' expectations, with important consequences for the institutional development of the House. Given that neither the Clay nor the Reed case fits very well within the basic logic of the contextual theory, in the third section of the chapter I draw on the evidence from these two cases to propose some possible new directions for the development of leadership theory. I do not, however, attempt to test the alternative theoretical ideas outlined in the third section, nor do I mean to suggest that these two cases alone provide anything like conclusive evidence in support of an alternative approach that assigns greater weight to the characteristics of individual leaders. My goal is simply to propose some ideas about how we might go about constructing a more satisfactory theory of the influence of leaders in congressional history.

Henry Clay and the Transformation of the Speakership

Henry Clay served as Speaker for most of the period from the 12th through the 18th Congresses (1811–25).[4] Students of the history of the House generally agree that two important institutional developments can be traced to this period: the transformation of the Speakership into an important leadership institution and the emergence of the main features of the modern standing committee system. At the outset of Clay's Speakership, the polarization of the House around issues tied to the initiation and prosecution of war with England created an opportunity for exercising active leadership from the Speaker's chair. Clay made the most of that opportunity. But of equal importance for the development of the Speaker's office during these years, Clay's political skill allowed him to sustain this more active mode of leadership for almost a decade after the war ended and his formerly unified Republican followers had fallen into factional conflict. Speaker Clay sought to advance certain strongly held public policy goals, as well as his own office-holding ambitions. And he continued actively to employ the prerogatives of the Speakership to pursue public policy goals, even after his House followers' preferences became quite heterogeneous. Rather than taking his guidance from followers' expectations or reining in his activity as Speaker after his followers fell into factional conflict, Clay appears instead to have succeeded in using his strategic advantages as leader to advance his own policy goals and redefine House members' expectations about the Speakership.

THE POLITICAL CONTEXT OF THE CLAY SPEAKERSHIP

The political context in the House changed significantly over the course of the Clay Speakership. Accounts of the congressional politics of this period coincide in describing a mostly unified Republican coalition during 12th and 13th Congresses (1811–15), followed by a period of intense factionalism over the period from 1815 to 1825 (see Nielsen 1968; Gamm and Shepsle 1989; Binder 1997: 53–55; Jenkins 1998: 504–507). During the 12th and 13th "war" Congresses, Clay wielded the Speaker's authority more actively in more areas than any of his predecessors had (Follett 1896: 69–80; Horsman 1962: 225–45; Cooper 1970: 47–49, 64; Hatzenbuehler 1976; Remini, 1991: 72–93; Peters 1997: 34–36). Given the unified condition of his Republican followers during the war Congresses, Clay's leadership during these years fits the proposition that strong legislative leadership will occur when followers' preferences are homogeneous. Clay's independent contribution to the early institutional development of the House was his ability to sustain the more activist Speakership beyond the crisis of the war years, thereby establishing a clear precedent for using the office as a position of political leadership. I turn now to the question of Clay's motivations and why he would have taken it upon himself to continue to wield the powers of the Speakership so actively after his followers fell into political disarray.

CLAY'S GOALS AS LEADER

Henry Clay evinced a clear set of public policy goals relatively early in his national political career and with only a few exceptions continued to pursue those same objectives throughout the period he served as Speaker of the House. From his earliest service in the Kentucky legislature, Clay had been an active supporter of government-sponsored public works. During two brief stints in the U.S. Senate in 1806 and 1810, he began to develop a national reputation as an articulate proponent of federally funded internal improvements. Clay had also begun to advocate tariff protection for domestic manufactures as early as 1810 (Baxter 1995: 4–5; Remini 1991: 48, 59–63; Peterson 1987: 16–17). His early service in the Senate also established Clay's reputation as an aggressive nationalist in foreign policy, a stance that was instrumental in his initial election to the Speakership of the House in 1811.

After the War of 1812, Speaker Clay continued to advocate a program of national economic development centered on internal improvements and protective tariffs. Clay did shift from opposing to supporting the Bank of the United States during the postwar period, a position more consistent with his program of federally sponsored economic development but not widely popular in his Western political base (Peterson 1987: 48; Remini 1991: 140–41; Baxter 1995: 35–37). With the exception of the bank question, however, Clay remained consistent in pursuing the same domestic policy goals throughout his Speakership.

The one major new issue Clay took up in the postwar years was promoting the cause of Latin American independence from Spain. Clay first took a public position on the issue in 1813 (Remini 1991: 154). After 1816, this stance placed him in direct conflict with the Monroe administration, which was seeking an agreement with Spain on the cession of Florida prior to recognizing the new Latin American states (Cunningham 1996: 45, 48–49, 52, 149–51). Historians have long debated whether Clay's motivation was hemispheric solidarity; republican idealism; resentment of Monroe and his secretary of state, John Quincy Adams; an attempt to associate himself with a popular issue; or some combination of these (Peterson 1987: 52–55, 57–58; Remini 1991: 154–157; Hoskins 1927).

Finally, while no etching has yet surfaced of the earnest young Kentuckian shaking hands with President Jefferson, the historical record leaves little doubt that Clay's ambitions became focused on the White House relatively early in his political career. One well-regarded history of the period concludes that Clay had begun to think seriously about gaining the office by 1814 and that after 1816, he "arranged every detail of his political behavior with reference to his succession to Monroe" (Dangerfield 1952: 102). By the early 1820s, Clay was openly polling his political allies regarding whether service in Congress would advance or hinder his prospects for winning the White House (Remini 1991: 212).

There can be little doubt that Clay valued holding the office of Speaker and hoped that it would be a stepping-stone to the White House. But he also sought consistently to advance a well-defined program of federally directed economic integration at home, as well as national and hemispheric autonomy in foreign affairs. In his House speeches, Clay presents his domestic program as a project that would complete the work of the Founders by creating a higher degree of economic interdependence and mutual interest among sections.[5] Overall, historian Daniel Walker Howe's (1979) assessment of Clay seems well supported by historical evidence: "There was a serious statesman in him along with the gamester-politician; behind his never-ending serious of plausible expedients there was a consistency of purpose" (124). In the aftermath of the War of 1812, Clay may have lost a unified coalition of Republican supporters, but he had reasons of his own to continue to exercise the newly expanded powers of the Speakership both to advance his program of national policy and to achieve his higher political ambitions.

Clay and the Speakership

Clay was the first American politician to gain a high degree of national political visibility as Speaker of the House. Most commentators on the period agree that Clay also wrought a transformation in the office itself. Note, for example, Joseph Cooper's (1970) assessment:

> Henry Clay . . . wrought basic and permanent changes in the role of the Speaker. Once he assumed the office in 1811 he transformed it from a weak and rather apolitical position into the focal point of leadership within the House. In contrast to his predecessors, he involved himself deeply and extensively in the decision-making process and employed his considerable talent and charm to assemble and maintain majority support for major policies that bore his stamp. Similarly, in the interests of his program he boldly began to exploit and even extend the various sorts of leverage the rules conferred on the Speaker (47).[6]

The most important features of this new Speakership included regular participation in debates in the Committee of the Whole, use of the Speaker's parliamentary authority to advance policy objectives, and use of the Speaker's committee appointment power to "stack" committees with members supportive of the policy views of the majority or in some cases of the Speaker himself. Elements of Clay's approach—certainly stacking of committees and speaking in floor debates—had been employed by previous

Speakers (see Risjord 1992; Stewart 1998: 16–24; Gunning and Strahan 2000). What was innovative about Clay's use of the office was the *scope* of his activity as partisan and policy leader and the *duration* over which it was exercised.

The active policy leadership witnessed during the war Congresses early in the Clay Speakership is precisely what the contextual theory would predict: follower homogeneity creating expectations of active leadership, which an ambitious leader supplies. And proponents of this theory have cited the politics of the war years as an important example of the conditions under which House members will expect strong leadership from their leaders (Rohde and Shepsle 1987: 112–15; Gamm and Shepsle 1989: 57–58). What is puzzling from this perspective is why Clay would continue in this mode after the unity of his Republican followers had broken down. "In a world of heterogeneous preferences, legislative leadership, animated as it is by a desire to retain office and position, must seek out instruments other than policy initiatives" (Rohde and Shepsle 1987: 113).

One interpretation of the politics of this period, first advanced by James Sterling Young (1966; see also Rohde and Shepsle 1987; Gamm and Shepsle 1989; Shepsle 1989b), holds that Clay did not seriously attempt to exercise policy leadership after the war Congresses, instead pursuing a strategy of maintaining followers' support by delegating more authority over policy to standing committees. However, new evidence on Clay's conduct of the Speakership in the period after 1815 shows that Clay did persist in exercising active policy leadership despite the increasingly heterogeneous preferences of his followers. This evidence appears in the committee appointments Clay made in the postwar Congresses and in his record of legislative success.

After the War of 1812 ended, Speaker Clay was most engaged in three policy areas: protective tariffs, internal improvements, and foreign policy matters involving support for new democracies and democratic movements abroad, especially in Latin America. Vincent Moscardelli, Moshe Haspel, Richard Wike, and I have assembled some new data on Clay's conduct of the Speakership during these years (Strahan and others 2000). First, we collected data on support for Clay's policy positions among all House members during the postwar Congresses in which he served as Speaker (14th, 15th, 16th, and 18th) and on support for his positions within the four main sectional factions that structured House politics during these years (New England, Mid-Atlantic, West, and South). We then compared the committees Clay appointed with the parent House chamber, looking both at sectional representation in the House and on committees and at levels of support among individual members for the Speaker's policy views. In two of the three main policy areas in which Clay was interested, Clay continued to use the powers of the Speakership to advance policy goals by stacking committees in a manner favorable to his own policy views. An overview of this evidence of Clay's continued activism as Speaker after the War of 1812 follows.[7]

First, it is important to note that there was significant variation across issue areas in terms of support for Clay's program in the House. Among all House members, Clay was least successful in attracting support on foreign policy issues, where mean chamber support on all votes on which he took a position during his postwar Speakership was only .40 (40 percent voting in support of the Speaker's position). On the other two issues in which he was most interested, the House appears to have been closely divided. Mean chamber support for the Speaker's positions on all postwar tariff votes was .50, and for all internal improvement votes, it was .53.

Table 9.1 shows sectional representation in the House and on the committees with jurisdiction over tariffs, internal improvements, and foreign affairs during the Congresses Clay served as Speaker after the War of 1812. The most striking evidence of committee stacking is the makeup of committees with jurisdiction over tariff legislation. During the 14th Congress, tariffs fell within the jurisdiction of the Southern-dominated Ways and Means Committee. However, when Southern members shifted toward more intense opposition to protective tariffs after 1816 (see Peterson 1987: 72–76; Vipperman 1989: 119–43, 204–32), Clay steered tariff jurisdiction from the Ways and Means Committee to the newly created Committee on Manufactures. The new panel, which reported major tariff bills passed by the House in the 16th and 18th Congresses, was clearly dominated in those Congresses by members from the two regions most supportive of Clay's tariff views—the Mid-Atlantic (.82) and the West (.80).[8] Members from these two regions constituted 71.5 percent of the panel's membership in the 16th Congress and 85.7 percent in the 18th Congress (recall that Clay did not serve as Speaker in the intervening 17th Congress). By contrast, the regions least supportive of Clay's protectionist views—New England (.43) and the South (.18)—were consistently underrepresented in the Speaker's appointments to the Committee on Manufactures.

Internal improvements measures were handled by select committees throughout Clay's Speakership. Here again, in every case, these panels were dominated by members from the most supportive regions, the Mid-Atlantic (.71) and the West (.78). Members from those two regions constituted majorities of all five select committees that exercised jurisdiction over the internal improvement measures on which Clay took a public position from the

Table 9.1
Sectional Representation in the Postwar Congresses in Which Henry Clay Served as Speaker (%)

			COMMITTEE		
Congress	Region[a]	House of Representatives	Ways and Means[b]	Bonus[c]	Foreign Affairs[d]
14th	New England	20.4	14.3	0.0	14.3
	Mid–Atlantic	32.0	28.6	40.0	42.9
	West	12.6	0.0	20.0	0.0
	South	35.0	57.1	40.0	42.9
Congress	Region[a]	House of Representatives	Ways and Means[b]	Internal Improvements[c]	Foreign Affairs[d]
15th	New England	21.7	14.3	14.3	28.6
	Mid–Atlantic	31.3	14.3	42.9	14.3
	West	12.1	14.3	14.3	0.0
	South	34.8	57.1	28.6	57.1
Congress	Region[a]	House of Representatives	Manufactures[b]		Foreign Affairs[d]
16th	New England	22.8	14.3		14.3
	Mid–Atlantic	30.7	42.9		14.3
	West	12.9	28.6		0.0
	South	33.7	14.3		71.4
Congress	Region[a]	House of Representatives	Manufactures[b]	Roads and Canals[c]	Foreign Affairs[d]
18th	New England	18.0	0.0	0.0	0.0
	Mid–Atlantic	32.0	71.4	57.1	42.9
	West	18.5	14.3	14.3	14.3
	South	31.5	14.3	28.6	42.9

[a] *New England:* Connecticut, Maine, Massachusetts, New Hampshire, Rhode Island, Vermont; *Mid-Atlantic:* Delaware, New Jersey, New York, Pennsylvania; *West:* Illinois, Indiana, Ohio, Kentucky, Missouri, Tennessee; *South:* Alabama, Georgia, Louisiana, Maryland, Mississippi, North Carolina, South Carolina, Virginia.
[b] Committee with jurisdiction over tariff issues.
[c] Main committee with jurisdiction over internal improvements issues.
[d] Committee with jurisdiction over foreign affairs.
SOURCE: Strahan and others (2000).

15th through the 18th Congresses.[9] Conversely, representatives from New England, who mostly opposed the Speaker's positions on internal improvements (.25 support), were underrepresented on four of the five committees and were completely shut out of appointments in three of the five.

However, patterns in appointments to the committees responsible for foreign policy issues look quite different. Foreign policy matters fell within the jurisdiction of a select committee until the 17th Congress, when a standing committee on Foreign Affairs was created. During the postwar years, Clay's foreign policy views received strong support only from Western members (.78). Members from the Mid-Atlantic states were fairly evenly divided (.50). Little support existed for Clay's postwar foreign policy views among Southerners (.29) and even less among New Englanders (.17). Majorities on the foreign affairs committees most often came from the regions *least supportive* of the Speaker's policy views—New England and the South. This occurred in three of the four cases. Also, no members from the West (the most supportive region) were even assigned in three of the four cases. Recall that mean support for Clay's foreign policy positions across all of the postwar Congresses was only .40, meaning that on average 60 percent of the chamber voted *against* the Speaker on these votes. Unlike the committees appointed to review tariff and internal improvements measures—issues over which the House was closely divided—Clay seems to have been careful in the foreign policy area to ensure that the regional factions *opposed* to his views were well represented.

Evidence on support for the Speaker's policy positions among the individual members who were appointed to these committees strengthens the conclusion that Clay continued stacking committees in an effort to advance his policy goals. With the exception of the committees with responsibility for foreign policy issues, panels with jurisdiction over recurring policy issues in which Clay was interested repeatedly took on a political complexion more favorable to the Speaker's policy views than the chamber as a whole (see Strahan and others 2000: 580–84). Given the variety of factors that may have come into play in making committee assignments, no single committee-chamber comparison can be considered conclusive evidence that Clay was stacking committees. But consistent patterns in appointments favoring Clay's positions on key committees seem very unlikely to have occurred as the result of the chance convergence of other factors.

The critical factor in Clay's attempts to exercise policy leadership through committee appointments appears to have been the factional balance in the chamber. In those issue areas where the House was most closely divided—

the most important being tariffs and internal improvements—Clay acted independently to pursue his own policy goals, using the Speaker's authority over committee appointments to attempt to control the legislative agenda and assemble majorities in support of his favored policies. In the one recurring issue area where the factional balance in the chamber consistently produced large majorities opposed to the Speaker's own views—foreign policy—Clay normally appointed committee majorities unsympathetic to his views. Clay was politically astute enough to realize that it was necessary to give away part, but *only* part, of the policy "store" in order to retain sufficient support among his House followers to win reelection to the Speakership. On other issues, he continued to use the prerogatives of the Speakership to pursue his own program of national policy.

Further evidence of Clay's continuing exercise of policy leadership is found in his record of legislative success in the postwar Congresses. In an earlier study of Clay's leadership, James Sterling Young (1966: 131) concluded that historical scholarship had exaggerated Clay's effectiveness. Others have questioned Young's reading of the historical evidence (Cooper 1970: 150, n. 197; 156, n. 262). A new survey of the extent and success of Clay's activity as a legislative leader in the postwar Congresses turned up twenty-four major issues introduced in the House in the form of bills or resolutions on which Clay took a position. Of these, the House voted in support of Clay's position on final passage on sixteen, a success rate of exactly two-thirds (Strahan and others 2000: 585–86).

Although it would be an oversimplification to attribute passage of all of these measures to Clay's leadership, it is clear that Clay not only continued to exercise active leadership from the Speaker's chair but also achieved some measure of legislative success on some of the most important issues on the national agenda during the postwar years. The most impressive cases were tariff measures in 1816, 1820, and 1824 and the Missouri Compromise legislation in 1820. Clay's postwar record on internal improvements and other economic measures was mixed but was hardly one of consistent failure. He succeeded in winning support to recharter the Bank of the United States in 1816 and won approval for using the "bonus" received for the bank charter as a fund for internal improvements. After President James Madison's veto of the bonus bill was sustained, Clay had to settle for a much less active program of internal improvements than he would have preferred. Still, he continued to advance his agenda in this area, winning approval in the 18th Congress for funds to conduct a major survey of future road and canal projects, to improve navigation on Western rivers, and to continue construction of the Cumberland Road (Baxter 1995: 46–54; Minicucci 1998: chap. 2). An interesting political irony is that the postwar House consistently rejected Clay's leadership in the area of foreign policy. Clay may have led the House forcefully on matters related to war with England during the 12th and 13th Congresses, but he found very limited support for his legislative efforts after the war to advance early recognition of the newly independent states in Latin America.

Still, there is still ample evidence here to indicate that Clay succeeded in sustaining much of the activism of his early years as Speaker by pursuing a strategy of independent leadership on issues where opportunities existed to advance his policy goals and deference to chamber majorities on other issues—what my colleagues and I have described as a "strategic majority" approach (Strahan and others 2000). What is truly remarkable about Clay's postwar leadership is not only that he survived as Speaker during a period of intensely factionalized House politics but also that he never encountered a serious challenge (Leintz 1978: 68–71). In a situation without clear precedent and in the face of heterogeneous preferences among his followers, Clay nonetheless used his extraordinary political skill to continue to exercise the expanded powers of the war Speakership for almost a decade. This case seems very hard to square with the basic logic of the new contextual theories and suggests instead that congressional leaders may sometimes encounter political situations in which they are free to act more independently of followers' preferences than those theories imply. I now turn to the question of Speaker Clay's role in the emergence of the standing committee system.

Clay and the Standing Committee System

Standing committees were already important bodies in some policy areas prior to Clay's Speakership, but three interrelated developments signaled a transformation in the committee system during the years Clay held the office. First, the total number of standing committees increased from nine in the 12th Congress (1811–13) to twenty-four in the 18th (1823–25) (Stewart and others 1995: tab. 1).[10] Second, the practice of referring substantial numbers of legislative proposals to select committees for review gave way to virtually exclusive use of standing committees.[11] Third, in contrast to earlier practice in which committees had required prior authorization from chamber majorities to report proposed legislation, committees were also granted broader discretion to introduce bills (Harlow 1917: 219–26; Cooper and Young 1989: 69–71). "By the early 1820s," Cooper and Young point out (1989: 71), "a new system of legislating had emerged in the House in which both major and minor subjects were typically referred to standing committees and standing committees possessed power to report by bill at their own discretion."

What, then, is the evidence of Clay's role in the development of the standing committee system between 1811 and 1825? There is strong circumstantial evidence that Clay orchestrated the creation of one new standing committee, the Committee of Manufactures, established during the 16th Congress (1819–21). This new committee was created after a period of jurisdictional conflict over tariff measures between the Committee on Commerce and Manufactures and the Committee of Ways and Means, neither of which was particularly favorably disposed toward Clay's preferred protectionist policies. Shortly after the opening of the 16th Congress, the existing Commerce and Manufactures Committee was renamed the Committee of Commerce, and a new Committee of Manufactures was established (*Annals of the Congress of the United States*, 1819: 708–10). It began immediately to receive referrals of tariff measures (Kennon and Rogers 1989: 86–88, 452). Clay appointed a strong protectionist, Henry Baldwin of Pennsylvania, as chair, and as noted earlier, a majority of its membership came from the protariff Mid-Atlantic and Western states.

A letter written by Clay some years later to a political ally, former Representative Peter B. Porter of New York, makes clear how the creation of this committee fit into the Speaker's broader political strategy on tariff legislation. During the first session of the 18th Congress, Clay wrote: "We entertain high hopes of passage of the Tariff. The South as usual is against it, but we trust that the coincidence of opinion which happily exists between the West and the middle states will ensure passage of that salutary measure" (Hopkins 1963: 629). The new standing committee on Manufactures provided the vehicle for Clay to ensure that the "coincidence of opinion" in favor of the tariff in the West and Mid-Atlantic sections would prevail at the committee stage in the 16th and later Congresses.

This is an important case, given that it involved jurisdiction over one of the most prominent national issues of the day, but only one piece of a much larger puzzle. And beyond this single case, there is little evidence that the emergence of the standing committee system was due primarily to Clay's leadership. Instead, the historical evidence on the early development of House committees assembled by Stewart and his colleagues now places the burden of proof on those who would contest the conclusion that "the drift in favor of standing committees began before Clay assumed the Speakership, made important gains during his occasional absences from the Speaker's office, and did not reach equilibrium until Clay left the House for good" (Stewart 1998: 29; see also Stewart and others 1995; Jenkins and Stewart 1997, 1998).

Clay's Leadership and the Institutional Development of the House

The significance of Clay's leadership for the early institutional development of the House lies primarily in influence on the development of the office of Speaker, rather than his role in the emergence of the standing committee system. In the former case, Clay's personal qualities—his political skill, personal appeal, moderation on the slavery issue, and strong interests in shaping public policy—were probably indispensable to sustaining the activist leadership mode Clay employed beyond the initial years surrounding the War of 1812. As Follett (1896: 80) noted in one of the earliest scholarly works to call attention to Clay's importance to congressional history, "few Speakers have known so well as Henry Clay how to measure their power so as to obtain the utmost possible and yet not go beyond that unwritten standard of 'fairness' which exists in every House of Representatives."

Henry Clay succeeded in establishing and sustaining a more activist Speakership when some earlier attempts to innovate in this direction—such as that by Federalist Theodore Sedgwick during the 6th Congress (1799–1801)—had mostly failed. The anomalous character of Sedgwick's Speakership is shown by the bitter controversy it engendered and the failure of the House to vote the customary thanks to the Speaker at the conclusion of his service. "Sedgwick's own feelings on the success of his Speakership may perhaps be judged from his closing speech, where he announced his intention to retire forever from Congress and public life" (Follett 1896: 68; see also Peters 1990: 30). By contrast, Clay was repeatedly reelected Speaker by large margins, regularly attracted praise from members of the minority party, and after leaving the House remained a major national figure until his death in 1852. Partly as a result of Clay's skill as a legislative leader, something important had changed in the politics of the House and the nature of the Speakership by the time of his departure from the chamber in 1825.

The politics of the Clay Speakership raise some important questions about contextual theories. Clay's aggressive leadership of the unified Republican coalition during the war years is entirely consistent with the behavior this theory predicts when a leader is "emboldened by a large, consensual coalition of supporters" (Rohde and Shepsle 1987: 112). However, Clay's activism in wielding the prerogatives of the Speakership during the postwar

Congresses, in pursuit of policy goals over which his followers were almost evenly divided, is not. Clay's conduct as leader demonstrates that for some leaders, at least, other goals may be of equal importance with being reelected to one's position and that some leaders will use the strategic advantages conferred by their leadership position to act independently of their followers in pursuit of those goals if opportunities arise to do so.

I turn now to a second important period of institutional change in the nineteenth-century House, the adoption of new rules in 1890 that established a foundation for the party government regime that structured House politics into the early years of the twentieth century.

Thomas Brackett Reed and Party Government

The development of the House during the second half of the nineteenth century was shaped by the strong political party organizations that held sway over American politics during these years. A trend toward placing greater control over the business of the House in the hands of the leader of the majority party reached its completion with the adoption of the "Reed Rules" in the Republican 51st Congress (1889–91). Some proponents of the contextual leadership theory have characterized these rules changes as an important case that supports this theory. As Rohde and Shepsle (1987: 116) put it, the 51st Congress . . . "found an ambitious leader acting as agent for a relatively homogeneous band of followers." However, a closer look at the politics of the adoption of the Reed Rules suggests that the contextual explanation may not be entirely sufficient. As with the transformation of the Speakership in the early years of the nineteenth century, the qualities of a particular leader may well have been an indispensable condition for the occurrence of such a major institutional shift in the House in 1890. Absent Thomas Reed's parliamentary skill and long-standing determination to establish a new form of majority party governance, it is not at all inconceivable that the history of the late-nineteenth-century House might have taken a different course.

The Political Context of the Reed Speakership

"The most distinctive feature of late 19th century American politics," historian Morton Keller (1977: 522) has written, "was its domination by highly organized parties and professional politicians." Peters (1997: 51) describes the period as the "partisan Speakership," an era "in which the Speakership of the House became an artifact and architect of party government in the

United States." Proponents of the contextual theory of leadership argue that the critical factor in the rise of strong party government in the House was increased Republican party unity during the 1880s and 1890s. This increased party cohesion is said to have occurred due to greater polarization of the two parties' electoral constituencies along agricultural and industrial lines (Cooper and Brady 1981; see also Rohde and Shepsle 1987).

However, new evidence collected by Eric Schickler calls into question this characterization of House Republicans' policy preferences at the time Reed was elected Speaker in 1889. The most important issues on the agenda of the 51st Congress were the tariff, the basis of the currency, and federal supervision of elections in the South. Based on a survey of historical accounts and contemporaneous sources, Schickler found "significant factional divisions" within the Republican majority on each of these issues (2001: 34–36). An analysis of manufacturing activity within House districts during this period also leads him to conclude ". . . that Republican districts did not become increasingly homogeneous, and that Republicans and Democrats did not become more polarized, until several years *after* passage of the Reed rules" (34).

Democrats, under the leadership of Speaker John G. Carlisle of Kentucky, had controlled the House for three Congresses (48th–50th, 1883–89) prior to Reed's election as Speaker. According to one account, "Carlisle had come to the Speakership with two fundamental principles: to carry out the will of his party as interpreted by himself in regard to tariff reform, and to protect the constitutional rights of the minority" (Barnes 1931: 151). Divisions within the Democratic majority and Carlisle's lack of interest in checking the proliferation of obstructionist tactics—especially the so-called disappearing quorum—frequently rendered the chamber immobile during these years. Peters (1997: 62) notes that Carlisle's years as Speaker "were among the most frustrating ever experienced in the post–Civil War House." Accounts critical of the parliamentary stalemate during the late 1880s proliferated in the national press, including stories titled "Slowly Doing Nothing" and "Legislative Lunacy"(Robinson 1930: 182, 189). After the final session of the 50th Congress adjourned, the *Washington Post* published "a mass of opinions, gathered from chambers of commerce, businessmen, State and Federal officials, editors, and many others, all extremely critical of the complexity, wastefulness and futility of House procedure" (189).

In the 1888 election, Republicans regained control of the House by a 17-vote margin. Along with the frustrations arising from legislative gridlock during the Carlisle Speakership, one additional contextual factor may have contributed to Republican members' willingness to entertain a major revision of House rules. With Benjamin Harrison's defeat of Grover Cleveland, the GOP controlled both houses of Congress and the White House for the first time in fourteen years, and the party would have an opportunity to enact and take credit for a party program. As we have seen, however, the Republican majority in the House may have been less than unified regarding what the content of that party program should be. Still, it seems clear that these conditions created some unusual opportunities for a leader willing to take the initiative in shaping how the Republican majority would respond. Well before he was elected Speaker in 1889, Thomas Reed had demonstrated a strong commitment to the principle of majority party governance of the House and a willingness to test the limits of support among his colleagues for rules changes that would allow it to be established.

Reed's Goals as Leader

Reed was first elected to the House in 1876, and by his second and third terms, he had become a frequent participant in floor debates on matters of procedure as well as policy. When Republicans took control of the House in 1881 (47th Congress), he was appointed to the Rules Committee. During the three Democrat-controlled Congresses (48th–50th) that followed, Reed served on both the Rules and Ways and Means Committees. He was a strong backer of the main tenets of Republican orthodoxy—protective tariffs, federal funding of public works, and a gold-backed currency—and rose to become leader of the Republican minority. Reed's views on governance of the House evolved over the course of his House career, but well before his election to the Speakership, he had begun a determined effort to establish a system of rules by which the Speaker and the majority party could control and be held responsible for the actions of the House.

In March 1882, as a majority member of the Rules Committee, Reed introduced a report proposing to change House rules to allow any measure to be brought to the House floor by a majority vote. There was insufficient support for this rules change among Republicans even to muster a quorum to debate the proposal. The following month, after members of the Democratic minority had blocked action for seven days on a contested election case, Reed brought forth another report from the Rules Committee establishing strict limitations on dilatory motions during consideration of election cases. When former Democratic Speaker Samuel J. Randall continued to offer delaying motions, Reed raised a point of order against dilatory motions during consideration of rules changes. The point of order was sustained by the House, and the rules change was adopted (Robinson 1930: 85–

90; Alexander 1916: 196–202). In the debate over the point of order, Reed explained the view of the Speakership that motivated his efforts: "Whenever it is imposed upon Congress to accomplish a certain work, it is the duty of the Speaker, who represents the House . . . to carry out that rule of law or of the Constitution. It then becomes his duty to see that no factious opposition prevents the House from doing its duty. He must brush away all unlawful combinations to misuse the rules and must hold the House strictly to its work" (*Congressional Record*, 47th Cong., 1st sess.: 4306).

In February 1883, Reed introduced another Rules Committee report that made it in order to suspend the rules and send a House-passed tariff bill to conference with a simple majority vote. The action was heatedly denounced by the Democratic minority and also apparently came very close to the limits of what the Republican majority was ready to accept in the way of procedural innovations. As Alexander (1916: 204) describes this situation:

> [Reed] was too shrewd to stake his growing prestige on this latest adventure without due warrant, so he spent several days in overcoming scruples and obtaining pledges. His precaution, however, scarcely justified his final action, for the disappearance of thirty-two members of his own party left him without a quorum. Even the next morning when he appeared with a file of recruits, failure stared him in the face until several Nationalists, suddenly seized with a desire to go on record in opposition, swelled the vote to a quorum.

In 1889, just before the 51st House convened with its new Republican majority, Speaker-elect Reed published two essays elaborating his views of party government. In both, he criticized the existing state of affairs in the House and advocated rules changes to allow the majority to govern. There is only one way to deal with the problem of minority obstruction, Reed (1889a, 794–95) wrote, . . . "and that is to return to the first principles of democracy and republicanism alike. . . . It is the old doctrine that the majority must govern. Indeed, you have no choice. If the majority do not govern, the minority will; and if tyranny of the majority is hard, the tyranny of the minority is simply unendurable. The rules, then, ought to be arranged to facilitate action of the majority."

"When a legislative body makes rules," Reed (1889b, 425) stated in the second essay, "it does not make them as the people make constitutions, to limit power and provide for rights. They are made to facilitate the orderly and safe conduct of business." He also predicted that when the House reconvened with a Republican majority, an effort would be made "to establish rules that will facilitate the public business—unlike those of the present

House, which only delay and frustrate action" (425). The story of what happened next is a familiar one to legislative scholars, but it merits retelling because its true significance for understanding the politics of congressional leadership has perhaps been less widely appreciated by students of legislative politics.[12]

The Reed Rules: Establishing Party Governance

Shortly after his election to the Speaker's chair for the 51st Congress, Reed seized the opportunity to complete the project of restructuring House rules he had been pursuing since the early 1880s. Rather than introduce new rules at the beginning of the session, he chose instead to operate for a time under general parliamentary law. On January 29, 1890, the question before the House was a vote to take up a contested election case from West Virginia, *Smith v. Jackson*. The vote was 162 yeas, 3 nays, and 163 not voting, when two Democratic members withdrew their votes. Because a quorum at the time consisted of 165 members and only 161 Republicans could be assembled on the floor, under existing House precedents, the change of two members to nonvoting status brought business to a halt for lack of a quorum. Amid cries from Democrats of "no quorum!" Reed broke with precedents traceable back to the 1830s by directing the clerk to record as present the names of members who were in the chamber but refusing to vote. Reed's ruling that a quorum was present provoked intense protest from the floor and was immediately appealed. The question was then debated before the House for two days. On the second day (January 31), Reed refused to entertain an appeal when he again counted a quorum on a vote to approve the *Journal* and, in response to a motion to adjourn offered by Democrat William Springer of Illinois, ruled that the Speaker would no longer entertain motions made only for purposes of delay. Each of the Speaker's rulings was sustained by the Republican majority, clearing the way for the enactment of a major revision of House rules.

The Reed Rules adopted in February 1890 consolidated the Speaker's ability to manage the business of the House by changing House procedures in four areas: dilatory motions would no longer be entertained, nonvoting members would be counted as present for purposes of establishing a quorum, procedures for debating and amending bills in the Committee of the Whole were restructured and the quorum reduced to one hundred members, and changes were made in the order of business, including granting the Speaker power to refer measures to committee without debate and formal recognition of the practice of allowing special orders from the Rules Committee to be adopted by a simple majority vote (see Alexander 1916: 206, 220–22; Robinson 1930: 223–31). The Reed Rules built on earlier organizational developments but had the effect of fundamentally transforming the politics of the House. Legislative productivity increased dramatically during the 51st Congress, with new tariff, currency, and electoral measures being passed by the Republican majority.

For its efforts, the newly productive Republican majority was rewarded with a massive defeat at the polls in 1890. Democrats regained control of the House for the 52d and 53rd Congresses (1891–95) and elected one of the most vocal critics of the Reed Rules, Charles F. Crisp of Georgia, to the Speakership. Crisp oversaw adoption of a modified version of the rules of the Democratic 50th Congress, repudiating the new prohibitions on dilatory motions and the disappearing quorum. Reed and the Republicans then turned the tables on their Democratic colleagues and repeatedly brought the business of the House to a halt by refusing to vote and by making motions requiring endless roll calls. Reed in effect forced Speaker Crisp to choose between losing control of the floor and reintroducing rules to check minority obstructionism. Finally, in April 1894, the Democratic majority chose to enact its own quorum-counting rule. As evidence that his motivation for restructuring House rules went beyond his or his followers' narrow partisan interests, Reed had led his party in voting with the Democrats to restrict the rights of his own Republican minority (see Binder 1997: 130).

Reed and the Institutional Development of the House

Viewed from the perspective of the contextual theory, Speaker Reed might appear to have been the agent of a unified Republican majority impatient to end minority obstruction and enact a party program. However, in addition to the growing body of evidence that calls into question the degree of homogeneity among Reed's followers on policy matters, there is also evidence that preferences among House Republicans were less than homogeneous regarding the extent to which the rules should be reformed. While most Republicans probably supported and expected some curtailment of minority obstructionism at the beginning of the 51st Congress (Reed had certainly signaled his intentions in that direction clearly enough), there was no consensus among Republicans in support of the most far-reaching of these changes—ending the disappearing quorum (Schickler 2001: 39–40). In fact, Reed actually *surprised* his partisan colleagues when he made this critical ruling (Robinson 1930: 220). As more historical evidence has emerged regarding the adoption of the Reed Rules, the creation of such a strong party government regime in the House in 1890 has begun to look much less like an inevitable consequence of underlying contextual factors and much more like a political outcome in need of some further explanation.

Some changes in House rules likely would have occurred in the 51st House regardless of who was Speaker, but Thomas Reed's parliamentary skill and personal commitment to end minority obstructionism were probably indispensable to the timing and scope of the institutional changes that actually did occur. The establishment of party government in the late-nineteenth-century House therefore appears to represent a second important case of a leader who failed to be deterred from using the powers of his office aggressively when followers' preferences were less than homogeneous. By publicly forcing the issue of the Speaker's authority to count a quorum and refuse dilatory motions in the intensely partisan atmosphere of a contested election case, Reed acted strategically to mobilize Republican support for institutional innovation under the most favorable possible conditions (Robinson 1930: 220; Riker 1986; Schickler 2001: 39–40). In this situation, Republican members faced two alternatives: supporting their Speaker or handing a major partisan victory to their Democratic opponents. Only after winning support of his surprise rulings from the chair did Reed attempt to bring to the House floor the report containing the formal revision of the rules, which, together with earlier developments involving the use of the Rules Committee and floor recognition, transformed the capacity of the Speaker to control the business of the House. Speaker Reed therefore appears to have succeeded both by manipulating his Republican followers' strong preferences to prevail in a partisan confrontation over a contested seat and by persuading at least some of the merits of his view of party governance (Schickler 2001: 38).

Finally, it is important to note that Reed's own understanding of the political situation at the beginning of the 51st Congress provides further support for the conclusion this was a case of a leader acting independently to advance strongly held personal goals, rather one of an agent inclined to take his bearings from his followers' expectations. Reed was uncertain that his Republican followers would support such radical changes in House procedures, and had quietly made arrangements to resign and join a New York law firm if they had failed to sustain his initial rulings (McCall 1914: 167). As he later recalled in an interview with the Lewiston, Maine, *Evening Journal* (quoted in Offenberg 1963: 95–96):

> I knew just what I was going to do if the House did not sustain me. . . .
> I should simply have left the chair, resigning the Speakership and my

seat in Congress. There were other things that could be done, you know, outside of political life, and for my own part I had made up my mind that if political life consisted of sitting helplessly in the chair and seeing the majority powerless to pass legislation, I had had enough of it and was ready to step down and out.

Toward a New Theory of Leadership

Neither Henry Clay's role in the emergence of the House Speakership as a leadership institution in the early decades of the nineteenth century nor Thomas Reed's in the establishment of a party government regime in the 1890s fits very well within the logic of the contextual leadership theories. Both actively wielded the powers of their leadership positions in situations where followers' preferences were far from homogeneous in support of the ends they were pursuing. These cases suggest that the new contextual theories of leadership may be incomplete in two respects. First, they may be grounded on overly narrow assumptions about why leaders lead. If goals other than ambition to remain in office are sufficiently important to congressional leaders, some may use their positions to advance these other goals, whether strictly consonant with followers' expectations or not. Second, the proposition that congressional institutions *always* place relatively narrow limits on leaders' actions under conditions of preference heterogeneity among followers may not capture the full range of political situations congressional leaders encounter. Stated in theoretical terms, congressional institutions undoubtedly *do* create strong incentives for leaders to be responsive to their followers, but it does not necessarily follow that congressional institutions completely solve the problems involved when multiple principals delegate authority to an agent. These cases, then, suggest two possible directions for developing a theoretical framework that can provide a more complete explanation for the role of leaders in congressional history.

Leaders' Goals

All social science explanations, whether employing ideal types, formal models, or less rigorous heuristic or explanatory frameworks, simplify reality in an effort to make sense of it. The critical question in considering different theoretical perspectives for explaining leadership is not whether, but how much, simplification is necessary. Where the question of leaders' goals has been addressed within the new contextual theories, leaders are assumed to be motivated primarily by ambition to retain office. As Sinclair argues: "To

the extent that leaders value their positions and want to retain them, they have an incentive to try to fulfill members' expectations" (Sinclair, 1995: 18, emphasis added).[13] But the politics of the leader-follower relationship may look different if we consider the possibility that some leaders have more complex motivations than simply retaining office. If this is true, incentives created by leadership selection processes would not necessarily impel a leader to take his or her bearings from followers' preferences in all situations.

Why might a House leader want to act independently of his or her followers' preferences? The first possibility is that a leader takes seriously some view of good public policy or the merits of some existing or proposed institutional arrangement. It would be naive in the extreme to assume that principled or public-spirited goals always motivate the behavior of leaders. But empirical research on Congress has also found repeatedly that concerns with advancing good public policy are an important motivation for rank-and-file members and leaders alike (Fenno 1973, 1978, 1991; Derthick and Quirk 1985; Strahan 1989, 1990; Arnold 1990). Leaders with strong views on policy or political principle may act independently of followers' views— even place a leadership position at risk—if deferring to followers might produce an outcome the leader considered personally unacceptable.

In addition, altruism, or a willingness to sacrifice personal ambition to political principle, is not the only motivation that might encourage congressional leaders to act independently of followers. Certain self-interested motives that go beyond officeholding ambition might also encourage leaders to act independently and take political risks if the result might be some political achievement that secures a national political reputation. A national (or even international) reputation as a statesman might be pursued as a means to higher office or as an end in itself—the desire to win the lasting esteem of others and leave a mark on history. Theorists of modern liberal democratic regimes, including the authors of *The Federalist*, considered this concern with a "place in history" to be an important motivation for individuals likely to be attracted to leadership positions (see Adair 1974; Manzer 1996; Epstein 1984: 183–85). Contemporary research on Congress has also found concerns about respect and reputation to be important motivations for members' behavior, particularly for those in leadership positions (see Derthick and Quirk 1985: 145–46, 239–42; Sabl 1997). Though the visibility of the House Speakership has waxed and waned throughout American history, the goal of winning a national reputation may be an important motive for some leaders during periods when national attention is focused on the office.[14]

To be sure, some legislators probably do seek out leadership positions

such as the House Speakership primarily to enjoy the prestige and perks of the office. These individuals could reasonably be expected to take their bearings from followers wherever possible. However, the motivations of other leaders may be more complex, and their responses to the incentives arising from leadership selection more conditional. Those with goals beyond officeholding may be motivated to act independently of followers in some political situations. In these cases, the leader's goals and skills, *along with* followers' preferences or other contextual factors, may be important causal factors in leadership politics and in the politics of institutional change. Along with the need for more realistic assumptions about leaders' goals, the Clay and Reed cases also suggest that theorists of legislative leadership need to consider the possibility that the institutional constraints congressional leaders work within may not be fixed but vary over time.

Opportunities to Lead: Critical Moments

The idea that the relationship between political structure and individual agency can vary over time has a long history in political science, from Machiavelli's treatment of the role of fortune in human affairs to Max Weber's progression of types of authority to works by contemporary political scientists, including Fred Greenstein and Stephen Skowronek. Greenstein (1969) proposed some years ago that the likelihood of a single individual influencing political outcomes will vary with the situation. He termed this question "action dispensability" and proposed that an individual's actions were most likely to be indispensable to political outcomes in situations involving a state of "precarious equilibrium" (40, 46). Greenstein also addressed the related question of "actor dispensability," meaning whether action taken by a strategically placed individual depended on the possession of certain personal qualities or would likely have been taken by any similarly situated person. Here again, he proposes that personal characteristics of individuals are more likely to be important in some political situations than others, including new organizational settings, where precedents and expectations have yet to be clearly established, and situations in which environmental cues contradict one another or suggest different courses for action (46–57).

Skowronek's theory of presidential leadership incorporates a similar view of temporal variation in structural constraints on individual agency. Presidents who assume office in opposition to vulnerable governing regimes encounter "the most promising of all situations for the exercise of political leadership"(1993: 37). However, these "reconstructive" situations contrast sharply with "the difficulties leaders in all other situations have had in try-

ing to assert authority over their moments in history . . ." (39). Along with this cyclical pattern in leadership opportunities deriving from the rise and decay of governing regimes ("political time"), Skowronek also finds in the history of presidential politics a secular decline over time in the range of action open to reconstructive leaders (56, 63, 413–14). Consistent with Greenstein's earlier proposition, presidents who served when the constitutional system was "newest" enjoyed the greatest leeway to innovate.

The politics of the Clay and Reed Speakerships also suggest that the constraints on leaders imposed by congressional institutions can vary over time, allowing greater leeway for independent action by leaders during some periods than others. These periods might be characterized as *critical moments* and periods of *equilibrium*. During equilibrium periods, institutional arrangements within the legislature are in rough balance with political conditions in the institution's environment. In the real world of congressional politics, change is almost always occurring along some dimension of congressional organization. But extended periods in the history of the institution witness relative stability and limited demands among members and outsiders for major institutional changes. Under these conditions of relative stability, most rank-and-file House members will have formed clear preferences about institutional arrangements, leaders will be selected who share those preferences, and those leaders will have limited opportunities to innovate or act independently. Contextual theories of leadership are undoubtedly useful for explaining the politics of leadership during these equilibrium periods.

But consider how the politics of congressional leadership may be different in another political situation that occurs from time to time in the history of the institution: when new contextual developments create support among members for change in the institution. Demands of this type often arise from shifts in electoral or partisan politics, the most common being the election of a new partisan majority. However, changes in any number of contextual factors may contribute to members' dissatisfaction with existing organizational arrangements. Joseph Cooper's work on the organizational development of the House remains one of the most careful and systematic efforts to identify the full range of these contextual factors and how they interact with more stable institutional forms. Along with shifts in electoral or partisan politics, Cooper identifies three additional contextual factors that may be important in generating support for organizational innovation: changes in the congressional agenda, in the state of relations with the executive branch, or in public or elite opinions about how democratic institutions should operate (1981: 331–36). Whether arising from electoral politics, new issues,

conflicts with the executive, or political reform movements, members' discontent with existing organizational arrangements may create unusual opportunities for institutional innovation on the part of leaders. During these critical moments, members' expectations of leaders may be ambiguous as preferences about what should replace existing institutional arrangements may be less clear than recognition that change is needed.

History suggests that the House can reach such a state of "precarious equilibrium" through combinations of contextual changes sufficiently complex to belie specification in advance.[15] However, the common feature of these political situations would seem to be a shift in one or more of these contextual factors that creates discontent with existing institutional forms among a majority of House members. While a critical moment may develop from a variety of contextual changes, the common feature should be unusually intense criticism of the institution or its performance from members and other political elites.

When considering the politics of congressional leadership throughout the history of the institution, there may also be a secular dimension that should be incorporated in leadership theories, reflecting the emergence of the main organizational features that structure congressional politics. Prior to the 1820s and 1830s, neither party organization nor standing committees were fixed in the institutional context for House leaders. Leaders had fewer established precedents to follow during this early period, and members had limited experience against which to judge new organizational arrangements. Also, those who might have been opposed to institutional innovation could mobilize few organizational resources to oppose it. Individuals such as Clay, who led the House in the earliest decades of its existence, surely encountered the fewest constraints on organizational innovation; those who led the chamber after the 1830s had to deal with a more complex and limiting institutional context.

A more complete leadership theory should incorporate variation over time in these two respects. Leaders should enjoy greater opportunities for acting independently during critical moments than during periods of institutional equilibrium. And those who served during critical moments in the very early history of the House may have encountered the fewest constraints and hence the greatest opportunities to influence the course of congressional development.

Critical moments appear to create two different types of leadership opportunities. The first type arises from a well-known quirk of majority rule institutions, which is that under some conditions, majority coalitions may be unstable.[16] Much theoretical work suggests, and some empirical studies

appear to confirm, that individuals who can control the framing of decisions in these settings can influence or even determine outcomes. For example, Aldrich (1995: 70–82) found that James Madison took skillful advantage of the instability of majorities in the early Congress to thwart Hamiltonian proposals that otherwise might have passed. It seems clear that Reed did something similar by initially bringing his most revolutionary procedural reforms before the House as rulings in a contested election case rather than offering them to the Republican majority in a straight up or down vote on new rules.

The second type of leadership opportunity that may arise during critical moments is the opportunity for leaders to persuade followers. When new political issues emerge or new institutional arrangements are being considered, unusual opportunities may be present for leaders to *shape* what followers want or will accept. Persuasion may take the form of building support among followers in advance of introducing an institutional or policy innovation or using the prerogatives of office to act unilaterally and then persuading followers to support the leader after the fact.

During critical moments in House politics, a range of alternative organizational responses may be possible, and by either manipulating House majorities or persuading them, leaders may have opportunities to influence which is chosen. However, when these critical situations arise, there is no guarantee that the individuals who occupy leadership positions will have the motivation or the political skill to take full advantage of them. Changes in contextual factors may be a *necessary* condition for major institutional changes to occur in Congress; but contextual change may not be *sufficient* in every case. During critical moments in congressional politics, the characteristics of individual leaders may assume unusual importance, and the motivation and skill of a leader may be the sufficient condition required for institutional change to occur. To use Greenstein's terminology, skillful political leaders may be indispensable in some important cases of institutional change.

The Clay and Reed Speakerships Revisited

Both Henry Clay and Thomas Reed were skillful politicians who assumed the Speaker's office during critical moments in House politics. When Clay was elected to the Speakership in November 1811, concerns among members about the adequacy of existing organizational arrangements were being driven primarily by the interplay between partisan politics and the congressional agenda—specifically, the growing agitation for war with England among Jeffersonian Republicans and increased obstruction of war-related measures by minority Federalists. As one Republican member described it, minority obstructionism in the previous Congress had produced "a scene which was, to say the least, disreputable to the House" (*Annals of the Congress of the United States*, 1811: 1094). We do not find the extensive criticism of the institution that marks later critical moments because the institutional remedies were close at hand in a House with few established precedents, few organizational resources in the hands of defenders of the status quo, and a talented Speaker inclined to use all means at his disposal to advance the cause of war. As noted, however, in pursuit of his own policy goals and a national reputation he hoped would secure him the presidency, Clay continued to assert the expanded powers of the Speakership even after the unity of his followers had broken down.

Clay was able to exercise such a large influence on the development of the Speakership because he led the House at a very early period in its institutional development. In comparing Clay to the Speakers who succeeded him, Peters (1997: 39) emphasizes the "fluidity" of early House politics: "It was the lack of institutional and political definition that enabled him to capitalize on his abilities." Occupying a leadership position at such an early point in the institutional development of the House, Clay encountered fewer institutional constraints than any of his successors would and as a result succeeded in transforming the nature of the Speaker's office.

The political context at the outset of the Reed Speakership also fits the definition of a critical moment in House politics. With frustrations running high over minority obstructionism in the previous Congress and a new Republican majority having just been elected, many Republicans were undoubtedly concerned about whether existing rules would allow the House to function and the Republican party to govern. However, there does not appear to have been any clear consensus among House Republicans about what types of rules changes should be enacted. Thomas Reed's strong personal commitment to party government and parliamentary skill were probably indispensable to the enactment of the sweeping rules changes that actually occurred in the 51st Congress.

Conclusion

The old-fashioned idea that leaders played an important part in shaping congressional history turns out to be partly correct. Although congressional leadership cannot be understood independently of the contextual factors that define constraints and opportunities for leaders, in some important cases, context alone may not provide a sufficient explanation for institutional change. Both Clay and Reed were elected Speaker at critical moments in House politics. Each had strongly held political goals beyond simply holding the office, and when the opportunity presented itself, each acted independently of his followers' preferences to pursue those goals, with important consequences for the institutional development of the House.

The behavior of Speakers Clay and Reed in orchestrating these institutional changes simply does not fit very well within the logic of the contextual theories advanced in recent congressional leadership studies. Neither leader took his bearings from followers' preferences to the extent that this perspective leads us to expect, and neither shied away from actively using the powers of his position when followers were divided over the ends being pursued. This does not mean that contextual theories should not be considered useful for explaining congressional leadership. Much of the time, congressional institutions *do* place fairly narrow limits on the independence of leaders, for precisely the reasons these theories suggest. These theories are not so much wrong as incomplete. A leadership theory that can account for the roles leaders such as Henry Clay and Thomas Reed have played in congressional history will need to pay greater attention to why leaders lead and to how opportunities for exercising leadership can vary over time.

Chapter 10

Institutional Evolution and the Rise of the Tuesday-Thursday Club in the House of Representatives

TIMOTHY P. NOKKEN AND BRIAN R. SALA

> Representatives and prospective representatives think about their constituencies because they seek support in their constituencies. They want to be nominated and elected, then renominated and reelected. For most members of Congress most of the time, this electoral goal is primary. It is the prerequisite for a congressional career and, hence, for the pursuit of other member goals. And the electoral goal is achieved—first and last—not in Washington but at home.
>
> —Richard Fenno, *Home Style* (1978: 31)

Richard Fenno's landmark 1978 study of the "home styles" of members of Congress began an onslaught of research on the incidence and effects of constituency services on legislators' electoral prospects.[1] In the book, Fenno argued that members of Congress (MCs) seeking reelection face a problem of how to allocate their resources optimally across different activities. Of the resources available to an MC, the most critical, he argued, was the member's personal time. Should the member's time be employed in Washington work or back in the district?

A compelling factor in determining the amount of time an MC spends back home in the district is the opportunity cost of time away from Washington. This cost is a function of how the member is scheduled by his or her staff and how committee work and floor work are scheduled by committee and party leaders. Hence the opportunity cost of home-style work is partly endogenous—determined by legislators' individual and collective choices —and partly exogenous—determined by transportation technology and the distance a member must travel to get home.

In this chapter, we explore issues of "Washington time" opportunity costs and how member responses to those costs have changed over time. We ar-

270

gue that during the "strong Speaker" period (roughly 1889–1911), the Speaker's control over scheduling legislative debates and floor votes gave him the opportunity to influence greatly the timing of important votes. Further, his control over committee assignments, floor recognition, and the Rules Committee empowered the Speaker to strongly shape majority party MC incentives vis-à-vis attendance on those votes. This combination of authorities empowered the Speaker to pursue his legislative agenda without much concern toward the timing with which issues were raised on the floor.

The Speaker's strong powers during this period stand in stark opposition to the growing incentives individual MCs faced to pursue *personal-vote* (Cain, Ferejohn, and Fiorina 1987) or *home-style* (Fenno 1978) reelection strategies. The switch to the secret ballot in Australia in the early 1890s, coupled with tremendous improvements in rail transportation to and from Washington, D.C., late in the nineteenth century, gave increasing numbers of incumbent MCs both the incentive and the means to go home regularly for two- or three-day working weekends of perpetual campaign activities.

The House's experience during the strong Speaker period contrasts with that of the Senate during the same period. We show that the timing of floor votes diverged in the two chambers during the strong Speaker era, whereas the chambers mirrored each other both before and after that period. Our study thus sheds new light on the motivation and consequences of the revolt against Speaker Joseph Cannon in 1910–11. In particular, we show that the distance between a member's district and Washington, D.C., was a significant predictor of weekend shirking before and after the Cannon Speakership but that the relationship broke down during Cannon's last three Houses as presiding officer. This finding is consistent with the conventional argument that Cannon abused his powers as presiding officer.

In this chapter, first we shall overview the data on the timing of recorded votes in the House and patterns of turnout on midweek and weekend votes over the post–Civil War era. Next we briefly review the history of the strong Speaker period, the rise of careerist MC strategies in the House, and the revolt against Cannon. We then test the hypothesis that House and Senate scheduling patterns deviated during the strong Speaker era but converged again after the revolt against Cannon and offer some concluding remarks.

The Tuesday-Thursday Club

Congressional scholars generally accept the notion that modern House members are driven by a desire for reelection and that they depend largely

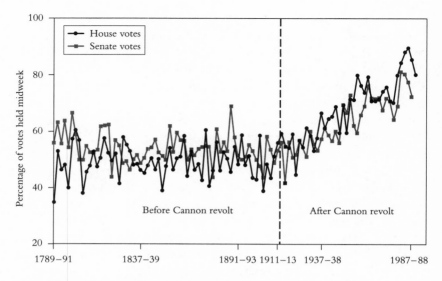

Figure 10.1. Timing of recorded votes in Congress, 1789–1988.

on their own efforts to win reelection. Candidate-centered campaigns are part and parcel of the "textbook Congress" of the post–World War II era.

A defining feature of the modern era is perpetual campaigning activities. House members are "running scared," in Jacobson's memorable phrase (1987). As a consequence, MCs are attentive to what Fenno (1978) called "home style" concerns, such as constituency service and personal appearances in the district. For example, Rivers and Fiorina (1991) show that incumbent MCs' reputations for being attentive to constituency problems play an important role in members' reelection success.

Modern floor management practices in Congress appear to accommodate members' desire to tend to home-style activities *during* congressional sessions. Figure 10.1 illustrates this tendency. The figure plots by Congress the proportion of House and Senate recorded votes held midweek (on Tuesdays, Wednesdays, and Thursdays) for the first 100 Congresses (1789–1988). As the figure indicates, about half of House and Senate recorded votes were held midweek and half during the Friday-through-Monday extended-weekend periods throughout the nineteenth century. Floor vote scheduling practices in both chambers then changed sometime in the early twentieth century, such that the share of votes held in midweek rose steadily until reaching nearly 90 percent by 1985–86. The focus of this chapter is on ex-

Table 10.1

Average House Midweek and
Weekend Abstention Levels, 1877–1997

Decade	Midweek Abstention	Weekend Abstention	T Statistic	Midweek N	Weekend N
1877–1888	91.5	98.1	−3.50	1058	1067
1889–1898	129.3	132.1	−1.06	762	655
1899–1908	132.2	148.5	−4.39	300	310
1909–1918	133.1	129.6	0.75	478	408
1919–1928	115.5	108.6	1.74	458	385
1929–1938	68.3	71.9	−0.98	403	276
1939–1948	68.0	77.1	−2.94	595	334
1949–1958	44.0	70.6	−8.55	664	281
1959–1968	44.1	80.1	−13.49	1116	408
1969–1978	41.2	72.1	−28.45	3595	1398
1979–1988	30.9	72.4	−24.60	4085	728
1989–1997	17.6	33.8	−16.95	4060	768

NOTE: We omitted from consideration all roll call votes held in a given Congress after December of the (even-numbered) election year. This eliminated nearly all lame-duck session votes. We counted ICPSR vote codes 7, 8, and 9 as "abstaining" and codes 1–6 (including actual votes, pairs, and announced positions) as participating.

plaining the origins and consequences of this change in scheduling regimes in the House.

Not only is a smaller share of floor votes held on weekends today than was true in the nineteenth century, but turnout differs sharply today between midweek and weekend votes. For example, of the 5,134 recorded votes held in the House during the 100th–104th Congresses (1987–96), absenteeism averaged 39.2 members (9.0 percent) on the 825 weekend votes and only 19.2 (4.4 percent) on the 4,309 midweek votes, a highly statistically significant difference. In contrast, for the 1,870 recorded votes held from 1887 to 1896, there was no significant difference in absenteeism between the 890 weekend votes (129.4, 38.5 percent) and the 980 midweek votes (126.8, 37.7 percent).

Table 10.1 displays, by decade, the abstention rates on non–lame-duck midweek and weekend votes for the period 1877–1997. We concentrate on non–lame-duck votes here primarily to avoid conflating the usual end-of-session crush of business with the "normal" pace and timing of floor activities that we believe characterized floor voting during the bulk of each long session of Congress in the early part of this period. Overall participation rates differed significantly between midweek and weekend votes in the 1870s and 1880s. We found no significant differences during the early 1890s, when the "disappearing quorum" tactic was at its peak (see Chapter 9). The turnout gap reemerged during the Cannon era but then disappeared in the wake of the revolt against Cannon, not to return until the opening of the Conservative Coalition era in the late 1930s.

Aggregate weekend absenteeism rates were stable from the 1930s through the 1980s, while midweek abstention was declining. Figure 10.1 and Table 10.1, taken together, strongly suggest that House leaders from at least the New Deal forward responded to members' desires to commute during sessions by shifting more and more of the important workload away from weekends to midweek.

Both practices—concentrating recorded votes during midweek and of differential turnout rates on midweek and weekend votes—reflect important aspects of modern congressional life. The fact that modern MCs are more likely to miss weekend votes than midweek votes even in spite of the dramatic reduction in the relative frequency of weekend roll calls strongly suggests that House leaders today successfully concentrate most of the important votes in midweek sessions. It further suggests that MCs are responsive to that strategic arrangement of the agenda.

Commuting between the home district and Washington during a session is a given in the modern Congress. Most House districts today are within a five- or six-hour airline ride of Washington. Nineteenth-century MCs faced more daunting travel costs than modern legislators do. Only districts that were close to Washington afforded their MCs the opportunity to commute during a session without missing substantial session time. But railroad technology and systems developed rapidly during and after the Civil War. By the opening of the strong Speaker period, the definition of "close by" districts had broadened significantly. According to railroad historian John F. Stover (1987: 176), the fastest schedule for the Baltimore and Ohio Railroad between New York City and Washington, D.C., in 1893, a trip of roughly 225 miles, "was five hours, including a twelve-minute ferry boat trip across the Hudson River to the foot of Liberty Street."

Of course, not all districts enjoyed the quality of service provided by the B&O between D.C. and New York City. But the spread of commuter-style turnout behavior is an empirical question that we can address indirectly in two ways. First, we can model overall turnout rates as a function of the distance between the member's district and Washington, D.C. If absenteeism is driven significantly by *home-style* activities rather than pure shirking behavior, members who face the lowest opportunity cost for commuting should be most likely to take advantage of commuting strategies. Hence absenteeism should decline as district distance from D.C. decreases.

Second, if the House leadership recognizes and accounts for commuting incentives, leaders should schedule important floor activities to accommodate commuting activities. One way to do so would be to establish a transparent scheduling regime that would inform MCs well in advance of when important issues were to be brought forward on the floor. A scheduling regime that tends to concentrate major activities on midweek days and minor events on weekends is a concrete example of such an incentive-compatible approach. We can explore whether House leaders are responsive in this way indirectly by comparing member turnout rates on midweek and weekend votes as a function of the distance between the member's district and Washington.

Table 10.2 shows the results of a series of simple regressions of MC abstention rates in a given Congress on logged district distance from D.C. and the member's party affiliation. The table shows a significant and growing inverse relationship between district distance and member abstention rates in the House throughout the postbellum nineteenth century and the early twentieth century. Distance from D.C. is already a significant predictor of abstention rates as early as the 45th House (1877–79). We estimate for the 45th House that a member whose district lay 100 miles from D.C. would abstain 27 percent of the time, whereas one whose district lay 500 miles away would abstain only 22 percent of the time, a decline of five percentage points. The estimated changes in abstention rates for this shift in district distance in subsequent Congresses were −8 points (50th House, 1887–89), −7 points (55th, 1897–99), −12 points (60th, 1907–09), −13 points (65th House, 1917–19), and −5 points (70th House, 1927–29). At the same time, we found no evidence that Democrats and Republicans differed in their abstention rates once we controlled for district distance.

If improvements in transportation technology had been wiping out the opportunity cost differences of shirking recorded votes perceived by members, at least over a nearby range of district distances, we should have found that district distance was declining over time as a determinant of participation. These regression results suggest that district distance was *not declining* as a determinant of participation in the period between the Civil War and

Table 10.2

House Member Abstention Rates by District Distance
from Washington, D.C.

Congress (Years)	Ln(Distance) (SE)	Democrat (SE)	Ln(Distance) × Democrat (SE)	Constant (SE)	N	R^2
45th 1877–79	−0.030 (0.016)	0.031 (0.125)	−0.0088 (0.020)	0.408 (0.101)	298	0.063
50th 1887–89	−0.048 (0.015)	0.061 (0.125)	−0.0021 (0.020)	0.663 (0.097)	312	0.088
55th 1897–99	−0.046 (0.011)	0.042 (0.158)	−0.0066 (0.024)	0.644 (0.071)	333	0.067
60th 1907–09	−0.071 (0.014)	0.103 (0.156)	−0.014 (0.024)	0.813 (0.088)	375	0.094
65th 1917–19	−0.084 (0.014)	−0.101 (0.121)	0.014 (0.018)	0.801 (0.090)	421	0.171
70th 1927–29	−0.031 (0.010)	0.098 (0.098)	−0.016 (0.015)	0.365 (0.063)	420	0.071

NOTE: OLS regression with robust standard errors. Dependent variable: Abstention rate for MC_i. We counted ICPSR vote codes 1–6 (yeas, nays, paired yea/nay, announced yea/nay) as participating and codes 7–9 as abstentions.

World War I. Hence they run contrary to the thesis that changes in turnout rates in this period were primarily a function of transportation technology and railroad expansion (Poole and Rosenthal 1997). Is there evidence of home-style commuting-driven abstention and strategic adaptation of floor agendas for this period?

Under an assumption that party leaders seek to accommodate their members' personal preferences vis-à-vis floor scheduling, we would expect individual MCs' turnout rates to be responsive to the timing of floor votes. Concentrating less important floor work in extended weekends would be incentive-compatible for MCs whose districts lie within a few hours' travel of D.C. Members whose districts lie closest to D.C. should show the greatest drop in participation on weekends relative to midweek, whereas members from more distant districts should be less affected by weekend roll calls.

We can illustrate the changing impact of distance from D.C. on home-style initiatives via simple, descriptive regressions of the difference between a member's weekend and midweek turnout rates on distance (expressed as a

Table 10.3

Estimated House Abstention Rate Differences
by Party, Selected Distances

Congress	Years	Party	100 mi.	200 mi.	300 mi.	400 mi.
45	1877–79	Rep.	6.15	5.46	4.81	4.21
		Dem.	**4.11**	**4.02**	**3.93**	**3.83**
51	1889–91	**Rep.**	**1.70**	**1.66**	**1.62**	**1.58**
		Dem.	3.58	3.21	2.85	2.52
53	1893–95	Rep.	2.61	1.98	1.39	0.84
		Dem.	**5.36**	**4.94**	**4.56**	**4.22**
55	1897–99	**Rep.**	**2.36**	**1.67**	**1.04**	**0.46**
		Dem.	−0.42	−0.74	−1.04	−1.32
57	1901–03	**Rep.**	**3.21**	**2.44**	**1.71**	**1.03**
		Dem.	6.48	5.40	4.38	3.44
59	1905–07	**Rep.**	**3.95**	**3.70**	**3.47**	**3.28**
		Dem.	9.03	7.00	5.27	3.88
61	1909–11	**Rep.**	**−3.01**	**−3.02**	**−3.07**	**−3.10**
		Dem.	−9.41	−8.34	−7.38	−6.50
63	1913–15	Rep.	7.38	6.11	4.92	3.81
		Dem.	**6.74**	**5.89**	**5.09**	**4.33**
65	1917–19	Rep.	6.32	5.24	4.22	3.26
		Dem.	**3.53**	**2.99**	**2.50**	**2.03**
70	1927–29	**Rep.**	**2.69**	**2.33**	**1.98**	**1.66**
		Dem.	7.54	6.70	5.93	5.22
75	1937–38	Rep.	1.57	1.11	0.68	0.27
		Dem.	**3.65**	**2.92**	**2.24**	**1.59**
80	1947–48	**Rep.**	**4.77**	**3.98**	**3.24**	**2.54**
		Dem.	3.95	3.54	3.16	2.81
90	1967–68	Rep.	12.61	11.80	11.04	10.34
		Dem.	**11.83**	**11.77**	**11.70**	**11.62**

NOTE: Rate difference is the weekend abstention rate for member *i* minus his or her mid-week rate. Majority party figures are in bold. Estimated differences were obtained by regressing (by party) rate difference on the distance and squared distance (in miles) between the member's district and Washington, D.C. A negative value indicates that midweek abstention rates were greater than weekend abstention rates. We thank Keith Poole for providing district distance data.

quadratic—including both miles and miles squared).[2] Table 10.3 shows predicted values from those regressions for selected Houses and district distances from D.C. Results for the majority party in a given House are shown in boldfaced type.

House members in the postbellum era frequently exhibited what we would today call "Tuesday-Thursday Club" behavior on recorded votes—participating less frequently in weekend votes (held Friday through Monday) than in midweek votes (held on Tuesdays, Wednesdays, or Thursdays). We found district distance to be a significant predictor of the abstention rate difference (weekend abstention rate for member i minus midweek abstention rate for that member) for the Republicans in the 53rd (1893–95) through 55th (1897–99) and for both parties for the 56th (1899–1901) through 58th (1903–05) Houses. The Tuesday-Thursday Club effect was relatively muted during the final years of the Cannon Speakership but reemerged strongly in the 62nd House, persisting for both parties throughout the Wilson administration.

The Strong Speaker Era

The regression results reported in Table 10.3 focus our attention squarely on the revolt against Speaker Joseph Cannon (R-Ill.) and the end of the strong Speaker era in House development. The history of the House of Representatives in the years following the Civil War is laden with the struggles of majority party leaders to gain firm control of the legislative agenda on the floor of the House (Bach 1990; Binder 1997; Dion 1997).

With the adoption and ratification of the Reed Rules in 1889 and 1894 (see Chapter 9), a new period of strong Speaker rule began. Reed's institutional innovations "arguably were the capstones of a nearly century-long struggle between majority and minority party rights" (Binder 1997: 125–26; see also Alexander 1916). We found in our discussion of the gap between member's abstention rates on midweek and weekend votes evidence to suggest that the strong Speakership was compatible with members' growing interests in home-style commuter behavior. Throughout the 1890s and early 1900s, as more members found themselves competing for reelection under the new Australian ballot voting rules and emerging direct primary nomination procedures, MCs whose districts lay closest to D.C. were taking advantage of weekends to shirk Washington work, presumably in order to attend to matters back home. Speakers Thomas Reed (R-Me., 1889–91, 1895–99), Charles Crisp (D-Ga., 1891–95), and David Henderson (R-Ia., 1899–1903) did not, it would seem, use their new powers to strong-arm attendance from members able to commute home on weekends.

In this new period, the Speaker, as chairman of the Committee on Rules, was able to write special rules to time and structure floor and Committee of the Whole consideration of bills as he saw fit, contingent on being able to hold majority support on the floor. Woodrow Wilson, reflecting on changes in the House since the first publication of his 1885 classic *Congressional Government*, wrote in 1900:

> The power of the Speaker has of late years taken on new phases. He is now, more than ever, expected to guide and control the whole course of business in the House—if not alone, at any rate through the instrumentality of the small Committee on Rules, of which he is chairman. That committee is expected not only to reformulate and revise from time to time the permanent Rules of the House, but also to look closely to the course of its business from day to day, make its programme, and virtually control its use of its time. . . . The Speaker himself—not as a member of the Committee on Rules, but by the exercise of his right to "recognize" on the floor—undertakes to determine very absolutely what bills individual members shall be allowed to bring to a vote, out of the regular order fixed by the rules or arranged by the Committee on Rules. (ix–x)

This new state of affairs, which Wilson regarded as a step toward but still falling short of "genuine party leadership" (xi), was not to last. Internal tensions within the majority Republican caucus spelled the end of the strong Speaker period barely two decades after its birth, in the famous revolt against Speaker Joseph Cannon, one of the best-known events of congressional history. Nonetheless, we argue, certain aspects of the revolt and its aftermath have been underappreciated.

According to Charles Jones (1968) and other students of the revolt, the so-called insurgent faction of the Republican party became increasingly disgruntled with Cannon's procedural and substantive direction of the House. In particular, Cannon elevated allies to important committee chairmanships over the heads of more senior but less loyal members (see Lawrence, Maltzman, and Wahlbeck 2001), and he jealously guarded his control over legislative scheduling. Members seeking passage of minor or private bills were forced to seek his prior approval before being recognized on the floor to ask unanimous consent for consideration of their pet bills. Disfavored or disloyal MCs had little prospect of receiving that approval.

Likewise, standing committees found themselves hamstrung in writing public bills they considered important because they could not be assured of floor time for consideration of their finished products. George Norris (R-Nebr.), a leading insurgent—and a principal figure in the revolt—later related in his autobiography that the ranking Democrat on the Committee on Public Buildings and Grounds during this period, Rep. William Bankhead (D-Ala.), "actually made a motion that the chairman of the committee should seek a conference with the Speaker and ascertain whether or not we should be allowed to have a public building bill at that session" (Jones 1968: 621).

While this comment no doubt carried a fair share of bitter jest, it illustrates a general problem likely facing members of the House under Cannon. Committee members were unlikely to exert a great deal of effort developing well-thought-out legislation if they had little hope of securing floor consideration for their efforts. Legislation inconsistent with Cannon's interpretation of the majority party's agenda was unlikely to receive floor consideration. Similarly, and more disturbing to insurgent Republicans, legislation that tended to set the Republican factions against one another, as well as "nonpartisan" proposals, were given lower priority than Republican party platform items.

This helps explain why "party votes" as a proportion of all recorded votes—and party cohesion on those votes—peaked during the Cannon Speakership despite growing evidence of internal divisions within the Republican party, before beginning a long, sustained decline (Brady, Cooper, and Hurley 1979). Floor voting patterns in the strong Speaker period suggest that this tendency to put nonpartisan and divisive intraparty bills on the back burner was more general to the era, rather than particular to Cannon's Speakership. Strong centralized control of the legislative schedule should have allowed the leaders to optimize floor time for the pursuit of their goals, which presumably revolved around keeping their party in firm majority control of the House and themselves in leadership positions (for a model of scheduling, see Cox and McCubbins 1993: chap. 9).

Katz and Sala (1996) noted that the beginning of the strong Speaker era coincided with a major innovation in the electoral connection—the widespread institution of Australian ballot laws in the states. They argued that the Australian ballot reforms induced MCs to increase their demand for resources and opportunities to curry favor with constituents. Increasing the stability of assignments to standing committees was one possible solution to this change in member incentives.

Katz and Sala (1996) argued that MCs would seek to exploit their committee assignments for ways to gain credit with constituents and that this arrangement could well be incentive-compatible for both the rank-and-file and party leaders. This conclusion depends on committee members' being allowed to do *something*, however, be it pass legislation or conduct significant oversight of the executive branch. Hence committees charged with legislative jurisdictions of high importance to the majority party agenda were most likely to be ones for which member efforts were rewarded by constituents.

With little or no prospect of obtaining floor time for their bills, what could disfavored rank-and-file members do to enhance their own reelection? The two candidates for credit-claiming opportunities would have been committee assignment–related oversight of the executive branch and more traditional constituency services. But Republican administrations were in place throughout 1889–92 and 1897–1912, significantly limiting the attractiveness of oversight activities for most Republicans.[3] Democrats, meanwhile, may have desired to conduct oversight but lacked the institutional resources with which to pursue that strategy. Hence reelection-seeking House members not among the party leadership should have been strongly motivated during the strong Speaker era to provide constituency services.

The evidence on the gap between midweek and weekend abstention rates during the pre-Cannon period of the 1890s and early 1900s is consistent with home-style commuter behavior. Members who could go home apparently were going home on weekends. Why, then, is there so little evidence in the voting patterns during the 59th–61st Houses of home-style commuting activities? We see the failure of House members, particularly of Republicans, to be responsive to district distance in their weekend shirking behavior during this period as supporting the general thesis that Speaker Cannon was indeed exercising what Jones (1968: 618) called "excessive leadership." Indeed, with the conclusion of the revolt and replacement of the Cannon regime with a Democratic majority in the 62nd House (1911–13), district distance once again was a significant predictor of differential (weekend versus midweek) shirking on floor votes for both parties.

The evidence on differential rates of turnout for weekend and midweek recorded votes is consistent with the conventional interpretation of the revolt against Cannon—that Cannon went too far in his efforts to control the House. For our purposes, the revolt consisted of two distinct sets of events. First, as Cannon and his allies sought to organize the House at the start of the 61st Congress, members anticipated a fight over the adoption of the standing rules of the House (on this episode, see *Congressional Record*, 44th Cong., 1st sess.: 19–34).

This contest was concluded by a deal struck between Cannon's allies and a faction of Democrats led by John J. Fitzgerald (D-N.Y.) and including several other Tammany Democrats. The main consequence of the deal was the creation of the unanimous consent calendar and its insertion as privileged on alternating Mondays, which gave MCs a new, incentive-compatible mechanism for arranging their personal schedules. Prior to this innovation, Speakers had used recognition for the presentation of unanimous consent requests as both a carrot and a stick. The carrot part is self-evident—an MC cannot request unanimous consent without being present. By holding out the prospect of recognition to many members, the Speaker could perhaps induce higher attendance than would otherwise have occurred. The stick part is only slightly more subtle—a member who wished to gain recognition to present a noncontroversial bill had to stay in the good graces of the Speaker personally. If one of the Speaker's goals was high attendance rates by rank-and-file majority party members and if MCs placed a high value on passing certain noncontroversial bills, the mere *threat* of disfavor from the Speaker for unexcused absenteeism could have induced higher turnout.

The rules change removed both carrot and stick from the Speaker's control. As a consequence, holding constant the scheduling choices made by the leadership for public bills, the opportunity cost of trips home should have declined. In turn, the Rules Committee should have become more inclined to coordinate legislative scheduling with members' plans for trips home.

Second, a year later, many of the same insurgent Republicans who had bucked their party's leaders on the adoption of the standing rules at the start of the Congress (only to be stymied in part by Tammany Democrats) moved again to rewrite the standing rules. This time, the Speaker was removed from the Rules Committee, and the committee was enlarged to raise the responsiveness of the floor scheduling process to the individual preferences of rank-and-file majority MCs.

As Jones (1968; see also Baker 1973) makes clear, Cannon's sin was insufficient responsiveness to the political needs of his own rank-and-file members more than the policy outcomes that resulted from his leadership. There is little evidence in the historical record that policy outcomes in the remainder of the 61st House were any more "progressive" than they had been prior to Cannon's removal from the Rules Committee. But the world after the revolt was distinctly different in terms of how floor activity was scheduled, as Figure 10.1 illustrated. As the figure showed, the proportion of recorded votes held in midweek was fairly constant throughout the nineteenth century but began a steady rise soon after the Cannon revolt.

This rising tide of midweek voting for the rest of the century of course reflects the tremendous changes in transportation technologies that evolved during the course of the twentieth century. Government investment in roads suitable for automobile travel exploded during the 1920s, as did automobile miles per capita traveled by Americans. Subsequently, air travel became feasible, and its costs declined significantly over the second half of the century. As transportation costs declined, the fixed or exogenous costs of going home declined steadily.

But this explanation is insufficient, because important transportation innovations were in place by the early 1890s that put as many as a quarter of House members within a five- or six-hour trip from home (Stover 1987). These members could easily leave Washington on Friday, perform constituency service activities on Saturday and Sunday, and return to Washington Sunday night or Monday morning.

Home Styles, Washington Work, and the Tuesday-Thursday Club

We asserted that changes in the electoral connection stemming from the Australian ballot reforms of the 1890s induced new demands from MCs for credit-claiming, position-taking, and advertising opportunities in the House (Mayhew 1974). With respect to home-style activities (Fenno 1978), we argued, transportation technology and infrastructure developments should have materially shaped members' incentives to take trips home during legislative sessions, holding constant the disincentives for such trips provided by the "Washington work" context.

Conventionally, the revolt against Cannon in 1909–10 is attributed to Cannon's "excessive leadership" vis-à-vis rank-and-file Republicans (Jones 1968: 618). The main evidence in favor of this argument has largely been anecdotal (although for new evidence relating to committee assignment practices under Cannon, see Lawrence, Maltzman, and Wahlbeck 2001; and Krehbiel and Wiseman 2001). Indeed, Krehbiel and Wiseman argue that the accusations of "tyrannical rule" by his contemporary opponents lack support in the data on committee assignments.

We focus on a different aspect of Cannon's leadership here to highlight the strong Speakers' influence over legislative scheduling and floor recognition as a potential source of rank-and-file discontent. The changes in the electoral connection arising from ballot law changes in the 1890s in the House and an associated rise in "careerist" legislators (Katz and Sala 1996; Price 1975) should have produced a greater incentive for MCs to shirk party-oriented Washington work in favor of constituency service activities. Members for whom extant transportation technologies made within-session commuting feasible should have been most tempted to substitute home-style work for Washington work.

But, we argue, scheduling patterns for floor votes did not adapt to this new incentive system. The House leadership during the strong Speaker period did not significantly rearrange recorded vote events to accommodate members seeking to commute.

To test this hypothesis, we model the proportion of recorded votes held on midweek days (Tuesdays, Wednesdays, and Thursdays) as a linear function of time. We divide congressional history into three eras for the purposes of this test: the period prior to the adoption of the Reed Rules (1789–1889), the strong Speaker era from the Reed Rules to the revolt against Cannon (1889–1911), and the postrevolt period (1911–98).

We expect there to be no systematic relationship between time and the frequency of midweek votes for the pre-Reed period. Transportation technology in the early and mid-nineteenth century limited commuting opportunities for legislators to only a very few members whose districts lay within a few hours' horse or carriage ride from Washington. For example, in the 26th Congress (1839–41), we found a small, significant difference in floor participation between the 10 percent of members whose districts lay closest to Washington and the other 90 percent.[4] But neither group changed behaviors between midweek and weekend votes, suggesting that there was no recognized core workweek in Congress that would allow close-by members to commute regularly between home and Washington without missing significant floor action.

Railroad technology and systems developed rapidly during and after the Civil War, broadening the definition of "close by" districts. In the 50th House (1887–89), members from the 25 percent of districts closest to Washington (within 330 miles) missed about 45 percent of floor votes, whereas members from farther away missed 37 percent of votes. We expect floor scheduling patterns to change after the Australian ballot innovations of the early 1890s to better accommodate nearby MCs' incentives to commute. But we allow for different slopes during the strong Speaker period and after the revolt in order to test the hypothesis that scheduling during the strong Speaker era didn't adjust in step with the expectations we drew from the changing electoral incentives.

In the regressions, the main time index is set equal to the Congress number. We then include separate time counters for the strong Speaker and postrevolt eras. The index for the strong Speaker period is set to 1 in the 52nd Congress (1891–93) and incremented by 1 each Congress through the 61st (1909–11). It is 0 for Congresses before and after that period. The index for the postrevolt period is 0 for the 1st through 61st Congresses and equal to the Congress number minus 61 thereafter. We also included step-function dummy variables for the strong Speaker and postrevolt periods (equal to 1 during the relevant era and 0 otherwise).

Figure 10.2 shows the results of these regressions for the House and the Senate. If the same process (e.g., changes in transportation costs) drives floor scheduling patterns in both chambers, there should be no difference in the general pattern of midweek versus weekend votes across the two houses. Al-

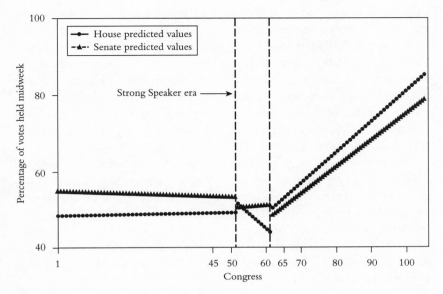

Figure 10.2. Percentage of votes held midweek, by era and chamber.

ternatively, if institutional rules matter, we would expect the House and Senate to have diverged during the strong Speaker period, as the strong Speakers tended to suppress changes in floor voting patterns arising from changes in transportation costs and members' electoral incentives. The figure does indeed show a divergence in voting patterns across the two chambers during the strong Speaker period. In the House, the proportion of votes held midweek (on Tuesdays, Wednesdays, and Thursdays) actually *declined significantly* during the period, whereas there was no significant time trend evident in the Senate during that period. Both chambers then exhibit a significant rising trend in the postrevolt period, again consistent with the notion that members increasingly desired to use weekends for home-style activities and that leaders increasingly accommodated those desires.

Conclusion

We have argued that the rising tide of Tuesday-through-Thursday voting during the postrevolt twentieth century reflects strong demands by MCs for floor scheduling of legislative activities that is consistent with members' incentives to provide increasing levels of both legislative output and home-style services. In contrast, the stability of pre—Reed Rules House voting practices, we argue, reflects relatively weak demands.

The strong Speaker period from the 51st House to 61st Houses (1889–1911) was a transitional period during which successful MCs adapted to the new electoral environment induced by Australian ballot election laws and direct primaries. Members demanded and received more reliable committee assignments (Katz and Sala 1996), expanded staff resources (Fox and Hammond 1977), and new office space with the opening of the first House office building (later named the Cannon Building) in 1908.

Our study suggests that the Tuesday-Thursday Club first arose early in the postbellum period as members from states close to Washington, D.C., began to vary their attendance on recorded votes according to whether the vote was held during midweek (Tuesday, Wednesday, or Thursday) or at the weekend (Friday through Monday). We found persistent evidence through the early strong Speaker period that district distance from D.C. was a significant predictor of weekend shirking of Washington work (as measured by roll call attendance).

This relationship appeared to break down late in the Cannon Speakership but reemerged strongly following the revolt against Cannon. Hand in hand with this reemergence, House scheduling patterns also began to change, shifting more and more of the important work of the House to midweek and away from extended weekends. We argue that the revolt, for whatever reasons it may have occurred, produced as one consequence more responsive floor management practices by House leaders. The Tuesday-Thursday Club is far from a purely modern, air-travel-driven development. It originated in the late-nineteenth-century changes in electoral incentives that encouraged the evolution of the career-oriented professional politicians that we see today. The apparent suppression of Tuesday-Thursday Club shirking we observed in the late Cannon Speakership and the resurgence of that shirking after the revolt speak both to the significance of legislative rules and procedures in shaping member behavior and, we contend, to the responsiveness of those rules and procedures to members' electoral incentives.

Chapter 11

Policy Leadership and the Development of the Modern Senate

GERALD GAMM AND STEVEN S. SMITH

Compared to their counterparts today, Senate party leaders of the mid-twentieth century were not policy leaders. In the "textbook Senate," the initiation, design, and promotion of policy proposals were left to others, primarily committee leaders. Reviewing the policymaking role of Senate leaders, Jones (1976: 19–20) observed that "strong substance-oriented policy leadership by party leaders is neither possible nor desirable in the United States Senate." And at least until recently, floor leaders have not been known for their public relations skills. The behavior of majority leaders from Alben Barkley (D-Ky.) to Mike Mansfield (D-Mont.) led such keen observers as Peabody (1976) and Ripley (1969) to give only token attention to their public relations responsibilities. To be sure, midcentury floor leaders were widely recognized and quoted. But from a contemporary perspective, they were managers, not policy leaders, whose primary responsibility was to expedite the flow of legislation that was drafted, introduced, negotiated, and promoted by others.

Recent leaders—Howard Baker (R-Tenn.), Robert Dole (R-Kans.), and Trent Lott (R-Miss.) on the Republican side, George Mitchell (D-Me.) and Tom Daschle (D-S.D.) on the Democratic side—have been more proactive in setting agendas, crafting legislation, and speaking for their parties. The polarization of the parties, changes in the media environment, and other factors have led senators to expect more policy leadership from floor leaders. In the 1980s, Democratic leader Robert Byrd (D-W.V.) was openly challenged on the basis of his ineffectiveness as a policy leader for the Democrats. Now senators regularly look to floor leaders for substantive policy agendas, for leadership in the negotiation of budget bills and other major legislation, and for the design and implementation of media strategies.

Still, these recent changes pale next to the dramatic development of party leadership at the end of the nineteenth century and the first decades of the twentieth. Between 1890 and 1940, the modern institutions of Senate leadership were invented and perfected. As late as the 1890s—one hundred years after the creation of the House Speakership—neither party in the Senate possessed any public spokesperson or an identified leader on the floor (Gamm and Smith 2001). "No one is *the* Senator," Woodrow Wilson observed in 1885. "No one may speak for his party as well as for himself" (213). The parties met regularly in caucuses, but the caucus chairmen exercised no obvious influence in or out of the caucus. Informal leaders existed, like Clay and Webster and Aldrich, but their leadership was not enshrined in institutional positions.

Formal changes came incrementally. In the 1890s, both parties created regular steering committees to set agendas and shape legislation. Meanwhile, the Democrats, in the minority from 1895 until 1913, came to rely on their caucus chairman to serve as their "party leader" on the floor. Though the Democratic caucus appears to have explicitly recognized the change only after the passage of many more years, by 1899, journalists and senators were routinely referring to the Democratic caucus chairman as the "minority leader." In 1913, when Democrats regained control of the Senate, they continued to regard their caucus chairman as their floor leader—the first "majority leader" in the Senate's history—and Republicans elected a minority leader. Also in 1913–15, both parties created the position of whip. Still, not until the 1920s and 1930s did floor leaders begin to assume modern responsibilities on the floor and enjoy the array of privileges now identified with the positions (Gamm and Smith 2002).

In this chapter, we explore the role of party leaders in the decades surrounding the creation of modern floor leadership early in the twentieth century. Typically, scholars have assumed that these were years of party decentralization. Ripley (1969) suggests that the period from 1905 to 1933 can be defined as six years of "decentralization," six years of "centralization," and sixteen years of "individualism." Similarly, Brady, Brody, and Epstein (1989) describe the first decades of the century as a period in which committee dominance took hold and, implicitly, central party institutions withered.

Our recent research on the emergence of formal leadership positions calls this account into question. A weakening of Senate party leadership in the early twentieth century could not have occurred if little regular floor leadership existed before then. In previous work, we have documented the development of formal leadership posts in the early twentieth century (Gamm and Smith 2000, 2002). But we realize that the creation of these new positions could have occurred without behavioral consequences. As the Senate's own position of president pro tempore demonstrates, lofty titles do not always coincide with real authority.

Drawing on both a survey of the *Congressional Record* (1875–1941) and the *Washington Post*'s day-by-day account of four long Senate sessions (1879–80, 1899–1900, 1919–20, and 1940–41), we test the hypothesis that creating the new positions of floor leadership changed the way senators did their business.[1] Specifically, we examine changing patterns of agenda setting, floor management, floor participation, and public spokesmanship. Taken together, these four activities form the foundation of the modern floor leader's role as a policy leader. We find a strong relationship between party and policy leadership in the decades surrounding the emergence of modern floor leadership in the Senate. The assumption of formal leadership posts by senators altered patterns of floor participation and access to the press in significant ways. The new leaders took the lead in managing floor activity, including the construction of unanimous consent agreements to limit debate and amendments. In this era, they became the chief spokesmen for their parties on the floor and in the press.

Emergence of Formal Leadership Positions

The formal position of floor leader emerged slowly, over the last decades of the nineteenth century and the first decades of the twentieth (Gamm and Smith 2000, 2001, 2002). For its first half-century, the Senate experimented with assigning powers to its presiding officer. At various times, the presiding officer named committees and enforced order. But with the rise of party caucuses in the 1840s, senators permanently took these powers away from the chair. By the end of the nineteenth century, the passive role of the presiding officer was firmly established.

Party-based leadership existed in the late nineteenth century, but it was leadership that senators assumed because of their ability and their activity, not because of their election to an official party position. In the 1890s, according to many observers, Nelson Aldrich (R–R.I.) and Arthur Pue Gorman (D–Md.) played major roles in setting their parties' agendas, shaping legislative strategies, and building coalitions, but neither was elected specifically to be his party's floor leader. Gorman served as Democratic caucus chairman, and Aldrich was a member of his party's steering committee. These were significant positions, but Gorman and Aldrich's stature as leaders initially existed independent of these offices. Apart from contributing to the creation of regular steering committees in the early 1890s, the two men exercised their leadership within preexisting institutions—though, through his aggressive leadership, Gorman transformed expectations for the role of Democratic caucus chairman. Their influence came not from structural innovation but from the sharpness of underlying party cleavages. The formal leadership positions were not decisively created until 1913–15, after Aldrich and Gorman had left the Senate.

Gorman left the Senate in 1899, one year after resigning the Democratic caucus chairmanship because of his opposition to the Spanish-American War. Since he, unlike Aldrich, had emerged as an active party manager while holding his caucus's chairmanship, Senate observers not only commented on the need for a new Democratic leader but also expected the new Democratic caucus chairman to fill that role. Newspapers devoted lengthy stories to Gorman's decision to resign as caucus chairman and to speculation about his successor. These stories, in 1898 and 1899, appear to represent the first news accounts in which the caucus chairman is described as the elected leader of one of the Senate parties.[2] As the *Washington Post* noted in 1899, "The Democrats recognized the leadership of Senator [James K.] Jones, of Arkansas, by making him their caucus chairman."[3]

Though not specifically identified as a floor leader, the Democratic caucus chairman after 1899 was regularly described as the "minority leader" of the Senate. Reflecting their new expectations, senators concerned about James K. Jones's abilities as minority leader called into question his competency as caucus chairman. "Senator J. K. Jones is expected to continue as chairman of the Democratic caucus, which carries with it official recognition as party leader," the *Baltimore Sun* reported in November 1901. "Toward the close of the last Congress considerable grumbling was heard within the ranks of the minority, and there was some talk of deposing Senator Jones and electing a new chairman of the Democratic caucus. A contest with this in view might have been begun but for the fact that those opposed to Senator Jones could not agree upon anyone whom they regarded as entitled to be his successor."[4] Gorman himself, who returned to the Senate and to the caucus chairmanship in 1903, was widely criticized for his inability to manage his party. And his immediate successors—Joseph Blackburn (D-Ky.), Charles Culberson (D-Tex.), and Hernando Money (D-Miss.)—were no better regarded.

By 1911, senators of both parties had come to expect effective management of their party's business. Although their leaders of the preceding decade had not met these evolving expectations, Democratic senators continued to regard the caucus chairman as their natural floor leader. Republicans, whose party leaders generally did not hold the caucus chairmanship, faced a serious succession crisis in 1911. Some Republicans, like the insurgent Senator Jonathan Dolliver (R–Ia.), hoped that the retirements of Aldrich and Eugene Hale (R–Me.) represented the end of disciplined party leadership. "When he was asked upon whom he thought the mantle of leadership would fall, he replied," according to the *Times*, " 'We are going to take it over to the Smithsonian Institution and keep it as a relic of an obsolete system.' "[5]

Party leadership and floor management were functions that senators could not discard so easily. With the transformation of the Democratic caucus chairman into the party's Senate leader, the old norm of uncontested elections for caucus chairman—long observed by both parties—had eroded in the Democratic caucus. The first open contest for Democratic leader occurred in 1911. When John Kern (D–Ind.) was elected Democratic caucus chairman in 1913, he was chosen by a divided caucus. "In the interest of party harmony," the incumbent caucus chairman, Thomas S. Martin (D–Va.), withdrew his name as a candidate for reelection, ensuring Kern's unanimous election.[6] Describing the election, the *New York Times* noted matter-of-factly that "this makes Mr. Kern the Democratic floor leader in the Senate."[7] Kern, the first Democratic leader since 1895 to preside over a majority party, was the first Senate leader consistently referred to as "majority leader."[8]

Republicans could no longer ignore the Democratic example. Jacob Gallinger (R–N.H.), elected caucus chairman in 1913, was described not only as Republican caucus chairman but also as the party's "floor leader."[9] And the practice continued after Gallinger's death. "Senator Henry Cabot Lodge of Massachusetts today was elected chairman of the republican conference of the Senate without opposition," the *Washington Star* reported in 1918. "This means that Senator Lodge is the republican leader of the Senate."[10] By 1921, when the *Times* reported that Lodge had been "re-elected floor leader," the designation was firmly established.[11] Through the mid-1940s— when Republicans formally created the separate positions of conference chairman and floor leader—their conference chairman assumed full responsibility for floor leadership.[12]

In the nineteenth century, the Republican and Democratic caucuses had elected only chairmen and secretaries.[13] Democrats created a new office, the whip, in May 1913.[14] The suggestion to establish the whip was made in the midst of a caucus meeting, as Democrats expressed their concern about the number of members who were planning to travel out of town. "Realizing how slender is their majority the democrats were practically unanimous in the demand that no chances be taken," the *Star* reported, and they quickly embraced the plan to choose a party whip "when plans were discussed for keeping members in line and getting them to the Senate when important votes were to be taken."[15] The Republicans established the position of whip in December 1915, at the start of the 64th Congress (Oleszek 1971: 959).[16]

Explaining Institutional Change

A variety of explanations have been offered for the emergence of formal party leadership in the Senate long after formal party leadership posts were established in the House. One possibility is that the Senate parties managed to find effective leaders, such as Aldrich and Gorman, without creating formal positions. The relatively small size of Senate parties may have made this possible. Moreover, given the Senate's rules, it is not clear what advantage would be gained in either party by creating floor leaders with little power. In addition, scholars have speculated and sometimes made empirical claims about the effects of senatorial careerism, party competition, interparty polarization, legislative workload, presidential intervention, and the influx of new and additional members.

Given the complex interactions that are likely to exist among these variables and the small number of Congresses, evaluating the independent influence of each factor on the emergence of the organizational features of Senate parties is difficult. In an earlier study, we analyzed the effects of these various factors on party structures (Gamm and Smith 2002). We found corroborating evidence only for party competition. Several major developments in Senate party organization and leadership occurred when the parties were nearly equal in strength and control over outcomes was most in doubt (Gamm and Smith 2002). The other factors, including the degree of polarization, were not timed closely with party innovations.

In this previous study, we postulated that senators turn to party-based solutions to solve acute collective action problems, except for those problems (like simple scheduling issues) that affect nearly all senators in similar ways. At times, the strategies may entail changes in party rules, organization, or leadership. At other times, a change in the choices made by an incumbent party leader is all that is required. Of course, a majority party may seek

changes in chamber rules to improve its circumstances, but a Senate majority party's ability to manipulate the rules is limited by inherited rules—
above all, the absence of a general rule limiting debate. And given the constitutional requirement that the vice president, rather than an agent
responsive to members, serve as the Senate's presiding officer, senators cannot look to the chamber's presumptive leader to solve problems. Therefore,
we contend, senators come to rely on party structures—and innovate accordingly when problems are especially severe. Over time, Senate parties
may build a capacity for collective action that enables central leaders to adjust to new problems by tactical changes of their own.

The difficulty of changing chamber rules in response to evolving collective action problems distinguishes the Senate from the House. As recent literature has emphasized (Binder 1997; Binder and Smith 1997; Dion 1997),
House majorities have frequently modified their chamber's rules to address
procedural and organizational problems. In the House, a minority disadvan-
taged by the change is unable to block the change. But Senate minorities,
particularly minority parties, can block the adoption of new rules by filibustering. Even the threat of a filibuster by a small minority can stall a rules
change because of the inconvenience and disruption that might result. One
consequence of this difference between the chambers is evident in the length
of their standing rules: the rules of the House are more than three times as
long as those of the Senate. Another consequence is that senators must seek
other ways to adjust to evolving collective action problems, such as modifying the practices of their party organizations.

We posit that senators have multiple goals (reelection, higher office, good
public policy, power, and so on) that generate three collective party goals—
building and maintaining a strong party reputation with the public, passing
or blocking legislation, and winning and maintaining majority party status.
Although we will not go into detail here about these party goals, we assume
that they are interdependent. A party's reputation influences its electoral
success, its electoral success influences its legislative success, and its legislative record influences its popularity. Interdependence of goals means that
parties will pursue all three goals even if one of the personal goals that un-
derpin them has little importance to rank-and-file senators. In fact, an even
stronger argument can be made: leaders will pursue all three party goals even
if rank-and-file senators are motivated exclusively by one of the personal
goals. Thus the priority given to any of the party goals by party leaders will
show less variability than variation in the importance or compatibility of individual goals suggests.

Although the goals are interdependent, the short-term tactics dictated by one party goal may be incompatible with the tactics dictated by the others. At a minimum, resources must be allocated among the efforts to achieve party goals. Making the necessary trade-offs—time spent on winning a legislative battle is time spent away from raising campaign funds, for example—is itself a collective action problem commonly assigned to party leaders. Even policy positions force important tactical decisions. A policy stance that is popular might have to be compromised in order to get legislation passed. This, too, is a trade-off among party goals that has collective consequences. It is precisely these trade-offs among collective goals, which go beyond the achievement of any single personal goal, that are uniquely the responsibility of parties and their leaders.

Interparty competition over elections, public policy, and power encourage collective efforts in the pursuit of party goals. As one party moves to coordinate collective action more effectively, competitive pressures are created for the other party to do so as well. Only at times when senators recognize that the benefits of collective action outweigh the costs they impose do innovations in party organization and leadership occur. As we demonstrated in this earlier study (Gamm and Smith 2002), the main periods of innovation—1875–79 (when party caucuses developed greater structure), 1892–93 (when permanent steering committees emerged), and 1913–15 (when both caucuses elected floor leaders)—coincided with fierce struggles for control of the Senate between evenly matched parties. Moreover, contemporary accounts of these three eras demonstrate that the new party institutions were created for electoral as much as internal legislative purposes.

Although we have chronicled and provided tentative explanations of the emergence of these new party positions, the effects of the emergence of formal party leadership is a subject that has gone untouched by political science. Did it matter that caucuses elected secretaries and chairs, developed steering committees, and created positions like floor leaders and whips? Or were the holders of these new formal positions invested with no greater authority than Clay, Webster, and Aldrich?

We approach the subject in four parts. First, we analyze the extent to which these new leadership positions centralized agenda-setting authority. Second, we establish that significant changes in floor management practices were associated with the new floor leadership positions. Third, we demonstrate that the innovations of floor leaders went beyond mere procedural innovations and extended to active participation in debate and amending activity. And fourth, we show that these changes occurred as floor leaders became public spokespersons for the Senate.

Agenda Setting

Perhaps the most important power of the modern floor leader is to coordinate and schedule the Senate's agenda. The floor leader grew out of the party caucus, and the caucus's chief function in the mid- and late nineteenth century—and the defining function of the caucus's steering committee—was to establish an "order of business." Nineteenth-century senators struggled to manage floor business without clear responsibility assigned to a floor leader. Majority party senators regularly found themselves in open competition with each other to get their legislation considered by the Senate, and misunderstandings about the agreed-on order of business were common (Gamm and Smith 2000). Filibusters became a regular parliamentary strategy (Binder and Smith 1997). Even the parliamentary status of unanimous consent agreements was unsettled. Until the rise of party leadership, the Senate's agenda was set by debate on the floor and by closed-door meetings of committee chairs.

Rothman (1966) contends that this era ended decisively with the rise of Aldrich, William Allison (R–Ia.), and Gorman in the 1890s. "The party caucus and its chieftains determined who would sit on which committees and looked after the business calendar in detail," Rothman writes. "Party leadership for the first time dominated the chamber's business, and the tactics of Allison, Aldrich, and Gorman were faithfully emulated by Lyndon Johnson" (4, 72). According to this account, the establishment of formal leadership positions in the 1910s—and the assumption of new formal powers by these leaders in the 1920s and 1930s—was an inconsequential aftermath of Aldrich's and Gorman's achievement in party discipline. Just as Lyndon Johnson (D–Tex.) set the Senate agenda in the 1950s, Aldrich set the agenda in the 1890s and 1900s.

To test that proposition, we examined the daily record of Senate business reported in the *Washington Post* at twenty-year intervals (1879–80, 1899–1900, 1919–20, and 1940–41). In all four Congresses, the *Post* regularly updated its readers on the Senate's agenda. The newspaper speculated about legislative priorities, the order of business, and possible strategies for bringing bills to a vote. Journalists interviewed senators and drew on sources, revealing how the agenda was set.

The stories for each of the four Congresses are internally consistent, and there was dramatic change over time. Of the four periods studied, 1919–20 was the first in which the agenda is noted to have been heavily influenced by individual senators—and these were the majority and minority leaders.

Table 11.1

Agenda Setters and Public Speakers, According
to Daily News Stories in the *Washington Post*

	Setting Senate Agenda	Meeting Regularly with President	Speaking Regularly to Press
1879–1880	No one	No one	No one
1899–1900	Republican Steering Committee	No one	No one
1919–1920	Henry Cabot Lodge (R, Mass.)		Lodge
	Gilbert Hitchcock (D, Nebr.)	Hitchcock	Hitchcock
	Oscar Underwood (D, Ala.)		Underwood
1940–1941	Alben Barkley (D, Ky.)	Barkley	Barkley
	Charles McNary (R, Ore.)		McNary
			Robert Taft (R, Ohio)
			Arthur Vandenberg (R, Mich.)

No one coordinated the 1879–80 agenda, and the 1899–1900 agenda was set, albeit loosely and amid conflict, by the Republican steering committee. Contrary to traditional understandings of Senate organization, Aldrich and Gorman did not resemble modern floor leaders in their ability to set legislative priorities. Aldrich's influence was not his alone. His influence was mediated by the steering committee, and the committee's authority was routinely challenged in ways that the authority of post-1913 floor leaders appears to have been rarely questioned. We summarize the results in the first column of Table 11.1.

Financial legislation dominated the business of the 1899–1900 session. Above all else, Republicans committed themselves to the passage of a gold standard bill. On this issue, Aldrich committed himself fully and adroitly. He was a masterful bill manager. Titling its story "Mr. Aldrich's Clever Move," the *Post* reported how Aldrich took advantage of a nearly empty Senate chamber to secure a "'unanimous' agreement" that the gold standard bill would be considered to the exclusion of all other business until it came to a vote eight days later. "The agreement was secured by Senator Aldrich yesterday afternoon," the *Post* stated, "when there were only eighteen Senators in the chamber, and when Senator Chandler, who is in charge of the Quay case; Senator Pettigrew, who is a persistent opponent of the administration's policy in the Philippines; and Senator Jones, the Democratic leader, were all absent." [17] That Aldrich acted in stealth, and behind James K. Jones's back, suggests that senators did not generally defer to Aldrich's leadership in setting an order of business.

Indeed, Aldrich's influence—and interest—in setting the Senate's agenda appears to have been generally restricted to financial bills. As chairman of the Finance Committee in an era when monetary and tariff issues were constantly under discussion, Aldrich was well positioned to shape important debates. But there, it appears, his main influence ended. Even as the Senate entered the final days of consideration of the gold standard bill, the *Post* reported that the chamber's remaining order of business remained unsettled. "After that measure is disposed of there will be a contest for precedence in the interest of several measures. These include the bills for providing forms of government for Hawaii and Porto Rico, the Nicaragua canal bill, and the resolution for the seating of Senator Quay. Which of these will take precedence remains to be determined. Just now there is some sharp sparring for first place." [18]

In 1899–1900, the "sparring" took place directly among bill sponsors and bill managers. The *Washington Post*, which thoroughly covered Aldrich's management of the gold standard bill, makes it clear that no individual senator coordinated the chamber's agenda. The *Post* described the chaos: "As soon as the Senate had disposed of the financial bill yesterday, Senator Cullom and Senator Chandler sought recognition, the former to press the Hawaiian bill and the latter to suggest consideration of the Quay case." [19] We have found the same general pattern in a review of typical weeks of Senate floor action reported in the *Congressional Record* (Gamm and Smith 2002).

To the extent that any senators coordinated legislative priorities in 1899–1900, that work was done by the Republican steering committee. The Republican caucus had appointed steering committees on an ad hoc basis for decades, but it had begun naming regular steering committees in the early 1890s (Gamm and Smith 2002). Meeting in February 1900, the Republican caucus was riven by conflict, with advocates for each bill arguing for precedence. "To preserve harmony in the Republican ranks," Allison, the caucus chairman, agreed to name a steering committee to sort out these competing claims. [20] Chairing the committee himself, Allison named eight other senators to the committee, including Aldrich. [21] But the steering committee was an imperfect coordination mechanism. Two weeks after it had been named, the Republican steering committee had reached no agreement "on any subject" except an adjournment date. [22]

Still, an imperfect solution to the collective action problem was better than no solution at all. No party leader and no regular steering committee existed in 1879–80. Consequently, the agenda in that session was in constant dispute on the Senate floor. Even a decision to set an adjournment date for the Christmas recess was an occasion for rambunctious discussion and decision making. "The question of the adoption of the House concurrent resolution to adjourn on the 19th inst. was the cause of quite a lively commotion in the Senate yesterday, as it developed considerable opposition, principally led by Senator Maxey, of Texas, who desired to have the resolution referred to the Committee on Appropriations," the *Washington Post* reported in December 1879. "It, however, was finally adopted by a decided vote."[23] A month later, describing Senate proceedings, a journalist for the *Post* contended that the chamber seemed incapable of setting priorities. "The proceedings are insipid and monotonous, because fully one-half the Senate's time is devoted to investigating claims," according to this writer. "It seems absurd that the legislature of a great nation should have to consider such petty matters, while questions of supreme importance to the people, as a whole, are postponed from week to week from want of time to consider them."[24]

It appears that only in the 1910s, with the creation of modern floor leadership, did senators establish a reliable institution for agenda setting. In both 1919–20 and 1940–41, as Table 11.1 shows, the Senate's majority and minority leaders assumed responsibility for the Senate's agenda. Henry Cabot Lodge (R-Mass.), majority leader in 1919–20, regularly announced the upcoming order of business, schedules for votes, and dates for adjournment and recess—and other senators generally deferred to Lodge on these issues. Frequently, Lodge coordinated his decisions with Gilbert Hitchcock (D-Nebr.), acting minority leader from November 1919 until April 1920, and Oscar Underwood (D-Ala.), who was elected minority leader in April 1920. Thus in February 1920, when Lodge agreed to a brief postponement of the debate over the Treaty of Versailles, he simultaneously demonstrated the substantial powers that he enjoyed as a majority leader and the respect that he accorded the minority leader. "I understood yesterday that the senator from Nebraska (Mr. Hitchcock) was not to be here today and I assented therefore to the senator from South Dakota (Mr. Sterling) taking up his bill (civil service retirement bill). I also, so far as I have the power, gave consent to taking up the dye-stuffs bill tomorrow," Lodge stated. "I now give notice that I shall call up the treaty on Thursday and shall ask the Senate to continue to consider it until a final disposition is made of it."[25]

Twenty years later, Alben Barkley (D-Ky.) and Charles McNary (R-Ore.) similarly cooperated in setting the Senate's agenda. In March 1940, when another Democrat tried to overrule Barkley's motion to call the Senate into session the next day, the *Washington Post* described the challenge as "an almost unprecedented move."[26] That July, in the days following the Democratic National Convention, the *Post* reported that "Democratic Leader Barkley of Kentucky and Republican Leader McNary of Oregon had a 'gentlemen's agreement' that no important legislation would be acted upon this week." Apparently, the Senate's business could now be stopped because "McNary, candidate for Vice President, has scores of personal details to handle while Barkley, along with many other Democrats, needs a few days to recuperate from the Chicago convention."[27]

The evidence from 1919–20 and 1940–41 suggests that the creation of formal leadership positions was a necessary precondition for establishing coordinated supervision of the Senate's agenda: Lodge and Barkley lived in very different worlds from Aldrich. The Senate had moved, first, from agenda setting by competition among bill managers to greater coordination by a majority party committee and then, finally, to the modern form of supervision by designated floor leaders.

Floor Management

Not only did floor leaders possess a newfound capacity for setting the agenda, but they also played an innovative role in the day-to-day management of the floor. Conventional accounts of parliamentary procedure in the Senate suggest that there has been little change since early in the nineteenth century. But these accounts have not been tested against the evidence: remarkably, there is no systematic review of floor practices in the literature. Our analysis of the *Congressional Record* suggests that the rise of floor leaders in the early twentieth century spawned a series of innovative procedural mechanisms to manage the Senate floor.

Until 1913, responsibility for floor management remained diffused. Not only was the position of majority leader not present, but the modern practices essential to floor leaders—unanimous consent agreements (UCAs) and the right of first recognition for the majority leader—were still unknown. Today, the right to be recognized gives the majority leader an opportunity to call up a bill or propose a UCA; a UCA provides an enforceable means to limit debate and amendments.

By 1913, UCAs had been used for several decades. Agreements that provided for a vote on a bill and pending amendments at a certain time were a regular part of floor management practice at the turn of the twentieth century. Yet the modern use and parliamentary status of UCAs was not established until the 1910s. Until then, responsibility for negotiating UCAs

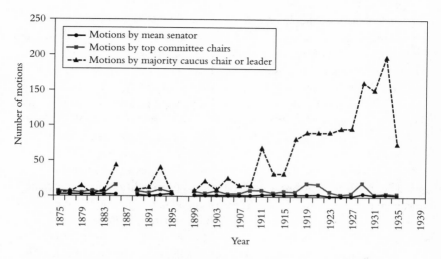

Figure 11.1.   Number of motions to close daily sessions, 1875–1939.

SOURCE: *Congressional Record* index.

NOTE: The majority whip performed most routine floor duties in the 72nd Congress (1931–33). The number of motions offered by the whip are included for that Congress.

rested with bill managers—typically, committee chairmen. Without a central leader, orchestrating agreements and managing several bills proved awkward and consumed considerable time on the floor. Moreover, UCAs were not enforced by the Senate's presiding officer and, strangely enough, could not be modified, even by unanimous consent. These circumstances limited the use of UCAs as devices for expediting the business of the chamber (Gamm and Smith 2000).

The functionality of UCAs improved greatly with the adoption of new provisions to Rule 12 in 1914, shortly after John Kern (D-Ind.) became the first majority leader. The new rule made UCAs orders of the Senate and therefore enforceable by the presiding officer, and it clarified that they could be modified by unanimous consent. The event precipitating the rules change occurred in the previous year, before the Democrats assumed majority control of the Senate and Kern became majority leader, but the solution was designed under Kern.[28]

Some crude indicators of the floor activities of floor leaders can be fashioned from the index to the *Congressional Record*.[29] In Figure 11.1, we report frequencies for motions to close daily sessions offered by senators.[30] Before 1913, these routine motions were offered by numerous senators over the

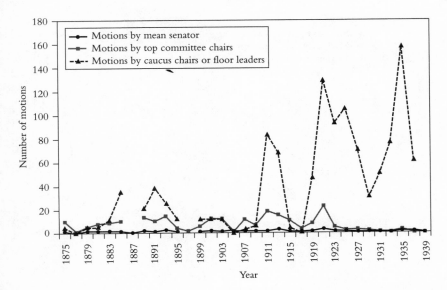

Figure 11.2. Mean number of motions to enter executive session, 1875–1939.

SOURCE: *Congressional Record* index.
NOTE: The majority whip performed most routine floor duties in the 72nd Congress (1931–33). The number of motions offered by the whip are included for that Congress.

course of a Congress, often by a senator managing a pending bill (usually a committee chairman) or by a senator who was simply tired and ready to go home. The few caucus chairmen in the nineteenth and early twentieth centuries who often offered motions to adjourn generally did so in their capacity as committee chairmen and bill managers. This changed in 1913 as the majority leader assumed responsibility for making most motions to adjourn or recess. As we show in Figure 11.2, motions on executive sessions, where treaties and nominations are considered, also shifted from the committee chairmen, who were managing specific bills, to the floor leaders. After the mid-1920s, when Charles Curtis (R-Kans.) became majority leader, committee chairmen no longer offered these motions with any frequency.

Other innovations became feasible once senators assigned floor leaders the task of finding solutions to collective action problems associated with floor activity. For example, as Figure 11.3 shows, from the 1910s onward, the Senate began the practice of frequently recessing at the end of daily sessions instead of adjourning. A recess kept the same legislative day in place,

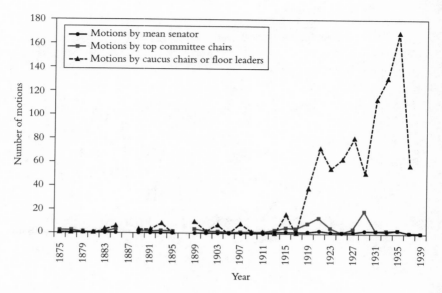

Figure 11.3. Mean number of motions to recess, 1875–1939.

SOURCE: *Congressional Record* index.

NOTE: The majority whip performed most routine floor duties in the 72nd Congress (1931–33). The number of motions offered by the whip are included for that Congress.

sidestepped obstructionist moves that might be used during morning hours, and set aside routine morning business. It became common in the 1920s and 1930s, under Curtis and Joseph Robinson (D-Ark.), to recess while a major bill was pending.

In 1879–80, at a time when caucus chairmen were not regarded as party leaders, William Wallace (D-Pa.), the Democratic caucus chairman, was invisible as a bill manager; similarly, no senator routinely assumed responsibility for opposing bills. Bill management remained entirely in the hands of committee chairmen and bill sponsors in 1899–1900. (Allison, the Republican caucus chairman, managed one bill in his capacity as chairman of the Appropriations Committee.) But the impact of even a minor formal change was evident in the frequency with which Jones led the opposition to an array of bills; elected soon after Gorman's resignation, Jones was the first Democratic caucus chairman to be called "minority leader" upon his election, and he appears to have modeled his behavior accordingly.

With the full establishment of the majority and minority leader positions in the 1910s, patterns of bill management and opposition continued to evolve. Lodge and Hitchcock led opposing forces on three major bills in 1919–20, though they probably did so in their capacities as the chairman and ranking minority member of the Foreign Relations Committee. Given the extent to which the Treaty of Versailles crowded out most other business, it is difficult to separate their roles as party leaders and committee leaders in this session. But behavior had changed decisively by 1940–41, when Barkley helped manage most of the major bills that came before the Senate and McNary was consistently visible in opposition. By the 1930s, the daily floor agenda had become the joint responsibility of the floor leaders and bill managers, with floor leaders exercising greater influence.

Notably, floor leaders gradually gave up committee chairmanships as their floor burdens increased. Before 1913, caucus chairmen kept old committee chairmanships and actively sought new chairmanships during their tenure. George Edmunds (R–Vt.) served as chairman of the Judiciary Committee throughout his tenure as Republican caucus chairman in 1885–91. John Sherman (R–Ohio), who in 1885 angrily announced his intention to resign his seat on the Finance Committee, was motivated in part by his failure to secure the committee chairmanship.[31] Sherman did serve as chairman of both the Republican caucus and the Foreign Relations Committee in the 1890s. Shelby Cullom (R–Ill.), in 1911–13, and Lodge, in 1919–24, also held the two positions. Thomas S. Martin (D–Va.) kept his chairmanship of the Appropriations Committee in 1917–19, when he served as Democratic leader. Curtis, who served as Republican leader and chairman of the Rules Committee in 1924–29, was the last party leader to serve simultaneously as chairman of a major committee.[32] James Watson (R–Ind.), who in 1929 succeeded Curtis as Republican leader, resigned his chairmanship of the Interstate Commerce Committee when he assumed his new post.[33] And Robinson declined to assume the chairmanship of the Rules Committee in 1933, citing his responsibilities as majority leader.[34]

Procedural innovation on the floor accompanied the creation of the new leadership posts. Aldrich and Gorman had done their work quietly in the 1890s, taking senators aside for discussions on the floor, in committee rooms, and in cloakrooms. Gorman did not "manifest any strong qualities as a floor leader," the *New York Times* noted in his 1906 obituary. "His success was entirely in the skillful arrangement of deals."[35] Aldrich, too, did not actively manage the Senate floor, except when financial bills were under consideration. "He knows when to 'bluff,' when to bully, when to flatter and when to anger," the *Baltimore Sun* observed in 1901. "The man who is lacking in alertness he bluffs, the timid man he bullies, the vain man he flatters and the man whose judgment is overturned when angry he torments and taunts until he loses his temper and is put at fault."[36] As Thompson (1906: 32) argued five years later, "Aldrich is a chess player with men." In principle, the innovations of modern floor management could have occurred without elected floor leaders. But in each case—in the use of enforceable but changeable UCAs, in the motions to adjourn daily sessions and enter executive sessions, in the routine use of recesses, in vigorous bill management and opposition, and in the clear separation between the powers of the floor leader and the prerogatives of committee chairmen—change came through the work of proactive floor leaders in the first decades of the twentieth century.

In one important way—in the sponsorship of complex UCAs that limit debate or amendments—modern floor management responsibilities devolved to floor leaders more slowly.[37] UCAs were far less common in the first half of the twentieth century than they were in the second half (Smith and Flathman 1989). Until Robinson became the Democratic majority leader in the 1930s, the vast majority of UCAs were offered by bill managers, who tended to be either committee chairmen or bill sponsors. There is little evidence that caucus chairmen or floor leaders played any role in coordinating UCAs before the 1930s, though it is possible that they occasionally intervened behind the scenes. Robinson, however, transformed the UCA into a powerful tool for the majority leader, becoming the first leader who routinely negotiated agreements to speed Senate action on legislation. Majority leaders after Robinson have adhered to this practice. Also under Robinson, the Senate established the precedent that the majority leader is recognized first when more than one senator seeks recognition, which, among other things, has guaranteed the majority leader an opportunity to make a motion to proceed or propound a UCA, both of which are central to the modern leader's ability to manage floor activity.

Floor Participation

Having examined the role of floor leaders in setting agendas and managing the floor, we now consider their involvement in the substance of floor debates and policymaking. As before, we compare the roles of floor leaders after 1913 with the activities of caucus chairmen in earlier years. We analyze two facets of leaders' involvement—their participation in floor debate and amending activity.

In Figure 11.4, we report the mean number of pages of floor remarks indexed in the *Congressional Record* for four groups: the caucus chairmen (and floor leaders), the whips, the chairmen of the top committees, and all sena-

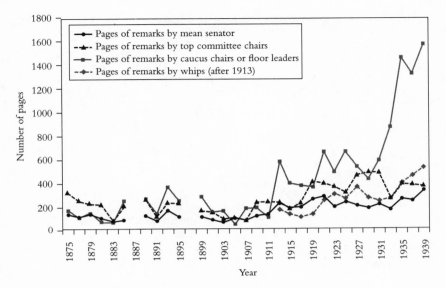

Figure 11.4. Mean number of entries for floor remarks recorded in the *Congressional Record* index, 1875–1939.

SOURCE: *Congressional Record* index.

tors. Simple motions unaccompanied by debate were not indexed as remarks. Before 1913, caucus chairmen were not distinctive in their frequency of floor speeches. Their participation in floor debate was typical of the chairmen of major committees. After 1913, floor leaders became more active in making floor remarks. For each Congress, we ranked all senators by number of pages, shown in Figure 11.5 (the higher the number, the higher the senator's ranking). Majority leaders are especially conspicuous. From 1913 onward, majority leaders were consistently ranked at or near the top of the Senate, while some minority leaders were not so active.

During the late nineteenth century, caucus chairmen did not usually speak as representatives of their parties when speaking in the Senate. In the 47th Congress (1883–84), for example, Henry Anthony (R–R.I.) addressed twenty-seven policy or legislative subjects, and nineteen of them related directly to his duties as a member of the committees on Printing, the Navy, and Revolutionary Claims. The Senate did not lack talkative members—Preston Plumb (R–Kans.), George Edmunds, George Hoar (R–Mass.), and others frequently addressed subjects beyond the jurisdictions of their committees. Edmunds may be the best example. While serving as Republican

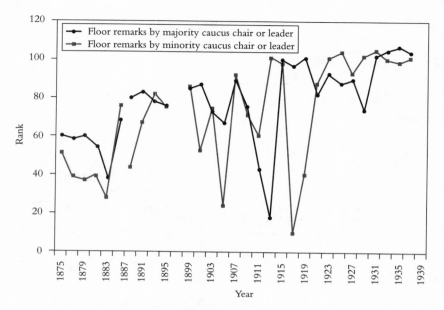

Figure 11.5.   Rank of party leaders in pages of floor remarks, 1875–1939.

SOURCE: *Congressional Record* index.

NOTE: Because of deaths and resignations, the number of senators serving over a two-year period is at least as great as the number (currently one hundred) in a full Senate.

caucus chairman in 1885–91, he was one of the most active senators in floor debate but was never (so far as we could determine) referred to as the Republican leader during debates.

In contrast, Curtis, McNary, and Robinson were regularly at or near the top of the list of senators most active on the floor. Their colleagues regularly referred to them as the party leaders and directed questions to them as the leading spokesmen for their parties on the floor. They addressed nearly every major measure debated on the floor and often offered commentary on the day's events, much like leaders at the end of the twentieth century.

Amending activity after 1913 does not show the sharp break that we see in floor remarks. As Figure 11.6 shows, Republican floor leader Jacob Gallinger (R-N.H.) was very active in the 1910s, but Kern and Lodge were more passive leaders and no more likely to offer amendments than important committee chairmen. Curtis was quite active on the floor but chose to offer few amendments, while McNary and Robinson were very active in offering amendments in the 1930s.

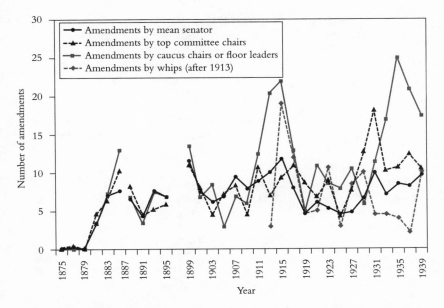

Figure 11.6. Mean number of measures to which amendments were offered, 1875–1939.

SOURCE: *Congressional Record* index.

Table 11.2 offers a summary perspective on leadership activism before and after 1913. The table shows estimates of the effects of party leadership, chairing a major committee, and majority party status on frequency of floor remarks and amendments. The estimates for the 1877–1913 period indicate that leaders were only slightly more active in speechmaking than other senators, controlling for committee chairmanships and party status, and were no more active in amending activity. During the 1913–41 period, however, leaders were much more active in speechmaking and significantly more active in amending activity.

The record of floor activity supports the view that the creation of floor leadership posts generated new behavior by the leaders that went beyond mere procedural participation. The new floor leaders assumed a strategic role in policymaking as well. The change was not instant—Kern was not an aggressive leader by modern standards, and Lodge proved active for only a short while. But even Kern and Lodge were dramatically more active on the floor than the preceding caucus chairmen, including Gorman. Curtis became the first floor leader engaged in full-time, personal management

Table 11.2

Relationship Between Formal Positions and Indicators
of Floor Activity, 1875–1913 and 1913–1941

| | DEPENDENT VARIABLES | | | |
| | *Number of Index Entries for Floor Remarks* | | *Number of Measures to Which Amendments were Offered* | |
	1877–1913	1913–1941	1879–1913	1913–1941
Constant	90.9	199.9	6.86	5.98
Leader	53.0	486.1	.30	6.11
	(20.1)	(45.0)	(1.16)	(1.24)
Top committee chair	70.1	124.2	−.34	2.49
	(13.3)	(26.0)	(.77)	(.72)
Party status	54.6	17.7	−2.73	2.95
	(9.6)	(13.1)	(.55)	(.36)
R^2	.05	.09	.02	.07

SOURCE: *Congressional Record* Index.

of floor activity. And McNary and Robinson extended the role to wide-ranging participation in debate and amending activity.

Public Spokesmanship

The establishment of formal floor leaders transformed not only the Senate's internal workings but its public face as well. Today, as Sinclair (1989b) observes, the majority and minority leaders speak for the Senate: "During 1985, Majority Leader Robert Dole appeared [on] or was mentioned 125 times by the three network news programs. Coverage of Dole was of an order of magnitude greater than that of the next most frequently mentioned senator. Dole was also the senator most frequently mentioned in stories in the New York *Times*" (189). The floor leader's public responsibility does not end with Sunday morning news shows and newspaper profiles. More than any other members of the Senate, the majority and minority leaders tend to represent the Senate in negotiations with the president and with House leaders.

This public role did not exist before the development of the formal positions. As Table 11.1 suggests, no senator regularly spoke to the press or consulted with the president in either 1879–80 or 1899–1900. This was not a routine job of caucus chairmen in the nineteenth century. In 1879–80, we found no references to meetings between any senator and President Rutherford B. Hayes, and we found only sparse, scattered accounts of public remarks by senators. In 1899–1900, the *Washington Post* quoted senators with greater frequency. During the debate over the gold standard bill, for example, the *Post* reported regularly on the strategies of Aldrich, the bill manager, and Jones, the leader of the opposition. "The Democrats will not agree to fixing a time for a vote until there has been ample debate," the *Post* stated in December 1899.

> Senator Jones, of Arkansas, said yesterday that the final vote would not be taken until the Democrats had had a full opportunity to present their views. "It would be useless," he said, "to attempt to prevent a vote, for this is but the beginning of a session which will last two years, but we propose to show that the Republican party has deluded the voters of this country with a promise of bimetallism which was never intended to be kept."[38]

Although the *Post* reported comments like these by Jones, the newly recognized "minority leader," and by bill managers and various other senators, there was no obvious pattern to the senators being quoted. Many senators, it appears, freely spoke to the press in 1899–1900, but none was especially distinctive as a Senate spokesman. The *Post* reported just one senatorial meeting with President William McKinley that year, a discussion between the president and Henry Cabot Lodge (the fourth-ranking Republican on the Foreign Relations Committee) about "civil government in Porto Rico."[39]

Patterns of spokesmanship seem to have changed dramatically with the creation of formal leadership positions. While many senators spoke to journalists in 1919–20, Lodge, Hitchcock, and Underwood were distinctive in the frequency of their remarks and in the clear presumption that they were speaking on behalf of the entire Senate—in Lodge's case—or at least on behalf of its majority or minority party. In addition to his remarks, Hitchcock, as acting minority leader in the Senate debate over the Treaty of Versailles, consulted regularly with President Woodrow Wilson. "The chances for ratification of the peace treaty dwindled again yesterday when it became known that President Wilson remains firm in his stand against effective reservations," the *Washington Post* reported, in one typical account, in February 1920. "The President's attitude has been communicated to Senator Hitchcock, the administration leader, and the latter made it known in response to inquiries yesterday evening." [40]

President Franklin Roosevelt met with the Democratic leaders of the House and Senate on a regular basis. Before delivering his State of the Union Address in January 1940, Roosevelt met with Barkley, the Senate majority leader, as well as the vice president, the Speaker of the House, and the House majority leader. After the meeting, Barkley talked with reporters about the upcoming legislative session. [41] In March, the president suggested the need for raising new taxes. According to the *Post*, "Senate Democratic leader Barkley revealed that Mr. Roosevelt brought the subject up at his regular legislative conference." [42] Three months later, Barkley announced plans to accelerate passage of defense legislation "after a visit to the White House." [43] Both Barkley and McNary, the minority leader, spoke regularly to reporters throughout the 1940–41 session. The floor leader's responsibility as party spokesman was now well established and widely recognized.

Concluding Observations

Between 1890 and 1940, the modern institutions of Senate leadership were invented. In this chapter, we set out to determine whether these inventions of the Senate parties had any "first order" effects on the operation of the Senate and the behavior of formal party leaders. We found substantial evidence of such effects. The incumbents of the new party posts took the lead in supervising the Senate's agenda, managed floor activity (including the construction of unanimous consent agreements to limit debate and amendments), became active participants in floor debates, and served as spokesmen for their parties on the floor and in the press. The leaders made a difference in the way the Senate conducted its business and in the way the Senate and its parties were treated in the press. We conclude with three observations.

First, we have not attempted to examine the "second order" effects of party leaders on the electoral success of the parties or on policy outcomes, although the Senate may seem to be a natural laboratory for such an investigation. With few changes in the formal rules, relatively stable membership, and the creation of leadership posts relatively late in its history, the connection between the basic collective action problems of congressional parties and leadership solutions to them would seem to be researchable. Unfortunately, a number of other developments of potentially great consequence— direct election of senators, the adoption of Rule 22, and so on—are roughly timed with the creation of formal floor leadership positions and greatly complicate an evaluation of leadership effects. Indeed, the altered incentives of popular election and the challenges of cloture may have contributed to the need for party leaders and influenced the strategies of leaders and followers.

Second, the data presented here provide a basis for optimism about the behavioral study of Senate leadership. Though more work remains to be done, we have successfully exploited the official record and contemporary press accounts to generate systematic comparisons of leaders on matters of significance. In doing so, we have been able to move beyond the secondary accounts, such as biographies, which themselves provide only a weak basis for characterizing leaders' behavior. Our behavioral measures have allowed us to provide circumstantial evidence that leadership posts made a difference.

Finally, we have demonstrated that party leadership is an integral and significant part of the development of the Senate. We have emphasized the dynamic character of Senate procedure and practice. The Senate has not been static. Instead, critical features of the modern Senate—supervision of the agenda, bill management, the use of UCAs, and leader recognition—evolved in important ways as the modern Senate emerged in the 1920s and 1930s. Rather than a minor chapter in that process, party leadership was a central feature of it.

Part III

Policy Choice and Congressional Institutions

Chapter 12

Why Congress? What the Failure
of the Confederation Congress and the Survival
of the Federal Congress Tell Us About
the New Institutionalism

JOHN H. ALDRICH, CALVIN C. JILLSON,

AND RICK K. WILSON

During 1783, Representatives to the Confederation Congress considered, neither for the first nor the last time, two significant issues. One was the fiscal plan submitted by Superintendent of Finance Robert Morris. Led on the floor by Reps. James Wilson (Pa.) and Alexander Hamilton (N.Y.), Morris's plan had been introduced in 1781 and had been subject to sporadic floor debate since, and there it remained all the while under threat of his resignation. On March 20, fiscal moderates led by Rep. James Madison (Va.) defected from the Morris coalition, defeating key provisions of the plan by a vote of 4 states aye, 7 nay, 1 divided, 1 abstain. While a more moderate measure proposed by Madison eventually passed the Confederation Congress, it included a provision that required approval by each state government before it would go into effect—a provision that all knew doomed the measure (Ferguson 1961).

The second issue, which occupied most of October, involved selecting a location for a new capital, preferably a permanent site, but failing that at least a temporary location. Between October 6 and 8 alone, fifteen roll call votes were taken, with votes on October 6 rejecting sites in seven states (in the order voted down, Rhode Island, New York, New Jersey, Pennsylvania, Delaware, Maryland, and Virginia—that is to say, all of the centrally located and therefore feasible states). Over the next two weeks, another eighteen roll call votes were taken, considering (sometimes several times) a variety of potential sites, including the banks of the Potomac. Also considered were dual capitals, rotating the honor for six months each year.

The inability of the Confederation Congress to resolve these two issues effectively meant that the Congress and its enabling Articles of Confederation would not long survive. Following its demise, the 1st Congress under the new Constitution took up these two matters again. For a considerable portion of that 1st Congress, Hamilton, Madison, and eleven others who were in Congress both in 1783 and in 1790, revisited their struggle over these issues, sometimes in identical form.

On January 9, 1790, Hamilton responded to the Congress' request and submitted the first of his Reports on the Public Credit. In contrast to the Confederation Congress, the new Congress at first readily agreed to provisions for the funding of the federal debt. The most contentious question involved federal assumption of state debt, and the outcome resembled the chaos seven years earlier. On March 8, the House endorsed assumption 31–26 on an unrecorded vote in the Committee of the Whole. This statement of principle was reversed on April 12, however, when Madison, after many earlier amendments had been defeated, finally succeeded in defeating this key aspect of Hamilton's plan by an unrecorded (but scholarly reconstructed) vote of 29–31, also in the Committee of the Whole.

The prognosis for the siting resolution also looked grim in 1790. Following much discussion but inconclusive action, Sen. Robert Morris (Pa.) proposed temporarily locating the new capital in Philadelphia, a move many believed would actually be final. His coalition lost 11–13, however, when Sen. Gunn (Ga.), Sen. Paterson (N.J.), and both North Carolina senators defected from their previous support. With the Senate now delaying action, Rep. FitzSimmons (Pa.) introduced Morris's motion in the House, and on May 31, the motion passed, 38–22. On June 8, the Senate again voted 11–13, defeating the House resolution. Finally, on June 11, the House voted 31–28 to replace Philadelphia with Baltimore. The bill thus amended passed the House easily, in large part because all understood that the Senate would never accept Baltimore and the House's "decision" was tantamount to a stalemate.

Thus as summer approached, both assumption and residency were blocked. This must have aroused concern that the new Congress (and its enabling Constitution) might fail, just as certainly, and over the same issues, as the earlier Congress and the Articles of Confederation had. But a scant two months later, both issues were resolved after Jefferson, Madison, and Hamilton struck a deal (which may or may not have been executed) over dinner at Jefferson's lodgings. Madison's defeat of assumption was reversed, and

Hamilton's plan was enacted in a form nearly identical to the one he had proposed—and in a form quite similar to what Morris had proposed nine years earlier. In August 1790, the new government also agreed to siting the capital temporarily in Philadelphia, awaiting construction of a permanent residence on the banks of the Potomac. Thus not only were these policies adopted, but unlike so many resolutions in the old order, they were settled once and for all.

Our purpose in this chapter is to demonstrate one central lesson of the new institutionalism. In spite of similar actors, preferences, and alternatives, different rules are sufficient to yield different outcomes. Our specific purposes are, first, to document the claim that "rules matter" as precisely as we can with available circumstances and data. Our second purpose is to demonstrate that the (sometimes formally, sometimes informally) derived properties of the rules explain why these different rules led to the different outcomes observed. Our third and final goal is to argue that these different combinations of rules led not just to adoption of most of Hamilton's plan and to the siting of the capital in Washington, D.C., but they also played an integral role in the failure of one attempt and the success of a second attempt at ensuring the success of the "Great Experiment in republican democracy." We view the events of the 1783 and 1790 as providing vivid documentation of the value of the new institutionalism. Rarely do we find historical circumstances that exhibit such clear commonality in people, preferences, and policy choices with such stark differences in institutions and outcomes. Even more rarely are we able to do so in circumstances where the stakes were— and were understood to be—so high.

Institutional Analysis and Design

Our theoretical analysis is derived from the rational choice branch of the "new institutionalism." Its central syllogism is that political outcomes are the consequence of the behavior of actors seeking to realize their preferences; the rules, laws, and procedures that govern the actions open to those actors; and the historical context in which the choice is set. In our cases, the actors, their goals, and the historical context were nearly identical in 1783 and 1790. Indeed, precisely because the Confederation Congress was unable to resolve these critical issues, the status quo of 1790 was quite like that of 1783. Therefore, or so we argue, the difference in outcomes between 1783 and 1790 must be due, at least primarily, to the different rules.

The logic of our hypothesis—that the differing outcomes can be traced to the different rules—would require that the actors, choices, and preferences be *exactly* the same. Obviously, none of those is "exactly" the same. There were, to be sure, many of the same actors involved in both cases (sometimes in a different office, and sometimes in the same one). Hamilton did use Morris's plan as the basis (and sometimes the actual wording) of his own plan, and the geographic possibilities for siting were, of course, the same, but we could hardly maintain that either the set of actors or the set of choices they faced were identical. As a result, all aspects undoubtedly differed in some degree, but the greatest differences were the rules, and we will demonstrate that the rules should be expected to have the consequences we argue they did. It therefore follows as a reasonable claim—but hardly as an empirical certainty—that the different outcomes were due largely to the different rules.

THREE RULES CONSIDERED

The literature of the new institutionalism offers a wide variety of specific results from which we can draw and a method for reasoning about particular rules not yet covered by formal derivations. In our case, the Articles and Constitution differed on three rules that proved critical. First, voting in the Confederation Congress was by state—what we call the "unit rule." Each representative announced his vote orally, in order, but the state vote was cast according to how a majority of its representatives voted.[1] By contrast, members of the Federal Congress voted as individuals.

Second, in the Federal Congress, legislation required a simple majority of the votes cast to pass. Under the Articles, "important" legislation, including all revenue bills, needed an extraordinary majority of nine positive votes to pass. Other legislation required at least seven positive votes. In our case, the revenue bills required the nine-vote extraordinary majority, while most of the siting votes required only seven. Yet even this seven-vote requirement was greater than a simple majority for those (individuals) present and voting in an institution prone to absenteeism (Jillson and Wilson 1994). Consequently, this seven-vote majority was effectively a supermajority rule, and the nine-vote majority for important bills often verged on unanimity.

Third, one of the long-term weaknesses of the Confederation Congress was its very limited ability to take action. In the case of Morris's plan, this point was made quite clearly. The plan as eventually adopted explicitly stated that each of the thirteen state legislatures would have to approve of this legislation and vote to supply its share of the funding before the plan would go into effect. Not only was there a pure unanimity requirement, but it required action after congressional passage. The Confederation Congress's vote was therefore not final. By contrast, no such constraint bound the first Federal Congress.

Thus the three key provisions for comparing the Confederation Congress and the Federal Congress are unit voting versus individual voting, supermajority versus simple majority voting, and provisional versus final legislating. Of what consequence are these features of the rules for understanding our political outcomes? The new institutionalist answer begins by considering equilibrium.

EQUILIBRIUM

The key question in the new institutionalism revolves around the existence and nature of equilibrium. An outcome is called an equilibrium outcome if, should it ever become the status quo, it remains the status quo. We cannot judge empirically whether a status quo policy *could* not be replaced, of course, but we can observe that it *was* not replaced, often (as in these cases) after many attempts. The inability of the Confederation Congress to pass legislation implies its inability to change the status quo, suggesting that the then current status quo was an equilibrium outcome.

The Federal Congress was able to pass legislation, often relatively quickly, implying that under *its* rules, the status quo ante was *not* an equilibrium. In particular, the outcomes of no residence for the capital and no (effective) fiscal plan were revealed to be in equilibrium in the Confederation Congress by virtue of their not being replaced despite extensive efforts to try to do so. Those same outcomes were replaced in the first Federal Congress by many of the same people pursuing the same goals. Thus no site and no fiscal plan were revealed *not* to be equilibrium outcomes under the rules of the 1st Congress.

SUPERMAJORITY VERSUS SIMPLE MAJORITY RULE

We begin with this rule because there are applicable formal results to consider. The study of voting by simple majority rule is dominated by questions flowing from Arrow's theorem. Generally, if preferences are unidimensional, an equilibrium exists (at the median voter, due to Black's theorem). Unless preferences of the actors are arrayed (or in principal arrayable) as single-peaked in *one* dimension, there is generally no equilibrium at all. But as Schofield (1985; Schofield, Grofman, and Feld 1988) has shown, as the size of the needed majority increases from a simple majority toward unanimity, the chances of an equilibrium existing increase. Indeed, at unanimity, an equilibrium is certain for preferences arrayed over any number of dimensions. Hence supermajority voting rules under the Articles would be expected to yield equilibria under a wider array of circumstances, while (except in unidimensional cases) we would expect equilibrium to be rare under pure, simple majority voting as in the Federal Congress—precisely the general pattern we observe.[2]

It is crucial to note that the supermajority results imply the existence of equilibria far more commonly than under simple majority. These results also demonstrate that the range of alternatives that are equilibria (should they ever be the status quo) is increasingly large and diverse. At unanimity, for example, every voter (here, every state delegation) can veto any change, so that only those outcomes that are disfavored by every state to some *specific* alternative are *not* in equilibrium. For example, all might have agreed that some capital was better than none, but if there was no one particular location that (nearly) every state preferred to wherever the Congress then sat, then that status quo would remain in effect and be an equilibrium outcome. Thus the formal result is that the chances of any equilibrium existing grows from virtually zero in multidimensional simple majority rule circumstances to certainty at unanimity. At the same time, the set of alternatives that are equilibria becomes increasingly large and more diverse.

STATE UNIT VOTING VERSUS INDIVIDUAL VOTING

When issues are hotly contested and divisions are expected to be close, every individual voter becomes important, because convincing only one or a few to change their minds can change the outcome. Every vote counts, in ordinary parlance, because every voter is pivotal, in technical parlance. In the Federal Congress, for example, the logroll over finance and siting involved Madison and Jefferson convincing only two (another account says four) Representatives to change their vote. Hamilton, for his part, may not have even needed to get *anyone* to change sides. In some versions, he only had to keep the Massachusetts senators from proposing "killer" amendments (Bowling 1971). By contrast, a voter in the Confederation Congress was a state. To change a single unit vote may therefore have required changing a number of individuals' votes.

Certainly it is possible for a single individual to be pivotal in the unit vote system.[3] It is equally clear, however, that close votes among individual voters are much more amenable to compromise and bargaining than when the voters are states. A standard method of demonstrating this claim theoretically would require complex calculations, typically based on ad hoc and unrealistic assumptions. The alternative, which we follow, is to apply the reasoning to the particulars of the cases.

FINALITY AND COMMITMENT

The third institutional change we consider is the finality of the vote result in determining the policy outcome. When the Federal Congress voted, the policy became the law of the land if passed by both chambers and signed by the president. This was true for the revenue bills under consideration and for the siting bills (the back-and-forth on siting was due to difficulties in getting the same bill through both chambers). When the Confederation Congress passed Morris's plan, it was not yet law and would not be so until adopted by every state legislature. This lack of finality makes bargaining and compromise much more difficult. While specific votes could be traded, any decisions based on preferences over actual outcomes could not be agreed to, because members could not deliver on their promises, no matter how much they might want to. The Congress itself could not deliver.

The absence of credible commitment was *the* problem of the Confederation Congress, and it is therefore even more evident that no individual could credibly commit, whether because his commitment might not change his state's vote or because he could not deliver on outcomes that the body in which he served could not credibly promise to deliver. Almost without a doubt, the modified version of Morris's plan eventually passed with full knowledge among members that passage was merely symbolic. They were almost certainly aware that at least one state (probably more) would fail to pass the plan and it would never be implemented. And it was not.

Next we develop the context of the two Congresses, the institutional forms that were similar, and the three rules that sharply differentiated the two. We examine the empirics of the relevant people, their preferences, leadership, and issues, all of which are similar. We then consider the impact of three of the rules that did change: the unit rule versus individual voting, supermajority compared to simple majority, and provisional instead of final commitment.

Institutional Structure and the Early Congresses

THE CONTINENTAL CONGRESSES

The Continental and succeeding Confederation Congresses were the national government between 1774 and 1789. The First Continental Congress, which met in the fall of 1774, was called to discuss concerns that the colonies had with England over changes in policies regarding trade and colonial autonomy. With no thought of American independence yet in the air, the delegates adopted a minimal set of rules that highlighted the parliamentary rights of individual delegates and the equality of the colonies. However, the crisis steadily deepened, leading first to increasingly strained relations, the Declaration of Independence, seven years of military conflict, and American independence.

From 1774 through 1781, the Congress had no explicit constitutional powers or limitations. Early in the First Continental Congress, John Rutledge was recorded by John Adams as observing that "we have no legal authority; and obedience to our determinations will only follow the reasonableness, the apparent utility and necessity of the measures we adopt. We have no coercive or legislative authority. Our constituents are bound only in honor to observe our determinations" (September 6, 1774; Burnett, 1921: 1:14). Nonetheless, as the crisis deepened and military conflict ensued, the Congress discovered that it could do anything it wanted, as long as things could be paid for with the paper money it printed. But by 1779, the paper money had lost all value (it was "not worth a Continental"). From then on, the Congress could ask for anything, but it could command nothing.

In the meantime, because it was a discussion body without formal authority, the Congress evolved a set of rules and norms that highlighted the principles of state sovereignty, equality of the sovereign states, universalism, open and extended discussion, and the search for consensus. Within the Congress, each colony, irrespective of its size or wealth, had a single vote. The president of the Congress had no power to appoint committees, to assign work to them, or to establish any form of an agenda. He was charged merely to manage debate on the floor and to ensure the equal treatment of all delegates.

The floor rules ensured that delegates had equal rights to speak on the floor, bills came up for floor consideration in the order that they were reported to the secretary, any amendment to any bill could be offered by any member (i.e., there was no germaneness rule), and the decisions made by Congress effectively took the form of recommendations to the states. Such rules created an open agenda, and these rules and norms remained in force throughout the history of the Congress.

THE ARTICLES OF CONFEDERATION

Only months before Cornwallis surrendered to Washington at Yorktown, Maryland approved the Articles of Confederation. They went into effect on March 1, 1781, and they made policymaking in the Congress more difficult on several key dimensions.

Article 2 declared that "each State retains its sovereignty, freedom, and independence, and every power, jurisdiction, and right, which is not by this confederation expressly delegated to the United States, in Congress assembled." Critically, the power to tax, which is the foundation for doing virtually anything else, was withheld from the Congress. As a result, even after the Articles took effect, the Congress could request that the states take action, but it could not order them to do so. This Article therefore guaranteed a lack of finality or commitment on the part of the Congress.

Delegates to the Confederation Congress recognized that adoption of the Articles did nothing to strengthen the hand of the Congress in relation to the states. Just one month after the Articles went into effect, delegates noted that "the United States have not vested Congress, or any Body, with the Power of calling out effectually the Resources of each state. The articles of Confederation gave only the Power of Apportioning. Compliance in the respective states is generally slow, and in many instances does not take place" (James Varnum to the governor of Rhode Island, William Greene, April 2, 1781; Burnett, 1921: 6:41). Soon James Madison was advising Thomas Jefferson of "the necessity of arming the Congress with coercive powers arises from the shameful deficiency of some of the States which are most capable of yielding their apportioned supplies" (April 16, 1781; Burnett, 1921: 6:59).

While the initial debates were taking place in the Congress over draft articles of confederation during the summer of 1776, John Adams wrote to his wife, Abigail, to observe that "if a confederation should take place, one great question is how shall we vote. Whether each colony shall count one? Or whether each shall have a weight in proportion to its number, or wealth, or exports, and imports, or a compound ratio of all?" (July 29, 1776; Burnett, 1921: 2:29). Less than a year later, Adams was providing his correspondents with specific examples of the ill effects, from his perspective, of voting by states in Congress. In describing a particular 5–5 tie vote, Adams said, "Here is an example of the inconvenience and injustice of voting by States. Nine gentlemen, representing about eight hundred thousand people, against eighteen gentlemen representing a million and a half nearly, determined this point" (John Adams to James Warren, February 12, 1777; Burnett, 1921: 2:246). Despite long-standing concerns with voting rules in Continental Congress, Article 5 retained voting by states in the Confederation Congress.

Article 5 further declared that "delegates shall be annually appointed, in such manner as the legislature of each State shall direct. . . . Each State shall maintain its own delegates" and recall ". . . its delegates, or any of them, at any time within the year, and to send others in their stead for the remainder of the year." Moreover, even though attendance was always a problem in the

Congress, the Articles declared that "no States shall be represented in Congress by less than two . . . members; and no person shall be capable of being a delegate for more than three years in any term of six years."

Article 9 declared that a seven-state majority was required to pass normal legislation, while a supermajority of nine states was needed to pass legislation in critical categories that included revenue and spending, military and foreign policy, and commercial regulation. As attendance lagged through the mid- and late 1780s, seven positive votes became increasingly difficult to gather, and nine-vote majorities became almost impossible without bargaining for every state vote and often for every individual vote. These legislative decision rules made the Continental Congress approximate a "unit veto" institution or, effectively, one that was governed by unanimity.

Delegates frequently complained that low attendance made it exceedingly difficult to create the majorities required by the Articles to do business in the Confederation Congress. "The small Representation for sometime past, of seven states, had occasioned a considerable delay in Business of Consequence as nothing could be done without unanimous consent" (Ezra L'Hommedieu to New York Governor George Clinton, September 26, 1781; Burnett, 1921: 6:228), and ". . . It is a rule observed since the Confederation was completed, that seven states are requisite in every question, and there are seldom more than 7, 8, 9, or 10 states present, even the opinion of a Majority of Congress is a very different thing than a constitutional vote" (James Madison to Thomas Jefferson, November 18, 1781; Burnett, 1921: 6:264–65). The nine-vote requirement made life that much more difficult: ". . . A ninth state appeared today, but eight of the nine being represented by two delegates each, all important questions will require not only an unanimity of states, but of members, for which we have no reason to hope" (Thomas Jefferson to Edmund Pendleton, March 2–4, 1784; Burnett, 1921: 7:458).

THE FIRST FEDERAL CONGRESS

In some important respects, the internal environment of the first Federal Congress was strikingly similar to that of the Continental Congresses. The Speaker, like the president of the Continental Congress, was merely a presiding officer; the committee system continued to be predominantly ad hoc (although see Cooper 1970); and floor rules still tended to ensure that members were treated equally. Although the Speaker was permitted to appoint committees of three members or less, those with more than three members were elected from the floor as they had been in the Continental Congress. These rules provided only a little more structure than the rules of the Continental Congress. Therefore, one close student of the period has described the first House as "a leaderless herd. . . . During the first session of April–September 1789, in a nearly free flow of legislative individualism, members had agreed or disagreed as issues came and went" (Chambers 1963: 38). His description, while not unique, is near the extreme of most unstructured conduct. Others (e.g., Aldrich and Grant 1993) find more order and structure in the conduct of the House but attribute it more to ideology and coalition politics than to formal institutional designs.

However, there were also important institutional differences. The new Congress was sovereign within the areas of its constitutional authority. The Federal Congress had full and definitive power to decide matters of taxation, commerce, foreign policy, and other substantive issues without reference to the states. Voting was by individual members rather than by state delegations. And a simple majority (50 percent plus 1) of a simple majority quorum could resolve most substantive issues. These differences, as we shall soon see, played a key role in resolving the issues of siting of the federal capital and of a fiscal policy for the United States.

Analysis of Roll Calls

Our focus here is on the voting behavior of members of the Continental and Federal Congresses. Recorded votes were routinely taken in the Continental Congress beginning in 1777. Whenever a recorded vote was requested and seconded, it was recorded, by delegate, in the *Journals of the Continental Congress*. A simple majority vote within the state delegation decided how that state's vote was cast. Votes in the Federal Congress were recorded in the *Journal of the House*.

REPRESENTATION OF MEMBERS' PREFERENCES

Here we shall demonstrate the similarity of actors' preferences in 1783 and 1790 through use of a well-known multidimensional scaling (MDS) technique. MDS is used to recover estimated proximities of individuals based on their votes and to produce a spatial map describing how delegates voted with respect to one another. Those closest in proximity voted together most frequently, while those farthest apart voted together least frequently across the full range of issues. MDS begins with an input matrix of pairwise values across individuals. In our analysis, we use a simple measure of agreement—the percentage of times each member voted in the same manner as another member.[4] A measure of "stress" is used to gauge the number of dimensions needed to represent the data. In these data, two dimensions are sufficient to

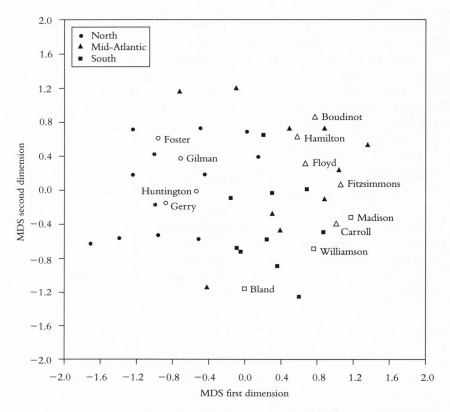

Figure 12.1. Voting preferences among members of the Confederation Congress, 1783.

NOTES: The North consists of New Hampshire, Massachusetts, Connecticut, and Rhode Island; the Mid-Atlantic states are New York, New Jersey, Pennsylvania, Delaware, and Maryland; the South is Virginia, North Carolina, South Carolina, and Georgia. Names identify individuals who served in both the 1783 Confederation Congress and the 1790 Federal Congress.

provide a very good fit (see Jillson and Wilson 1994: app. 1). This finding is consistent with that observed by Poole and Rosenthal (1997) using a different technique and in later Congresses.

Our analysis focuses on a two-dimensional representation of votes over time. The MDS estimates yield a picture of the alignment of delegates in 1783 and 1790. First, consider the map generated from 1783 (see Figure 12.1). In the figure, we identify the regional affiliation of every member and identify by name the members who served in both 1783 and 1790. The year 1783 marked the high point of nationalist influence and cohesion in the Continental Congress (Ferguson 1969). The nationalists from the Mid-Atlantic states and the upper South cluster in the upper right quadrant of the preference space. In the lower right quadrant is a small group of state advocates, mostly from the lower South. The left side of the figure is taken up by a diffuse set of New England delegates who, together with isolated supporters from New Jersey, New York, and South Carolina, stood firm in opposition to the New York, Pennsylvania, and Chesapeake nationalists.

The nationalist alliance, drawing strong support from members of the New York, Pennsylvania, Delaware, Maryland, Virginia, and North Carolina delegations, had a distinctly regional division within it. The northern wing was anchored by Alexander Hamilton of New York and James Wilson of Pennsylvania. The southern wing was anchored by Virginia's James Madison, with steady support from North Carolina's Hugh Williamson and Maryland's Daniel Carroll. The nationalist surge of 1781–83 attracted a number of moderates, men like James Duane, William Floyd, and Elias Boudinot, president of the Congress during 1783, to the nationalist program. Although these moderates would occasionally drift away, the real strength of the nationalist alliance was in its northern core, while its critical weakness was in its southern wing. Madison and Williamson sometimes had difficulty carrying their own delegations, and most of the lower South was deeply suspicious of Hamilton, Wilson, and the commercial elites of New York and Philadelphia.

Figure 12.2 shows the recovered positions of representatives from the House in 1790. The general distribution of members across the preference map for 1790 is remarkably similar to that for 1783. Again, regional clustering is evident in that the New England delegates are distributed across the left half of the space, the delegates from the Mid-Atlantic states are distributed through the upper right quadrant, and the delegates from the lower South are distributed through the lower right quadrant. Moreover, eight of the ten delegates who attended and voted frequently enough in both 1783 and 1790 to appear on both maps occupy very similar positions. This implies that the distribution of preferences in the two Congresses, in terms of both broad regional differences and the particular positions of individual members within their regions, was remarkably stable.

While the overall image is one of similarity between 1783 and 1790, there are a few differences. There were, for example, somewhat fewer members located in the middle, in between the regional groupings in 1790. The two who were in both Congresses and are estimated to have moved the most

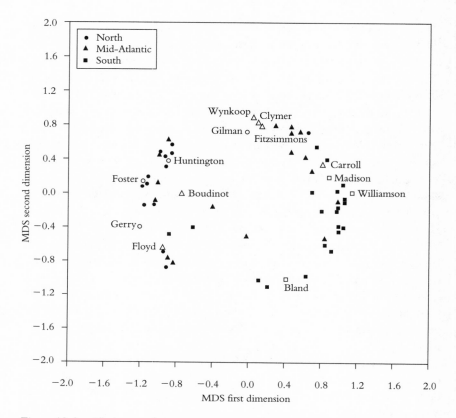

Figure 12.2. Voting preferences among members of the Federal Congress, 1790.

NOTES: The North consists of New Hampshire, Massachusetts, Connecticut, and Rhode Island; the Mid-Atlantic states are New York, New Jersey, Pennsylvania, Delaware, and Maryland; the South is Virginia, North Carolina, South Carolina, and Georgia. Names identify individuals who served in both the 1783 Confederation Congress and the 1790 Federal Congress.

are Floyd and Boudinot. They were moderates who apparently were swept up in the nationalist surge, aligning more closely with Hamilton and then reverting to their more normal positions near New Englanders by 1790.

We have shown to this point that the two Congresses faced nearly identical issues; many of the same people were involved in both Congresses and played similar leadership roles; and as we just saw, the mapping of voting-determined preferences was quite similar, with both cases yielding a two-dimensional solution with broadly similar locations of members' ideal points in those spaces. The mapping from 1783 is typical of those of the Continental Congresses in general (see Henderson 1974; Jillson and Wilson 1994). The mapping of 1790 is similar to those obtained by others and that of the 2nd Congress (see Hoadley 1986; Aldrich 1995).

VOTES

We turn now to consider the individual votes in the two Congresses on the two issues. Each vote may be located in the preference space as a vector based on regressing votes on the ideal point location of members in the two-dimensional MDS space. Each vector's origin is at the center of the space (centroid, or mean of the distribution of ideal points), and each points in the direction determined by those who voted aye. That is, the vector points in the direction that is predicted by the regression to be most likely to vote aye. Note, however, that direction is less important than the full line passing through the space, from highest likelihood of voting aye to lowest. Thus if a set of votes is determined by the same coalitions, the vectors of votes will fall on or near the same line through the space. If coalitions shift substantially, however, the vectors will go off in different directions. In the former case, the voting coalitions are more nearly unidimensional; in the later case, they are multidimensional. Thus in the former case, the median voter and related results would apply (barring sophisticated strategies), while in the multidimensional case, the results that yield the lack of equilibrium (such as the chaotic results under simple majority voting; see McKelvey 1976; Schofield 1985) would apply.

Figures 12.3 and 12.4 report the results of the votes on the financial plans for 1783 and 1790, respectively. Even if one were to reflect V942 in Figure 12.3 to run in the opposite direction (as one may freely do), the angle between the votes would cover nearly the full 90-degree range, indicating that the set of votes cover the full two-dimensional space. V957, the last vote in the series, runs almost directly through Madison's position, indicating just how successful he was in modifying (and effectively gutting) Morris's plan. The vote vectors for 1790 in Figure 12.4 show equally full dispersion and also indicate a full two-dimensional makeup of the voting coalitions. V90 is the reconstructed vote in the Committee of the Whole that defeated assumption. The vector points toward the Southern grouping, well away from the northeast quadrant, where Hamilton's support is located. The (presumably agreed-on) reversal of that defeat is visually apparent in the figure, as the vector points toward the New England and Mid-Atlantic Representative grouping, the core of Hamilton's support.

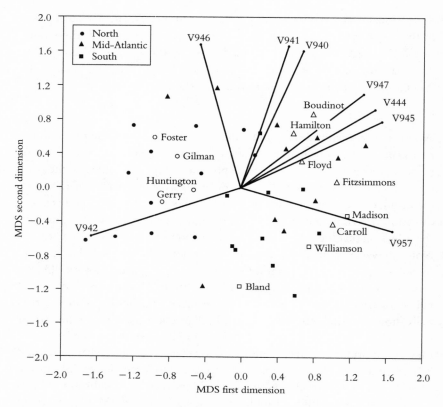

Figure 12.3. Votes on the financial plan, 1783.

NOTES: The North consists of New Hampshire, Massachusetts, Connecticut, and Rhode Island; the Mid-Atlantic states are New York, New Jersey, Pennsylvania, Delaware, and Maryland; the South is Virginia, North Carolina, South Carolina, and Georgia. Names identify individuals who served in both the 1783 Confederation Congress and the 1790 Federal Congress.

Figures 12.5 and 12.6 display the vectors for the numerous votes in the two Congresses on the siting of the capital. The multidimensional nature of these two sets of votes is even clearer. The vote vectors almost literally point in every direction, reflecting the dramatic shifts in the coalitions supporting one option and then the next. While also true for the votes over the financial plans, a clearer demonstration of actual cycling over a wide variety of majority coalitions is hard to imagine. In both Congresses, the results were in fact just like those the theory predicts: anything can pass, anything can be

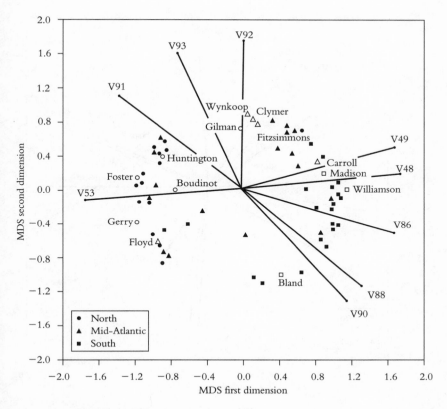

Figure 12.4. Votes on the financial plan, 1790.

NOTES: The North consists of New Hampshire, Massachusetts, Connecticut, and Rhode Island; the Mid-Atlantic states are New York, New Jersey, Pennsylvania, Delaware, and Maryland; the South is Virginia, North Carolina, South Carolina, and Georgia. Names identify individuals who served in both the 1783 Confederation Congress and the 1790 Federal Congress.

defeated, or in the cases of 1783 and 1790, before the vote-trading dinner, no alternative is ever actually and finally defeated.

Figure 12.7 displays a series of votes taken over another aspect of Hamilton's plan, his proposal to create a national bank. This proposal encountered plenty of opposition—indeed, some of the same opposition, led by Madison and others, as surfaced to assumption. Still, as Figure 12.7 illustrates, the vote vectors come extremely close to falling along a single line. Thus even with ideal points distributed over multiple dimensions, voting coalitions can

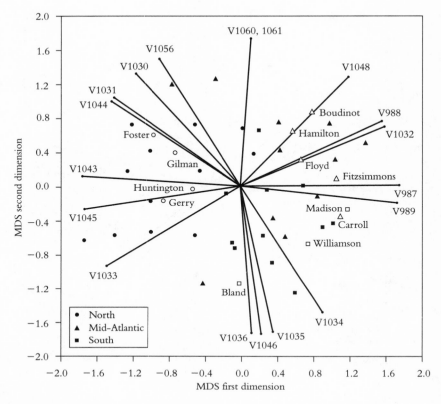

Figure 12.5. Votes on the siting of the U.S. capital, 1783.

NOTES: The North consists of New Hampshire, Massachusetts, Connecticut, and Rhode Island; the Mid-Atlantic states are New York, New Jersey, Pennsylvania, Delaware, and Maryland; the South is Virginia, North Carolina, South Carolina, and Georgia. Names identify individuals who served in both the 1783 Confederation Congress and the 1790 Federal Congress.

be reasonably fixed and unidimensional. Indeed, the smaller number of votes over the bank proposal also illustrates another expectation with a unidimensional basis of choice: fairly quick and certain resolution of the issue.

Analysis of the Rules

THE CONTINENTAL CONGRESS

We now turn to a more detailed analysis of the impact of the three rules. The members, of course, were well aware of the rules (as the quotations from the

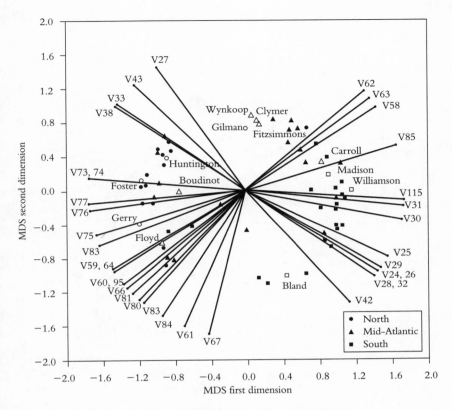

Figure 12.6. Votes on the siting of the U.S. capital, 1790.

NOTES: The North consists of New Hampshire, Massachusetts, Connecticut, and Rhode Island; the Mid-Atlantic states are New York, New Jersey, Pennsylvania, Delaware, and Maryland; the South is Virginia, North Carolina, South Carolina, and Georgia. Names identify individuals who served in both the 1783 Confederation Congress and the 1790 Federal Congress.

Confederation Congress illustrate). They may therefore well have conditioned their behavior in part on their expectations about the impact of the rules, and they might have behaved differently if the rules were different. Indeed, it was precisely the effects of the rules of the Confederation Congress that led its members to seek to change them—eventually into the rules of the Federal Congress.

Figures 12.8 and 12.9 report, along the vertical axis, the votes of individual members (these individual votes were recorded in the Confederation Congress, so the *y*-axis values are the actual votes as recorded for both Con-

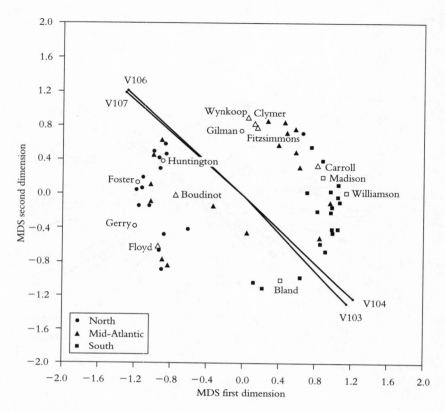

Figure 12.7. Votes on the Bank of the United States, 1790.

NOTES: The North consists of New Hampshire, Massachusetts, Connecticut, and Rhode Island; the Mid-Atlantic states are New York, New Jersey, Pennsylvania, Delaware, and Maryland; the South is Virginia, North Carolina, South Carolina, and Georgia. Names identify individuals who served in both the 1783 Confederation Congress and the 1790 Federal Congress.

gresses). The *x*-axes report the votes by state, using the rules as prescribed by the Articles of Confederation. In Figure 12.8, these are the actual and effective votes for 1783. In Figure 12.9 are the statewide votes that we constructed from applying the rules from the Articles (at least two representatives had to vote, and the state was recorded as voting however a simple majority of its delegation voted).[5] All votes throughout the 1st Congress (1789–91) are included in Figure 12.9. The diagonal line in each figure is estimated from regressing the individual on the unit vote percentages. Votes would fall on a 45-degree line from the origin if the individual representa-

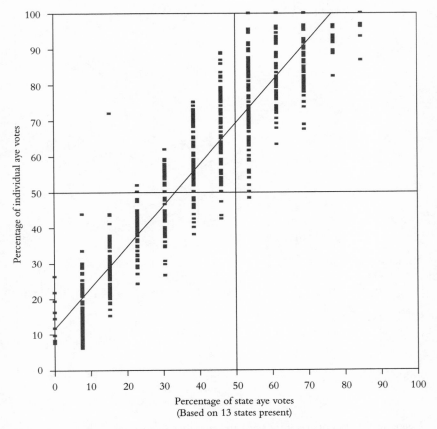

Figure 12.8. Comparison of state and member majorities, 1783.

tive and statewide unit vote were the same. They are not, as demonstrated by the fact that both regression lines have intercepts in the 10 to 20 percent range (i.e., even when 10 to 20 percent of individuals vote aye, no state is expected to vote aye).

Of most interest in the figures are points in the northwest quadrant. Votes in that quadrant are ones that received at least a simple majority of individual votes but less than a simple majority of unit votes. In other words, every such point represents a vote that would or actually did pass in the Federal Congress and would or did fail in the Confederation Congress (even if "only" seven aye votes were needed, instead of nine for major issues). There are a large number of such cases. In the Confederation Congress, nearly

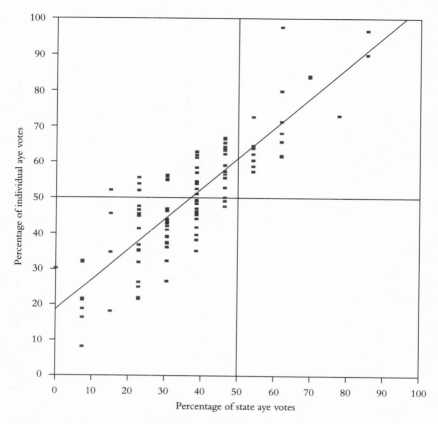

Figure 12.9. Comparison of state and member majorities, 1790.

three-quarters again (or 174 percent of the actual number) as many proposals would have passed under the federal rules as received seven votes in the
actual event. In the first Federal Congress, nearly two-thirds of the proposals that did pass in the House would have failed using the unit voting rule.
It does not follow by logical necessity that a proposal would receive a higher
percentage of individual than unit votes. In fact, there is but a single instance
in which a vote yielded less than a majority of individual votes but a majority of state votes. The consequence, therefore, is that, *ceteris paribus*, unit versus individual voting made a huge difference, with the unit voting rule defeating far more proposals.

This overall impact in the two Congresses affected the siting and fiscal issues as well. In 1783, twenty-five of the votes on siting would have been the

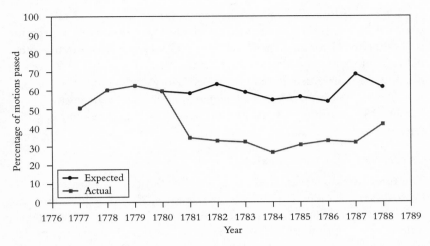

Figure 12.10. Actual and expected passage of legislation with adoption of the Articles of Confederation.

SOURCE: Jillson and Wilson (1994: fig. 5.1).

same under either rule (seventeen would have failed under either rule, and eight would have passed under both). Still, eight siting proposals had at least a simple majority of members who voted for them but failed (seven failed to get seven or more unit votes, and one that did get seven unit votes included a financial provision and therefore needed, and failed to receive, nine unit votes). Both the direct defeat of Morris's plan and the passage of Madison's moderate (and ineffective) alternative would have been the same under Federal congressional voting. The first failed 4 aye, 7 nay, 1 divided, 1 abstain, and the individual votes aggregating to that conclusion were 14 aye, 18 nay. Madison's alternative received 9 aye votes (and 1 nay, 1 divided, 1 not voting, 1 absent), with 25 members having voted aye, 4 nay. In between these two votes, however, three proposals failed to reach 7 aye votes (with 9 needed because these were fiscal proposals) but had a majority of delegates voting in their favor. In sum, we examined 41 votes on these two issues in 1783. One-quarter (11 of 41) that failed under unit voting would have passed under the rules of the new Congress.

It is apparent in Figure 12.8 that many more proposals received seven or eight than received nine votes in their favor. Thus if those were major proposals, they failed, even with a simple majority voting in their favor. The intention of this supermajority provision was to make it more difficult to pass "major" legislation. We cannot tell, of course, how many proposals, if any, were withdrawn before a vote was cast because supporters foresaw the inability to win at least nine votes. But Figure 12.10 suggests that of those that did make it to a recorded vote, the intention underlying Article 9 was satisfied. Before implementation of the supermajority rules under the Articles, two-thirds of all proposals passed, whereas after they went into effect in March 1781, nearly two-thirds still received a majority vote but only one-third passed with nine affirmative votes.

THE FEDERAL CONGRESS

The foregoing discussion made clear the difficulties that the rules of the Confederation Congress imposed on its members. The consequence was inaction and a turn to revision of the Articles that became the new Constitution. Siting and Morris's plan were central issues in this regard. The discussion also demonstrated that the rules of the new Congress enabled the House to pass considerably larger numbers of proposals. Upon reaching agreement with the Senate and receiving Washington's signature (the former of which was a new and sometimes crucial sticking point), a great number of the proposals that our data indicate passed through the House also became law. Here we look particularly at the issues of siting and Hamilton's plan and how the altered rules appear to have facilitated their passage in the summer and fall of 1790. We begin with a more detailed specification of the events surrounding the alleged vote trade.

In the two Congresses, there were many proposals for siting the capital. The final choice in 1790 came down to a temporary relocation to Philadelphia, which many worried would become permanent, versus an undeveloped site on the banks of the Potomac. Fiscal plans, both Morris's and Hamilton's (which was based heavily on the former's proposals from the early 1780s), contained a wide variety of choices. The key event in 1790, however, was Madison's ability to undermine federal assumption of state debt, at least in the House.

The dinner at Jefferson's in the summer of 1790, involving Hamilton, Jefferson, and Madison and at which a vote trade was proposed, was an attempt to resolve these two issues in particular. The agreed-on trade was that Madison (and Jefferson) would secure changes in votes on the assumption amendment in the House sufficient to remove it and allow assumption to proceed. If the trade were executed (and it is unclear that it was on either side), Maryland Representatives Daniel Carroll and George Gale and possibly Virginians Richard Bland Lee and Alexander White were to be convinced to switch their votes. These four did change their votes. Their reasons for doing so are unknown; their votes, however, changed the outcome. Their votes were pivotal under the rules of the Federal Congress, but they would not have been (*ceteris paribus*) under the rules of the Confederation Congress. In exchange for securing assumption (and as a result effectively securing adoption of his plan), Hamilton was to ensure that the capital would relocate temporarily to Philadelphia while a permanent home on the banks of the Potomac was prepared—or at least that is the most common understanding of the vote trade agreement. In this view, Hamilton may not have had to get anyone actually to change votes. He may have needed only to ensure, "perhaps through his Massachusetts supporters Fisher Ames and Theodore Sedgwick, who convinced the Massachusetts delegation not to interfere with the Philadelphia-Potomac residence bill" (Bowling 1971: 633), that no alternatives would be proposed to upset the agreement on location.

Cooke (1970) argues that although a trade was agreed (perhaps only over aspects of assumption), it was *not* consummated. He contends that there were numerous others involved in striking deals to change choices and that Hamilton held insufficient power over those who agreed with his views to implement a trade anyway. Instead, by Cooke's reconstruction, far too many deals were struck over these issues (typically separately, rather than as a package) to attribute the resulting resolution to Hamilton, Jefferson, and Madison. Whichever view is correct, it remains true that politicking occurred in ways unimaginable in the Congress under the Articles and that the key changes in votes reversed the results and resolved both issues in the House only under the Federal and not under the Confederation rules.

In Table 12.1, we report the results of five key votes, three on assumption and two on siting. The first vote, A1 in the table, is Bowling's reconstruction of the vote of April 12, 1790, in the Committee of the Whole that opposed federal assumption of state debt. This vote actually reversed an earlier one in the same committee (March 8) that had approved assumption. A1, therefore, is the vote that defeated assumption in the House. A2 was held on July 24, after the dinner at Jefferson's and after the Senate had adopted assumption. It defeated a proposal by James Jackson (Ga.) to reject the Senate bill. Gale, Carroll, White, and Lee all switched their position. A3 was the passage of assumption on July 26, marking what Jefferson declared to be the greatest ". . . of all the errors of my political life" (quoted in Cooke 1970: 545). S1, on June 11, is the vote on siting on which the House agreed to "strike out Philadelphia and insert Baltimore," noted earlier as the manner by which the House sent siting back to the Senate, knowing full well the upper chamber would object to Baltimore, as it had repeatedly in the past. Thus S1 reflects the decision of the House to leave the matter unresolved.

Table 12.1

Votes on Federal Assumption of State Debt
and Siting of the Federal Capital, 1790

	VOTES ON ASSUMPTION			VOTES ON SITING	
State	*A1 4/12*	*A2 7/24*	*A3 7/26*	*S1 6/11*	*S2 7/9*
Connecticut	5−0	0−5	5−0	0−5	0−5
Delaware	1−0	0−1	1−0	1−0	1−0
Georgia	0−3	3−0	0−3	2−1	3−0
Maryland	0−6	4−2	2−4	6−0	4−2
Massachusetts	8−0	0−8	8−0	0−8	0−8
New Hampshire	2−0	2−1	1−2	1−2	0−3
New Jersey	2−2	0−4	4−0	2−2	2−2
New York	3−3	3−3	3−3	0−6	0−6
North Carolina	0−3	5−0	0−5	3−1	5−0
Pennsylvania	3−4	4−3	3−4	7−0	7−0
South Carolina	4−1	1−4	5−0	1−4	1−3
Virginia	1−9	7−2	2−7	9−0	9−0
Total vote	29−31	29−32	34−28	32−29	32−29

	ROLL CALL VOTE				*Simple Majority Win*	*State Unit Rule Win*
Vote	*Yes*	*No*	*Divided*	*(Del.)*		
A1	5	5	2	(Yes)	No	No
A2	6	5	1	(No)	No	No
A3	5	6	1	(Yes)	Yes	No
S1	6	5	1	(Yes)	Yes	No
S2	5	5	1	(Yes)	Yes	No

S2, on July 9 (and after Jefferson's dinner), was the vote on passage of siting, putting it temporarily in Philadelphia but permanently on the banks of the Potomac (on land carved from Carroll and Lee's districts and about 10 miles north of George Washington's Mount Vernon).

The state-by-state reports are, of course, the actual votes cast by the representatives (as reconstructed by Bowling). Note that all five votes were relatively close. The bottom panels develop the results by applying the rules from the Confederation Congress.[6] Madison's strategizing on assumption would have succeeded under either rule (i.e., A1 was a defeat under either method). The same was true for A2, so that Jackson's attempt to reject the Senate bill would have been defeated under unit voting (assuming that all representatives would have voted as they did under simple majority individual voting). A3, however, passed under the actual rules but would have failed under unit voting on no better than a 6-to-6 tie. Even if New York had broken its tie in favor, assumption involved finances and under the Articles would have needed nine votes to pass. Thus assumption, and quite possibly Hamilton's plan, would have been defeated, just as Morris's plan was eight years earlier.

Both of the capital location votes passed in the House. Neither would have passed using the rules of the Confederation Congress. Of course, S1's failing meant that Philadelphia would not have been stricken and Baltimore substituted. Perhaps the Senate would have defeated a bill designating Philadelphia in June, as it did the actual bill for Baltimore. But then, the resolution that was adopted by the Senate in July, S2, would have failed in the House under unit voting, leaving the issue unresolved.

The key individuals in the Hamilton-Jefferson-Madison vote trade, if it were implemented, were Carroll and Gale of Maryland and Lee and White of Virginia. All four voted no on A1 and A2 and yes on A3, S1, and S2. They were therefore collectively pivotal on all five votes and thus on both issues. Had they voted aye on A1, it would have passed (if no one else changed his choice). They all voted nay on A2, thereby being pivotal in the defeat (*ceteris paribus*) of Jackson's proposal to reject the Senate bill with assumption included. They all voted yes on A3, once again providing the difference in votes between passage and failure. Of course, their switch in sentiment on assumption between A1 and the subsequent two votes and between S1 and S2 may have been due to Madison and Jefferson's prevailing on them or to other reasons. Whatever their reasoning, the crucial point is that they were pivotal in blocking assumption and siting and then pivotal in resolving them.

Under the statewide unit vote, these four representatives would have been pivotal on *none* of these votes. Had they voted differently (and had none of the remainder of their delegations changed any votes), Maryland and Virginia would have voted exactly the same. The central concern was assumption. All four voted with the majority of their state before the dinnertime talk of trade but afterward voted against all others in their state (and virtually the whole of the Southern delegation) on assumption. Thus they were pivotal and decisive as individuals, but they would have been ineffective as members of their state units, because their switch would not change either of their states' votes (and even if they did, they still would have fallen short of nine positive votes on A3).

Conclusion

The point of calling for the Annapolis Convention in 1786 was the widely shared belief that the rules of procedure specified in the Articles of Confederation rendered its Congress ineffective. Unit voting, the size of the required majority, and the finality of its decisions—the rules and procedures we have considered here—were precisely some of the central features that the delegates and others expressed frustration over, in virtually the same words that scholars of the new institutionalism might use today. In the end, it took change in each of the three rules—to individual voting, simple majority rule, and sovereignty (within the domain specified in the new Constitution and as amended by the Bill of Rights)—before the two central issues of the day were able to be resolved.

One final note is in order. Some observers believed that only minor revision of the Articles was necessary to make them effective, and indeed that was the charge to the delegates in the Constitutional Convention. Others— a majority of those delegates, it turned out—believed that a whole new and radically altered constitution was necessary. They believed that a confederation was infeasible and that a federal republic was required. The issue was what Aldrich (1995) calls the "Great Principle," the balance of power between the central government and the various states. Our findings indicate that federation was necessary or at least that confederation was insufficient.

Whether one trade was made among Hamilton, Jefferson, and Madison, as Bowling believes, or whether there were many, as Cooke would have it, no trade or set of trades would have been possible under the Articles. Under the Constitution, Carroll, Gale, White, and Lee were collectively decisive.[7] But there would have been no ability to make a trade if the states were sovereign, as they were under the Articles and would have been if the Articles had been revised only slightly. The federal government had to be effective and act with finality for the trade or trades to have been possible, and with no trades, there almost certainly would have been no effective fiscal plan adopted and perhaps no site for the capital would have been selected. The crisis of the Articles would therefore have continued into the 1790s and possibly the Great Experiment in representative democracy in an extended republic would have failed.[8]

Chapter 13

Agenda Manipulation, Strategic Voting, and Legislative Details in the Compromise of 1850

SEAN M. THERIAULT AND BARRY R. WEINGAST

Three crises threatened antebellum America, all intimately involving the expansion of slavery: the crisis over the admission of Missouri (1818–20), the crisis over the land gained in the War with Mexico (1846–50), and the crisis triggered by the Kansas–Nebraska Act (1854–61). Americans resolved the first two crises with what comparative political scientists call "pacts," agreements among contending elites to resolve mutual differences (Higley and Gunther 1992). The first two pacts became known as the Missouri Compromise and the Compromise of 1850, respectively. Americans failed to resolve the third crisis, and the result was the Civil War.

Historians widely regard the first pact as a success, ushering in sectional peace for much of a generation. Efforts to resolve the third crisis obviously failed. Historians give mixed reviews to the Compromise of 1850. Although this compromise ended a four-year state of crisis, for several reasons historians do not judge it a long-term success. Circumstantial evidence, for example, appears to weigh against this compromise's success: not only did the Civil War break out a decade later, but the next sectional crisis erupted only four years later. More important, factors internal to the crisis have led some historians to question whether the Compromise of 1850 settled anything. Potter (1976) argues that the 1850 pact is not rightly called a compromise but should instead be thought of as a "truce" or "armistice" between the sections. Regarding the compromise's several components, passed as separate bills, Potter argues the "armistice thesis":

Consistently, the preponderant strength of one section opposed the preponderant strength of the other; yet in each case the measure passed. . . .

These facts raise a question of whether the so-called Compromise of 1850 was really a compromise at all. If a compromise is an agreement between adversaries, by which each consents to certain terms desired by the other, and if the majority vote of a section is necessary to register the consent of that section, then it must be said that North and South did not consent to each other's terms, and that there was really no compromise—a truce perhaps, an armistice, certainly a settlement, but not a true compromise. Still, after four years of deadlock, any positive action seemed a great accomplishment. (113–14)

McPherson (1988: 71) states a similar conclusion: "The 'Compromise' that finally emerged was not really a compromise in which all parties conceded part of what they wanted. . . . The Compromise of 1850 undoubtedly averted a grave crisis. But hindsight makes clear that it only postponed the trauma." In short, these historians question the ultimate value and success of the Compromise of 1850.[1]

In this chapter, we take issue with the armistice thesis. This thesis and its underlying logic hinge in large part on a dramatic set of events at the center of the compromise's passage, including the central role of Henry Clay and Stephen A. Douglas in creating the compromise.

The conclusion reached in the armistice thesis rests on inferences about how the compromise was passed. Clay sought compromise along six dimensions, attempting a delicate balance of benefits to each section. His proposal included organizing the Utah and New Mexico territories, admitting California as a state, resolving the Texas boundary and debt issues, abolishing the slave trade in the District of Columbia while affirming the existence of slavery there, and improving the enforcement of the Fugitive Slave Law. Clay combined the first four components—Utah, New Mexico, California, and Texas—in an omnibus. By the end of July, Clay and many others thought he had succeeded. In a dramatic moment on July 31, however, Clay's omnibus unraveled. Exhausted, Clay left Washington in defeat. Stephen A. Douglas then assumed leadership of the compromise. By dividing Clay's omnibus into its components, Douglas steered the passage of the compromise as six separate bills.[2]

The logic underlying the armistice thesis hinges on the inference that Douglas could pass Clay's measures only by separating the omnibus into its components. The implication, often made explicit, is that the entire compromise could not command a majority. By inference, had the Senate faced the choice of approving the whole package, a majority would have voted against the complete compromise.

Proponents of the armistice thesis argue that the Compromise of 1850 did not resolve the underlying sectional tensions (Potter 1976: 120). As such, the compromise only delayed the inevitable. The unstated counterfactual in this argument appears to be that had the Compromise of 1850 been a true compromise, it would have done more than delay the Civil War; it would have forestalled it.

Because these arguments hinge on this critical set of congressional events, we focus on the question of why the effort by Clay failed but Douglas's leadership succeeded. This question lies at the intersection of congressional politics and the larger politics of fashioning compromise. We now turn to a range of possible answers to our central question, intimately involving congressional procedure, agenda control, strategic voting, and manipulation of the legislative content.

Historians provide three different explanations for Douglas's success following Clay's defeat. By far the most common is what we call the *procedural hypothesis* or *omnibus-unites-the-opposition hypothesis*:

> *Procedural hypothesis*: Clay failed because he sought to pass his measures as an omnibus. Instead of uniting the friends of compromise, the omnibus united its enemies, leading to defeat. Douglas succeeded because he broke the omnibus into its components and then passed each component as a separate bill.

The procedural hypothesis holds that the omnibus would not pass, in part because it contained too many controversial components. Extremists in both sections united against the omnibus, opposing any legislation containing benefits to the opposite section, even if this risked losing benefits for their own section. By separating the measures, Douglas divided the extremists. Although they continued to oppose measures benefiting the other section, many extremists supported Douglas's measures that exclusively gave benefits to their section.

One of the principal proponents of the omnibus-unites-the-opposition hypothesis was Douglas himself, who said in a letter on August 3, 1850, "I regret [the failure of the omnibus] very much, although I must say that I never had very strong hopes of its passage. By combining the measures into one Bill the Committee united the opponents of each measure instead of securing the friends of each" (quoted in Johannsen 1973: 294).[3]

A second hypothesis in the literature is the *abstention hypothesis*:

Abstention hypothesis: Clay failed because the omnibus could not pass. In order to pass the separate measures, Douglas and others persuaded sufficient opponents to abstain rather than vote against a measure benefiting the opposite section.

According to the abstention hypothesis, the omnibus would not pass. Douglas, perhaps with the help of President Millard Fillmore, used an intermediate strategy for passage. Instead of persuading opposing senators to vote for compromise, Douglas divided the measures and induced some of the opponents to abstain from particular measures so that the measures could pass. Consistent with this view, Hamilton (1964: 142) suggests that "nothing is more arresting than the enormous number of absentees" (see also McPherson 1988: 75).

A third hypothesis, perhaps the least developed in the literature, is at first glance an obvious one: Douglas's sequence of measures passed because they differed in substance from Clay's measures. We call this the *pivot misjudgment hypothesis*:

Pivot misjudgment hypothesis: Clay lost because the substance of his measures failed to attract the pivotal senator necessary for passage. Douglas succeeded not because he divided Clay's omnibus but because several of his bills differed substantively from Clay's.

According to this hypothesis, Clay failed to assess accurately the pivotal senator's views. His omnibus came close, but not close enough, to obtaining the pivotal senator's support. Douglas succeeded because he gained the pivot's support by adjusting the content of several measures, especially legislation dealing with the potentially explosive issue of the Texas boundary (Stegmaier 1996; Smith 1988) and with the fugitive slave law (Freehling 1990: 501). Holt (1978: 72–86) comes closest to articulating this hypothesis when he argues that Douglas and the Democrats sought to put their own stamp on the compromise so as to differentiate themselves from Clay and the Whigs. He concludes that "it is important to note that Clay's resolutions differed from the final Compromise in several significant respects." Further, "what began as a congressional Whig alternative to [President Zachary] Taylor's California plan was changed by the Democratic majority into a Democratic compromise" (82, 86).

Although the literature advances these three different explanations for why Clay failed but Douglas succeeded, it provides no means for adjudicating among them.

We evaluate the three hypotheses theoretically and empirically. The analysis supports the misjudgment hypothesis. Our theoretical results show the existence of a true compromise. Clay failed to reach this, not because he used the omnibus, but because his legislative provisions failed, if but barely, to attract the support of a majority. The key to Douglas's success was that he adjusted the details of several of the bills to attract the support of more senators. We also show that although there are circumstances under which the procedural hypothesis would be true, these circumstances did not hold for the 1850 Senate.

Our perspective also shows that the Potter test for a true compromise is inadequate. Using standard models of legislative voting, we show that if a true compromise exists, it can be reached either in one step (as an omnibus) or in a sequence of steps (as a series of separate bills). Yet the patterns of voting coalitions differ markedly under these two agendas. The omnibus unites the broad middle of the political spectrum against the extremes, so that a true compromise gains a majority of both sections. In contrast, passing that same compromise as a series of separate measures, each benefiting one section, consistently unites a majority of one section against a majority of the other. The omnibus agenda therefore satisfies the Potter test while the sequential agenda fails this test. Because both agendas reach the *same outcome*, a true compromise, the Potter test cannot be used to judge whether a set of measures was a true compromise.

Our empirical results support our theoretical contentions. First, we show how the contents of several measures differed in critical details between the Clay and Douglas versions, notably the Texas, New Mexico, Utah, and fugitive slave bills. Second, we show the existence of regular and predictable voting blocs. Voting behavior by these blocs corresponds to that predicted by our voting model. Third, we derive predictions about the change in coalition structure for the bills voted on under both Clay and Douglas (the New Mexico, Texas, and California bills). This analysis supports the misjudgment and not the procedural hypothesis. Finally, we also provide evidence against the abstention hypothesis.

Our conclusion emphasizing the substantive differences between Clay's and Douglas's measures questions the logic underlying the armistice thesis of the Compromise of 1850 (see also Stegmaier 1996: 321). At several key junctures during the debate on the Douglas bills, opponents of compromise could have foiled Douglas through a variety of means: by voting no on the first Douglas measure, a filibuster, a cross-sectional extremist pact, or a plethora of damning legislative procedures. Because a majority could have prevented compromise but did not do so, voting theory implies that a majority preferred compromise to no compromise. Although mutual sectional acceptance may not have occurred on any of the six bills, we argue that it did occur on the compromise in toto. Consistent with this argument is the observation that two years later, the House passed a resolution calling the Compromise of 1850 a "finality." The resolution enjoyed the support of a majority of Whigs, Democrats, Northerners, and Southerners (Holt 1978: 97).

A final observation weighs against the armistice thesis. We show that the Missouri crisis had precisely the same characteristics that proponents of the armistice thesis use to claim that the Compromise of 1850 was not a true compromise. First, in the 1820 House of Representatives, a majority never voted on the entire package, which like the Compromise of 1850 had to be split into separate components to pass (Moore 1953: 102); second, sectional majorities consistently opposed one another on the separate provisions in the House; and third, in the Senate, the vast majority of Northerners voted against the package. Because historians widely agree that the Missouri Compromise was a success, these same factors cannot be used to suggest that the Compromise of 1850 failed.

We develop our argument in a series of steps. The next part of the chapter provides a narrative of events in the compromise's passage as well as some preliminary statistical results. We end this part by considering the important differences between Clay's and Douglas's measures. We then turn to the main theoretical results about voting on an omnibus measure versus a series of separate measures, proving our main results. After that, we provide the empirical tests of our hypotheses, showing considerable support for our pivot misjudgment hypothesis against both the procedural and abstention hypotheses. We conclude with a discussion of the larger meaning of the compromise.

A Description of the Compromise of 1850

Here we briefly review the events leading to Clay's failure and Douglas's success in passing the Compromise of 1850. It is not our intention to compete with the historians' descriptions but rather to provide a foundation for our theoretical and empirical work.[4]

The Wilmot Proviso initiated a national crisis in 1846. For a variety of reasons, Northerners insisted on the proviso, requiring that any new territory gained from Mexico be free from slavery (Holt 1978: chap. 3; Potter 1976: chap. 4). In the House of Representatives, where Northerners had a majority, the proviso passed on a purely sectional vote. Deadlock occurred when the proviso failed in the Senate, where equal representation with

Northerners allowed Southerners to reject it. As the war was initiated in part to gain more territory for slavery, Southerners considered the proviso an anathema. Despite numerous attempts at compromise, the crisis worsened. As 1850 began, the compromise's passage was not obvious (Silbey 1967: 108).

COMPROMISE UNDER CLAY'S LEADERSHIP

Remarkable for its "unusual brilliance" (Hamilton 1957: 332), the Senate in 1850 included the venerable Henry Clay, Daniel Webster, and John C. Calhoun, as well as two intelligent and articulate younger leaders, Stephen A. Douglas and Jefferson Davis. Not surprising, the Senate overshadowed its political counterparts. The inexperienced House had trouble organizing, requiring fifty-nine ballots to elect a Speaker. The president, whose election hinged in part on his opaque views, was a political neophyte.

When the attempt to resolve the sectional crisis took center stage in the Senate, all eyes focused on Henry Clay, the architect of peace in the Missouri Compromise. On January 29, Clay offered an outline for sectional peace. After debating his and other proposed solutions, the Senate delegated the responsibility of fashioning a compromise to the specially established Committee of Thirteen, who chose Clay as its chair. The committee's final report included compromise along six separate dimensions: organizing the Utah and New Mexico territories, admitting California as a state, reconstructing the poorly administered Fugitive Slave Law, assuming the bonded debt that Texas had accumulated as an independent republic between 1836 and 1845 in exchange for the withdrawal of Texan claims to disputed land, and prohibiting the slave trade while reaffirming slavery's existence in the District of Columbia. As noted earlier, Clay, in a fateful move, wrapped the portions dealing with Utah, New Mexico, California, and Texas together into an "omnibus" bill.[5]

In the eleven weeks following the committee's report, the Senate became a theater, its members posturing and grandstanding to the delight of the Washington audience. Through July 23, twenty-seven roll calls were taken on amendments to the omnibus; only three succeeded. Each altered the ability of the territorial legislatures to affect slavery. Although Clay succeeded in protecting his omnibus from amendment—Clay lost only one of the twenty-seven roll call votes—an unholy alliance between compromise opponents from both regions seemed to control enough votes to defeat it. Stegmaier (1996: 177) explains, "Clearly, any amendment satisfactory to most Southerners would have lost more votes for the Omnibus than the Southerners it attracted to the bill." The same held in reverse for an amendment satisfactory to most Northerners.

Beginning on July 23, Clay and the compromisers set out on an ambitious effort to obtain the votes of pivotal members. They appealed to border and Northern senators by proposing the establishment of a commission to hammer out an agreement between Texas and the federal government on the former's western and Southern boundary. After two votes ended in ties on July 29, however, the compromisers realized that although they had come close to gaining majority support, they were still short. Setting their sights on the two moderate senators from Texas, the group proposed amending the Texas boundary commission legislation in favor of Texas by preventing New Mexico from setting up a government east of the Rio Grande until the commission had completed its work. Offered by William Dawson (Whig-Ga.), the amendment passed, 30–28. Following this close vote, the commission amendment passed by the same margin (although several senators switched sides). With this delicate balance achieved, historians agree that Clay believed he had won (Hamilton 1964: 109; Stegmaier 1996: 193).

Clay's buoyant mood, however, did not last long. By the end of the following day, Clay's omnibus was "smashed—wheels, axles and body—nothing left but a single plank termed Utah" (from Horace Greeley, quoted in Hamilton 1964: 111). The commission solution to the Texas boundary proved to be the omnibus's vulnerable link. Although James A. Pearce favored the commission solution, he maintained that Dawson's amendment tilted the delicate balance too much toward Texas and the South (*Appendix to the Congressional Globe*, July 31, 1850: 1473).[6]

In an attempt to remove the Dawson provision, Pearce embarked on an intricate and seemingly foolhardy strategy. He proposed first to delete the Texas and New Mexico parts from the omnibus and then to reinsert them without the Dawson amendment.[7] Clay feared that the Pearce maneuver would destroy the fragile balance achieved the previous day. He scolded Pearce on the floor: "I certainly cannot repress my regret and surprise at this motion. What is its effect? It is to destroy one of the most valuable features of the bill" (*Appendix to the Congressional Globe*, July 31, 1850: 1473). Other senators joined Clay in begging Pearce to withdraw his motion, warning that it would cause its defeat. Pearce retorted with a striking statement of principle before compromise: "If it does [cause the bill's defeat], then I cannot help it. . . . No, sir, when we are engaged in a work of compromise, I am not to be overawed and told that I must pursue a given course. If the thing is in my judgment right, I will sustain it—if not, I shall do my duty" to defeat it (1474). Pearce's first motion to delete the Texas and New Mexico parts of Clay's bill passed, 33–22.

Having succeeded with the first half of his intricate move, Pearce then moved to reinsert the Texas and New Mexico language without the Dawson provision. At this point, Northern and Southern extremists sabotaged Pearce's efforts. Before permitting another vote, they offered an amendment to delete everything having to do with Texas from Pearce's second motion. It passed by one vote, causing the omnibus to unravel (Poage 1936). According to Stegmaier (1996: 199), "Thus imbalanced, the whole edifice of the bill came tumbling down." Two votes later, the amended Pearce amendment, now only establishing the commission to resolve the boundary dispute, was defeated, 25–28. Eight votes later, California was removed from the omnibus. By the end of the day, only the Utah portion of the omnibus remained; it passed, 32–18. Journalist Lizzie Blair Lee wrote, "The Mormons alone got thru' living—the Christians all jumped out" (Stegmaier 1996: 201).

COMPROMISE UNDER DOUGLAS'S LEADERSHIP

Defeated, Clay left for his seaside resort. Most moderate senators blamed Clay's defeat on the omnibus. Clay's fellow senator from Kentucky, Joseph Underwood, complained that it was a serious "error to attempt to unite . . . the various measures . . . in one bill. That course arrayed all the malcontents . . . into a formidable phalanx against the whole" (Hamilton 1964: 117). Stephen A. Douglas also advocated this view. In addition to commencing a new procedural strategy that separated what was unified under the omnibus, he also initiated several substantive changes. Five days after Clay's defeat, Douglas worked with Pearce—who "was very anxious to shake off the yoke of being known as the principal destroyer of the Omnibus"—to propose a new solution to the Texas boundary dispute (Stegmaier 1996: 205). Leaving the commission solution in the ashes of the omnibus, their new proposal altered the border in such a way that both North and South could claim victory. The new proposal granted Northerners their desire to remove the Mexican communities North of El Paso from Texas's claim. In exchange, Southerners got a new tract of land, the Texas panhandle. Three days later, after some last-minute minor alterations, the bill passed, 30–20.

With the passage of the pro-Southern Utah portion[8] on the fateful July 31 and after achieving a genuine compromise on the Texan boundary dispute, Douglas next brought up the pro-Northern California statehood bill. With exactly the same language as that proposed by Clay's Committee of Thirteen, the bill passed on August 13, by a vote of 34–18. Two days later, an unaltered New Mexico territory bill passed, 27–10. Having achieved victory on the territorial provisions, Douglas next passed the largely rewritten Fugitive Slave Bill on August 23, 22–13. The last component dealing with the status of slavery in Washington passed on September 16, 33–19.

The House adopted each measure, making only minor changes. In addition to removing some appropriations, the House joined the Texas and New Mexico bills. The creation of the "little omnibus" attempted to keep Southern moderates on the side of compromise. Southerners feared that the Texan debt forgiveness would never reach the Texans but would be used to "make splendid fortunes" for the "speculators in Wall Street and borers in Washington" (Hamilton 1964: 155). By combining the Texas and New Mexico bills, Southerners knew for certain that the latter would benefit the South even if the former did not. Most of the compromise debate in the House centered on the little omnibus. Once it passed on September 6, the House approved the remaining four bills in the succeeding eleven days. On September 9, 18, and 20, President Fillmore signed the disparate parts of the Compromise of 1850 into law.

PRELIMINARY VOTING ANALYSIS

Before analyzing the substantive changes made to fashion compromise, we first present scores that summarize Senate voting on legislation under the leadership of both Clay and Douglas.

To provide an understanding of how the compromise passed, we compute a series of different voting scores to summarize senators' voting behavior. Voting scores have a long history in political science and in political history. Alexander (1967) and Silbey (1964) represent pioneering roll call voting applications of quantitative methods to the antebellum era.[9]

As we have described, in a series of votes, three of the four components were stripped from the omnibus on July 31. We use these three votes to compute our first compromise support score; each senator's score reflects the proportion of time he voted the pro-compromise position.[10] Table 13.1 shows the mean of the compromise support scores by region and party. For example, the mean pro-compromise score of Northern Democrats was 80 percent. Clay's own Southern Whigs were somewhat less supportive, at 60 percent. Southern Democrats and especially Northern Whigs led the effort to defeat Clay's compromise in both strategy and votes. In fact, Northern Whigs cast only three of thirty-seven votes in favor of compromise (all three were in favor of California statehood). Reflecting Clay's failure, the average support among all senators was 44 percent.

Table 13.2 parallels Table 13.1, providing pro-compromise scores for the

Table 13.1

Compromise Scores by Party and
Region Under Clay (the number
of observations are in parentheses)

| | REGION | | |
	North	South	All
Party			
Free Soil	.42 (2)		.42 (2)
Democrats	.80 (15)	.28 (18)	.52 (33)
Whigs	.10 (13)	.60 (12)	.34 (25)
All	.47 (30)	.41 (30)	.44 (60)

Table 13.2

Compromise Scores by Party
and Region Under Douglas

| | REGION | | |
	North	South	All
Party			
Free Soil	.42	.00	.42
Democrats	.85	.55	.70
Whigs	.48	.69	.58
All	.67	.61	.64

passage of the six individual bills that succeeded the failed omnibus. Again, Northern Democrats and Southern Whigs were most supportive of compromise, though both at increased levels. Under Douglas, however, Southern Democrats cast more pro-compromise votes than anti-compromise votes, while Northern Whigs, at just under .50, were nearly evenly divided. In fact, under Douglas's leadership, both major parties and both regions cast more votes for compromise than against.

The conventional wisdom among historians is that the Compromise of 1850 passed because of the support of Northern Democrats and Southern Whigs.[11] Hamilton (1964: 143) is a primary defender of the Democratic party:

Table 13.3

Difference in Compromise Scores
Under Douglas and Under Clay,
by Party and Region

	REGION		
	North	*South*	*All*
Party			
Free Soil	.00	.00	.00
Democrats	.05	.27	.18
Whigs	.38	.09	.24
All	.20	.20	.20

A tabulation of the roll calls on the various Compromise measures shows . . . the positive contribution made by the Democratic party and by individual Democrats. . . . In the totality of affirmative ballots cast on the six tests, the numerical difference [between Democrats and Whigs] is 46 and the percentage difference 26. Both figures favor the Democrats quantitatively in the role of compromisers, vis-à-vis the Whigs.

Although we do not dispute this finding, a more careful examination of the votes reveals a subtlety missed by this judgment. An examination of the voting behavior shows that these groups also supported the omnibus. Because it failed and because these two groups voted similarly on the omnibus and on individual measures, they did not make the difference between success and failure. A closer examination reveals that the conversion of Northern Whigs from their anti-compromise position under the omnibus to their pro-compromise position under Douglas's leadership primarily accounts for the latter's margin of victory.

Table 13.3 highlights our point that Northern Whigs and, to a lesser extent, Southern Democrats were pivotal. The table reports the difference between the compromise scores under the leadership of Douglas and Clay. It shows that the Free Soilers, Northern Democrats, and Southern Whigs voted similarly under both Clay and Douglas. Northern Whigs, however, were much more supportive of compromise under Douglas. So too were Southern Whigs, though not to the same extent as their Northern partisans.

SUBSTANTIVE CHANGES IN THE LEGISLATION

We now examine the principal difference between the failed and the passed measures. In this endeavor, we follow Holt (1978: 72–86), who suggests that in addition to Douglas's procedural changes, we attend to the differences in the legislation. "Almost every measure was altered and realtered," Holt notes (86).

Our first observation is that the changes under Douglas's leadership were at the margin. Although these changes altered important components of several bills, with the exception of the Fugitive Slave Bill, they did not alter the bill's main character. Perhaps that is why most historians have not analyzed or even described these differences—the changes seem like details rather than the essence. And yet as the new literature on "pivotal politics" suggests, the critical difference between success and failure is often in exactly these details (see Brady and Volden 1998; Krehbiel 1998; and McNollgast 1994). These critical differences may alter at the margin who supports the legislation. This implies that small legislative changes can sometimes swing the pivotal legislator from opposition to support, thus changing the fate of the legislation from failure to success.

Four bills had significant changes: the Texas, New Mexico, Utah, and Fugitive Slave bills. The California statehood bill had minor changes, and the District of Columbia legislation had none.

Utah and New Mexico Territory Organization. The Douglas measures organizing the Utah and New Mexico territories differed from Clay's omnibus measures in one important respect. The difference involved the heart of the debate of congressional legislation over the territories from the mid-1840s through the Civil War, namely, the future of slavery in the territories, including the specific question of at what stage and by whom could this decision be made. These questions were central to the Wilmot Proviso, the Compromise of 1850, the Kansas-Nebraska Act of 1854, and the controversy over the attempt to admit Kansas as a slave state in 1858. As noted earlier, the Wilmot Proviso represented the extreme Northern view on slavery in the territories, while Calhoun's common property argument represented the Southern extreme.

In the late 1840s, some Northern Democrats, such as Lewis Cass, attempted to articulate new a middle ground between the two extremes. Douglas became a major champion. Sometimes known as popular sovereignty, the doctrine reserved the right to determine slavery's status in a territory to the people of the territory. Of course, members of Congress still debated whether this decision could be made by the territorial legislature or whether the territory could decide only when it proposed a constitution as part of the statehood process. The answer to this question had significant implications for the future of slavery.[12] A newly organized territory was unlikely to have any slaves. If the territorial legislature could prohibit slavery, it could prevent any chance for slavery to take hold. Absent slaveholders, the territory would lack any political commitment to slavery. In contrast, prohibiting the territorial legislature from legislating on this topic would allow slaveholders to bring their slaves into the territory, potentially establishing support for making slavery legal.[13]

The Committee of Thirteen's language on both the Utah and New Mexico bills held that "no law shall be passed interfering with the primary disposal of the soil, nor in respect to African slavery" (*Congressional Globe*, May 8, 1950: 944). Russel (1972), who calls the slavery provisions of the territorial acts the "ones most frequently misunderstood," suggests that "this wording recognized that slavery was a 'rightful' subject of legislation but forbade the territorial legislatures to touch it" (5, 7). On June 5, the Senate agreed to the Berrien amendment, which struck out "in respect to" and inserted "establishing or prohibiting." This change was deleted from the bill on July 31 when the entire phrase was removed from the omnibus. Following this action, "it was understood by all concerned that the territorial legislatures were left entirely free to legislate on slavery" (10). Douglas's version that became part of the compromise did not include the controversial phrase (see Table 13.4).[14]

Texas Legislation. The Douglas measures concerning the Texas boundary and debt portion differed from Clay's in two ways. First, the Committee of Thirteen left blank the amount paid to Texas debtors. Eventually, the sum became $10 million. On August 9, Pearce successfully offered an amendment that stipulated how the money would be distributed. This amendment also transferred the authority for distributing part of the money from Austin to Washington (see Table 13.4). Although both Texas senators voted against the amendment, it did not stop them from ultimately supporting the bill.

The second set of substantive changes had to do with Texas's western and southern boundaries. No less than ten different solutions were proffered to resolve the boundary dispute. Figure 13.1 displays some of the proposed solutions. As is readily apparent from the map, these solutions differed significantly. Clay originally proposed cutting Texas in half (the horizontal dashed-and-dotted line in Figure 13.1). The Committee of Thirteen con-

Table 13.4

Changes Made by Douglas to the Six Measures

Measure	Clay Provision	Douglas Provision
Utah and New Mexico	Prohibited the territorial legislature from legislating on slavery	Allowed the territorial legislature to legislate on slavery
Texas	(1) Delegated the boundary decision to a commission	(1) Settled the boundary
	(2) Granted Texas the authority to distribute funds	(2) Transferred authority to distribute funds to Washington
Fugitive slaves	Fines for wrongful accusations; Northern juries may be involved	Court appointee to be paid $10 if he ruled that the accused was a runaway, $5 if not
California	Statehood	Minor change involving the Eastern border
District of Columbia	Abolished slave trade but retained slavery	No change

sidered at least five different solutions, three of which proposed dividing Texas into at least two states.

The committee ultimately proposed a diagonal border from just north of El Paso to the intersection of the Red River and the 100° longitude (the short dashed line in Figure 13.1). After lengthy debates showed the inability of that line to garner a majority, the compromisers opted to delegate the decision to a commission. In the meantime, New Mexico sought statehood with an eastern boundary relatively far to the east (the boundary from its proposed constitution is represented as the dotted line in Figure 13.1). After the commission solution led to the collapse of the omnibus, Pearce with Douglas's help proposed the long-dashed line. In an attempt to appease both regions, he altered the line to the thick line, which he then introduced on August 5. This border eventually passed and remains in effect today.

The Fugitive Slave Measure. The Fugitive Slave Law also exhibited major changes (Basinger 1999; Freehling 1990). As is so often the case with congressional legislation, the devil is in the details of enforcement. Clay's wording favored the North. Enforcement involved fines for wrongly accusing an African American. Also included was a provision involving juries. The leg-

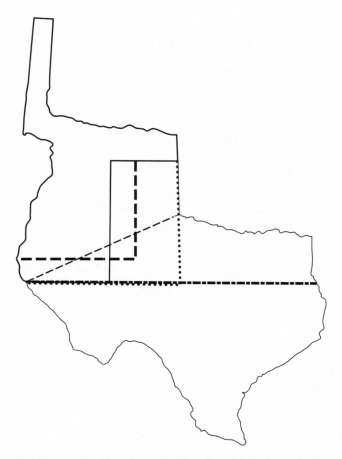

Figure 13.1. Proposed solutions to the Texas boundary dispute.

islation under Douglas replaced Clay's provisions with what members called a "bribe." In an explicit attempt to bias Northern magistrates in favor of finding against the accused, the legislation set the fee for a court appointee at $5 if the accused person was found not to be the runaway in question and $10 if so. Whereas Clay's provisions biased the legislation against slaveholders, Douglas's language biased it in favor.

California Statehood Legislation. The language for California's admission to the United States did not change significantly from introduction to final passage. The only change involved an insignificant change to the eastern border. Although senators proposed many amendments, none passed.

District of Columbia Legislation. The District of Columbia portion of the Compromise of 1850 was unlike the other components in two respects. First, the language adopted by the Senate on September 16, 1850, did not differ from the language initially proposed by the Committee of Thirteen on May 8. Second, significantly fewer amendments were offered and voted on in the Senate relative to the other components of the compromise.

CONCLUSIONS

By focusing on Douglas's procedural changes as necessary for passing the Compromise of 1850, most historians deemphasize the substantive changes in the legislation. Following Freehling (1990), Holt (1978), and Stegmaier (1996), we argue that these changes were not insignificant in understanding how Douglas formulated the compromise. Although the individual legislation steered to success under Douglas did not provide wholesale revisions to any legislation, in four cases—the Texas boundary and debt bill, Utah, New Mexico, and the Fugitive Slave Bill—the legislation differed in important respects from Clay's omnibus.

Theoretical Evaluations of the Hypotheses

Here we present a model of Senate's votes on the Compromise of 1850. The model helps assess the plausibility of the various hypotheses discussed earlier in the chapter. First, we develop a spatial model illustrating the strategic political dynamics facing the Senate. The model suggests a set of circumstances under which the pivot misjudgment hypothesis holds but the procedural hypothesis does not. The model also yields a range of predictions about voting behavior, which we test later in the chapter. Second, we delineate the circumstances under which the procedural hypothesis holds. We then argue that the circumstances for the procedural hypothesis were unlikely to have held for the 1850 Senate.

THE SPATIAL MODEL

To help visualize the strategic problem facing the Senate under Clay and Douglas, we employ the well-known spatial model of legislative voting (see, for example, Shepsle and Bonchek 1997; Hinich and Munger 1997). We represent the policy options facing the Senate with two dimensions, benefits to Northerners along the horizontal axis and benefits to Southerners along the vertical axis in Figure 13.2.

We represent each type of legislator as an *ideal point*, or a policy that he prefers to all other policies, and a *preference function* giving his preference ranking over all policies. For the time being, we assume standard prefer-

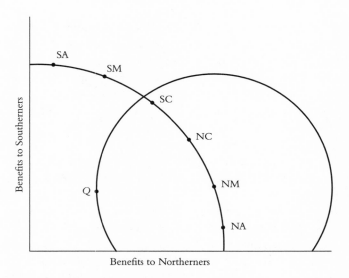

Figure 13.2. Spatial model: Preferences and the status quo.

NOTES: SA, Southern anti-compromiser; SM, Southern moderate; SC, Southern compromiser; NA, Northern anti-compromiser; NM, Northern moderate; NC, Northern compromiser.

ences, meaning that legislators prefer policies closer to their ideal points to those farther away. The assumption of standard preferences has an important implication. Legislators see a trade-off between the two policy dimensions such that they are willing to tolerate something they do not like along one dimension if they obtain something sufficiently valuable along the other. This assumption implies that legislator indifference curves are circular—for a given policy, the set of points to which a legislator is indifferent is a circle through that policy with a center at the legislator's ideal point. This legislator prefers all policy alternatives inside the circle to all alternatives on the circle; further, he prefers all policies on the circle to all outside the circle.

We illustrate these types of preferences in the figure by considering the legislator with an ideal point at NM. The circle through policy alternative Q represents the set of alternatives to which NM is indifferent. NM prefers all points inside the circle to any point on the circle because these points are closer to his ideal point. We consider alternative forms of preferences shortly. In Figure 13.2., we employ six types of senators in our model: an anti-compromiser or extremist, a moderate, and a compromiser from each section. Our placement of the ideal policies reflects the following logic. Of the three types in each section, the extremist prefers the most for his section and is the least tolerant of benefits going to the other section. We thus place the extremist's ideal policy highest on his section's dimension and lowest on the other's section's dimension than the ideal point of any of the other five types.

We represent compromisers in both sections as having ideals that are less extreme concerning policies favoring their own section than extremists and considerably more favorable than extremists to policies benefiting the other section. These senators prefer compromise policies that benefit both sections to extreme policies benefiting their section alone. The difference in location between the SC and NC ideal policies shows that each set of compromisers holds a bias for compromise toward its section, but this bias is modest in comparison with their preference for compromise over extreme policies.[15]

We represent moderates from both sections with ideal points that are less extreme on the dimension benefiting their section than extremists; that is, they are more willing than extremists to tolerate benefits going to the other section. In contrast, compromise legislators would rather have policies benefiting solely their section over compromise; nevertheless, they will tolerate benefits to the other section if they gain sufficient benefits to theirs.

The legislators' ideal points are located along a convex curve representing the set of feasible alternatives. Any policy alternative on or below the curve is possible; those above and to the right of the curve are not feasible.

Figure 13.2 also shows the location of the status quo, Q. We locate Q well below the set of ideal points, reflecting the crisis following the Wilmot Proviso. All types of senators could be better off than the status quo if only they could resolve the crisis and move policy from Q upward and to the right. For example, Southern extremists (SA) are worse off when policy moves horizontally from Q toward the Northerners. A similar argument holds, *mutatis mutandis*, for Northern extremists (NA). Compromisers prefer compromise, a move from Q toward their ideal points. In contrast to extremists, moderate senators also prefer compromise to the status quo. Figure 13.2 also shows the indifference curve of a Northern moderate (NM) through the status quo. Such a senator prefers all policy alternatives within this circle to Q.

The purpose of the model is not to make exact predictions about the legislation's content but to make predictions about which senators should favor various measures. As is common in these models, what matters for our predictions is not the exact location of the various policy alternatives but their location *relative* to one another and to the status quo.

To demonstrate the veracity of our model, we examine the preferences

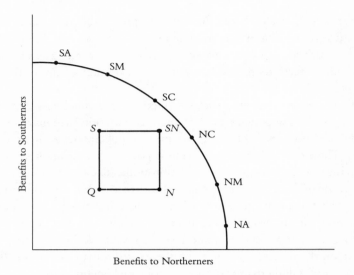

Figure 13.3.   Status quo, Southern and Northern benefits, and a true compromise.

NOTES: SA, Southern anti-compromiser; SM, Southern moderate; SC, Southern compromiser; NA, Northern anti-compromiser; NM, Northern moderate; NC, Northern compromiser.

of the three types of senators over the various policy combinations. In Figure 13.3, we depict three policy alternatives to the status quo: a move from *Q* to *S* provides benefits solely to Southerners, while a move from *Q* to *N* provides benefits solely to Northerners. We represent the combination of both components as the potential compromise policy, *SN*.

Consider first the extremists. Although each set of extremists prefers the proposal benefiting their section alone to the status quo, each is worse off under compromise than under the status quo. Of the four policies, an extremist least prefers the policies benefiting the other section alone. SA therefore prefers the policy alternatives in the order *S*, *Q*, *SN*, *N*. For similar reasons, NA ranks the alternatives *N*, *Q*, *SN*, *S*. Because compromise inevitably provides too much benefit to the other side, both sets of extremists dislike it.

Next consider the moderates. As with extremists, moderates are best off under the policy benefiting solely its section. In contrast to extremists, a moderate is better off under compromise than under the status quo. Similarly, each moderate group is worse off with the policies that benefit the other section alone. SM orders the alternatives S, SN, Q, N, while NM orders them N, SN, Q, S.

Third, although compromisers from each section prefer policies benefiting their own section to the status quo, they prefer the combined policies to the other three alternatives. In contrast to all other senators, compromisers prefer policies that benefit solely the other section to the status quo. To summarize, SC prefers the alternatives in the order SN, S, N, Q, while NC orders them SN, N, S, Q.

A final result, implicit in the foregoing discussion, is the existence of a true compromise, SN. We discuss this possibility next, along with Clay's failure to attain it.

VOTING BEHAVIOR GIVEN STANDARD PREFERENCES

The model's payoff derives from a series of implications about voting behavior and coalition formation. Because the model assumes that legislators prefer policies closer to their ideal point to those farther away, a simple geometric principle allows us to predict how the various senators will vote when faced with a choice between two alternatives. For a given pair of alternatives, the perpendicular bisector between them separates legislator ideal points for those who vote for one alternative from those who vote for the other. The reason is that the ideal points on one side of the bisector are closer to the alternative on its side, so these legislators thus favor it over the other alternative. In contrast, legislators on the other side of the bisector are closer to the second alternative and thus favor it over the first.

Consider the two sectional proposals, S and N. A choice between N and Q yields a perpendicular bisector or cutting line, as in Figure 13.4. The figure shows that the ideal points of all Northerners are closer to N than Q, so they are better off under N. The figure also reveals that Southern compromisers prefer N to Q. The other two groups of Southern senators, SA and SM, are worse off under N and so oppose a move from Q to N. The model predicts that when facing the decision of N against Q, all Northerners and Southern compromisers would vote for N, while Southern extremists and moderates would vote for Q.

Similarly, suppose that S is posed against Q. The perpendicular bisector in Figure 13.5 shows that all Southerners are better off under S than Q, as are Northern compromisers. Northern extremists and moderates, by contrast, are worse off under S than Q. The model predicts that when facing the decision of S against Q, all Southerners and Northern compromisers

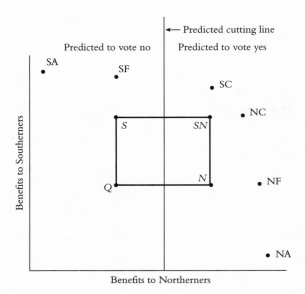

Figure 13.4. Predicted vote for a pro–Northern measure.

NOTES: SA, Southern anti-compromiser; SM, Southern moderate; SC, Southern compromiser; NA, Northern anti-compromiser; NM, Northern moderate; NC, Northern compromiser.

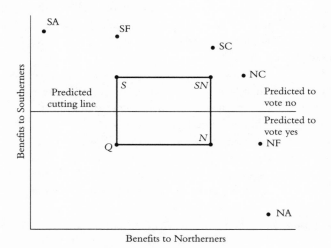

Figure 13.5. Predicted vote for a pro-Southern measure.

NOTES: SA, Southern anti-compromiser; SM, Southern moderate; SC, Southern compromiser; NA, Northern anti-compromiser; NM, Northern moderate; NC, Northern compromiser.

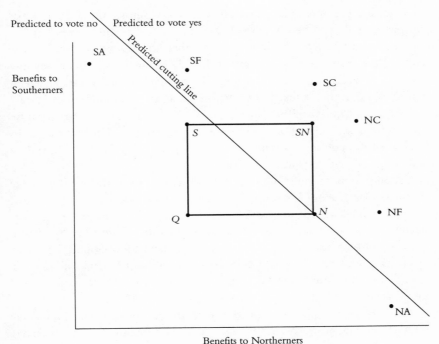

Figure 13.6. Predicted vote for a compromise measure.

NOTES: SA, Southern anti-compromiser; SM, Southern moderate; SC, Southern compromiser; NA, Northern anti-compromiser; NM, Northern moderate; NC, Northern compromiser.

would vote for *S*, while Northern extremists and moderates would vote against it.

Next consider a choice between the compromise package *SN* and *Q*. The perpendicular bisector is now a line that slants down from the upper left to the lower right (see Figure 13.6). This shows that both sets of compromisers and both sets of moderates have ideal points closer to *SN* than to *Q*, and so they favor the compromise package over the status quo. In contrast, the extreme senators from both sections are worse off under the compromise and will oppose it.

With the addition of two assumptions, we can calculate majorities among various proposals: the number of Northerners equals the number of Southerners; extremists are a minority of both sections and therefore in the Senate.

Several important implications follow for the Compromise of 1850. First, the procedural hypothesis is false. There exists a compromise proposal, *SN*, favored by a majority of both sections. Further, the Senate can move to the compromise combination, *SN*, either directly in one step or indirectly in a two-step sequence of votes.[16] To see this, consider the *Clay agenda*, which pits the compromise package *SN* against Q. Then all moderates and compromisers, a majority of the Senate, vote in favor of *SN*, so the compromise passes outright. The support coalition that forms under this vote is the broad middle of the political spectrum, which is opposed by the two (seemingly united) groups of extremists.

Second, suppose the compromise is considered under the stepwise *SAD agenda*—that is, a vote between Q and S and then a vote between S and *SN*. Under the SAD agenda, the voting pattern differs from that under the Clay agenda. A majority of Southerners support the move from Q to S, while a majority of Northerners oppose it; and then a majority of Southerners vote against a move from S to *SN*, while a majority of Northerners vote in favor of it. At no time under the SAD agenda does a majority of both sections support any piece of legislation or the entire compromise.

Our first two implications yield a third and more important one. As is standard in legislative voting models, our model reveals that the observed coalition pattern is in part a function of the agenda, or how the alternatives arise for a vote. Under the Clay agenda, a majority of both sections supports compromise, and *SN* passes as an omnibus. Voting under this agenda thus meets the Potter test for a true compromise. You will recall that a true compromise, according to Potter, requires majority support from both sections. Under the SAD agenda, a majority of one section consistently opposes a majority of the other; never do majorities of both sections support the same measure. The SAD agenda for attaining compromise thus fails the Potter test for a true compromise.

This discussion demonstrates that the Potter test provides an inadequate guide to whether a set of measures is a true compromise. Under both the Clay and SAD agendas, the final legislative outcome is the same, *SN*, the true compromise. Yet the coalition formation under the two agendas differs sufficiently that voting under one passes the Potter test while voting under the other fails it. Because both agendas yield the same outcome, the model demonstrates that we cannot use the Potter test or the underlying coalition pattern to make inferences about whether a true compromise was achieved.

Next we test these predictions of coalition formation and voting behavior against the actual patterns of data.

THE PIVOT MISJUDGMENT HYPOTHESIS

Because the model predicts that a true compromise will pass in omnibus form, we need an explanation of why Clay's omnibus failed. We shall use the spatial model to explain the pivot misjudgment hypothesis and why Clay's omnibus failed. Historians have employed the same logic we use here. Consider Stegmaier's (1996: chap. 7) analysis of the events in July 1850, leading to Clay's dramatic failure on July 31, in which the drama of July 15–31 focuses on Clay's uncertainty about winning and his slow movement from seeming failure to near success. Virtually every element of the drama used by Stegmaier, with the exception of a few events involving the border dispute between Texas and New Mexico, concerns Clay's maneuvering the coalition by tinkering with the provisions of the bill. As we will see, Stegmaier focuses on the pivotal or "swing" voters.

As noted, by the last few days of July, Clay believed he had come close to success. To gain additional support, Clay courted the Texas senators by altering the provision concerning the Texas boundary. On July 30, James Bradbury (D–Me.) proposed an amendment that would place the boundary dispute in the hands of a commission. Some Northerners opposed this amendment because it would only prolong the dispute and because the provision gave Texas a veto over the any commission proposal. The Texan senators were evidently pleased. Following Bradbury's amendment came another pro-Southern amendment: Dawson sought to prohibit the territory of New Mexico from operating in the disputed region east of the Rio Grande, tacitly allowing Texas to do so.

With these two amendments, Clay thought he had succeeded in building a majority in favor of his omnibus. He then sought one additional change, which Moses Norris (D–N.H.) introduced. Along with most Northerners, Clay "now supported" that the legislation allow the territorial legislatures to legislate on slavery (Stegmaier 1996: 193). The Committee of Thirteen's legislation, however, prohibited the territorial legislature from doing so. The distinction is nontrivial and involved one of the hottest aspects of the sectional dispute over the territories. If the territorial legislature could prohibit the introduction of slavery, it could guarantee an absence of slavery and slaveholders and hence become a free state. In contrast, if the congressional legislation prohibited the territorial legislature from legislating on slavery, slaveholders could enter, potentially gaining sufficient support to allow slavery in its state constitution. When Clay and Norris sought to change the territorial bills from the pro-Southern to the pro-Northern language, Clay lost several votes. "Southern radical disdain for the Norris amendment was per-

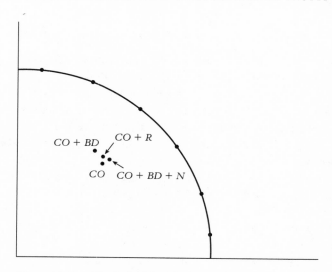

Figure 13.7.   Clay's final legislative maneuvers.

fervid. Clay did not realize how badly he had overestimated his control over Southern votes" (193).

A supporter of compromise until the Bradbury amendment, Pearce chose this moment to defect. A long-standing critic of Texas in its boundary dispute with New Mexico (see Stegmaier 1996: 195; Steiner 1921–22: 18: 260, n. 169), Pearce disliked the Dawson amendment sufficiently that he sought to remove it. Although Clay believed that Pearce's amendment began the unraveling, paralleling Stegmaier's analysis, our model suggests instead that Clay never had a majority in favor of his omnibus. Clay's maneuvers may have gained him the Texas senators, but they also lost Pearce and some Southerners.

To provide additional insights into Clay's misjudgment, we translate these details into the spatial model. We represent Clay's omnibus as it stood on the morning of July 30, prior to the critical amendments of that day and the next, as the point CO in Figure 13.7. Again, what matters for the model is not the exact location of the alternatives but their location relative to one another. Because we can analyze the net effect of each amendment, we can easily specify the alternatives' relative location.

We represent the various amendments as movements in particular directions from CO. Consider Bradbury's amendment on the Texas boundary. We model this amendment as a small movement in the pro-South direction (i.e., upward from CO to $CO + B$). This provision provides Southerners with a modest benefit, as it also involved some uncertainty that might be resolved in one or the other section's favor. Dawson's amendment was more complex. This benefited Texas and harmed New Mexico. By tacitly granting Texas rights over the disputed area, the amendment increased the likelihood that this land would become part of Texas and the slaveholding South. By reducing the size of New Mexico, Dawson's amendment also reduced the prospects that New Mexico would become a free state in the near or intermediate future. We thus model this amendment as a movement upward and to the left $(CO + BD)$. Norris's amendment moved policy at once away from Southerners and gave to Northerners, hence a movement toward the lower right $(CO + BD - N)$.

Clay's last minute maneuvers largely moved the contents of the compromise along a 45° line moving from the upper left to the lower right. Although the addition of the Bradbury amendment moved the compromise toward the compromisers $(CO$ to $CO + B)$, the next two amendments moved along the 45° line $(CO + B$ to $CO + BD$ and then to $CO + BD + N)$.

This sequence of amendments has a direct consequence for the groups who would potentially support a compromise in the form of the omnibus. The model shows that attempting to gain support by moving toward one section's compromisers and moderates risks losing support from the other section's compromisers and moderates. Movements along this line are therefore not likely to result in net gains in support.[17] Put simply, Clay's final maneuvers were not focused in the right way to gain more support.

We underscore this conclusion by contrasting Clay's maneuvers with Douglas's legislative changes. Douglas omitted the Bradbury and Dawson provisions but retained that of Norris. In Figure 13.8, this represents a move downward and to the right (from CO to $CO + N$). Douglas's next two changes, however, moved policy off the 45° line along which Clay maneuvered toward the ideal points of all four compromise support groups. First, Douglas gave more territory to New Mexico, a benefit to Northerners and thus a movement to the right (from $CO + N$ to $CO + N + NN$). Second, in compensation for Texas's loss of territory to New Mexico, Douglas gave Texas the panhandle, a movement benefiting the South and thus upward in the figure (from $CO + N + NM$ to $CO + N + NM + TX$). Douglas's last major change provided a considerably more pro-Southern Fugitive Slave Bill than Clay (from $CO + N + NM + TX$ to $D = CO + N + NM + TX + FSL$). We represent the net effect of Douglas's major changes by the arrow, a movement from CO to D. In combination, Douglas's changes moved policy upward and to the right. These changes made compromisers

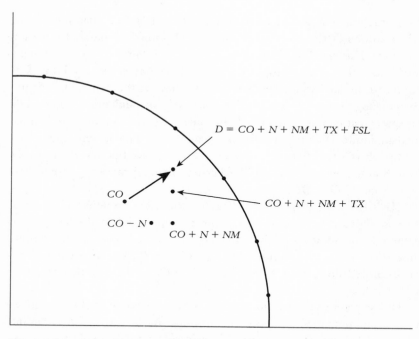

Figure 13.8. Douglas's legislative changes.

and moderates from both sections better off, thus solidifying the majority in favor of compromise.

The model implies that the key to Douglas's success was his finding a better combination of provisions than Clay to solidify support for compromise. Whereas most of Clay's last-minute legislative changes maneuvered policy along the zero-sum line from the upper left to the lower right, Douglas's major changes moved policy upward and to the right.

Clay had come quite close to securing a majority for compromise. This "near miss" allowed Douglas to make marginal but essential modifications in the legislation and thus succeed. Clay's fault was not in the omnibus strategy. Although often repeated by participants in the compromise and by historians, the issue of the omnibus versus separate measures is a red herring. Instead, Clay's flaw was in failing, just barely, to assemble a set of provisions that would garner majority support. The extremist coordination against the omnibus is epiphenomenal because the coalition pattern generated by Clay's omnibus united the middle against the extremes. Clay lost not because the omnibus inevitably made the extremes stronger but because his provisions were slightly off. Extremists were insufficient in number to defeat Clay. Failure instead required that sufficient numbers of moderates and compromise senators vote against the omnibus. Historians' appeal to the omnibus uniting the extremes fails to explain the defection of the moderates and compromisers. Instead, their logic about the swing voters, as with our analysis here, supports the pivot misjudgment hypothesis as the explanation.

THE THEORY OF PROCEDURAL HYPOTHESIS: PRINCIPLED VOTERS

The analysis thus far has relied on standard assumptions about preferences in which legislators vote for alternatives instrumentally—to achieve the best policy outcome. Other forms of preferences imply a different form of voting behavior. Some students of the modern Congress argue that in certain circumstances, elections constrain representative voting behavior in a way that violates the standard assumptions. Federal aid to education in the 1950s provides a classic example. According to Denzau, Riker, and Shepsle (1985), Republicans defeated Democratic proponents of this legislation by attaching a civil rights amendment, saying that none of the money could go to segregated schools. Northern Democrats felt compelled to vote for civil rights even though this doomed the bill because it caused Southern Democrats to defect.[18] We call this form of preferences "principled" because legislators vote on principle, sometimes at the expense of their own interests.

In the 1850 Senate, principled preferences correspond to a senator who opposed any measure that contains benefits to the opposite section, regardless of how much he valued the legislation's component benefiting his section. This type of preference distinguishes principled from standard legislators' preferences because the latter will favor an alternative containing benefits to the other section, provided that benefits to their own section are sufficiently large.

Several conclusions follow when all senators have principled preferences. First, in a direct vote against the status quo, the omnibus cannot pass—every legislator votes for Q over the package SN because the omnibus contains benefits for the other section. Second, under the SAD agenda, each measure fails by virtue of a tie. For a Senate divided exactly in half between two groups with principled preferences, Q is the equilibrium choice under both the Clay and the SAD agendas. Third, it is possible to use the SAD agenda to get to the compromise, but this requires that some legislators from each section abstain instead of voting against benefits to the other group. This also implies that no measure garners absolute majority support: measures benefiting Southerners pass by plurality (not a majority) $N/2$ votes to $N/2 - A_n$

votes, where A_n is the number of Northerners who abstain; and measures benefiting Northerners pass by a plurality of $N/2$ votes to $N/2 - A_s$ votes, where A_s is the number of Southerners who abstain. Under principled preferences and strategic abstention, no measure gains any support from the other group, and none gets more than a plurality of support.

Third, the results so far have assumed that all legislators had principled preferences. Suppose instead that each section still contains three types of senators—extremists, moderates, and compromisers—but only the extremists are principled. Under these conditions, we obtain two further results. Fourth, for the moment, suppose that the Senate contains extreme and moderate preferences from each section but no compromisers. Then passing the measures under the SAD agenda requires strategic abstention by some members of the opposite section, and no measure garners an absolute majority of votes. Without compromisers, all members of one section oppose legislation benefiting the other, so the only way legislation benefiting one section can pass is if at least one of the opponents abstains. The omnibus will pass if the number of moderate legislators exceeds that of extreme legislators: all moderate legislators vote for the omnibus, while all extreme legislators vote against.

Fifth, suppose that all six types are represented in the legislature and that extreme senators are a minority in each section. Then under the SAD agenda, measures benefiting each section pass with an absolute majority: all senators from the benefiting section plus the compromisers from the other section vote in favor while the remaining senators from the other section vote against. The omnibus will pass by a vote of $N - p$ to p, where p is the number of extreme senators. All moderate and compromise legislators support the omnibus while all extreme legislators oppose it. No measure requires abstaining to pass. Alternatively, if the number of extreme legislators is an absolute majority, the omnibus cannot pass.

These conclusions bear directly on our hypotheses. First, given our estimates, the Senate of 1850 contained too few extreme senators for strategic abstention to be necessary to pass the compromise measures. The strategic abstention hypothesis therefore seems theoretically false. Second, because passage of the package under the SAD agenda implies that the omnibus will also pass, the procedural or omnibus-unites-the-opposition hypothesis is also false. As will soon be made clear, we estimate the number of extreme senators p at twenty-one, too few to produce the circumstances where extreme senators affect voting outcomes.

Implications

Our theoretical results favor the pivot misjudgment hypothesis. We derive seven major implications to supports this thesis. First, the model implies that the 1850 Senate preference configuration afforded a true compromise. A fair-sized, absolute majority of the Senate favored compromise.

Second, we show that the true compromise could be reached using either the Clay or the SAD agenda. The issue of the omnibus as the source of Clay's failure is a red herring.

Third, Clay's failure was not in using the omnibus but in failing to arrive at the right combination of legislative provisions; he just barely failed to attract the pivotal senator's support. Under different circumstances, Clay might have adjusted his measures so that they would have succeeded. His last-minute maneuvers, designed to increase support, failed to do so: In passing the Bradbury and Dawson amendments, Clay lost Pearce, and—in passing the Norris amendment—Clay appears to have lost a few critical Southern votes. The counterfactual prediction is that had Clay used the same provisions as Douglas, the unraveling would not have taken place.

Fourth, Douglas's legislative adjustments proved superior to Clay's. Clay's final maneuvers were such that provisions benefiting one section harmed the other. Douglas's adjustments made compromise supporters better off, gaining him the support of the majority and hence passage of the compromise measures.

Fifth, our approach also suggests why, despite the existence of a true compromise, Clay seemed to have been defeated so decisively on July 31. By coming very close to attracting the pivot, but not quite, Clay's measure failed by one or a few votes. Pearce sought to make a unilateral change in one of the measures. The Pearce and Norris amendments made Southerners feel that part of their benefits were being cut out. Once Pearce had begun his maneuvers, the entire package unraveled as first Southerners and then Northerners took out other pieces. The unraveling should be seen as a series of mutual defections from compromise, not as massive dissatisfaction with the omnibus. Defecting is perfectly rational once the first step was taken. Our prediction is that had Clay attracted the pivot, the first step in the unraveling would not have succeeded.

Sixth, we showed that there are circumstances under which the procedural hypothesis is true. But we are also convinced that these circumstances did not hold for the 1850 Senate.

Finally, we showed that the Potter test is inappropriate for gauging a true compromise. Our construction of the Senate preference configuration, with the existence of a true compromise, implies that moving from the status quo to the compromise under the Clay agenda would satisfy the Potter test while moving there under the SAD agenda would fail that test. Since the two agendas arrive at the *same* outcome, this proves that the Potter test is inconsistent and ineffective.

Statistical Results

We shall now test the hypotheses developed at the start of the chapter. The results suggest that Clay failed to pass the omnibus because he critically, but just barely, misjudged the preferences of the pivotal legislators. Douglas succeeded by altering the legislation consistent with their wishes. Our test has five components. First, we offer evidence against the strategic abstention hypothesis. Second, through an examination of senator roll call behavior, we present evidence substantiating the spatial analysis presented in this chapter. Third, we present divergent predictions resulting from the pivot misjudgment and procedural hypotheses. Fourth, we provide evidence validating the misjudgment hypothesis. Fifth, we argue that Clay's omnibus might have passed if it had contained Douglas's solution to the Texas boundary dispute.

EVIDENCE AGAINST THE STRATEGIC
ABSTENTION HYPOTHESIS

Historians have long speculated about the high number of abstentions on the final passage votes of the bills comprising the Compromise of 1850. Several claim that Douglas achieved passage only because he convinced the opponents of particular components to abstain rather than voting against the measures (Hamilton 1964: 142; McPherson 1982: 67; 1988: 175). Fewer yes votes would be needed for passage if Northern senators who opposed, for example, the New Mexico bill abstained rather than voting against it. Likewise for the Southern senators on pro-North components.

Table 13.5 offers some evidence supporting the strategic abstention argument. Half of the final Compromise of 1850 measures did not gain an absolute majority of senators (these votes are highlighted in bold in the table). On these three bills, an average of 18 senators abstained. Had all 10 Texas abstainers, 17 New Mexico abstainers, and 15 Fugitive Slave abstainers voted against these measures, they could have defeated the compromise. As our theoretical discussion indicates, a defeat on any one of these bills could have unraveled the entire compromise.

An analysis of who abstained and when, however, seriously undermines the strategic abstention hypothesis. Consider the Texas bill. Only one of the

Table 13.5
The Vote Totals Under Clay and Douglas

	CLAY'S LEADERSHIP				DOUGLAS'S LEADERSHIP				
	TX	*NM*	*CA*	*UT*	**TX**	*CA*	**NM**	**FSL**	*DC*
Pro–compromise votes	28	22	25	32	**30**	34	**27**	**27**	33
Anti-compromise votes	29	33	34	18	**20**	18	**10**	**12**	19
Total abstentions	3	5	1	10	**10**	8	**23**	**21**	10
Were abstentions potentially pivotal?	Yes	No	No	No	**Yes**	No	**Yes**	**Yes**	No

ten abstainers would have needed to vote in favor of the bill for it to achieve an absolute majority. All present Southern senators voted in favor of Texas, and four of the six who were absent supported Texas under Clay's omnibus. It is therefore unlikely that all six abstaining Southern senators would have voted against it (incidentally, one of the absent senators was Clay, who most assuredly would have voted for it). These observations suggest that the Texas measure certainly would have passed had all senators voted.

The other two bills, New Mexico and the Fugitive Slave Law, are more difficult to disprove. We therefore turn to more sophisticated statistical tests to provide evidence against the abstention hypothesis. A logistic regression equation containing two independent variables accurately predicts both of these votes: the two Poole-Rosenthal scores for the senators in the 31st Congress. These two variables predict 34 of the 37 votes on New Mexico and 37 of the 39 votes on the slave law. Furthermore, the pseudo R^2 is a resounding 0.73 and 0.81, respectively.

We can use these estimations to predict the probability that each of the absent senators would vote in favor of the compromise bills had they been present. These parallel tests allow us to assess the probable voting behavior of the absent senators. For the New Mexico bill, we predict that 13 of the 23 abstainers have probabilities greater than .997 of supporting the bill. An additional 3 have probabilities greater than .88. It is doubtful that the remaining 7 would have supported the bill, but even if they hadn't, the opponents of New Mexico would still have only secured 17 no votes. For the opponents to have been victorious, they would have had to convince all of the senators with probabilities of supporting the bill below .9999999 to vote against it. With a high degree of certainty, we can be sure that abstention on New Mexico did not change the result.

The evidence for the Fugitive Slave Bill is nearly as convincing. We predict that five of the abstainers had probabilities of supporting the bill of over .97. An additional six have probabilities greater than .75. Even if all the other abstainers had voted against the bill, the opponents would still have fallen short by 8 votes. For the opponents of compromise to have defeated the bill, they would have had to attract the votes of all the senators who had below .98 probability of supporting the bill. Again, this analysis suggests that abstentions did not affect the outcome of the compromise.

These results cast doubt on the hypothesis that the high number of abstentions altered the outcome on the final passage votes under Douglas's leadership. The results are consistent with the theoretic predictions of Cohen and Noll (1991). They suggest that abstainers typically come from the winning side. In this theory, abstainers have constituents on both sides of the issue. Abstention allows these legislators to give something to each side: the bill passes, so constituents favoring the bill get what they want, and for constituents who are opposed, the legislators can argue that by abstaining, they did not help the bill pass.

CATEGORIES OF SENATORS

Our theoretical model used six categories of senators, three each for both the North and the South. We now develop these categories by analyzing the senators' roll call votes on the three Clay leadership and six Douglas leadership votes discussed earlier.[19] This exercise has two purposes. First, we demonstrate that the theoretical categories make sense by showing that senators are easily categorized. Second, we draw some conclusions from the analysis. To the extent that categories of senators were distinct and readily identifiable, they would likely be visible to the participants. Although there may be some doubt as to a few senators, by and large, well-defined categories correspond to visible voting blocs. We consider these two purposes in turn.

The spatial analysis from Figures 13.5, 13.6, and 13.7 can be used to predict the voting behavior of the categories based on the votes' content. As long as benefits to one region were tied to benefits from the other region, both anti-compromise groups will oppose compromise. They will be aligned with the regional moderate group that does not get the benefit. For example, on the vote to delete the California language from the omnibus, for example, both anti-compromise groups will join with the Southern moderate group. On the omnibus's New Mexico and Texas votes, however, it should be the Northern moderates who join with the anti-compromisers to defeat Clay's plan.

Table 13.6

Hypothesized Votes on the Compromise of 1850 by Senate Category

		CLAY			DOUGLAS					
	n	*NM*	*TX*	*CA*	*UT*	*TX*	*CA*	*NM*	*FSL*	*DC*
SA	11	−	−	−	+	**+**	−	+	+	−
SM	14	+	+	−	+	**+**	−	+	+	−
SC	5	+	+	+	+	**+**	+	+	+	+
NC	13	+	+	+	+	**+**	+	+	+	+
NM	7	−	−	+	−	−	+	−	−	+
NA	10	−	−	−	−	−	+	−	−	+

+ denotes a pro-compromise vote

− denotes an anti-compromise vote

When each of the components are voted on separately, the compromisers should be joined by the anti-compromise and moderate groups from the region receiving the benefit. For example, the compromisers should be joined with the Southern anti-compromisers and Southern moderates for the Utah, Texas, New Mexico, and Fugitive Slave portions of the compromise. Conversely, anti-compromise and moderate Northerners will vote with the compromisers on California and the D.C. slave trade. These predictions are summarized in Table 13.6.

By matching these voting predictions with the actual votes, the senators can be divided into the six categories by implementing an algorithm. For each senator, we computed the number of voting errors between the prediction for each category and his actual votes. We then placed the senator in the category that minimized the number of errors.[20] For example, Senator Houston voted in favor of compromise on every vote except Texas under Clay. A comparison of this voting record against each of the three Southern categories' predictions reveals the following: he had four prediction errors in the Southern anti-compromise category (Clay's New Mexico and California votes and Douglas's California and D.C. votes), four errors in the Southern moderate category (Clay's Texas and California votes and Douglas's California and D.C. votes), and one error in the Southern compromiser category (the vote against Texas under Clay). We therefore placed Houston in the Southern compromiser category, which best fits his voting record.

The fewest-errors classification criterion leads to relatively clean and accurate categories. The classification method accurately predicts 415 out of 449 votes (92.4 percent), for an error rate of only 7.6 percent.

Further evidence for this conclusion arises when we compare our fewest-errors criterion with extant roll call analyses. Stegmaier (1996: app. B) develops regional pro-compromise and anti-compromise groups based on twenty-five roll call votes centered around the border dispute between New Mexico and Texas. His four categories and our six categories have a correlation coefficient of .971.[21] Furthermore, Poole and Rosenthal (1997) calculate multidimensional voting scores by analyzing all roll call votes within a Congress. During the antebellum period, they argue that economic issues cluster on the first dimension and that slavery issues cluster on the second dimension. Our analysis suggests that the Compromise of 1850 involved both dimensions nearly equally. Our categories correlate with the first dimension at .671 and the second dimension at .667. Again, these results suggest that voting under the Compromise of 1850 occurred within explicit and consistent patterns.

The main conclusion of the analysis is that the infrequency of errors suggests that senators voted according to visible patterns during the debate, patterns that were highly likely to be visible to participants. These results call into question the historians' claims that the votes on the Compromise of 1850 were "kaleidoscopic" (Hamilton 1964: 109; Remini 1991: 757) or exhibited "considerable confusion" (Smith 1988: 177). To the contrary, the voting blocs must have been quite visible to Clay as he tinkered with the legislation in July 1850.

VOTING BLOC PREDICTIONS

We now combine our predictions of voting behavior by category and our categorization of senators illustrated in Table 13.6. We compare these predictions with the actual senators' votes on the specific components of the compromise.

Table 13.7 shows the accuracy of the categories predicting each of the Compromise of 1850 votes. The cells contain the proportion of senators who voted in favor of compromise out of the total number who voted (we again exclude abstentions). The proportions that are boxed are those predicted by our spatial model to be in the pro-compromise voting coalition.

We highlight in bold the proportions that are inconsistent with our predictions. In total, the spatial model correctly predicted the voting majority for 52 out of the total 54 categories (six categories multiplied by nine votes). The difference in voting between the categories just inside the pro-

Table 13.7

Category Proportions for Those Supporting
the Compromise of 1850

	CLAY			DOUGLAS					
	NM	TX	CA	UT	TX	CA	NM	FSL	DC
SA	.00	.00	.00	1.00	.00	.10	1.00	1.00	.10
SM	.85	.86	.00	.80	.90	.10	1.00	1.00	.00
SC	.60	.80	1.00	1.00	.75	1.00	1.00	1.00	1.00
NC	.80	1.00	1.00	1.00	1.00	1.00	1.00	.60	1.00
NM	.00	.25	1.00	.00	.00	1.00	.00	.00	1.00
NA	.00	.00	.00	.00	.60	1.00	.00	.00	1.00

compromise coalition is stark. On average, .90 separates these proximate groups. These results, again, suggest that the senate voting blocs were quite clearly defined in the 31st Congress.

PREDICTIONS BY THE OMNIBUS–UNITES–THE–OPPOSITION AND THE MISJUDGMENT HYPOTHESES

According to historians who support the omnibus-unites-the-opposition hypothesis, the strategy to defeat the compromise depended integrally on including benefits to both regions in the same bill. By combining Northern and Southern benefits, the omnibus united the extremists against the compromise. When the measures were separated, coordination between the extremists became more difficult. Cooperation between Northern and Southern extremists broke down as the sequencing of votes replaced the omnibus mechanism that had allowed extremists to coordinate to defeat the compromise. By offering exclusive benefits to one region at a time, Douglas made it difficult for the extremists to vote against benefits to their respective regions. When these extremists, according to the procedural hypothesis, switched to supporting benefits to their region, the compromise was forged.

The misjudgment hypothesis, by contrast, suggests that the actual process by which the compromise was fashioned is irrelevant. Rather, the key to understanding why Douglas succeeded after Clay failed depended on the substance of the compromise. This argument suggests that if Clay had found the appropriate language, he could have passed the omnibus with a coalition of moderates and compromisers against the extremists (see Figure 13.7). Earlier we outlined several changes that Douglas made to Clay's proposals. It was only after the language was changed that the compromise was achieved.

The procedural hypothesis predicts that the New Mexico and Texas voting coalitions under Douglas would become more pro-Southern. The reason is that the Southern extremists would not vote for any measure containing benefits for Northerners. Southern extremists would favor New Mexico and Texas once they were separated from the California provisions. Likewise, the procedural hypothesis predicts that the California coalition would become more pro-Northern as the Northern extremists vote for passage.

The misjudgment hypothesis, however, predicts that the coalitions change as a result of changes in legislation's substance. Earlier we argued that Douglas proposed nearly the exact same language as Clay for the California and New Mexico bills. The Texas measure, however, underwent major changes. If the support coalition for Texas was more pro-Southern, we would not be able to deduce if the procedural change or the change in legislative provisions led to its passage. A pro-Northern tilt in the support coalition, however, can only be explained by the substantive changes made in the Texas measure.

TESTING THE HYPOTHESES' PREDICTIONS

We use the senator category analysis to adjudicate among these hypotheses. Consider first the compromise coalition on the New Mexico bill. According to Table 13.7, the Southern moderates and the Northern and Southern compromisers supported Clay on the New Mexico vote. The Southern extremists voted against the pro-Southern New Mexico component because it was tied to the pro-Northern California statehood provision. This latter component was anathema to Southerners because it would destroy regional balance in the Senate. The procedural hypothesis suggests that if the New Mexico language were isolated from pro-Northern benefits, the Southern extremists would join this coalition, and New Mexico would pass. According to Table 13.7, this predicted scenario played out. Not only did Clay's supporting coalition became proportionately more supportive of compromise, but every Southern extremist who had previously voted against New Mexico voted for it. We see a similar result for California, except this time with Northern extremists joining the pro-compromise coalition. The ten votes against compromise under Clay became nine votes in favor of compromise when Douglas separated California from the pro-Southern benefits.

If the language changes enacted by Douglas on the Texas bill were immaterial to the passage of the compromise as the procedural hypothesis sug-

Table 13.8
A Comparison of the Predicted Supporters and Opposers Under Douglas

	PROPORTION OF PRO–COMPROMISE VOTES			
	Procedural Hypothesis Supporters	Procedural Hypothesis Opposers	Difference	Probability That the Difference Is Insignificant
New Mexico	1.000	.000	1.000	*
California	1.000	.100	.900	*
Texas	.667	.429	.238	.061

*Indicates that the statistical significance cannot be ascertained because of a lack of variability in one or both of the groups.

gests, then the same voting pattern that was present with New Mexico should be present again with Texas. The supporting coalition for Texas under Douglas, however, does not resemble the coalition under New Mexico. Every Southern extremist continued to vote against Douglas's Texas, just as they had under Clay. Northern extremists, by contrast, gave six out of their ten votes for its passage. These six votes were pivotal for its passage. If all six Northern extremist senators who supported Texas under Douglas had again opposed the bill as they had under Clay, this component of the compromise would have lost, 24–26. As Holt (1999: 535) argues, the Texas component was "the key to the passage of all the other compromise measures." The procedural hypothesis cannot explain why these pivotal senators would have switched sides. Not only does the pivotal misjudgment hypothesis explain this switch, but the historical record of Douglas's making wholesale changes in the Texas language substantiates this explanation. Indeed, during the debate, Senator Winthrop, one of the pivotal Northern extremists, claimed, "I desire to say, in a word, that it is my earnest desire to vote for this [Texas] bill. I do believe that it is the precise measure, and that it is more calculated to bring peace to the country, to reconcile the differences which have so long divided it, and to restore it to unity and concord, than almost any bill which has been proposed" (*Appendix to the Congressional Globe*, August 9, 1850: 1568).

Table 13.8 offers a comparison of the hypotheses' predictions on the three Douglas votes that were also voted on under Clay. It shows that for

New Mexico and California, the difference in the proportion voting in favor of Texas between the predicted supporters and the predicted opponents is stark. In fact, we cannot compute a statistic measuring the probability of difference because of the lack of variation in one or both predicted groups (no predicted supporter of California and New Mexico voted against them, and no predicted opponent of New Mexico voted for it). The difference in the proportion between the two groups for Texas, however, is much smaller. Although it still achieves a high degree of statistical significance, it indicates that a different voting dynamic may underlie the Texas component—the only component that may be used to differentiate the hypotheses.

We offer another visual depiction of how the supporting coalitions for Texas, New Mexico, and California changed under the leadership of Clay and Douglas. Using the votes analyzed in Table 13.5, we ordinally ranked the senators from the greatest supporter of the South to the least supporter of the South (and hence greatest supporter of the North). Barnwell, who never voted for a Northern benefit, is first in the ranking, and Upham, who never voted for a Southern benefit, is last. Southerners Clay and Spruance and Northerners Sturgeon and Cass, all of whom never cast a vote against the compromise, are in the middle of the ranking.

Using these rankings, we can determine the supporting coalitions for each of the three pieces of compromise that were voted on under Clay and Douglas. The supporting coalition is determined by minimizing the number of errors dividing the supporters and the opponents into two groups. In Figure 13.9, the supporting coalitions under Clay are represented by the thin line and the supporting coalition under Douglas by the thick line. The respective lines in the middle of the coalitions are the midpoints of the coalitions, defined as the points at which exactly half of the supporters are above the line and half are below the line (these may not necessarily be the midpoints of the coalitions due to rampant abstentions).

According to the procedural hypotheses just outlined, the New Mexico and Texas components should become more pro-Southern as these pieces are separated from the anti-Southern California statehood issue. Inversely, California should become more pro-Northern when it is separated from the pro-Southern components. Yet the pivotal misjudgment hypothesis predicts that the coalition will change as the substance of the compromise changes. Table 13.9 summarizes the visual depiction offered in Figure 13.9.

Our findings in Table 13.7 are confirmed. Again, the New Mexico coalition becomes more pro-Southern and the California coalition becomes more pro-Northern. The hypotheses cannot distinguish between these findings. Texas, on the other hand, becomes much more pro-Northern. The

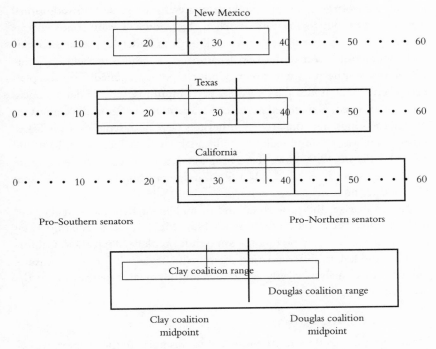

Figure 13.9. Differences in coalition midpoint and range during the Clay and Douglas votes.

Table 13.9

The Midpoint Analysis Under Clay and Douglas

	NEW MEXICO		TEXAS		CALIFORNIA	
	Clay	*SAD*	*Clay*	*SAD*	*Clay*	*SAD*
Coalition midpoint	24–25	26	28–29	33–34	38	42–43
Coalition range	14–39	1–43	12–42	12–56	26–50	25–60

midpoint shifts down five senators and the coalition extends in the pro-Northern direction by fourteen senators while not changing on the Southern side of the rankings. These findings again are only consistent with the pivotal misjudgment hypothesis.

To ensure that the results from the Texas votes are not an artifact of our senator category and ordinal ranking analyses, we present an additional perspective on which senators switched their votes. Twenty-one senators supported Texas under both Clay's and Douglas's leadership; seventeen senators opposed it under both. Two senators—a Southern moderate (Atchison) and a Southern compromiser (Underwood)—switched from the pro-compromise side under Clay to the anti-compromise side under Douglas. Eight other senators switched in the opposite direction. Six of the eight were Northern Whigs. The only two Southerners were both senators from Texas. These switches, in combination with the analyses from Table 13.7, 13.8, and 13.9 and Figure 13.9, show that Douglas's Texas bill was decidedly more Northern than Clay's bill. Only the misjudgment hypothesis is consistent with this result.

To summarize, the procedural and misjudgment hypotheses make predictions about the coalition shifts on the New Mexico, California, and Texas measures. Because they predict the same shift on New Mexico and California bills, the key to differentiating them is the Texas bill. On this measure, our empirical analysis clearly favors the misjudgment hypothesis over the procedural hypothesis.

A NEW EXPLANATION

Using the results and narrative presented to this point in the chapter, we offer the following new interpretation of the demise of Clay's omnibus. We argue that Clay's omnibus strategy might have worked had the substance of his measures differed modestly. We conjecture that had Clay used Douglas's solution for the Texas boundary dispute, the omnibus might have passed.

Suppose that Clay had used Douglas's text for the Texas measure and that an amendment was offered to delete Texas from the omnibus. We assert that this amendment would have barely failed. We know that the twenty-one principled senators from both regions would have voted in favor of the amendment. Assuming that the compromisers would unanimously oppose any compromise-defeating amendment, we have eighteen pro-compromise votes. The moderate senators, again, are the pivotal group. We know from observing their behavior under both Clay and Douglas that they voted for compromise when their region benefited. In fact, their voting behavior is impervious to Douglas's procedural change. Under both strategies, they supported measures benefiting their region.[22] On Douglas's Texas bill, the Southern standard senators were nearly unanimous in support, voting 9–1 in favor (with four not voting); the four Northern moderate senators who were present voted against Texas (three abstained). Even if we assume that Atchison and Underwood as well as all the Northern moderate senators would continue to oppose Texas, the amendment to strip it from the omnibus still would have failed on a tie vote, 30–30. As Holt suggests, if compromise on this component was struck, so was the comprehensive compromise package.

Clay's omnibus came within a hair of passing, failing first by one vote on the amendment to delete the Texas provisions. Even with his commission solution, Clay almost kept the omnibus intact. Suppose that Pearce's first procedural motion to delete all the New Mexico and Texas provisions passed as it did on July 31. The following motion to delete Texas from Pearce's commission-without-Dawson-amendment initially passed, 29–28, with three abstentions. The abstainers were Borland, who missed the entire compromise debate; Cooper, who was classified as a Northern compromiser; and Hale, a Northern moderate. If only one of these senators had been present to vote against the amendment, it would have failed. The amendment to bring New Mexico back into the omnibus (Pearce's revised amendment) was defeated, 25–28. The seven abstentions came from one Southern extremist, one Southern moderate, one Southern compromiser, three Northern compromisers, and one Northern moderate. The pivotal four votes necessary for the amendment to have succeeded could have come exclusively from the compromisers. This analysis supports our contention that Clay came close—very close—to winning the votes on Texas and New Mexico. Had he done so, he could have stopped the omnibus from unraveling. Revisions in the Texas boundary solution might have saved Clay and the omnibus.

Our purpose here is not to argue that Clay's omnibus was the best mechanism for achieving compromise. Instead, we analyze historians' claim that Clay failed *because of his omnibus strategy*. Seen in light of the spatial model, these empirical results suggest that the procedure of fashioning compromise was not nearly as important as the substance of the legislation.

Conclusions

In this chapter, we challenge Potter's armistice thesis, the predominant interpretation of the Compromise of 1850. The armistice thesis relies on inferences drawn from congressional voting behavior. Proponents of this thesis advance three related arguments to support it. First, they argue that the failure of Clay's omnibus shows that no majority favored the compromise. Second, Douglas succeeded where Clay had failed because he divided the measures, avoiding a vote on the entire package. Finally, Potter suggests that the compromise fails what he suggests should be a necessary condition for a true sectional compromise, that members from both sides grant mutual recognition to the concessions granted to the other side. The compromise fails this condition, Potter argued, because a preponderance of strength from one side consistently opposed the preponderance of strength from the other side. Neither side accepted the concessions to the other with majority support.

Because of the central role of inferences from congressional voting behavior and agenda setting in the armistice thesis, we undertook an in-depth analysis of Clay's failure and Douglas's defeat. With a few notable exceptions—our close look at the differences between the Clay and Douglas measures and some of our voting analysis—much of the debate is not about facts. By and large, everyone agrees on the drama and votes. Instead, the debate is about what we infer from what we observe.

This conclusion is nowhere more evident than in the three separate hypotheses for explaining Clay's failure and Douglas's success. Historians have failed to adjudicate among these different explanations; moreover, it is not obvious that the traditional methods of research are sufficient to do so. The central role of congressional voting in assessing these hypotheses implies that doing so is ripe for social science analysis, particularly using the modern tools from political science of voting theory and statistical analyses of congressional voting behavior.

We summarize our contribution as follows. First, we articulate the logic underlying the three separate hypotheses about why Clay failed and Douglas succeeded. The *procedural hypothesis* holds that Clay failed because he combined several separate measures together in an omnibus (Hamilton 1964; McPherson 1988; Milton 1934; Remini 1991). Douglas succeeded because he divided the omnibus into its separate components, allowing a majority to form on each bill. The *abstention hypothesis* argues that Douglas succeeded because he and others persuaded sufficient opponents of these measures to abstain rather than oppose each measure (Hamilton 1964; McPherson 1988). Finally, the *pivot misjudgment hypothesis* holds that Clay failed because he did not quite gain the pivotal senator's support. Douglas succeeded by altering Clay's measures, picking up sufficient additional support to command a majority for his measures (Holt 1978; see also Freehling 1990; Stegmaier 1996).

We also provide a more careful analysis of the differences between the Clay and Douglas measures. This reveals significant differences in four of the six measures, the Utah and New Mexico territorial bills, the Texas debt and boundary measure, and the Fugitive Slave Bill. On the Texas bill, Douglas's measure substituted a specific boundary solution for Clay's clause delegating the boundary issue to a commission, thus avoiding possible violence between Texas and New Mexico, possibly with the intervention of the federal government (Stegmaier 1996). The territorial bills differed on one of the hottest issues of the time, whether the territorial legislature in a territory organized without reference to slavery could prohibit the introduction of slaves. Clay's measures prohibited the territorial legislature from legislating on slavery, whereas Douglas's measures allowed the territorial legislature to do so. On the Fugitive Slave Bill, Douglas's measure substituted enforcement provisions biased in favor of slaveholders for those biased against.

Although none of these changes altered the overall outline of Clay's compromise, they altered sufficient details to induce a few senators to switch sides. Given that the omnibus's unraveling began on an amendment defeated by a single vote, marginal changes could easily have induced a small number of senators to switch from opposition to support. Indeed, this behavior is commonly observed in the literature on Congress.

Our theoretical approach favors the misjudgment hypothesis. The model shows that given the preference configuration of the 1850 Senate, a true compromise existed. Further, this compromise could be reached via the omnibus or through a sequence of separate measures. Clay failed because he just barely failed to attract the support of the pivotal senator. By adjusting four of the six measures, the individual bills under the guidance of Douglas succeeded because the new language gained the support of the pivot. In this view, the issue of whether the omnibus doomed to failure Clay's efforts is a red herring.

Our theory implies that the conditions under which the sequence of votes led to the final compromise also allow the omnibus to pass. This implies that had Clay's omnibus contained the substance of Douglas's measures, it would have passed. Thus had Douglas used the omnibus instead of his sequential agenda, it too would have passed.

Our statistical results combine with the theoretical results to test the various hypotheses explaining why the omnibus failed and the individual bills succeeded. We found little support for the strategic abstention hypothesis. Although we agree with many historians that certain senators probably strategically abstained, we argue that their votes were never pivotal. We also found some support for the procedural hypothesis. Consistent with its prediction, the California measure enjoyed more Northern support and the New Mexico measure enjoyed more Southern support under Douglas than Clay. It does not adequately explain why the omnibus necessarily failed, however.

Our statistical tests strongly point to the pivot misjudgment hypothesis. To differentiate between the procedural and pivot misjudgment hypotheses, we examine votes where they make differential predictions about the coalitions supporting each measure, namely, the three measures voted on under both legislative procedures. The procedural hypothesis says that the coalitions supporting each bill should be largely the same under Clay and Douglas. The pivot misjudgment hypothesis, in contrast, argues that Douglas's adjustments to the measures should lead to somewhat different support coalitions. We find significant changes in the support coalition from Clay to Douglas on the Texas measure, which underwent substantial changes. This supports only the pivot misjudgment hypothesis. Clay's omnibus came within a razor's edge of passing. Our evidence suggests that had he offered a slightly different proposal—for example, that later proposed by Douglas—it is likely that the Texas portion of the omnibus would not have been defeated, which would have stopped the omnibus from unraveling. In combination, this series of theoretical and empirical results support the pivotal misjudgment hypothesis.

Before turning to the larger implications of the analysis, we raise a fourth hypothesis, the *partisan sabotage hypothesis*. Did the omnibus fail because the Democrats sabotaged the efforts of Clay (a Whig) so that they could pick up the pieces, save the compromise, and then claim political credit? This hypothesis has a surface plausibility: if Clay had built the coalition to support the omnibus, a few well-placed Democrats could have withheld their support on the key votes so that the Democrats could then take over.

Circumstantial evidence provides some support for this hypothesis. The Democrats rode the wave of the compromise's success in both the 1850 and 1852 elections, not only recapturing the presidency but amassing their largest-ever proportion of members among all Northerners in the House. Had Clay instead succeeded, the Democrats' electoral prospects would have been dampened. Johannsen (1973) makes an intriguing comment on this last point: "The identification of the omnibus bill with Henry Clay, Douglas felt, had been one factor in its defeat. The Taylor administration was jealous of Clay's leadership, and some democrats feared his presidential ambitions if his bill should succeed" (295). Whether Douglas or the Democrats intentionally attempted to kill Clay's compromise is debatable; that Clay failed and Douglas succeeded is not. On the fateful last day of July in 1850, when Clay's omnibus unraveled, Douglas voted the opposite of Clay twice during the debate on the compromise (on Dawson's provision that increased the power of the Texas legislature in their ongoing territorial dispute with New Mexico and Pearce's motion to delete all the New Mexico and Texas portions of the omnibus).

Yet besides these votes and the fact that Douglas was an early critic of

Clay's omnibus strategy, we have uncovered no evidence suggesting that Douglas quietly or explicitly sabotaged Clay's efforts. The most likely place to uncover substantiating evidence is in various personal archives, especially Clay's and Douglas's. Given that the papers of each have been thoroughly examined, we doubt that further efforts would prove valuable. Moreover, had there been any hint of partisan sabotage, it is likely that Clay would have mentioned it.

Further, one piece of evidence casts doubt on the partisan sabotage hypothesis. The data from Table 13.3 show that Northern Whigs more than any other group switched from voting against Clay's omnibus to supporting Douglas's individual bills. Although the idea of a partisan or Douglas sabotage may appeal to conspiracy theorists, they must come up with an explanation of why Northern Whigs would conspire with Douglas to defeat Clay. Indeed, the Northern Whigs' switch in support remains a major puzzle in the compromise.

These findings have implications for Potter's armistice thesis. We contest two inferences underlying the armistice thesis about Clay's failure and Douglas's success: first, that a majority never favored the full compromise, and second, that Douglas succeeded only by manipulating the agenda to prevent a vote on the entire package. We argue instead that a majority in the Senate did favor the compromise. This is not as strong a statement as saying a majority of senators from both sections approved the compromise. In contrast to the proponents of the procedural hypothesis, we argue that the compromise passed because a majority favored it and hence Douglas's procedural manipulation was not necessary for passage.

We now turn to a set of stronger claims about the armistice thesis. First, we argue that Potter's test for a true compromise is inadequate. We showed that when a true compromise exists, it can be reached using either the omnibus or a sequence of votes. Yet the voting patterns differ significantly under these two agendas for passage. Under the omnibus, a majority of both sections supports compromise, thus meeting the Potter test. Under a sequence of votes, however, a majority of one section consistently opposes a majority of the other, thus failing the Potter test. Because both procedures reach the true compromise, the Potter test cannot be used to judge whether a set of measures is a true compromise.

A second problem with the armistice thesis is that the succession of votes leading to the passage of the Missouri Compromise is nearly identical to those passing the Compromise of 1850. Although the 1820 compromise passed by a majority of 24–20 in the Senate, 80 percent of Northerners voted against. This observation led Moore (1953), in his classic treatment of the Missouri controversy, to draw a conclusion similar to Potter's: "It has often been said that the compromise of 1820 was a solemn compact between the North and South. From this analysis, however, it is evident that it was merely an agreement between a small majority of Southern members of Congress and a small minority of the Northern ones" (111).

Paralleling arguments made about Clay's omnibus, Moore reports (1953) that the Missouri Compromise could not be passed in total in the House. Regarding a vote on the package: "Such a vote could have produced only a negative decision. . . . Only by splitting the compromise into sections and voting separately on each one was it possible to push the measure through the House" (102).[23]

In sum, the Missouri Compromise shares with the Compromise of 1850 the same characteristics cited by proponents of the armistice thesis as supporting their view. As with the Compromise of 1850, the Missouri Compromise fails what Potter suggests should be a necessary criteria for a true sectional compromise, that it be accepted by majorities in both sections.

Because the Compromise of 1820 is widely regarded as a success in ushering in sectional peace and because both compromises share the same characteristics, these characteristics cannot be used to explain the two compromises' differential success. In particular, these characteristics cannot explain why the Compromise of 1850 failed to create lasting sectional peace.

We thus reject the principal logic underlying the armistice thesis. The Compromise of 1850 may not have been a true compromise (though see Stegmaier 1996: 321). But if the 1850s measures failed to provide a lasting compromise, the armistice thesis does not explain why. Along with the new political historians (Holt 1978; Silbey 1964), we argue that explanation of the outbreak of the third sectional crisis and its failure in the Civil War lies elsewhere.

Although sectional conflict reemerged after the Kansas–Nebraska Act of 1854, nothing inherent in the Compromise of 1850 made that inevitable. Our interpretation is consistent with the account of new political historians who offer two interrelated criticisms of the traditional historical narrative. First, they argue that traditional historians tend to view the period from the mid-1840s through the Civil War as an inexorable move toward war (see Silbey 1964; Swierenga 1975). In contrast, new political historians argue that the peace following the compromise was more than a mere uneasy quiescence. According to Holt (1978: 102):

> The historians who argue that sectional conflict over slavery disrupted the old bisectional parties detect a clear progression of events between

1848 and 1854. Hence they jump from divisions over the Proviso to the Compromise of 1850 to the uneasy acquiescence in the Compromise in 1851 and 1852 and finally to the Kansas–Nebraska Act, which polarized North against South and completed the destruction of the Whigs while fragmenting the Democrats along sectional lines. The cogency of that interpretation, however, depends largely on skipping over periods *between* slavery-related events and ignoring other developments in those same years.

Second, new political historians emphasize the importance of factors other than slavery for undermining the second party system and hence for the crisis that emerges in 1854. In particular, they emphasize the role of immigration and nativism (Holt 1978; Silbey 1964, 1985; Swierenga 1975).

Our argument combines with those of the new political historians to suggest a decoupling of the events in 1850 from those of the third crisis emerging in 1854. Although the Compromise of 1850 may not have resolved the sectional crisis for a generation, the reasons for this failure do not involve those given by proponents of the armistice thesis.

Chapter 14

Congress and the Territorial Expansion of the United States

NOLAN MCCARTY, KEITH T. POOLE,

AND HOWARD ROSENTHAL

There has been a renewed emphasis in political science on the role of institutions in shaping political outcomes. This emphasis has led many scholars to the tougher question of how institutions, so prized for their durability and predictability, do in fact undergo fundamental transformations.

The entry of new states into the American Union is one process by which our political institutions have undergone radical changes. Apart from changes in the terms of the Constitution through amendment and judicial decision, few experiences have altered the political terrain of the United States as much as the process of adding new land and people. Between 1789 and 1912, the United States expanded from a confederation of thirteen former British colonies along the Atlantic coast to a union of forty-eight states spanning the North American continent (see Table 14.1). All but three of the forty-eight contiguous states had entered by 1896 (the two noncontiguous ones, Alaska and Hawaii, entered the Union in 1960). These changes were instrumental not only in enhancing the power of the national state but also in reallocating power within it.

The politics of statehood lies squarely within the legislative domain. Article 4, section 3, of the U.S. Constitution gives Congress the authority to add new states to the Union with only the restriction that they not be carved out of existing states without the existing states' consent.

The exercise of this authority is in many ways similar to the acceptance

Table 14.1
The Inclusion of New States

State	Date of Admission	Slavery Status	Total Free States	Total Slave States	Population at Entry	U.S. Population at Previous Census
Original thirteen states	1787– 1790	Varied[a]	7	6	3,000,000+[b]	
Vermont	1791	Free	8	6	92,329	3,929,214
Kentucky	1792	Slave	8	7	103,133	3,929,214
Tennessee	1796	Slave	8	8	77,638	3,929,214
Ohio	1803	Free	9	8	100,984	5,308,483
Louisiana	1812	Slave	9	9	91,926	7,239,881
Indiana	1816	Free	10	9	98,115	7,239,881
Mississippi	1817	Slave	10	10	62,205	7,239,881
Illinois	1818	Free	11	10	46,625	7,239,881
Alabama	1819	Slave	11	11	116,016	7,239,881
Maine	1820	Free	12	11	298,335	9,638,459
Missouri	1821	Slave	12	12	73,973	9,638,459
Arkansas	1836	Slave	12	13	70,700	12,886,020
Michigan	1837	Free	13	13	158,079	12,886,020
Florida	1845	Slave	13	14	70,961	17,069,453
Texas	1845	Slave	13	15	212,592	17,069,453
Iowa	1846	Free	14	15	132,573	17,069,453
Wisconsin	1848	Free	15	15	360,577	17,069,453
California	1850	Free	16	15	92,597	23,191,876
Minnesota	1858	Free	17	15	138,834	23,191,876
Oregon	1859	Free	18	15	48,428	23,191,876
Kansas	1861	Free	19	15	132,925	31,443,321
West Virginia	1863	Free	20	15	296,286	31,443,321
Nevada	1864	Free	36	0[c]	21,111	31,443,321
Nebraska	1867	Free	37	0	94,747	31,443,321
Colorado	1876	Free	38	0	132,542	39,818,449
North Dakota	1889	Free	39	0	175,576	50,155,783
South Dakota	1889	Free	40	0	323,567	50,155,783
Montana	1889	Free	41	0	132,548	50,155,783
Washington	1889	Free	42	0	329,020	50,155,783
Idaho	1890	Free	43	0	88,548	62,947,714
Wyoming	1890	Free	44	0	62,555	62,947,714
Utah	1896	Free	45	0	250,361	62,947,714

(continued)

Table 14.1
(continued)

State	Date of Admission	Slavery Status	Total Free States	Total Slave States	Population at Entry	U.S. Population at Previous Census
Oklahoma	1907	Free	46	0	1,396,900	75,994,575
Arizona	1912	Free	47	0	230,000	91,972,266
New Mexico	1912	Free	48	0	333,600	91,972,266
Alaska	1960	Free	49	0	226,000	178,464,236
Hawaii	1960	Free	50	0	633,000	178,464,236

SOURCE: Population figures from Stewart and Weingast 1992: 256; Morison and Commager 1950: 790.

[a]In 1776, slavery had been abolished in only two of the original thirteen states. By 1849, it had been abolished in all of the seven "free" states among the original thirteen. However, abolition was often restricted only to those born after a certain date. In 1860, eighteen slaves remained in New Jersey, a "free" state (Freehling, 1990: 133, 480). Slavery also existed in the form of "black apprentices" in the "free" states. Apprentices continued in Illinois until 1824 (Freehling, 1990: 149).

[b]The first census was conducted in 1791; earlier figures are estimated.

[c]President Lincoln's Emancipation Proclamation of 1863 freed slaves only in Confederate states but, for simplicity, all states are treated as "Free" beginning in 1864. Slavery was ended in all of the United States by the 13th amendment, ratified December 18, 1865.

of new partners in a business or legal partnership.[1] On the one hand, a new partner is entitled to a share of profits, diluting the return for existing partners. Similarly, in congressional politics, the entry of new states changes the allocation of seats in both Houses. This dilutes the power of all existing states. This fact should make all existing states reluctant to take in new members. On the other hand, a new partner has the capacity to increase the total profits of the firm, increasing the return for existing partners. Analogously, the loss of power to existing states might not deter accepting new members if "manifest destiny" brought scale economies and continental power advantages to the union. How the partnership decision relates to profits is shaped by the exit options of the potential partner. Even if adding the partner diluted profits, profits might be even lower were the candidate to join another firm. A candidate state might likewise set up shop on its own (Texas) or engage in disliked behaviors that could be bargained away in a statehood negotiation (Utah).

The business partnership analogy should not be carried too far, however.

In a pure partnership model, all actors have a common interest in maximizing the present value of the firm. Thus the decision is likely to turn mainly around "efficiency" considerations. But statehood decisions also have important distributive implications that are not easily bargained out by compensating side payments. Some of these distributive implications may be narrowly economic. A potential entrant may be a complement to the economy of one state but a competitor to another. A potential entrant may be expected to be relatively poor for some time, a likely ally for states inclined to support government policies that redistribute via taxation, spending, and regulation. Interest may also diverge over issues, such as the extension of slavery, that are as much a question of ideological preference as economic interests.[2] On these distributive issues, the congressional delegation of an entrant may be a potential ally or an enemy of an individual member of Congress. Thus in our own times, Democrats are eager to see the District of Columbia represented in Congress, but Republicans are opposed.

Our central hypothesis is that the distributive aspects of statehood dominate the factors that push all members to take a common position on statehood. Rather than view institutional change as a mechanism to promote efficiency, we argue that how statehood changes the political balance in the short run is the key to understanding when and which new states are added to the Union. Thus we also hypothesize that the entry of new states is likely to create a great deal of conflict within Congress.

The roll call voting record of Congress is our main source of data for investigating this hypothesis of distributive or ideological conflict. We emphasize ideology because economic and noneconomic issues are tightly bundled. The conflict expressed in most votes, regardless of the underlying policy issues, can be accounted for by a single dimension (e.g., liberal-conservative; see Poole and Rosenthal 1997). Consequently, we further hypothesize that members of Congress are likely to judge a new entrant by where its congressional delegation is likely to locate on this dimension. Indeed, we will show that conflicts over entry always relate to the important political issues of the era.

We focus on the politics of entry in the nineteenth and early twentieth centuries. Until the Civil War, the dominant political issue was slavery (Weingast 1991). Subsequently, entry was determined by the Republicans' objective of maintaining the policies they enacted during the Civil War and Reconstruction (Stewart and Weingast 1992). The major economic issues that pitted industrial versus agricultural interests were also important factors in the admission politics of this era.

We argue that patterns of settlement influenced the demand for statehood by the territories while national political controversies determined the federal government's willingness to grant statehood. Demand certainly had an important endogenous component that reflected policies adopted by Congress. Settlement, for example, was affected by the terms of sale of public lands and the subsidies afforded to railroads. But much was exogenous. Settlements in Texas and California took place on foreign lands. The supply of settlers was affected by fertility in New England, war and pestilence in Europe, the world price of cotton, and numerous other factors. The uncertainty of the demand side often worked to undermine the ability of political actors to use statehood to promote their goals. This was true for antebellum attempts at regional balance as well as postbellum attempts to establish Republican hegemony. To support our claims, we analyze the politics of statehood from the perspective of the spatial model of congressional voting (Poole and Rosenthal 1997). We establish that roll call voting on statehood and related issues map onto the partisan and regional cleavages that defined congressional coalitions in each relevant era.

Land Tenure and the Formation of States

The European settlers in the North American British colonies took it for granted that they could move inland to the west at will and settle there. The form of land tenure [3] in the British colonies was much freer than in England because of the simple necessity of attracting colonists. By the time of the Revolution, the prevailing form of land tenure was *free and common socage*, or what is referred to in more modern language as *title in fee simple*. This was, in effect, the modern form of land ownership free of the old feudal burdens. [4] The landowner could freely sell his land, pass it to his heirs, cut down the trees or dig up the minerals on the land, and so on. [5] Land quickly became a commodity that was bought and sold for profit rather than a family estate that was preserved for one's heirs (Carstensen 1963; Harris 1970).

One of the most important questions the victorious American revolutionaries faced was how to dispose of the public lands belonging to (or claimed by) the newly sovereign states. Thomas Jefferson provided the answer in the great Land Ordinances of 1785 and 1787. He regarded the government's tenure as being fee-simple. Consequently, the government could transfer that fee-simple title to a private buyer through a sale. Jefferson's system was a model of simplicity. The land would be properly surveyed and sold at public auction.

The Northwest Ordinance of 1787 banned slavery from the territory north of the Ohio River and embraced Jefferson's basic scheme. By 1793, all

Table 14.2

Size of Congressional Delegations of States Admitted in the Decade Prior to the Reapportionment Year

Reapportionment Year	New State Representatives	New State Senators	New States
1793	4	4	VT, KY
1803	2	2	TN
1813	2	4	OH, LA
1823	16	12	IN, MS, IL, AL, ME, MO
1833	0	0	
1843	3	4	AR, MI
1853	10	10	FL, TX, IO, WI, CA
1863	4	6	MN, OR, KS
1873	5	6	WV, NV, NE
1883	1	2	CO
1893	6	12	ND, SD, MT, WA, ID, WY
1903	1	2	UT
1913	6	6	OK, AZ, NM
1923–53	0	0	
1963	3	4	AK, HI

the territory from the Allegheny Mountains to the Mississippi was, at least in theory, organized according to Jefferson's principles.

One of these principles covered entry to the Union. By the Ordinance of 1787, new territories would be organized with a governor and court appointed by the president. These federal officials also served as de facto legislatures that had the power to enact territorial statutes, generally drawing on existing statutes in other states and territories. Upon reaching five thousand inhabitants, territories would have the right to set up a bicameral legislature and send a nonvoting delegate to Congress.[6] When a territory reached a population of sixty thousand, it could apply for statehood.

The low population threshold meant that concern about how entry would modify the ideological or partisan balance centered on the Senate.[7] Each entrant could elect two senators. When Vermont entered in 1791, the Senate expanded significantly, from 26 to 28 members. The entry of Arizona and New Mexico in the early twentieth century was still a substantial expansion, from 92 to 96. Additions to the House were proportionately much smaller. Table 14.2 shows the additions in the year of each reapportioned Congress (Congresses elected in years ending in 2), represented by states admitted in the previous decade. Typically, the new entrants had even fewer representatives than senators. Only once did new states' representatives outnumber new states' senators, by just one-third, yet the House always had at least twice as many members as the Senate. In the short run, new states would have only a marginal effect on the composition of the House. In contrast, they had an immediate impact on the Senate.

Because of these large effects on the Senate, entry of new states was always caught up in the major political conflict of the existing Union. Yet many other factors also shaped statehood politics at different times, including economic conflicts, the demands of the party patronage system, the uncertainties of political development, and religious and ethnic issues.

Because of differences in the major dimension of political conflict, we break the politics of statehood into two distinct eras. First was the antebellum period to 1861, during which the balance between slave and free states in the Senate influenced the status quo on slavery. Second was the period from the beginning of the Civil War in 1861 through 1890. During this period, eleven new states were admitted, primarily to the benefit of the Republican party (Stewart and Weingast 1992).

Slavery and the Balance of Political Power, 1789–1861

The admission of new states during the antebellum period was tied to the conflict over slavery, an issue that was compromised but not resolved at the Constitutional Convention of 1787. Both the compromise and the potential for tension on the issue were clearly evident in the provision that apportioned the House of Representatives on the basis of the Caucasian population plus *three-fifths* of all Negroes and Indians. Although slavery was clearly left at the discretion of the states by the Constitution, the Constitution could be amended by a two-thirds vote in both houses of Congress plus ratification by three-fourths of the states. Nevertheless, and this is the key to the slavery controversy, the Constitution explicitly prohibits amendments that would deprive a state of its seats in the Senate.[8] In other words, no matter how few people live in a state, it retains its two seats in the Senate. So as long as there were as many slave states as free states, slave states could block any legislation, such as the admission of new states, that might affect the slave economy. *A fortiori*, they could block abolition, which would require the two-thirds vote necessary to amend the Constitution.

The Senate was all the more critical because even though the three-fifths clause advantaged Southern whites, the population balance favored the free states in the House of Representatives (the slave states *never* had a majority of House seats). Thus the South's best hope lay in preserving parity in the Senate. Consequently, the admission of each new free state was typically compensated by the admission of a slave state (see Table 14.1).

Weingast (1991) argues that the North had to make a credible commitment to the South via the balance rule, under which one slave state was admitted for every free state, preserving the South's veto power with regard to slavery.[9] He sees the admission of California as an uncompensated free state in 1850 as breaking this commitment and precipitating the Civil War a decade later. Weingast (1998) also emphasizes that the loss of House seats by the Northern Democrats in the 1854 elections made it impossible to balance California with Kansas.

Our view of the role of balance is more nuanced. Between 1790 and 1860, Southern demands for balance were probably increasing. In the last decade of the eighteenth century and the first of the nineteenth, Northern abolitionist pressure on the South was virtually absent. Northern states were still adopting *post-nati* emancipation, freeing only children of slaves, during this period. Slavery was fully abolished in New York, for example, only in 1827 (Freehling 1990: 133). With the gradual abolition of slavery in the North, abolitionists increasingly took the fight directly to the South, including attempts at mass mailings of propaganda. A second and more debatable factor affecting Southern demand for a guarantee was fear of slave revolts in the South. Consequently, we see Southern demands for balance increasing almost continuously, consistent with the steadily increasing appearance of slavery as a distinct issue dimension in congressional roll call voting during the 1830s and 1840s (Poole and Rosenthal 1997: chap. 5).

A more direct indication that balance was not initially needed as part of a credible commitment is that Ohio was admitted as a noncompensated free state in 1803 under a Southern president, Thomas Jefferson. Ohio was compensated by Louisiana only nine years later, in 1812. Balance was maintained for the next eight years by admitting two slave states and two free states. This balance proved impossible to maintain when Missouri applied for admission in 1818.

Alabama's petition for statehood was already under consideration when Missouri applied for statehood. Alabama was clearly going to enter as a slave state, and it was admitted in December 1819. The admission of Alabama as the twenty-second state produced an even balance of eleven free and eleven slave states.

MISSOURI AND THE EMERGENCE OF THE BALANCE RULE

The problem Missouri posed was that although it was not a Deep South cotton producer, it had a large enough slave population (16.4 percent) to cause slavery proponents to seek its admission as a slave state. (Missouri's slave population was smaller than any of the eleven slave states.) [10] Missouri was sufficiently populated to seek admission, but there was no other newly settled area that could enter as a free state. The next states to be admitted, Arkansas and Michigan, entered fifteen years later. They were virtually unpopulated in 1820 — 8,896 people resided in Michigan and 14,273 in Arkansas. No state had been admitted (or was ever admitted) with a population this small. The remainder of the territory of what is now the United States was in 1820 essentially uninhabited by Caucasians.

Admitting Missouri as an uncompensated slave state would unbalance the Senate twelve to eleven in favor of slavery. Opponents of the entry of Missouri also voiced concerns about its entry on the balance in the House, particularly in light of the South's ability to draw advantage from the three-fifths clause. But these concerns were probably largely rhetoric. Missouri's slave population was small. The state entered with only one House seat. Four decades later, at the outbreak of the Civil War, its delegation had risen to seven — still smaller than, say, Indiana's eleven. In any event, an increasingly strident abolitionist movement intensified concerns about the balance of power.

The North's legislative attack on Missouri slavery came in the House. In February 1819, amendments by James Tallmadge of New York passed in nearly purely sectional votes (see Figure 14.1 and Table 14.3). These amendments would have banned future imports of slaves into Missouri and freed all slave children in Missouri born after 1825. The North in fact enjoyed a two-vote edge in the Senate at the time, as Alabama had not yet entered the Union. But the amendments failed in the Senate when a unanimous South was joined by five Northern defectors, including two from Illinois, where slavery was present in the form of black apprenticeships (Freehling 1990: 149).

At the time of voting on Missouri, slavery represented the principal conflict in congressional politics. Later statehood votes also reflect the major lines of conflict of their historical periods. We quantify how the inclusion of new states reflects congressional politics by examining roll call voting in the House and Senate. The model used is the spatial model of voting (Enelow and Hinich 1984) estimated by the D–NOMINATE model of Poole and Rosenthal (1991, 1997).

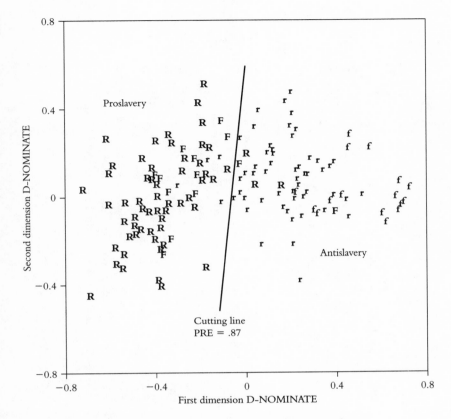

Figure 14.1. Voting in the House on the Tallmadge Amendment.

NOTES: R, r = Jeffersonian Republican; F, f = Federalist. The capital letters indicate representatives who voted on the proslavery side; lowercase, those who voted on the antislavery side. PRE = proportionate reduction in error (see text).

In the spatial model, each legislator is represented as a point on an ideological map. For example, a map might have two dimensions. Left and right on the map might represent economic liberals versus economic conservatives; up and down might represent proslavery versus antislavery positions. Not only legislators but also roll calls are represented on this map. Two points represent each roll call. One corresponds to the outcome identified with a yea vote, the other to the outcome identified with a nay vote. Each legislator votes probabilistically over the two outcomes, the probabilities being functions of the distances between the legislator and the outcomes. A legislator who is much closer to the yea outcome than to the nay outcome

Table 14.3

Statehood and Slavery Roll Calls in the House of Representatives, 1817–21

Congress	States	Date	Margin[a]	Republican[a]	Federalist[a]	Class. Errors[b]	PRE[c]	Vote Description
15	n/a	1/30/1818	69–84	53–69	16–15	25	.64	Pass fugitive slave bill
15	Missouri	2/16/1819	87–76	65–64	22–12	5	.93	Tallmadge amend, no new slaves in MO
15	Missouri	2/16/1819	82–78	63–66	19–12	10	.87	Free MO slaves at age 25
15	Arkansas	2/18/1819	70–71	54–61	16–10	7	.90	No slavery in Arkansas
15	Arkansas	2/18/1819	75–73	58–63	17–10	7	.90	Free Arkansas slaves at age 35
15	Arkansas	3/2/1819	86–90	64–76	22–14	10	.88	No new slaves in Arkansas
15	Missouri	3/2/1819	78–76	56–65	22–11	4	.95	Strike free MO slaves at age 25
16	Missouri	1/24/1820	86–88	73–78	13–10	11	.87	Postpone MO bill
16	Maine	2/19/1820	107–70	90–61	17–9	16	.77	Commit Maine admission
16	Missouri	2/23/1820	93–72	77–64	16–8	9	.88	Disagree with Senate amendments
16	Missouri	2/23/1820	102–68	86–60	16–8	14	.79	Disagree with Senate amendments
16	Missouri	2/28/1820	97–76	82–68	15–8	7	.91	Insist on disagreement
16	Missouri	2/29/1820	98–82	84–71	14–11	9	.89	Abolish future slavery in MO/fugitive slaves
16	Missouri	2/29/1820	94–86	80–75	14–11	6	.93	Abolish future slavery in MO
16	Missouri	3/1/1820	87–90	73–78	14–12	10	.89	Concur to Senate amendment
16	Missouri	3/2/1820	134–42	115–36	19–6	28	.33	No slavery north of 36° 30'
16	Missouri	2/12/1821	61–107	46–97	15–10	16	.74	Ban slavery in MO

[a]The first entry in the vote splits shows the votes for the *anti-slavery* position.
[b]Total classification errors of the D-NOMINATE model for the roll call.
[c]Proportionate-reduction in error with respect to the margins.

votes yea with a probability close to 1.0. A legislator who is exactly equidistant from the yea and nay outcomes votes yea with probability .5. The D-NOMINATE method, basically, provides maximum likelihood estimates of the legislator and roll call points.

Poole and Rosenthal found that two dimensions were sufficient to describe roll call voting behavior through American history. The first dimension—horizontal in the figures that follow—is always far more important than the second (vertical) dimension. The first dimension accounts for about 83 percent of the individual decisions. The second dimension adds another 2 or 3 percent.[11] All figures used in this paper come from a simultaneous estimation using all 8,110,702 individual voting decisions in the House from 1789 to 1985 and 2,317,915 decisions in the Senate for the same period.

The vote depicted in Figure 14.1 is on the Tallmadge motion to free all newly born slaves in Missouri on their twenty-fifth birthday. The tokens represent the legislators; R denotes members of the Jeffersonian Republican party, and F denotes members of the Federalist party. In all the figures, an uppercase letter indicates a proslavery vote and a lowercase letter indicates an antislavery vote. The line is the cutting line for the roll call, the perpendicular bisector of the line joining the yea and nay outcomes. Legislators to the right of the cutting line are predicted to vote antislavery; those to the left of the line, proslavery.

The classification errors are represented by uppercase tokens to the right of the cutting line and lowercase tokens to the left. Because the voting model is one in which probabilities depend on distances between legislator points and outcomes, errors should be most likely among nearly indifferent voters close to the cutting line. This is in fact the case for the Tallmadge motion.

We also present statehood roll call vote outcomes in tabular form. Table 14.3 is typical.[12] The column labeled "Margin" contains the total vote breakdown. To facilitate comparison across roll calls, the vote in support of a position, such as antislavery, appears first for every roll call. Thus the first number is not always the yea votes. The columns contain the same breakdowns for the major political parties. The second-to-last column shows the classification errors for the spatial model—figuratively, the number of tokens on the wrong side of the cutting line. The next-to-last column contains a summary measure of fit, the proportionate reduction in error (PRE). In the PRE, the classification errors are benchmarked relative to the total number of votes cast for the minority position on the roll call. When there are no classification errors, PRE = 1. When there are as many classification errors as minority votes, PRE = 0.

The vote on *post-nati* emancipation in Missouri shown in Figure 14.1 took place in an atypical period of American history, one without a strong two-party system (Poole and Rosenthal 1997, chap. 5). This period was known as the "Era of Good Feelings," commonly dated as running from 1815—the end of the Napoleonic Wars and their North American offshoot, the War of 1812—to 1822. The country had been badly divided over siding with Britain or France and over the economic program of Alexander Hamilton. The Republicans, triumphant in the presidency with Jefferson, Madison, and Monroe from 1801 to 1824, had moved toward Hamilton's ideas, and the foreign policy conflict was settled. Only a single electoral vote was cast against Monroe's reelection to the presidency in 1820. In the 16th House, which passed the Missouri Compromise, the Jeffersonian Republicans held over 85 percent of the seats.

Moreover, as can be seen in Figures 14.1 through 14.4, the parties were not well differentiated ideologically. There are no distinct clusters of R and F tokens, although the Federalists, more represented in the North, were more to the "right" end of the spectrum. On most issues, voting had no ideological structure. But votes on slavery, and especially, slavery related to the inclusion of new states, were highly structured. In fact, Figures 14.1 and 14.2 show that slavery votes were votes on the first dimension. That is, they were votes on the principal dimension of political conflict in this period, which is largely a North-South vote.

In the Era of Good Feelings, party itself does not predict roll call voting particularly well. As seen in Table 14.3, the parties themselves were badly split internally on Missouri. In contrast, the spatial model of voting accurately picks up the internal North-South divisions of the parties. There are relatively few classification errors. Table 14.3 illustrates two important points about the inclusion of new states:

- The table shows that voting on slavery in the 15th Congress centered on the two vital issues that were to come up time and again until the Civil War. One was the South's interest in forcing free states to capture and return fugitive or runaway slaves. The other was that slavery in territories about to become states had, as we have seen, enormous implications for the distribution of political power in the country. The Fugitive Slave Law votes in 1818 fit the model well, and the Missouri-Arkansas votes in 1819 fit exceptionally well. The inclusion of new states was the central issue in American politics at this time.

- There was a nearly even division in the House over extension of slavery at this time. The antislavery forces experimented with finding the

toughest law that could command a majority. Tallmadge first succeeded in passing an amendment that banned further importation of
slaves into Missouri. He then managed, by a narrower margin, to pass
the *post-nati* amendment (see Figure 14.1). Encouraged by these suc-
cesses, the antislavery forces tried to press even harder, to secure the
same bans in the to-be-formed Arkansas territory, to the *south* of Missouri in the latitudes of Mississippi and Tennessee. This effort failed
when Speaker Henry Clay of Kentucky, a slavery moderate, broke a
tie vote.

No legislation passed the 15th Congress, however, as the Senate took a
proslavery position. The impasse was resolved by the famous Missouri Compromise that was formulated in the 16th Congress, seated following the
1818 elections.

There were two essential elements to the Missouri Compromise. Maine,
a noncontiguous portion of Massachusetts, was made a separate free state
and admitted in March 1820. Missouri was then admitted as a slave state in
August 1821, producing a balance of twelve free and twelve slave states.

Even more important than the Maine-Missouri trade-off was the agreement that slavery would be prohibited in the remainder of the Louisiana
Purchase north of 36°30′ latitude (the southern border of Missouri). The
Missouri Compromise clearly unraveled the balance rule if the South were
at all forward-looking. In the forty-year period between the admission of
Missouri and the outbreak of the Civil War, only three slave states south of
36°30′ latitude were admitted to the Union. In contrast, six free states, including three in the area closed to slavery by the Missouri Compromise,
were admitted by 1859.[13] Eventually, eight more states entered the Union
from the territory closed to slavery by the Missouri Compromise.[14]

Table 14.3 also shows the roll calls on the Missouri Compromise in the
16th House, and Figure 14.2 shows the crucial vote on March 1, 1820, that
cemented the compromise in place. The spatial structure is very clear. The
voting was largely along the first dimension, which at the time was essentially sectional—North versus South (Poole and Rosenthal 1997, chap. 5).

As we noted earlier, the spatial structure of congressional voting during
this period was very weak. The best-fitting issues (in terms of PRE, classification, and log-likelihood measures) were related to slavery and territory.
Next best were tariff issues, on which there was also a North-South split.
But the tariff cutting lines, rather than vertical, were at a −45° angle to the
horizontal axis, as illustrated by the passage vote on the 1820 tariff bill,
shown in Figure 14.3. This tariff vote can be compared to the critical vote

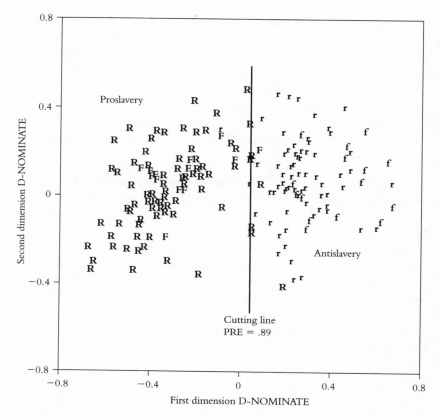

Figure 14.2. Voting in the House on the Missouri Compromise.

NOTES: R, r = Jeffersonian Republican; F, f = Federalist. The capital letters indicate representatives who voted on the proslavery side; lowercase, those who voted on the antislavery side. PRE = proportionate reduction in error (see text).

on the Missouri Compromise, which has a vertical cutting line, shown in Figure 14.2. The distinction arises because on the one hand, some coastal Southern districts and districts in the Ohio River valley in Kentucky were on the high-tariff side, while districts in rural New England, in New Hampshire and Vermont, favored low tariffs. By having the −45° angle, the tariff cutting line is able to put the Ohio River valley districts on the high-tariff side and the rural New England districts on the low-tariff side.

The second dimension, because it is relatively weak, is more difficult to interpret than the first. It appears to distinguish supporters for a larger role for the federal government (up) from more traditional small-government

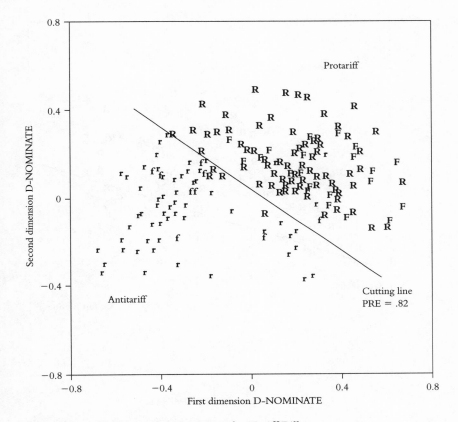

Figure 14.3. Voting in the House on the Tariff Bill.

NOTES: R, r = Jeffersonian Republican; F, f = Federalist. The capital letters indicate representatives who voted on the protariff side; lowercase, those who voted on the antitariff side. PRE = proportionate reduction in error (see text).

Jeffersonians (down). For example, Figure 14.4 shows a roll call on increasing military expenditure. The cutting line is nearly horizontal. Support for tariffs is also linked to support for a larger government, because the tariff was the main source of government revenue. Thus the tariff vote shown in Figure 14.3 was a blend of the two dimensions, since tariff votes also responded to the same sectional divisions as occurred on slavery. Other, less important, issues did not fit the model as well.

In any event, the critical votes on slavery in new states remained along the first dimension and were captured by the spatial model, as shown in Table 14.3. The important votes fit very well:

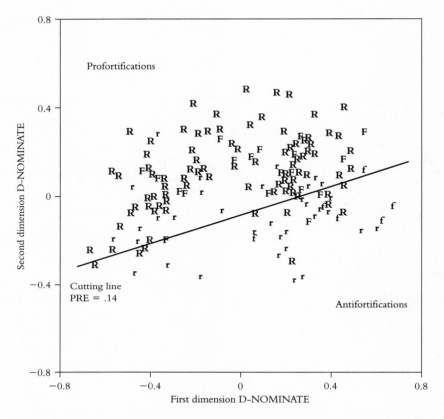

Figure 14.4. Voting in the House on increasing military spending on fortifications.

NOTES: R, r = Jeffersonian Republican; F, f = Federalist. The capital letters indicate representatives who voted on the profortification side; lowercase, those who voted on the antifortification side. PRE = proportionate reduction in error (see text).

- A vote on January 24, 1820, in which the North failed, by 2 votes, to block consideration of the statehood bill (PRE = .87).
- A vote on February 19, 1820, that allowed Deep South representatives to oppose Maine statehood. This vote has a large antislavery majority because the North was solidly in favor, and some representatives from the Middle South and border states, mainly Kentucky, Maryland, North Carolina, and Virginia, voted for Maine, as required by the Missouri Compromise (PRE = .77).

- Votes in which the House "postured" in its negotiations with the Senate by rejecting amendments to its bill that were contained in the Senate bill. These votes were not knife-edge but were still reasonably close, with the antislavery side winning by margins of 20 to 30 votes (PRE = .88, .79, .91, .89, and .93).[15]
- The crucial vote on the Missouri Compromise, the first vote shown in bold in Table 14.3 (PRE = .89).

The Missouri Compromise was actually packaged as two votes. First, the House concurred in the Senate amendment allowing Maine and Missouri to enter, with Missouri as a slave state. This passed by a 3-vote margin, with the North in opposition. Thus Northern representatives were allowed to go on record as opposing slavery. Next the 36°30′ line was passed. (This is also shown in bold in Table 14.3.) The PRE is low because the vote was not close. The most proslavery Southerners were allowed to take positions against. A few Northerners, presumably not satisfied with the entire package, also voted against. But the important observation is that many Southerners voted in favor. In essence, the South traded away slavery in a huge chunk of the nation in future years for slavery in Missouri. The Southern representatives had to be aware that the free part of the Louisiana Purchase would eventually be formed into many states. The South was, almost literally, giving away the ranch to the North rather than obtaining a credible commitment on the future composition of the Senate.

Thus the Missouri Compromise did not maintain a credible commitment by the North that suddenly disappeared in 1850 with California's admission. On the contrary, the South appeared to have traded away the future in 1820 for the short-term gain of the admission of Missouri as a slave state.

Initially, the slow pattern of settlement in the North meant that the South could regard imbalance as relatively remote. But after the balanced admissions of Arkansas in 1836 and Michigan in 1837 (much before the admission of California in 1850), the slave states became aware "that they had got the small end of the Missouri Compromise" (Morison and Commager 1950: 583). In a Christmas Day resolution in 1837, the Alabama legislature noted: "It needs but a glance at the map to satisfy the most superficial observer that an overbalance is produced by the extreme northeast, which as regards territory would be happily corrected and counterbalanced by the annexation of Texas" (583–84). In addition to Texas, Florida was admitted in 1845, producing an imbalance of fifteen slave to thirteen free states. The "compensating" free states, Iowa and Wisconsin, were admitted only in 1846 and 1848, respectively. In 1840, Iowa had 43,112 residents and Wisconsin

30,945, so there was no case for earlier admission. Yet the admission of these states, Minnesota, and, eventually, the plains states could have been anticipated by the South.[16]

In agreeing to the Missouri Compromise in 1820, the South indeed had no immediate concern. Southerners could have noticed that the Panic of 1819 and the collapse of the Western economy would greatly slow down the expansion of the frontier (see Rothbard 1962). The compromise succeeded perhaps not by the craft of Henry Clay and other politicians but by the very slow rate of settlement of the West in this period.

After the Missouri flare-up, slavery was not an important part of the congressional agenda until after the formation of the Whig-Democratic political party system in the early 1830s. The collapse of the Federalist–Jeffersonian Republican party system during the Era of Good Feelings was due not to slavery but to economic issues.

The controversy over Missouri fell in the middle of a period of democratization of American politics that can be roughly dated from about 1810 to 1828. The six states admitted before Missouri between 1810 and 1820 all entered the Union with constitutions that dropped property qualifications for voting and had popularly elected governors. Universal white male suffrage and direct elections in these states placed pressure on the older states to liberalize their qualifications for voting (Hofstadter, Miller, and Aaron 1959: chap. 13). By 1841, only Rhode Island retained some property qualifications for voting. All the remaining states had universal white male suffrage. In addition, by 1828, every state except Delaware and South Carolina allowed popular election of presidential electors, and only New Jersey, Maryland, Virginia, North Carolina, and South Carolina did not have popular election of governors. "The election of Jackson in 1828 was not the beginning, but rather the climax, of the strong impulse toward democracy that swept through the American states" (390).

By the end of Jackson's first term in 1832, a coherent two-party system had emerged in Congress. The primary dimension of conflict was economic, but a clear second dimension divided both political parties along sectional lines. Voting on slavery-related issues during this period was not concerned with the admission of new states but rather over mostly symbolic issues related to slavery, like the infamous "gag rule." These tensions over slavery did not affect the regional bases of the two parties. As Figures 14.5 and 14.6 demonstrate, the parties were extremely well balanced along North-South lines as measured by success in both presidential and House contests. In fact, through the 1830s, there were proportionately more Whigs from slave states than from nonslave states. Only in the 1840s did the Whigs

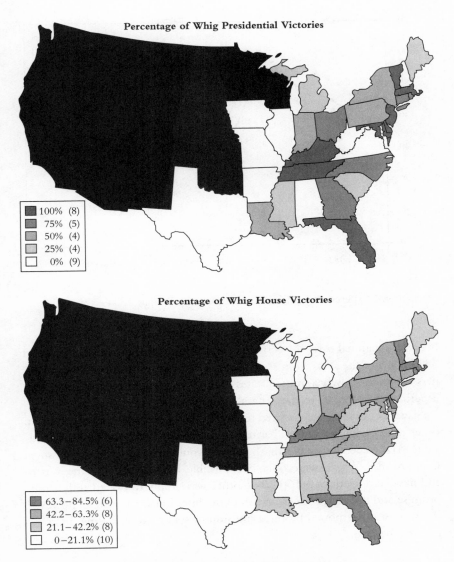

Percentage of Whig Presidential Victories

■	100% (8)
	75% (5)
	50% (4)
	25% (4)
□	0% (9)

Percentage of Whig House Victories

■	63.3–84.5% (6)
	42.2–63.3% (8)
	21.1–42.2% (8)
□	0–21.1% (10)

Figure 4.5. Whig electoral victories, 1836–48.

NOTE: Black indicates areas not yet admitted to the Union as states.

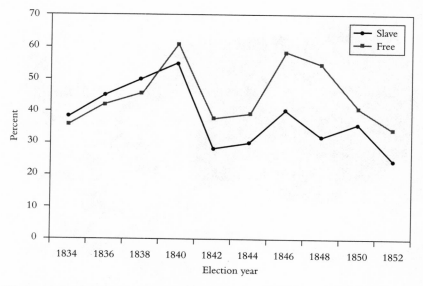

Figure 14.6. Percentage of House seats won by Whigs, 1834–52.

become a regional party. Nevertheless, the Whigs continued to hold around 30 percent of the seats from slave states. The primary area of Whig weakness was in the newly admitted states of the West—slave and nonslave. This is perhaps attributable to the general Whig hostility to expansion.

Slavery could not be confined to largely symbolic issues for very long. In order to maintain long-term balance in the Senate given the territorial advantage conceded to the North, the South would need to undo the Missouri Compromise. There were only two possible lines of attack. One was to add new land south of 36°30′. The other was simply to overturn the compromise and introduce slavery north of the line. In the meantime, however, the issue was postponed by the admission of states two at a time, in cross-regional pairs.

ARKANSAS AND MICHIGAN

The first states to enter after the Missouri Compromise were Arkansas and Michigan. Their admission appears linked to a balance rule. The Senate bills authorizing state conventions were successive bills, S. 81 and S. 82. The debate on admission began with an "Anti-Jacksonian," Ewing of Ohio, trying to table both bills. The split on Arkansas-Michigan statehood was always partisan, with Jacksonians favorable and the incipient Whigs opposed. The

Senate votes are shown in Table 14.4. There is never a hint of regional voting. The votes have high fits to the spatial model with the exception of two procedural votes.

One consequence of highly partisan voting is that the Jacksonians lost only two statehood votes in the 24th Congress. One was an adjournment vote, on January 3, 1837. It is not clear if this loss had political relevance, signifying a possible unraveling of a Jacksonian logroll, or if the defectors simply wanted to adjourn for the day. On the following vote, the next day, nine Jacksonian senators changed sides. Although two switched to voting with the Whigs, seven switched back to their party majority. Passage of the bill followed on January 5.

Most of the Senate votes prior to passage concerned Michigan. The Anti-Jacksonians, including Henry Clay, and the South Carolina Nullifiers, led by John C. Calhoun, fought to delay a final vote. The issues were the state boundaries and land policy.

The boundary issue reappeared in the House votes, shown in Table 14.5. The boundary question must have been favorable to Ohio. Of the nine defecting Anti-Jacksonians in the House on the motion of April 14, 1836, to take up the statehood bills, seven were representatives from Ohio. In contrast, on the vote to order the main question with regard to Arkansas on June 13, all five Anti-Jacksonian defectors are from slave states. The Ohio defections on boundary issue votes lower some of the PREs in Table 14.5. Nevertheless, important votes on third readings have high PREs. As in the Senate, the division was partisan, not regional.

We should emphasize that slavery was an important issue in the 24th Congress, with many votes on the slave trade in the District of Columbia, on sending slaves back to Africa, and on the petition rights of slaves. On these votes, there was a clear regional pattern. In contrast, "balance" on the admission issue meant that admissions were not used to debate slavery. This was apparent in the absence of a regional pattern, even on the two House votes concerning slavery in Arkansas.

FLORIDA, IOWA, AND WISCONSIN

The admissions of Florida and Iowa were clearly linked in a common bill, H. R. 497, passed with relatively little debate and few roll calls in the 29th Congress. Procedural roll calls were along party lines in the Senate, but on other roll calls, both sides raised the slavery issue. In the House, Southern Democrats tried to add a provision that would have allowed Florida eventually to become two states. It was killed on an almost purely regional vote

Table 14.4

Statehood Roll Calls in the Senate, 1834–46

Congress	States	Date	Margin[a]	Anti-Jackson or Whig[a]	Jackson or Democrat	Class. Errors[b]	PRE[c]	Vote Description
23	Michigan	5/9/1834	20–14	7–12	13–1	7	.50	Table authorization to form state
23	Arkansas	5/12/1834	20–22	4–20	16–1	4	.80	Table authorization to form state
23	Arkansas	6/26/1834	17–15	4–12	13–1	2	.87	Authorize people of AR to form state govt.
24	Michigan	4/1/1836	28–9	9–6	22–0	8	.11	Congress, not pres., decides MI admission
24	Michigan	4/1/1836	23–12	1–12	22–0	2	.83	Do not seat MI delegation immediately
24	Michigan	4/1/1836	23–14	1–12	22–0	2	.86	Do not let aliens vote in MI
24	Michigan	4/1/1836	24–7	2–7	22–0	1	.86	Designate only part of MI as state
24	Michigan	6/9/1836	24–20	19–4	5–15	5	.75	No tax on MI lands
24	Michigan	1/3/1837	22–16	1–13	21–1	2	.88	Adjourn during debate
24	Michigan	1/4/1837	25–12	1–10	24–1	2	.83	Amend MI admission, re preamble and boundaries
24	Michigan	1/5/1837	25–10	2–9	23–0	1	.90	Pass MI admission bill
28	Texas	5/13/1844	18–23	5–17	13–5	5	.72	Make Texas debate non-secret
28	Texas	6/6/1844	12–27	4–19	8–7	4	.67	Receive Friends slavery report
28	Texas	6/8/1844	16–35	1–27	15–7	4	.75	Ratify annexation

28	Texas	6/13/1844	20–25	1–23	19–1	2	.90	Table annexation bill
28	Texas	2/5/1845	23–22	1–21	22–0	1	.96	Refer annex. bill to committee
28	Florida, Iowa	2/14/1845	23–24	1–23	22–0	1	.96	Refer FL–IA to committee
28	Texas	2/24/1845	30–11	10–10	20–0	4	.64	Consider H.J. Res. 46
28	Texas	2/27/1845	33–16	9–15	23–1	11	.31	No debt assump., slavery decided by people of state
28	Texas	2/27/1845	27–25	3–24	24–0	3	.88	Request president to negotiate with Texas
28	Texas	2/27/1845	33–11	9–10	24–0	6	.46	Divide texas into slave and non-slave states
28	Florida, Iowa	2/28/1845	23–26	0–25	23–0	0	1.00	Postpone order of day
28	Florida	3/1/1845	35–12	11–11	24–0	1	.92	Amend FL constitution slavery provision
28	Florida, Iowa	3/1/1845	36–9	12–8	24–0	3	.67	Pass H.R. 497
29	Texas	3/11/1845	23–20	1–20	22–0	1	.95	Postpone consideration
29	Texas	3/12/1845	32–9	11–9	21–0	5	.44	Amend resolution
29	Texas	12/22/1845	31–13	5–13	26–0	0	1.00	Order third reading, admit Texas
29	Iowa	12/24/1846	40–2	17–1	23–1	5	−1.50	Amend H.R. 557

[a] For the votes on Michigan and Arkansas, the first entry in the vote splits shows the votes for the *Jacksonian* position. The votes for the two factions do not equal the margin because of the presence of two Nullifiers from South Carolina. As many as two Whig votes are included with the Anti-Jacksons for 1837 votes.

For all other votes, the first entry in the vote splits shows the votes for the *Southern Democratic* position. Party votes do not total the margins because of Law and Order, Independent Democratic, and Independent Whig members.

[b] Total classification errors of the D-NOMINATE model for the roll call.

[c] Proportionate-reduction in error with respect to the margins.

Table 14.5

Statehood Roll Calls in the House of Representatives, 1835–45

Congress	States	Date	Margin[a]	Anti-Jackson or Whig[a]	Jackson or Democrat[a]	Class. Errors[b]	PRE[c]	Vote Description
24	Michigan	12/30/1835	133–47	31–25	88–16	41	.13	Admit elected MI member as spectator
24	Michigan	1/5/1836	110–101	11–58	95–29	45	.55	MI memorial
24	MI, AR	4/14/1836	119–70	9–51	108–5	17	.76	Introduce resolution on AR and MI bills
24	Michigan	6/13/1836	153–45	29–35	115–2	24	.47	Third reading of S. 177
24	Arkansas	6/13/1836	126–67	15–45	108–9	15	.78	Third reading of S. 178
24	Arkansas	6/13/1836	143–50	30–30	107–8	18	.64	Pass S. 178
24	Michigan	6/13/1836	96–59	4–42	91–3	11	.81	Proper election on Michigan representative
24	Michigan	1/25/1837	140–57	20–37	116–5	24	.58	Third reading of S. 81
24	Michigan	1/25/1837	132–43	22–32	103–2	24	.44	Pass S. 81
28	Texas	3/15/1844	121–39	18–35	103–2	5	.87	Do not annex Texas
28	Texas, Oregon	3/25/1844	66–106	4–54	62–48	24	.64	Table annexing Texas and Oregon
28	Texas	6/13/1844	123–56	10–54	113–0	5	.91	Texas annex. unconstitutional
28	Texas	12/19/1844	109–61	6–56	103–2	7	.89	Refer Tex. to Committee of the Whole
28	Texas	1/10/1845	81–92	21–41	60–49	25	.69	Divide Texas into two states
28	Texas	1/15/1845	127–31	31–24	94–5	31	.00	Introduce Texas annex. bill

28	Texas	1/22/1845	119–63	23–40	95–21	42	.33	Reject annexation
28	Texas	1/25/1845	120–98	9–66	111–28	27	.72	Pass H.J. res. 46
28	Florida	2/13/1845	75–121	20–50	55–67	10	.87	Do not allow two states in Florida
28	Florida, Iowa	2/13/1845	144–48	27–41	117–5	13	.73	Pass H.R. 497 Florida-Iowa admission
28	Texas	2/28/1845	134–77	2–72	132–2	3	.96	Accept Senate amendment
29	Texas	12/16/1845	142–52	20–48	120–1	6	.90	Table admission of Texas
29	Texas	12/16/1845	141–58	20–50	120–3	6	.90	Admit Texas
29	Wisconsin	2/16/1847	81–58	9–45	72–11	19	.67	Give education land grant to WI
29	Wisconsin	2/19/1847	41–92	4–41	37–49	17	.59	Public works in Wisconsin
30	Wisconsin	5/11/1848	94–46	43–31	50–15	49	–.07	WI adm. to exclude public lands from sale

[a]For the votes on Michigan and Arkansas, the first entry in the vote splits shows the votes for the *Jacksonian* position. The votes for the two factions do not equal the margin because of the presence of Anti-Masonics and Nullifiers. As many as two Whig votes are included with the Anti-Jacksons for 1837 votes.

For all other votes, the first entry in the vote splits shows the votes for the *Southern Democratic* position. Party votes do not total the margins because of Law and Order, Independent Democratic, and Independent Whig members.

[b]Total classification errors of the D-NOMINATE model for the roll call.

[c]Proportionate-reduction in error with respect to the margins.

with a horizontal cutting line. Northern Democrats clearly felt the South had gone too far in this case. In the Senate, Northern Whigs sought to influence the slavery provision of the Florida constitution. On this issue, Northern Democrats stayed in the party coalition and supported slavery in Florida. Finally, the bill passed easily in the House. Nevertheless, all but one Northern Whig vote was cast against passage. The Northern Whigs were thus on record as willing to hold up statehood in the North to prevent slavery in the South. This position may have further weakened their political viability on the frontier.

The entry of Wisconsin engendered very few roll calls in the House and none in the Senate. The votes generally divide one or both parties along regional lines (see Table 14.5).

TEXAS

The strategy of adding land was first undertaken with respect to Texas. Texas annexation was a project not of the South but of the Democratic party. At the time of annexation, the Democrats had a hefty majority in the House, but the Whigs controlled the Senate.

Tables 14.4 and 14.5 contain the roll call votes dealing with admission of Texas into the union. The admission of Texas was first taken up by the Senate in the context of ratifying a treaty (which required a two-thirds vote). Action on the treaty ran from May 1844 to the end of the year. The Democrats, who were a minority, offered many amendments and motions to delay a final vote. The majority Whigs were almost always more disciplined than the Democrats, but party unity was not strong enough to get the necessary two-thirds vote. Northern Democrats were free to desert the party and do position taking by casting anti-Texas votes. Also in 1844, the House (Table 14.5) conducted position-taking votes on the Texas issue. Every roll call in both houses fits the spatial model quite well. Roll call voting on Texas reflected both party discipline and North–South splits.

The proponents of Texas admission, most notably lame-duck President John Tyler, then decided that Texas could be admitted by a resolution that required only a simple majority in both houses. During the lame-duck session of December 1844, the House began its deliberations on the terms of the U.S. annexation offer.[17] With a large Democratic majority, the House on January 25, 1845, voted to admit Texas. Because the Democratic majority was substantial, both parties could allow defections.

Votes on Texas that had partisan defections from Southern Whigs and Northern Democrats have cutting lines angled about 45° in the D-NOMI-NATE estimation. These votes express a mixture of party pressures (vertical

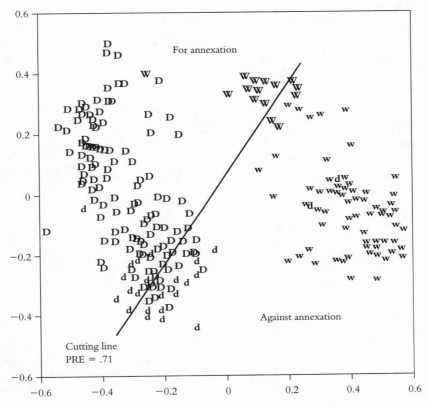

Figure 14.7. Voting in the House on the Brown amendment on Texas annexation.

NOTES: D, d = Democratic; W, w = Whig. The capital letters indicate representatives who voted for annexation; lowercase, those who voted against annexation. PRE = proportionate reduction in error (see text).

cutting lines) and regional pressures (horizontal cutting lines). One such vote is the famous Brown amendment (Freehling 1990: chap. 25), shown in Figure 14.7. After their stinging defeat in the 1844 elections, Southern Whigs sought to shore up their proexpansionist and proslavery credentials. On January 13, 1845, Milton Brown of Tennessee proposed allowing Texas to be split into as many as five states, with only the caveat that any state created north of 36°30' must be a free state. The amendment respected the Missouri Compromise line, which showed that the line was still a binding commitment by the South a quarter-century after the compromise.[18] With-

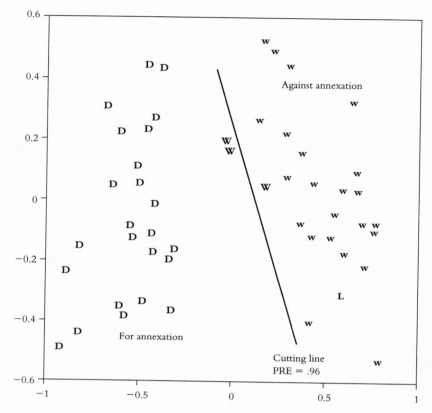

Figure 14.8. Voting in the Senate on Texas annexation, February 1845.

NOTES: D, d = Democratic; W, w = Whig, l = Law and Order. The capital letters indicate representatives who voted for annexation; lowercase, those who voted against annexation. PRE = proportionate reduction in error (see text).

out the support of Brown and eight other Southern Whigs, the vote on the amendment and the bill might have been extremely close. But it is likely, given what happened later in the Senate, that the Southern Democrats could have pressured enough Northern Democrats to support the bill, so the Whig support in the House was perhaps less essential than it seems.

When the bill reached the Whig-dominated Senate, the Democrats required perfect party discipline and a few Whig defections to get to a third reading. Such a vote, illustrated by the third-reading vote in Figure 14.8, has a nearly vertical cutting line. (Note that the classification of the model would remain at one error if the cutting line were made vertical.) The map in the figure illustrates how party, not region, dictated the vote. State delegations that were split along party lines split in the vote. The vote was so close that every senator voted. The delegations from seven of the twenty-six states split.

The Senate was less inclined to go along with such a proslavery provision as the Brown amendment. Missouri's Thomas Hart Benton, the only Southern Democrat to vote against the annexation treaty in the previous session, was particularly determined to prevent Texas from becoming a major victory for "slave power" (Freehling 1990: 446). He proposed an alternative amendment requiring any division of Texas to correspond to the balance rule. Therefore, two additional slave states and two additional free states could be carved out of Texas. Pressure from his own state legislature forced him to drop this proposal, however, and offer an amendment that was silent about future division but required a reopening of negotiations with Texas over boundary disputes. Ultimately, the Senate opted to leave it to the president's discretion whether to offer the Texans the Brown formula or the Benton formula. After the House voted to accept the Senate "no decision," Tyler and then Polk chose the Brown plan.[19]

The Texas Convention voted overwhelmingly in support of statehood. Admission occurred as soon as the 29th Congress convened, in December 1845. As Figures 14.9 and 14.10 show, the final passage vote was ideological, splitting the Whig party along regional lines. The Senate vote in fact showed no classification errors. Note that the Democrats had more senators voting than the Whigs in the 29th Senate. Southern Whigs felt free to defect and go with the majority proslavery position. Northern Whigs cast the only Senate votes opposed to the admission of Texas. The situation in the House is very similar. There were only six classification errors. These included the three Northern Democrats who voted against Texas, the one Northern Whig who voted in favor, and the one member of the American party who voted in favor. The maps in the House figure show that Northern opposition had no strong regional base but was determined solely by whether a Whig or a Democrat had won the House seat in the elections of 1844.

The Democratic logroll, however, continued the strategy of adding land by undertaking the Mexican War. President Polk had tried to buy New Mexico and California from Mexico for $40 million in November 1845 (Presidents Jackson and Tyler had earlier tried to buy California), but the Mexican government rebuffed his offer. American expansionists including Polk wanted California badly because of the excellent ports at San Francisco

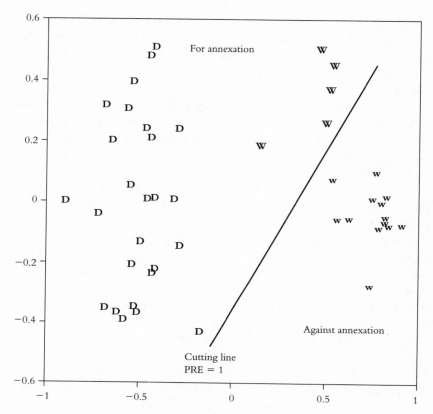

Figure 14.9. Voting in the Senate on Texas annexation, December 1845.

NOTES: D, d = Democratic; W, w = Whig. The capital letters indicate representatives who voted for annexation; lowercase, those who voted against annexation. PRE = proportionate reduction in error (see text).

and San Diego (Oregon had no harbors of comparable quality). This desire, coupled with a continuing dispute with Mexico over the southern border of Texas, led to the outbreak of war in 1846.

After the victory of the American forces at Buena Vista and Vera Cruz, Polk sent an envoy, Nicholas Trist, to Mexico in 1847 with instructions to demand the Rio Grande as the southern boundary of Texas and the cession of New Mexico and California. During Trist's absence in the summer of 1847, considerable sentiment built up in the Polk administration for a prolonged occupation and perhaps the eventual annexation of all of Mexico. This led Polk to change his instructions to Trist, who was in the middle of

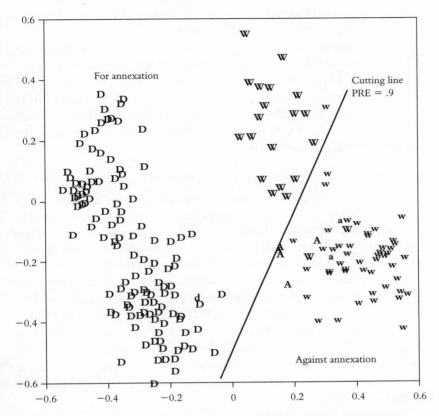

Figure 14.10.　Voting in the House on Texas annexation, December 1845.

NOTES: D, d = Democratic; W, w = Whig, A, a = American. The capital letters indicate representatives who voted for annexation; lowercase, those who voted against annexation. PRE = proportionate reduction in error (see text).

negotiations. Trist ignored Polk's new instructions and went on to negotiate a very favorable treaty that conformed to his original instructions. Polk promptly fired Trist when he returned to Washington but sent the treaty to Congress anyway. The treaty passed on a vote of 38–14 in the Senate on March 10, 1848. Both Whigs and Democrats supported the treaty (11–7 and 26–7, respectively); majorities of Northerners and Southerners also voted for the treaty. The fact that there was no sharp regional split on the treaty with Mexico and no strong appetite to annex all of Mexico was due to the Southerners' misgivings about continued conflict with Free Soilers about the disposition of such large territories and the fear that an armed occupation would surely increase the power of the federal government in the long run (Hofstadter, Miller, and Aaron 1959: chap. 15).

A large chunk of the territory acquired from Mexico was below the 36°30' Missouri Compromise line, so in theory, slavery might have been extended to these territories. President Taylor proposed extending the 36°30' line westward, which, assuming a split of California, could have eventually given rise to three slave and three free states. But even this proposal would not have allowed the South to maintain balance, given that most of the United States was north of 36°30'.

CALIFORNIA AND THE COMPROMISE OF 1850

The South's long-run problems were further worsened by Northern settlement of the Oregon country in the Pacific Northwest. The South could do little with respect to this free land (eventually three more states) other than to block any urge to fight a war with the British over the northern boundary. Again the pattern of settlement was important to the status quo.

Moreover, nonslaveholders settled California after the discovery of gold in 1848. The North was now adamant about blocking any extension of slavery. The Compromise of 1850 admitted California as a free state. The North also succeeded in abolishing the slave trade in the District of Columbia and having substantial Texas land claims ceded to the federal government. The South got a fugitive slave law, federal assumption of the Texas debt, and a nondecision on slavery in the Utah and New Mexico territories created on former Mexican land.

The ideological map of voting on the Compromise of 1850 resembled Figure 14.7, but with an important difference. Many Northern Whigs abstained rather than vote against the compromise, thus allowing the principal elements to pass. The strain of the compromise on the party system was nonetheless too great. The political parties fragmented along regional lines, and the Whig party simply imploded. The result was that roll call voting in the 32nd Congress was completely disorganized—indeed, it was essentially spatially chaotic (Silbey 1967; Poole and Rosenthal 1997).

The Compromise of 1850 was unacceptable to all sides. It left slavery present in much of the nation. Furthermore, Southern beliefs that the annexation of Texas and the war with Mexico would correct the imbalance implicit in the Missouri Compromise were not fulfilled. In 1850, the Union contained thirty-one states. Of the remaining seventeen states that would eventually fill out the "lower forty-eight," only two, Arizona and New Mexico, could conceivably have been slave if the 36°30' rule were maintained.

The Compromise of 1850 also represented the rejection of any plans to maintain balance via the subdivision of Texas into multiple slave states as allowed by its annexation treaty. Plans for such a subdivision were hatched by Daniel Webster in February 1849. Concerned that the preservation of the Union required a pro-Southern compromise championed by a Northerner, he proposed dividing Texas into three states while admitting only the portions of California above 36°30′. When other Whig leaders convinced him that the plan made too many concessions to the South, he backed off his proposal, only to have it carried forward by the future presidential nominee, John Bell from Tennessee. The plan was a nonstarter, however, not only because of intense opposition from the North, but also because the opposition of Texas whose acquiescence was required to carry out the plan. To the Texans, there were a number of issues that trumped increasing the representation of slave states. Many were concerned about the economic and trade implications of subdividing the state. The western land (which it retained at annexation) was also Texas's only source of state revenue (Fehrenbacher 2001), so the state would have demanded steep compensation for subdivision. However, even more important, it was considered doubtful that states carved out of southwestern Texas would remain slave states.[20] This area had few slaves, and many Texans feared the consequences of having a free state on their border. This area was also the home of a movement that sought to be separated from Texas. In particular, many of the region's residents of Mexican descent felt that the state would abrogate any preindependence land claims. As a result, many Texans felt that any effort to subdivide Texas was a placation of the separatists (Stegmaier 1996).

MINNESOTA

Votes on Minnesota were the first statehood votes after the balance rule had been broken. The South does not appear to have fought further admissions vigorously. Indeed, the votes on passing S. 86 were "Hurrah" votes (see Tables 14.6 and 14.7). If there was a commitment in American politics, it was not to balance admissions but to admit new states once they had reached a sufficient population. Minnesota was hardly held back. Its population at admission was less than that of Wisconsin and Michigan when they were admitted. The debate on Minnesota concerned voting rights for aliens, a salient issue for the American party, and the number of representatives to be seated before the 1860 census. These votes were not along party lines. The issues related partly to nativism, which does not fit well in the two-dimensional space. The South did vote almost as a bloc on several amendments dealing with the number of representatives, but there were always some defections. On the whole, the South sought only to make a tempo-

Table 14.6

Statehood and Slavery Roll Calls in the House of Representatives, 1857–76

Congress	States	Date	Margin[a]	Republican[a]	Democrat[a]	Amer.	Class. Errors[b]	PRE[c]	Vote Description
34	Minnesota	1/31/1857	98–76	60–19	30–29	7–27	25	.57	Pass authorization for people of Minn. to form state
35	Minnesota	5/11/1858	117–72	48–29	69–30	0–13	64	.11	Only one house seat for Minn.
35	Minnesota	5/11/1858	51–141	38–40	0–99	12–2	49	.04	New constitution + two Reps.
35	Minnesota	5/11/1858	157–39	57–21	100–3	0–14	44	−.13	Pass S. 86
35	Oregon	5/18/1858	115–104	15–71	98–20	0–11	38	.64	Pass S. 239
36	Kansas	4/12/1860	135–72	105–0	21–48	—	23	.68	Pass H.R. 23
36	Kansas[d]	1/28/1861	119–41	92–0	16–22	—	19	.54	Consider amendment to H.R. 23
36	New Mexico	3/1/1861	71–115	27–77	28–20	—	57	.20	Table H.R. 1008
37	W. Virginia	7/16/1862	70–45	61–18	2–11	—	25	.44	Table S. 365
37	W. Virginia	12/10/1862	97–58	84–10	4–32	—	20	.66	Pass S. 365
37	CO, NV[d]	3/3/1863	65–47	60–5	1–27	—	9	.81	Consider S. 523 & S. 524
38	Colorado	3/17/1864	88–18	64–0	9–15	—	2	.89	Amend S. 97, striking prohibition of slavery in CO
38	Nebraska	3/17/1864	72–43	58–0	2–36	—	1	.98	Amend H.R. 14 to require census before entry
39	Colorado	5/3/1866	109–29	102–5	0–24	—	6	.79	Table S. 74

39	Colorado	5/3/1866	74–64	67–37	1–25	—	36	.44	Refer S. 74 to committee
39	Colorado	5/3/1866	82–58	74–31	0–25	—	31	.47	Pass S. 74
39	Nebraska	1/15/1867	105–55	99–10	0–34	—	12	.78	Pass S. 456
39	Colorado	1/15/1867	94–60	87–17	0–32	—	18	.70	Pass S. 462
39	Nebraska	2/9/1867	122–44	112–5	0–33	—	6	.86	Pass S. 456 over Johnson veto
42	Colorado	1/29/1873	65–122	53–42	7–73	—	48	.26	Table H.R. 148
43	New Mexico	5/21/1874	161–55	122–26	37–27	—	46	.16	Pass H.R. 2418
43	Colorado	6/8/1874	170–66	138–24	30–40	—	44	.33	Pass H.R. 435
43	CO, NM[d]	3/3/1875	164–83	153–13	10–67	—	21	.75	Pass resolution regarding admission of CO & NM
43	CO[d]	3/3/1875	166–78	152–7	11–66	—	16	.80	Concur in Senate amendments to H.R. 435
43	NM[d]	3/3/1875	155–86	146–16	7–67	—	18	.79	Concur in Senate amendments to H.R. 2418
44	Colorado	12/4/1876	95–147	77–0	145–14	—	16	.83	Previous question on resolution admitting Colorado
44	Colorado	12/4/1876	99–142	78–0	144–15	—	16	.84	Pass resolution to determine if CO is a state

[a]The first entry in the vote splits shows the votes for the *pro-expansion* position. The breakdown is shown first for the entire House (Margin) and then for the Republican, Democratic, and American parties. See note to Table 14.2 for explanation of errors and PRE.

[b]Total classification errors of the D-NOMINATE model for the roll call.

[c]Proportionate-reduction in error with respect to the margins.

[d]Two-thirds vote required.

Table 14.7

Statehood Roll Calls in the Senate, 1857–76

Congress	States	Date	Margin[a]	Republican[a]	Democrat[a]	Amer.[a]	Class. Errors[b]	PRE[c]	Vote Description
34	Minnesota	2/21/1857	24–27	9–8	15–18	0–1	11	.54	Amend H.R. 642, only citizen vote
34	Minnesota	2/21/1857	47–1	15–1	31–0	1–0	0	1.00	Pass H.R. 642
34	Minnesota	2/24/1857	21–35	6–13	14–22	1–0	13	.38	Reconsider vote on H.R. 642
34	Minnesota	2/25/1857	31–24	12–9	19–15	0–1	14	.42	Reconsider vote to restrict vote to American citizens
34	Minnesota	2/25/1857	31–22	13–6	18–15	0–1	11	.50	Pass H.R. 642
35	Minnesota	4/1/1858	21–29	18–0	2–26	1–2	5	.76	Two Reps. until next apportionment
35	Minnesota	4/7/1858	49–3	19–0	26–2	3–1	3	.00	Pass S. 86
35	Minnesota	4/13/1858	24–30	19–0	3–27	2–2	0	1.00	Disagree with House version and request conference
35	Oregon	5/18/1858	35–17	11–6	23–7	1–3	5	.38	Pass S. 239
36	Kansas	6/7/1860	27–32	25–0	2–32	0–0	2	.93	Proceed to consider H.R. 23
36	Kansas	1/21/1861	36–16	26–0	9–15	1–1	2	.88	Pass H.R. 23
37	West Virginia	7/7/1862	17–18	12–13	1–3	—	17	.000	Consider S. 365
37	West Virginia	7/14/1862	25–11	19–7	1–3	—	9	.18	Consider S. 365
37	West Virginia	7/14/1862	23–17	21–7	1–5	—	9	.47	Pass S. 365
37	West Virginia	2/26/1863	28–12	25–0	1–8	—	0	1.00	Consider S. 531, supplement to S. 365

37	Nevada	3/3/1863	24–16	18–7	4–5	—	9	.44	Pass S. 524
37	Colorado	3/3/1863	16–20	14–11	0–6	—	12	.25	Postpone consideration of S. 522
37	Colorado	3/3/1863	18–17	14–9	2–4	—	9	.47	Pass S. 253
37	Nebraska	3/3/1863	25–11	14–8	7–1	—	11	.00	Consider S. 522
37	Nebraska	3/3/1863	12–23	3–21	6–0	—	4	.67	Postpone consideration of S. 522
39	Colorado	3/13/1866	16–22	12–13	2–6	—	16	.00	Order third reading of S. 74
39	Colorado	4/25/1866	21–17	17–7	0–6	—	4	.77	Reconsider vote refusing third reading of S. 74
39	Colorado	4/25/1866	21–14	17–7	0–6	—	4	.72	Pass S. 74
39	Nebraska	7/27/1866	24–7	21–5	2–2	—	5	.29	Consider S. 447
39	Nebraska	1/9/1867	24–15	21–8	0–6	—	6	.60	Pass S. 456
39	Colorado	1/16/1867	23–11	20–5	0–5	—	4	.64	Amend S. 462
39	Nebraska	2/8/1867	31–9	28–4	0–4	—	2	.78	Override veto of S. 456
39	CO	3/1/1867	29–19	26–10	0–8	—	7	.63	Sustain veto; Pass S. 462
43	Colorado	6/23/1874	20–33	20–15	3–11	—	16	.20	Table motion to consider H.R. 435
43	Colorado	2/24/1875	47–17	39–0	2–12	—	5	.71	Pass H.R. 435
43	New Mexico	2/24/1875	31–11	26–5	4–6	—	6	.46	Pass H.R. 435
44	New Mexico	3/8/1876	21–29	21–11	0–28	—	6	.72	Consider S. 229

[a]The first entry in the vote splits shows the votes for the *pro-expansionist* position. In the case of Minnesota, there is some ambiguity in what is proadmission. Some of the votes on the number of representatives may have been strategic. The vote corresponding to the majority vote among opposition Republicans is taken as proadmission. A yea vote has been coded proadmission.

[b]Total classification errors of the D-NOMINATE model for the roll call.

[c]Proportionate-reduction in error with respect to the margins.

rary limit to the effect of Minnesota's admission (because the census would shortly determine the number of representatives). Further changes in the ratio of slave states to free states were not resisted.

OREGON

Oregon was the last state to be admitted before the Civil War, and the Oregon Territory is an interesting case study of how the Missouri Compromise undid the South. The American claim to the Oregon Territory came through the Louisiana Purchase of 1803, but England, Spain, and Russia also made claims to the area. In the 1844 presidential election, the Oregon boundary question ("54°40' or fight!") was almost as important as the issue of Texas annexation (Hofstadter, Miller, and Aaron 1959: chap. 15). This dispute was the result of a large influx of Americans into Oregon via wagon trains beginning in 1843. This continuing influx made British control impossible over the long run.

In an 1818 treaty, the United States and Britain had set the northern border at 49°. In 1827, the treaty was extended another ten years with a one-year "opt out" clause. On the eve of the Mexican War, in 1846, Congress reduced tariffs on British manufactures, and there was a change of government in Britain. This pair of events considerably reduced the tension between the two countries. The British proposed a compromise to President Polk—extend the 49° northern boundary to the Pacific Ocean, and in exchange, the British would keep all of Vancouver Island and would retain navigation rights on the Columbia River. President Polk and Congress were on the verge of war with Mexico (declared on May 13, 1846), and the British offer seemed like a good deal, given that most of the high-quality farmland was south of the 49th parallel. Consequently, the deal was struck on June 15, 1846.

The moral of the Oregon story is that the slavery issue played no important part in the politics of annexation. Rather, it was a mix of pure American nationalism and the desire to avoid a two-front war. However, it was inevitable that the states carved out of the Oregon Territory (Oregon, Washington, and Idaho) would be free states.

Given this history, it is not surprising that the admission of Oregon as a free state appears to have been largely uncontested. The Democratic majorities in the Senate managed the bills. The manager in the Senate appears to have been Stephen Douglas of Illinois, sponsor of the Kansas-Nebraska Act that undid the Missouri Compromise. The manager in the House was the future Confederate vice president, Alexander Stephens of Georgia. Voting was not along party lines in the Senate, where, with the exception of one procedural vote, PREs were low. Perhaps Republicans were dissatisfied with the terms of the bill. Moreover, Oregon's admission appears to have been premature, as it had a lower population than any state previously admitted, with the exception of Illinois forty years earlier. PREs were higher in the House. The Democrats voted against an alternative Republican bill, and the Republicans voted against passage of the Democratic bill.

KANSAS AND NEBRASKA

The South's only possible salvation lay in undoing 36°30'. Congress did so with the Kansas-Nebraska Act in 1854. Senator Stephen Douglas, an Illinois Democrat, bought Southern votes for a Northern, rather than Southern, route for the transcontinental railway with a measure that would have allowed the Nebraska Territory, which was north of the Missouri Compromise line, to enter as two states. One, Kansas, would be slave, even though slavery was almost certainly economically not viable in Kansas. The other, Nebraska, would be free.

The bill passed, pushed by the long-standing Democratic party alliance in which the current Midwest traded votes on slavery for votes on economic matters (Weingast 1991). But it was the last hurrah. Northern politicians, unwilling to trade away the slavery issue, displaced the old political class of the second party system.

The structure of congressional voting changed completely. The primary dimension of conflict was now over the extension of slavery to the territories. The second dimension of the Democrat-Whig party system was now the first dimension of the new system that emerged with the voting in 1853–54 (Poole and Rosenthal 1997). The losing coalition that fought the Kansas-Nebraska Act eventually became the Republican party.

With the emergence of the Republican party, any hope of maintaining balance vanished. This was true even for lands south of 36°30'. Cuba had been the focus of American expansionists for a long time. Cuba was a potentially large and highly profitable slave territory. President Polk offered Spain $100 million for Cuba in 1848, but Spain turned it down. In 1854, during the Pierce administration, another abortive attempt was made to acquire Cuba that touched off the Ostend Manifesto incident. By this time, however, the combination of free-soil sentiment and the passions raised by the Kansas-Nebraska Act doomed the effort to annex Cuba (Hofstadter, Miller, and Aaron 1959: chap. 18, Merk 1963). There would be no future senators from the slave state of Cuba to balance those from the territories north of 36°30'.

Like Weingast (1991), we conclude that balance in the Senate was a major issue in the admission of new states before the Civil War. Our view, however, is that politicians in Washington did not and could not vote in Congress to make credible commitments on slavery via balance in the Senate. They did not, because the Missouri Compromise promised imbalance in the long run. They could not, because ordinary citizens were voting with their feet, moving to new lands that then demanded representation in the Union. Jefferson's Land Ordinances helped undo slavery. Indeed, although historians have focused on the political conflict over the Kansas-Nebraska Act in 1854, neither Kansas nor Nebraska was admitted before the Civil War. In contrast, Minnesota and Oregon were rather quietly admitted as free states, under a Democratic president and Congress, strengthening the imbalance in the Senate initiated by California's admission in 1850.

The Period of Partisan Admissions, 1861–1912

Almost as soon as shots were fired at Fort Sumter, the Republican party began the process of making its tenuous hold on the American government more permanent. This was not a cynical goal. After all, winning the war involved not only the preservation of the Union but also the faithful implementation of Republican policies in its aftermath. It is often easy to forget how fragile Republican control was at the outbreak of hostilities. Lincoln had been elected with a mere 40 percent of the popular vote against a badly split Democratic opposition. Even after the secession of eleven states that had cast very few Republican votes in 1860, Lincoln gathered only 55 percent of the 1864 vote in spite of a dramatic pro-Union turn in the tide of the war.[21] As a concession to its uncertain electoral situation, the party went so far as to give the second position on its national ticket to Andrew Johnson, a slaveholding Democrat from a border state.

Just as before the war, political necessity played a large part in the incorporation of territories as states. The Republicans moved quickly to grant statehood to Kansas, Nevada, and the Unionist counties of western Virginia. Congress also voted in 1864 to offer statehood to Colorado, but its voters rejected the state constitution and so Colorado remained outside the Union for another twelve years.

In the cases of West Virginia and Nevada, the Republicans broke decisively with constitutional doctrine and prior practice. Maintaining the illegality of Virginia's ordinance of secession, the congressional Republicans fudged the constitutional restriction against altering a state's borders without its consent. Whereas the creation of West Virginia was a onetime constitutional deviation, the entrance of Nevada deviated from the patterns of antebellum statehood politics. Nevada was admitted even though it fell well short of the admission criteria that had been applied before the war —most notably a population large enough to entitle it to a single House seat.[22] The Republicans' political ingenuity was quickly repaid in electoral votes.

At war's end, the Republican party's future was made more precarious by the impending return of the Confederate states. Given that its success had probably peaked in its core states of the Northeast and Midwest, its survival as the majority party hinged on expanding its sphere of influence. There were two directions it could go: south or west.

A major goal of radical Reconstruction was an attempt to build up the Republican party in the South. The main components of this strategy were black enfranchisement and the reinstitution of Southern Whiggery. The powers of the federal government were forcefully turned in both of these directions. The military was to enforce black voting rights and, equally important, deny them to former Confederates. Federal patronage was used to draw northern Republicans to the South and encourage Southern whites to identify with the party.

With the increasing probability that this original "Southern strategy" would fail, the Republicans turned westward (Stewart and Weingast 1992). This strategy had its own problems. Not the least was that few areas had a substantial population. None of the Republican areas of the West had a population that would support statehood based on prewar standards. Only Mormon (and presumably Democratic) Utah would have qualified. Although the entrance of Nevada showed that the statehood criteria were "suggestions" at best, admitting underpopulated states posed a number of problems for Republicans. The population of the new states remained a potent (though rarely decisive) issue for the Democratic opponents of expansion. Furthermore, the small population bases would be little help in electing substantial numbers of Republicans to the House and be only marginal help in the electoral college. The one salvation was that the malapportionment of the Senate would allow for Republican dominance of that body with the help of newly admitted Western states. The Republicans' best hope was to preserve the status quo via control of the Senate.

There were many other impediments to the new state strategy as well. President Johnson's conflicts with the radical Republicans over Reconstruction policy led him to oppose Western statehood on political grounds. To this end, he vetoed bills calling for Nebraska and Colorado statehood. To complicate matters further, the Republican economic policies were as unpopular with agricultural interests in the West as they were in the South.

The Republicans' hope was that Union veterans living on homesteads and receiving generous pensions would be reluctant to vote for the party of "rum, romanism, and rebellion" regardless of the GOP's other policies.

To better relate statehood to the politics of the era, Tables 14.6 through 14.9 contain all of the major votes on expansion for both houses until 1911. Before we turn to analyzing each statehood controversy, a few comments about general patterns are in order. First, the extent of partisan division grew tremendously. Judging either by the PREs of the unidimensional model or by the partisan voting margin, the issue was far more partisan in the 1880s and 1890s than in the 1860s. In the 1860s, the Democrats were often monolithic, but the Republicans were substantially divided, especially on Colorado. Perhaps because the failure of Southern Republicanism was not yet imminent, other issues also influenced voting decisions before 1876. As the party system became more competitive, however, short-term political considerations came to be dominant. Second, the parties were often inconsistent about which territories they supported for statehood. Republicans went from being the biggest supporters of New Mexico statehood to being diehard opponents just as Democrats picked up its cause.

A final puzzle relates to the extent to which the Democrats emulated the partisan strategies of the Republicans. The Democrats had obviously fewer opportunities in terms of both territories with Democratic leanings and periods of control of the federal government. Furthermore, it would appear that the Democrats failed to move on the entry of Democratic states on the occasions when they had the opportunity. For example, they held both chambers of the 46th Congress but did not record a vote on the admission of the Democratic territories. Although the inaction may be attributable to the fact that there was a Republican in the White House, it does not explain similar inactivity in the Democratic Senate during unified Democratic control of both branches in the 53rd Congress.[23] However, the Democrats did use their control of the House and the presidency to gain admission for Montana with a population well below a House quota as part of the Omnibus Bill in 1888.[24] We shall employ a statistical test to compare the strategies of each party.

THE INTERNAL POLITICS OF THE TERRITORIES

Perhaps the biggest impediment to the implementation of the partisan strategies was the often tumultuous politics of the territories themselves. The powers of territorial assemblies were quite limited. Both Congress and the territorial governor had absolute vetoes over territorial legislation. In this way, the territorial policies of the United States were not that different

Table 14.8

Statehood Roll Calls in the House, 1882–1911

Congress	States	Date	Margin[a]	Republican[a]	Democrat[a]	Class. Errors[b]	PRE[c]	Vote Description
47	Dakota	7/17/1882	103–45	98–3	0–72	4	.95	Adopt H.R. 4456
47	Dakota	2/5/1883	152–110	139–1	6–106	7	.95	Pass H.R. 4672
49	Dak, MT, WA	2/18/1887	112–123	111–0	1–121	1	.99	Fix day to hear bills on admission of Dak, WA, MT
50	South Dakota	1/18/1889	119–122	113–0	2–120	3	.98	Amend S. 185
50	ND, MT, WA, NM	1/18/1889	133–120	0–120	129–0	1	.92	Amend S. 185 with new bill, H.R. 8466
50	South Dakota	1/18/1889	118–131	118–0	0–127	1	.99	Recommit S. 185
50	South Dakota	1/18/1889	145–98	12–98	129–0	12	.88	Pass S. 185
50	South Dakota	1/18/1889	91–108	91–2	0–102	1	.99	Adopt preamble to S. 185
50	South Dakota	2/14/1889	137–103	127–0	7–38	7	.93	Agree to second division of amend. to S. 185
50	South Dakota	2/14/1889	145–110	127–0	15–108	15	.86	Table motion to reconsider vote on second division
50	SD, ND, MT, WA	2/14/1889	148–102	128–0	17–99	16	.84	Agree to third division of amend. to S. 185
51	Wyoming	3/11/1890	125–119	122–0	0–116	0	1.00	Consider H.R. 982
51	Wyoming	3/26/1890	142–139	141–1	0–128	1	.99	Recommit H.R. 982 to Committee on Territories (Nay is proexpansion)

(continued)

Table 14.8
(*continued*)

Congress	States	Date	Margin[a]	Republican[a]	Democrat[a]	Class. Errors[b]	PRE[c]	Vote Description
51	Wyoming	3/26/1890	139–127	138–1	0–126	1	.99	Pass H.R. 982
51	Idaho	4/3/1890	126–112	124–0	0–111	0	1.00	Amend H.R. 4562 to provide for convention
51	Idaho	4/3/1890	121–104	118–0	2–104	2	.98	Require constitutional referendum (Nay is proexpansionist)
51	Idaho	4/3/1890	130–2	127–0	1–1	—	—	Pass H.R. 4562
52	New Mexico	6/6/1892	174–13	2–13	164–0	2	.85	Pass H.R. 7136
53	Utah	12/8/1893	148–6	1–2	137–4	5	.17	Consider H.R. 352
53	Utah	12/8/1893	158–33	9–29	140–4	12	.64	Call of the House during debate on H.R. 352
53	Arizona	12/15/1893	187–62	27–56	150–6	21	.66	Pass H.R. 4393
53	New Mexico	6/27/1894	117–84	1–72	113–7	11	.87	Amend H.R. 353 to req. English in schools (nay is pro–exp.)
53	New Mexico	6/27/1894	115–81	0–70	112–5	7	.91	Amend H.R. 353 to req. English in schools (nay is pro–exp.)
58	OK, AZ, NM	4/19/1904	151–112	148–2	0–109	2	.98	Agree to H. Res. 331, ordering consideration of H.R. 14749

58	OK, AZ, NM	4/19/1904	148–104	144–2	0–102	2	.98	Pass H.R. 14749
58	OK, AZ, NM	4/19/1904	151–112	148–2	0–109	2	.98	Agree to H. Res. 331, ordering consideration of H.R. 14749
58	OK, AZ, NM	4/19/1904	148–104	144–2	0–102	2	.98	Pass H.R. 14749
58	OK, NM	2/17/1905	160–127	159–0	0–127	0	1.00	Previous ques. H. Res. 497, discharge petition on H.R. 14749
58	OK, NM	2/17/1905	161–127	158–1	0–126	1	.99	Pass H. R. 497
59	Oklahoma	1/24/1906	192–165	192–43	0–122	29	.82	Previous question on H.R. 192
59	Oklahoma	1/24/1906	188–158	188–36	0–122	28	.82	Adopt H. R. 192
59	Oklahoma	1/24/1906	195–150	195–33	0–177	25	.83	Pass H.R. 12707
59	Oklahoma	3/22/1906	173–153	173–42	0–111	32	.77	Prev. quest, on H.res. 372 (Remove H.R. 12707 from speaker)
59	Oklahoma	3/22/1906	175–156	175–41	0–115	32	.78	Adopt H.Res. 372 (Remove H.R. 12707 from speaker)
62	NM, AZ	5/23/1911	225–65	36–58	177–0	19	.71	Recommit H.J. Res. 14 (Nay is proexpansionist)

[a]The first entry in the vote splits shows the votes for the *proexpansionist* position.

[b]Total classification errors of the D-NOMINATE model for the roll call.

[c]Proportionate-reduction in error with respect to the margins.

Table 14.9
Statehood Roll Calls in the Senate, 1884–1911

Congress	States	Date	Margin[a]	Republican[a]	Democrat[a]	Class Errors[b]	PRE[c]	Vote Description
48	South Dakota	3/24/1884	35–26	29–0	2–23	2	.92	Make special order for S. 1682
48	South Dakota	12/9/1884	34–25	33–0	0–25	0	1.00	Consider S. 1682
48	South Dakota	12/16/1884	36–32	33–0	0–28	0	1.00	Pass S. 1682
49	South Dakota	2/5/1886	39–27	31–0	1–22	1	.96	Pass S. 967
49	WA, MT	4/8/1886	22–27	0–23	19–0	0	1.00	Amend S. 67
49	Washington	4/10/1886	39–15	26–0	4–13	4	0.73	Pass S. 67
50	South Dakota	4/19/1888	36–26	26–0	0–23	0	1.00	Pass S. 185
51	AZ, ID, NM, WY	6/27/1890	23–35	0–29	18–0	0	1.00	Amend H.R. 982, substitute new bill
51	AZ, ID, NM, WY	6/27/1890	18–34	0–29	18–0	0	1.00	Amend H.R. 982
51	WY, ID	6/27/1890	35–20	29–0	0–18	0	1.00	Pass H.R. 982
58	OK, AZ, NM	1/5/1905	32–19	31–1	0–16	1	.95	Consider H.R. 14749
58	OK, AZ, NM	1/5/1905	32–19	31–1	0–16	1	.95	Recommit H.R. 14749
58	OK, AZ, NM	2/7/1905	36–40	11–26	0–28	8	.78	Amend H.R. 14749, eliminating NM and AZ
61	AZ, NM	6/16/1910	42–22	42–0	0–19	0	1.00	Agree to amendment to H.R. 18166
61	AZ, NM	6/16/1910	65–0	44–0	21–0	—	—	Pass H.R. 18166
61	AZ, NM	3/4/1911	39–45	14–42	25–3	6	.85	Amend H.J. Res. 295
62	AZ, NM	8/8/1911	56–19	23–16	30–2	11	.42	Pass H.J. Res. 14
62	AZ, NM	8/18/1911	59–9	26–7	27–2	7	.22	Pass S.J. res. 57

[a]The first entry in the vote splits shows the votes for the *pro-expansionist* position.
[b]Total classification errors of the D-NOMINATE model for the roll call.
[c]Proportionate-reduction in error with respect to the margins.

from the policies of Britain toward its North American colonies. One major difference was that the federal government paid the salaries of territorial officials. Thus unlike the colonial assemblies, which used salary threats to force the accommodation of royal governors, territorial assemblies had little leverage over the territorial governors. When some territorial assemblies began to "supplement" gubernatorial salaries, Congress banned the practice in 1873 (Pomeroy 1947). Beyond a lack of formal authority, these assemblies also suffered from inexperience, personal opportunism, and corruption, as Lamar's (1956) description of the Dakota assembly illustrates: "The average assemblyman . . . was first of all an opportunist, flexible in his ambitions and shifting in his loyalties. [He] was such a young and active man that the sessions often resembled a college fraternity meeting. On various occasions these frontier solons brandished pistols to get recognition from the Speaker, or had drinks sent in by a nearby saloon" (79).

Given the weaknesses of assemblies, the quality and experience of the federal appointees was a crucial factor in the smooth governing of the territories. Unfortunately, this key to good territorial government was undermined by patronage politics of the postwar era and a general ambivalence in Washington about territorial affairs. Unlike the antebellum era, when such prominent figures as Andrew Jackson, William Henry Harrison, and Lewis Cass served as territorial governors, the Western territories were often governed by spoilsmen and speculators from the East. Only in the late 1880s did a large share of these appointments begin to go to territorial residents.

Given the relatively low salaries the positions commanded, most federal appointees were motivated either by extramural economic opportunities or by political opportunities accompanying statehood, especially election to the Senate. However, given that many governors became extremely unpopular within the territories, the economic opportunities afforded by continuing territorial status dominated the political opportunities of statehood. Thus many governors fostered "federal factions" opposed to statehood.

Territorial delegates, by contrast, tended to support statehood. Since they had proved popular among the territories' voters, they could reasonably expect to remain powerful in a newly formed state government. Thus they were often the foci of pro-statehood factions. Given that these divisions rarely mapped neatly into the national party system, the territorial political system was rife with intraparty factionalism.

Other sources of political conflict were provided by land speculation and the railroads. In the earliest days of newly settled territories, one of the main speculative activities was town site speculating. Various syndicates would claim land and organize it as a town on paper by subdividing it into lots. If a railroad happened to be built through one of these "towns" or a territorial capital were sited there the lots could be sold quickly at an immense profit. The stakes involved exacerbated regional factionalism. It also undermined the collective goal of statehood, as at various times, different factions opposed it for fear that a state government might charter competing rail lines or relocate the capital.

In spite of a general desire for self-government and local control of political offices and patronage, a number of factors undermined desires for statehood. The first was the imminent loss of the federal subsidy given to territories.[25] The second was that many economic interests in the territories benefited from federal control. This was especially true of railroad interests, who feared that state governments might regulate more heavily than the federal government and that they might be tempted to charter competing lines. Creditors also feared that state governments might adopt laws more favorable to debtors. In fact, adopting debt exemption laws was one technique that Western states used to lure immigrants from the East (Lamar 1956).

Congressional Voting on Statehood

To take a closer look at the politics of statehood, we now turn to the history of roll call voting on admissions.

THE WAR YEARS

The debate on the admission of Kansas as a free state began in advance of the secession crisis and wrapped up slightly more than a month after South Carolina passed its articles of secession. In its first session, the 36th House passed H.R. 23. The vote fit nicely into the pattern of statehood voting established in prior episodes. The pattern of the voting on the roll call was primarily regional. Whereas Republicans were unified in support of Kansas as a free state, the Democratic party was deeply split along regional lines. All forty Southern Democrats voted against the bill; Northern Democrats went 21–8 in favor.

Because of Democratic opposition, the Senate did not take up Kansas statehood until January 1861, during the lame-duck session of Congress. A motion in June 1860 by Benjamin Wade to bring the Kansas bill (S. 261) to the floor was defeated on a party-line vote with only two Democratic defections. By the time the bill reached the Senate floor, the secession crisis led many Northern Democrats to break with their Southern colleagues and vote overwhelmingly in favor of statehood. Interestingly, Andrew Johnson was the lone Southerner voting for Kansas. By the time the House voted to concur with the Senate's technical amendments, support was so overwhelming that it was brought to the floor by a two-thirds vote to suspend the rules and then passed on a voice vote.

The absence of Southern representation in Congress gave the Republicans an opportunity to expand the Union. The first opportunity was to create a new state in the mountainous pro-Union areas of Virginia. This was accomplished despite some splits in the Republican party over the details. One split vote took place in the Senate on July 14, 1862, on the West Virginia statehood bill S. 365 (roll call no. 529). Seven Republican senators sided with the Democratic opposition. The opposition came in part from prominent abolitionists such as Preston King and Charles Sumner. Although other abolitionists were strong supporters—notably the bill's sponsor, Benjamin Wade—it was clearly troubling to abolitionists to admit a new state that allowed slavery. The Senate on the same day voted down an amendment to ban slavery in the state (not shown). Four of the seven senators who voted against the bill voted for the amendment. Perhaps the antislavery commitment symbolized by the Emancipation Proclamation issued in September 1862 quelled abolitionist concerns, as Republicans were far more unified on the final passage votes between December 1862 and February 1863.

With the link of slavery to expansion severed, the Republicans turned westward to Nebraska, Nevada, and Colorado. As Stewart and Weingast (1992) point out, these territories failed to meet the prewar criteria for statehood on almost every dimension. Not only were their populations a fraction of that required for a House seat in the established states, but the territories themselves were new creations. The Republicans pushed enabling acts for these territories at the end of the 37th Congress. Nevada passed easily, and Colorado passed by a single vote. However, Nebraska statehood was tabled with Republican votes. The Nevada and Colorado bills reached the House in the shadow of adjournment, forcing supporters to move to suspend the rules to bring the Nevada and Colorado bills to the floor. The motion fell well short of the required two-thirds vote.

The setback was temporary for Nevada, as its enabling act was passed on voice votes early in the 38th Congress. Colorado's act passed on a voice vote in the Senate and a lopsided roll call in the House. To the chagrin of its supporters, Colorado voters rejected the constitution crafted at the territorial convention and so remained outside the Union.[26] A Nebraska bill passed the House with Republican support, but no action was taken in the Senate.

RECONSTRUCTION

After Lincoln's death, statehood politics became intimately entwined with the controversies over Reconstruction. President Johnson was disinclined to help his radical opponents increase their representation in the Senate. He also felt that it was inappropriate to admit new states until the Southern states were returned to their former status. Therefore, when Johnson was presented with bills for Colorado and Nebraska statehood in May 1866, he vetoed them. Colorado statehood had insufficient support for an override, and Nebraska was the victim of a pocket veto. Johnson's stated justification for the vetoes was that the proposed constitutions guaranteed suffrage only to whites, although he was otherwise no champion of the rights of blacks (Sefton 1980). In the case of Nebraska, this strategy backfired, as a new statehood bill was passed that guaranteed black suffrage. It shored up support among Republican radicals such as Charles Sumner and Benjamin Wade. The more unified Republicans easily overrode a second veto. The same tactic failed to gain Colorado statehood. The veto override fell just three votes short. From the D-NOMINATE estimation, it appears that the defection of New York's Senate delegation and a couple of New England senators was pivotal. The tumultuous nature of Colorado politics undoubtedly contributed. It was likely that the same conflicts that had sunk statehood three years earlier could be rekindled.[27]

Colorado's statehood struggle continued until the final days of Reconstruction. In the lame-duck session after the loss of the House in the 1874 elections, Republicans sought to admit Colorado and New Mexico. The bills passed the Senate easily (Colorado, 47–17; New Mexico, 31–11). Though unified on Colorado, the Republicans were somewhat split over New Mexico. As there was unified Democratic opposition, it seems unlikely that New Mexico was considered less reliably Republican. Opposition to a state with a Spanish-speaking majority was more likely a cause. New Mexico's Hispanic population was strongly Union during the war and sympathetic to radical Reconstruction, but the fact that only two New Mexico counties could feasibly hold jury trials in English gave nativists a potent issue (Larson 1968). Debates over whether the state constitution should make English the official language and require English instruction in public schools dominated the deliberations. The critical votes in the House came as the lame-duck session wound down. Because of time constraints, supporters of both bills sought to avoid a referral to the Committee on Territories. They therefore sought to bring the bills to the floor under a suspension of the rules, which required a two-thirds majority (Larson 1968). The first motion, which sought to bring both bills to the floor, failed by one vote (164–83). The motions were then split. Colorado's motion passed (166–78), and New Mexico's failed (155–86). Six Republicans voted yes on Colorado and no on New Mexico, and four Democrats did the same. Colorado entered the Union just in time to cast its three electoral votes for Hayes in the 1876 elections.[28]

THE ERA OF PARTISAN BALANCE

The elections of 1876 ushered in an era of partisan balance and recurring divided government. The stakes involved in statehood politics had increased, but neither party had sufficient control of the federal government to push the admission of its preferred states. No serious attempt at expansion was mounted until the late 1880s. Bills on behalf of the Dakotas often passed one house only to die in the other. In the elections of 1888, however, both political parties had strong expansionist planks. The Democrats called for statehood for Montana, Dakota, Washington, and New Mexico, and the Republicans added Wyoming, Idaho, and Arizona (Spence 1975). When the Republicans swept both branches of government, the Democrats were eager to act in order to deny the Republicans all the credit. In the following lame-duck session, the Democratic House and president and the Republican Senate were able to reach agreement on the admission of North and South Dakota, Washington, and Montana. The Democrats saw the admission of the Republican Dakotas and Washington as a fait accompli. Rather than obstruct, they were able to secure admission of Democratic Montana. The Democrats also sought the admission of New Mexico, but that proposal was eliminated in conference because of Republican opposition. In 1890, the now dominant Republicans pushed Wyoming and Idaho on strict party-line voting. The Democrats' only feasible defense was to attempt to insert delays into the ratification process of the state constitutions, but these amendments were voted down each time. By the time Idaho came up for final passage in the House, all but two Democrats had left the floor in an attempt to withhold quorum.

In spite of years of Democratic support for Utah statehood, two factors delayed its admission. The first was Mormon opposition to federal laws against plural marriage, and the second was the fact that the Mormons tended to support their own local political party rather than the national parties (Lyman 1986). The way for statehood was finally paved by the Woodruff Manifesto, which declared that polygamy violated Mormon doctrine, and by the disbanding of the Mormon political party.[29] When these events combined with the Democratic victories in 1892, Utah was granted statehood.

The enabling bill passed the House with Republican opposition on procedural roll calls. Final passage occurred on a voice vote on December 12, 1893. By the time the bill reached the Senate, the Republicans were fully on board lest they completely alienate the citizens of the future state of Utah. At the same time, Democratic leaders became hesitant after a dramatic shift to the Republicans in the previous territorial assembly elections. Because they could no longer blame the Republicans' intransigence on Utah, however, they eventually allowed the bill to come to the floor. It passed on a voice vote. The Democrats were rewarded with three electoral votes for Bryan, and the Republicans got two more Senators.

THE SOUTHWEST

After the admission of Idaho and Wyoming, the only remaining territories in the contiguous United States were New Mexico, Arizona, and Oklahoma. Once again, partisanship played a big role in forming preferences over statehood. The Republicans were keen to admit Oklahoma, whereas Arizona and New Mexico were considered Democratic projects.

After the House was restored to Democratic control by the 1890 midterm elections, the House passed New Mexico and Arizona bills, but the Republican Senate was not interested.[30] When similar bills passed the House in 1893, they surprisingly died in a Democratic Senate.[31]

The three remaining territories made the next major push for statehood jointly in the 58th Congress. The proposal called for Oklahoma and the Indian Territory to be admitted as one state and for New Mexico and Arizona to be admitted as the state of Montezuma. Presumably, the proposal was designed to generate enough partisan balance to get through a unified Republican government. While Republican attempts to sever the proposal into separate bills for each state failed, the desired effect was achieved through the bitter political rivalries between Arizona and New Mexico. After the bill was passed, Oklahoma moved quickly toward statehood; Arizona and New Mexico residents had to vote on the controversial jointure proposal. An overwhelmingly antijointure vote in Arizona led to the referendum's defeat.

Finally, in 1911, a Democratic House, with the help of many Republicans, especially in the Senate, passed an act calling for separate statehood for Arizona and New Mexico. But the completion of the continental forty-eight was not achieved without some controversy. The proposed Arizona state constitution was a manifesto for the progressive movement that contained many of the movement's favorite political institutions and reforms. Most controversial was the provision for voter recall of state judges. This proposal enraged not only conservatives like President Taft but some leading progressives as well. Ironically, New Mexico's constitution was attacked as being too conservative because its amendment procedures were too demanding. Taft vetoed the first resolution accepting the state constitutions. When a resolution passed to accept the Arizona constitution if voters struck the offending provision, Taft signed it. Arizona and New Mexico soon joined the Union.

The Effects of Partisanship on Admissions: A Statistical Analysis

To test the partisan hypothesis, we collected data on the populations of each organized territory from 1863 to 1913 as well as the partisan identifications of the territorial delegate to the U.S. Congress. We then estimated a model of the probability that a given territory was admitted during a particular congressional session as a function of its size, its partisanship, and party control of the federal government. As Beck, Katz, and Tucker (1998) suggest, this setup has a close resemblance to duration or hazard analysis. Per this analogy, the organized territories are the "risk set," and admission constitutes a "failure." Thus the data set is composed of 171 territory and Congress observations, twelve of which are the admission of a new state.[32] Unlike standard duration analysis, this approach easily lends itself to an analysis of independent variables that change over time, such as territorial population and partisanship. To capture any possible duration dependence, we include a variable that indicates how long a territory has been organized. For example, if the length of the organizational phase increases self-governing capacity, we might expect that the longer a territory has been organized, the more likely it is to be admitted. However, alternatively, the fact that a territory has been organized without admission for a long time may indicate that there are unmeasured factors preventing its entry. In this case, the length of time since organization may lower the likelihood of admission.

The basic model, which we estimate via probit, is therefore

$$\text{Prob\{Admit\}} = \beta_1 + \beta_2 REPCONTROL + \beta_3 DEMCONTROL + \beta_4 POPRATIO + \beta_5 YRSORG$$

The first two independent variables are constructed from interactions of the partisanship of the territorial delegate and control of the federal government. *REPCONTROL* is an indicator for a Republican delegate multiplied by the number of branches (House, Senate, presidency) controlled by the Republicans. The variable *DEMCONTROL* is defined similarly. Implicit in

Table 14.10
Results of the Statistical Analysis Model

	Coefficient	Mean	SD	Min	Max
Constant	−4.042 (1.001)	—	—	—	—
REPCONTROL	0.356 (0.168)	1.129	1.313	0.000	3.000
DEMCONTROL	0.500 (0.245)	0.234	0.635	0.000	3.000
POPRATIO	0.265 (0.166)	0.624	0.770	0.015	5.584
YRSORG (natural log)	0.550 (0.283)	2.651	0.930	0.000	0.930
N	171				
Log-likelihood	−34.161				
Pseudo R^2	0.214				

this specification is that territories represented by independents receive no partisan benefits toward admission.[33] It also assumes linear effects for the number of branches each party controls. *POPRATIO* is the territorial population divided by the Vinton ratio established by the most recent apportionment act. Due to the lack of data on annual population changes, the territorial population was linearly extrapolated between decennial censuses. The final variable *YRSORG* is just the natural logarithm of the number of years for which the territory has been organized.[34] The results of the model are given in Table 14.10.

These results show the mixture of partisan and efficiency motivations. Both *POPRATIO* and *YRSORG* have positive substantively large coefficients, although the coefficient for *POPRATIO* falls just short of conventional significance levels. Not surprisingly, given the extent of partisanship on statehood roll calls, the partisan control variables are strongly significant. The substantive importance of these effects is underscored by the fact that a territory with an apportionment ratio of 1 and an average organizational period has only a 1.6 percent chance of being admitted when the opposite party is in power. Alternatively, when the Republicans are in complete control, a territory with a Republican delegate has a 14.4 percent chance of statehood. When the Democrats are in charge, Democratic territories get admitted with a 26.4 percent chance. While the differences between Republican and Democratic control fail to reach statistical significance, they are substantively large and robust across different specifications.[35] Given that the pattern of admissions generally favored the Republicans, it is interesting

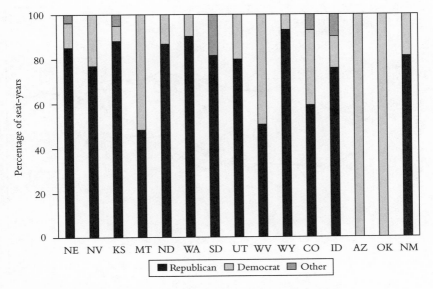

Figure 14.11. State representation in the Senate, 1861–1920.

that the Republican standard for admission of its states was so much more stringent than that of the Democrats. If the Republicans had used the Democratic standard, its advantage would have been certainly earlier and possibly larger.

THE POLITICAL AND POLICY EFFECTS OF EXPANSION

How successful was partisan expansion in promoting its political and policy goals of the Republican party? Let us first look at the effects of expansion on the composition of the Senate. While we agree with Stewart and Weingast (1992) that partisanship of territorial delegates helped predict party positions on statehood controversies, we wish to stress how *ex post* uncertain these partisan loyalties were. Figure 14.11 shows the percentage of seat-years of new states that each party controlled in the Senate. Although Democrats were relatively rewarded for their efforts on Montana statehood, they were burned by Utah and New Mexico. Republicans were also guilty of major miscalculations on Colorado, Arizona, West Virginia, and Oklahoma. This reasonably low correlation between territorial and state patterns of partisanship reinforces exactly how fluid politics were in the West.[36]

To get a better sense of the policy effects, we look at the relationship of

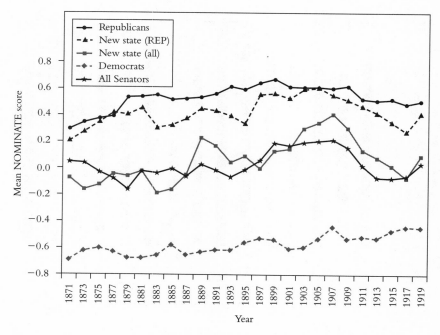

Figure 14.12. D-NOMINATE scores for representation in the Senate, 1871–1919.

the new entrants to old state Republicans on the first-dimension D-NOM-INATE scores. Then we examine two issues that were important to the Republicans and distinguished them from the Democrats: tariffs and currency (see Poole and Rosenthal 1997). Did members of Congress from the new states support the Republicans on these issues? We examine voting patterns on these issues from 1871 to 1919 to see if the new states were sources of support for Republican policies.

Figure 14.12 shows the mean D-NOMINATE score in the Senate for each party juxtaposed against that of the Republicans from the new states (as shown in Figure 14.11) for the years 1871–1919. Clearly, senators from the new states occupied the central part of the political spectrum. This pattern is due to two factors: some of the new senators were affiliated with the Democrats; and Republican senators from the Western states were systematically more moderate than Republicans elsewhere. The net effect of expanding statehood on the political center of the Senate is negligible except for two periods of slight Republican advantage around 1890 and 1910.

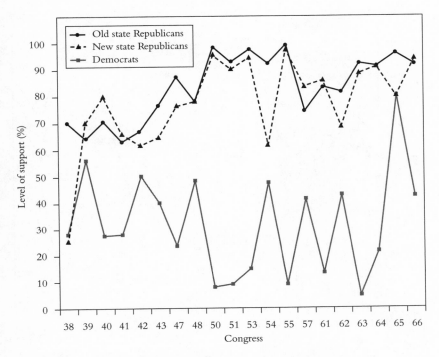

Figure 14.13.   Support of Republican positions on tariffs, 38th–66th Congresses.

We now turn to the effects on the salient issues of trade and currency. Figures 14.13 and 14.14 show the support scores for the Republican majority (old states') position on tariff and currency votes.[37] Because these issues define the postwar party alignment, we find that Republican support on these issues is very high and Democratic support very low. However, new state Republican support is quite mixed. Tariff support does not differ significantly between the new and old states. In fact, Westerners were occasionally a bit more supportive of the Republican position. Thus statehood politics probably did help the Republican bid to maintain high tariffs. Currency is quite a different story. After 1880, Western Republican support for hard money was always well below that of the Eastern Republicans and occasionally below that of Democrats. When the Democratic and Populist senators are added to the mix, the Republican admissions policy moved monetary policy decidedly toward the position of the Democrats.

It is unclear to what extent Republicans were aware of or anticipated these

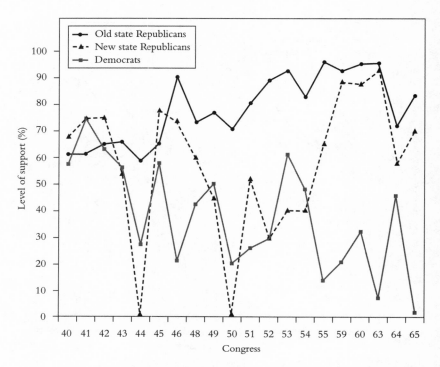

Figure 14.14. Support of Republican positions on hard money, 40th–65th Congresses.

policy trade-offs, but the net policy effect of Western expansion seems to have been higher tariffs and softer money. One should not, however, exaggerate the effects of the new states on the Republican party. The difference between new-state Republicans and the overall party, shown in Figure 14.12, is generally small, particularly in the 52nd Congress, when the party split before the presidential election. The reason is that agrarian or progressive Republicans were not confined to the new states. For example, the ten most liberal Republican D-NOMINATE scores in the 60th Senate (1911–13) were evenly divided between Republicans from antebellum admits (Lafollete, Wis.; Clapp, Minn.; Works, Calif.; Kenyon, Ia.; and Cummins, Ia.) and those from new states (Poindexter, Wash.; Bristow, Kans.; Borah, Idaho; Gronna, N.D.; and Crawford, S.D.). The intersectional rivalry was not between the thinly populated new states and older ones but between the farm belt and the industrial states.

Conclusion

Territorial expansion and the incorporation of new states is one of the most important institutional changes that the United States has endured since its inception. The politics of statehood has had substantial effects on the historical development of American political institutions and policies. The debates over these institutional changes, however, were not couched in broad, principled terms but rather in terms of short-run political expediency. The inability of statehood politics (or any other institutional change) to commit the nation to any particular policy course meant that short-term considerations always dominated. Thus statehood was always tied to the political concerns and party systems of the day. Just as the so-called balance rule was a set of short-term fixes rather than a long-term commitment, postbellum Republican dominance through expansion proved elusive.

The politics of statehood provides many lessons for the study of the processes of institutional change. The analogies to other federations undergoing potential expansion, such as the European Union, are clear. We also learn much about institutional change in general. It is rarely carried out through a "veil of ignorance." It is difficult to use institutional mechanisms to generate long-term commitments. Given these conditions, the battle over short-term advantage is rarely likely to lead to the most efficient set of institutions.

Chapter 15

Representation of the Antebellum South in the House of Representatives: Measuring the Impact of the Three-Fifths Clause

BRIAN D. HUMES, ELAINE K. SWIFT,
RICHARD M. VALELLY, KENNETH FINEGOLD,
AND EVELYN C. FINK

During the Constitutional Convention, Southern ambivalence toward the Constitution was resolved through a number of sectional compromises. One of the most important was the three-fifths clause" of Article 1, which provided that three-fifths of all slaves be counted as part of a state's population when apportioning congressional seats. The clause reads as follows:

> Representatives and direct Taxes shall be apportioned among the several States which may be included within this Union, according to their respective Numbers, which shall be determined by adding to the whole Number of free Persons, including those bound to Service for a Term of Years, and excluding Indians not taxed, three fifths of all other Persons.

Enforcement of this clause enabled the South to receive significantly more House seats than would have been the case had it been apportioned on the same basis as the North. This malapportionment in turn created ripple effects inside and outside the institution, further magnifying the section's seat advantage.[1]

Between 1795 and 1861, the three-fifths clause openly and systematically gave the South a disproportionate share of seats in the House. This overrepresentation allowed Southerners to wield tremendous power over House decisions; in addition to influencing legislative battles, the clause also affected the outcomes of two critical presidential elections. Thus it played an important part in shaping the course of antebellum U.S. history.

In this chapter, we advance two counterfactual thought experiments as a means of measuring the impact of the three-fifths clause.[2] In our first counterfactual, we estimate how representatives would have been apportioned in the antebellum era if slaves in the South had not been counted for purposes of apportionment. We then apply these apportionment figures in several ways. First, we look at roll call votes in the House, presenting data on the number of outcomes altered by the enforcement of the three-fifths clause. Next, we look to see whether any "major" legislation that passed during this period would have been defeated. Finally, we examine the collateral effects of the clause on the electoral college.

In our second counterfactual, we imagine an antebellum United States where slaves were counted in the same way as women and children. That is, we count slaves as whole persons for the purpose of apportionment.[3] We then repeat the analysis of the first counterfactual, looking at both the number of roll call vote outcomes altered and the collateral effects of the clause on the electoral college. *Whereas both counterfactuals yield significant departures from the historical record, our first counterfactual represents a more drastic change from actual outcomes.* Had slaves not been counted for purposes of apportionment of House seats in the antebellum South, nearly half of the roll call votes could have had different outcomes, including a number of "major" pieces of legislation. Further, we find that the outcomes of two critical presidential elections—1800 and 1824—would likely have been reversed without the enforcement of the three-fifths clause.

To conclude, however, that these findings represent the *actual* effect of the three-fifths clause would require the strong assumption that aside from the method of counting blacks, all else would have remained constant. In particular, three aspects of the lawmaking process—the types of Southern representatives elected, the way those representatives voted, and the legislative agenda—would have to have been the same in order for our counterfactuals to accurately portray the alternative outcomes that would have been obtained without the three-fifths clause (see Appendixes A and B to this chapter for further discussion of our assumptions). We do not assert that all else would have been constant. Rather, the findings in this chapter should be understood as the maximum possible effect of the three-fifths clause. We contend that the magnitude of our results, particularly in the first counterfactual, demonstrates a clear and substantial effect.

The chapter proceeds as follows. First, we show how the apportionment of House seats would have changed if slaves had not been counted for apportionment. Next, based on the new apportionment, we predict the outcomes of all roll call votes in the House from 1795 to 1861, followed by a more specific investigation of some of the major legislation of that era. We then turn to our second counterfactual and again perform an analysis of legislative outcomes between 1795 and 1861. Following that, we apply both of our counterfactual apportioning procedures to the electoral college and look at how each might have changed the outcomes of presidential elections.

Counterfactual 1: Slaves Are Not Counted for Apportionment Purposes

In order to estimate the South's gains from the three-fifths clause, we must first define what constituted the South in antebellum politics. Although the postbellum South was, and is, commonly defined as the former states of the Confederacy (Black and Black 1992; Key 1984; Kousser 1974), antebellum political actors included other states — typically border states with significant slave populations — in their view of that region. Adopting the construction of contemporaries, we define the South as the "slave states " that Congress sought to evenly balance with "free states" in the composition of the antebellum Senate: Alabama, Arkansas, Delaware, Florida, Georgia, Kentucky, Louisiana, Maryland, Mississippi, Missouri, North Carolina, South Carolina, Tennessee, Texas, and Virginia (Swift 1996: 108–110).

CONGRESSIONAL APPORTIONMENT

In Appendix A, we detail our methods for assessing the number of representatives the South gained from the three-fifths clause. Here, suffice it to say that in apportioning seats to Southern states, we applied the same formulas used to allot House members to Northern states. Table 15.1 presents our results. The three-fifths clause awarded the South significant extra representation. Between the 4th (1795–97) and 36th (1859–61) Congresses, the South gained anywhere from 14 to 30 seats per Congress, with an average gain of 20 seats.

Further, the seats the South gained from the three-fifths clause were fairly evenly distributed between the parties of the period. In sharp contrast to the Solid Democratic South that would take root in the late nineteenth and early twentieth centuries, the antebellum period was far more competitive, particularly after the emergence of the Jacksonian Democrats and the Whigs. Unsurprisingly, then, our estimates of the impact of the clause on party and factional strength show that it had limited impact on their relative proportions in the House.[4] In the 4th through 17th Congresses (1795–1823), the

Table 15.1

Impact of the Three-Fifths Clause on Slave and Nonslave State Representation, 4th–36th Congresses (1795–1861)

Census Used for Apportionment	Congresses Affected	WITH THREE-FIFTHS CLAUSE		WITH SLAVES NOT COUNTED[a]		Slave State Gains from Three Fifths Clause
		Slave States[b]	Nonslave States[b]	Slave States[b]	Nonslave States[b]	
1790	4th–7th	49 (46.2%)	57 (53.8%)	35 (38.5%)	56 (61.5%)	14 (7.7%)
1800	8th–12th	66 (46.2%)	77 (53.8%)	50 (39.4%)	77 (60.6%)	16 (6.8%)
1810	13th–17th	81 (43.5%)	105 (56.5%)	63 (37.7%)	104 (62.3%)	18 (5.6%)
1820	18th–22nd	90 (42.3%)	123 (57.7%)	68 (35.6%)	123 (64.4%)	22 (6.7%)
1830	23rd–27th	100 (41.3%)	142 (58.7%)	75 (34.6%)	142 (65.4%)	25 (6.7%)
1840	28th–32nd	89 (38.4%)	143 (61.6%)	74 (32.5%)	154 (67.5%)	15 (6.1%)
1850	33rd–36th	95 (41.8%)	132 (58.2%)	75 (33.1%)	152 (66.9%)	30 (12.6%)

[a]See Appendix A for the method by which representation was estimated in the absence of the three-fifths clause.

[b]Slave and nonslave states were defined by the antebellum conventions used to balance representation of these interests in the U.S. Senate (Swift 1996). The following were considered slave states: Alabama, Arkansas, Delaware, Florida, Georgia, Kentucky, Louisiana, Maryland, Mississippi, North Carolina, South Carolina, Tennessee, Texas, and Virginia.

Jeffersonian Republicans gained 1.1 percent more adherents, while the Federalists lost the same proportion. In the 18th through 24th Congresses (1823–37), a period marked by competition between an emerging Jacksonian party and less organized anti-Jacksonian factions, the Jacksonians gained just 0.7 percent more seats, while the opposition lost 1.6 percent. From the 25th through 33rd Congresses (1837–55), the high tide of competition between the Jacksonians and the Whigs, the former gained 0.9 percent more seats, while the latter lost 1 percent.[5]

LEGISLATIVE OUTCOMES

The South's inflated House delegation made its numbers felt in legislative outcomes. As Table 15.2 shows, we find that the clause changed the results in 41.3 percent of the roll calls in the antebellum period, changing winning coalitions into losers and losing coalitions into winners (see Appendix B for a discussion of the procedures behind these results). The percentage of roll calls that changed ranges from 26.3 percent in the 34th Congress (1859–61) to 55.3 percent in the 6th Congress (1799–1801). Analyzing the roll call results on a decade-by-decade basis, we find that the clause affected almost half of the roll calls in the 1790s; the proportion of bills affected is 28.9 percent in the first decade of the 1800s, 37.8 percent in the 1810s, and 36.5 percent in the 1820s. This figure then increases, peaking at 51 percent in the 1840s. While these numbers seem to show a trend in the clause's impact, there is a considerable amount of variation within each decade. However, it is clear from this analysis that a large number of roll call votes were affected.[6]

Our analysis further suggests that the South's bonus seats had an impact on a wider variety of issues than just those traditionally associated with the region, including government management, social welfare, agricultural assistance, civil liberties, and international involvement. We found that there is little variation in the degree to which the clause reversed outcomes in each of the categories.

Of course, one might inquire whether these were important votes or not. Although we cannot directly answer this question, we can begin to address it by looking at the impact of the three-fifths clause on major legislation. We use Dell and Stathis (1982) to identify important measures in each Congress from the 4th through the 36th.[7] For each Congress, Dell and Stathis identify two to six pieces of legislation. A large number of the measures identified did not have recorded votes on final passage. However, this list is not intended as an exhaustive analysis. Rather it is presented as an illustration of the types of measures that could have been defeated with a change in apportionment. For measures where there are final recorded votes, we note

Table 15.2

Roll Call Votes Affected by the Three-Fifths Clause,
4th–36th Congresses (1795–1861)

Congress (years)	Affected Votes	Total Votes	Percentage of Votes Affected
4 (1795–1797)	25	83	30.1
5 (1797–1799)	86	155	55.5
6 (1799–1801)	54	96	56.3
7 (1801–1803)	44	142	31.0
8 (1803–1805)	41	132	31.1
9 (1805–1807)	52	158	32.9
10 (1807–1809)	54	237	22.8
11 (1809–1811)	77	293	26.3
12 (1811–1813)	97	314	30.9
13 (1813–1815)	112	352	31.8
14 (1815–1817)	41	113	36.3
15 (1817–1819)	48	106	45.3
16 (1819–1821)	66	147	44.9
17 (1821–1823)	26	95	27.4
18 (1823–1825)	40	94	42.6
19 (1825–1827)	49	111	44.1
20 (1827–1829)	76	233	32.6
21 (1829–1831)	98	273	35.9
22 (1831–1833)	212	462	45.9
23 (1833–1835)	138	327	42.2
24 (1835–1837)	150	459	32.7
25 (1837–1839)	197	475	41.5
26 (1839–1841)	327	751	43.5
27 (1841–1843)	474	974	48.7
28 (1843–1845)	278	597	46.6
29 (1845–1847)	331	642	51.6
30 (1847–1849)	273	478	57.1
31 (1849–1851)	293	572	51.2
32 (1851–1853)	239	455	52.5
33 (1853–1855)	290	607	47.8
34 (1855–1857)	403	729	55.3
35 (1857–1859)	274	548	50.0
36 (1859–1861)	167	433	38.6

the measures that could have been defeated if the South did not receive apportionment based on its slaves. The measures discussed here are the only ones that are identified by Dell and Stathis for which a roll call vote was taken on final passage.

In the 4th through 6th Congresses, five measures would have been defeated with a change in apportionment. In the 5th Congress, there were three measures: an act to establish a Department of the Navy, the Alien Act, and the Sedition Act. The latter two acts were parts of the Alien and Sedition Acts that encouraged and reinforced in the split between the Federalists and the Jeffersonian Republicans. In the 6th Congress, a change in apportionment would have resulted in the defeat of the First Federal Bankruptcy Law and the Judiciary Act of 1801. The latter act reduced the number of Supreme Court justices from six to five, increased the number of district courts, and established six circuit courts.

In the 7th through 11th Congresses, there were only two acts that would have been defeated. Both occurred in the 9th Congress: the Cumberland Road Act and the Judiciary Act of 1807. The former was the first major internal improvement project funded by the federal government and created the most important route for immigration to the Northwest until 1840. The latter increased the number of Supreme Court justices from six to seven.

In the 12th through 16th Congresses, only one major piece of legislation would have been affected. In the 14th Congress, the Second National Bank of the United States was established. The creation of the bank, of course, led to major political battles in the 1830s between President Jackson and the supporters of the National Bank.

In the 17th through 21st Congresses, only the Indian Removal Act, passed in the 21st Congress, met our criteria. This act arranged for the removal of Native Americans to lands west of the Mississippi. It resulted in the forcible relocation of the Chickasaws, Choctaws, Creeks, Cherokees, and Seminoles to present-day Oklahoma. Thus this act authorized what is now referred to as the "Trail of Tears."

In the 22nd through 26th Congresses, only one act would have been affected. This was the Tariff Act of 1832, passed in the 22nd Congress. This act was expected to appease the antiprotectionist South. However, soon after its passage, South Carolina adopted the Ordinance of Nullification. This resulted in President Jackson's call for a "force bill."

In the 27th through 31st Congresses, two pieces of legislation would have been affected, both in the 31st Congress. The Texas and New Mexico Act established boundaries between the United States and Texas, compensated Texas for relinquishing claims to New Mexico, and made provisions to allow the citizens of New Mexico to decide if it would be admitted as a slave state or a free state. The Utah Act established the boundaries of that state and let its voters decide whether it was to be a free or slave state.

In the 32nd through 36th Congresses, only the English Bill passed in the 34th Congress with a sufficiently small margin that it could have been defeated without the three-fifths clause. This bill concerned the admission of Kansas to the statehood. It stated that Kansas would be admitted immediately if its citizens accepted the Lecompton Constitution. If its citizens rejected this measure, the state would not be admitted until it met the minimal size required for apportionment of a member of the House of Representatives.

The foregoing discussion clearly shows that policy was affected by the three-fifths clause. We have shown that the outcomes of numerous votes would have changed had apportionment been done without counting slaves as part of a state's population. We have also shown that several important pieces of legislation would have been defeated without the additional representation given to the South through the implementation of the clause. Although some of these measures were not as important as others, some clearly defined the political landscape of the time. As such, it is clear that the North yielded something real to the South when it agreed to the three-fifths clause.

Counterfactual 2: Slaves Count as Whole Persons for Apportionment Purposes

Of course, because the three-fifths clause was a compromise, the South also made concessions to the North; let us now consider what the South yielded when it agreed to the compromise by examining what would have happened if slaves had been counted as whole persons for apportionment purposes.

CONGRESSIONAL APPORTIONMENT

We repeat our earlier analysis, with one change. Instead of not counting slaves toward apportionment at all, we count slaves as whole persons. Except for the weightings, the process is identical to that discussed earlier and in Appendix A.

Table 15.3 presents our results. As we can see, the three-fifths clause reduced the proportion of seats awarded to the South. Between the 4th (1795–97) and 36th (1859–61) Congresses, the South lost anywhere from 6 to 15 seats, with an average loss of 10.9 seats.

Once again, the seats that the South lost from the three-fifths clause were fairly evenly distributed between the parties of the period. Unsurprisingly,

Table 15.3

Impact of the Three-Fifths Clause on Slave and Nonslave State Representation, 4th–36th Congresses (1795–1861), with Slaves Counted as Whole Persons

Census Used for Apportionment	Congresses Affected	WITH THREE-FIFTHS CLAUSE		WITH SLAVES NOT COUNTED[a]		Slave State Gains from Three Fifths Clause
		Slave States[b]	Nonslave States[b]	Slave States[b]	Nonslave States[b]	
1790	4th–7th	49 (46.2%)	57 (53.8%)	55 (49.1%)	57 (50.9%)	6 (5.7%)
1800	8th–12th	66 (46.2%)	77 (53.8%)	75 (49.3%)	77 (50.7%)	9 (13.6%)
1810	13th–17th	81 (43.5%)	105 (56.5%)	95 (47.3%)	106 (52.7%)	14 (17.2%)
1820	18th–22nd	90 (42.3%)	123 (57.7%)	104 (45.8%)	123 (54.2%)	14 (15.6%)
1830	23rd–27th	100 (41.3%)	142 (58.7%)	115 (34.6%)	142 (65.4%)	15 (15.0%)
1840	28th–32nd	89 (38.4%)	143 (61.6%)	100 (44.7%)	137 (55.3%)	11 (12.4%)
1850	33rd–36th	90 (40.5%)	132 (59.5%)	97 (43.7%)	125 (56.3%)	7 (7.8%)

[a]See Appendix A for the method by which representation was estimated in the absence of the three-fifths clause.

[b]Slave and nonslave states were defined by the antebellum conventions used to balance representation of these interests in the U.S. Senate (Swift 1996). The following were considered slave states: Alabama, Arkansas, Delaware, Florida, Georgia, Kentucky, Louisiana, Maryland, Mississippi, Missouri, North Carolina, South Carolina, Tennessee, Texas, and Virginia.

then, our estimates of the impact of the clause on party and factional strength show that it had limited impact on their relative proportions in the House.[8]

LEGISLATIVE OUTCOMES

The South's deflated delegation weakened its influence on legislative outcomes. As Table 15.4 shows, we find that the clause changed the results in 26.3 percent of the roll calls in the antebellum period (again, see Appendix B for a discussion of the procedures behind these results). The percentage of roll calls affected ranges between 10.8 percent in the 4th Congress (1795–97) to 36.2 percent in the 18th (1823–25). Decade by decade, the pattern is as follows: the clause affected almost one-quarter of the roll calls in the 1790s, 22.1 percent of its roll calls in the next decade, and 29.7 percent in the 1810s, which is the high point of the number of roll calls affected; the level declined to 25.7 percent in the 1820s and rose slightly to 27 percent in the 1830s and 27.5 percent in the 1840s and 1850s. While these numbers seem to show a slight trend in the clause's impact, there is a considerable amount of variation within each decade. However, it is clear from this analysis that a significant number of roll call votes were affected.[9]

As in our first counterfactual, further analysis suggests that the South's loss of seats had an impact on a wider variety of issues than just those traditionally associated with the region. Looking at the same issue areas—government management, social welfare, agricultural assistance, civil liberties, and international involvement—we again found little variation in the degree to which the clause reversed outcomes in each of the categories.

Collateral Effects of the Three-Fifths Clause

House apportionments determine the size of a state's delegation in Congress, as well as the size of its delegation in the electoral college.[10] The South therefore reaped dividends from the enforcement of the three-fifths clause not only in its number of representatives but also in the number of its electors. In general, the clause increased the importance of the South in presidential contests, inflating the extent to which the region had to be courted in order to secure an electoral college victory. As we can see from Table 15.5, the impact of the three-fifths clause on the electoral college was especially important in the formative stages of the first party system, affording a decisive advantage to the Jeffersonians, who were stronger in the South. Moreover, it undoubtedly encouraged that party to maintain its

Table 15.4

Roll Call Votes Affected by the Three-Fifths Clause,
4th–36th Congresses (1795–1861) with Slaves Fully Counted

Congress (years)	Affected Votes	Total Votes	Percentage of Votes Affected
4 (1795–1797)	9	83	10.8
5 (1797–1799)	46	155	29.7
6 (1799–1801)	34	96	35.4
7 (1801–1803)	24	142	16.9
8 (1803–1805)	27	132	20.5
9 (1805–1807)	31	158	32.9
10 (1807–1809)	23	237	19.6
11 (1809–1811)	46	293	15.7
12 (1811–1813)	56	314	17.8
13 (1813–1815)	87	352	24.7
14 (1815–1817)	33	113	29.2
15 (1817–1819)	44	106	41.5
16 (1819–1821)	52	147	35.4
17 (1821–1823)	17	95	17.9
18 (1823–1825)	34	94	36.2
19 (1825–1827)	36	111	32.4
20 (1827–1829)	49	233	21.0
21 (1829–1831)	57	273	20.8
22 (1831–1833)	140	462	30.3
23 (1833–1835)	97	327	29.7
24 (1835–1837)	88	459	19.2
25 (1837–1839)	129	475	27.2
26 (1839–1841)	214	751	28.5
27 (1841–1843)	320	974	32.9
28 (1843–1845)	140	597	23.5
29 (1845–1847)	166	642	25.9
30 (1847–1849)	143	478	29.9
31 (1849–1851)	145	572	25.3
32 (1851–1853)	106	455	23.3
33 (1853–1855)	149	607	24.5
34 (1855–1857)	263	729	36.1
35 (1857–1859)	184	548	33.6
36 (1859–1861)	88	433	20.3

Table 15.5

Impact of the Three-Fifths Clause on the Electoral College, 1792–1860

Census Used for Apportionment	Congresses Affected	WITH THREE-FIFTHS CLAUSE		WITH SLAVES NOT COUNTED		Slave State Gains from Three Fifths Clause
		Slave States	Nonslave States	Slave States	Nonslave States	
1790	4th–7th	65 (47.1%)	73 (52.9%)	51 (41.5%)	72 (58.5%)	14 (5.6%)
1800	8th–12th	81 (46.0%)	95 (54.0%)	65 (40.6%)	95 (59.4%)	16 (5.4%)
1810	13th–17th	103 (44.0%)	131 (56.0%)	85 (39.5%)	130 (60.5%)	18 (4.5%)
1820	18th–22nd	114 (43.7%)	147 (56.3%)	92 (38.5%)	147 (61.5%)	22 (5.2%)
1830	23rd–27th	126 (42.9%)	168 (57.1%)	101 (37.5%)	168 (62.5%)	25 (5.3%)
1840	28th–32nd	117 (39.8%)	177 (60.2%)	102 (26.0%)	291 (74.0%)	15 (13.8%)
1850	33rd–36th	135 (44.6%)	168 (55.4%)	128 (42.2%)	175 (57.8%)	7 (2.3%)

Southern roots, which it did by nominating only Southerners as presidential candidates.

The three-fifths clause not only consistently strengthened Southern influence in presidential contests but also, in two elections, actually altered the outcome. These elections were among the most significant of the antebellum period: that of 1800, which set in motion the dominance of the Jeffersonian party, and that of 1824, which launched the Jacksonian party.

In the famous election of 1800, Jefferson captured 52.9 percent of the electoral college votes.[11] However, had the three-fifths clause not been a factor, John Adams would have captured 51.5 percent of the electoral college and therefore the presidency.[12] The role that the three-fifths clause played in Jefferson's narrow victory was well recognized by contemporaries (see Miller 1959: 563–64; Lynd 1967: chap. 7). Years later, the memory was still fresh: the Federalists who gathered at the 1814 Hartford Convention had not forgotten the devastating impact and included a call for abolition of the clause in the first of their reform planks. Abolitionists, too, recognized its significance and pointed to the election as an example of how the South might sway national politics through what they viewed as an unholy advantage (Lynd 1967: chap. 7).

The role that the clause played in the election of 1824 was subtler but just as crucial. In that fractious presidential contest, no candidate won a majority of the electoral college. The House, therefore, had to choose the president from among the top three electoral college vote-getters; this meant that the fourth-highest vote-getter, Speaker of the House Henry Clay, was eliminated from consideration, leaving the House to choose among Andrew Jackson, John Quincy Adams, and William Crawford. Although Clay's role in influencing the ultimate selection of Adams was—and is—disputed, he vetted the candidates and played an active role in guiding the House's selection (Remini 1991). If the three-fifths clause had not been in effect, the three names forwarded to the House for decision would have been Clay, Adams, and Jackson. Given Clay's strong presidential ambitions and the extent of his support in the House, he undoubtedly would have pursued the prize and would have had a plausible chance of winning it.[13]

What if slaves had been counted as whole persons for the purpose of apportionment? Table 15.6 illustrates the change in representation in the electoral college if slaves had been counted as whole persons. In the first two decades of apportionment, representation of slave states was nearly equal to that of nonslave states. Although the margin increased over time, with nonslave states always dominating the process, this margin would have been significantly smaller had slaves been counted as whole persons.

Table 15.6

Impact of the Three-Fifths Clause on the Electoral College, 1792–1860, with Slaves Fully Counted

Census Used for Apportionment	Congresses Affected	WITH THREE-FIFTHS CLAUSE		WITH SLAVES NOT COUNTED		Slave State Gains from Three Fifths Clause
		Slave States	Nonslave States	Slave States	Nonslave States	
1790	4th–7th	65 (47.1%)	73 (52.9%)	71 (48.6%)	73 (51.4%)	6 (8.5%)
1800	8th–12th	81 (46.0%)	95 (54.0%)	93 (49.5%)	95 (50.5%)	12 (12.9%)
1810	13th–17th	103 (44.0%)	131 (56.0%)	117 (47.4%)	130 (52.6%)	14 (12.0%)
1820	18th–22nd	114 (43.7%)	147 (56.3%)	128 (46.5%)	147 (53.5%)	14 (10.9%)
1830	23rd–27th	126 (42.9%)	168 (57.1%)	147 (46.7%)	168 (53.3%)	21 (14.3%)
1840	28th–32nd	117 (39.8%)	177 (60.2%)	128 (42.8%)	171 (57.2%)	11 (8.6%)
1850	33rd–36th	135 (44.6%)	168 (55.4%)	142 (45.9%)	167 (54.1%)	7 (4.9%)

However, only one election would have been affected by this change. In the election of 1796, the order of finish would have been reversed: instead of Adams becoming president and Jefferson serving as vice president, Jefferson would have defeated Adams by one vote in the electoral college. With the election of Jefferson at that time, it is unlikely that the Federalists would have pushed for the Alien and Sedition Acts. Without these acts, one can only conjecture about whether or when there would have been a split between the Federalists and the Jeffersonians.

Conclusion

We turn now to a brief recapitulation of our findings. Like many of the authors in this book, we illustrate a way in which a particular institution affected congressional history. We have done so by examining the impact of the three-fifths clause of Article 1 of the U.S. Constitution, using two counterfactual premises about counting slaves for apportionment purposes. Under both counterfactuals, we find that congressional seat apportionment, legislative battles, and presidential elections would have differed from those that actually occurred. In particular, we find dramatic differences in the first counterfactual scenario (slaves are not counted at all), estimating that nearly half of all roll call votes would have had different outcomes, including a number of pieces of major legislation. In addition, we find under the first counterfactual that two crucial presidential elections—those of 1800 and 1824—would likely have had different outcomes. Although these findings should be taken as a "maximum possible effect" of the three-fifths clause, we argue that the magnitude of our results is large enough to substantiate our point.

Appendix A

Method for Calculating the Impact
of the Three-Fifths Clause on Apportionment

To assess the impact of the three-fifths clause, we estimated how many representatives slave states would have received if they had been apportioned without counting slaves. To do so, we first compiled U.S. census data on the number of slaves in each of the states, which we then subtracted from each state's total population, since even some nonslave states had appreciable numbers of slaves, particularly in the early antebellum era. Next, we consulted *Congressional Quarterly's Guide to Congress* (Wormser 1982) for the apportionment formula employed after each census. Using these formulas, we then calculated how many total representatives each state would have received if slaves were not counted as part of the state's population for apportionment purposes. *Fixed ratio with rejected fractions* formulas were used after the censuses of 1790, 1800, 1810, 1820, and 1830; employing the same ratios only to the free population yields smaller-sized Houses overall. Due to rounding, the *fixed ratio with major fractions* formula, used after the 1840 census, yields a House of approximately the same size. The *Vinton formula*, used after the census of 1850, was based on a fixed size, which we assume would have been the same in the absence of the three-fifths clause. We also assumed that states entering the Union after reapportionment for that decade would have been allocated the same number of seats regardless of the status of the three-fifths clause.

To determine the party affiliations in our equitably apportioned Congresses, we assumed that each state's delegation would have identified with parties in the same proportion in which they identified under the three-fifths clause. For example, in the 28th Congress, Alabama, under the three-fifths clause, was apportioned seven representatives and elected one Whig and six Democrats. Applying the same ratio and policy on fractions adopted by Congress while adjusting for the number of Alabama slaves, we determined that without the clause, Alabama would have received five representatives and elected a Whig to one-seventh of the five, or 0.71 seats, and elected a Democrat to six-sevenths of the five, or 4.29 seats. We thus did not round the number of party members but preserved the fractions. This practice observes the minimal-rewrite rule (Tetlock and Belkin 1996) and also minimizes distortion in estimating the impact of the absence of the three-fifths clause on roll call voting outcomes.

Appendix B

Method of Calculating the Impact
of the Three-Fifths Clause on Legislation

To assess the impact of the three-fifths clause, we first created a subset of the roll call votes for the period being examined. For each Congress, we found those votes where the vote margin was small enough that the outcome could have changed if the three-fifths clause had not been in place. After identifying this subset of roll calls for each Congress, we then examined each vote separately. With the change in apportionment, we weighted each state's vote to be in line with the new apportionment. Thus if a state lost seats, the state's votes would be smaller than originally but would still be cast in the same manner, with the division between ayes, nays, and those not voting remaining constant. In the case of a state gaining seats, the state's votes would be larger than originally but would still be cast in the same manner, with the division between ayes, nays, and those not voting remaining constant. In most cases, these transformations led to fractional votes. We left these fractional votes intact in order to keep constant as many factors as possible. The ayes and nays were then counted. Only on votes where the outcome changed was it concluded that the three-fifths clause had an affect on the legislative outcome. This provided the information for Tables 15.2, 15.3, 15.5, and 15.6 as well as our analysis of specific pieces of legislation.

Afterword: History as a Laboratory

DAVID W. BRADY AND MATHEW D. MCCUBBINS

Twenty years ago, Cooper and Brady (1981) argued that history should be used as a laboratory to test theories of legislative behavior, organization, and policymaking. This book is a culmination of that recommendation; indeed, its primary characteristic is that the authors herein used the historical record of Congress to test contemporary legislative theories.

The studies included here, however, are not the only recent works to use history as a laboratory for improving our understanding of Congress. In recent years, a number of political scientists have begun to study congressional history in this way. For example, Stewart and Jenkins have studied the development of the committee system (Stewart 1989, 1992, 1998; Jenkins 1998; see also Gamm and Shepsle 1989); Gamm and Smith (2000a, 2000b, 2001) have written several studies concerning the rise of party leadership positions in the Senate; Binder (1997) and Schickler (2000, 2001) have examined the role of partisan interests in the evolution of the standing rules in the House and Senate; and Weingast (1991, 1998) has provided us with new understandings of the origins of the Civil War. These studies, and others referenced throughout this volume, have not only informed us about the dynamics of important historical events but also aided our understanding of our contemporary theories of the workings of Congress.

An inference that can be drawn from these studies and the chapters in this volume, however, is that we do not yet have general theories of institutional and behavioral change. Therefore, to Brady and Cooper's call for greater use of history in our studies of Congress, we add a second call: that legislative scholars develop more dynamic theories that account for institutional and behavioral change. This may entail the development of a strand of congressional scholarship that is the analogue of the economics literature explaining the evolution of economic institutions (e.g., Coase 1937; North and Thomas 1973; Williamson 1985). Given that the congressional organization literature already owes deep intellectual debts to transaction cost economics, the theory of the firm, and the industrial organizations literature, this would seem a natural extension.

Chapter 1

1. For a thorough survey of the congressional organization literature, see Shepsle and Weingast (1995).

2. See Krehbiel (1993, 2000) and Shepsle and Weingast (1995) for further elaboration of the observational equivalence among leading theories.

3. Again, see Shepsle and Weingast (1995) for a comprehensive comparison of the various theories, including the assumptions that they make about parties.

4. See the individual chapters that follow for more detailed literature reviews.

5. See, for example, McKelvey (1976) and Riker (1980).

6. In this case, "demand" refers to demand for the "goods" produced by Congress—which can mean particularistic benefits, policy, constituent service, and so on. It is commonly assumed that reelection motivates legislators (Mayhew 1974) and that this leads them to adopt their constituents' preferences as their own, even if their "unconstrained" preferences differ from their constituents' preferences. Thus it is sometimes assumed that legislators' goals reflect demand for the things Congress produces. The "supply" considerations faced by members largely consist of facilitating the production of desired congressional goods and services.

7. Ironically, in more recent work, Krehbiel (1998) has moved away from the supply aspect of the analogy and has primarily emphasized legislator preferences.

8. For an explicit rebuttal to this "workload hypothesis," see Binder (1997).

9. For examples of works that *do* explicitly test the effects of institutional change on policy change in Congress, see Stewart (1989) and Rohde (1991).

10. An illustration is the literature on realignments, in which broad changes in policy are linked to significant changes in voters' party alignments (cf. Burnham 1970; Brady 1988).

11. For more on this effect, see Campbell (2001).

Chapter 2

1. These were weighted by dividing by 2 times the standard deviation of the distribution of all ideal points in that Congress, as a "standardized" measure, to facilitate comparison across Congresses and between measures. Two times the standard deviation was used for scaling purposes (and, of course, corresponding to a range that if done at the floor median would effectively encompass about two-thirds of all members' ideal points). We do the same in this chapter.

2. This ratio is subtracted from 1 in order to have it on a scale comparable to that of the first measure.

3. We ran a principal components analysis. In both the House and the Senate data, the four estimates formed one component (e.g., the eigenvalues of the first factor are large, while they fall well short of 1 on the second factor).

4. This divergence might be caused by the passage of the Seventeenth Amendment, as we hope to explore further.

Chapter 3

1. The categorization of rules for the 100th and 101st Congresses was done by examining the text of the rule and, where necessary, the debate in the *Congressional Record*. In close calls, I relied on Wolfensberger's judgment (see source note to Table 3.1), and my categorization is very close to his. For the 103rd and 104th Congresses, I use Wolfensberger's categorization. The 102nd Congress is not included because much of the data used in this analysis was initially gathered for another project for which that Congress did not fit the criteria for inclusion.

2. This captures those cases where the committee process was highly partisan but the minority party did not call for a recorded vote on approving the bill in committee. For legislation reported from several committees, the action of the lead committee, if such existed, was coded; if there were several committees with more or less equal responsibility, those committees all had to have met the criteria for committee partisanship. In a few cases where the committee was bypassed, the variable was coded for the drafting entity rather than the committee: for example, a Democratic leadership task force drafted the Democrats' Contra aid measure in the 100th Congress, which was coded partisan; the ethics and pay raise package drafted by bipartisan joint leadership task force in the 101st Congress was coded not partisan.

3. The measure was constructed as follows. First, I distinguished some involvement from none based on answers to the following questions: (a) Was the bill a part of the leadership's agenda? (b) Did the Speaker or the majority

leader advocate passage during floor debate? (c) Did *Congressional Quarterly's* account report the leadership as being involved? If any one of the answers is yes, the leadership is considered as having been involved. Second, I distinguish major from minor involvement on the basis of the mode or modes of involvement reported by *Congressional Quarterly*. Four modes are distinguished: (a) the leadership uses its control over scheduling, the Rules Committee, or other procedure to advantage the legislation; (b) the leadership is involved in a floor vote mobilization effort; (c) the leadership is centrally involved in some other aspect of legislative strategy; or (d) the leadership participates in shaping the content of the legislation by talking or negotiating with or among the committee or committees, with the Senate, or with the president. Major leadership involvement is defined as engaging in shaping legislation (d) or in any two of the other activities (a, b, or c). The variable is coded 0 for no involvement, 1 for minor involvement, or 2 for major involvement. For more detail, see Sinclair 1995, chap. 3.

    4. The results are much the same if the omnibus variable without these cases is used; there are simply a few more errors of classification.

    5. These are measures that leaders vowed to pass immediately—the clean water and highway bill at the beginning of the 100th Congress and the congressional compliance measure at the beginning of the 104th. The results are much the same if the variable excludes these cases; there are simply a few more errors of classification.

    6. Voice votes on the rule and on passage were coded as 100 percent yes votes.

Chapter 4

    1. See also Krehbiel (1991: 101–103, 261). For a discussion of positivism, see Blaugh (1992).

    2. It should be noted that there are several variants of NOMINATE scores due to Poole and Rosenthal's efforts over the years to improve comparability across Congresses. The most recent variant and the one Poole and Rosenthal now recommend for comparison across time are the DW-NOMINATE scores. In addition, several sets of political scientists have sought to improve on the NOMINATE scores and have devised different scores or measures to capture the structure of preferences in roll call votes. See, for example, Heckman and Snyder (1997). Nonetheless, at present, the NOMINATE scores are by far the measures most frequently relied on by students of congressional voting patterns.

    3. The NOMINATE scores appear both to underweight and overweight the role of party in structuring voting patterns. On the one hand, restriction to one dimension disregards other dimensions where the structure of opinion

correlates less well with party affiliation. On the other hand, methods taken to provide comparability over time involve carrying a member's voting pattern in past Congresses into subsequent Congresses with the result that votes in a particular Congress are discounted if they do not meet certain parameters. Hence the full impact of party in structuring voting patterns in particular Congresses may not be captured (see Schickler 2000). A further complication is introduced by treating all votes equally. A consequence is that very similar NOMINATE scores are associated with very different levels of party voting. Yet preference theory would expect similar scores in both, assuming that the NOMINATE scores capture preference distributions. So too would party theory, assuming that these scores are a good measure of party strength. However, note the level of the party vote as compared to the difference in Poole and Rosenthal DW-NOMINATE party medians in the following categories. For differences in the median greater than .900, Houses with a party vote of 56.7 percent and a party vote of 90.8 percent produce scores of .950 and .920. For differences between .800 and .899, Houses with a party vote of 48.0 percent and a party vote of 83.5 percent produce scores of .820 and .839. For differences between .700 and .799, Houses with a party vote of 46.6 percent and a party vote of 67.4 percent produce scores of .770 and .780. Similar anomalies exist in the remaining categories.

4. The traditional measures include the party vote score, the party unity score, the Rice likeness and difference scores, and the Rice cohesion scores. For recent examples of their use see Rohde (1991), Binder (1997), and Hurley and Wilson (1989).

5. On the development of traditional aggregate measures of party voting and the contributions of Lowell, Rice, and Turner, see Shannon (1968: 3–23). On some more recent variants, see Cooper, Brady, and Hurley (1977); Brady, Cooper, and Hurley (1979); and Cox and McCubbins (1994b). For a variety of measures based on DW- or W-NOMINATE scores, see Poole and Rosenthal (2001) and Aldrich and Rohde (1998).

6. Keith Krehbiel (1999a, 1999c, 2000) has argued on both theoretical and measurement grounds that aggregate party scores produce artificial or arbitrary findings.

7. It should also be noted that Krehbiel's finding that the party vote does not vary in relation to party voting but rather in relation to the area defined between the median positions of the two parties on a continuum of member ideal points is tied to the assumptions of the model he posits. This model, among other things, assumes that the relationship between intraparty homogeneity and interparty-heterogeneity is inverse—that the more parties become alike or homogeneous internally, the more different or heterogeneous they become in relation to one another. That is true as a matter of logic when majorities of the two parties oppose one another. It is not true when majorities vote in concert. Thus, for example, in a case in which party A votes

80 percent–20 percent yea-nay and party B votes 20 percent–80 percent on one vote and respectively 90 percent–10 percent yea-nay and 10 percent–90 percent on a second vote, the relationships are inverse. In contrast, in a case in which both parties vote 80 percent–10 percent yea-nay on one vote and 90 percent–10 percent yea-nay on a second vote, the relationships are not inverse. The parties become more alike or unified internally and no more different or heterogeneous in relation to each other. This is true absolutely in terms of the distance between them and relatively in terms of the distance from a 50 percent–50 percent split. In the former regard, there is no change, and in the latter regard, their "likeness" is enhanced. It is quite probable then that whatever problems this model has in predicting voting scores when the parties split will be compounded when they vote in concert.

8. Indeed, it may well be asked how, in a model that assumes in a variety of ways that voting patterns rest on preference distributions, could party voting fail to reduce to patterns of preference distribution?

9. This method of adjusting the scores responds to the need to temper the simple structuring scores in relation to the proportionate size of their domains. It should be noted that an analysis of the fit or relation of individual House simple structuring and party vote scores to one another indicates that a substantial amount of variance exists, although the correlation across all Houses is high.

10. The average difference in Poole and Rosenthal DW-NOMINATE median party scores for the Reed-Henderson, Cannon, Clark, 1920s, New Deal, and Foley-Gingrich Houses are as follows: 0.945, 0.934, 0.767, 0.745, 0.599, and 0.705. It may also be noted that Aldrich and Rohde's results differ in a number of significant regards from our results and from those of Poole and Rosenthal (see Chapter 2). This is particularly true of their measure of the difference in party medians, which is based on D-NOMINATE scores they have standardized in a fashion they find compelling. Their differences in party median scores establish the New Deal Houses as the most partisan Houses of all and record so little variation in partisanship from the 1870s through the 1930s that Houses are virtually indistinguishable. Thereafter a decline occurs, but of lesser proportions and with less variance than our structuring scores or the Poole and Rosenthal DW-NOMINATE scores capture. However, their composite measure, which involves all four of their measures, comes somewhat closer to matching our results as displayed in Figure 4.3.

11. The Senates from 1969 to 1999 can be categorized as follows: four truncated, three cross-partisan, four bipartisan, two partisan, one mixed, and one hybrid. For the periods 1889–1919, 1919–41, 1941–69, and 1969–99, the average party vote was 68.3, 57.3, 57.8, and 46.6 percent, respectively. The average partisan residual scores for these periods were 27.9, 38.6, 50.0, and 42.6 percent. In contrast, the average bipartisan residuals were 44.3, 45.1, 40.0, and 29.6 percent. The simple structuring scores are the reciprocals of

these scores. Once again, our simple and overall partisan structuring scores for the Senate show far more variation than the Aldrich and Rohde difference in party median scores and also, to a lesser extent, than their composite measure (see Chapter 2).

12. Poole and Rosenthal NOMINATE scores can nevertheless be used to great effect in measuring ideological orientations at the individual level in particular Congresses and assessing this factor as an explanation of outcomes in regression models vis-à-vis other factors such as length of service, committee positions, region, and even party label. However, results from models that also include party label must be interpreted with care, given the overlap between party and ideology, the ways in which roll call votes confound party and preference effects, and the differences that exist between explaining individual votes and behavior and collective impacts and behavior. For an intelligent use of NOMINATE scores to assess the factors involved in votes to reform the rules, see Schickler 2001.

13. Although we have not reported the simple bipartisan win score in Table 4.3, the percentage of bipartisan wins is equal to the percentage of bipartisan votes in both our simple and adjusted scores. This is true because whether one is measuring wins only on bipartisan votes or across all votes, there are by definition no cross-partisan wins on bipartisan votes. Hence the simple bipartisan win score is always 100 percent. Similarly, when measuring bipartisan wins across all votes, the adjusted win score is equal to the percentage of bipartisan votes. The situation with respect to partisan wins is different. In measuring wins only on party votes (our simple score), the partisan win score is the absolute percentage of the time the majority party wins on party votes, and this number subtracted from 100 percent is necessarily the cross-partisan win score on party votes. In measuring partisan wins across all votes (our adjusted score), the total is set by the proportion of party votes. There can be no greater percentage of party wins than party votes. The percentage of adjusted partisan wins is thus the absolute number multiplied by the party vote, and the percentage of cross-partisan votes is equal to the difference between the party vote and the adjusted percentage of partisan wins.

14. The partisan win scores for the remaining three periods were 67.7, 70.8, and 67.4 percent, respectively. The cross-partisan win scores for these periods were thus 32.3, 29.2, and 32.6 percent, as contrasted with the score for the period of the Party Senate which, given a win score of 77.2 percent, was 22.8 percent. The party rule scores for these remaining three periods were 34.4, 30.0, and 32.2 percent.

15. The adjusted or overall win scores for the four periods were as follows: 50.5, 40.1, 40.6, and 33.6 percent for adjusted wins; 17.8, 17.2, 17.2, and 13.3 percent for adjusted cross-partisan wins; and 31.7, 42.7, 42.2, and 53.3 for adjusted bipartisan wins. The adjusted party rule scores were 37.0, 21.6, 17.4, and 16.1 percent.

16. See also Binder (1999), which concerns the explanation of gridlock, and Schickler (2000), which concerns the explanation of rule changes.

17. For a discussion of the impacts of not taking margin into account, see Dodd and Oppenheimer (1997).

18. Aldrich and Rohde (2001) attempt to encompass the electoral process comprehensively in a theory of conditional party government. See also Cooper, Brady, and Hurley (1977); Cooper and Brady (1981); Rohde (1991); and Dodd and Oppenheimer (1997). On the impact of executive factors relative to electoral factors, see Brady, Cooper, and Hurley (1979) and Hurley and Wilson (1989).

19. On changes in roll call behavior, see Nokken (2000) and Stratmann (2000). On the leverage of party leaders, see Cox (2000, 2001); see also Bawn (1998) and Sinclair (1998a). On the treatment of roll call data to test for party effects, see Jenkins (1999, 2000); see also Snyder and Groseclose (2000); Burden and Clausen (1999); and Hager and Talbert (2000). On the use of simulation to test for party effects, see Lawrence, Maltzman, and Smith (1999) and Wilson (1998).

20. For suggestive insights along these lines, see Hall (1996: 1–48) and Weaver (2000: 23–54).

21. It should be noted that Aldrich and Rohde (2000a) have retreated somewhat on the question of whether party moves the median.

Chapter 5

The authors thank Rod Kiewiet, Keith Krehbiel, Ken Shepsle, Barry Weingast, and the discussants and participants at the History of Congress Conference for their comments. In addition, we thank the National Science Foundation (SES-9905224) and the Committee on Research at the University of California, San Diego, for their generous financial support.

1. In this volume, both Aldrich, Berger, and Rohde (Chapter 2) and Cooper and Young (Chapter 4) argue that party control and centralization of authority are in fact a function of two things: homogeneity within party and the heterogeneity, or distance, between majority and minority parties.

2. On the agenda-setting role of committees, see Cox (1999); on the Rules Committee as "traffic cop," see Oleszek (1989: 120); on the Speaker's scheduling powers, see Oleszek (1989: 138), Hinckley (1988: 174), and Sinclair (1994: 45). Some evidence that the majority's seeming institutional powers translate into real advantages comes in the literature that shows that majority party status brings with it (1) greater campaign contributions (Cox and Magar 1999) and (2) greater levels of pork for a member's district (Murphy 1974; Levitt and Snyder 1995).

3. With these assumptions about members' preferences, the model is slightly more general than the standard unidimensional spatial model—in-

deed, if $n = 1$, that model emerges as a special case. Although more general, the model is just about as easy to deal with analytically: one can consider each dimension in isolation and use ordinary unidimensional results, such as the median voter theorem (Black 1958). The "city block" utility assumption is not necessary for our results. Much the same results could be derived assuming strictly quasi-concave utilities, although in this case germaneness restrictions would play a crucial role (see Cox 1999).

4. Formally, m_j is the median of the set $\{x_j^k: k$ is a member of the minority party$\}$, with similar definitions for M_j and F_j. For convenience, we shall assume that each median is always a unique point rather than an interval.

5. The legislators' ideal points on each dimension might also be time-indexed (although we do not keep track of that notationally here): the legislator from a given district may be new or have undergone an ideological conversion. So even if there is no shock to the status quo on a particular dimension, it may be nonmedian due to changes in the location of the median legislator.

6. This in turn sets up a delegation problem with respect to the central authority, which is the topic of Kiewiet and McCubbins (1991).

7. To identify final passage votes—as opposed to votes on amendments and the like—we conducted a systematic search through ICPSR roll call codebooks. ICPSR has collected information on roll calls for every Congress from 1789 to the present. The codebooks contain a one-paragraph description of every motion that received a roll call vote in the House. The descriptions for most final passage votes contain the words *to pass*; however, because not every final passage vote was described with these words, we also selected votes described with the word *passage* for our analysis. Party divisions and rolls are only observable for recorded (i.e., roll call) votes. It has been suggested that the resulting censoring problem may bias our findings. We have no means to evaluate this claim, but we do note that our results may be affected by censoring.

8. This is true as long as the probability density function of status quo points, g in Figure 5.1, has positive support over the entire policy space.

9. Although we don't report our estimates of Equation 1 using a logistic regression, we did estimate Equation 1 and found these results to be quite similar to those using the MLCS and OLS.

10. The standard deviation is based on the set of legislators who were either the first or only occupant of their congressional seat and who received a nonzero D-NOMINATE score; a D-NOMINATE score of zero indicates that the legislators' voting record could not be scaled by the Poole-Rosenthal method.

11. We included dummy variables for each type of division in a reestimation of Equation 2 and found no systematic and significant effect for these dummy variables.

12. The three bills on which Democrats were rolled in committee in these Congresses came from committees with Northern chairs.

13. We thank David Rohde for the data on which we base our conclusions in the next three paragraphs and that appear in Table 5.5. Note that Rohde's data include both House and Senate bills. Thus the figures in this section are not precisely comparable to the figures elsewhere in this chapter, where we focus solely on House bills.

14. Included in the final passage category are votes on ordinary bills, resolutions, concurrent resolutions, joint resolutions, and conference reports.

15. Excluded from the "prefinal" category are votes on veto overrides and Speakership elections.

16. In fact, the left endpoint of the majority roll region, $2M_{jt} - F_{jt}$, is to the left of M_{jt}. It is not possible to say in general how much farther left, in terms of the distribution of ideal points, the endpoint will be, but we know it will be to the left of the 25th percentile when there is a bare majority.

17. Under the cartel model, if preferences shift right and there are no status quo shocks by nature, then the only status quo points that fall outside the new (time t) majority block zone are those on the left; thus the only bills that pass will win with bipartisan support (majorities of both parties, typically larger majorities from the minority party).

18. However, sufficiently large rightward preference shifts eventually decrease P (if congressional preferences shift far enough right, then the only status quo points that remain will tend to be so far left of the new congressional preference distribution that even the majority party median wishes to change them; thus although there will be change on these dimensions, the majority party will not be rolled on them).

19. A caveat is in order similar to that registered in note 18. For sufficiently large leftward preference shifts, even the minority party may favor changing the status quo.

20. More precisely, let $S_t = F_t - F_{t-1}$, where F_t denotes the median D-NOMINATE score in Congress t. Then $PrefShift_{ct} = S_t$ if c = Democrats and $PrefShift_{ct} = -S_t$ if c = Republicans.

21. Estimating the model using a block logit technique produces qualitatively similar results.

Chapter 6

The authors thank the National Science Foundation (SES-9905224) and the Committee on Research at the University of California, San Diego, for their generous financial support.

1. Because the Senate is considered a continuing body, the rules are not made anew at the beginning of each congressional session; the previous session's rules carry forward.

2. Rule 22, however, stipulates that a motion to proceed to consideration of a matter on the executive calendar is not debatable. This means that nominations and treaties have one less hurdle to clear.

3. As in Chapter 5, a "roll" is an instance where a majority of a party opposes a bill or nomination but it passes nonetheless.

4. To identify final passage votes—as opposed to votes on amendments and the like—we conducted a systematic search through ICPSR roll call codebooks. ICPSR has collected information on roll calls for every Congress from 1789 to the present. The codebooks contain a one-paragraph description of every motion that received a roll call vote. The descriptions for most final passage votes contain the words *to pass*; however, because not every final passage vote was described with these words, we also selected votes described with the word *passage* for our analysis. A similar procedure was conducted to compile all final nomination votes searching on language, such as *consent, confirm, appoint,* and *nomination.* Not included are votes with supermajority requirements. This includes votes on treaties and presidential veto overrides. Party divisions and rolls are observable only for recorded votes (roll call votes). It has been suggested that the resulting censoring problem may bias our findings, but to our knowledge, there are no means of evaluating this claim.

5. In every Congress between the 52nd and 57th with the exception of the 54th, the House overwhelmingly passed five separate resolutions calling for the submission of an amendment for popular election. With significant external pressure and a substantial portion of the Senate membership owing their positions to some form of popular will by 1911, the Senate finally allowed the issue to come up for vote. The issue failed twice on the Senate floor before a House-Senate deadlock was broken in May 1912 with the House conceding to the Senate's version (Haynes 1960).

6. "Even before its adoption, the direct primary movement had already diminished the power of the legislatures, and by 1913 three-fourths of the candidates for the Senate were being nominated in direct primaries" (Congressional Quarterly 1976: 217).

7. Empirically, there were no cases in which the majority party median fell within the pivot zone. If this were the case, the pivot model would also predict that the majority party would never be rolled.

8. This is true as long as the distribution of status quo points has no areas of zero density.

9. The dependent variable has the value of either 0 or 1 for each vote, whereas the independent variables do not vary by vote but rather by Congress. For a complete discussion of the estimation challenges implied by the data, see Chapter 5.

10. This result is limited to the D-NOMINATE scoring system. Using

Poole and Rosenthal's DW-NOMINATE scores, the majority party distance coefficient is not significant regardless of technique or control variables.

11. Details of these estimations are reported in Campbell (2001).

Chapter 7

1. By delaying the appointment of most committees until after key party legislation had been approved, the Speaker could enforce greater party discipline on those measures to the degree that MCs desired committee assignments. Further, with the relative lack of office space prior to the opening of the Cannon House Office Building in 1908 and the very low ceilings placed on pay for professional staffing for rank-and-file members prior to 1899, members coveted appointment to committee chairmanships for the resources such appointments afforded them (Fox and Hammond, 1977: 15–18).

2. Responsibility for the annual appropriations bills was recentralized in the Committee on Appropriations in 1921. It had been divided across eight committees since 1887, with Appropriations handling the bills for Legislative, Executive, and Judicial; Sundry Civil; Fortifications; District of Columbia; Pensions; and Deficiencies (McConachie 1998).

3. In contrast, the Republicans vested the committee appointment responsibility in a special Committee on Committees beginning with the 65th House (1917–19). As I note later in the chapter, this caucus committee was dominated by party leaders.

4. See, for example, the ideological mappings of member ideal points for the 62nd–65th Houses provided by Poole and Rosenthal's Voteview program (http://voteview.uh.edu).

5. The sponsorship data are derived from the texts of ICPSR roll call voting studies.

6. My count of committee-leader sponsored motions in the 60th House is only a lower bound. Many of the motions offered by "rank-and-file" majority party MCs were undoubtedly made at the behest of leaders. For example, Rep. Walter Smith (R-Ia.) made ten motions leading to recorded votes in the 60th House. Smith was the sixth ranking Republican on the Appropriations Committee. Of his ten motions, seven were to resolve into the Committee of the Whole to consider HR 21260, the 1909 Sundry Civil Appropriations bill, strongly suggesting that Smith was that bill's floor manager.

7. There are two general circumstances under which a motion sponsor would seek defeat of his or her motion. First, some procedural motions— such as a motion to adjourn—can trigger consequences desired by the sponsor if the motion is defeated. Second, in this period, recorded votes on amendments to bills could be obtained only on the floor of the House. Members retained the right to demand separate floor votes on amendments *adopted*

in the Committee of the Whole, but only rarely could attempt directly to amend a bill. Hence MCs who opposed an amendment adopted in the Committee of the Whole could seek to have that amendment excised with a separate vote on the floor. Thus when committee leaders or the majority party leaders got rolled in the Committee of the Whole, they could try to reverse their defeat later on the floor in a more public forum.

8. I excluded the 76th House from the sample period. The ICPSR roll call data sets changed coding practices significantly in the late 1930s, such that motions to pass or adopt a bill, resolution, conference report, or rule that formerly would have designated a sponsor no longer have a sponsor listed. In the 76th House, these anonymous motions accounted for 73 of the 87 motions to pass or adopt, one-third of the 229 recorded votes in the session.

9. This definition is more restrictive than the one originally employed by Cox and McCubbins (1993), who would count a vote as part of the Democratic agenda when both Democrats and one Republican vote yea but the other Republican leader abstained, for example. I thus count 278 *fewer* party agenda votes in the 1921–40 period than would have been identified by Cox and McCubbins's original definition (from a high of 91 in the 67th House to a low of 7 in the 70th).

10. For the purposes of these statistics, I dropped all members eligible for fewer than ten agenda votes (33 Democrats and 12 Republicans).

11. I used a two-tailed test here to reflect both the explicit "textbook Congress" hypothesis that committee leaders should be *less* loyal than other party members and the implicit alternate, following the work of the partisan theorists, such as Rohde and Cox and McCubbins, that committee leaders should be loyal.

12. McReynolds died July 11, 1939. He was absent on 71 of 118 Democrat agenda votes in the 76th House and 69 of 88 in the 75th. He supported the party agenda 60 percent of the time in the 74th and 83 percent in the 73rd.

13. I coded the eleven states of the Confederacy plus Oklahoma and Kentucky as Southern.

14. A "leadership vote" is a recorded vote falling in *both* parties' partisan agendas; see Cox and McCubbins (1993).

15. Green had not been an enthusiastic supporter of Treasury Secretary Andrew Mellon's tax proposals. The motions were made as part of extending debate surrounding the Revenue bill. Prior to the cigarette tax motion, Garner had successfully trumped the Republican leadership by offering a substitute bill that increased tax cuts but made the measure more progressive. Republican leader Longworth then offered a compromise income tax rate structure, which won back enough support from progressive Republicans to pass. The battle over tax rates primarily reflected the fact that the faction of progressive Re-

publicans was pivotal, or nearly so, in this closely divided House. For a thorough discussion of the Revenue Act of 1924, see Blakey and Blakey (1940: 223–50).

Chapter 8

1. On such problems in the twentieth century, see Kiewiet and McCubbins (1991).

2. The data used to analyze committee membership patterns can be accessed via anonymous FTP at cabernet.mit.edu.

3. The greatest bulk of legislative business before the Civil War came in the form of private claims, not public legislation. From 1789 to 1851 (1st–31st Congresses), the House received an average of nineteen hundred private claims petitions per Congress. Virtually all of these petitions were referred to a House committee. Private petitions dominated the dockets of virtually all committees, including those with general legislative jurisdiction, such as Ways and Means and Military Affairs. An exhaustive summary of these petitions can be found in *Congressional Serial Set*, ser. 653–55, 32nd Cong., 1st sess.

4. The best example of demand-side views of committee development in recent times has been research into the congressional committee reforms of the 1970s, most of which places the impetus for these reforms squarely on the shoulders of dissatisfied liberals within the House Democratic caucus (see Rohde 1991).

5. Krehbiel (1991: 122–23) asserts that his information theory "accommodate[s] the supply side as well as the demand side."

6. On the financing of the War of 1812, see Bolles (1894: 219–300), Studenski and Krooss (1963: chap. 7), and Perkins (1994: chap. 15).

7. Separate select committees on retrenchment in the government were appointed in the 17th, 20th, 21st, 27th, and 28th Congresses.

8. A fourth standing committee, Indian Affairs, was also created in the 17th Congress. Its creation, however, occurred separately from the others and did not result directly from the comprehensive changes in the standing rules.

9. Stewart and others (1995) trace the first select committee on Foreign Affairs back to the 10th Congress, Military Affairs to the 1st, and Naval Affairs to the 4th. It was not until the 10th Congress that these committees were regularly associated with the president's message, however.

10. Quotes abound among the principals in the army debate that are consistent with the Crawford-versus-Calhoun view. For instance, Samuel Smith, chairman of the Ways and Means Committee, believed that "several members of the House . . . had allowed their enthusiasm for crucifying Calhoun to get the best of their judgment" (Pancake 1972) and that "friends of reduction . . . rally around a bill, right or wrong, good or bad" (*Annals of the Congress of the*

United States, 1820: 903). John Quincy Adams, the secretary of state, echoed this general theme in his diary entries.

11. We use Poole's common-space W-NOMINATE estimates here because we are interested in assessing the spatial proximity of Military Affairs Committee members to two administration politicians—Crawford and Calhoun—who did not have voting records in the 16th Congress but who had congressional careers. Under the assumption that MCs exhibit ideological consistency throughout their congressional careers, including changes from one chamber to the other, Poole's (1998) common-space estimation procedure creates a single set of ideal-point coordinates for each MC, incorporating his *entire* congressional career in the calculation. Keith Poole was extremely generous in providing us with W-NOMINATE scores for this time period.

12. Thompson, like Calhoun, blamed Taylor and his appointments to the Naval Affairs select committee for the reductions in his departmental budget, in which the annual allotment for the construction of new ships was cut in half, from $1,000,000 to $500,000 (*Annals of the Congress of the United States*, 1820: 1830; Adams 1875: 437–39).

13. Unfortunately for us, voting for Speaker during this period was via secret ballot. Therefore, we cannot directly corroborate the spatial accounting of these events. However, the events as they unfolded are entirely consistent with this spatial account, and we are therefore confident in it.

14. Party codes are taken from Martis (1989).

15. We limit our discussion to seven-man standing committees here. Similar results are obtained in an analysis of the eight three-man standing committees.

16. The debate stretched from January 11 to February 6, 1822, and is amply documented in the *Annals of Congress*.

17. In writing this, we are aware that the structure of the problem facing House members in the early 1820s is identical to that facing coalition governments: it is not enough to distribute ministerial portfolios to junior coalition partners; it is also necessary to guarantee that these portfolios come bundled with some sort of legislation initiation powers. This is a line of argument that we will pursue in future research.

Chapter 9

1. Neither Rohde's nor Sinclair's explanations of leadership behavior is purely or strictly contextual. Both acknowledge that individual characteristics of leaders can have some effect on leadership power and style. Rohde (1991: 172) notes that even when contextual conditions permit strong leadership, "leaders who are aggressive and enthusiastic will likely exhibit substantially more activist behavior than will leaders who are reluctant about the exercise of their powers." Although her theoretical framework is almost entirely con-

textually driven, Sinclair's (1999) analysis of the Gingrich Speakership seems to suggest that some leaders may be able to shape followers' expectations in ways that permit greater leeway in the exercise of policy leadership.

2. Sinclair's theory of leadership also incorporates some other contextual factors that may affect the costs and benefits of centralized leadership for individual members. However, the degree of homogeneity among followers' preferences appears to be the single most important determinant of leadership power in this theory (see Sinclair 1995: chap. 2).

3. In fairness to Sinclair and Rohde, these theories have been developed primarily to explain leadership in the contemporary House, not the House of the nineteenth century. Because of the many important differences in congressional politics in these two periods—including differences in parties and rules during the late nineteenth century and the virtual breakdown of partisan organization during part of the Clay Speakership—it may be asking too much of a theory to explain leadership politics in both centuries. Still, because the underlying logic of these theories does not seem particularly tied to a specific political context—and because one of the authors of this theory proposed in an early statement (Rohde and Shepsle 1987) that it might apply to the nineteenth-century institution—how well these theories apply to congressional history remains an interesting question to consider.

4. Clay left the position during 1814 and 1815 (part of the 13th Congress) to participate in the American delegation that negotiated the Treaty of Ghent, and again from 1820 to 1823 (part of the 16th and all of the 17th Congresses) to attend to his finances in the aftermath of the Panic of 1819.

5. Clay argued that existing "political" and "moral" ties among sections would inevitably weaken over time and would have to be reinforced by economic interest for the Union to survive. See, for example, his speeches on internal improvements in 1818 and on tariff policy in 1820 (*Annals of the Congress of the United States*, 1818: 1164–80; 16th Cong., 1st sess. 1820: 2034–52).

6. Other scholars who have noted Clay's transformation of the office include Follett (1896: 70–82), Harlow (1917: 207–208, 219), Polsby (1968: 155–56), Peters (1997: 34–39), and Swift (1998). However, some remain skeptical of the conclusion that Clay's Speakership represents a major discontinuity in the development of the office; see Young (1966: 131–35), Risjord (1992), and Stewart (1998).

7. For a more detailed treatment of the evidence discussed in this section, see Strahan and others (2000).

8. Numbers in parentheses are mean sectional support scores for Clay's positions on all votes in the issue area during the postwar Congresses.

9. Three select committees exercised jurisdiction over internal improvements issues in the 18th Congress. All three had majorities appointed from Mid-Atlantic and Western states. For purposes of clarity in presentation, only

the most important of these, the Select Committee on Roads and Canals, is included in Table 9.1.

10. Clay presided over the creation of eleven of the standing committees created between 1811 and 1825, but only two were substantive legislative committees. Another five were created during his absences in the 13th and 17th Congresses (see Jenkins and Stewart 1997; Stewart 1998).

11. Referral data collected by Gamm and Shepsle (1989: 51) show that the percentage of measures referred to standing committees increased from 53 percent in the first session of the 12th Congress (1811–13) to 89 percent in the first session of the 18th (1823–25). It is important to note, however, that important measures continued to be referred to select committees throughout this period, including most measures involving internal improvements.

12. Important exceptions include Riker 1986 and Schickler 2001.

13. In some statements of the contextual theory, officeholding ambition is explicitly assumed to take precedence over other goals (see Rohde and Shepsle 1987: 113, 128–30). Rohde (1991: 37–38, 172) does note that a leader's behavior may be influenced by his or her willingness to exercise power when followers' preferences are homogeneous. Beyond this one qualification, how leaders' behavior might be influenced by goals other than retaining office has not been addressed systematically by the proponents of this approach.

14. The frequency of serious presidential bids by Speakers, would-be Speakers, and former Speakers during the nineteenth century (including Clay, Polk, Blaine, Reed, and McKinley) indicates that the office was regularly sought and held by figures whose political horizons transcended merely continuing to preside over the House.

15. On the variety of collective interests that may be evoked during these periods of institutional change, see Schickler (2001) and Forgette (1997).

16. See especially Riker (1980, 1986). On opportunities for institutional innovation that may exist because of the instability of congressional majorities, see Aldrich and Shepsle (2000).

Chapter 10

1. One crude indicator of the changing academic tastes is the frequency with which the phrase "constituency service" shows up in political science journal articles indexed on J-Stor. Of 108 articles containing that phrase published during 1960–99, only 13 appeared during 1960–78, with the balance of 95 appearing after the publication of Fenno's book. Similarly, of 105 articles containing the word *casework* published in that period, only 15 appeared in 1960–78 but 90 during 1979–99.

2. We use these regressions mostly for their descriptive effects and do not claim that the specifications chosen are optimal for fitting the data. The quadratic specification for the effects of distance used here gives results that are

similar to those obtained using the natural log of distance, but the different specifications allow for very different nonlinear effects. The log specification implies a greater change in the distance effect over the first few hundred miles than is true for the quadratic specification. Our estimated quadratic effects are very nearly linear over the first several hundred miles. A fuller model would perhaps control for end-of-session, special-session, and lame-duck session voting (by lame-duck MCs).

3. Note as well that both Cannon and his predecessors made strategic use of committee assignments to induce party cohesion on key party proposals. For example, Hasbrouck (1927: 37) recounts the case of the 61st House (during which the revolt took place). Cannon appointed Rules and Ways and Means committee members on March 16, 1909, the second day of the opening session. He did not appoint the other standing committees until August 5, 1909, "the last day of the session, after the Payne-Aldrich tariff had passed the conference stage."

4. We thank Keith Poole for providing district distance data. Poole estimated distances between Washington and district midpoints, based on Ken Martis's district maps (1989). The closest 10 percent of districts in 1839–41 lay within 127 miles of D.C.

Chapter 11

1. As figures in this chapter suggest, there are a few years that we must still glean from the *Congressional Record* to complete the data series. Also, we— or, more precisely, our research assistants—have not yet finished identifying stories from the *Washington Post*. For this chapter, we draw on a complete record of the *Post's* stories on the Senate for the time periods November 15, 1879–February 2, 1880 (partial session); November 16, 1899–March 17, 1900 (partial session); November 16, 1919–June 9, 1920 (complete session); and December 15, 1939–April 2, 1940, and June 1, 1940–August 6, 1940 (partial session). So far we have read, copied, and coded at least two thousand news stories on Senate business.

2. "Mr. Gorman Resigns," *Baltimore Sun*, April 30, 1898; "Turpie Succeeds Gorman," *New York Times*, April 30, 1898; "Democratic Senators Caucus," *Washington Star*, April 30, 1898; "Mr. Gorman Retires," *Washington Post*, April 30, 1898; "Why Mr. Gorman Was Not Chosen," *Baltimore Sun*, May 4, 1898; "Will Succeed Mr. Gorman," *Baltimore Sun*, February 2, 1899.

3. "Both Parties in Caucus," *Washington Post*, December 6, 1899.

4. "No One Yet to Lead," *Baltimore Sun*, November 24, 1901.

5. "Insurgents Wary of Aldrich Move," *New York Times*, April 20, 1910.

6. "Martin Drops Out," *Washington Star*, February 28, 1913.

7. "Radicals Control Senate," *New York Times*, March 6, 1913.

8. The caucus minutes, which are brief and formal, lag long behind

newspaper accounts in this regard. Not until March 1917 do the caucus minutes mention "leader" and "chairman" together, and then it appears to be a self-reference by Martin. On March 5, 1921, the caucus minutes refer to the unanimous selection of Oscar Underwood as "Minority Leader" (Ritchie 1998: 258, 303).

9. "Radicals Control Senate," *New York Times*, March 6, 1913; "Dean of Senators, J. H. Gallinger, Dies," *New York Times*, August 18, 1918.

10. "Republicans Name Lodge as Leader," *Washington Star*, August 24, 1918.

11. "Re-Elect Senate Leaders," *New York Times*, March 6, 1921.

12. "Senate Republicans Pick Temporary Slate of Leaders," *Washington Star*, January 18, 1944; "GOP Senators Vest Leadership in Three Men," *Washington Star*, March 15, 1944; "Republicans in Senate Decide to Continue 3-Man Leadership," *Washington Star*, December 24, 1944.

13. See, for example, "Senatorial Caucuses," *Washington Star*, March 5, 1885; "Notes from Washington," *New York Times*, March 6, 1885; *New York Times*, December 4, 1887; *Washington Post*, December 4, 1887; "A Democratic Caucus," *Washington Star*, March 7, 1889; "First Day in Congress," *New York Times*, December 8, 1891; "Democrats in Caucus," *New York Times*, March 8, 1893; "Republican Senate Caucus," *New York Times*, December 9, 1896; "The Senate Organization," *New York Times*, March 7, 1897; "Only Talk in Caucus," *Washington Post*, March 7, 1897; "Both Parties in Caucus," *Washington Post*, December 6, 1899; "Democratic Caucus," *Washington Star*, March 6, 1903; "Republican Senators Hold a Brief Caucus," *Washington Post*, December 6, 1905; "Senate Dozen Win," *Washington Post*, April 5, 1911; "Gallinger Heads Party," *Washington Star*, March 5, 1913.

14. "Senator J. Ham. Lewis Elected Party Whip," *Washington Star*, May 28, 1913.

15. "Senator J. Ham. Lewis Elected Party Whip," *Washington Star*, 28 May 1913; also see the Democratic caucus minutes that report that attendance was a serious problem in 1913 and stimulated the move to appoint a whip (Ritchie 1998: 76–79).

16. "Senate Republicans Perfect Organization," *Washington Star*, December 6, 1915.

17. "Mr. Aldrich's Clever Move," *Washington Post*, February 7, 1900: 4.

18. "Vote on Finance Bill," *Washington Post*, February 12, 1900: 3.

19. "Hawaiian Bill Taken Up," *Washington Post*, February 16, 1900: 4.

20. "Programme in the Senate," *Washington Post*, February 15, 1900: 4.

21. "Order of Business in the Senate," *Washington Post*, February 25, 1900: 4.

22. "To Bring About an Early Adjournment," *Washington Post*, March 8, 1900: 4.

23. "In the Senate," *Washington Post*, December 11, 1879: 1.

24. "In the Senate," *Washington Post*, January 13, 1880: 1.

25. "Lodge to Force Pact," *Washington Post*, February 25, 1920: 1.

26. "Barkley Stakes Job as Leader on Hatch Act," *Washington Post*, March 9, 1940: 1.

27. "Roosevelt Signs 2-Ocean Navy Measure," *Washington Post*, July 21, 1940: 1, 8.

28. We have not been able to determine Kern's role in fashioning the new rule. More important, the lack of adequate indexing to the *Congressional Record* and the *Journal* have slowed our effort to systematically review the use of UCAs before and after 1913. This is left for the future.

29. Unfortunately, indexing practices in the *Record* are not consistent throughout the period under examination. However, the indexes are reasonably consistent for simple motions. Even for entries that require more judgment, the indexes are good enough to make accurate cross-sectional comparisons and fairly accurate longitudinal comparisons. We avoid making precise comparisons over time in order to avoid giving the impression of greater precision than is possible.

30. For Senate Democrats, the positions of caucus chairman and floor leader have been merged since 1899; before that date, the caucus chairman was never called a floor leader. For Senate Republicans, the positions of caucus chairman and floor leader were merged from 1913, when floor leadership began, until 1944. In all figures, the top committee chairs are the chairs of the committees on Appropriations, Banking, Finance, Foreign Relations, Judiciary, and the various forms of commerce. The 50th and 55th Congresses are missing from our data at the moment.

31. "Reorganization of Senate Committees," *Washington Post*, December 8, 1883; "Mr. Sherman Declines to Serve," *New York Times*, March 14, 1885.

32. For a list of major committees in the nineteenth- and early-twentieth-century Senate, we referred to a Senate resolution offered in 1909 by Sen. Elmer Burkett. That list includes Appropriations, Commerce, Finance, Foreign Relations, Interstate Commerce, Judiciary, and Rules; see "A Few Men in Control," *Baltimore Sun*, February 26, 1909. For a list of major committees since the 1940s, we referred to the five committees identified in the "Johnson rule": Appropriations, Finance, Armed Services, Foreign Relations, and Judiciary (Shuman 1991: 212–13).

33. *Washington Star*, March 4, 1929; "Interest Stirred in Watson Plans," *Washington Star*, March 14, 1929.

34. "King Named Head of D.C. Committee in New Senate," *Washington Star*, March 8, 1933.

35. "Gorman Dies Suddenly; Was Seemingly Better," *New York Times*, June 5, 1906.

36. "Aldrich as a Leader," *Baltimore Sun*, December 29, 1901.

37. This paragraph is based on an extensive analysis of complex unanimous

consent agreements for the period 1876–1940, which we will soon be reporting in greater detail. We are grateful to John La Boda for conducting much of this research.

38. "Month's Debate in Senate," *Washington Post*, December 12, 1899: 4.

39. "Foraker Gains Point," *Washington Post*, March 13, 1900: 1.

40. "Wilson Firm on Pact," *Washington Post*, February 7, 1920: 1.

41. *Washington Post*, January 3, 1940: 1.

42. "Roosevelt Sees New Tax Need in Farm Parity," *Washington Post*, March 12, 1940: 2.

43. "Army Supply Bill Passed by House," *Washington Post*, June 11, 1940: 1.

Chapter 12

1. At least two delegates had to vote before a state's vote could be counted, and in case of a tie, the state cast no vote.

2. Much of the new institutionalism literature is about rules that, when added to pure, simple majority voting, yield equilibrium in multidimensional spaces.

3. For example, if a state has seven delegates with six divided evenly, the remaining delegate will be pivotal for the state, and the state's vote may well be pivotal for the outcome also.

4. There is always a problem with missing data when examining roll call votes. Absenteeism was a serious problem in the Continental Congress, which generally met without interruption. Although the Congress had yearly sessions, which began in November, often the states' appointments of delegates ran beyond or otherwise cut across the "congressional year." Delegates themselves often seemed to serve at their own leisure, with many appointments never served. In this analysis, individuals who did not vote on at least 25 percent of the issues for a particular congressional year were excluded from the analysis.

5. States with only a single representative present were excluded. Thus Delaware, with only one member, is never included in the analysis.

6. Delaware, with a single representative, is listed separately, but it is included as a unit vote based on how its single representative voted.

7. In fact, Carroll and Gale were decisive on siting and the first two votes on assumption, and if they had voted differently and the second assumption vote were reversed, there would have been no third option (no A3) on which to vote.

8. The Founders were generally pessimistic about the prospects of success under the new Constitution, just as they were under the older Articles, and most generally felt that its failure would lead to selection of a nondemocratic national government or to the breakup of the Union.

Chapter 13

The authors thank Scott Basinger, David Brady, Ethan Bueno de Mesquita, Eric Dickson, Gerald Gamm, Stephen Haber, Jeffrey Hummel, Patricia Hurley, Morton Keller, Nolan McCarty, Mathew McCubbins, Paul Peterson, Kenneth Shepsle, Theda Skocpol, and Charles Stewart for their helpful comments.

1. Fehrenbacher (1980: 44) echoes some of these themes: "The Compromise legislation of 1850, though apparently resolving a number of vexatious and even dangerous problems, had scarcely touched the deeper, ineluctable conflict over slavery. . . . It was, in the words of one southern editor, 'the calm of preparation, and not of peace.'"

2. Throughout this chapter, we frequently refer to the "Clay" and "Douglas" bills, as though Clay and Douglas were the only authors and only promoters. We use this shortcut for expository purposes. Clay and Douglas, as the historical record makes clear, relied upon the wisdom and efforts of their allies in passing what became known as the Compromise of 1850.

3. Many historians echo Douglas's logic. McPherson (1988: 74), for example, argues that "as the legislators labored through the heat of a Washington summer it became obvious that the omnibus strategy was backfiring." See also Hamilton (1964: 117), McPherson (1982: 67), Milton (1934: 72), Morrison (1997: 125), Nichols (1963: 77), and Smith (1988: 181, 191).

4. For major accounts of the passage of the compromise, see Freehling (1990: chap. 28), Hamilton (1964), Holt (1978: chap. 4), Nevins (1947: chaps. 7–10), Potter (1976: chaps. 4–5), and Stegmaier (1996).

5. Although Clay's decision to create the omnibus represents a major development in the success and failure of the compromise, his reason for this move remains unclear. Potter argues that Clay put together the omnibus to increase the separate bills' chances of passage in the House (Potter 1976: 103). Stegmaier (1996: 103; see also 113) suggests that Clay joined the territorial measures because some Southerners feared that if the California legislation were not bound with the other territorial measures, Northerners might impose the Wilmot Proviso.

6. Other senators in favor of the compromise felt uneasy about the Dawson amendment. Shields defended Pearce: "But since I have reflected on the effect of the vote I gave yesterday, and on the effects of that amendment, I am really gratified that my friend from Maryland has presented a mode by which I can redeem myself" (*Appendix to the Congressional Globe*, July 31, 1850: 1475).

7. Senator Yulee, a Southern extremist, convinced him to separate the two steps.

8. The Utah portion is considered pro-Southern because it was organized without the Wilmot Proviso.

9. For a modern methodology for computing voting scores, including a comprehensive analysis of the entire history of congressional roll call voting, see Poole and Rosenthal (1997).

10. As each of these amendments stripped sections from the omnibus, a no vote is a vote *in favor of* the compromise.

11. A notable exception is Holt (1999: 537), who credits the New England Whigs for securing passage of the Texas bill and subsequently the compromise.

12. Indeed, many historians claim that this ambiguity causes problems later, dividing Northern and Southern Democrats (Potter 1976).

13. Holt (1978: 81–82) argues that this issue also characterized the difference between President Taylor's plan and that of Douglas. By advocating immediate statehood for New Mexico, Taylor's proposal precluded any possibility of slaveholders' gaining a political foothold. This, in turn, caused considerable opposition among Southerners.

14. Another amendment, offered by Pierre Soulé of Louisiana on June 17, added, "And when the said Territory, or any portion of the same, shall be admitted as a State, it shall be received into the Union with or without slavery, as their constitution may prescribe at the time of their admission" (*Congressional Globe*, June 6, 1850: 1239). This amendment "was a promise by one Congress that a later Congress would not refuse to admit" the territories as states even if they included provisions for slavery (Russel 1972: 15).

15. Other configurations of preferences are possible but less plausible. For example, we might depict extremists as extreme on both dimension: Southerners near zero on the Northern dimension but very high relative to their sectional compatriots on the Southern dimension, and vice versa. The conceptual problem with this configuration is that all six groups of voters are better under a compromise, including extremists, so extremists will not work against compromise, in this configuration.

16. For the present, we consider *SN* a true compromise. In a subsequent subsection, we study why Clay's omnibus failed to be a true compromise.

17. Technically, there can be net gains in support if the distribution of ideal points is not symmetric.

18. Krehbiel and Rivers (1988) provide an alternative account. Since we are only illustrating the principle and not relying on a claim that this actually occurred, the debate about aid to education need not concern us.

19. Numerous scholars have developed scores and categories for representatives in Congress based on their roll call votes (see Poole and Rosenthal 1997; Alexander 1967). Inevitably, these scores will contain some anomalies when the reality of a member's voting score does not live up to his reputation. Nonetheless, these scores help serve useful purposes far exceeding the costs of some misclassified members or senators. It is with this caveat that we present our scores.

20. Because abstentions are excluded, they do not affect the categorization of the senators. Borland is placed in the Southern anti-compromise category even though he did not vote during the Compromise of 1850 debate. This placement is consistent with how historians believed he would have voted (Hamilton 1964: 116). Four senators scored evenly between two categories. Berrien, Pearce, Rusk, and Sebastian all had an equal number of errors between the Southern anti-compromise category and the Southern moderate category. If they were in fact true anti-compromisers, they would not have supported any of the votes under Clay's leadership, yet Berrien and Pearce voted for Texas, and Rusk and Sebastian voted for New Mexico. Consequently, we categorized all four as Southern moderates.

21. For purposes of determining the correlation coefficient, we coded the most extreme Southern group for both our category and Stegmaier's category as a 1. For more pro-Northern senators, the number assigned to each category increased by 1. Thus we coded the extreme Northern group for our categories as a 6 and for Stegmaier as a 4.

22. For the pro-Northern votes, Northern standard senators voted 7−0 (Clay's California), 6−0 (Douglas's California), and 6−0 (D.C. slave trade). On the pro-Southern votes, the Southern standard senators voted 11−2 (Clay's New Mexico), 12−2 (Clay's Texas), 8−2 (Utah), 10−0 (Douglas's New Mexico), and 12−0 (Fugitive Slave Bill).

23. Milton (1934) quotes Douglas as drawing the same conclusion: "'If it was intended to be a compact,' he commented, 'the North never agreed to it. The Northern Senators voted to insert the prohibition of slavery in the Territories; and then, in the proportion of more than four to one, voted against the passage of the bill. The North, therefore, never signed the compact, never consented to it, never agreed to be bound by it'" (136).

Chapter 14

We thank Erik Berglöf for suggesting that we write this chapter. We also thank David Brady, Noah Kaplan, Jonathan Katz, Mathew McCubbins, Steven Solnick, Greg Wawro, and Barry Weingast for comments, Kathleen Much for editing, and Matthew Atlas for research assistance. This chapter was written while Howard Rosenthal was a Fellow at the Center for Advanced Study in the Behavioral Sciences. He is grateful for financial support provided by National Science Foundation Grant SBR-9022192. The research was also supported by National Science Foundation Grant SBR-9730335 to Carnegie Mellon University and Princeton University.

1. For theoretical work that formalizes many of the considerations in the remainder of this discussion, see Bolton and Roland (1997), Alesina and Spoloare (1997), and Farrell and Scotchmer (1988).

2. Since distributive issues arise in firms with regard to nepotism, gender,

racial and religious discrimination, and interpersonal liking, the distinction between firms and Congress is a matter of degree.

3. Technically, *land tenure* refers to the manner in which *rights in land are held* and the period for which they are held. In this regard, property is *rights*, not *things*. "The things are property objects, and tenure is concerned with rights in these things" (Harris 1970: 2). Tenure in land is a *bundle of rights*, and rights in land held by a private party constitute an *estate in land*. See Harris (1970: 1–10) for a full discussion of these definitions.

4. In feudal England, these burdens were homage, fealty, wardship, marriage, relief, *primer seisin*, aids, fines for alienation, and escheat. See Harris (1970: 25–27) for definitions and discussion.

5. Technically, the characteristics of *free and common socage* were as follows: it was perpetual, it could be inherited, it could be passed on in a will, obligations were fixed and certain (see note 2), the owner had the right to waste, and it was freely alienable (it could be sold or given away).

6. Initially, only the lower house of the territorial assembly was directly elected. The upper house was chosen by federal appointees and Congress, and the delegate was elected by the assembly. After 1816, these practices gave way to direct election of the upper house and the delegate (Pomeroy 1947; Lamar 1956).

7. As Stewart and Weingast (1992) point out, this threshold was approximately the population of Delaware, the smallest state. However, it was much more than sufficient to justify a single house seat. The quota for the 1790 apportionment was only thirty-three thousand. In fact, Rhode Island had two representatives following 1790 for a population of only sixty-nine thousand.

8. Article 5 states that "no State, without its Consent, shall be deprived of its equal Suffrage in the Senate."

9. Note that the balance rule, were it a credible commitment, was likely to be more symbolic than linked to any actual considerations of institutional rules. First, the South could have blocked ratification of any constitutional amendment dealing with slavery with only one-fourth, not one-half, of the states. Second, a sufficiently large minority can successfully filibuster any legislation in the Senate.

10. The percentage of the total state population accounted for by slaves in 1820 (counting slaves as whole persons) was as follows: Alabama, 33 percent; Delaware, 23 percent; Georgia, 44 percent; Kentucky, 23 percent; Louisiana, 52 percent; Maryland, 36 percent; Mississippi, 44 percent; North Carolina, 34 percent; South Carolina, 53 percent; Tennessee, 20 percent; and Virginia, 50 percent (*Historical Statistics of the United States*: ser. A, 195–209).

11. See Poole and Rosenthal (1997: chap. 3) for a detailed discussion of the fit of the model.

12. For space reasons, we are presenting only the votes that we feel are important or that illustrate a central feature of the politics of statehood. Therefore, many procedural motions and minor amendments are not included.

13. Michigan was part of the old Northwest Territory, which was closed to slavery by the Land Ordinance of 1787.

14. In the area bounded by the 1818 Treaty with Great Britain (that set the northern boundary), the 1819 Treaty with Spain (that set the southern boundary), and the original Louisiana Purchase, the states formed after Missouri were Iowa, Minnesota, North Dakota, South Dakota, Nebraska, Kansas (portion), Arkansas, Oklahoma (portion), Wyoming (portion), Montana (portion), and a small piece of Colorado. Arkansas and Oklahoma were below 36°30'.

15. The larger margins on these votes may reflect members who normally vote proslavery but are close to the cutting line voting to uphold the House as an institution vis-à-vis the Senate.

16. Obviously, it is difficult to know with any certainty what Southern expectations were about the acquisition of new slave territories after the Missouri Compromise. A number of factors suggest that pessimism was more likely than optimism. First, there was little consensus even among Southerners as to what the natural boundaries of slavery were. As of 1820, the prime possibilities for expansion were Texas, Spanish Florida, Mexico, and the Caribbean. However, a number of events make it fairly safe to assume that these acquisitions were either considered as low in probability or extremely distant in the future. Filibustering expeditions in West Florida in 1810 and in Texas in 1819 generated very little enthusiasm even in the South (Merk 1963). Second, until the controversy of the Wilmot Proviso erupted, the South was probably the region most opposed to seeking territory from Mexico. Merk's study of Southern editorials during the Mexican War reveals that most Southerners viewed Mexico as free territory. Finally, the public hostility to the Ostend Manifesto demanding that Spain sell Cuba to the United States suggests that there probably never would have been sufficient support for that acquisition.

17. It is important to note that at this time, the Republic of Texas had not committed itself to annexation. For negotiating purposes, it still held out the possibility of signing a treaty with Britain that would have guaranteed its independence from Mexico and the United States.

18. Opponents did not see this as much of a compromise, as Texas could forgo that territory, which many felt it was not legitimately entitled to, while creating four states below the compromise line.

19. It is not clear whether this choice was made primarily to expand slavery or to avoid reopening negotiations at a time when delay could have led to an increase in British influence in North America.

20. Both the Webster and Bell plans called for a state stretching from the Colorado River in the north and the Rio Grande in the south.

21. There was, however, a 6 percentage point increase over his performance in the same states in 1860.

22. As Stewart and Weingast (1992) point out, Nevada would have satis-

fied such a population criterion only in 1970. The only previous state to be admitted without a population exceeding a House seat quota was Oregon in 1859.

23. In spite of House passage of New Mexico and Arizona statehood bills, an endorsement from President Cleveland, and a favorable (bipartisan) committee report, the bills never were brought up on the Senate floor (Larson 1968).

24. The admission of the state of Washington was more politically ambiguous. Though it was traditionally supportive of the Republican party, the Democrats had won the previous two elections for territorial delegate.

25. A Dakota newspaper estimated the incremental cost of statehood to be about $100,000 per annum, and opponents of statehood often pointed to Nevada's financial problems as evidence of the burden that these costs entailed (Lamar 1947). However, these arguments probably distorted the extent of the federal government's financial contribution to the territories. Pomeroy (1947) estimates that each territory in the 1880s received about $25,000 to $30,000 from the federal government per annum, and this amount generally constituted about a tenth of the territorial budget. In per capita terms, this subsidy represents about three to five times the transfer to the state governments for that period.

26. One possible reason for this failure was the opposition of the territorial governor to statehood (see Larson 1968). However, Sanford (1927) attributes it simply to the fact that the people of Colorado were not yet ready to assume the obligations of statehood.

27. Another factor may well have been residual Eastern indignation over the territorial government's role in a well-publicized massacre of Indians at Sand Creek in 1864. In the minds of Easterners, the incident undermined confidence in Colorado's ability to govern itself.

28. As a form of retribution, the Democratic-controlled House voted in December 1876 to investigate the legality of Colorado's statehood.

29. Church leaders did not want to alienate Democratic supporters of statehood. They also sought to build Republican support for statehood. Consequently, they carefully orchestrated the mobilization of the church's followers into roughly equal Republican and Democratic contingents (Lyman 1986).

30. It was reported out of the Republican-controlled Committee on Territories (Larson 1968).

31. New Mexico's Democratic delegate blamed the defeat on a Republican filibuster of an appropriations bill unrelated to statehood.

32. Since Alaska and Hawaii were not admitted during the sample period, they are excluded.

33. Arizona and Utah were routinely represented by independents or delegates elected on tickets of local third parties. An issue arises as to how to treat the Dakota Territory, which was split only at admission; the results provided

are those where North and South Dakota are treated as distinct territories with the population apportioned according to the geographic split that took place at admission. The results are robust to treating Dakota as a single territory and to dropping the Dakotas altogether.

34. Many of specifications of *YRSORG* were tried, but the natural log fit the best. In particular, a quadratic function was fitted, but the squared term was small and statistically insignificant.

35. It is also true that territories represented by Republican delegates had significantly larger populations ($t = 2.54$).

36. We should note that Figure 14.11 probably gives an overstated view of Republican prescience since many states that defected from the Republicans were brought back into the fold by the realignment of 1896.

37. These support scores are calculated simply as the percentage of each set of votes each that senator cast with the majority of his party.

Chapter 15

1. The richest vein of research on the three-fifths clause concerns its constitutional origin, with only a small amount of research devoted to its impact beyond 1787 (Lynd 1967; Ohline 1971, 1980; Potter 1972; Robinson 1971; Simpson 1941).

2. In each counterfactual, to explore the impact of the three-fifths clause, we adopt a comparative statics approach. Commonly used by economists but increasingly applied by political scientists, it estimates the impact of an independent variable on the dependent variable by holding all other independent variables constant. To conduct this historical comparative statics exercise of estimating the impact of the three-fifths clause, we adhered as much as possible to the minimal-rewrite rule, which calls for "altering as few 'well-established' historical facts as possible" (Tetlock and Belkin 1996: 18).

3. At first glance, it may seem odd that we would consider this latter alternative. However, one must remember that the three-fifths clause was a compromise. Southerners pushed in the Constitutional Convention, briefly and unsuccessfully, for apportionment to be based equally on the slave and free population. Although this proposal was defeated, it did offer one end of the spectrum from which the eventual compromise was developed; the other was not counting slaves for apportionment at all. Thus to understand the effects of the compromise, one must examine both what the South *gained* and what it *lost*.

4. For brevity, we have chosen not to provide a detailed discussion of the impact of the three-fifths clause on political parties since no political party was clearly harmed or benefited from the impact of this clause.

5. We use the party and factional identifications made by Martis (1989). In the 18th Congress, Jacksonian Federalists and Republicans were classified

as Jacksonians. All Adams- and Crawford-affiliated factions were classified as anti-Jacksonians. In later Congresses, anti-Masonics, Nullifiers, and Whigs were classified as anti-Jacksonians. Majority party and factional percentages are affected by rounding and by the presence of minor party and faction members that fall outside of the dominant pro- and anti-Jefferson and pro- and anti-Jacksonian cleavages of the period.

6. We make no attempt to distinguish between types of votes here (votes on final passage, procedural issues, amendments, etc.), for two reasons. First, eliminating all votes but those on final passage would leave very few votes to examine during this era. And second, although some of the votes included in our analysis might have been frivolous or dilatory, we have no way of judging this without studying the circumstances of each vote carefully. Since we cannot reasonably make such judgments, we have decided to include all roll call votes in the analysis. However, some of the more obvious purely procedural roll calls are eliminated through Clausen's (1973) coding scheme.

7. These authors note only major pieces of legislation that passed. However, it is clearly the case that if these measures had been defeated in the House, national policy would have changed, since the measures either had passed or eventually passed the Senate. Clearly, some of these measures would not have passed if the South had not been overrepresented by the impact of the three-fifths clause.

8. See note 4.

9. See note 6.

10. We should also note that national political party conventions for much of the nineteenth and twentieth centuries allocated delegates to states on the basis of their electoral college apportionments. However, we do not treat the implications of the Three-Fifths Clause because in single-ballot conventions, their enforcement or nonenforcement did not affect the outcomes, and in multiballot conventions, it is difficult to say how they would have affected the complex web of timing, dealmaking, momentum, and section-oriented voting rules that influenced the nomination process. For the fullest treatment of the influence of the South on Republican and Democratic party nominations in this era, see Bain (1960) and David, Goldman, and Bain (1960).

11. Aaron Burr, the Jeffersonian Republican's candidate for vice president, captured the same percentage, necessitating a final decision in the House.

12. Adams would have become president, and Thomas Pinckney would have become vice president, having received one less electoral vote than Adams.

13. By 1824, Clay had already sought the presidency twice and would wage aggressive campaigns two more times; also by 1824, he had been elected Speaker each of the five nonconsecutive terms he sought the office, and each time he won on the first ballot.

Abramson, Paul R., John H. Aldrich, and David W. Rohde. 1999. *Change and Continuity in the 1996 and 1998 Elections*. Washington, D.C.: Congressional Quarterly Press.

Adair, Douglas. 1974. "Fame and the Founding Fathers." In *Fame and the Founding Fathers: Essays by Douglas Adair*, ed. Trevor Colbourn. New York: Norton.

Adams, John Quincy. 1875. *Memoirs of John Quincy Adams, Comprising Portions of His Diary from 1795–1848*, vol. 5, ed. Charles Francis Adams. Philadelphia: Lippincott.

Alchian, Armen, and Harold Demsetz. 1972. "Production, Information Costs, and Economic Organization." *American Economic Review* 62: 777–95.

Aldrich, John, H.1994. "A Model of a Legislature with Two Parties and a Committee System." *Legislative Studies Quarterly* 19: 313–41.

———. 1995. *Why Parties? The Origin and Transformation of Party Politics in America*. Chicago: University of Chicago Press.

———. 1999. "Political Parties in a Critical Era." *American Politics Quarterly* 27: 9–32.

Aldrich, John H., and Ruth Grant. 1993. "The Antifederalists, the First Congress, and the First Parties." *Journal of Politics* 55: 295–326.

Aldrich, John H., and Richard G. Niemi. 1993. "The Sixth American Party System: Electoral Change, 1952–1992." In *Broken Contract: Changing Relationships Between Americans and Their Government*, ed. Steven Craig. Boulder, Colo.: Westview Press.

Aldrich, John H., and David W. Rohde. 1997a. "Balance of Power: Republican Party Leadership and the Committee System in the 104th House." Paper presented at the annual meeting of the Midwest Political Science Association, Chicago, April 10–13.

———. 1997b. "The Transition to Republican Rule in the House: Implications for Theories of Congressional Politics." *Political Science Quarterly* 112: 541–67.

———. 1998. "Measuring Conditional Party Government." Paper presented at the annual meeting of the Midwest Political Science Association, Chicago, April 23–25.

————. 2000a. "The Consequences of Party Organization in the House: The Role of Majority and Minority Parties in Conditional Party Government." In *Polarized Politics: Congress and the President in a Partisan Era*. ed. Jon Bond and Richard Fleisher. Washington, D.C.: Congressional Quarterly Press.

————. 2000b. "The Republican Revolution and the House Appropriations Committee." *Journal of Politics* 62: 1–33.

————. 2001. "The Logic of Conditional Party Government: Revisiting the Electoral Connection." In *Congress Reconsidered*, 7th ed., ed. Lawrence C. Dodd and Bruce I. Oppenheimer. Washington, D.C.: Congressional Quarterly Press.

Aldrich, John H., and Kenneth A. Shepsle. 2000. "Explaining Institutional Change: Soaking, Poking, and Modeling in the U.S. Congress." In *Congress on Display, Congress at Work*, ed. William Bianco. Ann Arbor: University of Michigan Press.

Alesina, Alberto, and Enrico Spoloare. 1997. "On the Number and Size of Nations." *Quarterly Journal of Economics* 112: 1027–56.

Alexander, De Alva Stanwood. 1916. *History and Procedure of the House of Representatives*. Boston: Houghton Mifflin.

Alexander, Thomas Benjamin. 1967. *Sectional Stress and Party Strength: A Study of Roll-Call Voting Patterns in the United States House of Representatives, 1836–1860*. Nashville, Tenn.: Vanderbilt University Press.

Altman, O. R. 1937. "First Session of the Seventy-Fifth Congress, January 5, 1937, to August 21, 1937." *American Political Science Review* 31: 1071–93.

Arnold, R. Douglas. 1990. *The Logic of Congressional Action*. New Haven, Conn.: Yale University Press.

Bach, Stanley. 1990. "Suspension of the Rules, the Order of Business, and the Development of Congressional Procedure." *Legislative Studies Quarterly* 15: 49–63.

Bach, Stanley, and Steven S. Smith. 1988. *Managing Uncertainty in the House of Representatives*. Washington, D.C.: Brookings Institution.

Bain, Richard C. 1960. *Convention Decisions and Voting Records*. Washington, D.C.: Brookings Institution.

Baker, John D. 1973. "The Character of the Congressional Revolution of 1910." *American Journal of Political Science* 60: 679–91.

Barnes, James A. 1931. *John G. Carlisle: Financial Statesman*. New York: Dodd, Mead.

Bartels, Larry M. 2000. "Partisanship and Voting Behavior, 1952–1996." *American Journal of Political Science* 44: 35–50.

Basinger, Scott J. 1999. "Deckstacking in the Pre–Civil War Era: The Case of the Fugitive Slave Law." Paper presented at the annual meeting of the American Political Science Association, Atlanta, September 2–5.

Bawn, Kathleen. 1998. "Congressional Party Leadership: Utilitarian Versus Majoritarian Incentives." *Legislative Studies Quarterly* 23: 219–45.

Baxter, Maurice G. 1995. *Henry Clay and the American System.* Lexington: University of Kentucky Press.

Beck, Nathaniel, Jonathan N. Katz, and Richard Tucker. 1998. "Taking Time Seriously: Time-Series Cross-Section Analysis with a Binary Dependent Variable." *American Journal of Political Science* 42: 1260–88.

Berger, Mark M. 1999. "The Role of Political Parties in Senatorial Elections and Governance." Ph.D. dissertation, Duke University.

Berkson, J. 1953. "A Statistically Precise and Relatively Simple Method of Estimating the Bio-Assay with Quantal Response, Based on the Logistic Function." *Journal of the American Statistical Association* 50: 565–99.

Bianco, William T., David B. Spence, and John D. Wilkerson. 1996. "The Electoral Connection in the Early Congress: The Case of the Compensation Act of 1816." *American Journal of Political Science* 40: 145–71.

Binder, Sarah A. 1995. "The Partisan Basis of Procedural Choice: Allocating Parliamentary Rights in the House, 1789–1990." *American Political Science Review* 90: 8–20.

————. 1997. *Minority Rights, Majority Rule: Partisanship and the Development of Congress.* New York: Cambridge University Press.

————. 1999. "The Dynamics of Legislative Gridlock:, 1947–96." *American Political Science Review* 93: 519–33.

Binder, Sarah A., and Steven S. Smith. 1997. *Politics or Principle?: Filibustering in the United States Senate.* Washington: Brookings Institution.

Biographical Directory of the United States Congress, 1774–1989. 1989. Washington, D.C.: Government Printing Office.

Black, Duncan. 1958. *The Theory of Committee and Elections.* Cambridge: Cambridge University Press.

Black, Earl, and Merle Black. 1992. *The Vital South: How Presidents Are Elected.* Cambridge, Mass.: Harvard University Press.

Blakey, Roy G., and Gladys C. Blakey. 1940. *The Federal Income Tax.* New York: Longmans, Green.

Blaugh, Mark. 1992. *The Methodology of Economics.* New York: Cambridge University Press.

Bolles, Albert S. 1894. *The Financial History of the United States from 1789 to 1860.* New York: Appleton.

Bolton, Patrick, and Gerard Roland. 1997. "The Breakup of Nations: A Political Economy Analysis." *Quarterly Journal of Economics* 112: 1057–90.

Bowling, Kenneth R. 1971. "Dinner at Jefferson's: A Note on Jacob E. Cooke's 'The Compromise of 1790.'" *William and Mary Quarterly* 28.

Brady, David W. 1973. *Congressional Voting in a Partisan Era.* Lawrence: University Press of Kansas.

————. 1988. *Critical Elections and Congressional Policymaking*. Stanford, Calif.: Stanford University Press.

Brady, David W., Richard Brody, and David F. Epstein. 1989. "Heterogeneous Parties and Political Organization: The U.S. Senate, 1880–1920." *Legislative Studies Quarterly* 14: 205–23.

Brady, David W., Joseph Cooper, and Patricia A. Hurley. 1979. "The Decline of Party in the U.S. House of Representatives, 1887–1968." *Legislative Studies Quarterly*. 4: 381–407.

Brady, David W., and David F. Epstein. 1997. "Intraparty Preferences, Heterogeneity, and the Origins of the Modern Congress: Progressive Reformers in the House and Senate, 1890–1920." *Journal of Law, Economics and Organization* 13: 26–49.

Brady, David W., and Mark Morgan. 1987. "Reforming the Structure of the House Appropriations Process: The Effects of the 1885 and 1919–1920 Reforms on Money Decisions." In *Congress: Structure and Policy*, ed. Mathew D. McCubbins and Terry Sullivan. New York: Cambridge University Press.

Brady, David W., and Craig Volden. 1998. *Revolving Gridlock: Politics and Policy from Carter to Clinton*. Boulder, Colo.: Westview Press.

Brown, Everett S., ed. 1926. *The Missouri Compromises and Presidential Politics, 1820–1825*. St. Louis. Mo.: St. Louis Historical Society.

Brown, George R. 1974. *Leadership of Congress*. New York: Arno Press.

Burden, Barry, and Aage R. Clausen. 1999. "The Unfolding Drama: Party and Ideology in the 104th House." In *Great Theatre: The American Congress in the 1990s*, ed. Herbert Weisberg and Samuel Patterson. New York: Cambridge University Press.

Burnett, Edmund C., ed. 1921. *Letters of the Members of the Continental Congress*. 8 vols. Washington, D.C.: Carnegie Institution.

Burnham, Walter Dean. 1970. *Critical Elections and the Mainsprings of American Politics*. New York: Norton.

Cain, Bruce E., John Ferejohn, and Morris P. Fiorina. 1987. *The Personal Vote: Constituency Service and Electoral Independence*. Cambridge, Mass.: Harvard University Press.

Cameron, Charles M. 2000. *Veto Bargaining: Presidents and the Politics of Negative Power*. New York: Cambridge University Press.

Campbell, Andrea C. 2001. "Party Government in the U.S. Senate." Ph.D. dissertation, University of California, San Diego.

Canon, David, and Charles H. Stewart III. 1998. "The Development of the Senate Committee System, 1789–1879." Paper presented at the annual meeting of the American Political Science Association, Boston, September 3–6.

Carstensen, Vernon, ed. 1963. *The Public Lands: Studies in the History of the Public Domain*. Madison: University of Wisconsin Press.

Cater, Douglas. 1964. *Power in Washington*. New York: Random House.

Chambers, William Nisbet. 1963. *Political Parties in a New Nation: The American Experience, 1776–1809*. New York: Oxford University Press.

Chambers, William Nisbet, and Walter Dean Burnham, eds. 1967. *The American Party Systems: Stages of Development*. New York: Oxford University Press.

Chiu, Chang-wei. 1928. *The Speaker of the House of Representatives Since 1896*. New York: Columbia University Press.

Clausen, Aage R. 1973. *How Congressmen Decide*. New York: St. Martin's Press.

Coase, Ronald H. 1937. "The Nature of the Firm." *Economica* 4: 386–405.

Cohen, Linda R., and Roger G. Noll. 1991. "How to Vote, Whether to Vote." *Political Behavior* 13: 97–127.

Cole, Donald B. 1984. *Martin Van Buren and the American Political System*. Princeton, N.J.: Princeton University Press.

Collie, Melissa P. 1988a. "The Rise of Coalition Politics: Voting in the U.S. House, 1933–1980." *Legislative Studies Quarterly* 13: 321–42.

———. 1988b. "Universalism and the Parties in the U.S. House of Representatives, 1921–80." *American Journal of Political Science* 32: 865–83.

Collie, Melissa P., and David W. Brady. 1985. "The Decline of Partisan Voting Coalitions in the House of Representatives." In *Congress Reconsidered*, 3d ed., ed. Lawrence C. Dodd and Bruce I. Oppenheimer. Washington, D.C.: Congressional Quarterly Press.

Committee on Rules, U.S. House of Representatives. 1983. *A History of the Committee on Rules*. 97th Cong., 2d Sess. Washington, D.C.: Government Printing Office.

Congressional Quarterly. 1976. *Origins and Development of Congress*. Washington, D.C.: Congressional Quarterly.

Cooke, Jacob E. 1970. "The Compromise of 1790," *William and Mary Quarterly* 27: 523–45.

Cooper, Joseph. 1970. *The Origins of the Standing Committees and the Development of the Modern House*. Houston, Tex.: Rice University Studies.

———. 1981. "Organization and Innovation in the House of Representatives." In *The House at Work*, ed. Joseph Cooper and G. Calvin Mackenzie. Austin: University of Texas Press.

———. 1988. *Congress and Its Committees: A Historical Approach to the Role of Committees in the Legislative Process*. New York: Garland.

Cooper, Joseph, and David W. Brady. 1981. "Institutional Context and Leadership Style: The House from Cannon to Rayburn." *American Political Science Review* 75: 411–25.

Cooper, Joseph, David W. Brady, and Patricia A. Hurley. 1977. "The Electoral Basis of Party Voting." In *The Impact of the Electoral Process*, ed. Louis Maisel and Joseph. Cooper. Beverly Hills, Calif.: Sage.

Cooper, Joseph, and Martin Hering. 2001. "Party Theory Versus Preference Theory: Premises, Propositions, and Tests." Unpublished manuscript.

Cooper, Joseph, and Rick K. Wilson. 1994. "The Role of Congressional Parties." In *Encyclopedia of the American Legislative System*, vol. 2,: ed. Joel H. Silbey and others. New York: Scribner.

Cooper, Joseph, and Cheryl D. Young. 1989. "Bill Introduction in the Nineteenth Century: A Study of Institutional Change." *Legislative Studies Quarterly* 14: 67–105.

Cooper, Joseph, and Garry Young. 1997. " Partisanship, Bipartisanship, and Crosspartisanship in Congress Since the New Deal." In *Congress Reconsidered*, 6th ed., ed. Lawrence C. Dodd and Bruce I. Oppenheimer. Washington, D.C.: Congressional Quarterly Press.

Cox, Gary W. 1987. *The Efficient Secret: The Cabinet and the Development of Political Parties in Victorian England*. Cambridge: Cambridge University Press.

———. 1999. "Agenda Setting in the U.S. House: A Majority-Party Monopoly?" Paper presented at the annual meeting of the American Political Science Association, Atlanta, September 2–5.

———. 2000. "On the Effects of Legislative Rules." *Legislative Studies Quarterly* 25: 169–93.

———. 2001. "Agenda Setting in the U.S. House: A Majority-Party Monopoly." *Legislative Studies Quarterly* 25: 185–211.

Cox, Gary W., and Eric Magar. 1999. "How Much Is Majority Status in the U.S. Congress Worth?" *American Political Science Review* 93: 299–310.

Cox, Gary W., and Mathew D. McCubbins. 1993. *Legislative Leviathan: Party Government in the House*. Berkeley: University of California Press.

———. 1994a. "Bonding, Structure, and the Stability of Political Parties: Party Government in the House." *Legislative Studies Quarterly* 19: 215–31.

———. 1994b. "Party Coherence on Roll Call Votes in the U.S. House of Representatives." In *Encyclopedia of the American Legislative System*, vol. 2, ed. Joel H. Silbey and others. New York: Charles Scribner's Sons.

Cox, Gary W., and Keith T. Poole. 2001. "On Measuring Partisanship in Roll Call Voting: The U.S. House of Representatives, 1877–1999." Paper presented at the annual meeting of the American Political Science Association, San Francisco, August 30–September 2.

Cunningham, Noble, Jr. 1996. *The Presidency of James Monroe*. Lawrence: University Press of Kansas.

Dangerfield, George. 1952. *The Era of Good Feelings*. New York: Harcourt, Brace.

David, Paul T., Ralph M. Goldman, and Richard C. Bain. 1960. *The Politics of National Party Conventions*. Washington, D.C.: Brookings Institution.

Davidson, Roger H. 1981. "Subcommittee Government: New Channels for Policy Making." In *The New Congress*, ed. Thomas E. Mann and Norman J. Ornstein. Washington, D.C.: American Enterprise Institute.

———. 1985. "Senate Leaders: Janitors for an Untidy Chamber?" In *Congress Reconsidered*, 3d ed., ed. Lawrence C. Dodd and Bruce I. Oppenheimer. Washington, D.C.: Congressional Quarterly Press.

———. 1989. "The Senate: If Everybody Leads, Who Follows?" In *Congress Reconsidered*, 4th ed., ed. Lawrence C. Dodd and Bruce I. Oppenheimer. Washington, D.C.: Congressional Quarterly Press.

Dell, Christopher, and Stephen W. Stathis. 1982. *Major Acts of Congress and Treaties Approved by the Senate, 1789–1980*. Report No. 82–156 GOV. Washington, D.C.: Library of Congress.

Denzau, Arthur, William H. Riker, and Kenneth A. Shepsle. 1985. "Farquharson and Fenno: Sophisticated Voting and Home Style." *American Political Science Review* 79: 1117–35.

Derthick, Martha, and Paul J. Quirk. 1985. *The Politics of Deregulation*. Washington, D.C.: Brookings Institution.

Dewey, Davis R. 1934. *Financial History of the United States*. New York: Longmans, Green.

Dion, Douglas. 1997. *Turning the Legislative Thumbscrew: Minority Rights and Procedural Change in Legislative Politics*. Ann Arbor: University of Michigan Press.

Dodd, Lawrence C. 1989. "The Rise of Technocratic Congress: Congressional Reform in the 1970s." In *Remaking American Politics*, ed. Richard A. Harris and Sidney M. Milkis. Boulder, Colo.: Westview Press.

Dodd, Lawrence C., and Bruce I. Oppenheimer. 1997. "Congress and the Emerging Order: Conditional Party Government or Constructive Partnership?" In *Congress Reconsidered*, 6th ed., ed. Lawrence C. Dodd and Bruce I. Oppenheimer. Washington, D.C.: Congressional Quarterly Press.

Downs, Anthony. 1957. *An Economic Theory of Democracy*. New York: Harper.

Drew, Elizabeth. 1996. *Showdown: The Struggle Between the Gingrich Congress and the Clinton White House*. New York: Simon & Schuster.

Enelow, James, and Melvin Hinich. 1984. *The Spatial Theory of Voting*. New York: Cambridge University Press.

Epstein, David F. 1984. *The Political Theory of the Federalist*. Chicago: University of Chicago Press.

Eulau, Heinz, and Vera McCluggage. 1984. "Standing Committees in Legislatures: Three Decades of Research." *Legislative Studies Quarterly* 9: 195–217.

Evans, Lawrence, and Walter J. Oleszek. 1997. "Analyzing Party Leadership in

Congress: An Exploration." Paper presented at the annual meeting of the Midwest Political Science Association, Chicago, April 10–13.

Farrell, Joseph, and Suzanne Scotchmer. 1988. "Partnerships." *Quarterly Journal of Economics* 103: 279–97.

Fehrenbacher, Don E. 1980. *The South and the Three Sectional Crises.* Baton Rouge: Louisiana State University Press.

————. 2001. *The Slaveholding Republic: An Account of the United States Government's Relations to Slavery.* New York: Oxford University Press.

Fenno, Richard F. 1966. *The Power of the Purse.* Boston: Little, Brown.

————. 1973. *Congressmen in Committees.* Boston: Little, Brown.

————. 1978. *Home Style: House Members in Their Districts.* Boston: Little, Brown.

————. 1991. *The Emergence of a Senate Leader: Pete Domenici and the Reagan Budget.* Washington, D.C.: Congressional Quarterly Press.

Ferguson, E. James. 1961. *The Power of the Purse: A History of American Public Finance, 1776–1790.* Chapel Hill: University of North Carolina Press.

————. 1969. "The Nationalists of 1781–83 and the Economic Interpretation of the Constitution." *Journal of American History* 56: 241–61.

Fiorina, Morris P. 1977. *Congress: Keystone of the Washington Establishment.* New Haven, Conn.: Yale University Press.

Fiorina, Morris P., David W. Rohde, and Peter Wissel. 1975. "Historical Change in House Turnover." In *Congress in Change: Evolution and Reform,* ed. Norman J. Ornstein. New York: Praeger.

Fisher, Louis. 1975. *The Constitution Between Friends.* New York: St. Martin's Press.

Follett, Mary Parker. 1896. *The Speaker of the House of Representatives.* New York: Longmans, Green.

Forgette, Richard. 1997. "Reed's Rules and the Partisan Theory of Legislative Organization." *Polity* 29: 375–96.

Fox, Harrison W., and Susan Webb Hammond. 1977. *Congressional Staffs: The Invisible Force in American Lawmaking.* New York: Free Press.

Freehling, William W. 1990. *The Road to Disunion,* vol. 1, *Secessionists at Bay,: 1776–1854.* New York: Oxford University Press.

Fuller, Hubert Bruce. 1909. *The Speakers of the House.* Boston: Little, Brown.

Galloway, George B. 1976. *History of the House of Representatives,* 2d ed. New York: Crowell. Originally published in 1962.

Gamm, Gerald, and Kenneth A. Shepsle. 1989. "Emergence of Legislative Institutions: Standing Committees in the House and Senate, 1810–1825." *Legislative Studies Quarterly* 14: 39–66.

Gamm, Gerald, and Steven S. Smith. 1998. "Emergence of Senate Party Leadership." Paper presented at the annual meeting of the Midwest Political Science Association, Chicago, April 23–25.

————. 2000a. "Last Among Equals: The Senate's Presiding Officer." In *Es-*

teemed *Colleagues: Civility and Deliberation in the U.S. Senate*, ed. Burdett A. Loomis. Washington, D.C.: Brookings Institution.

———. 2000b. "Steering the Senate: The Consolidation of Senate Party Leadership, 1892–1913." Unpublished manuscript.

———. 2001. "The Senate Without Leaders: Senate Parties in the Mid-Nineteenth Century." Paper presented at the annual meeting of the American Political Science Association, San Francisco, August 30– September 2.

———. 2002. "Emergence of Senate Party Leadership." In *Senate Exceptionalism*, ed. Bruce I. Oppenheimer. Columbus: Ohio State University Press.

Gertzog, Irwin N. 1976. "The Routinization of Committee Assignments in the U.S. House of Representatives." *American Journal of Political Science* 20: 693–712.

Gilligan, Thomas, and Keith Krehbiel. 1989. "Asymmetric Information and Legislative Rules with a Heterogeneous Committee." *American Journal of Political Science* 33: 459–90.

———. 1990. "Organization of Informative Committees by a Rational Legislature." *American Journal of Political Science* 34: 531–64.

Goodwin, George. 1970. *The Little Legislatures: Committees of Congress*. Amherst: University of Massachusetts Press.

Greenstein, Fred I. 1969. *Personality and Politics: Problems of Evidence, Inference, and Conceptualization*. Chicago: Markham.

Greenstone, J. David. 1993. *The Lincoln Persuasion: Remaking American Liberalism*. Princeton, N.J.: Princeton University Press.

Gronke, Paul. 2000. *The Electorate, the Campaign, and the Office: A Unified Approach to Senate and House Elections*. Ann Arbor: University of Michigan Press.

Groseclose, Tim, and James M. Snyder. 1996. "Buying Supermajorities." *American Political Science Review* 90: 303–15.

Gunning, Matthew, and Randall Strahan. 2000. "The Emergence of the U.S. House Speaker as a Policy Leader, 1789–1841." Paper presented at the annual meeting of the Southern Political Science Association, Atlanta, November 13–15.

Hager, Gregory, and Jeffrey Talbert. 2000. "Look for the Party Label: Party Influences on Voting in the U.S. House." *Legislative Studies Quarterly* 25: 75–101.

Hall, Richard. 1996. *Participation in Congress*, New Haven, Conn.: Yale University Press.

Hamilton, Alexander, James Madison, and John Jay. 1961. *The Federalist*, ed. Clinton Rossiter New York: New American Library. Originally published in 1787–88.

Hamilton, Holman. 1957. "'The Cave of the Winds' and the Compromise of 1850." *Journal of Southern History* 23: 331–53.

————. 1964. *Prologue to Conflict: The Crisis and Compromise of 1850*. New York: Norton.

Harlow, Ralph Volney. 1917. *The History of Legislative Methods in the Period Before 1825*. New Haven, Conn.: Yale University Press.

Harris, Marshall. 1970. *Origin of the Land Tenure System in the United States*. Westport, Conn.: Greenwood.

Hasbrouck, Paul DeWitt. 1927. *Party Government in the House of Representatives*. New York: Macmillan.

Hatzenbuehler, Ronald L. 1976. "The War Hawks and the Question of Leadership in 1812." *Pacific Historical Review* 43: 1–22.

Haynes, George H. 1960. *The Senate of the United States: Its History and Practice*. New York: Russell & Russell.

Heale, M. J. 1982. *The Presidential Quest: Candidates and Images in American Political Culture, 1787–1852*. New York: Longman.

Heckman, James, and James M. Snyder. 1997. "Linear Probability Models of the Demand for Attributes with an Empirical Application to Estimating the Preferences of Legislators." *Rand Journal of Economics* 28: S142–S148.

Hemphill, William E. 1971. *The Papers of John C. Calhoun*. Columbia: University of South Carolina Press.

Henderson, H. James. 1974. *Party Politics in the Continental Congress*. New York: McGraw-Hill.

Hennig, Robert A. 1996. "Between the Margins: Party Politics and Committee Power in Conference Committees of the U.S. House of Representatives." Unpublished Ph.D. dissertation, University of California, Berkeley.

Hicks, John D. 1960. *Republican Ascendancy, 1921–1933*. New York: Harper & Row.

Higley, John, and Richard Gunther. 1992. *Elites and Democratic Consolidation in Latin America and Southern Europe*. New York: Cambridge University Press.

Hill, Jeffrey S., and Kenneth C. Williams. 1993. "The Decline of Private Bills: Resource Allocation, Credit Claiming, and the Decision to Delegate." *American Journal of Political Science* 37: 1008–31.

Hinckley, Barbara. 1988. *Stability and Change in Congress*, 4th ed. New York: Harper & Row.

Hinich, Melvin J., and Michael C. Munger. 1997. *Analytical Politics*. New York: Cambridge University Press.

Hoadley, John F. 1980. "The Emergence of Political Parties in Congress, 1789–1803." *American Political Science Review* 74: 757–79.

————. 1986. *Origins of American Political Parties, 1789–1803*. Lexington: University of Kentucky Press.

Hofstadter, Richard, William Miller, and Daniel Aaron. 1959. *The American Republic*, vol. 1. Englewood Cliffs, N.J.: Prentice Hall.

Holt, Michael F. 1978. *Political Crisis of the 1850s*. New York: Norton.

———. 1999. *The Rise and Fall of the American Whig Party: Jacksonian Politics and the Onset of the Civil War*. New York: Oxford University Press.

Hopkins, James F., ed. 1963. *The Papers of Henry Clay*, vol. 3. Lexington: University of Kentucky Press.

Horsman, Reginald. 1962. *The Causes of the War of 1812*. Philadelphia: University of Pennsylvania Press.

Hoskins, Halford L. 1927. "The Hispanic American Policy of Henry Clay, 1816–1828." *Hispanic American Historical Review* 7: 460–78.

Howe, Daniel Walker. 1979. *The Political Culture of the American Whigs*. Chicago: University of Chicago Press.

Huitt, Ralph K. 1961. "Democratic Party Leadership in the Senate." *American Political Science Review* 55: 333–44.

Hurley, Patricia A., David W. Brady, and Joseph Cooper. 1977. "Measuring Legislative Potential for Policy Change." *Legislative Studies Quarterly* 2: 385–99.

Hurley, Patricia A., and Rick K. Wilson. 1989. "Partisan Voting Patterns in the U.S. Senate, 1877–1986." *Legislative Studies Quarterly* 14: 225–50.

Jacobson, Gary C. 1987. "Running Scared: Elections and Congressional Politics in the 1980s." In *Congress: Structure and Policy*, ed. Mathew D. McCubbins and Terry Sullivan. New York: Cambridge University Press.

Jenkins, Jeffery A. 1998. "Property Rights and the Emergence of Standing Committee Dominance in the Nineteenth Century House of Representatives." *Legislative Studies Quarterly* 23: 493–519.

———. 1999. "Examining the Bonding Effects of Party: A Comparative Analysis of Roll Call Voting in the U.S. and Confederate Houses." *American Journal of Political Science* 43: 1144–65.

———. 2000. "Examining the Robustness of Ideological Voting: Evidence from the Confederate House of Representatives." *American Journal of Political Science* 44: 811–22.

Jenkins, Jeffery A., and Brian R. Sala. 1998. "The Spatial Theory of Voting and the Presidential Election of 1824." *American Journal of Political Science* 42: 1157–79.

Jenkins, Jeffery A., and Charles H. Stewart III. 1997. "Order from Chaos: The Transformation of the Committee System in the House, 1816–1822." Paper presented at the annual meeting of the American Political Science Association, Washington, D.C., August 28–31.

———. 1998. "Committee Assignments as Side Payments: The Interplay of Leadership and Committee Development in the Era of Good Feelings." Paper presented at the annual meeting of the Midwest Political Science Association, Chicago, April 23–25.

Jillson, Calvin C., and Rick K. Wilson. 1994. *Congressional Dynamics: Structure,*

Coordination, and Choice in the First American Congress, 1774–1789. Stanford, Calif.: Stanford University Press.

Johannsen, Robert W. 1973. *Stephen A. Douglas.* New York: Oxford University Press.

Jones, Charles O. 1968. "Joseph G. Cannon and Howard W. Smith: An Essay on the Limits of Leadership in the House of Representatives." *Journal of Politics* 30: 617–46.

———. 1976. "Senate Party Leadership in Public Policy." In *Policymaking Role of Leadership in the Senate.* Compilation of papers prepared for the Commission on the Operation of the Senate, 94th Cong., 2d Sess. Washington, D.C.: Government Printing Office.

Katz, Jonathan N., and Brian R. Sala. 1996. "Careerism, Committee Assignments, and the Electoral Connection." *American Political Science Review* 90: 21–33.

Keller, Morton. 1977. *Affairs of State: Public Life in Late Nineteenth Century America.* Cambridge, Mass.: Harvard University Press.

Kennon, Donald R., and Rebecca M. Rogers. 1989. *The Committee on Ways and Means: A Bicentennial History.* Washington, D.C.: Government Printing Office.

Key, V. O. 1984. *Southern Politics in State and Nation.* Knoxville: University of Tennessee Press. Originally published in 1949.

Kiewiet, D. Roderick, and Mathew D. McCubbins. 1991. *The Logic of Delegation: Congressional Parties and the Appropriations Process.* Chicago: University of Chicago Press.

King, David C. 1997. *Turf Wars: How Congressional Committees Claim Jurisdiction.* Chicago: University of Chicago Press.

Kousser, J. Morgan. 1974. *The Shaping of Southern Politics: Suffrage Restrictions and the Establishment of the One-Party South, 1880–1910.* New Haven, Conn.: Yale University Press.

Krehbiel, Keith. 1991. *Information and Legislative Organization.* Ann Arbor: University of Michigan Press.

———. 1993. "Where's the Party?" *British Journal of Political Science* 23: 235–66.

———. 1997a. "Rejoinder to 'Sense and Sensibility.'" *American Journal of Political Science* 41: 958–64.

———. 1997b. "Restrictive Rules Reconsidered." *American Journal of Political Science* 41: 919–44.

———. 1998. *Pivotal Politics: A Theory of U.S. Lawmaking.* Chicago: University of Chicago Press.

———. 1999a. "Paradoxes of Parties in Congress." *Legislative Studies Quarterly* 24: 31–64.

———. 1999b. "The Party Effect from A to Z and Beyond." *Journal of Politics* 61: 832–41.

————. 1999c. "Party Voting in a Nonpartisan Legislature." Paper delivered at annual meeting of the Public Choice Society, New Orleans, March 12–14.

————. 2000. "Party Discipline and Measures of Partisanship." *American Journal of Political Science* 44: 212–27.

Krehbiel, Keith, and Douglas Rivers. 1988. "The Analysis of Committee Power: An Application to Senate Voting on the Minimum Wage." *American Journal of Political Science* 32: 1151–74.

Krehbiel, Keith, and Alan Wiseman. 2001. "Joseph G. Cannon: Majoritarian from Illinois." *Legislative Studies Quarterly* 26: 357–89.

Lamar, Howard R. 1956. *Dakota Territory, 1861–1889: A Study of Frontier Politics*. New Haven, Conn.: Yale University Press.

Larson, Robert W. 1968. *New Mexico's Quest for Statehood, 1846–1912*. Albuquerque: University of New Mexico Press.

Lawrence, Eric D., Forrest Maltzman, and Steven S. Smith. 1999. "Who Wins? Party Effects in Legislative Voting." Paper presented at the annual meeting of the Midwest Political Science Association, Chicago, April 16–19.

Lawrence, Eric D., Forrest Maltzman, and Paul J. Wahlbeck. 2001. "The Politics of Speaker Cannon's Committee Assignments." *American Journal of Political Science* 45: 551–62.

Leintz, Gerald R. 1978. "House Speaker Elections and Congressional Parties, 1789–1860." *Capitol Studies* 6: 63–89.

Levitt, Steven D., and James M. Snyder. 1995. "Political Parties and the Distribution of Federal Outlays." *American Journal of Political Science* 39: 958–80.

Lyman, Edward L. 1986. *Political Deliverance: The Mormon Quest for Utah Statehood*. Urbana: University of Illinois Press.

Lynd, Staughton. 1967. *Class Conflict, Slavery, and the United States Constitution*. New York: Bobbs-Merrill.

Maddala, G. S. 1983. *Limited-Dependent and Qualitative Variables in Econometrics*. New York: Cambridge University Press.

Manzer, Robert A. 1996. "Hume on Pride and Love of Fame." *Polity* 18: 333–55.

Martin, Joseph G. 1871. *Seventy-Three Years' History of the Boston Stock Market, from January 1, 1798, to January 1, 1871*. Boston: Joseph G. Martin.

Martis, Kenneth C. 1989. *The Historical Atlas of Political Parties in the United States Congress, 1789–1989*. New York: Macmillan.

Mayhew, David. 1974. *Congress: The Electoral Connection*. New Haven, Conn.: Yale University Press.

————. 1991. *Divided We Govern*. New Haven, Conn.: Yale University Press.

McCall, Samuel W. 1914. *The Life of Thomas Brackett Reed*. Boston: Houghton Mifflin.

McConachie, Lauros G. 1998. *Congressional Committees: A Study of the Origin and Development of Our National and Local Legislative Methods.* New York: Franklin Reprints.

McCormick, Richard P. 1966. *The Second American Party System: Party Formation in the Jacksonian Era.* Chapel Hill: University of North Carolina Press.

————. 1982. *The Presidential Game: Origins of American Politics.* New York: Oxford University Press.

McCubbins, Mathew D., and Thomas Schwartz. 1984. "Congressional Oversight Overlooked: Police Patrols Versus Fire Alarms." *American Journal of Political Science* 28: 165–79.

McKelvey, R. D. 1976. "Intransitivities in Multidimensional Voting Models and Some Implications for Agenda Control." *Journal of Economic Theory* 12: 472–82.

McNollgast. 1994. "Legislative Intent: The Use of Positive Political Theory in Statutory Interpretation." *Law and Contemporary Problems.* 57: 3–37.

McPherson, James M. 1982. *Ordeal by Fire: The Civil War and Reconstruction.* New York: Knopf.

————. 1988. *Battle Cry of Freedom: The Civil War Era.* New York: Oxford University Press.

Merk, Frederick. 1963. *Manifest Destiny and Mission in American History.* Cambridge, Mass.: Harvard University Press.

Miller, John C. 1959. *Alexander Hamilton and the Growth of the New Nation.* New York: Harper & Row.

Milton, George F. 1934. *The Eve of Conflict: Stephen A. Douglas and the Needless War.* Boston: Houghton Mifflin.

Minicucci, Stephen. 1998. "Finding the Cement of Interest: Internal Improvements and American Nation-Building, 1790–1860." Ph.D. dissertation, Massachusetts Institute of Technology.

Mooney, Chase C. 1974. *William H. Crawford, 1772–1834.* Lexington: University Press of Kentucky.

Moore, Glover. 1953. *The Missouri Controversy: 1819–1821.* Lexington: University of Kentucky Press.

Morison, Samuel Eliot, and Henry Steele Commager. 1950. *The Growth of the American Republic,* 4th ed., vol. 1. New York: Oxford University Press.

Morrison. Michael A. 1997. *Slavery and the American West: The Eclipse of Manifest Destiny and the Coming of the Civil War.* Chapel Hill: University of North Carolina Press.

Morrow, William L. 1969. *Congressional Committees.* New York: Scribner.

Murphy, James T. 1974. "Political Parties and the Porkbarrel: Party Conflict and Cooperation in House Public Works Committee Decision-Making." *American Political Science Review* 68: 169–86.

Nevins, Allan. 1947. *Ordeal of the Union*, vol. 1, *Fruits of Manifest Destiny, 1847–1852*. New York: Scribner.

Nichols, Roy F. 1963. *American Leviathan: The Evolution and Process of Self-Government in the United States*. New York: Harper Colophon.

——. 1967. *The Invention of the American Political Parties*. New York: Macmillan.

Nielsen, George R. 1968. "The Indispensable Institution: The Congressional Party During the Era of Good Feelings." Ph.D. dissertation, University of Iowa.

Niven, John. 1983. *Martin Van Buren: The Romantic Age of American Politics*. Oxford: Oxford University Press.

——. 1988. *John C. Calhoun and the Price of Union*. Baton Rouge: Louisiana State University Press.

Nokken, Timothy P. 2000. "Dynamics of Congressional Loyalty: Party Defection and Roll Call Behavior, 1947–1997." *Legislative Studies Quarterly* 25: 417–44.

North, Douglass C., and Robert P. Thomas. 1973. *The Rise of the Western World: A New Economic History*. New York: Cambridge University Press.

Offenberg, Richard Stanley. 1963. "The Political Career of Thomas Brackett Reed." Ph.D. dissertation, New York University.

Ohline, Howard A. 1971. "Republicanism and Slavery: Origins of the Three-Fifths Clause in the United States Constitution." *William and Mary Quarterly*, series 3, 28: 562–84.

——. 1980. "Slavery, Economics, and Congressional Politics, 1790." *Journal of Southern History* 46: 333–42.

Oleszek, Walter J. 1971. "Party Whips in the United States Senate." *Journal of Politics* 33: 955–79.

——. 1989. *Congressional Procedures and the Policy Process*, 3d ed. Washington, D.C.: Congressional Quarterly Press.

Oppenheimer, Bruce I. 1994. "The Rules Committee: The House Traffic Cop." In *Encyclopedia of the American Legislative System*, vol. 2, ed. Joel H. Silbey and others. New York: Scribner.

Palazzolo, Daniel J. 1992. *The Speaker and the Budget: Leadership in the Post-Reform House of Representatives*. Pittsburgh, Pa.: University of Pittsburgh Press.

Pancake, John S. 1972. *Samuel Smith and the Politics of Business: 1752–1839*. University: University of Alabama Press.

Patterson, James T. 1967. *Congressional Conservatism and the New Deal*. Lexington: University of Kentucky Press.

Peabody, Robert. 1976. *Leadership in Congress: Stability, Succession, and Change*. Boston: Little, Brown.

Perkins, Edwin J. 1994. *American Public Finance and Financial Services, 1700–1815*. Columbus: Ohio Status University Press.

Peters, Ronald M. 1990. *The American Speakership: The Office in Historical Perspective*. Baltimore: Johns Hopkins University Press.

———. 1996. "The Republican Speakership." Paper presented at the annual meeting of the American Political Science Association, San Francisco, August 29–September 1.

———. 1997 *The American Speakership: The Office in Historical Perspective*, 2d ed. Baltimore: Johns Hopkins University Press.

Peterson, Merrill D. 1987. *The Great Triumvirate: Webster, Clay, and Calhoun*. New York: Oxford University Press.

Poage, George Rawlings. 1936. *Henry Clay and the Whig Party*. Chapel Hill:, University of North Carolina Press.

Polsby, Nelson W. 1968. "The Institutionalization of the U.S. House of Representatives." *American Political Science Review* 62: 144–68.

Polsby, Nelson W., Miriam Gallaher, and Barry S. Rundquist. 1969. "The Growth of the Seniority System in the U.S. House of Representatives." *American Political Science Review* 63: 787–807.

Pomeroy, Earl S. 1947 *The Territories and the United States, 1861–1890: Studies in Colonial Administration*. Philadelphia: University of Pennsylvania Press.

Poole, Keith T. 1998. "Recovering a Basic Space from a Set of Issue Scales." *American Journal of Political Science* 42: 954–93.

Poole, Keith T., and Howard Rosenthal. 1985. "A Spatial Model for Legislative Roll Call Analysis." *American Journal of Political Science* 29: 357–84.

———. 1991. "Patterns of Congressional Voting." *American Journal of Political Science* 35: 228–78.

———. 1997. *Congress: A Political-Economic History of Roll Call Voting*. New York: Oxford University Press.

———. 2001. "D-NOMINATE After Ten Years: A Comparative Update to *Congress: A Political-Economic History of Roll Call Voting*." *Legislative Studies Quarterly* 26: 5–31.

Potter, David M. 1972. *The South and the Concurrent Majority*, ed. Don E. Fehrenbacher and Carl N. Degler. Baton Rouge: Louisiana State University Press.

———. 1976. *The Impending Crisis,: 1848–1861*, ed. Don E. Fehrenbacher. New York: Harper & Row.

Powell, Fred Wilbur, comp. 1939. *Control of Federal Expenditures: A Documentary History, 1775–1894*. Washington, D.C.: Brookings Institution.

Price, H. Douglas. 1971. "The Congressional Career: Then and Now." In *Congressional Behavior*, ed. Nelson W. Polsby. New York: Random House.

———. 1975. "Congress and the Evolution of Legislative 'Professionalism.'" In *Congress in Change: Evolution and Reform*, ed. Norman J. Ornstein. New York: Praeger.

————. 1977. "Careers and Committees in the American Congress: The Problem of Structural Change." In *The History of Parliamentary Behavior*, ed. William O. Aydelotte. Princeton, N.J.: Princeton University Press.

Reed, Thomas B. 1889a. "Obstruction in the National House." *North American Review*, October.

————. 1889b. "Rules of the House of Representatives." *Century Magazine*, March.

Remini, Robert V. 1991. *Henry Clay: Statesman for the Union*. New York: Norton.

Riker, William H. 1980. "Implications form the Disequilibrium of Majority Rule for the Study of Institutions." *American Political Science Review* 74: 432–46.

————. 1986. *The Art of Political Manipulation*. New Haven, Conn.: Yale University Press.

Ripley, Randall B. 1969. *Power in the Senate*. New York: St. Martin's Press.

Risjord, Norman K. 1992. "Partisanship and Power: House Committees and the Powers of the Speaker, 1789–1801." *William and Mary Quarterly* 49: 628–51.

Ritchie, Donald A. 1998. *Minutes of the Senate Democratic Conference: Fifty-Eighth Congress Through Eighty-Eighth Congress, 1903–1964*. 105th Congress. S. Doc. 105-20. Washington, D.C.: U.S. Government Printing Office.

Rivers, Douglas, and Morris P. Fiorina. 1991. "Constituency Service, Reputation, and the Incumbency Advantage." In *Homestyle and Washington Work: Studies of Congressional Politics*, ed. Morris P. Fiorina and David W. Rohde. Ann Arbor: University of Michigan Press.

Robinson, Donald L. 1971. *Slavery in the Structure of American Politics, 1765–1820*. New York: Harcourt Brace Jovanovich.

Robinson, William A. 1930. *Thomas B. Reed,: Parliamentarian*. New York: Dodd, Mead.

Rohde, David W. 1991. *Parties and Leaders in the Postreform House*. Chicago: University of Chicago Press.

————. 1994. "Parties and Committees in the House: Member Motivations, Issues, and Institutional Arrangements." *Legislative Studies Quarterly* 19: 341–61.

Rohde, David W., and Kenneth A. Shepsle. 1987. "Leaders and Followers in the House of Representatives: Reflections on Woodrow Wilson's *Congressional Government*." *Congress and the Presidency* 14: 111–33.

Rothbard, Murray N. 1962. *The Panic of 1819: Reactions and Policies*. New York: Columbia University Press.

Rothman, David J. 1966. *Politics and Power: The United States Senate, 1869–1901*. Cambridge, Mass.: Harvard University Press.

Rubin, Alissa J. 1995. "Finishing the 'Contract' in Style, House Passes Tax-Cut Bill." *Congressional Quarterly Weekly Report*, April 8, pp. 1010–14.

Russel, Robert R. 1972. "What Was the Compromise of 1850?" In *Critical Studies in Antebellum Sectionalism: Essays in American Political and Economic History*. Westport, Conn.: Greenwood.

Sabl, Andrew. 1997. "Political Offices and American Constitutional Democracy." Ph.D. dissertation, Harvard University.

Sala, Brian R. 1999. "Party Loyalty and Committee Leadership in the House." Paper presented at the History of Congress Conference, Stanford University, January 15–16.

Sanford, Albert B. 1927. "The Organization and Development of Colorado Territory." In *The History of Colorado*, ed. James H. Baker and LeRoy R. Hafen. Denver, Colo.: Lindeman.

Scharpf, Fritz. 1997. *Games Real Actors Play: Actor-Centered Institutionalism in Policy Research*. Boulder, Colo.: Westview Press.

Schickler, Eric. 2000. "Institutional Change in the House of Representatives, 1867–1998: A Test of Partisan and Ideological Power Balance Models." *American Political Science Review* 94: 285–86.

———. 2001. *Disjointed Pluralism: Institutional Innovation and the Development of the U.S. Congress*. Princeton, N.J.: Princeton University Press.

Schickler, Eric, and Andrew Rich. 1997. "Controlling the Floor: Politics as Procedural Coalitions in the House." *American Journal of Political Science* 41: 1340–75.

Schofield, Norman. 1985. *Social Choice and Democracy*. Heidelberg, Germany: Springer Verlag.

Schofield, Norman, Bernard Grofman, and Scott Feld. 1988. "The Core and the Stability of Group Choice in Spatial Voting Games." *American Political Science Review* 82: 195–211.

Sefton, James E. 1980. *Andrew Johnson and the Uses of Constitutional Power*. Boston: Little, Brown.

Shannon, W. Wayne. 1968. *Party, Constituency, and Congressional Voting*. Baton Rouge: Louisiana State University Press.

Shea, Daniel M. 1999. "The Passing of Realignment and the Advent of the 'Baseless' Party System." *American Politics Quarterly* 27: 33–57.

Shepsle, Kenneth A. 1978. *The Giant Jigsaw Puzzle*. Chicago: University of Chicago Press.

———. 1979. "Institutional Arrangements and Equilibrium in Multidimensional Voting Models." *American Journal of Political Science* 23: 27–59.

———. 1989a. "The Changing Textbook Congress." In *Can the Government Govern?* ed. John E. Chubb and Paul E. Peterson. Washington, D.C.: Brookings Institution.

———. 1989b. "Studying Institutions: Some Lessons from the Rational Choice Approach." *Journal of Theoretical Politics* 1: 131–47.

Shepsle, Kenneth A., and Mark S. Bonchek. 1997. *Analyzing Politics: Rationality, Behavior, and Institutions.* New York: Norton.

Shepsle, Kenneth A., and Barry R. Weingast. 1981. "Structure Induced Equilibrium and Legislative Choice." *Public Choice* 37: 509–19.

————. 1984a. "Legislative Politics and Budget Outcomes." In *Federal Budget Policy in the 1980s*, ed. Gregory B. Mills and John L. Palmer. Washington, D.C.: Urban Institute.

————. 1984b. "Uncovered Sets and Sophisticated Voting Outcomes with Implications for Agenda Institutions." *American Journal of Political Science* 29: 49–74.

————. 1987a. "The Institutional Foundations of Committee Power." *American Political Science Review* 81: 85–104.

————. 1987b. "Reflections on Committee Power." *American Political Science Review* 81: 35–104.

————. 1994. "Positive Theories of Congressional Institutions." *Legislative Studies Quarterly* 19: 149–78.

————. 1995. "Positive Theories of Congressional Institutions." In *Positive Theories of Congressional Institutions*, ed. Kenneth A. Shepsle and Barry R. Weingast. Ann Arbor: University of Michigan Press.

Shuman, Howard E. 1991. "Lyndon B. Johnson: The Senate's Powerful Persuader." In *First Among Equals: Outstanding Senate Leaders of the Twentieth Century*, ed. Richard A. Baker and Roger H. Davidson. Washington, D.C.: Congressional Quarterly Press.

Sieberer, Ulrich. 2001. "The Margin of the Majority Party, Party Unity, and Party Effectiveness: Evidence from the U.S. Congress, 1889–1999." Unpublished manuscript.

Silbey, Joel H. 1964. "The Civil War Synthesis in American Political History." *Civil War History* 10: 130–40.

————. 1967. *Shrine of Party: Congressional Voting Behavior, 1841–52.* Pittsburgh, Pa.: University of Pittsburgh Press.

————. 1985. *The Partisan Imperative: The Dynamics of American Politics Before the Civil War.* New York: Oxford University Press.

Simpson, Albert F. 1941. "The Political Significance of Slave Representation, 1787–1821." *Journal of Southern History* 7: 315–42.

Sinclair, Barbara. 1983. *Majority Leadership in the U.S. House.* Baltimore: Johns Hopkins University Press.

————. 1989a. "House Majority Party Leadership in the Late 1980s." In *Congress Reconsidered*, 4th ed., ed. Lawrence C. Dodd and Bruce I Oppenheimer. Washington, D.C.: Congressional Quarterly Press.

————. 1989b. *The Transformation of the U.S. Senate.* Baltimore: Johns Hopkins University Press.

————. 1990. "Congressional Leadership: A Review Essay and a Research Agenda." In *Leading Congress: New Styles, New Strategies*, ed. John J. Kornacki, ed. Washington, D.C.: Congressional Quarterly Press.

————. 1992a. "The Emergence of Strong Leadership in the 1980s House of Representatives," *Journal of Politics* 54: 657–84.

————. 1992b. "Strong Party Leadership in a Weak Party Era: The Evolution of Party Leadership in the Modern House." In *The Atomistic Congress,* ed. Allen D. Hertzke and Ronald M. Peters Jr. Armonk, N.Y.: Sharpe.

————. 1994. "The Speaker as Party Leader." In *The Speaker: Leadership in the U.S. House of Representatives,* ed. Ronald M. Peters Jr. Washington, D.C.: Congressional Quarterly Press.

————. 1995. *Legislators, Leaders, and Lawmaking.* Baltimore: Johns Hopkins University Press.

————. 1997. *Unorthodox Lawmaking.* Washington, D.C.: Congressional Quarterly Press.

————. 1998a. "Do Parties Matter?" Paper presented at the annual meeting of the Midwest Political Science Association, Chicago, April 23–25.

————. 1998b. "The Plot Thickens: Congress and the President." In *Great Theatre: The American Congress in the 1990s,* ed. Herbert Weisberg and Samuel Patterson. New York: Cambridge University Press.

————. 1999. "Transformational Leader or Faithful Agent? Principal Agent Theory and House Majority Party Leadership in the 104th and 105th Congresses." *Legislative Studies Quarterly* 24: 421–50.

Skladony, Thomas W. 1985. "The House Goes to Work: Select and Standing Committees in the U.S. House of Representatives, 1789–1828." *Congress and the Presidency* 12: 165–87.

Skowronek, Stephen. 1993. *The Politics Presidents Make: Leadership from John Adams to George Bush.* Cambridge, Mass.: Harvard University Press.

Smith, Elbert B. 1988. *The Presidencies of Zachary Taylor and Millard Fillmore.* Lawrence: University Press of Kansas.

Smith, Steven S. 1989. *Call to Order: Floor Politics in the House and Senate* Washington, D.C.: Brookings Institution.

Smith, Steven S., and M. Flathman. 1989. "Managing the Senate Floor: Complex Unanimous Consent Agreements Since the 1950s." *Legislative Studies Quarterly* 14: 349–74.

Snyder, James M., and Tim Groseclose. 2000. "Party Pressure in Congressional Roll Call Voting." *American Journal of Political Science* 44: 193–211.

Spann, Edward K. 1960. "The Souring of Good Feelings: John W. Taylor and the Speakership Election of 1821." *New York History* 41: 379–99.

Spence, Clark C. 1975. *Territorial Politics and Government in Montana, 1864–1889.* Urbana: University of Illinois Press.

Stegmaier, Mark J. 1996. *Texas, New Mexico, and the Compromise of 1850: Boundary Dispute and Sectional Crisis.* Kent, Ohio: Kent State University Press.

Steiner, Bernard C. 1921–22. "James Alfred Pearce." *Maryland Historical Magazine* 16: 319–39; 17: 33–47, 177–90, 269–83, 348–63; 18: 38–52, 134–50, 257–73, 341–57; 19: 13–29, 162–79.

Stewart, Charles H., III. 1989. *Budget Reform Politics: The Design of the Appropriations Process in the House of Representatives, 1865–1921.* New York: Cambridge University Press.

———. 1992. "Committee Hierarchies in the Modernizing House, 1875–1947." *American Journal of Political Science* 36: 835–856.

———. 1998. "Architect or Tactician? Henry Clay and the Institutional Development of the U.S. House of Representatives." Paper presented at the annual meeting of the American Political Science Association, Boston, September 3–6.

Stewart, Charles H., III, David Canon, Greg Flemming, and Brian Kroeger. 1995. "Taking Care of Business: The Evolution of the House Committee System Before the Civil War." Paper presented at the annual meeting of the American Political Science Association, New York, August 31–September 3.

Stewart, Charles H., III, and Barry R. Weingast. 1992. "Stacking the Senate, Changing the Nation: Republican Rotten Boroughs, Statehood Politics, and American Political Development." *Studies in American Political Development* 6: 223–71.

Stid, Daniel. 1996. "Transformational Leadership in Congress?" Paper presented at the annual meeting of the American Political Science Association, San Francisco, August 29–September 1.

Stover, John F. 1987. *History of the Baltimore and Ohio Railroad.* West Lafayette, Ind.: Purdue University Press.

Strahan, Randall. 1989. "Members' Goals and Coalition-Building Strategies in the U.S. House: The Case of Tax Reform." *Journal of Politics* 51: 372–84.

———. 1990. *New Ways and Means.* Chapel Hill: University of North Carolina Press.

———. 1994. "Congressional Leadership in Institutional Time: The Case of Henry Clay." Paper presented at the annual meeting of the American Political Science Association, New York, September 1–4.

Strahan, Randall, Vincent G. Moscardelli, Moshe Haspel, and Richard S. Wike. 1998. "Leadership and Institutional Development in the Early U.S. House: The Clay Speakership." Paper presented at the annual meeting of the Midwest Political Science Association, Chicago, April 23–25.

———. 2000. "The Clay Speakership Revisited." *Polity* 34: 561–93.

Stratmann, Thomas. 2000. "A Congressional Voting over Legislative Careers: Shifting Positions and Changing Constraints." *American Political Science Review* 94: 665–77.

Studenski, Paul, and Herman E. Krooss. 1963. *Financial History of the United States*. New York: McGraw-Hill.

Sundquist, James L. 1981. *The Decline and Resurgence of Congress*. Washington, D.C.: Brookings Institution.

Swierenga, Robert P. 1975. *Beyond the Civil War Synthesis: Political Essays of the Civil War Era*. Westport, Conn.: Greenwood.

Swift, Elaine K. 1996. *The Making of an American Senate: Reconstitutive Change in Congress, 1787–1841*. Ann Arbor: University of Michigan Press.

———. 1998. "The Start of Something New: Clay, Stevenson, Polk, and the Development of the Speakership, 1789–1869." In *Masters of the House: Congressional Leadership over Two Centuries*, ed. Roger H. Davidson, Susan Webb Hammond, and Raymond W. Smock. Boulder, Colo.: Westview Press.

Swift, Elaine K., and David W. Brady. 1994. "Common Ground: History and Theories of American Politics." In *The Dynamics of American Politics: Approaches and Interpretations*, ed. Lawrence C. Dodd and Calvin C. Jillson. Boulder, Colo.: Westview Press.

Tetlock, Philip E., and Aaron Belkin. 1996. "Counterfactual Thought Experiments in World Politics: Logical, Methodological, and Psychological Perspectives." In *Counterfactual Thought Experiments in World Politics*, ed. Philip E. Tetlock and Aaron Belkin. Princeton, N.J.: Princeton University Press.

Thompson, Charles Willis. 1906. *Party Leaders of the Time*. New York: Dillingham.

Tiefer, Charles. 1989. *Congressional Practice and Procedure: A Reference, Research, and Legislative Guide*. New York: Greenwood Press.

Vipperman, Carl J. 1989. *William Lowndes and the Transition of Southern Politics, 1782–1822*. Chapel Hill: University of North Carolina Press.

Wander, W. Thomas. 1984. *Congressional Budgeting*. Baltimore: Johns Hopkins University Press.

Weaver, R. Kent. 2000. *Ending Welfare as We Know It*. Washington, D.C.: Brookings Institution.

Weingast, Barry R. 1989. "Floor Behavior in Congress: Committee Power Under the Open Rule." *American Political Science Review* 83: 795–815.

———. 1991. "Institutions and Political Commitment: A New Political Economy of the American Civil War Era." Unpublished manuscript, Stanford University.

———. 1998. "Political Stability and Civil War: Institutions, Commitment, and American Democracy." In *Analytical Narratives*, ed. Robert H. Bates and others. Princeton, N.J.: Princeton University Press.

Weingast, Barry R., and William Marshall. 1988. "The Industrial Organization of Congress." *Journal of Political Economy* 96: 132–63.

White, Leonard D. 1951. *The Jeffersonians: A Study in Administrative History, 1801–1829*. New York: Macmillan.

Williamson, Oliver E. 1985. *Economic Institutions of Capitalism: Firms, Markets, and Relational Contracting*. New York: Free Press.

Wilmerding, Lucius, Jr. 1943. *The Spending Power: A History of the Efforts of Congress to Control Expenditures*. New Haven, Conn.: Yale University Press.

Wilson, Rick K. 1998. "Here's the Party: Group Effects and Partisan Advantage." Paper presented at annual meeting of the Midwest Political Science Association, Chicago, April 23–25.

Wilson, Woodrow. 1885. *Congressional Government*. Boston: Houghton Mifflin.

Wilson, Woodrow. 1900. *Congressional Government*, 2d ed. Boston: Houghton Mifflin.

Wormser, Michael D., ed. 1982. *Congressional Quarterly's Guide to Congress*, 3d ed. Washington, D.C.: Congressional Quarterly Press.

Young, James Sterling. 1966. *The Washington Community, 1800–1828*. New York: Columbia University Press.